# Dear Readers,

When we set out to revise *Reading and Learning to Read,* our goal was to update this seventh edition with the latest thinking in the field of literacy while adhering to our core beliefs about literacy learning. We hope you conclude that we have done that. Below we share with you some of the critical issues that have driven us to craft this new edition. These new issues are not in any particular order of importance; we invite you to think about them as you expand your knowledge and expertise regarding your current preclinical, clinical, and professional teaching experiences.

In this edition of *Reading and Learning to Read* we address the critical issues of diversity in more depth. We recognize the importance of educating teachers with a core knowledge base that includes a focus on issues that address linguistic, cultural, and cognitive diversity. After all, it is very probable that you will have students in your classrooms who come to you with various backgrounds, languages, and learning abilities. In addition to inviting you, the reader, to think about contemporary topics regarding diversity issues, this edition provides you with practical strategies for engaging diverse students in the process of learning to read.

We also introduce "new literacies." This concept embraces experiences that many of you have probably experienced as you learned to read. Essentially new literacies include reading that goes beyond linear print to include knowledge of fluid print such as Internet hypertext, graphic design, visual literacy, music, and film interpretation. This is a fast-growing area in reading due to the abundance of technology available to today's students. Throughout the text we offer classroom strategies that will broaden your understanding of literacy and the new skills you will need to address as teachers of reading.

Another new feature that we address in this edition is the role of a literacy coach. The idea of employing literacy coaches primarily focuses on assisting classroom teachers in the teaching of reading. We provide information on what coaching might look like in schools, explore how coaches help teachers develop effective skills for literacy instruction, and provide examples of techniques coaches use. At the end of each chapter we suggest ways for you to examine common teaching practices as a literacy coach.

Finally, we are excited about the new Viewpoint boxes in many of the chapters. We asked colleagues and students to share their stories and experiences on particular features of reading instruction in order to provide you with authentic anecdotes and classroom-tested strategies from real educators.

There is so much more included in this redesign that we hope you will take time to explore it and find new features for yourself. We are excited about this new edition and hope it serves you well in your quest to make a difference in the ways in which you teach children to read!

Our best,
Linda C. Burkey
Lisa A. Lenhart
Christine A. McKeon

SEVENTH EDITION

# Reading and Learning to Read

Jo Anne L. Vacca
*Kent State University*

Richard T. Vacca
*Kent State University*

Mary K. Gove
*Cleveland State University*

Linda C. Burkey
*Mount Union College*

Lisa A. Lenhart
*The University of Akron*

Christine A. McKeon
*Walsh University*

Boston • New York • San Francisco

Mexico City • Montreal • Toronto • London • Madrid • Munich • Paris

Hong Kong • Singapore • Tokyo • Cape Town • Sydney

Executive Editor: Aurora Martínez Ramos
Senior Development Editor: Mary Kriener
Associate Editor: Barbara Strickland
Series Editorial Assistant: Kara Kikel
Executive Marketing Manager: Krista Clark
Editorial Production Service: Omegatype Typography, Inc.
Composition Buyer: Linda Cox
Manufacturing Buyer: Megan Cochran
Electronic Composition: Omegatype Typography, Inc.
Interior Design: Carol Somberg
Photo Researcher: Omegatype Typography, Inc.
Cover Administrator: Linda Knowles

For related titles and support materials, visit our online catalog at www.pearsonhighered.com.

Between the time website information is gathered and then published, it is not unusual for some sites to have closed. Also, the transcription of URLs can result in typographical errors. The publisher would appreciate notification where these errors occur so that they may be corrected in subsequent editions.

**Library of Congress Cataloging-in-Publication Data**

Reading and learning to read / Jo Anne L. Vacca . . . [et al.] — 7th ed.
    p. cm.
Includes bibliographical references and index.
ISBN-13: 978-0-205-57112-3 (hardcover)
ISBN-10: 0-205-57112-3 (hardcover)
1. Reading (Elementary) 2. Language arts (Elementary) I. Vacca, Jo Anne L.

LB1573.V32 2008
372.4—dc22

                2008002490

Printed in the United States of America
10 9 8 7 6 5 4 3 2 1    RRD-OH    12 11 10 09 08

Credits appear on page 592, which constitutes an extension of this copyright page.

**Allyn & Bacon**
**is an imprint of**

www.pearsonhighered.com

ISBN-10:  0-205-57112-3
ISBN-13:  978-0-205-57112-3

# About the Authors

## Richard and Jo Anne Vacca

Richard and Jo Anne Vacca are professors emeriti in the Department of Teaching, Leadership, and Curriculum Studies in the College and Graduate School of Education, Health, and Human Services at Kent State University. They met as undergraduate English majors at SUNY–Albany and have been partners ever since. Jo Anne taught middle school language arts in New York and Illinois and received her doctorate from Boston University. Rich taught high school English and earned his doctorate at Syracuse University. He is a past president of the International Reading Association.

The Vaccas have a daughter, Courtney; son-in-law, Gary; and grandsons, Simon, Max, and Joe. They live with pets Tiger Lily and Jasmine in Vero Beach, Florida.

## Mary K. Gove

Dr. Mary Gove is an associate professor at Cleveland State University in the graduate literacy education program and served as a co-author on the early editions of *Reading and Learning to Read.* Her research interests include action research and how teachers' beliefs about teaching and learning influence classroom practice and teacher efficacy. Dr. Gove has also presented papers at various conferences and seminars worldwide. A recent area of focus for Dr. Gove has been ecological critical literacy (ECL), an approach to enhance how we read and critically think about published and broadcasted information about the present environmental depletion of natural resources.

## Linda C. Burkey

Dr. Linda Burkey is a professor and chair of the Education Department at Mount Union College in Alliance, Ohio. She also serves as the coordinator of the teacher education program at Mount Union and teaches courses on reading methods and reading assessment. Prior to receiving her Ph.D. from Kent State University, Dr. Burkey taught special education and elementary school. Her areas of interest in research include reading methods, reading assessment, and the teaching of reading in international countries. Dr. Burkey enjoys traveling and spending time with her family.

## Lisa A. Lenhart

Dr. Lisa Lenhart is an associate professor of literacy in the College of Education at The University of Akron teaching both undergraduate and graduate courses. She also serves as the co-director of the Reading First–Ohio Center for Professional Development and Technical Assistance, overseeing content development of the State Institutes for Reading Instruction (SIRI) and statewide implementation of SIRI e-learning courses. As a former elementary school teacher and Title I Reading teacher, Dr. Lenhart focuses her research on early literacy development and has co-written a book entitled *Oral Language and Early Literacy in Preschool.* Dr. Lenhart received her Ph.D. from Kent State University.

## Christine A. McKeon

Dr. Christine McKeon is a professor of middle childhood and reading education at Walsh University in North Canton, Ohio. She holds a Ph.D. from Kent State University and teaches Methods of Teaching and Developmental Reading and Reading Assessment and Intervention at Walsh University. She is also currently the co-editor of the *Ohio Reading Teacher Journal,* an IRA-affiliated professional journal. Dr. McKeon focuses her research on technology and new literacies, as well as on assessment and intervention strategies for struggling readers. As a former second-grade teacher, Title I reading teacher, and high school reading teacher, Dr. McKeon has developed a particular interest in adolescent literacy. When not writing textbooks and articles for peer-reviewed journals, Dr. McKeon spends her quiet time writing poetry and short stories.

May all who embrace literacy
as an integral part of life
look upon this book as one avenue
to *begin* the adventure
of teaching *everyone* how to read.

Thank you to all who have supported our writing
about *reading and learning to read, especially:*

Jo Anne and Rich Vacca
John, Jimmy, and Matthew McKeon
Bob and John Burkey
Matt, Hannah, and Emma Lenhart

# Brief Contents

# Contents

## CHAPTER 3

# Meeting the Literacy Needs of Diverse Learners   56

## CHAPTER 4

# Early Literacy: From Birth to School    92

## CHAPTER 5

# Inviting Beginners into the Literacy Club    122

**CHAPTER 6**

## Assessing Reading Performance    160

**CHAPTER 7**

## Word Identification    200

CHAPTER **8**

# Reading Fluency

246

## CHAPTER 11

# Reading–Writing Connections　350

CHAPTER **12**

# Bringing Children and Literature Together    388

CHAPTER **13**

# Basal Readers and Instructional Materials    424

## CHAPTER 14

# Making the Transition to Content Area Texts   454

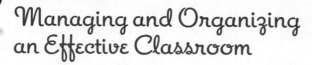

# CHAPTER 15
## Managing and Organizing an Effective Classroom     492

# Features

## New Literacies

## Research-Based Practices

## Step-by-Step Lesson

## Straight from the Classroom

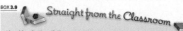

## Viewpoint

## Viewpoint: The Literacy Coach

# Preface

$\mathcal{E}$vidence-based reading research, the essential components of reading instruction, data-driven decision making, new literacies, and literacy coaching—these concepts represent the direction in which literacy professionals currently focus attention. Fortunately, *Reading and Learning to Read* has always included philosophies, teaching strategies, and assessment practices that reflect the beliefs that underscore these concepts. In this seventh edition of *Reading and Learning to Read*, we continue to recognize research-based practices and update the reader with new strategies that reflect alternative reading methodologies that we consider to be best practices. In addition, we highlight the essential components of effective literacy instruction (phonemic awareness, phonics, fluency, vocabulary, and comprehension) and demonstrate how each component can be taught within meaningful contexts.

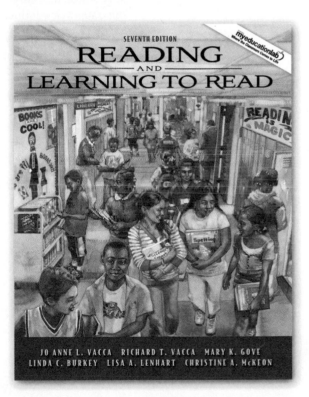

The seventh edition continues to feature technology applications as they relate to literacy instruction, and also highlights *new literacies*. The concept of new literacies goes beyond linear print to include knowledge of *fluid print* such as hyper text, graphic design, visual literacy, music, and film interpretation. We recognize that new literacies are transforming the way children comprehend and express their understanding of the world. This seventh edition features examples of lessons that develop teacher–student connections with new literacies, as well as thoughtful comments that can serve as springboards for discussion.

In addition, the seventh edition reflects our dedication to struggling readers. We include features that demonstrate the role of reading coaches and how they can assist teachers as they master teaching skills that will help all children succeed.

## Core Beliefs at the Center of This Text

$\mathsf{T}$his seventh edition of *Reading and Learning to Read* is based on research and current thinking about how children become literate. We continue to use our core beliefs about literacy learning to frame important questions related to the teaching of reading.

In addition, we craft our beliefs to reflect topics that address current educationally related literacy issues relevant to the twenty-first century. We believe the following:

- Children use language to seek and construct meaning from what they experience, hear, view, and read.

- Reading, writing, speaking, listening, and viewing are interrelated and mutually supportive as children learn to become literate.

- Learning to read involves learning how to decode words quickly and accurately with comprehension as the main goal of word recognition instruction.

- Children learn to read as they read to learn. They need to view reading as enjoyable, a process of communication, a process of gathering knowledge, a venue for expressing opinions, and so much more.

- Children need to be exposed to a broad spectrum of reading materials and literature, including fiction, nonfiction, electronic texts, and texts that reflect *new literacies* (art, music, dance, graphics, comics, etc.).

- Children develop skills and strategies through explicit instruction in purposeful, meaningful ways.

- Assessment techniques and processes need to mirror the authentic ways children demonstrate their continually developing literacy, and assessments should inform instruction.

- Children benefit from classroom communities in which materials, curricula, instruction, practice, and assessment recognize diversity.

- Teachers, parents, and administrators should work together as they make decisions based on how children learn and how they can best be taught.

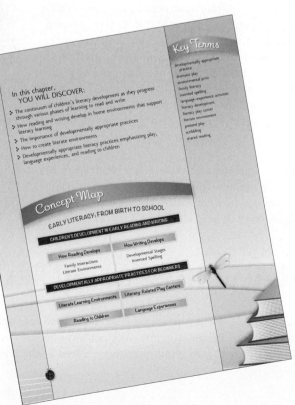

# Changes to the Seventh Edition

The seventh edition of *Reading and Learning to Read* continues to emphasize a comprehensive approach to teaching reading and writing. In maintaining this standard of excellence, this edition includes a number of additions that reflect the changes in the field of literacy.

● A **reorganization** of content moves Chapter 3, "Meeting the Literacy Needs of Diverse Learners," toward the front of the book, reflecting a greater emphasis on the importance of understanding concepts of diversity in all aspects of the literacy classroom.

● The burgeoning concept of new literacies is explored in the general text and in the **New Literacies** boxed features, offering classroom strategies that broaden the understanding of literacy beyond print, including multimodal forms of graphic design, visual literacy, music, film, and even advertising.

● New coverage of literacy coaches in schools explores how coaches help teachers to develop effective skills for literacy instruction. **Viewpoint: The Literacy Coach** boxes provide examples of techniques coaches use. **Through the Lens of a Literacy Coach** action items at the end of each chapter ask readers to examine common teaching practices as a literacy coach might.

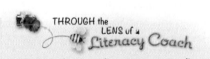

THROUGH the
LENS of a
Literacy Coach

4. Take time to observe a reading or content area reading teacher. What is the teacher doing well? What evidence did you see? How might you guide the teacher to improve his or her skills?

BUILDING
TEACHING SKILLS:
VIDEO

Go to this section in Chapter 1 of the Vacca MyEducationLab site to view the "Encouraging Social Interaction" video and see how affect and motivation are often closely connected.

● **MyEducationLab marginal activities** throughout every chapter signal the readers to go to the MyEducationLab web site. This rich online resource created specifically for this edition of *Reading and Learning to Read* offers prospective teachers the opportunity to assess their knowledge, view live classroom footage, evaluate classroom artifacts, and much more.

In addition to these global changes, discussions have been enhanced and new topics have been introduced within each chapter of the seventh edition to reflect the latest trends and research in literacy education. Go to www.pearsonhighered.com/vacca7einfo to view a complete breakdown of changes to the seventh edition. Here is a sample of the additions to this edition:

## CHAPTER 1

- Introduction of concepts of *literacy coaches* and *new literacies* in reading instruction
- New Teacher Action Research activities, including Through the Lens of a Literacy Coach activity
- New Literacies box, "Dr. William Kist on New Literacies"
- Viewpoint box, "What Is a Literacy Coach?"

## CHAPTER 2

- The addition of digital-language-experience approach (D-LEA) into the discussion of LEA
- The section "Technology-Based Instruction" discusses how to incorporate e-mail and blogs in instruction
- New minilesson on modeling
- New Literacies box, "Using Blogs in Classroom Center Activities"

## CHAPTER 3

- Discussion of the impact of No Child Left Behind and high-stakes instruction for English language learners.
- New information on Mora's four-by-four model of language arts instruction
- New subsections in "Instructional Strategies for Students Speaking Diverse Languages": "Response Protocol," "Content Area Practices," and "Thematic Teaching"
- New information on personal considerations of beliefs and experiences with other cultures
- New section, "Technology-Enhanced Instruction"
- Updates based on IDEA 2004 legislation
- The section "Instructional Principles for Academic and Cognitive Diversity" discusses literacy coaches and their work in the classroom
- The section "Instructional Strategies for Students with Diverse Academic and Cognitive Abilities" incorporates information on differentiated instruction, new literacies, and response to intervention
- New section, "Programs and Strategies for Struggling Readers Who Are Academically and Cognitively Diverse"
- New Literacies boxes, "Employing Visual Literacy" and "Enhancing Instruction with Technology"
- Viewpoint: The Literacy Coach box, "Important Questions to Ask"
- Research-Based Practices box, "KWLQ"
- Straight from the Classroom box, "How Mrs. R. Uses Differentiated Instruction"

## CHAPTER 4

- Revised section on the importance of invented spelling
- New section, "Designing Literacy-Related Play Centers," discusses critical roles teachers assume in children's play
- Research-Based Practices box, "The Five Essentials for Families"
- Viewpoint: The Literacy Coach box, "Coaching Teachers and Caregivers of Young Children"
- New Literacies box, "Using Wikis Effectively in Early Literacy"

## CHAPTER 5

- New chapter-opening vignette
- More information on the digital-language-experience approach (D-LEA)
- New Literacies box, "Podcasts in the Classroom"
- Updated information on the Concepts About Print Test

- Revised information on tasks children should be able to perform before moving on to phonics and spelling instruction
- New book suggestions for read-alouds

## CHAPTER 6

- Updated information on formative assessment
- New Literacies box, "Assessment and New Literacies"
- Updated information on miscue analysis based on recent research of McKenna and Picard

- New section, "Assessment Today and Tomorrow"
- New Teacher Action Research activities
- Straight from the Classroom box, "Narrative Retelling Rubric"

## CHAPTER 7

- New chapter-opening vignette
- New section, "Using Structural Analysis to Identify Words"
- New Teacher Action Research activities
- Research-Based Practices box, "Five-Day Sequence for Teaching Word Families"

- New Literacies box, "Words for Today's Students"
- Viewpoint: The Literacy Coach box, "Using Phonics Instruction Effectively"
- Table 7.1, "Developmental Stages of Word Learning and Spelling," based on the latest research of Bear, Invernizzi, Templeton, and Johnston

## CHAPTER 8

- New chapter-opening vignette
- Guidelines for conducting reader's theater
- New section on involving parents in oral reading development
- The section "Monitoring Oral Reading Fluency" examines ways to monitor and assess student progress

- Viewpoint box, "Andrew: My Reading History"
- New Literacies box, "Practicing Fluency Online"
- Viewpoint: The Literacy Coach box, "Coaching for Fluency"
- New reader's theater script, "The Gifts of Wali Dad"

## CHAPTER 9

- New chapter-opening vignette
- Updated information on connecting vocabulary instruction and assessment
- New information on utilizing media to help learning words be more fun and interesting

- New section, "Dictionary Usage"
- New Teacher Action Research activities
- New Literacies box, "The Motivation of Technology"

## CHAPTER 10

- New chapter-opening vignette
- Figure 10.1 provides examples of types of questions that reinforce comprehension
- New "What About Struggling Readers and Reading Comprehension?" explores the relationship between word recognition, fluency, and comprehension
- New Teacher Action Research activities

- Step-by-Step Lesson box, "Scaffolded Instruction"
- Straight from the Classroom box, "Model of a Think-Aloud Lesson"
- New Literacies box, "'Thinking Aloud' with Hypertext"
- Figure 10.2 identifies sample question prompts for ReQuest

## CHAPTER 11

- New section, "Alternative Strategies That Motivate Students to Write," offers ways to encourage student writing
- Guidelines for planning and organizing a writing workshop
- New section, "Children's Books and Technology," discusses the organization of web-based resources for use in teaching writing
- New "What About Struggling Readers and Reading–Writing Connections?" discusses creating an environment that fosters writing

- New Teacher Action Research activities
- Step-by-Step Lesson box, "Plot Scaffolding"
- Straight from the Classroom box, "Using Social-Issue Texts as a Springboard for a Writing Workshop"
- Research-Based Practices box, "Revising Using the Focused Question Card Strategy"
- Viewpoint: The Literacy Coach box, "Organizing Writing Instruction"
- New Literacies box, "The Earth Day Groceries Project"

## CHAPTER 12

- Viewpoint box, "Literature and Multiple Perspectives"
- New Literacies box, "Collaborative Literature Project, Peer Response, and New Literacies"
- New Teacher Action Research activities

- New suggestions of award-winning, contemporary selections of multicultural literature

## CHAPTER 13

- New section, "Making Instructional Decisions," discusses the role of literacy coaches in these decisions
- Revised information on the options for electronic materials for the classroom
- New Literacies box, "Integrating Technology into Basal Programs"
- Viewpoint box, "Coaching the Use of a Basal Program"

- Viewpoint box, "A Conversation with Three District Leaders," discusses the decision-making process behind selecting a basal reading program for the district
- New sample pages from a major basal reading program

## CHAPTER 14

- New chapter-opening vignette
- New information on qualities that characterize effective teachers of reading
- New section, "Vocabulary Building," discusses using realia and guidelines for engaging readers in content area lessons using literature
- New section, "Curriculum-Based Reader's Theater"
- New "What About Struggling Readers and Content Area Texts?"
- New "What About Standards, Assessment, and Content Area Texts?"

- New Teacher Action Research activities
- Viewpoint: The Literacy Coach box, "Leading Content Area Teachers Toward Excellence"
- Research-Based Practices box, "Guidelines for Choosing Literature to Enhance Content Area Reading Instruction"
- Step-by-Step Lesson box, "Implementing a Curriculum-Based Reader's Theater"
- New Literacies box, "Using the Internet for Developing Comprehension Skills"

## CHAPTER 15

- Information about grouping patterns that aid instructional management

- Viewpoint box, "Thoughts About Flexible Grouping"
- New Literacies box, "Incorporating Technology"

# Features of the Seventh Edition

With superior coverage of standards and an emphasis on comprehensive reading instruction, *Reading and Learning to Read*, Seventh Edition, remains an active learning tool that encourages future teachers to teach reading in ways that are both meaningful and reflective. Notable features of *Reading and Learning to Read* include the following:

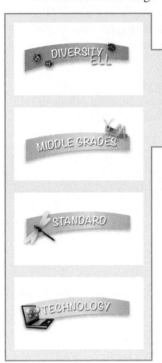

- **User-friendly marginal icons** highlight point-of-reference text material focused on International Reading Association standards, diverse learners, English language learners, technology, and middle-grade students.

- **Research-Based Practices** boxes throughout the text highlight relevant research that is supported by theoretically sound rationales and/or evidence-based research. These boxes provide general suggestions, strategies, and approaches that are supported by theory or scientific research for reading instruction.

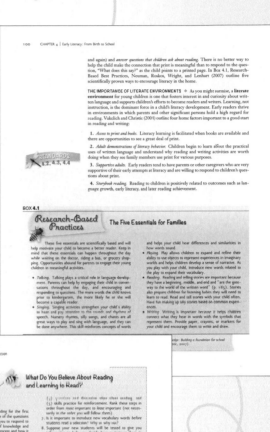

- **Viewpoint** boxes introduce the reader to the research and opinions of respected teacher-educators, researchers, and authors about particular facets of reading instruction.

- **Straight from the Classroom** boxes provide authentic anecdotes and classroom-tested strategies from real teachers.

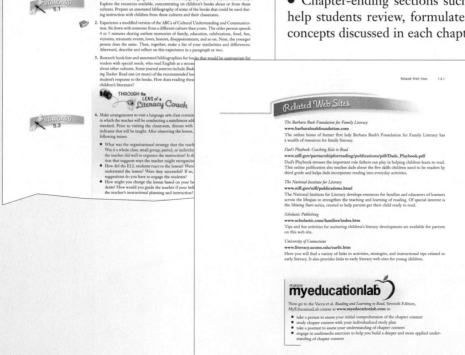

- **Step-by-Step Lesson** boxes offer teacher-directed lessons that can be imported directly into the classroom as specific lessons or as a series of lessons.

- **A focus on standards and assessment** can be found throughout every chapter. Meeting standards—state, local, and those developed by professional organizations—plays a major role in helping teachers meet the challenge of accountability for student performance on standards-based tests. In addition to marginal icons that correlate content with the latest International Reading Association (IRA) standards, applicable IRA standards are also listed at the beginning of each chapter and special sections at the ends of Chapters 3–15 tie the content of each chapter to some aspect of standards and assessment.

- An emphasis on **diverse learners** and **struggling readers** reflects current realities and concerns in today's schools. This emphasis includes **What About Struggling Readers** sections at the end of each chapter. These sections highlight the importance of accommodating those who struggle with reading and comprehension.

- Chapter-ending sections such as Summary and Related Web Sites help students review, formulate, and extend their thinking about the concepts discussed in each chapter. In particular, **Teacher Action Research** projects challenge the reader to think critically about the information covered. Icons indicate those activities that are appropriate for inclusion in **National Board Certification** portfolios.

# Supplements for Instructors and Students

The following supplements provide an outstanding array of resources that facilitate learning about reading instruction. For more information, speak with your local Allyn & Bacon Merrill Education representative about obtaining these supplements for your class, or contact the Allyn & Bacon Merrill Faculty Field Support Department at 1-800-526-0485. Many of the supplements are available for download at the Instructor Resource Center at www.pearsonhighered.com/irc. For technology support, call 1-800-677-6337 or go to http://247.pearsoned.com.

**INSTRUCTOR'S RESOURCE MANUAL.** Written by co-author Dr. Lisa Lenhart of The University of Akron, the Instructor's Resource Manual includes a wealth of instructional tools designed to help instructors teach the course. Each chapter includes a chapter-at-a-glance grid; key terms; purpose and underlying concepts; student objectives; activities and discussion questions; critical thinking questions about technology, diverse learners, middle school students, and struggling readers; and suggested readings and media. (Available for download from the Instructor Resource Center at www.pearsonhighered.com/irc.)

**TEST BANK.** Written by co-author Dr. Lisa Lenhart of The University of Akron, the Test Bank for *Reading and Learning to Read*, Seventh Edition, includes multiple choice, true/false, and essay questions. For this edition, page references to the main text, suggested answers, and skill types have been added to each question to help instructors create and evaluate student tests. (Available for download from the Instructor Resource Center at www.pearsonhighered.com/irc.)

**COMPUTERIZED TEST BANK.** The printed Test Bank is also available electronically through the Allyn & Bacon computerized testing system, TestGen. Instructors can use TestGen to create exams in just minutes by selecting from the existing database of questions, editing questions, and/or writing original questions. (Available for download from the Instructor Resource Center at www.pearsonhighered.com/irc.)

**POWERPOINT™ PRESENTATION.** Ideal for lecture presentations or student handouts, the PowerPoint™ Presentation created for *Reading and Learning to Read*, Seventh Edition, provides dozens of ready-to-use graphic and text images. (Available for download from the Instructor Resource Center at www.pearsonhighered.com/irc.)

**ALLYN & BACON DIGITAL MEDIA ARCHIVE CD-ROM FOR LITERACY, 2002.** This CD-ROM offers still images, video clips, audio clips, web links, and assorted lecture resources that can be incorporated into multimedia presentations in the classroom.

**VIDEOWORKSHOP FOR READING METHODS, VERSION 2.0.** An easy way to bring video into your course for maximized learning! This total teaching and learning system includes quality video footage on an easy-to-use CD-ROM plus a Student Learning Guide and an Instructor's Teaching Guide—both with questions and activity suggestions. The result? A program that brings textbook concepts to life with ease and that helps students understand, analyze, and apply the objectives of the course. VideoWorkshop is available for students as a value-pack option with this textbook.

**COURSE MANAGEMENT.** Powered by Blackboard™ and hosted nationally, Allyn & Bacon's own course management system, CourseCompass, helps you manage all aspects of teaching your course. For colleges and universities with WebCT™ and Blackboard™ licenses, special course management packages can be requested in these formats as well. The test item file for this text is available in the appropriate format for importing into your system. (Speak with your sales representative for additional information.)

# PEARSON
# myeducationlab

## Where the Classroom Comes to Life

*Your Class. Your Career. Everyone's Future.*

Teacher educators who are developing pedagogies for the analysis of teaching and learning contend that analyzing teaching artifacts has three advantages: it enables new teachers time for reflection while still using the real materials of practice; it provides new teachers with experience thinking about and approaching the complexity of the classroom; and in some cases, it can help new teachers and teacher educators develop a shared understanding and common language about teaching. . . .[1]

As Linda Darling-Hammond and her colleagues point out, grounding teacher education in real classrooms—among real teachers and students and among actual examples of students' and teachers' work—is an important, perhaps even essential, part of training teachers for the complexities of teaching today's students in today's classrooms. For a number of years, we have heard the same message from many of you as we sat in your offices learning about the goals of your courses and the challenges you face in teaching the next generation of educators. Working with a number of our authors and with many of you, we have created a web site that provides you and your students with the context of real classrooms and artifacts that research on teacher education tells us is so important. Through authentic in-class video footage, interactive simulations, rich case studies, examples of authentic teacher and student work, and more, **MyEducationLab** offers you and your students a uniquely valuable teacher education tool.

MyEducationLab is a research-based learning tool that brings teaching to life. Through authentic in-class video footage, interactive simulations, rich case studies, examples of authentic teacher and student work, and more, MyEducationLab prepares you for your teaching career by showing what quality instruction looks like.

BUILDING
TEACHING SKILLS:
VIDEO

Go to this section in Chapter 1 of the Vacca MyEducationLab site to view the "Encouraging Social Interaction" video and see how affect and motivation are often closely connected.

**MyEducationLab** is easy to use! In the textbook, look for the MyEducationLab logo in the margins and follow the simple link instructions to access the multimedia "Homework & Exercises" and "Building Teaching Skills" assignments in MyEducationLab that correspond with the chapter content. Homework & Exercises assets offer opportunities to understand content more deeply and to practice applying content. Building Teach-

ing Skills assignments help you practice and strengthen skills that are essential to quality teaching through your analysis and response to student and teacher instructional encounters and artifacts. The rich, thoughtful, and interactive elements you will encounter throughout MyEducationLab include the following:

- **Video.** Authentic classroom videos show how real teachers handle actual classroom situations.
- **Case Studies.** A diverse set of robust cases illustrates the realities of teaching and offers valuable perspectives on common issues and challenges in education.
- **Simulations.** Created by the IRIS Center at Vanderbilt University, these interactive simulations offer hands-on practice at adapting instruction for a full spectrum of learners.
- **Individualized Study Plan.** The study plan is designed to help students perform well on exams and to promote deep understanding of chapter content. Readers have the opportunity to take tests before and after reading each chapter of the text. Test results automatically generate a personalized study plan that identifies areas of the chapter that students must reread to fully understand chapter concepts, as well as interactive multimedia exercises to help ensure learning.
- **Readings.** Specially selected, topically relevant articles from ASCD's renowned *Educational Leadership* journal expand and enrich your perspectives on key issues and topics in literacy.
- **Student & Teacher Artifacts.** Authentic preK–12 student and teacher classroom artifacts are tied to course topics and offer you practice in working with the actual types of materials you will encounter daily as teachers.
- **Lesson & Portfolio Builders.** With this effective and easy-to-use tool, you can create, update, and share standards-based lesson plans and portfolios.
- **News Articles.** Looking for current issues in education? Our collection offers quick access to hundreds of relevant articles from the New York Times Educational News Feed.

**MyEducationLab is easy to assign, which is essential for providing the greatest benefit to your students.** Visit www.myeducationlab.com for a demonstration of this exciting new online teaching resource.

[1]Darling-Hammond, L., & Bransford, J. (Eds.). (2005). *Preparing Teachers for a Changing World*. San Francisco: John Wiley & Sons.

# Acknowledgments

This edition has evolved not only from the new information in the field of literacy, but also from the thoughtful response of our reviewers. We wish to thank Beverly Boulware, The University of Texas at Arlington; Carolyn Jaynes, California State University, Sacramento; Patricia Jenkins, Albany State University; Claudia McVicker, Southern Illinois University Edwardsville; Edward F. Sacco, Framingham State College; Corlis Snow, Delta State University; Yvonne D. Taylor, Shippensburg University; and Renata M. Ziolkowska, California State University, Northridge. Throughout the revision process, each of us returned to their comments and feedback many times to focus our writing.

We also wish to thank the teachers and colleagues who contributed to this seventh edition. Thanks to Dr. Michelle Lenarz of Walsh University; David Anderson, the literacy lead teacher at the Canton McKinley High School Freshman Academy in Canton, Ohio; Jeremy Brueck of The University of Akron; Kimberly Hartman Brueck of Green Local Schools, Ohio; Jane Hallisy, an independent literacy coach; Michele Evans-Gardell of Canton City Schools in Ohio; Andrew P. of Aurora, Ohio; William Kist of Kent State University; Maryjo Hepler, Peter Schneller, and Mandy Capel of Mount Union College; and Alicia Jackson, a graduate student at Walsh University.

In addition, we would like to thank all of the professionals at Allyn & Bacon who have guided us through the process of writing this seventh edition of *Reading and Learning to Read*. Genuine thanks to Executive Editor, Aurora Martínez; Senior Development Editor, Mary Kriener; Executive Marketing Manager, Krista Clark; Associate Editor for Supplements, Barbara Strickland; and Production Coordinator, Judy Fiske. We would also like to thank the team at Omegatype Typography for helping march this book through production. Thank you for all of your support.

And, of course, we would like to thank our families for their loving support as we researched, crafted, and developed major changes in this seventh edition. Their patience with us has indeed made the process a family affair. Thank you to our husbands—Bob, John, and Matt.

Finally, we need to thank Jo Anne and Rich Vacca for the opportunity to continue the professional challenge of crafting this new edition of *Reading and Learning to Read*. Their initial invitation to write has motivated us to continue to develop literacy collaboratives, research based inquiry, and a friendship that is priceless. Thank you, Jo Anne and Rich!

L.C.B.
L.A.L.
C.A.M.

## CHAPTER 1

# Knowledge and Beliefs About Reading

Standards found in this chapter:
- 1.1
- 1.2
- 1.3
- 2.2
- 4.1
- 4.2
- 4.4
- 5.1
- 5.2
- 5.3
- 5.4

## In this chapter,
### YOU WILL DISCOVER:

- How beliefs about literacy learning influence instructional decisions and practices
- How teachers use and construct personal, professional, and practical knowledge about literacy learning
- How language, social, and psychological perspectives on reading inform knowledge and beliefs about literacy learning
- How different theoretical models of the reading process describe what humans do when they engage in reading

## Concept Map

### KNOWLEDGE AND BELIEFS ABOUT READING

**THE IMPORTANCE OF BELIEF SYSTEMS**

**Ways of Knowing About Reading and Learning to Read**

Personal Knowledge
Practical Knowledge
Professional Knowledge

**Perspectives on Learning to Read**

Cognitive Insights
Language Perspective
Models of Reading

On an unusually warm and humid day in May, the furnace at Lincoln Elementary School is blasting hot air into one of the first-grade classrooms. Two building custodians are trying to turn off the heat while the teacher and the students are trying to work despite the physical discomfort. The windows are wide open; a fan moves the hot air around the room, to little avail.

Lincoln Elementary, built in the 1940s, is an inner-city school. Although the physical plant shows its age, temporary inconveniences such as the heating system going haywire don't get in the way of teaching and learning. In the midst of all the commotion in the first-grade classroom, one of the students is at her desk, busy with paper and pencil, as she writes a note to the teacher. She folds it in half, writes "Mrs. H" on the front, and delivers it posthaste. The teacher, Mrs. Henderson, opens the note and much to her delight, reads:

Plese turn of the fan Then guys smell like my brother when he mos the grass.

Toni P.

The note to Mrs. Henderson has a great deal to say about "literacy in the making." As lighthearted as it may seem on the surface, it reveals much about Toni's literacy development. Just ask yourself, for example, "Does Toni know what writing and reading are for? Does she get her message across effectively? Does she have a sense of the teacher as a reader?" And as a language user, "Is Toni empowered? Is she willing to take risks?" The answers to questions such as these are as revealing about Toni's literacy development as the grammatical and spelling errors she made.

Although the school year is rapidly coming to a close, Mrs. Henderson recalls Toni's first day in her class. She hardly spoke a word. Yet today, Toni has blossomed into a confident and competent reader and writer. Some of her literacy strengths are mirrored in the note she has written to Mrs. H. Not only does Toni express a strong, clear, concise message, but her writing also exhibits good sentence structure, word usage, and—for the most part—mechanics (spelling, punctuation, and grammar). In a small but significant way, the note reflects the progress she has made since the beginning of the school year.

Although she misspelled three words, Toni's written approximations of *please, off,* and *mows* are phonetically regular and close to the conventional spellings of the words. Though she neglects to use a period at the end of the first sentence, Mrs. Henderson attributes the omission to fast writing rather than Toni's lack of understanding of a punctuation mark at the end of a sentence. Developmentally, Toni writes the way she talks. In time, she'll understand why it is grammatically inappropriate to use *them* when she means *those.*

Throughout the year, Mrs. Henderson's literacy program has centered on the development of confident and competent readers and writers. She wants her students to be motivated, thoughtful, and skillful as they engage in literacy learning. Toni is motivated and thoughtful, and she is in the process of becoming skillful as a reader and writer. Mrs. Henderson makes a mental note to work with Toni on learning the conventional spellings of *please, off,* and *mows.* She plans to teach these words explicitly because of their irregular letter–sound patterns. But not immediately.

Instead, Mrs. Henderson reads Toni's note and acts on the plea—quickly, we might add—by turning off the fan. And at the same time, she can't help but appreciate Toni's use of language to communicate. Mrs. Henderson recognizes that a powerful and authentic literacy event has just taken place between a writer and a reader. She decides, on the spot, to extend the transaction that has just occurred between the two of them.

So she writes a note to Toni thanking her. She tells Toni that the way the day has begun reminds her of the story she had read to the class a while ago about Alexander, who had a *terrible, horrible, no good, very bad day!* And because of Toni's note, she will read the story again to the class "so we can all feel better about this morning!" Mrs. Henderson's decision to continue and extend the communication reflects not only what she knows about reading and learning to read but also what she believes about teaching, learning, and the process of becoming literate.

How teachers come to know and develop beliefs about reading and learning to read is the subject of this chapter. Examine the chapter overview. It depicts the connections among several key concepts related to the role of teacher knowledge and beliefs in reading instruction. A **belief system** represents a teacher's informed philosophy of reading and learning to read. What teachers believe about reading and learning to read is closely related to what they know about literacy learning and the teaching of literacy. As you study this chapter, pay close attention to how teachers come to know about literacy learning through (1) personal experiences—past and present—as readers and writers, (2) practical experiences and knowledge of their craft as they work with and learn from children, and (3) professional study that allows them to develop and extend their knowledge base about teaching and learning literacy.

Also in this chapter, we emphasize how different perspectives related to reading and learning inform teachers' knowledge and beliefs about literacy learning. Language, social, and psychological perspectives are not mutually exclusive domains of knowledge. Often, effective literacy practice, sometimes referred to as **best practice**, requires teachers to use multiple perspectives as they plan and enact literacy instruction in their classrooms. As suggested in the Concept Map, the final section of this chapter describes various theoretical models of the reading process. Understanding reading and learning to read within the context of theoretical models will enable you to connect knowledge and beliefs about reading to issues and approaches related to instructional practice in Chapter 2.

## The Importance of Belief Systems

Knowledge and beliefs about reading and learning to read are wedded in ways that influence almost every aspect of a teacher's instructional decisions and practices. To illustrate, consider what Mrs. Henderson does after she writes her reply to Toni's note.

Connecting the events of the morning to *Alexander and the Terrible, Horrible, No Good, Very Bad Day* by Judith Viorst is an opportune, authentic way to demonstrate one of the *language functions* that reading serves. As we

The main goal of reading instruction is teaching children to become independent readers and learners.

discuss later in the chapter, reading can be put to use in different ways for different purposes, one of which is to entertain—or, in the classroom situation that the first graders find themselves, to provide some relief from the smell in the room.

In addition, sharing the book with the class results in a "commercial" for another book, Patricia Reilly Giff's *Today Was a Terrible Day*, which is part of the classroom library collection. This is a story about a boy named Ronald who has a terrible day in school until he discovers that he can read (without any help) a personal note written to him by the teacher. Toni's teacher previews the story with the class and makes a connection between the notes that she and Toni have exchanged and the note that the teacher in the story writes to Ronald. She then builds anticipation for the story by inviting the students to think about the "terrible days" experienced by Alexander and Ronald, what contributes to making a day terrible, and what people can do to turn a bad day into a good one.

Throughout the remainder of the day, as you might anticipate, children asked if they could leaf through or read *Today Was a Terrible Day* between class activities. Some of them even wrote about terrible days in their journals, which are an integral part of the literacy curriculum in this first-grade classroom.

All of the reading and writing activities that evolved from the unanticipated events of the morning provided children with a demonstration of the *intertextuality* of stories. Stories are products of the imagination, but the problems and themes they portray reflect the human experience. *Intertextuality* is a word used by literary theorists to describe the connections that exist within and between texts. Think about the personal connections made by Toni and her classmates. They were able to build on the morning's heating crisis to make connections between the two stories shared by the teacher, as well as the texts that some of them created by writing in their journals. The children in Toni's class are exploring what it means to be *meaning-seekers* and *meaning-makers*. Their use of texts to construct meaning is the nexus by which they link the stories and explore a theme that will recur throughout their lives.

Not a bad day's work on a hot, muggy day in May. The work of teachers sometimes takes unexpected twists and turns—"teachable moments," if you will, that usually beget reasons for reading and writing. Yet taking advantage of a teachable moment, as Toni's teacher did, requires a philosophy of reading and learning to read. Some educators call a teacher's philosophical stance a *worldview*; others call it a *belief system*.

For one reason or another, some teachers would probably have reacted differently to Toni's note. Perhaps a teacher would have praised Toni for her effort in writing the note but rather than extend the **literacy event,** concentrate on the misspellings or punctuation error. Another teacher might have been too busy or preoccupied with the heating crisis or other matters to respond to the note in a manner that connects literacy learning to life in the classroom. Other teachers might simply have been oblivious to the teachable moment because they did not understand or appreciate the literacy event that occurred. Our point, therefore, is that a teacher's knowledge and beliefs about the nature and purposes of reading and the ways in which it should be taught contribute significantly to whatever decisions a teacher makes in a given situation.

## Different Beliefs, Different Instructional Decisions

Just about every teacher we've ever talked to agrees on the main goal of reading instruction: to teach children to become independent readers and learners. Differences among teachers, however, often reflect varying beliefs and instructional perspectives on how to help children achieve independence. Because they view the reading process through different belief systems, teachers have different instructional concerns and emphases. The decisions they make will vary.

In addition, effective reading teachers use their knowledge and beliefs about reading to adapt instruction to individual differences among children in their classrooms. The

STANDARD
4.1

**HOMEWORK EXERCISE: VIDEO**

Go to the Homework and Exercises section in Chapter 1 of MyEducationLab to watch the "Teaching to Diverse Learning Styles" video about how different belief systems can inform different instructional decisions.

DIVERSITY

students they work with may have different academic, language, cultural, or physical needs. Student diversity in today's classrooms, as we explain more fully in Chapter 3, is greater today than at any time in this century. There is an increasing number of students whose first language is not English and whose culture does not reflect the beliefs, values, and standards of the mainstream culture in U.S. society. Moreover, inclusive classrooms, where students with "special needs" are included in regular classrooms, make it necessary that teachers become knowledgeable about the nature and purposes of reading acquisition.

The Viewpoint in Box 1.1, written by a parent, is a poignant reminder of the importance of teachers who know *how* to respond to students' literacy needs and *why*.

No two teachers, even if they work with children at the same grade level and in classrooms next door to each other, teach reading in exactly the same way. Even though they may share the same instructional goals and adhere to literacy guidelines established within the school district or state department of education standards, teachers often make decisions and engage in practices based on what they know and believe to be worthwhile. Observe how Arch and Latisha, two first-grade teachers, introduce beginners to reading and learning to read.

Arch invites his first graders to explore and experience the uses of oral and written language in a variety of instructional situations. He chooses all kinds of authentic and functional reading material—"anything that's real and important to the kids"—for reading and learning to read: signs, boxtops, labels, poems, nursery rhymes, children's books, interactive stories, and computer games. His students also create their own texts, and these become the basis for reading. They write in journals about what they read, make books from original stories that they share with one another, and dictate stories that Arch captures on chart paper. In addition, Arch uses "big books" and storybooks to build concepts and skills related to reading. Often he begins a big-book lesson by reading the story aloud and discussing it with the class. Over the course of several days, he rereads the story in unison with the children once, twice, or even more times and then invites individual students to read parts of the story on their own.

Arch pays some attention to letter–sound relationships in the context of the writing and reading activities that children engage in. He encourages students to invent spellings during journal writing and other writing activities by helping them "spell the words the way they sound." In doing so, he responds individually to children's invented spellings. For words that he thinks a child should know how to spell correctly, he provides explicit intervention. For others, he accepts the child's invention if it approximates the conventional spelling. In addition, during big-book readings, Arch will periodically stop to point out and discuss initial letters and sounds, letter combinations, or endings. When students read aloud, Arch places little importance on word-perfect reading. He says, "I tell my kids not to let one or two words prevent them from reading; they might be able to understand what the story is about and to enjoy it without identifying all of the words."

Latisha also teaches reading to 6-year-olds. But her approach is different from Arch's. She believes quite strongly that beginning readers must start with letter–sound correspondences, translating print into speech. Other than occasional "experience charts" in the first weeks of the school year, Latisha doesn't attempt to introduce writing until most of her children make the monumental "click" between the black squiggly marks on a page (print) and the sounds they represent (speech).

Of the "click," Latisha says, "You can't miss it." When she sees children making the connection between print and speech, Latisha begins to aim for mastery.

The study of words in Latisha's class centers around story selections from the basal reading program that her school adopted several years ago. The basal program provides Latisha with "great literature, big books, everything that you need to teach reading." When she began teaching 15 years ago, Latisha taught letter–sound relationships by relying heavily on workbooks and worksheets from the basal program. Her students spent a lot of time on isolated drill and rote memorization of phonics rules. "I didn't

BOX **1.1**

# Viewpoint

## Adam's Journey

Karen A. Whitmer

*In addition to being a mom, Karen Whitmer is an elementary school principal.*

I don't know if we can teach your son to read if he cannot hear the difference between sounds.

Your son will have to learn to read in a special class because he learns differently.

Why do you read aloud to your son if he cannot hear you?

Adam can skip library time to go to speech. He's probably not interested in books anyway.

These are the types of comments my hearing-impaired son and I have heard when he entered school. At times we have been upset and discouraged by the way some people have written him off as a reader and a learner. Today, however, we are able to laugh at such narrow ways of thinking because my son, Adam, is learning. Adam *is* reading—and he is loving it! Adam's journey into reading clearly illustrates what is, for me, an important principle underlying reading and learning to read: *When reading is meaningful, children learn to read.*

When my son was 4 years old, we had an established ritual each evening, which we would go through before his bedtime. Adam would take his bath, and while he was doing that, we would take time to name every object around him: soap, water, boat, shampoo, towel. We would also use the objects to show action: boat floats, water splashes, soap sinks. We would use the dressing ritual to show sequence: first, we put on underwear; next, we put on our bottoms; last, we put on our top. We would end the evening with a story, which I would read aloud. Adam would try to read along with me, and sometimes he could, if he had the text memorized. I noticed that his language was improving and that his articulation errors were fewer and fewer, but he wasn't transferring this knowledge to the decoding of printed words. Silently, I worried. Being a teacher, I knew what was to come for him.

This frustration remained my own until Adam entered school. Once he saw everyone else learning to read, he began to feel that same frustration. One night he left me a note by his bed (something he had never done before). On that note was a picture of a boy with tears rushing down his face. Next to the boy's head was the word "Adam." Without even thinking, I found a pencil and drew a picture of me with tears and wrote "Mom" next to it.

The next morning, Adam and I cuddled in his bed and talked about the reason for our tears. We were both sad that Adam was having trouble with reading. I assured Adam that I would talk to his teacher and that I would help him myself.

We began labeling everything in his room with index cards. This was the same thing we had been doing verbally, but now we were putting those utterances into print. Each evening, we would quiz each other on several of the cards. We also kept writing to each other in that notebook by his bed. Pictures and one-word labels eventually turned into phrases and sentences. I am sure these actions helped Adam on the road to becoming a reader. We capitalized on his strengths (memory and writing) as we fine-tuned his weakness (hearing sounds in words).

However, the thing that sparked Adam's reading was his desire to learn. I truly believe Adam had a need to read. He wanted to be successful in school. He wanted to be included, to be a part of the community of readers in his classroom. He had to find a way to read that made sense to him, his own way.

Adam's way was through writing. It still is. We are still writing to each other on a daily basis. We no longer have his room full of index cards, however. Instead, Adam attempts to label unfamiliar objects or subjects that he needs for his writing. Adam also writes to his teacher, a pen pal, and his favorite professional baseball player. He writes to find out information. He reads now because those people are writing back with the information he asked for. If they write words he cannot decode, we work together to figure them out. Then Adam writes those words in a notebook and illustrates them, if appropriate. He uses that notebook for future reference and for future writings.

Adam still has trouble hearing the difference between sounds, but he can tell you all kinds of words that contain those sounds. He can also tell you what your mouth looks like when you produce those sounds, and he can make them himself. This "sounding-out" process is a slow and frustrating one for Adam. He prefers to read through a visual modality. He relies heavily on remembering what he writes. It is very common to see Adam running up to his room saying, "I've got to write that down!"

It takes a special teacher to allow Adam to "do it his own way," but we have been fortunate to find several teachers like that. Adam is not in a special class, and he is reading on grade level. He is in control of his learning. His desire to learn drives his journey into reading and learning to read. Recently, Adam drew another picture of himself. The picture shows a happy boy on a soccer field scoring a winning goal for his team. The caption under the picture reads, "Adam's the winner!" What more can I possibly say?

know better then. Using workbook exercises was accepted practice by the teachers in my building, and I thought I was doing the right thing."

Today, however, Latisha bases much of what she does on research related to how children learn words. Each day she blocks out 15 to 20 minutes for word study. She still goes about the teaching of letter–sound relationships in a direct and systematic manner but relies more on *explicit instruction*. That is, Latisha makes it a practice to *model* skills and strategies that children need to decipher unknown words, *explain* why it is important for students to learn the skill or strategy under study, and *guide* students in their acquisition of the skill or strategy. She makes sure, for example, at the beginning of the school year that her students have rudimentary skills related to hearing sounds in words, recognizing letters and sounds, and blending sounds into words. Latisha uses story selections from the basal reading anthology and big books to identify words for study and to provide practice and application in the use of the skill or strategy. Rather than dispense worksheets that require students to circle letters or draw lines to pictures, Latisha says, "I do a lot more teaching about phonics skills and strategies so that it makes sense to students as they learn to decode words."

The perspectives from which Latisha and Arch teach reading reflect different beliefs about learning to read that result in different instructional emphases and practices. Arch uses authentic, real-world literature such as children's books and functional materials such as signs and boxtops. Latisha relies on materials from a basal reading program that includes literature anthologies and a wide range of ancillary materials. Latisha begins instruction with an emphasis on phonics skills and strategies. Arch begins with immersion in reading and writing. Comprehension is as important to Latisha as it is to Arch, but the two differ in belief. Latisha's understanding of reading suggests that when children decode words accurately and quickly, they are in a better position to comprehend what they read than children who are not accurate and automatic decoders. Arch's view is that children who engage in authentic literacy experiences will search for meaning in everything they read and write.

## Reading Instruction and Teachers' Belief Systems

Latisha's style of teaching reading reflects beliefs that employ a systematic instructional approach. A systematic instructional approach includes direct teaching and a logical instructional sequence. This structure includes ample opportunities to practice specific skills and move along a defined trajectory related to the sequencing of skills. Arch's methods are the product of a belief system that reflects a broader constructivist view. This model is focused on the needs of the individual child. In this perspective, the role of the teacher is a facilitator who helps the child negotiate text by addressing the most immediate instructional needs. The progression of instruction or sequencing of skills is often centered around the student's individual progress. Language skills are practiced through application or embedded skills instruction.

In examining these two approaches to reading, it is clear that the implementation of reading instruction can be viewed from multiple perspectives. (Refer to the Viewpoint in Box 1.2 on page 8.) This ambiguity is further complicated as we look at the current movement at the national level that emphasizes standards and demands that educators be accountable for results.

In April 1997, the National Institute of Child Health and Human Development (NICHD), in consultation with the Secretary of Education, was charged to convene a National Reading Panel (NRP) that would assess the status of research-based knowledge, including the effectiveness of various approaches to teaching children to read. The panel was asked to provide a summary of findings that included the application of this work to classroom-based instruction. The NRP built upon the previous work of the National Research Council (NRC) published in *Preventing Reading Difficulties in Young Children* (Snow, Burns, & Griffin, 1998). In April of 2000, the panel released its findings and made

BOX **1.2**

# Viewpoint

### Controversy in the Teaching of Reading: What Else Is New?

Richard T. Vacca

*Richard T. Vacca is past president of the International Reading Association and the author of many books and articles on reading instruction.*

Will the controversies over how to teach reading, especially to beginners, ever subside? Probably not in our lifetimes. Reading and learning to read are tied too closely to human emotion and belief. After all, reading is a covert and complex human process that takes place in the head and heart of the reader. Who really knows what happens within a child or adult who picks up a book and engages in the activity that we call *reading?* The best that teachers can do is to engage in instructional practices based on the best evidence from research and inquiry.

Attempting to accomplish learning to read through a single method or approach never made much sense to me. There is no single approach to the teaching of reading that works best for all children. In its position statement on evidence-based instructional practices, the International Reading Association (2002b, p. 1) put it this way: "there is no single instructional program or method that is effective in teaching all children to read. Rather, successful efforts . . . emphasize identification and implementation of evidence-based practices. . . ." Given the human complexities associated with learning to read, a "one size fits all" mentality is not in the best interest of all children.

Yet the debate and criticism over the teaching of reading continue to be stronger today than ever. I first became aware that controversies existed in the teaching of reading when, as a doctoral student, I read Nila Banton Smith's (1965) classic historical study, *American Reading Instruction.* Smith's review and analysis of reading instruction in America reveal how every major educational epoch, from the religious emphasis of our Puritan forefathers to the onset of the technological revolution in the latter half of the twentieth century, has generated its fair share of debate and criticism over how children should be taught to read.

In the past 50 years, the debate over how reading should be taught to beginners seems to have intensified, becoming as much a political issue as an educational controversy. Beginning with the popular book *Why Johnny Can't Read—And What You Can Do About It* by Rudolph Flesch (1955), the debate has focused on the role of phonics in the teaching of reading. *Why Johnny Can't Read* remained on the *New York Times* bestseller list for more than 30 weeks. Flesch, who was not considered

to be a reading expert, railed against established instructional practice, which espoused an eclectic approach to teaching reading rather than a heavy phonics emphasis. His book, while popular with the general public, had little impact on established practice and was generally discounted by reading professionals as the work of a cranky malcontent. Yet it was the first book to bring the controversy over the teaching of reading to the public's attention, creating the impression that something was wrong with schools and the educational establishment because they did not teach reading using a strong phonics emphasis. It wasn't until Jeanne Chall wrote *Learning to Read: The Great Debate* (1967) that the controversy over how to teach reading really began to heat up among reading professionals within the educational community. Chall, a much-respected Harvard-based reading researcher, reviewed a large number of studies and came to the conclusion that phonics or decoding should be emphasized from the very beginning.

The "Great Debate" among reading professionals turned into the "Reading Wars" of the 1990s. The so-called Reading Wars were largely a media-driven phenomenon. A battle between the proponents of phonics and whole language was waged in newspapers, magazines, television news reports, and eventually in state legislatures where laws were enacted in several states to teach phonics intensively. Vilified in the media and by some legislatures, instructional practices associated with whole language instruction were abandoned by many school districts.

I don't get it. I am a proponent of phonics instruction for beginners. I am also a proponent of whole language practices. Phonics is a tool needed by all readers and writers of alphabetically based languages such as English. While I am not a proponent of isolated drill, overreliance on worksheets, or rote memorization of phonics rules, I support the teaching of phonics that children actually need and use to identify words quickly and accurately. Effective classroom teachers make a difference in the teaching of reading by asking how, how much, to whom, and when it is most appropriate to teach phonics. Phonics is an important part of literacy instruction and needs to be taught well in classrooms where children read and write each day. Although phonics is a tool needed by readers and writers, the teaching of phonics—as necessary as it is—isn't sufficient to develop thoughtful, comprehending readers who value reading and its many uses.

recommendations about teaching methods that are scientifically proven to increase student learning and achievement. The reauthorization of the Elementary and Secondary Education Act (ESEA) in 2001 includes the scientifically based reading instruction recommendations for preschool and primary grades.

Scientifically based reading research, as defined in the federal legislation, is the body of scientific evidence about reading methodologies drawn from experimental and quasi-experimental work. These include rigorous data analysis and measurements that provide valid data across observers and evaluators. The research must be accepted by a peer-reviewed journal or be approved by an independent panel of experts.

With the reauthorization of ESEA in 2001, the federal government set forward initiatives in an attempt to ensure that no child is left behind. This legislation challenges educators to use evidence-based research as a guide in the development of high-quality reading programs for students in preschool and the primary grades. Programs such as Reading First and Early Reading First clearly define the parameters and expected outcomes for our work as educators and charge us to examine our teaching practices, tools, and materials. These programs challenge us to rethink what it means to "teach and learn."

Continuing dialogue related to these current trends has resulted in recommendations from high-level reading organizations. The International Reading Association raises questions about the notion of scientific research and calls for a broader perspective. This point of view stresses that "No single study ever establishes a program or practice as effective; moreover, it is the convergence of evidence from a variety of study designs that is ultimately scientifically convincing" (IRA, 2002b, p. 1). The International Reading Association supports evidence-based reading instruction as the way to enhance literacy development.

In light of the various positions on reading research, teachers need to be aware of programs and practices based on multiple types of research studies with a broad scope of topics reviewed. Research provides the reading professional a foundation for effective reading instruction. It should broaden reading professionals' beliefs, not narrow them. With more and more external mandates and narrowing views of reading instruction, teachers now more than ever need to make informed decisions based on their beliefs of reading and learning to read. Teachers—not programs—produce effective reading instruction and achievement. It is ultimately the teacher who is responsible for providing successful reading experiences.

This is especially true when focusing on **new literacies.** Although difficult to define due to various interpretations of what constitutes "new" literacies in the context of changing textual media, the definition that best represents the viewpoint of this text is that of Karchmer, Mallette, Kara-Soteriou, and Leu (2005), who suggest that "new literacies" are the knowledge, skills, strategies, and dispositions needed to use and adapt to constantly changing information and communication technologies. Developing new literacies is dependent on teachers' belief systems and relies on their professional expertise and their evaluation of current technology to successfully integrate technology in their classrooms.

Being able to use, locate, and evaluate information from a web page, participate in an online discussion, listen to a podcast, and develop a video production are a few examples of new technologies that require students to be critical, active readers. Readers rely on their foundational literacies to develop the skills and strategies needed to be critical readers (Leu, Kinzer, Coiro, & Cammack, 2004). William Kist provides further insights and reading instruction in Box 1.3, New Literacies, on page 10.

STANDARD
2.2

Why isn't there more consensus on how to teach children to read? Although it is perfectly natural to want to know the "right way" to do something, a comprehensive reading program—using several methods instead of just one approach—gives teachers the freedom to use their own professional expertise and judgment. The danger of buying into the "right way" to teach reading is that teachers can become dependent on others telling them how to help children develop as readers. If teachers are to be empowered as professionals, they must apply their knowledge and beliefs about reading and learning to read in deciding what practices are best for their students.

In the pressured world of teaching, it is sometimes easy to lose sight of what we know and believe about children, reading, and how children learn to read. The common thread that runs through the literacy practices of Mrs. Henderson, Arch, Latisha, and countless other reading professionals is that they view reading and learning to read through belief systems that define and shape their roles as classroom teachers. Through

BOX **1.3**

## New Literacies

# DR. WILLIAM KIST ON NEW LITERACIES

*Dr. William Kist, associate professor of education at Kent State University and author of* New Literacies in Action: Teaching and Learning in Multiple Media *(2005), shares his perspectives on the concept of "new literacies" in schools.*

### What does the term "new literacies" mean?

The term "new literacies" is just one of several terms that have been used by literacy educators to talk about the rapidly changing nature of "reading" and "writing." One of my favorite definitions is by Elliot Eisner.

> In order to be read, a poem, an equation, a painting, a dance, a novel, or a contract each requires a distinctive form of literacy, when literacy means, as I intend it to mean, a way of conveying meaning through and recovering meaning from the form of representation in which it appears. (Eisner, 1997, p. 353)

People who refer to "new literacies" or "multiliteracies," or "multimodal literacy" or "media literacy," are generally talking about a broadened conception of literacy that still, of course, includes print literacy, but also includes a knowledge of graphic design, visual literacy, and even music and film literacies as well as advertising.

Reading/language arts teachers have historically been focused on print exclusively. The new ways we read and write today are pushing us to help our students be better readers and writers not only of print but of other forms of representation as well.

### What do students of all ages need to learn in order to create (output) what they know about literacy, learning, and content knowledge via new literacies?

To put it simply, our students will probably be "writing" using a greater variety of media than people have in the past. In the "old days" of schooling—way back in the twentieth century—students most often represented their knowledge by writing something in print, perhaps a book report, or essay questions on a paper-and-pencil test. (My dad still talks about creating a diorama model of Shakespeare's Globe Theatre many decades ago. So I think they have always allowed their students to represent knowledge using alternatives to print.)

As we move from a page-based society to a screen-based society (Kress, 2003), students will need to be able to represent what they know not only on paper, in a linear fashion, using print, but on a screen, still using print, but also using graphics, sound, and motion, and doing so in a nonlinear way. When I say "nonlinear," I'm thinking of the old *Choose Your Adventure* books, in which the reader got to choose how the plot progresses and the choices made led to alternative page numbers to continue the story. Writing a text that is embedded with hyperlinks is challenging! Try it sometime!

The writer has to be content with the knowledge that a hyperlink that is embedded in the text will take the reader to different texts, and that reader may never return to the original text. Are there similarities to writing on paper? Yes; both certainly involve a knowledge of print communication including organization and mechanics (conventions). But there are additional layers that must be understood by someone who wants to communicate effectively in this new, nonlinear way. The writer of a hyperlinked text must know something about the affordances provided by this new form of communication.

### What do today's teachers need to know about these new literacies?

It's hard to pin down exactly what teachers should know about these new literacies, because they are multiplying so rapidly. Perhaps the best thing for teachers to know about new literacies is that they don't have to know everything about them! I think what scares some teachers about these new literacies is that they feel that the students will know more about these new media than they will. We teachers have to let that fear go. I have let go in my own classrooms, as I routinely encounter students who know much more than I do about desktop video editing, for example, or building a web page. Teachers (at all levels and of all subjects) should at least be open to allowing their students to both "read" and "write" using these new media. There are an increasing number of books and online resources that are out there to help teachers with ideas for assignments and assessments that incorporate these new media. But probably the best thing is for teachers to become readers and writers of these new media themselves, right in there with the kids.

### What are some alternative ways to develop student comprehension via new literacies?

Currently, there are many students who are challenged to comprehend a printed text in a textbook. Now, we are throwing at these students not only print, but also visual art, motion pictures, sound, and advertising. And we're also asking them to be much more critical of the source than we have in the past, especially with the development of volunteer-produced web sites such as Wikipedia. Speaking of Wikipedia, we're also asking students to construct knowledge in a different way than they have in the past. These new media have a more social nature to them. In a more traditional school environment, we have tended to equate "comprehension" with "memorization" done in isolation. (If anything, these new media are probably pushing us to make changes in schools that should have been made long ago.) In short, these new literacies are transforming the way people "comprehend" their world. There are many

*(Continued)*

## New Literacies *(Continued)*

more layers, I believe, to teaching comprehension skills than there have been in the past.

The good news is that these new media texts may be more engaging for students than the old-fashioned textbook has been. These new media may draw in students who, in the past, have been left in the cold by a textbook representation of the Civil War, for example, or the migratory patterns of the starling. In a new media environment, a student might be able to play a multiplayer Civil War role-playing game online, re-enacting a battle with other players. That student might also be able to follow the flight pattern of a starling in a motion video

that is linked to GoogleMaps, and might even see the starling fly over his or her home town!

If anything, one of the main comprehension skills that our students will need to have is the ability to sort through the immense amount of material that is out there on any given subject. No matter what is being studied, thousands and thousands of words (and images and sounds) are instantaneously available and downloadable. One of our main tasks as reading/language arts teachers will be to help our students navigate this world of texts, even as it is constantly changing.

---

what set of beliefs do you view reading and learning to read? How do you believe reading and writing should be taught in an effective literacy program? Throughout your teaching career, from the time you begin studying to become a teacher and all the while you practice your craft, you will be continually developing answers to these questions as you build and refine your knowledge and beliefs about what counts as literacy learning in your classroom.

Are some belief systems better than others? The answer to the question lies not with the authors of this or any comprehensive textbook on reading telling you the "right way" to think about teaching and learning to read but in the process of coming to know about literacy learning. The more you know about what readers and writers do and the roles that reading and writing play in the lives of children, the more empowered you are to respond to a question of such personal and professional importance.

Belief systems related to literacy learning are not a collection of naive assumptions and presuppositions but rather a set of beliefs that are grounded in research and current thinking about reading and writing. As suggested in the International Reading Association's *Standards for Reading Professionals* (2003), beliefs are built on an organized and specific set of knowledge, skills, and dispositions that are needed to influence students' reading achievement. In the preface to this book, we outlined the core beliefs that underlie the writing of this book. Suffice it to say that what we, as authors of this book, believed about some aspects of reading and learning to read has changed considerably since we entered the teaching field, primarily because the *knowledge base* has changed. Nevertheless, there are some beliefs about children, teachers, teaching and learning, and how children learn to read and use reading to learn that have remained constant since we entered the teaching profession. If we were to characterize our worldview of reading and learning to read today, we would affirm that our beliefs are rooted in an *interactive* view of the reading process and a comprehensive view of reading instruction—concepts that will be developed in this chapter and the next.

# How Teachers Come to Know About Reading and Learning to Read

Teachers come to know in different ways. For example, in a lifetime of interaction with the world about us, we acquire knowledge about reading and learning to read by *building it from the inside* as we interact with people, processes, ideas, and things. Jean Piaget's theory of **constructivism** provides a compelling explanatory framework for understanding the acquisition of knowledge. Piaget, one of the preeminent child psychologists of the twentieth century, theorized that children do not internalize knowledge directly from the outside but construct it from inside their heads, in interaction with the environment (Kamii, 1991). When constructivist thinking is applied to the acquisition of knowledge about teaching and learning, it holds that teachers engage in a process of seeking and making meaning from personal, practical, and professional experiences.

## Constructing Personal Knowledge

**HOMEWORK EXERCISE: VIDEO**

Go to the Homework and Exercises section in Chapter 1 of MyEducationLab to watch the video "Becoming A Teacher" about one person's motivation to become a teacher.

Personal knowledge of reading and learning to read grows out of a teacher's history as a reader and a writer. Consider, for example, the influences in your life that have shaped the literate person you are. From birth, you have interacted with *people* (parents, teachers, siblings, friends, and significant others) and *things* (all kinds of literacy artifacts and texts, including books, signs, letters, labels, pencil and paper, word processors, e-mails, and the Internet) to construct knowledge about the *processes* of reading and writing. By engaging in reading and writing, you come to know in a very personal way what readers and writers do and the contributions that reading and writing make to a life. You belong to what Frank Smith (1988) calls the "literacy club" by virtue of the fact that you read and write.

The development of an **autobiographical narrative** is a powerful tool that helps you link your personal history as a reader to instructional beliefs and practices. Not all teachers like to read, even though they know how. Some may read well and be well read. But others may have struggled as readers and bear the emotional scars to prove it. How do these realities affect what teachers do in classroom situations?

An autobiographical narrative helps you inquire into the past in order to better understand what you do in the present and what you would like to do in future classroom situations. Teachers who engage in narrative inquiry explore mental pictures of memories, incidents, or situations in their lives. The inquiry allows you to reflect, make connections, and project. As Connelly and Clandinin (1988) put it, "Where we have been and where we are going interact to make meaning of the situations in which we find ourselves" (p. 6).

To develop a reading autobiography, consider the questions in Figure 1.1. You may wish to share your narratives with others. What beliefs, values, and attitudes are an integral part of your stories? How do your personal histories of reading and learning to read influence where you are in your thinking about reading and where you would like to be?

## Constructing Practical Knowledge

Teachers also construct practical knowledge, which is closely related to personal knowledge in that it grows out of experience both in and out of the classroom. The

---

**Figure 1.1  Developing a Reading Autobiographical Narrative**

Reflect on how you learned to read, the reading habits you have formed, home and school influences on your reading development, and the kinds of reading you do. Prepare an autobiographical sketch that captures these personal memories. How did you learn to read? What home reading experiences do you recall? What kinds of instructional activities and practices were you involved in as an elementary school student? Which ones do you recall fondly? Which, if any, do you recall with regret? In retrospect, what belief systems and views of reading and learning to read did your elementary school teachers seem to hold? Were you effectively taught how to handle the variety of reading tasks you face in the real world?

more that you work with and observe children in literacy situations in classroom and community contexts and reflect on their behavior *and* your own, the more you develop theories about what is the best practice for the readers and writers with whom you work. Practical knowledge is characterized by the beliefs, values, and attitudes that you construct about readers and writers, texts, reading and writing processes, learning to read and write, and the role of the teacher in the development of children's literate behavior.

In teacher education programs, field experiences and student teaching are vehicles for acquiring practical knowledge. In addition, interactions with and observations of practicing teachers influence the way you might think about reading and learning to read in classroom situations. At times, preservice teachers may find incongruities between what is taught in education courses and what they observe in the field. These incongruities create conceptual conflict. This conflict is healthy because it helps reflective students of literacy think more deeply about their own understandings, beliefs, and practices.

The construction of practical knowledge extends beyond classroom situations and includes interactions within the cultural context of school and community. For example, a teacher's beliefs about reading and learning to read may be affected by the beliefs of colleagues and administrators, school board policies, curriculum guidelines, the publishing and testing industry, public opinion, and standards for teaching reading.

## Constructing Professional Knowledge and Expertise

As an integral part of their professional development, teachers interact with the world of ideas. Professional education organizations, such as the International Reading Association, refer to what teachers ought to know and be able to do in order to teach reading well as *standards* or the *knowledge base*.

**Professional knowledge** is knowledge acquired from an ongoing study of the practice of teaching. What teacher education programs do best is help preservice and inservice teachers build a knowledge base that is grounded in current theory, research, and practice. Throughout their professional development, the books and journals teachers read, the courses and workshops they take, and the conferences they attend contribute to the vision they have of reading and learning to read.

The instructional differences among teachers reflect the knowledge they put to use in classroom situations. While few would argue that nothing is as practical as a good theory, we embrace the notion that "there's nothing so theoretical as a good practice." Teachers construct theories of reading and learning to read based on their ways of knowing, which influence the way they teach, including the ways they plan, use and select texts, interact with learners, and assess literate activity. In turn, the decisions teachers make about instruction influence students' reading performance and their perceptions of and attitudes toward reading, as illustrated in Figure 1.2 on page 14.

Coming to know what readers do is no easy matter. Part of the challenge that teachers encounter comes from the complex, elusive nature of the reading process. Who can ever really know a process that takes place in the mind? The best we can do is investigate reading and learning to read by inquiring into literacy teaching and learning. The inquiry process can be made easier with assistance from a **literacy coach.** (See the Viewpoint in Box 1.4 on page 15.) Using their expertise in reading and learning to read, literacy coaches provide professional development opportunities and resources. Literacy coaches help develop expertise in the classroom.

The role of the literacy coach varies. As reported in the International Reading Association's position statement, The Role and Qualifications of the Reading Coach in the United States (2004), in-class coaching and support define the role of literacy coach. Coaches provide a variety of activities while in a nonevaluative role. Such activities include developing curriculum with colleagues, making professional development

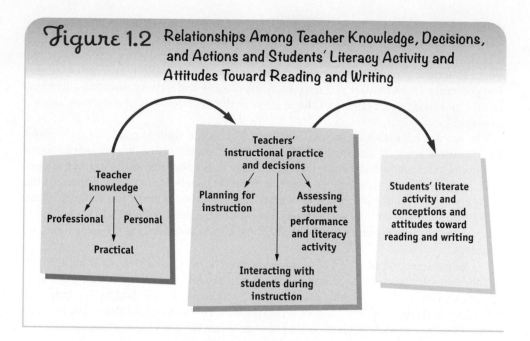

*Figure* 1.2  Relationships Among Teacher Knowledge, Decisions, and Actions and Students' Literacy Activity and Attitudes Toward Reading and Writing

presentations to teachers, modeling lessons, providing resources, and visiting classrooms to provide feedback.

The responsibility of the literacy coach also varies across ages. According to Puig and Froelich (2007), the elementary coach's role focuses on promoting a more comprehensive literacy program, whereas in the middle and high schools, literacy coaches support the teachers using reading and writing to develop content area knowledge. No matter how reading is taught, constructing professional knowledge is essential. Personal, practical, and professional experiences are the stepping-stones to knowing about reading and learning to read.

A reading professional, whether novice or veteran, continually needs to study the knowledge base from *multidisciplinary* perspectives. Because reading and learning to read are complex processes, no one field of study provides all the answers. Understanding reading from multiple perspectives allows teachers to affirm, change, or let go of what they believe and value in light of new knowledge and research. Multidisciplinary perspectives on reading and learning to read enrich and broaden the knowledge base so that teachers are in the very best position to use their professional expertise and judgment to make instructional decisions.

A single discipline cannot provide a teacher with the insights and understandings needed to guide and support literacy learning in the modern world. The fields of education, linguistics, cognitive psychology, technology, sociology, and anthropology, to name a few, contribute in important ways to knowledge and beliefs about reading and learning to read. From a *cognitive* perspective, for example, an elementary teacher needs to understand, among other things, how children learn words in an alphabetic system of writing such as English; from a *language* perspective, how children's knowledge of written language emerges and develops naturally in early childhood to form the basis for literacy learning; and from a *sociocultural* perspective, how children's home language and community values influence language use and literacy learning.

Research on reading in the past 3 decades has centered primarily on the roles of cognition and language in reading acquisition. Cognitive studies have provided insights into how people comprehend and learn as they process written symbols. Cognitive scientists and researchers are interested in how reading works inside people's minds—how readers learn to *decode* words accurately and automatically in an alphabetic writing system, how readers use prior knowledge *(schemata)* to understand what they are reading,

BOX **1.4**

# *Viewpoint*

## What Is a Literacy Coach?

*The relatively recent phenomenon of literacy coaches in schools has arisen from recognition of literacy as the critical basis for all learning. From this understanding, more and more education officials acknowledge that "a cornerstone of implementing any successful school reform model is having knowledgeable literacy coaches" (Puig & Froelich, p. v). In* The Literacy Coach: Guiding in the Right Direction *(2007), Enrique Puig and Kathy Froelich further explain the roles of literacy coaches in a school system.*

There are many different definitions for literacy coaching, and the definition of *literacy coach* can be considerably different from that of a mentor. We believe a literacy coach is different from a mentor. . . .

We see the mentor as someone who supports new teachers as they begin their work in the classroom. Additionally, we see mentors as having protégés, whereas literacy coaches are co-learners. Literacy coaches learn and support teachers as they continue in their [own] careers. *Reading Today* ("Coaches, Controversy, Consensus," 2004) expands on the definition of *literacy coach:* "When most people talk about literacy coaches, they are understood to mean educators who spend at least part of their time providing professional development to other teachers in a school or district setting." These literacy coaches are co-workers who work with their colleagues over a period of time.

In our definition, literacy coaches are certainly mentors, but mentors may not necessarily be coaches. Coaches are ones that assist in shifting classroom teachers to better understand critical pedagogy and the need for change based on evidence. According to Lyons and Pinnell (2001), the literacy coach, through observation and co-learning, helps the teacher see beyond what is in the classroom to what can improve it, and helps the teacher expand her or his knowledge base by becoming an ongoing learner, while offering support and encouragement as needed.

The Continuum of Coaching figure outlines the range of support a literacy coach can provide. In a typical workweek, a literacy coach's work hours may be broken down as follows:

- 40%   Work with students
- 20%   Engage in dialogic conversations with teachers and observations
- 10%   Provide observation lessons
- 20%   Plan and prepare for training sessions
- 10%   Engage in professional book study

## CONTINUUM OF COACHING
### A Comprehensive Landscape of Support for Professional Development

**Interactive Coaching** ←————————————————————→ **Intraactive Coaching**

| Facilitate a **workshop** or **session** to improve instruction and student learning. | Provide an **observation lesson** to improve instruction and student learning. | **Co-teach** with a host teacher to improve instruction and student learning. | **Confer, observe, and debrief** to improve instruction and student learning. | Facilitate a **study group or literacy leadership council** investigating common interest topics to improve instruction and student learning. | Facilitate **action research** to seek resources after reflection to improve instruction and student learning. |

**Increased external scaffolding** ←————————————————————→ **Decreased external scaffolding**

**Subject-centered pedagogy**          **Problem-centered andragogy**

Transformations may occur when teachers/coaches are provided opportunities to observe, co-teach, confer, study, research, and reflect on practices based on behavioral evidence.

*Note:* The term *observation lesson* has been used to replace *demonstration lesson* to denote the opportunity being provided versus a model lesson to emulate.

and how readers use and develop *strategies* to *regulate* and *monitor* comprehension as they learn from written language.

Language and literacy learning are inseparable. Learning to read needs to be understood in terms of learning to use written language effectively. One of the most important ways people learn is through the use of language—spoken, written, or signed. Goodman (1986) puts it this way: "Language enables us to share our experiences, learn from each other, [and] plan together, and greatly enhances our intellect by linking our minds with others of our kind" (p. 11). Children are inherently social. If children perceive little use for written language, they will have a difficult time learning to read and write. However, if written language is meaningful, the social and cultural situations in which it is used allow children to discern what reading and writing are all about.

# Cognitive Insights into Reading and Learning to Read

STANDARDS
1.1, 1.2

A university colleague of ours, a cognitive psychologist by training, says he's been researching and studying the reading process for more than 2 decades because he's interested in "how the mind works." How the mind works is another way of saying that he's interested in understanding *cognitive* and *meta-cognitive processes* in reading. His inquiries into the reading process embrace a psychological perspective. One of the important contributions from cognitive psychology focuses on beginning readers' discovery of the **alphabetic principle** in languages such as English. Learning to read English involves learning how an alphabetic writing system works.

## The Alphabetic Principle and Learning to Read

**BUILDING TEACHING SKILLS: ARTIFACTS**

Go to the Homework and Exercises section in Chapter 1 of MyEducationLab to complete the exercise in which you examine student artifacts as they relate to learning to read.

The alphabetic principle suggests that there is a correspondence between letters *(graph-emes)*, which are the basic units of writing, and sounds *(phonemes)*. Pearson (1996) likens the discovery of the alphabetic principle to learning a great secret: When children "have learned the great secret—that English writing represents sounds—two entire worlds open to them: first, that well-spring of inner oral language; and second, through that language, a seemingly unending world of books" (p. 270). A teacher needs to understand how beginning readers come to master the alphabetic system and use their knowledge of English writing to identify words.

However, before you consider how beginners learn to identify words accurately and quickly, participate in the two demonstrations that follow. These demonstrations make clear what *skilled* readers know about the alphabetic system and how they use their knowledge for accurate and automatic word identification.

Suppose the following lines were flashed on a screen in half-second intervals, and you were asked to write down what you could remember after each line was flashed.

Line 1    —○— □ ⊗ ⌐ ⊔ ‡ ⌐⊔

Line 2    xmrbacdy

Line 3    boragle

Line 4    institution

Line 5    flour wiggle come stove investigate girl door yell

Line 6    the beautiful girl ran down the steep hill

When we have conducted this demonstration with preservice teachers in reading methods classes, here's what usually happens.

Most class members are unable to recall accurately the squiggly marks on line 1. They are able to remember some, but not all, of the letters in line 2. Both the nonword *boragle* in line 3, which follows conventional English spelling patterns, and the word *institution* in line 4 are usually recalled. Students are unable to recall all the words in line 5, but the whole string of words in line 6, which makes a sentence, is usually recalled.

What can we learn from this demonstration? Human beings can make about four fixations per second with their eyes (Smith, 1985). When looking at the flashed items, skilled readers use about 50 milliseconds of visual intake and then use 200 milliseconds to process the intake. During the intake, they can probably attend to only about five to seven items—the range of items most human beings can hold in short-term memory. When looking at each of the six lines for a half-second, the limitations of short-term memory (being able to recall five to seven items) operate. What changes line by line is the nature of the items. Skilled readers are able to recognize some of the items quickly and accurately because they are able to perceive them as letter patterns or units of written language. These patterns are recognized by skilled readers as familiar *spelling patterns* or *sight words*.

In line 1, skilled college-level readers are unable to group the marks, which we'll call "squiggles," into meaningful patterns. The reason is simple: They have no prior knowledge of the squiggles. These squiggles have not been learned as an *orthography*. Skilled readers have internalized the shapes of alphabetic letters, their names, and the sounds they symbolize. But they aren't the least bit familiar with the shapes of the individual squiggles in line 1 or whether the squiggles function as written symbols that represent sounds.

In line 2, the black squiggly marks are recognized as individual letters in English writing. However, within the time constraints of a half-second interval, college readers cannot group all of the letters into meaningful letter patterns. As a result, they have difficulty holding all the letters in short-term memory.

In lines 3, 4, and 5, skilled readers can group the letters into familiar spelling patterns. *Boragle* and *institution* are easily recalled by most college students when flashed on a screen. Even though *boragle* is a nonsense word, the letter patterns are consistent and predictable. *Institution* is recalled as a known sight word.

Most of the college students in our classes cannot in a half-second recall all of the words in line 5 because these words cannot be strung together into a meaningful utterance. However, the students stand a greater chance of recalling line 6 precisely because the string of words makes a meaningful sentence that they are able to decode, based on their immediate sight recognition of known words.

Now read these two lists, both containing nonwords:

| List 1 | List 2 |
| --- | --- |
| scrass | tblc |
| sook | gfpv |
| tolly | oeaiu |
| amittature | rtbm |
| lanfication | gdhtaiueo |

Which list is easier to read? Use what you learned from the first demonstration to respond to the question.

List 1, of course, is fairly easy for skilled readers to read, but list 2 is nearly impossible. The reason why list 1 is easier to read than list 2, as you might have surmised, involves your skill at identifying letter patterns. Written English contains predictable letter patterns that skilled readers are able to associate with sounds very rapidly and accurately (Juel, 1988; Venezky & Massaro, 1979). Skilled readers know that *scr* is likely to occur in English writing but that *tblc* is not likely to occur. When skilled readers encounter multisyllable words (or even nonwords that contain common orthographic patterns), they depend on their ability to group these patterns into syllables. This is done by using their knowledge of likely and unlikely letter sequences. We know that the letters *lan* would go together to pronounce "lan," and that *fi, ca,* and *tion* should be treated as clusters of letters that we chunk together or treat as a group. Cognitive studies show that skillful readers chunk words into syllables automatically, *in the course of perceiving letters.* Skilled readers are able to do this because of their knowledge of likely spelling patterns, or **orthographic knowledge.** This knowledge is so thoroughly learned that skilled readers do not have to put any energy into identifying words (Adams, 1990).

From an instructional perspective, then, it is important to know how to help beginning readers develop into skilled readers who can identify words quickly and accurately as they read. When young children begin reading, their eyes encounter three units of written language: letters, words, and sentences. Although Holdaway (1979) notes the importance of the alphabetic principle in learning to read, he also points out that the visual display of print on the page makes the learning of words critical:

> We think of the alphabet principle as a wonderful invention. **BUTWEOVERLOOKANINVENTIONALMOSTASBRILLIANTAND CERTAINLYMORESIMPLE**—namely the visual display. . . . Indeed, written language is perceived as words, not as a series of individual letters. (p. 83)

Because of the use of spaces—a print convention that evolved with Gutenberg's invention of the printing press in the fifteenth century—the visual display of written language creates a system of distinct, perceptual units called *words.* According to Ehri (1995), during the course of learning to read, the eyes come to favor written words over letters and sentences: "The advantage of words over sentences is that words can be assimilated in one glance. The advantage of words over letters is that written words correspond more reliably to spoken words than letters correspond to sounds" (p. 171). Because words are the primary units of written language, helping beginners develop word-reading skill is one of the important instructional responsibilities of teachers in learning to read. Although beginners have developed some knowledge of written language prior to first grade, explicit instruction becomes essential as children progress through various phases of word-reading development and develop strategies to read words quickly and accurately.

How children think and reason with print is an important concern in this book. A cognitive view of reading suggests that the reader's ability to construct meaning is at the core of the process. The constructive processes characteristic of reading comprehension have been of intense interest to cognitive psychologists and reading researchers for more than a decade. In particular, they have studied the role that schemata play in comprehending texts.

## Schema Theory and Reading Comprehension

**Schemata** reflect the prior knowledge, experiences, conceptual understandings, attitudes, values, skills, and procedures a reader brings to a reading situation. Children use what they know already to give meaning to new events and experiences. Cognitive psychologists use the singular term *schema* to describe how humans organize and construct meaning in their heads. Schemata have been called "the building blocks of cognition" (Rumelhart, 1982) and "a cognitive map to the world" (Neisser, 1976) because they represent elaborate networks of concepts, skills, and procedures that we use to make sense of new stimuli, events, and situations.

For example, do you possess the schemata needed to interpret the passage in Figure 1.3? Upon first reading, Bransford and Johnson's passage may seem difficult to understand unless you were able to activate an appropriate schema. How many of you recognized that the passage had to do with washing clothes? Once a schema for washing

## Figure 1.3   What Is the Passage About?

The procedure is quite simple. First you arrange things into different groups. Of course, one pile may be sufficient depending on how much there is to do. If you have to go somewhere else due to lack of facilities that is the next step; otherwise you are pretty well set. It is important not to overdo things. That is, it is better to do too few things at once than too many. In the short run this may not seem important but complications can easily arise. A mistake can be expensive as well. At first the whole procedure will seem complicated. Soon, however, it will become just another facet of life. It is difficult to foresee any end to the necessity for this task in the immediate future, but then one can never tell. After the procedure is completed one arranges the materials into different groups again. They can be put into their appropriate places. Eventually they will be used once more, and the whole cycle will then have to be repeated. However, this is part of life.

*Source:* Reprinted from "Considerations of Some Problems of Comprehension," by J. D. Bransford and M. K. Johnson, in *Visual Information Processing*, edited by W. C. Chase, copyright © 1973, with permission from Elsevier.

clothes is activated, the words and phrases in the passage take on new meaning. Now try rereading the passage. Upon rereading, you will probably react by saying, "Aha! Now that I know the passage is about washing clothes, it makes sense!" Ambiguous words such as *procedure* and word streams such as "A mistake can be expensive" are now interpreted within the framework of what you know about washing clothes. The more you know about washing clothes, the more comprehensible the passage becomes. When readers activate appropriate schemata, *expectations* are raised for the meaning of the text. Your expectations for the passage help you anticipate meaning and relate information from the passage to things you already know.

The more we hear, see, read, or experience new information, the more we refine and expand existing schemata within our language system.

Schemata, as you can see, influence reading comprehension and learning. For comprehension to happen, readers must activate or build a schema that fits with information from a text. When a good fit occurs, schema functions in at least three ways to facilitate comprehension. First, schema provides a framework that allows readers to *organize* text information efficiently and effectively. The ability to integrate and organize new information into old facilitates retention. Second, schema allows readers to *make inferences* about what happens or is likely to happen in a text. Inferences, for example, help children predict upcoming information or fill in gaps in the material. And third, schema helps readers *elaborate* on the material. Elaboration is a powerful aspect of reasoning with print. When children elaborate on what they have read, they engage in cognitive activity that involves speculation, judgment, and evaluation.

## Metacognition and Learning

**Metacognition,** defined generally by Ann Brown (1985), refers to knowledge about and regulation of some form of cognitive activity. In the case of reading, metacognition refers to (1) *self-knowledge*—the knowledge students have about themselves as readers and learners; (2) *task knowledge*—the knowledge of reading tasks and the strategies that are appropriate given a task at hand; and (3) *self-monitoring*—the ability of students to monitor reading by keeping track of how well they are comprehending.

Consider the following scenario, one that is quite common when working with reading beginners: A first grader, reading orally, comes to a word in the text that he doesn't recognize. Stymied, he looks to the teacher for help. The teacher has at least four options to consider in deciding how to respond to the reader: (1) tell him the word, (2) ask him

Teachers sometimes engage readers in brief discussions on metacognitive strategies.

to "sound it out," (3) ask him to take an "educated guess," or (4) tell him to say "blank" and keep on reading.

What would you do? A rationale, based on what you know and believe about teaching reading, can be developed for each of the options or for that matter, a combination. For example, "First, I'd ask him to sound out the word, and if that didn't work, I'd tell him the word." Or, "First, I'd ask him to take a good guess based on what word might make sense, and if that didn't work, I'd ask him to say 'blank' and keep on reading."

Options 2 through 4 represent strategies to solve a particular problem that occurs during reading—identifying an unfamiliar word. Sounding out an unfamiliar word is one strategy frequently taught to beginners. When using a sounding-out strategy, a reader essentially tries to associate sounds with letters or letter combinations. An emphasis on sounding out in and of itself is a limited strategy because it doesn't teach or make children aware of the importance of monitoring what is read for comprehension. A teacher builds a child's metacognition when sounding out is taught in conjunction with making sense. For example, a teacher follows up a suggestion to sound out an unfamiliar word by asking, "Does the word make sense? Does what you read sound like language?"

Option 3, taking an educated guess, asks the reader to identify a word that makes sense in the context of the sentence in which the word is located or the text itself. The **implicit** message to the reader is that reading is supposed to make sense. If a child provides a word other than the unfamiliar word but preserves the meaning of the text, the teacher would be instructionally and theoretically consistent by praising the child and encouraging him to continue reading.

The fourth option, say "blank" and keep on reading, is also a metacognitive strategy for word identification because it shows the reader that reading is not as much a word-perfect process as it is a meaning-making process. No one word should stop a reader cold. If the reader is monitoring the text for meaning, he may be able to return to the word and identify it or decide that the word wasn't that important to begin with.

The teacher can make the implicit messages about reading strategies **explicit.** Throughout this book, we will use terms associated with explicit instruction: *modeling, demonstrating, explaining, rationale-building, thinking aloud, reflecting.* From an instructional point of view, these terms reflect practices that allow the teacher to help students develop *metacognitive awareness* and *strategic knowledge*. For example, Arch, the first-grade teacher discussed earlier in this chapter, chooses to engage the reader—after she has taken a good guess at the unfamiliar word and completes reading—in a brief discussion of the importance of identifying words that "make sense" and "sound like language" in the context of what's being read. Such metacognitive discussions have the potential to build self-knowledge and task knowledge and also to strengthen the reader's self-monitoring abilities.

**SELF-KNOWLEDGE** ◆ Do children know what reading is for? Do they know what the reader's role is? Do they know their options? Are they aware of their strengths as readers and learners? Do they recognize that some texts are harder than others and that all texts should not be read alike? Questions such as these reflect the self-knowledge component of metacognition. When readers are aware of *self* in relation to *texts* and *tasks*, they are in a better position to use reading strategies effectively (Armbruster, Echols, & Brown, 1982).

**TASK KNOWLEDGE** ◆ Experienced readers are strategic readers. They use their task knowledge to meet the demands inherent in difficult texts. For example, they know how to analyze a reading task, reflect on what they know or don't know about the text to be read, establish purposes and plans for reading, and evaluate their progress in light of purposes for reading. Experienced readers are often aware of whether they have understood what they have read. And if they haven't, they know what to do when comprehension fails.

**SELF-MONITORING** ◆ Reading becomes second nature to most of us as we develop experience and maturity with the process. Experienced readers operate on "automatic pilot" as they read, until they run into a problem that disrupts the flow. For example, read the following passage:

> The boys' arrows were nearly gone, so they sat down on the grass and stopped hunting. Over at the edge of the woods they saw Henry making a bow to a little girl who was coming down the road. She had tears in her dress and also tears in her eyes. She gave Henry a note, which he brought over to the group of young hunters. Read to the boys it caused great excitement. After a minute but rapid examination of their weapons, they ran down the valley. Does were standing at the edge of the lake, making an excellent target. (author unknown)

Now reflect on the experience. At what point during reading did a "built-in sensor" in your head begin to signal to you that something was wrong? At what point in the passage did you become aware that some of the words you were misreading were homonyms and that you were choosing the inappropriate pronunciations of one or more of the homonyms? What did you do to rectify your misreadings? Why do you suppose the "sensor" signaled disruptions in your reading?

As experienced readers, we expect reading to make sense. And as we interact with a text, the metacognitive "sensor" in each of us monitors whether what we're reading is making sense.

What reader hasn't chosen an inappropriate pronunciation, come across a concept too difficult to grasp, or become lost in an author's line of reasoning? What experienced reader hasn't sensed that a text is too difficult to understand the first time around? The difference, of course, between the experienced and inexperienced reader is that the former knows when something's wrong and often employs correction strategies to get back on track. The strategic reader also has the confidence and belief that he or she can succeed in understanding what is read, leading to more motivation and engagement in the reading process (Vacca, 2006). This is what monitoring comprehension is all about.

Metacognitive ability is related to both age and reading experience (Stewart & Tei, 1983). Older students are more strategic in their reading than younger students, and

MIDDLE GRADES

**HOMEWORK EXERCISE: READING**

Go to the Homework and Exercises section in Chapter 1 of MyEducationLab to read "The Sweet Work of Reading" to further explore the reading processes children bring to the classroom.

STANDARDS
1.1, 1.3

good readers demonstrate more ability to use metacognition to deal with problems that arise during reading than readers with limited proficiency. Nevertheless, the instructional implications of metacognition are evident throughout this book. Becoming literate is a process of becoming aware not only of oneself as a reader but also of strategies that help solve problems that arise before, during, and after reading. A classroom environment that nurtures metacognitive functioning is crucial to children's literacy development.

# Reading from a Language Perspective

Cognition and language are crucial components in human development. Although the acquisition of language is a complex process, many children understand and use all of the basic language patterns by the time they are 6 years old.

A child's apparent facility with language is best understood by recognizing the active relationship between cognition and language.

Jean Piaget (1973) spent most of his life observing children and their interactions with their environment. His theory of cognitive development helps explain that language acquisition is influenced by more general cognitive attainments. As children explore their environment, they interpret and give meaning to the events they experience. The child's need to interact with immediate surroundings and to manipulate objects is critical to language development. From a Piagetian view, language reflects thought and does not necessarily shape it.

Lev Vygotsky (1962, 1978), the acclaimed Russian psychologist, also viewed children as active participants in their own learning. However, at some point in their early development, children begin to acquire language competence; as they do so, language stimulates cognitive development. Gradually, Vygotsky believed, they begin to regulate their own problem-solving activities through the mediation of egocentric speech. In other words, children carry on external dialogues with themselves. Eventually external dialogue gives way to inner speech.

According to both Piaget and Vygotsky, children must be actively involved in order to grow and learn. Merely reacting to the environment isn't enough. An important milestone in a child's development, for example, is the ability to analyze means–ends relationships. When this occurs, children begin to acquire the ability to use language to achieve goals.

The linguistic sophistication of young children cannot be underestimated or taken for granted. Yet the outdated notion that children develop speech by imitation still persists among people who have little appreciation or knowledge of oral language development. The key to learning oral language lies in the opportunities children have to explore and experiment with language toward purposeful ends. As infants grow into toddlers, they learn to use language as an instrument for their intentions: "I want" becomes a favorite phrase. No wonder M. A. K. Halliday (1975) described learning oral language as a "saga in learning to mean."

STANDARDS
1.1, 1.3

When teachers embrace reading as a language process, they understand the importance of learning oral language but are also acutely aware that written language develops in humans along parallel lines. Children learn to use written language in much the same manner that they learn to use oral language—naturally and purposefully. As Goodman (1986) put it, "Why do people create and learn written language? They need it! How do they learn it? The same way they learn oral language, by using it in authentic literary events that meet their needs" (p. 24).

Ultimately, there's only one way to become proficient as a writer and reader, and that's by writing and reading. When opportunities abound for children to engage in real literacy events (writing and reading), they grow as users of written language.

When language is splintered into its parts and the parts are isolated from one another for instructional purposes, learning to read becomes more difficult than it needs to be. The whole language concept, originated by Kenneth and Yetta Goodman, reflects the way some teachers think about language and literacy. They plan teaching activities that support students in their use of all aspects of language in learning to read. Keeping language "whole" drives home the point that splintering written language into bits and pieces, to be taught and learned separately from one another, makes learning to read harder, not easier. According to Kenneth Goodman (1986):

> Many school traditions seem to have actually hindered language development. In our zeal to make it easy, we've made it hard. How? Primarily by breaking whole (natural) language up into bite-size, but abstract little pieces. It seemed so logical to think that little children could best learn simple little things. We took apart the language and turned it into words, syllables, and isolated sounds. Unfortunately, we also postponed its natural purpose—the communication of meaning—and turned it into a set of abstractions, unrelated to the needs and experiences of the children we sought to help. (p. 7)

Support for more holistic teaching comes from two areas of language inquiry: **psycholinguistics** and **sociolinguistics.**

## Psycholinguistics and Reading

A psycholinguistic view of reading combines a psychological understanding of the reading process with an understanding of how language works. Psycholinguistic inquiries into the reading process suggest that readers act on and interact with written language in an effort to make sense of a text. Reading is not a passive activity; it is an active thinking process that takes place "behind the eyes." Nor is reading an exact process. All readers make mistakes—"miscues" as Kenneth Goodman (1973) calls them. Why? Miscues are bound to occur because readers are continually *anticipating* meaning and *sampling* a text for information cues based on their expectations. In fact, readers search for and coordinate *information cues* from three distinct systems in written language: the **graphophonemic,** the **syntactic,** and the **semantic.**

STANDARD 1.1

**GRAPHOPHONEMIC SYSTEM** ◆ The print itself provides readers with a major source of information: The graphic symbols or marks on the page represent speech sounds. The more experience readers have with written language, the more they learn about regular and irregular letter–sound relationships. Experienced readers acquire enough knowledge of sounds associated with letter symbols that they do not have to use all the available graphic information in a word in order to decode or recognize it.

**SYNTACTIC SYSTEM** ◆ Readers possess knowledge about how language works. *Syntactic information* is provided by the grammatical relationships within sentence patterns. In other words, readers use their knowledge of the meaningful arrangement of words in sentences to construct meaning from text material.

The order of words provides important information cues during reading. For example, although children may be able to read the words *"ran race the quickly children the,"* they would make little sense out of what they read. The meaning is not clear until the words are arranged like so: *"The children quickly ran the race."* In addition, readers use syntactic information to anticipate a word or phrase that "must come next" in a sentence because of its grammatical relationship to other words in the sentence. For example, most children reading the sentence *"I saw a red ___ ."* would probably fill in the blank with a noun because they intuitively know how language works.

**SEMANTIC SYSTEM** ◆ The semantic system of language stores the schemata that readers bring to a text in terms of background knowledge, experiences, conceptual understandings, attitudes, beliefs, and values.

## Sociolinguistics and Reading

In the child's first several years, skill in spoken language develops naturally and easily. Children discover what language does for them. They learn that language is a tool they can use and understand in interactions with others in their environment. They also learn that language is intentional; it has many purposes. Among the most obvious is communication. The more children use language to communicate, the more they learn the many special functions it serves.

Halliday (1975) viewed language as a reflection of what makes us uniquely human. His monumental work explored how language functions in our day-to-day interactions and serves the personal, social, and academic facets of our lives. Frank Smith (1977) expanded Halliday's functions of language by describing ten of its uses. He proposed that "the uses to which language is put lie at the heart of language comprehension and learning" (p. 640). The implications of this proposition for learning to read will become apparent throughout this book.

These are the ten uses of language Smith (1977, p. 640) described:

1. *Instrumental.* "I want." (Language as a means of getting things, satisfying material needs)
2. *Regulatory.* "Do as I tell you." (Controlling the behavior, feelings, or attitudes of others)
3. *Interactional.* "Me and you." (Getting along with others, establishing relative status) Also, "Me against you." (Establishing separateness)
4. *Personal.* "Here I come." (Expressing individuality, awareness of self, pride)
5. *Heuristic.* "Tell me why." (Seeking and testing knowledge)
6. *Imaginative.* "Let's pretend." (Creating new worlds, making up stories, poems)
7. *Representational.* "I've got something to tell you." (Communicating information, descriptions, expressing propositions)
8. *Divertive.* "Enjoy this." (Puns, jokes, riddles)
9. *Authoritative/contractual.* "How it must be." (Statutes, laws, regulations, agreements, contracts)
10. *Perpetuating.* "How it was." (Records, histories, diaries, notes, scores)

Children recognize the meaningfulness of written language once they become aware of its uses. As Halliday (1975) noted, if children have difficulty learning to read, it is probably because beginning instruction often has had little to do with what they have learned about the uses of oral language.

The work of Harste, Woodward, and Burke (1984), which explores the literacy development of preschool children, reveals that even 2-year-olds use language strategies, often in concert, to make sense of written language. Four strategies in particular characterize the literacy expectations of beginners:

1. *Text intent.* Children expect written language to be meaningful. Their encounters with text support the expectation that they will be able to re-create and construct an author's message.
2. *Negotiability.* Because children expect print to make sense, they use whatever knowledge and resources they possess to negotiate meaning—to create a meaningful message. Negotiation suggests that reading is a give-and-take process between reader and author.
3. *Risk-taking.* Children experiment with how written language works. They take risks. They make hypotheses and then test them out. Risk-taking situations permit children to grow as language users.
4. *Fine-tuning.* An encounter with a written language becomes a resource for subsequent literacy events and situations. The more children interact with authors and texts, the better they get at constructing meaning.

Because reading is uniquely human, learning to read requires sharing, interaction, and collaboration. Parent–child, teacher–student, and student–student relations and participation patterns are essential in learning to read. To what extent do children entering school have experience operating and communicating in a group as large as that found in the typical classroom? Children must learn the ropes. In many cases, kindergarten may be the first place where children must follow and respect the rules that govern how to operate and cooperate in groups. Not only must they know how and when to work independently and how and when to share and participate, but they must also learn the rules that govern communicative behavior. This is essential for students of all ages.

*Communicative competence*, as defined by Hymes (1974), develops differently in different children because they have not all had the same set of experiences or opportunities to engage in communication in the home or in the community. Some preschoolers have acquired more competence than others as to when and when not to speak and as to what to talk about, with whom, where, and in what manner. The sociolinguistic demands on a 5- or 6-year-old are staggering. As students age more communicative competence develops. However, although middle school students have increased communication competence, motivation to participate in the social context of the classroom may be lacking. Therefore, "reading instruction must be rooted in the connections of texts to engagement in and simulations of actions, activities, and interactions—to real and imagined material and social worlds" (Gee, 2004, p. 119).

Because a large part of learning to read will depend on the social and cultural context of the classroom, opportunities must abound for discussions and conversations between teacher and student and among students. Within this context, students must demonstrate (1) an eagerness to be independent; (2) an unquenchable zest to explore the new and unknown; (3) the courage to take risks, try things out, and experience success as well as some defeat; (4) the enjoyment of being with others and learning from them; and (5) a willingness to view themselves as readers.

# Models of Reading

Models of the reading process often depict the act of reading as a communication event between a sender (the writer) and a receiver of information (the reader). Generally speaking, language information flows from the writer to the reader in the sense that the writer has a message to send and transmits it through print to the reader, who then must interpret its meaning. Reading models have been developed to describe the way readers use language information to construct meaning from print. *How* a reader translates print to meaning is the key issue in the building of models of the reading process. This issue has led to the development of three classes of models: *bottom-up*, *top-down*, and *interactive*.

**BOTTOM-UP MODELS OF READING** ◆ **Bottom-up models** assume that the process of translating print to meaning begins with the print. The process is initiated by **decoding** graphic symbols into sounds. The reader first identifies features of letters; links these features together to recognize letters; combines letters to recognize spelling patterns; links spelling patterns to recognize words; and then proceeds to sentence-, paragraph-, and text-level processing.

**TOP-DOWN MODELS OF READING** ◆ **Top-down models** assume that the process of translating print to meaning begins with the reader's prior knowledge. The process is initiated by making predictions or "educated guesses" about the meaning of some unit of print. Readers decode graphic symbols into sounds to "check out" hypotheses about meaning.

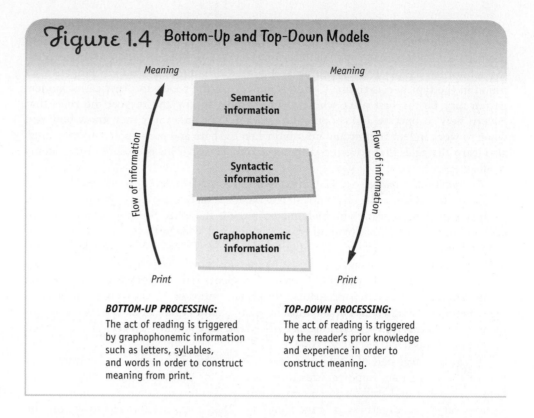

**Figure 1.4** Bottom-Up and Top-Down Models

*Meaning*                          *Meaning*

Semantic information

Syntactic information

Graphophonemic information

Flow of information

Flow of information

*Print*                            *Print*

**BOTTOM-UP PROCESSING:**
The act of reading is triggered by graphophonemic information such as letters, syllables, and words in order to construct meaning from print.

**TOP-DOWN PROCESSING:**
The act of reading is triggered by the reader's prior knowledge and experience in order to construct meaning.

**INTERACTIVE MODELS OF READING** ◆ **Interactive models** assume that the process of translating print to meaning involves making use of both prior knowledge and print. The process is initiated by making predictions about meaning and/or decoding graphic symbols. The reader formulates hypotheses based on the interaction of information from semantic, syntactic, and graphophonemic sources of information.

The terms *top-down, bottom-up,* and *interactive* are used extensively in the fields of communication and information processing. When these terms are used to describe reading, they also explain how language systems operate in reading.

Models of reading attempt to describe how readers use semantic, syntactic, and graphophonemic information in translating print to meaning. It is precisely in these descriptions that bottom-up, top-down, and interactive models of reading differ. Figures 1.4 and 1.5 show the flow of information in each reading model. Note that these illustrations are general depictions of information processing during reading and do not refer specifically to models such as those in Singer and Ruddell's *Theoretical Models and Processes of Reading* (1985).

## Bottom-Up Models

As illustrated in Figure 1.4, the process of deriving meaning from print in bottom-up models is triggered by graphic information embedded in print. This is why bottom-up models are described as being "data-driven." Data in this case are the letters and words on the page. A prototype model for bottom-up processing was constructed by Gough (1985), who attempted to show what happens in "one second of reading." In Gough's model, reading involves a series of steps that occur within milliseconds in the mind of the reader. The reader takes one "linguistic step" after another, beginning with the recognition of key features in letters and continuing letter by letter, word by word, and sentence by sentence until reaching the top—the meaning of the text being read.

The reading model by Samuels (1994) is also essentially bottom-up. However, the Samuels model incorporates the idea of *automaticity*. The concept of automaticity suggests

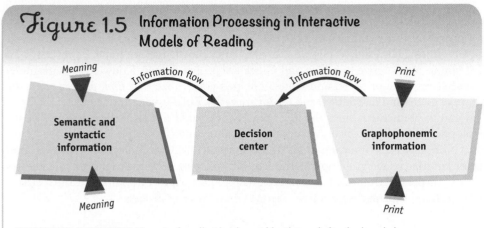

**Figure 1.5  Information Processing in Interactive Models of Reading**

Meaning

Information flow

Information flow

Print

**Semantic and syntactic information**

**Decision center**

**Graphophonemic information**

Meaning

Print

**INTERACTIVE PROCESSING:** The act of reading is triggered by the reader's prior knowledge and experience as well as graphophonemic information in order to construct meaning.

that humans can attend to only one thing at a time but may be able to process many things at once as long as no more than one requires attention. Automaticity is similar to putting an airplane on automatic pilot and freeing the pilot to direct his or her attention to other things.

In reading, *decoding* and *comprehending* vie for the reader's attention. Readers must learn to process graphophonemic information so rapidly that they are free to direct attention to comprehending the text material for meaning.

The young reader is similar to the novice automobile driver. When learning to drive a car, the beginner finds the mechanics of operating the automobile so demanding that he or she must focus exclusively on driving. However, with practice, the skilled driver pays little conscious attention to the mechanics of driving and is able to converse with a passenger or listen to the radio. Likewise, the beginning reader must practice decoding print to speech so rapidly that decoding becomes automatic. As beginners become more fluent in decoding, they can devote their attention to comprehending the writer's message.

## Top-Down Models

Top-down models emphasize that information processing during reading is triggered by the reader's prior knowledge and experience in relation to the writer's message. Obviously, there are no pure top-down models because readers must begin by focusing on print. As opposed to being data-driven, top-down models are said to be conceptually driven. That is to say, ideas or concepts in the mind of a reader trigger information processing during reading. As Frank Smith (1985) put it, "The more you already know, the less you need to find out" (p. 15). In other words, the more readers know in advance about the topic to be read, the less they need to use graphic information on the page.

To get a better idea of how reading is conceptually driven, read the following story:

FLAN AND GLOCK
Flan was a flim.
Glock was a plopper.
It was unusual for a flim and a plopper to be crods, but
Flan and Glock were crods. They medged together.
Flan was keaded to moak at a mox. Glock wanted to kead
there too. But the lear said he could not kead there.
Glock anged that the lear said he could not kead there
because he was a plopper.

Although you've never heard of Flan and Glock and don't know what a flim or a plopper is, it is not difficult to interpret from this short story that Glock was discriminated against. How did you figure this out? Your knowledge of capitalization may have led you to hypothesize that Flan and Glock are proper names. Knowledge of grammar, whether intuitive or overt, undoubtedly helped you realize that *flim, plopper, crods,* and *mox* are nouns and that *medged* and *keaded* are verbs. Finally, your knowledge of the world led you to predict that since the lear said, "Glock could not kead there because he was a plopper," Glock is probably a victim of discrimination.

Note that these interpretations of the story are "educated guesses." However, both prior knowledge and graphophonemic information were required to make these guesses. From our perspective, reading is rarely totally top-down or bottom-up. A third class of models helps explain the interactive nature of the reading process.

## Interactive Models

Neither prior knowledge nor graphophonemic information is used exclusively by readers. Interactive models as illustrated in Figure 1.5 suggest that the process of reading is initiated by formulating hypotheses about meaning *and* by decoding letters and words. According to Kamil and Pearson (1979), readers assume either an active or a passive role, depending on the strength of their hypotheses about the meaning of the reading material. If readers bring a great deal of knowledge to the material, chances are that their hypotheses will be strong and that they will process the material actively, making minimal use of graphophonemic information. Passive reading, by contrast, often results when readers have little experience with or knowledge of the topic to be read. They rely much more on the print itself for information cues.

Effective readers know how to interact with print in an effort to understand a writer's message. Effective readers adapt to the material based on their purposes for reading. Purpose dictates the strategies that readers use to translate print to meaning. Two of the most appropriate questions that readers can ask about a selection are "What do I need to know?" and "How well do I already know it?" These two questions help readers establish purposes for reading and formulate hypotheses during reading. The questions also help readers decide how to *coordinate* prior knowledge and graphophonemic information.

Note that the models of reading just described don't take into consideration the social nature of reading and learning to read. In this sense, they're incomplete. However, models are useful in some respects: They help you reflect on your beliefs, assumptions, and practices related to reading instruction—the topic of Chapter 2.

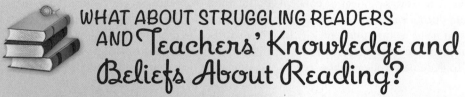

WHAT ABOUT STRUGGLING READERS AND *Teachers' Knowledge and Beliefs About Reading?*

Many children struggle with reading and learning to read. They appear to apply strategies in somewhat less efficient and effective ways. They also are often insecure about their reading abilities. Therefore struggling readers require modified instruction that meets their particular needs.

Teachers' instructional practices and decisions (planning, interactions, and assessments) directly influence all students' literate activities and attitudes toward reading and writing. It is important for teachers to recognize their beliefs about reading and learning to read and to articulate those beliefs. Only after this self-reflection and

STANDARD
5.1

awareness can teachers develop a belief system that will influence instructional practices and strategies for all readers, including those who struggle, focusing on their individual needs.

Consider your overall beliefs about reading and learning to read. Do your beliefs change when you think about struggling readers? Why or why not? If so, how? These are important questions that teachers need to ask themselves regarding children who find reading difficult.

## Summary

We organized this chapter around knowledge and beliefs about reading to suggest that teachers view what they do in the classroom through belief systems that focus and clarify their instructional decisions and practices. Belief systems bring into focus what teachers know, believe, and value—not only about their roles as classroom teachers of reading but also about reading, readers, curriculum, and instruction. Teachers develop belief systems about reading and learning to read through personal, practical, and professional study and experience.

Because we believe that all teachers are theorists in that they have reasons for their instructional decisions, we examined the reading process from cognitive, linguistic, and social perspectives and described three models that involve the processing of language information.

The next step in thinking about reading and learning to read is to study how belief systems influence instructional practices and strategies. Chapter 2 explores the concept of comprehensive reading.

## Teacher Action Research

Teachers who engage in reflection and inquiry find themselves asking questions and observing closely what goes on in their classrooms. Action research is a way for teachers who want to reflect and inquire to better understand within the context of their own teaching more about themselves as teachers and their students as learners. At the end of each chapter, several ideas for action research are presented. Some are intended to be done in the field; others are for the classroom.

STANDARD
5.3

1. Observe a teacher in an elementary school. Record what you see and hear during reading instruction time. Based on the interactions recorded between teacher and students, what did you learn about the teacher's knowledge and beliefs about literacy?

2. Using the idea of the reading autobiography, prepare an autobiographical narrative following the directions in Figure 1.1. Share your autobiographical sketch with other members of the class or with colleagues in your school, or with a family member or roommate. What differences in reading development and attitude are evident? What similarities exist?

3. Suppose you are going to be a guest speaker to a group of preservice teachers. The topic is "Influences on Reading Instruction." You have time for a 15 minute presentation. What would you say?

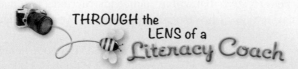

THROUGH the
LENS of a
Literacy Coach

**4.** Take time to observe a reading or content area reading teacher. What is the teacher doing well? What evidence did you see? How might you guide the teacher to improve his or her skills?

## Related Web Sites

*International Reading Association*
**www.reading.org**
Information is provided on membership, online resources, programs, articles, and other professional development opportunities.

*Literacy Coaching Clearinghouse*
**www.literacycoachingonline.org**
This site provides information and research about the practice of literacy coaching.

*National Council of Teachers of English*
**www.ncte.org**
Information is provided on membership, online resources, programs, articles, and other professional development opportunities.

*Public Law 107-110*
**www.ed.gov/policy/elsec/leg/esea02/index.html**
The U.S. Department of Education provides information on Public Law 107-110, the No Child Left Behind Act of 2001.

*Reading First*
**www.ed.gov/programs/readingfirst/index.html**
The U.S. Department of Education provides information for the Reading First initiative of 2002.

*Reading Online*
**www.readingonline.org**
This site links to an electronic journal of the International Reading Association.

*Standards for Reading Professionals, Revised 2003*
**www.reading.org/resources/issues/reports/professional_standards.html**
This site on the International Reading Association's web site links to the standards for reading professionals.

*Teaching Children to Read*
**www.nichd.nih.gov/publications/nrp/intro.htm**
The National Reading Panel reports on teaching reading.

*What Is Evidence-Based Reading Instruction?*
**www.reading.org/positions.html**
The International Reading Association gives its position statement on evidence-based reading instruction.

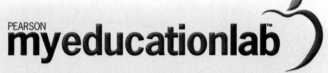

Now go to the Vacca et al. *Reading and Learning to Read,* Seventh Edition, MyEducationLab course at **www.myeducationlab.com** to

- Take a pretest to assess your initial comprehension of the chapter content
- Study chapter content with your individualized study plan
- Take a posttest to assess your understanding of chapter content
- Engage in multimedia exercises to help you build a deeper and more applied understanding of chapter content

# CHAPTER 2

# Approaches to Reading Instruction

Standards found in this chapter:
- ► 1.1
- ► 1.2
- ► 1.3
- ► 1.4
- ► 2.1
- ► 2.2
- ► 2.3
- ► 4.1
- ► 4.2
- ► 4.3

## In this chapter,
### YOU WILL DISCOVER:

- The relationship between comprehensive instruction and beliefs about reading
- How beliefs are connected to different theoretical models of reading
- Curricular differences among bottom-up and top-down models of reading
- Instructional approaches in the teaching of reading
- What it means to achieve a comprehensive program

## Concept Map

### APPROACHES TO READING INSTRUCTION

**BELIEF SYSTEMS AND APPROACHES TO INSTRUCTION**

**CURRICULUM PERSPECTIVES**

Bottom-Up          Top-Down

**INSTRUCTIONAL APPROACHES**

Literature-Based          Integrated Language Arts

Language-Experience          Basal Reading

Technology-Based

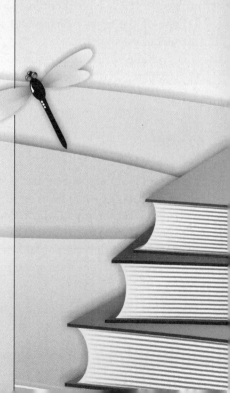

Katie attended a suburban private college. The college offered a small teacher education program. Katie's reading and reading-related courses included elementary reading, children's literature, language arts, and a class on reading diagnosis and evaluation. Katie participated in numerous hours of field experience throughout her junior and senior years. She especially enjoyed her reading courses because the instructor "challenged us to think about reading as a language, not just skills to be taught in itsy-bitsy pieces. She taught us how to align the curriculum with the standards and to select appropriate materials." During many of her visits in the field Katie noticed the instruction wasn't congruent with what she was learning in her reading classes. Many of the teachers were teaching right out of the basal reader and using worksheets to teach critical skills to children. The incongruity of what she was seeing in the field was the subject of much inquiry and debate: Should future teachers maintain the status quo, or should they be innovators who bring new ideas into the teaching profession?

Katie's school is situated in the inner city. About 70 percent of the children are from minority backgrounds with 20 percent English language learners (ELLs). The principal is considered a "strong instructional leader." She believes that an "effective school must maintain high expectations for student achievement, an orderly climate, and a rigorous assessment program to monitor the children's progress." As a result, the principal is a proponent of the teach, test, teach model for instruction. She indicates that it is OK to try out new teaching strategies, "as long as you are teaching the skills the children need." How well children score on achievement tests is one of the main indicators of a teacher's success in the school.

Katie feels the pressure of "having to teach skills in isolation." This approach, she admits, is "not what I believe in," but she feels obligated to "follow the lead of all of the other teachers." She is especially concerned about her ELL students being taught in this manner. "I know that if I start with the children's native language and build on it, I'll help them expand their English vocabulary. I can't do that with a skills workbook."

DIVERSITY

Prior to the opening of school Katie spent two weeks planning what she was going to do. One of her first tasks was to fix up the room so that it would "invite kids to learn." The room has a reading corner and a writer's nook. Both areas are stocked with children's books, paper, pencils, markers, scissors, and posters. The reading corner has an area rug, a book rack, and an old couch that Katie got from her parents. The writer's nook has a round table and several computers. She remembers being excited about getting the children in the writing nook and on the Internet: "I have some ideas for using online discussion boards and I read about how some classes are publishing podcasts about what they are learning. I'd like to try that in my classroom."

The reality of teaching reading skills is omnipresent, despite Katie's attempts to provide meaningful experiences for her second graders. Frequently she is required to test children to determine mastery of the skills, and she must also use a test preparation booklet to prepare them for the standards-based state achievement tests. The principal requires that weekly lesson plans be in her office in advance on Friday afternoons. Katie's plans are returned on Monday morning, before the start of school, with comments and notations.

In practice, Katie tries to teach a dual reading curriculum. She teaches the skills using the workbooks in the morning and then she "smuggles in the good stuff" whenever she can find the time. Needless to say, Katie goes home each day exhausted and frustrated. She complains that she spends more time assessing children than she spends on instruction. The reading corner and writer's nook are underused, and she hasn't even had time to think about the notion of creating a class podcast. "At least," Katie says, "I still read the class a story every day. I know this is important for building vocabulary for all of the children, especially the English language learners."

Although she tries to combine skills teaching with more top-down activities, Katie's instruction is out of balance. Her philosophical stance is in direct conflict with the principal's beliefs about learning to read. The external pressure to conform to the principal's expectations for skills instruction and required assessments forces Katie to put her knowledge and beliefs about learning to read on hold. Although she attempts to mesh literature and language-rich activities and new ways to use technology with skills instruction, it simply doesn't work for her because she is caught between contrasting instructional methodologies. Her efforts to be "eclectic" simply create a disjointed mishmash of instructional activity.

This chapter helps you make connections between theory and practice as you explore issues related to achieving a comprehensive approach to the teaching of reading. First, we explore theoretical perspectives and belief systems related to the teaching of reading. Next, you will learn how curricular issues and approaches to teaching reading have emerged. In the final section, you will read about approaches to teaching a comprehensive reading program. As you study the concept map, note the relationships among beliefs, curricular perspectives, and approaches to instruction.

# Belief Systems and Approaches to Literacy Instruction

In the search to build a comprehensive literacy program, it is critical for teachers to be aware of the needs of students. Consider this quote from the International Reading Association's (IRA) position statement "Using Multiple Methods of Beginning Reading Instruction" (1999b), which is still distributed today:

STANDARDS 1.1, 1.2

> There is no single combination of methods that can successfully teach all children to read. Therefore, teachers must have a strong knowledge of multiple methods for teaching reading and a strong knowledge of the children in their care so they can create the appropriate balance of methods needed for the children they teach. (para. 2)

Literacy programs require an informed philosophical stance. A teacher's philosophical stance, or belief system, is crucial to achieving balance in the teaching of reading because instruction involves the kinds of decisions that teachers make based on how children learn to read and how they can best be taught.

As noted in Chapter 1, what teachers do to teach reading usually reflects what they know and believe about reading and learning to read. One way to examine your beliefs about reading and learning to read is to connect them to theoretical models of the reading process. Does your philosophical stance reflect a bottom-up view of reading? Top-down? Or interactive? Throughout this book, we contend that teachers who use a more **comprehensive approach** to teaching reading will meet the needs of their students when their instructional decisions and practices reflect the interactive nature of the reading process. Interactive models underscore the important contributions that both the reader *and* the text make in the reading process.

One important way to define who we are as teachers of reading is by talking about *what* we do and *why* we do it or by observing one another in a teaching situation and asking *why* we did what we did. Another way is through self-examination and reflection. The tools that follow will help you inquire into your beliefs about reading in relation to instructional practices.

**HOMEWORK EXERCISE: VIDEO**

Go to the Homework and Exercises section in Chapter 2 of MyEducationLab to view the video entitled "Developing a Philosophy of Education" and reflect on your own philosophy as it applies to literacy instruction.

## Beliefs About Reading Interview

Your beliefs about how students learn to read in all likelihood lie on a continuum between concepts that reflect bottom-up, interactive, and top-down models of reading. By participating in the Beliefs About Reading Interview (see the Viewpoint in Box 2.1), you will get a *general indication* of where your beliefs about learning to read lie on the continuum illustrated in Figure 2.1 on page 37.

Your responses in the interview will often mirror **units of language** emphasized for instructional purposes. For example, the smallest units of written language are

# BOX 2.1

# Viewpoint

## What Do You Believe About Reading and Learning to Read?

*Use this opportunity to express your views and beliefs about reading.*

If you are a preservice teacher studying reading for the first time, you may find it difficult to answer some of the questions in Question Set A. However, we encourage you to respond to all of the questions based on any sources of knowledge and beliefs you currently hold about the reading process and how it should be taught. Knowledge sources may include your own school experiences, observations in the field, experiences as a reader, and previous study. Toward the end of the semester, you may wish to respond to the interview questions again. This will provide a good measure of the growth you have made in thinking about reading and learning to read. Team up with a partner, if possible, and take turns interviewing each other. Study the directions and respond to the appropriate set of questions in the Beliefs About Reading Interview.

Use Appendix A to analyze and interpret your beliefs about reading and learning to read. Appendix A will provide you with a general framework for determining whether you view reading and learning to read from a bottom-up, interactive, or top-down perspective.

## Beliefs About Reading Interview

*Directions:* Select Question Set A if you are preparing to become a teacher. Select Question Set B if you are presently a teacher. Respond to each question, thinking in terms of *your own* classroom—either the one in which you plan to teach or the one in which you now teach. As you respond to each question, explain *what* you (would) do and *why* you (would) do it.

### QUESTION SET A: PRESERVICE TEACHERS

1. You have just signed a contract for your first teaching position in an elementary school. Which goals for reading instruction do you feel most confident about making progress in during the school year?
2. Suppose that a student is reading orally in your class and makes a reading error. What is the first thing you will probably do? Why?
3. Another student in your class is reading orally and doesn't know a word. What are you going to do? Why?
4. You have read about and probably tried out different kinds of strategies and activities for teaching students to read. Which ones do you feel will be the *most* important in your classroom? Why?
5. What kinds of activities do you feel your students should be involved in for the *majority* of their reading instructional time? Why?
6. Here are the typical steps in a directed reading activity as suggested in basal reader manuals: (1) introduction of vocabulary, (2) motivation or setting purposes, (3) reading,

(4) questions and discussion after silent reading, and (5) skills practice for reinforcement. Rank these steps in order from *most* important to *least* important (not necessarily in the order you will follow them).
7. Is it important to introduce new vocabulary words *before* students read a selection? Why or why not?
8. Suppose your new students will be tested to give you information to help you decide how to instruct them in reading. What would this diagnostic test include, and what kind of information would you hope it gives you about your students?
9. During silent reading, what do you hope your students will do when they come to an unknown word?
10. Look at the oral reading mistakes that are underlined below on these transcripts of three readers. Which of the three readers would you judge as the best or most effective reader (Harste & Burke, 1977)?

channel
*Reader A:* I live near this <u>canal</u>. Men haul things up
channel
and down the <u>canal</u> in big boats.

2. candle
1. ca
*Reader B:* I live near this <u>canal</u>. Men haul things up
candle
and down the <u>canal</u> in big boats.

2. candle
1. ca
*Reader C:* I live near this <u>canal</u>. Men haul things up
cannel
and down the <u>canal</u> in big boats.

### QUESTION SET B: INSERVICE TEACHERS

1. Of all the goals for reading instruction that you have in mind as a teacher, which do you think you have made good progress toward accomplishing this year? Cite one or more and, for each, explain why.
2. What do you usually do when a student is reading orally and makes an oral reading error? Why?
3. What do you usually do when a student is reading orally and doesn't know a word? Why?
4. You probably use different kinds of strategies and activities in teaching reading. Which ones do you feel are the *most* important for your students? Why?
5. What kinds of activities do you feel students should be involved in for the *majority* of their reading instructional time? Why?
6. Here are the typical steps in a directed reading activity as suggested in basal reader manuals: (1) introduction of

*(Continued)*

## Viewpoint *(Continued)*

vocabulary, (2) motivation or setting purposes, (3) reading, (4) questions and discussion after silent reading, and (5) skills practice for reinforcement. Rank these steps in order from *most* important to *least* important (not necessarily in the order you follow them).

7. Is it important to introduce new vocabulary words before your students read a selection? Why or why not?

8. Assuming that your students were tested to provide you with information that helped you decide how to instruct

them in reading, what did diagnostic testing include? What kind of information did it give you about your individual students?

9. During silent reading, what do you hope your students do when they come to an unknown word?

10. Look at the oral reading mistakes that are underlined on the transcripts of three readers in item 10 of Question Set A. Which of these three readers do you deem the best or most effective reader?

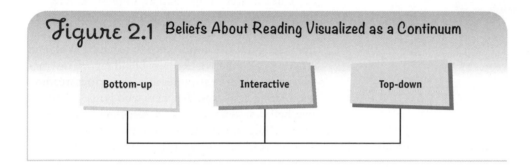

## Figure 2.1  Beliefs About Reading Visualized as a Continuum

letters; the largest unit is the text selection itself. In Figure 2.2 on page 38, concentric boxes help illustrate units of written language. The largest box represents the text as a whole. It may be a story, a poem, or an article on the Civil War. This unit of language is made up of *paragraphs*, which are made up of *sentences*, which are made up of *words*, which are made up of *letters*.

Teachers who possess a bottom-up belief system believe that students must decode letters and words before they are able to construct meaning from sentences, paragraphs, and larger text selections. Consequently, they view reading acquisition as mastering and integrating a series of word identification skills. Letter–sound relationships and word identification are emphasized instructionally. Because recognizing each word is believed to be an essential prerequisite to being able to comprehend the passage, accuracy in recognizing words is seen as important. If you hold a bottom-up set of beliefs, you may consider the practice of correcting oral reading errors as important in helping children learn to read. Or you may believe that helping students read a passage over and over is an important instructional activity because they develop accurate word recognition. Teachers who hold bottom-up belief systems often emphasize the teaching of skills in a sequential and systematic manner.

Teachers who have a top-down belief system consider reading for meaning an essential component of all reading instructional situations. They feel that the majority of reading or language arts instructional time should involve students in meaningful activities in which they read, write, speak, and listen. These teachers may also emphasize the importance of students' choosing their own reading material and enjoying the material they read. Sentences, paragraphs, and text selections are the units of language emphasized instructionally. Because recognizing each word is not considered an essential prerequisite to comprehending the passage, word errors during oral reading may not be corrected. Instead, the teacher may advocate noninterference during oral reading or encourage a student to use the context or meaning of the passage to identify unrecognized words.

STANDARD
1.4

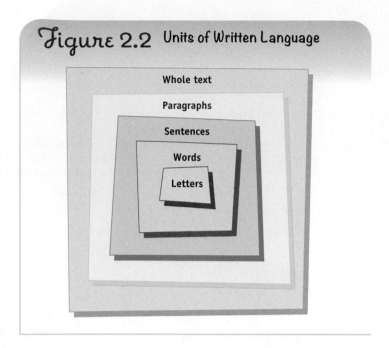

**Figure 2.2** Units of Written Language

Whole text

Paragraphs

Sentences

Words

Letters

Teachers who hold an interactive view of reading and learning to read fall between bottom-up and top-down belief systems on the beliefs continuum. Such teachers recognize that a reader processes both letter–sound cues and meaning cues during reading. Reading as a meaning-making activity is utmost in their thoughts about reading and learning to read, but they also believe that readers must be able to identify words quickly and accurately if they are going to make sense of what they read. Moreover, teachers with interactive belief systems integrate reading, writing, speaking, and listening activities; in the process of doing so, they *scaffold* children's literacy experiences. Scaffolding, as you will learn in more detail later in the chapter, suggests that teachers provide instructional support and guidance in the development of skills and strategies. Because they recognize the importance of teaching skills and strategies, interactive teachers blend *explicit* instruction with children's immersion in various reading and writing activities. Teachers who possess interactive belief systems are likely to achieve balance in the teaching of reading because they strike an equilibrium between children's immersion in reading and writing experiences and their development as skillful and strategic readers and writers.

Table 2.1 summarizes the beliefs defining bottom-up, top-down, and interactive belief systems.

## Theoretical Orientation to Reading Profile

The Theoretical Orientation to Reading Profile (TORP), designed by Diane De Ford in 1985, continues to be a highly reliable survey instrument used to determine teacher beliefs about practices in reading instruction. De Ford identifies three belief systems or theoretical orientations associated with instructional practices in beginning reading: *phonics*, *skills*, and *whole language*. Phonics and skills orientations are equivalent to bottom-up beliefs about reading. A whole language orientation is associated with top-down beliefs.

Appendix B contains the TORP survey and guidelines for determining your theoretical orientation toward reading. We invite you to complete the TORP survey because it will help you extend your thinking about instructional practices associated with learning to read. A teacher who holds a bottom-up orientation, for example, is likely to enact a curriculum that is quite different from a teacher who maintains a top-down orientation. Understanding the difference is essential to a teacher's approach to teaching reading.

## Curriculum Perspectives

The term *curriculum* has various shades of meaning in education. The word as it is defined from its early Latin origins means literally "to run a course." In its broadest sense a curriculum may refer to all courses offered at a school—a set of courses and their content. One way to think about curriculum is that it represents

## Table 2.1  Defining Bottom-Up, Top-Down, and Interactive Beliefs About Reading

| STANDARD 1.1 | BOTTOM-UP BELIEFS ABOUT READING | TOP-DOWN BELIEFS ABOUT READING | INTERACTIVE BELIEFS ABOUT READING |
|---|---|---|---|
| Relationship of Word Recognition to Comprehension | Believe students must recognize each word in a selection to be able to comprehend the selection. | Believe students can comprehend a selection even when they are not able to identify each word. | Believe students can comprehend by identifying words quickly and accurately. |
| Use of Information Cues | Believe students should use word and letter–sound cues exclusively to identify unrecognized words. | Believe students should use meaning and grammatical cues in addition to letter–sound cues to identify unrecognized words. | Believe students process letter–sound and meaning cues simultaneously to identify unrecognized words. |
| View of Reading | Believe reading requires mastering and integrating a series of word identification skills. | Believe students learn to read through meaningful and authentic activities in which they read, write, speak, and listen. | Believe students learn to read by developing skills and strategies in meaningful contexts. |
| Units of Language Emphasized Instructionally | Emphasize letters, letter–sound relationships, and words. | Emphasize sentences, paragraphs, and text selections. | Emphasize letters, letter–sound relationships, words, sentences, paragraphs, and text selections. |
| Where Importance Is Placed Instructionally | View accuracy in identifying words as important. | View reading for meaning as important. | View accurate word identification as contributing to meaningful reading. |
| Assessment | Think students need to be assessed on discrete skills. | Think students need to be assessed on the kind of knowledge constructed through reading. | Think students need to be assessed on the basis of their performance in meaningful contexts. Assessment informs instruction. |

courses of study that are based on national, state, and local school district standards and policies. In the United States, the basic curriculum is established by each state with individual school districts making adjustments. This curriculum course of study provides a blueprint for instruction that teachers are expected to follow.

A more dynamic conception of curriculum, however, is that it reflects what teachers and students *do* as they engage in classroom activity. If curriculum represents what teachers and students actually do in the classroom, a teacher's beliefs about literacy learning invariably contribute to curriculum decisions. These decisions involve, among other things, (1) the instructional objectives the teacher emphasizes for the classroom literacy program; (2) the materials the teacher selects and uses for instruction; (3) the learning environment the teacher perceives as most conducive to children's development as readers and writers; (4) the practices, approaches, and instructional strategies the teacher uses to teach reading and writing; and (5) the kinds of assessment the teacher perceives are best to evaluate literacy learning.

Curriculum-related questions every teacher has struggled with (or is struggling with) concern the teaching of literacy skills and strategies: What should children know and be able to do as readers and writers? Which skills and strategies are important? How do I teach skills and strategies? Answers to these questions will differ, depending on the curriculum perspective underlying the literacy program. Two curriculum perspectives— bottom-up and top-down—each supported by differing assumptions and principles about learning to read and write, have resulted in dramatically different objectives, materials, practices, and decisions related to literacy instruction.

## Bottom-Up Curricula

**READERS AND TEXTBOOKS** ◆ *The New England Primer*, published for American colonists in the late 1600s, followed a strong bottom-up model of instruction. The alphabet was taught first; then vowels, consonants, double letters, italics, capitals, syllables, and so on were presented for instruction, in that order. Words were not introduced systematically in basal readers until the mid-1800s. Colonial children might meet anywhere from 20 to 100 new words on one page!

By the mid-1800s, the word method, silent reading, and reading to get information from content were introduced in basals. The classics, fairy tales, and literature by U.S. authors became the first supplementary reading materials. Colored pictures, subjects appealing to children's interests, and the teacher's manual had all been introduced by the 1920s. It was then that a work pad was used for seatwork and skills practice in grades 1 through 3.

Publishing companies began to expand and add new components or features to their basal reading programs around 1925. The preprimer, for example, was added to the basal program to introduce beginning readers to the series and build a beginning reading vocabulary (i.e., words recognized on sight). Inside illustrations and outside covers also became increasingly colorful. Word lists became the standard for choosing readers' vocabulary.

As the major author for the publishing house Scott Foresman, William S. Gray was probably responsible for much of the structure associated with the reading instruction that we experienced as children. Workbooks accompanied our reader. First we worked on skills; then we read for enjoyment. Each book had a different title, and much of the story content was supposed to be "realistic" narrative. Whether the content was or is realistic is an issue both publishers and classroom teachers continue to debate.

As the concept of reading readiness became more popular, teacher's manuals began adding more detail, and readiness books provided opportunities to practice prerequisite skills. One preprimer proliferated into two, three, or even four preprimers.

Instruction in basal reading programs depended in part on a strict adherence to the scope and sequence of reading skills. The terminology evolved from the 1948 *Ginn Basic Reader*, the objective of which was to provide a *vertical* arrangement of skill development and to ensure continuity in skill development (Smith, 1965, p. 285). Teacher's editions were keyed to the children's books, and diagnostic and achievement tests were developed. Basal reading programs had become more sophisticated and, to many teachers, unwieldy.

Until the 1960s, books in reading series were arranged according to grade placement. Grades evolved into levels (anywhere from 15 to 20) or, as it became known, the management system. By the 1970s, teachers and curriculum committees in general sought clarification about levels in relation to grades. As a result, publishers used the term *level* and cross-referenced this with its traditional grade equivalent.

Management systems became necessary when publishers significantly overhauled their reading series in the 1970s. The majority of textbook publishers added new components, particularly in the area of assessment, such as pre- and postskill tests, section tests, and end-of-book tests.

The reading series used in schools in the twenty-first century are a far cry, in both appearance and substance, from the first readers. Nevertheless, current reading books retain some of the features that were once innovative. The new basal reading series have grown noticeably in size and price. Though not prescribing the bottom-up teaching approach that was used in the 1600s, today's teacher's manual presents a dilemma that is at the same time intriguing, interesting, and a bit daunting: It often purports to include *everything* that any teacher will ever need to teach reading.

**THE FIRST-GRADE STUDIES** ◆ While publishing companies were busy overhauling their programs, the federal government founded the United States Cooperative Research Program in First-Grade Reading Instruction (Bond & Dykstra, 1967), a large government-funded study commonly referred to as the "First-Grade Studies." These studies were launched nationally in an effort to identify the best approaches to the teaching of reading. It was one of the most influential and ambitious undertakings in reading research during the twentieth century. The First-Grade Studies compiled data from 27 individual research projects examining the effects of instructional approaches on beginning reading and spelling achievement. These instructional approaches included phonics, linguistic readers, basal programs, initial teaching alphabet, literature-based reading, language experience, and various grouping schemes and combinations of instruction. The First-Grade Studies found that *no instructional approach was superior to the others* for students at either high or low levels of readiness. Instead, the findings suggest "that although no single method proved best, combinations of methods were associated with the highest achievement" (Shanahan & Neuman, 1997).

The First-Grade Studies, more than anything else, underscored the importance of the "teacher variable" in children's reading achievement. Teachers make a difference. The more informed and knowledgeable they are, the more teachers are able to deal with the complexities of literacy learning as they respond to the how, when, and why of instruction. A significant by-product of the studies was the redirection of instruction away from materials being used by teachers to teachers and their craft (Robinson, Faraone, Hittleman, & Unruh, 1990).

## Top-Down Curricula

Late in the twentieth century the bottom-up perspective was seriously challenged by educators whose belief system came from a whole language orientation. **Whole language** was a progressive, child-centered movement that took root in the 1960s and blossomed in the 1980s. A whole language curriculum reflects the belief that students learn to read through meaningful experiences. These experiences include students' reading, writing, speaking, and listening about things important to them.

Teachers who maintain a whole language perspective believe in weaving into their teaching the use of authentic texts for children to read, discuss, listen to, or write about. One of the main goals of a whole language curriculum is to support children in the skillful use of language. They develop skills and strategies, but they do so in the context of meaningful learning. The development of skills and strategies is not assumed to occur in linear progression as in a skills-based curriculum. Instead, children grow as readers and writers, both vertically and horizontally. Some children will experience periods of accelerated learning followed by plateaus in their development. Some may need more time than others to "roam in the known" before they make noticeable progress in their use of language. Teachers provide the type of supportive environment that enables learners to develop confidence and competence with language and its many uses.

**SOME PRINCIPLES UNDERLYING TOP-DOWN PRACTICES** ◆ Although classroom descriptions of whole language practices vary from teacher to teacher, some basic principles guide every teacher's actions. For example, teachers believe that language serves personal, social, and academic purposes in children's lives. Language therefore cannot be

**HOMEWORK EXERCISE: READING**

Go to the Homework and Exercises section in Chapter 2 of MyEducationLab to read "Whole Language Works: Sixty Years of Research" and develop a deeper understanding of the whole language approach to reading instruction.

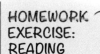

STANDARDS 1.1, 1.2, 1.3, 4.3

STANDARD 1.3

severed from a child's quest to make sense; language and meaning-making are intertwined. In addition, top-down teachers recognize that oral and written language are parallel; one is not secondary to the other. Language, whether oral or written, involves a complex system of symbols, rules, and constructs that govern the content and form of language in the context of its use. For the teacher, keeping language "whole" means not breaking it into bits and pieces or isolating the subsystems of language for instructional emphasis.

Respect for the child as a learner is paramount to a successful classroom environment. Top-down teachers believe that children are natural learners who learn how to read and write best under natural conditions. Because learning to read and write involves trial and error, top-down teachers hold firm to their convictions that children must learn to take risks in classroom contexts.

Classrooms are "communities" in a top-down curriculum. Teacher and students come together as a community of learners to engage in reading, writing, and other collaborative acts of meaning-making. Language learners help one another. They talk to each other about what they are writing and what they are reading. They engage in partnerships around projects and thematic studies. They share their understandings of how to solve problems encountered while reading and writing.

Although whole language has transformed the way many of today's teachers think about and enact a literacy curriculum in their classrooms, educators and policymakers in the late twentieth century questioned the effectiveness of a whole language curriculum to develop skillful and competent readers and writers and called for its removal as a basis of reading instruction. Some called for a return to a skills-based curriculum. Others called for balanced instruction in which teachers drew on the best practices of both skills-based curricula and a whole language curriculum, embroiling educators in the so-called "Reading Wars" referred to in Chapter 1.

Today, we find ourselves still seeking answers to the same questions. The recent national efforts to identify key research on difficulties in learning to read (Snow, Burns, & Griffin, 1998) and on best practices for reading instruction (National Institute of Child Health and Human Development, 2000) have become part of the enduring debate on how best to teach reading.

In a top-down curriculum, students and teachers work together as a community. They engage with one another in an effort to share understandings and to learn to solve problems together.

In the twenty-first century, however, the debate has continued to shift. Instead of arguing whether reading instruction should be *phonics-based, whole language, or balanced*, literacy experts currently debate what characterizes "scientifically based" reading instruction and what does not (Krashen, 2004; Lyon & Chhabra, 2004).

In addition, contemporary reading discussions focus on what have been coined *the essential components of a comprehensive reading program:* phonemic awareness, phonics, vocabulary, comprehension, and fluency. Reutzel and Cooter (2002) describe a comprehensive reading program as one that is "inclusive, research based, and meets the needs of learners so that no child is left behind" (p. 5). Although there is relative consensus that these components are important, discussion continues regarding *how much* and *how to* instruct children in each area, particularly with respect to those who struggle in reading (Allington, 2004). Regardless of where you stand on these issues, one thing is clear: Literacy experts continue to discuss, debate, and ask questions in the twenty-first century.

**CLASSROOM CONDITIONS FOR LEARNING** ◆ In the 1980s, Brian Cambourne conducted research on the origins of literacy and oral language development. In his research, he discovered that certain conditions must be in place for oral language acquisitions to take place. These conditions, since described by Cambourne (2001) and other theorists and educators (Goodman, 1986; Smith, 1989), hold true to a top-down philosophy. We contend that these conditions are critical for all classrooms. Cambourne's conditions have also influenced "thinking about working with adults as literacy coaches" (Puig & Froelich, 2007). Table 2.2 highlights these universal conditions.

## Table 2.2 Enhancing Literacy Learning

STANDARDS 1.1, 4.1, 4.2, 4.3

| | |
|---|---|
| Immersion | Must be immersed in written language. As learners, they need to engage in explorations of a wide range of texts, including those they produce by writing and those they use for reading. |
| Authenticity | Authentic texts may include children's actual writings as well as books representing different literary genres. Books may be big or little in size, wordless or predictable. Genuine texts may also serve the functional, everyday needs of children and may include "environmental print" (street signs, posters, boxtops, labels), reference materials, textbooks, newspapers, and magazines. |
| Engagement/Expectation | Engagement suggests the learner's commitment, mental involvement, and willingness to participate in a demonstration. Teachers create environments that reinforce the expectation that children will be successful and then provide the means for them to succeed. |
| Ownership | Children take ownership for their own learning, but teachers play an important role in helping children assume responsibility for their learning. For example, teachers may plan and gather resources for a thematic unit, but they include their students in setting goals and making decisions about texts, activities, and patterns of participation. |
| Time | Time to read and write also is essential. Children need time to engage in literacy events. Opportunities for reading, writing, speaking, and listening should occur throughout the day. |
| Response | If children are to realize their potential as language users, they need time not only to read and write but also to respond and share what they are reading or writing. |
| Approximation | Cambourne (1984) suggests that children approximate written language as they learn to read and write. With trial comes error. Conditions that favor trial-and-error learning help children become risk-takers. |
| Demonstration | Teachers and students alike demonstrate the role that literacy plays in their lives. Children need to encounter numerous demonstrations of reading and writing in use. |

# Instructional Approaches

Approaches to reading represent general instructional plans for achieving goals and objectives in a literacy curriculum. Instructional approaches respond to curriculum-related questions concerning content, methods, and materials in the teaching of reading. Skills-based curricula, for example, have spawned approaches to the teaching of reading that emphasize content, methods, and materials that are quite different from approaches associated with whole language curricula. When striving for a comprehensive program, teachers are likely to draw on their knowledge of different approaches in order to make decisions about instruction. Often, however, these decisions are consistent with teachers' beliefs about reading.

Several major approaches have dominated classroom literacy practice at various times in history and are still prevalent today. These include the basal reading approach, the language-experience approach, integrated language arts, literature-based instruction, and technology-based instruction. Figure 2.3 depicts these instructional approaches. No matter what approaches a teacher takes, each of the essential components of reading must be taught.

## The Basal Reading Approach

Contemporary basal reading programs, a prominent approach to classroom reading instruction, are examined at length in Chapter 13. Teachers who traditionally use the reading lesson or story with a small group of students during a specified time in a regular location are most likely to use the **basal reading approach.** They constitute the majority in terms of numbers of classroom teachers around the country using a particular approach.

Most of today's basal programs contain both narrative and expository text that encompass a wide variety of genres. They now feature anthologies and journals while

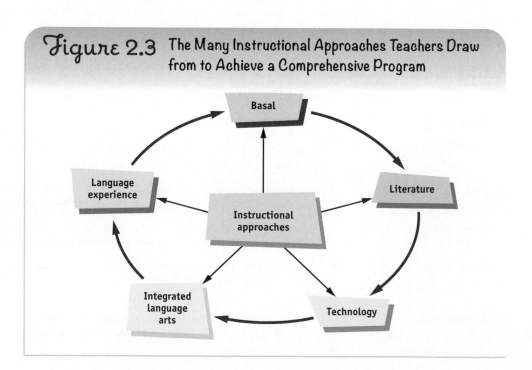

**Figure 2.3**   The Many Instructional Approaches Teachers Draw from to Achieve a Comprehensive Program

providing a scope and sequence of skills and strategies to be taught at various levels and grades. Depending on your beliefs, basal instruction could be considered a bottom-up approach, presenting skills to be taught in a sequence, or an interactive program, featuring unedited children's literature selections, strategy instruction, and writing opportunities.

In addition to having scope and sequence charts, the basal reading approach outlines a standard lesson framework with slight variations in differing programs. The *directed reading activity* (DRA) is the common label for the lesson framework in basal series. Components of a basal lesson are discussed in Chapter 13 and are important because they are based on the assumption that students learn to read by reading, writing, and talking about meaningful topics. As a major approach to reading instruction, basal reading is easily observable in elementary classrooms in small reading groups. Basal reading, frequently described as *eclectic*, runs the gamut from word recognition skills to extended and meaningful reading, discussing, and writing.

## The Language-Experience Approach

Teachers often use language-experience activities in combination with other approaches to reading instruction. However, the **language-experience approach (LEA)** is especially prevalent in kindergarten and first-grade classrooms. We will examine LEA in more depth later in chapters related to emergent literacy and beginning instruction.

LEA is often associated with *story dictation*, recording the language of children on chart paper or newsprint and using what they say as the basis for reading instruction. There is more to LEA, however, than just recording the ideas of students after they have taken a trip to the school nurse or the zoo. LEA includes planned and continuous activities such as individual- and group-dictated stories, the building of word banks of known words, creative writing activities, oral reading of prose and poetry by teacher and students, directed reading–thinking lessons, the investigation of interests using multiple materials, and keeping records of student progress. Computer technologies can play an important role in facilitating and transforming LEA into the digital-language-experience approach or D-LEA (Labbo, Love, & Ryan, 2007; Labbo, Eakle, & Montero, 2002). Multimedia features of word processing, digital cameras, and creativity software offer unique means of support for children's efforts to compose meaningful stories using descriptive language.

Allen (1976), an early proponent of LEA, summed up the theory behind the language experiences from the young reader's point of view: "What I think about, I can talk about; what I can say, I can write or someone can write for me; what I can write, I can read; and I can read what other people write for me to read." Labbo and her associates (2002) enhanced Allen's words this way: "What I think about, I can talk about. What I can see in a digital photograph, I can talk about and remember. What I can say, I can write down. What I can write down, I can revise on screen. What I can write I can read or have read to me by the computer. I can read what others write for me to read."

Teachers who subscribe to LEA have common viewpoints about children and their language. For example, they would probably agree that children's oral and written expression is based on their sensitivity to classroom and home environments. Further, they would support children working with their *own* language.

Thus the language-experience approach is based on the idea that language should be used to communicate thoughts, ideas, and meaning. How to use dictated stories and word banks, the directed reading–thinking procedure with comprehension strategies, and ways to extend children's writing and reading into more writing and reading are all examples of related instruction.

## Integrated Language Arts

An **integrated language arts approach** to instruction extends the concept of language experience throughout the grades by immersing students in reading, writing, talking, listening, and viewing activities. Just as teachers believe that systems of language should not be separated and taught as isolated skills, so too do they believe that reading, writing, speaking, listening, and viewing should be taught in concert, not in separate lessons. In this approach the language arts support one another and are connected through the use of informative and imaginative literature.

Teachers preserve the powerful bonds that exist among the various language arts by helping children make connections. The IRA/NCTE *Standards for English Language Arts* (1996) underscore the importance of preparing students at all grade levels for the literacy demands of today and tomorrow. Literacy expectations have accelerated in this century and are likely to increase dramatically in coming decades. When the process of developing national standards began, IRA and NCTE recognized that being literate means being active, critical, and creative users not only of printed and spoken language but also of visual language. The IRA/NCTE standards underscore the importance of integrating the language arts so that students will learn how to use language to think clearly, strategically, critically, and creatively.

Language is for learning. One of the more visible aspects of an integrated approach is the use of language as a tool for disciplinary learning. Teachers integrate language learning across the curriculum by organizing instruction around themes, inquiry-based project learning, and literature study. Various chapters throughout this book highlight the connections among the language arts, content area learning, and literature study.

In literature-based reading programs, students are encouraged to personally select their own trade books to read.

## Literature-Based Instruction

**Literature-based instruction** approaches accommodate individual student differences in reading abilities and at the same time focus on meaning, interest, and enjoyment. In literature-based instruction, teachers encourage their students to select their own trade books (another name for popular books).

In classrooms using literature in this way, children delight in the exploits of Curious George, Junie B. Jones, Encyclopedia Brown, and Harry Potter. The rationale is that an important part of classroom life should be *reading:* reading literature that makes children wonder, weep, laugh, shiver, and gasp.

Pieces of literature are used as springboards for writing. Children can write different endings for stories or incidents in their own lives that reflect conflicts similar to ones about which they have read. Students also look at story structures such as the repetitive structure in "The Three Little Pigs" and devise stories using the same kind of structure. Further, the conflicts between characters in literature can be used to help students gain insights into their own life situations. Students are encouraged to write about these also. Some teachers are using a piece of literature as a core book and then creating inquiry-oriented activities in which some (or all) of the information that learners interact with is online.

Students might download activities to complete such as Venn diagrams, create a new book cover for the story using online software, or link to other resources such as a piece of art or music associated with the story.

Self-selection of trade books or literature books is part of personalizing reading through the individualized approach. Teachers hold conferences with individual students about the books they are reading. Other forms of organization are also used. For example, a group of students reads and responds to the same piece of literature. Or students read different books with similar themes and then share and compare insights gained. Often, based on ongoing teacher assessment and observation of students' needs, teachers assemble flexible groups of students of similar abilities to develop strategies for strengthening reading skills. Reading instruction delivered in this way emanates from assumptions about the reading process that are interactive and top-down. Literature-based approaches depend on teachers who know children's literature and classroom organization. These topics are discussed in Chapters 12, 13, and 15.

## Technology-Based Instruction

**Technology-based instruction** in today's schools can make a dramatic difference in children's literacy development. Computers have changed the way we communicate and disseminate information, how we approach reading and writing, and how we think about people becoming literate (Reinking, 1995, 1998). Learning to read with computers is becoming as commonplace in twenty-first-century classrooms as basal reading programs were in the twentieth century.

In the early 1980s, when computers began to play an increasingly important role in classrooms, computer-related technologies were primitive compared to the powerful technologies that are available today. The computer's potential for classroom learning revolved mainly around word processing and computer-assisted instruction (CAI). CAI programs in the 1980s included the use of drills, tutorials, games, and simulations. Some computer programs were engaging and interactive, but many weren't. Drill and tutorial software, for example, often provided students with dull, uninviting "electronic worksheets" to practice skills and reinforce concepts.

In the 1990s, technology-based instruction changed the face of literacy learning and instruction. The development of the CD-ROM, for example, made learning to read with computers highly engaging and interactive. One example was the electronic, or "talking," book, a digital version of a story. These books were readily available on CD-ROM and provide another way to support children's literacy development (Labbo, 2000).

Today, computers allow students to access and retrieve information, construct their own texts, and interact with others. The Internet is having a tremendous impact on classroom learning. Online opportunities abound that can greatly enhance student learning yet be easily integrated into the classroom. E-mail and blogs allow students to have ongoing written correspondence with students from around the world. The Internet also provides immediate access to information on virtually any topic. In Box 2.2, technology specialists Kim and Jeremy Brueck share some examples of new literacies using technology-based instruction in the classroom.

In addition, computers as word processors allow children to create texts that can serve as the basis for learning to read. As they become more sophisticated in the use of word processing programs, children become skillful in their ability to organize, revise, and edit what they write. Young authors can also use computers to readily access free online resources to create covers for books they write.

Palm Pilots and computer tablets are being used in classrooms today to store, retrieve, and send information between students and teachers. These tools are also used to address classroom assessment mandates because they provide ongoing assessment data to monitor student progress. Smart Boards (interactive whiteboards), web cams,

BOX **2.2**

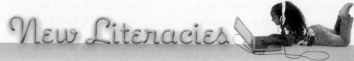

*New Literacies*

## USING BLOGS IN CLASSROOM CENTER ACTIVITIES

*Jeremy Brueck and Kimberly Hartman Brueck*

*Curriculum and technology specialists Jeremy Brueck and Kimberly Hartman Brueck of Akron, Ohio, share some strategies for using technology in the classroom to encourage reading and writing. Here they discuss using blogs as part of reading instruction.*

Our work focuses on development of and support for preK–3 teachers in their use of technology as they cultivate twenty-first-century content knowledge and skills in their students. Recently at the early childhood level, we have observed children coming to school with a basic knowledge of the desktop computer and possessing the skill set needed to keyboard, mouse, and navigate the World Wide Web. Since this generation of students has been connected to the Internet since birth, they do not respond as well as their parents did to a linear method of thinking and learning. Rather, these youngsters arrive at school comfortable with multitasking and in tune with the social context and experience the Web offers. From preschool through their elementary years, we see students thrive when teachers find ways to educate them in a more flexible, hypertext manner. That's why we encourage teachers to integrate new literacies like blogs into their reading curriculum.

Blogs can be incorporated into the early childhood classroom in a variety of ways. Most often, we see students using blogs to draft, edit, and publish writing responses. In the early childhood classroom, student blogging has been most successful when integrated into classroom center activities. This approach also helps teachers overcome one perceived obstacle to classroom technology integration: a limited number of classroom computers available for student use.

At center time, send a group of 3–4 students to the computer station together. Students of varied reading levels can support each other as they work to access the blog web site through a bookmark, log in, then compose and submit their blog. At the earliest levels, integrating predictable books with

blogging works well. For example, a teacher might begin by posting the phrase "Brown bear, brown bear what do you see?" The students would use the blog to compose their predictable response, "I see a _____ looking at me."

In any classroom, establishing routines is a crucial component to student success. During reading instruction, we observed teachers taking time to explain to students what good readers look like, to model strategies (chunking, using picture clues, skipping a word), and to tell students to seek help when needed. It is no different with blogging. Teachers should take time to explain what good bloggers do, what they look like, what strategies students can use when they encounter difficulty, as well as give examples of inappropriate blogging behaviors. When the teacher takes time to explain and model the blogging process to students before immersing them in this new literacy, a successful blogging community will result.

Teachers can effectively model the blogging process for students by developing a blog to post a classroom calendar, newsletter, or announcements and happenings. Within a kindergarten room, this might mean simply posting a picture of a paintbrush and the word *art* on the calendar days that students go to art class. Instead of checking a chart or a bulletin board for this information, students refer to the classroom blog, something they can do at home or at school. A teacher's blog can become an important and easily accessible resource used to communicate with students, parents, the community, and the world!

One important thing for teachers to keep in mind when using blogs in the classroom is student confidentiality. Since the content is online, student names and pictures should never appear in blog entries. Instead, we work with teachers to help them develop a student code that identifies the author of a post or comment. That way, students can post journals, reflections, dialogue, or group author with other students and the teacher in a safe, supportive, and—to the outside world—anonymous but productive learning environment.

electromagnetic LCD pen monitors, and iPods are among other technological advances changing the face of literacy instruction in the twenty-first century.

## Approaches and Strategies in Comprehensive Instruction

Eclectic instruction, a teacher's use of a combination of approaches and strategies, is not self-defeating when it is grounded in teachers' understanding of theoretical and research-based principles from the knowledge base on reading and learning to read. *Principled eclectic instruction* allows teachers to flexibly use approaches and strategies associated with different curricular perspectives. Effective teachers achieve a comprehensive literacy program by integrating reading and writing instruction throughout the school day.

Weaving approaches and strategies into a seamless pattern of instruction is one of the hallmarks of a comprehensive literacy program. Pressley (2006) contends that "balanced elementary instruction—that is, a balancing of whole-language and skills components—seems more defensible than instruction that is only immersion in reading and writing, on the one hand, or predominantly skills driven, on the other" (p. 417). He also says that teachers who teach in an eclectic, balanced way "combine the strengths of whole-language and skills instruction, and in so doing create instruction that is more than the sum of its parts" (p. 1).

Research supports the notion that highly effective teachers are an informative source of knowledge about exemplary literacy practices (Pressley, Rankin, & Yokoi, 1996; Pressley, Wharton-McDonald, Rankin, Yokoi, & Ettenberger, 1996). A research project conducted by a team of researchers from the National Reading Research Center investigated the nature of outstanding literacy instruction in primary classrooms. In a series of studies, the research team conducted surveys, interviews, and extensive observations of primary teachers who were considered by their supervisors to be outstanding teachers of literacy. As a result of the project, the researchers determined that highly effective first-grade teachers strike a balance between children's immersion in literacy experiences and explicit instruction. The characteristics of highly effective literacy teachers include the thorough integration of reading and writing activities and the extensive use of **instructional scaffolding** to support the development of children's literacy skills and strategies.

When teachers scaffold instruction, students become aware of and competent in the use of skills and strategies that they need to be successful. Used in construction, scaffolds serve as supports, lifting up workers so that they can reach areas they could not otherwise reach. The scaffold metaphor suggests helping students do what they cannot do on their own at first. Instructional scaffolding allows teachers to support literacy learning by showing students how to use skills and strategies that will lead to independent learning.

Instructional scaffolding means giving students a better chance to be successful with reading and writing. Teachers provide literacy scaffolds through the use of well-timed questions, explanations, demonstrations, practice, and application. These scaffolds provide instructional support for children in two ways: (1) the application of skills and strategies *at the point of actual use* during reading and (2) explicit instruction in the development of skills and strategies through minilessons.

Minilessons allow the teacher to provide **explicit strategy instruction** for students who need instructional guidance in the development and use of skills and strategies. The minilesson can be a short, unanticipated interchange between the teacher and students lasting a minute or two. Or it can be a planned lesson that may take 5 to 10 minutes to complete. Minilessons, regardless of duration, allow teachers to share insights and knowledge that students might otherwise never encounter. See, for example, Box 2.3's description of how Lauren Schultz uses minilessons to enrich her students' reading, composition, and spelling skills. Explicit lessons create a framework that will unify skill and strategy development by making provisions for children to become aware of, use, and develop control over skills and strategies that can make a difference in their literate lives.

Explicit instruction helps students by providing an alternative to what we have called direct instruction in a skills-based curriculum. A direct instruction model, as we noted earlier, is rooted in behavioral principles of learning. Students are taught what to do, given immediate feedback, and afforded extensive practice until discrete skills become habitual and automatic in their use. Students seldom grasp the rationale or payoff underlying the particular skills that are taught.

When teachers make instruction explicit, however, students construct knowledge about the use of skills and strategies. Explicit instruction involves strategic learning, not habit formation. Minilessons follow a pattern that usually includes (1) creating awareness of the strategy, (2) modeling the strategy, (3) providing practice in the use of the strategy, and (4) applying the strategy in authentic reading situations. Awareness of

BOX **2.3**

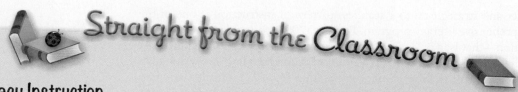

*Straight from the Classroom*

## Literacy Instruction

### LAUREN SHULTZ

*Lauren Shultz is an educator in Mayfield, Ohio. Lauren's literacy philosophy is reflected in her classroom. Following is a description of Lauren's program.*

I teach reading, writing, and word study in a daily 80-minute literacy block. Reading and writing workshop alternate days, while word study is integrated in minilessons and direct instruction 2 days per week. Although days are labeled "Reading" or "Writing," there is constant integration of both; in my classroom, reading and writing always go together.

I begin each literacy block with "status of the class," a way of recording the number of pages students read the previous evening. This not only provides a quick check for accountability, but assessment data for independent reading. Using informal conversation, I comment on book choices and recommend future reading selections. This lets students know I am knowledgeable about the books they are reading.

I use minilessons to focus on strategies students can utilize to become good readers and writers. During minilessons, modeling of teacher thinking is crucial. My students keep notes from minilessons in a literacy binder. I use newspapers, magazines, novel excerpts, poetry, nonfiction texts, short stories, picture books, and teacher and student writing samples for minilesson text.

After the minilesson, students work independently for approximately 40 minutes. During reading workshop, students read independently, have a teacher conference, or participate in a guided reading or literature study group. Students choose independent reading books across genres and according to interests. Teacher conferences are held at least twice a month to evaluate how successful students are at applying reading strategies in their independent reading. Struggling readers often need more frequent conferences. Students participating in guided reading meet with me and discuss or respond in writing to the assigned text. Literature study is stressed in sixth grade and can consist of a group reading the same book, books by one author, or a certain genre. Reading journals are an integral part of the assessment process. Whatever a student is working on independently will be reflected on in their reading journals at least once a week. I work in a collaborative classroom, so my teaching partner is able to help me accomplish all this in such a short time period.

During the 40-minute writing workshop, students work on writing pieces and have teacher–student writing conferences.

Sometimes students choose their writing topic, but other times they must write on a certain topic or in a particular genre. When needed, short-term guided writing groups are formed to support students struggling with a previously modeled writing concept. The writing process is directly modeled through minilessons and is a constant in writing workshop.

After independent work time, students present book talks, or we review the day's minilesson. During the last 15 minutes of each class, I read aloud. I select novels or short stories that stretch the students' ability to infer meaning and apply reading strategies. We often relate to the read-aloud as authors. This is great discussion time.

During word study, students are divided into four developmentally appropriate (fluid) groups. I meet with the groups on a rotating basis for approximately 20 minutes each. Groups are assigned group work and individual work to support their understanding. Spelling journals are used to record students' knowledge concerning word patterns. Some groups have tests that focus on patterns and words they wish to learn from their writing or reading. This testing decision depends on the group and what they struggle to understand about words and how they work. Vocabulary enrichment is integrated for all students during reading and writing workshop.

The support students need to become successful readers and writers drives my instructional decisions. Our schedule often changes during the year to accommodate student needs and interests.

### REFLECTIVE INQUIRY

- How does Lauren's program provide opportunities for children to read and write daily?
- How does Lauren provide explicit strategy instruction for students?
- What approaches described in this chapter contribute to Lauren's overall program?

a strategy often involves a give-and-take exchange of ideas between teacher and students. These exchanges may include explanations and strategy tips and are built around questions such as "Why is the strategy useful?" "What is the payoff for students?" "How does this improve learning?" and "What are the rules, guidelines, or procedures for being successful with the skill or strategy?" Students should come away from these discussions recognizing the rationale and process behind the use of the skill or strategy under consideration.

Once students understand the what and how of the skill or strategy, the teacher might want to extend a minilesson by modeling its use and providing students with practice. Modeling may include walking students through the steps and raising questions about the procedures.

Notice how Matt uses modeling in this minilesson to engage his second graders in a process discussion and then scaffolds and expands their strategies for figuring out unknown words.

| | |
|---|---|
| *Matt:* | Before we start reading today, I want to take a few minutes and find out what you do when you come to a word you don't know. I'm curious to know how you handle that. |
| *Sajit:* | Well, sometimes, I skip the word, read on, and then go back and see if I can figure it out. |
| *Matt:* | That's good, Sajit. But how do you know if the word is right or not? Do you think of any word that will make sense? |
| *Anna:* | No. You have to think of a word that makes sense AND starts with the same letter. Then when you guess, you make sure *all* of the letters make sense. |
| *Matt:* | Right. When you read for meaning you try to make guesses that make sense and go along with what you are reading. You know that reading has to make sense. What else do you do when you come to a word you don't know? |
| *Javon:* | Sometimes I look to see if there is a little word inside of a big word. Like if the word is *airplane*. I look and see the little words *air* and *plane*. Then I just figure it out. |
| *Matt:* | Oh. You look for little words in big words. That's because you know that often big words are made up of smaller words. You just gave an example of *compound* words. Compound words are made up of two smaller words together. Any other ways you figure out unknown words? |
| *Kris:* | I sound it out. |
| *Matt:* | Sound it out? Tell us about that. |
| *Kris:* | I look at the first letter, and then I look at the last letter. Then I look at the middle of the word and see if I can figure it out. |
| *Matt:* | These are all good strategies for figuring out unknown words. It's important to remember that there isn't just one way to figure out a word you don't know. You can look at the letters, look for patterns, look for little words inside big words, and even think about words that make sense. Readers rely on a lot of different strategies for figuring out words they don't know. Today I want to mention another strategy. Sometimes when you don't know a word, you can see if it looks like another word you know. For example, look at this sentence: |

He used a *quill* to write the letter.

| | |
|---|---|
| | You might not know the word *q-u-i-l-l* but you do know other words in the same family, like *bill, fill,* and *pill.* So you know *quill*. |
| *Matt:* | Let's practice. |

There was a *throng* of people on the stage.

| | |
|---|---|
| | What other words do you know that are like *throng*? |
| *Jessica:* | I know! *Song* and *long*! |
| *Matt:* | That's right. If you know *song* and *long* then you know *throng*. Next time you're reading and you come to a word you don't know, I'd like you to try this strategy and let us know how it goes. See if you can match it to words you do know that are in the same family. |

The hallmark of comprehensive instruction is the integration of reading and writing experiences with scaffolded instruction in the use of skills and strategies, which are best learned through meaningful use. When students are engaged in meaningful and authentic reading and writing activities, there are numerous opportunities to scaffold their literacy experiences.

Remember how Katie, the beginning teacher who opened our chapter, was confused about her theoretical orientations to reading? She exhibited confusion and inconsistency in her teaching. Now read how Gay, a veteran teacher, aligns her classroom instruction with her philosophical beliefs about how children learn to read and write. Gay is confident with her philosophy, methods, and beliefs.

Gay's gift wasn't what she had expected. Her mother's Christmas present in years past had always been unusual, but this year the woman had outdone herself. Wrapped in shiny foil, much to Gay's surprise, was a worn-out, overstuffed, red-covered notebook. There it was—Gay's old red notebook, which she hadn't seen for more than 20 years—reunited once again with its owner.

Between the covers of the red notebook were those wonderful, creative, misspelled stories that Gay had written as a child. She was about 8 years old when she penned her first story, "Hankie and the Hawk." Story after story filled hundreds of pages now yellowed with time. And then the idea struck her. Gay could hardly wait to get back to the students she taught and share her childhood stories with them.

Since then, Gay introduces "the old red notebook" to her students on the opening day of each school year. In her own words, "the book" has become the centerpiece of a strategy she uses to introduce her third-grade class to reading and writing: "Here I am, starting the morning of the first day of the school year by reading stories to my class that sound like something the children would have written. The book is falling apart, the pages are yellow, and the crazy teacher is grinning like a fool! Soon, however, an 'ah ha' or two can be heard as I read the author's name with each story: 'Hankie and the Hawk' by Miss Gay Wilson, April 3, 1957; 'How the Pig Got a Curly Tail' by Miss Gay Wilson, December 10, 1959; 'Sue's Birthday' by Miss Gay Wilson, February 21, 1958.

"The dates and the name Wilson carry little meaning, but a few of my students recognize the name Gay as mine and soon catch on to what's happening. 'These are stories *you* wrote when you was a little girl,' blurts a precocious listener. The looks on the children's faces are worth their weight in gold. Sheer delight!

"They beg for more, and I promise more another day. There are enough stories to read every day for most of the school year. So I make a promise to them that I will not break: 'Every day this year you'll get to read, and every day this year you'll get to write.' I want them to feel the specialness of this promise. Then we discuss the author in each of them.

"What do we do next? Write, of course. Do any of the children say, 'I don't know what to write about?' Not at all. Of course, not all of them do write; some, on the first day, draw. But all the children approach writing with confidence. What do they do next? Read, of course. Since I read to them what I had written as a child, they now read to one another."

First days are important. Why did Gay make the decision to use her childhood writings on the first day of school as an instructional tool? "It was a natural decision to make," says Gay, "because I believe strongly in my role as a model. What better way to model what it means to be an author and a reader than to use my own childhood stories?" So the old red notebook became part of a strategy—a plan of action—designed to build community, set expectations, and contribute to a classroom environment that supports a literacy program.

In this chapter, you learned about the importance of a comprehensive approach to reading instruction. There are many variables to be taken into consideration as teachers strive to meet students' needs. Instruction evolves from teachers' knowledge and beliefs about reading and learning to read. Gay's story closes this chapter because it illustrates how a teacher's beliefs about learning to read and write influence what she does in the classroom.

How does Gay's "old red notebook" strategy build a learning environment that contributes to a complete literacy program? We raise this question to guide your search for what it means to achieve a classroom literacy program that employs a variety of instructional approaches. As a third-grade teacher, Gay's goal is to immerse students in authentic literacy experiences. But she also attempts to balance these experiences with explicit teaching in the skills and strategies that her students need to use to be successful readers and writers. Teachers like Gay recognize that skills and strategies are learned best through meaningful use.

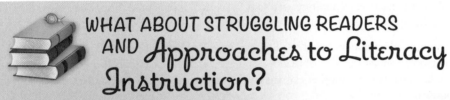

## WHAT ABOUT STRUGGLING READERS AND *Approaches to Literacy Instruction?*

There are no "quick fixes" for students who find learning to read and write difficult. However, students who struggle can benefit from a literacy program that is grounded in teachers' understanding of research-based principles. In comprehensive programs, children are engaged in authentic reading and writing activities daily, and have many opportunities to receive specific instruction in their area of need. Guided reading and writing groups naturally address struggling readers because they are small groups formed to target areas of need while allowing the student to be part of a community of learners. The teacher provides a scaffold for these groups, by constantly modeling strategies effective readers employ. Shared reading and writing activities also scaffold instruction and address the needs of nonreaders and English language learners by allowing them to take part in important experiences they might not otherwise be able to accomplish on their own. These are the types of activities that are built into a balanced literacy program to help students become competent readers and writers. Knowledgeable teachers who use flexibility in their approaches and strategies achieve balanced literacy programs that benefit *all* students.

## Summary

An underlying assumption in this book is that when teachers are in touch with their beliefs about reading and learning to read, they are in a better position to balance literacy instruction in the classroom. When you analyze your beliefs, connecting what you practice with what you know and believe, you are better able to understand what you do and why. The reading autobiography suggested in Chapter 1 lends itself to a narrative inquiry that helps teachers discover some of the events and experiences that contribute to the development of beliefs and attitudes related to reading and learning to read. In this chapter, the Beliefs About Reading Interview and the TORP survey were suggested as tools that also permit teachers to inquire into their beliefs.

We explored two predominant curricula, one founded on a bottom-up perspective and the other on a top-down perspective. We showed different instructional approaches to reading. These approaches include basal reading programs, language experience, integrated language arts, technology-based instruction, and literature-based programs.

Teachers enact curricula in varied and complex ways, based on their perspectives of the reading curriculum, the particular context in which they teach, and the desire to achieve a complete literacy program.

## Teacher Action Research

1. Is there someone you now work with, a teacher who stands out in the school in which you are interning, or a fellow classmate, who you believe has a comprehensive literacy program? Describe the teacher and his or her literacy program. Organize your description of this teacher with the following: (a) background information including some personal history, (b) beliefs about reading, (c) the school context, and (d) how he or she balances literacy instruction.

2. Interview a teacher who uses technology in the classroom. How does the teacher make use of the Internet? Is technology used to differentiate instruction? If so, how? How does the teacher use other technologies, such as web cams or smart boards?

3. Interview a fellow student using the Beliefs About Reading Interview (Box 2.1). Analyze the person's implicit theories of reading as suggested in this chapter. If there is time, ask her or him to interview another classmate and form a small group to compare the various responses.

**THROUGH the LENS of a Literacy Coach**

4. Interview a literacy coach. How does the coach work with teachers to build relationships and support their different beliefs about reading? How does the coach forge ongoing relationships with the teachers being coached? Ask the coach to describe a conflict between a teacher's belief system and the way he or she was expected to teach. What did the coach do to support this teacher?

## Related Web Sites

*Book Cover Creator*

**www.readwritethink.org/materials/bookcover**

Book Cover Creator is designed to allow users to type and illustrate front book covers, front and back covers, and full dust jackets. Students can use the tool to create new covers for books that they read as well as to create covers for books they write individually or as a class.

*Center for the Improvement of Early Reading Achievement (CIERA)*

**www.ciera.org/library/instresrc/principles/index.html**

CIERA is a national center for research on early reading. It features ten research-based, downloadable principles for improving reading achievement.

*Learning to Read: Resources for Language Arts and Reading Research*

**www.toread.com**

This web site is devoted to improving the quality of reading instruction through the study of reading. It serves as a clearinghouse for the dissemination of reading research.

*North Central Regional Educational Laboratory (NCREL)*

**www.ncrel.org/sdrs/areas/issues/content/cntareas/reading/li300.htm**

NCREL explores critical issues online in a multimedia document that synthesizes research using technology to enhance literacy instruction. It sets goals and an action plan and provides examples of schools that have succeeded in using technology in this way.

*ReadWriteThink*

**www.readwritethink.org**

This partnership between the International Reading Association (IRA), the National Council of Teachers of English (NCTE), and the Marco Polo Educational Foundation works to provide educators access to high-quality practices and resources in reading and language arts instruction.

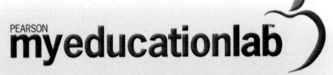

Now go to the Vacca et al. *Reading and Learning to Read,* Seventh Edition, MyEducationLab course at **www.myeducationlab.com** to

- Take a pretest to assess your initial comprehension of the chapter content
- Study chapter content with your individualized study plan
- Take a posttest to assess your understanding of chapter content
- Engage in multimedia exercises to help you build a deeper and more applied understanding of chapter content

# CHAPTER 3

# Meeting the Literacy Needs of Diverse Learners

Standards found in this chapter:

- ▶ 1.1
- ▶ 1.2
- ▶ 2.1
- ▶ 2.2
- ▶ 3.1
- ▶ 3.2
- ▶ 4.1
- ▶ 4.2
- ▶ 4.3
- ▶ 5.1
- ▶ 5.2
- ▶ 5.3
- ▶ 5.4

## In this chapter,
## YOU WILL DISCOVER:

:• Linguistic, cultural, cognitive, and academic factors that influence individual diverse learners

:• Issues about learning to read and write in relation to definitions of literacy and diversity

:• Illustrations of linguistic, dialectical, cultural, and academic and cognitive diversity in instructional situations

## Concept Map

### MEETING THE LITERACY NEEDS OF DIVERSE LEARNERS

**INSTRUCTIONAL BELIEFS AND PRINCIPLES**

**INSTRUCTIONAL STRATEGIES**

| Linguistic Diversity | Cultural Diversity |
|---|---|
| Sheltered English | Collaborations |
| Conversations | Image Making |
| Response Protocol | Technology-Enhanced Instruction |
| Thematic Teaching | |
| Other Literacy Practices | |
| Dialects | |

**Academic and Cognitive Diversity**

Inquiry Learning
Differentiated Instruction
New Literacies
Response to Intervention

eth Arnold is the principal of an urban elementary school located in the Midwest. The students come from homes in which the primary language is Spanish, Arabic, or French, as well as homes in which various African American dialects are spoken. On a tour of the school on Community Day, visitors might see classes taught in Spanish, family members in classrooms sharing their language and culture, and the school librarian sharing picture books and children's literature written in the students' first language. They might chat with an African American child who learned to speak and read in Arabic from listening to instruction for students with limited English proficiency (LEP). As the principal, Beth, an energetic African American woman, works hard to keep every student and every parent feeling involved and part of the school community.

"Our job here isn't just to teach students to speak English," Ms. Arnold says. "Part of our job is also to help these students *feel welcome* in school. Feeling welcome is essential for learning, and feeling welcome can't happen if no one understands you or if you can't understand anyone. Our language is totally connected to our sense of who we are. If people don't value our language, they devalue us."

In a rural school, Kelly Stone is proud of the cooperative and collaborative atmosphere in her classroom. Her kindergarten students have had few literacy experiences to prepare them for school. Their families struggle to live at subsistence levels, due to the area's economic difficulties. Consequently, the school has limited resources and materials. Soon after arriving in the district several years ago, Kelly called for help from her students' families. Together they designed and created classroom centers that were relevant to the children's lives and supported their emerging literacy. A family center, animal center, block center, take-apart center, garden center, fishing center, book center, writing and drawing center, and math center provided the kindergartners with a wide variety of meaningful experiences with literacy. Families donated items from closets, garages, cellars, fields, and forest. Junk became treasure, and sisters, brothers, aunts, uncles, cousins, mothers, fathers, and neighbors shared their time, materials, and talents. "The children's families seem to understand the culture of the school and literacy development better when the activities for their children relate to their environment. They read stories, tell stories, assist children at the centers, and give what they can to the kindergarten program. They say it takes a whole village to raise our children—well, that's exactly what we are doing."

Emily Simons teaches eighth grade in an economically and culturally diverse neighborhood in the Northeast. During language arts, she challenges her students with multiple opportunities to respond to literature from various cultural and historical perspectives. During a 4-week thematic unit on slavery, for example, she uses picture books to explore the topic from multiple points of view. A favorite story is *Christmas in the Big House; Christmas in the Quarters,* a picture book that contrasts the experiences of African Americans and of whites. Ms. Simons believes that her middle school students learn to understand cultural differences through children's literature. She thinks that students of all ability levels can relate to picture books; not only are they are beautifully illustrated, but also they can foster a sensitivity to ethnic diversity through visual representation.

Jim Brown's third-grade class begins the morning language arts block with a literature read-aloud. After that experience, his room is buzzing as 24 students interact in centers that develop reading, writing, listening, and speaking. Eight of Jim's students are reading below grade level. At the computer cluster, Jonathan, a student with deficits in written and oral language, is creating silly stories using rhyming words with Lindsey, his skill buddy, who is reading at a second-grade level. Seven other students of varying literacy levels are working with computer programs individually or in pairs.

When the teacher's bell rings for the next rotation, Jonathan moves to the response table, where he will select and complete an activity related to the morning's read-aloud. Materials in this area include Lego blocks, straws, toothpicks, clay, paint, two easels, glitter, scissors, paper, glue, magazines, cloth, yarn, and buttons. A teaching assistant spends an hour during the language arts block working with students at the response table.

In the last 35 minutes of the block, Jonathan meets with Mr. Brown to prepare for a story with three other students at his reading level. They study story background, analyze vocabulary, make predictions, and ask questions. Then they move to a table with earphones to listen and read along with copies of the story. Tomorrow they will read different parts of the story and discuss them in a group.

Jim Brown is delighted with his classroom this year. He explains, "This is the first time in 20 years of teaching that I think I am actually meeting the diverse needs of my students. Technology and block scheduling have helped me do it."

These stories illustrate how four educators strive to meet the diverse needs of students in their classrooms. Multiple factors contribute to the diverse nature of today's classrooms and the challenges that teachers face in the twenty-first century. Generally, these factors fall into three categories:

- *Linguistic diversity.* The language in which the student feels most comfortable communicating is not the language of instruction in the school.
- *Cultural diversity.* The student's home, family, socioeconomic group, culture, and/or society differs from the predominant (usually middle-class) culture of the school.
- *Cognitive and academic diversity.* The child learns at a pace or in a style different from that expected at the school.

These factors influence how, when, and under what circumstances students will best learn to read and write.

In addition to linguistic, cultural, and cognitive and academic diversity, socioeconomic diversity compounds the complex nature of today's classrooms. Although school success or failure is not exclusively determined by economic factors such as poverty, students who come from family contexts in which they do not have easy access to books may be at risk for reading failure. Moreover, limited access to meaningful print in schools may also contribute to low reading achievement for students with linguistic, cultural, and/or cognitive differences (Lazar, 2004). Students whose family contexts include a cycle of low literacy miss early literacy experiences such as shared reading. The more knowledge about literacy that students gain before entering school, the more likely they will experience success. Children from low-literacy families tend to lack experiences with print and hence tend to be at risk.

In this chapter, we examine diversity and literacy from these multiple perspectives. Teachers need to be aware of the nature of diversity and what it means for teaching reading so that *all* students have equal opportunities to become literate.

# The Complexity of Diversity in Literacy Classrooms

Complicating the choices teachers must make in helping students learn to read and write are the differing definitions both of literacy and of diversity. Kame'enui (1993b) notes that reading research refers to "critical literacy," "occupational literacy," and "pragmatic literacy," as well as "literacy as cultural form." In addition, evolving notions of "new literacies" include the ever-changing roles of technology and the multiple forms of cultural and visual literacy (Cummins, Brown, & Sayers, 2007; Leu, 2002b; Williams, 2007). Each definition of literacy implies different purposes for becoming literate and appropriate instructional strategies suited for those purposes. Box 3.1 on page 60 offers an adaptation of how one teacher incorporated visual literacy into her reading program.

Further complicating the choices teachers must make in the classroom is the complex nature of diversity (Garcia, Pearson, & Jimenez, 1990). The range of needs in learning to read is reflected in the range of children who compose our classrooms. There is no one African American experience, just as there is no one Hispanic American experience or European American experience. Moreover, no two students who are identified with learning disabilities are alike. Students come from different socioeconomic backgrounds, geographic locations, levels of parental education, and cultural backgrounds, and have varying levels of verbal skills. All of these factors influence student success or lack of success in learning to read.

HOMEWORK EXERCISE: VIDEO

Go to the Homework and Exercises section in Chapter 3 of MyEducationLab to watch the video "Strategies for Teaching Diverse Learners" to observe how some teachers accommodate the diverse needs of their students.

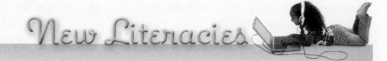

## BOX 3.1

### EMPLOYING VISUAL LITERACY

*Inspired by a children's exhibit at the National Gallery in London and her belief in the value of engaging students in multiple forms of literacy, T. Lee Williams adapted a project entitled "Tell Me a Picture" that fostered personal responses to artwork. Although Williams implemented the strategy with second graders, we suggest that the nature of the project holds much promise for learners of all ages, abilities, languages, and cultures. Here we synthesize and adapt Williams's strategy.*

#### VISUAL LITERACY

Step 1. Begin with an author study using picture or chapter books. Conduct literature discussions that focus on the author's style of writing.

Step 2. Continue with an illustrator study using picture books. Share background knowledge about the illustrator. Examine the artwork and discuss the artist's style and modes of expression.

Have the students draw their own pictures that capture the illustrator's style. Allow time to share.

Step 3. As a whole group, examine selected pieces of the artwork and encourage the students to brainstorm what they see in the pictures. Model through "think-alouds" and suggest how one can "read pictures" by interpreting them in personal ways. Use prompts such as "What do you think is happening in the picture?" "How does the illustrator make you feel when you look at the picture?"

Step 4. Partner the students. Have each pair examine other illustrations by the artist and write questions for the illustrator, an adaptation of "questioning the author" (Beck, McKeown, Hamilton, & Kucan, 1997). Follow up with a variation of KWL (Ogle, 1986) by focusing on the W, what the students want to know about the picture (e.g., Why is it raining?).

Step 5. Have the students write stories about the illustrations either individually or with a partner. Allow time to share.

*Source:* Adapted from "'Reading' the Painting: Exploring Visual Literacy in the Primary Grades," by T. L. Williams, 2007, *The Reading Teacher, 60,* pp. 636–642.

---

**HOMEWORK EXERCISE: VIDEO**

Go to the Homework and Exercises section in Chapter 3 of MyEducationLab to watch the video "Teacher Rigidity" and consider the instructional strategies you would apply.

To further complicate matters, the terminology associated with diversity has been debated and thus changed over time. In the past, for example, *Black English* was often referred to as *broken English;* the Linguistic Society of America, however, now refers to this form of nonstandard English as *Ebonics* or *Black Vernacular English,* among other names, and it is defined as an authentic linguistic system (Garcia, 2002). The reference to *children with learning disabilities* is often replaced with the more inclusive term, **exceptional children,** which refers to children with learning difficulties as well as children with superior abilities or talents (Heward, 2000). Table 3.1 lists and defines some of the contemporary terminology associated with diversity.

In the next sections of this chapter, we discuss instructional beliefs associated with linguistic, cultural, and academic diversity. We also suggest teaching principles and strategies for teachers as they address the diverse needs of their students.

## Linguistic Diversity in Literacy Classrooms

The demography of the United States has changed dramatically over the decades, and the **linguistic diversity** of our nation has had a tremendous impact on our schools. The increasingly large number of immigrants from non-European nations has influenced how we approach literacy instruction. Over 50 languages are spoken, for example, in some urban school districts (Banks, 2001) and nationwide over 400 languages are spoken (Hadaway & Young, 2006). According to the U.S. Census Bureau (2004) there will be an approximate 88 percent increase in immigrant population by 2050,

**Table 3.1** Terminology Associated with Diversity

| TERM | DEFINITION | REFERENCE |
|---|---|---|
| Ethnic group | People who share a common history, identity, values, and behavioral characteristics | Banks, J. A. (2002). *An Introduction to Multicultural Education.* Boston: Allyn & Bacon. |
| Sheltered English | Teaching strategies that maximize nonverbal communication for students whose primary language is not English | Garcia, E. (2002). *Student Cultural Diversity: Understanding and Meeting the Challenge* (3rd ed.). Boston: Houghton Mifflin. |
| Limited English proficient (LEP) | Nonproficient in English based on language usage at home and school and low academic performance in English | Garcia, E. (2002). *Student Cultural Diversity: Understanding and Meeting the Challenge* (3rd ed.). Boston: Houghton Mifflin. |
| English language learner (ELL) | A broad term that refers to people who are learning the English language. Some ELL students are more proficient than others. | Fitzgerald, J., & Graves, M. F. (2004). *Scaffolding Reading Experiences for English-Language Learners.* Norwood, MA: Christopher-Gordon. |
| Standard English | Grammar, vocabulary, and pronunciation that are appropriate for public oral and written discourse | Garcia, E. (2002). *Student Cultural Diversity: Understanding and Meeting the Challenge* (3rd ed.). Boston: Houghton Mifflin. |
| Inclusion | A classroom environment that fosters academic and social activities in which students with disabilities interact in general education settings | Scala, M. C. (2001). *Working Together: Reading and Writing in Inclusive Classrooms.* Newark, DE: International Reading Association. |
| Assistive technology | Equipment of any kind used to improve the functional capabilities of students with disabilities | Heward, W. L. (2000). *Exceptional Children: An Introduction to Special Education* (6th ed.). Columbus: Merrill. |
| Attention deficit/ hyperactive disorder (ADHD) | Diagnostic category for children who exhibit developmentally inappropriate inattention, impulsivity, and hyperactivity | Heward, W. L. (2000). *Exceptional Children: An Introduction to Special Education* (6th ed.). Columbus: Merrill. |
| Exceptional children | Includes children who experience difficulties in learning, as well as superior performance and/or talent. A more inclusive term than *students with disabilities.* | Heward, W. L. (2000). *Exceptional Children: An Introduction to Special Education* (6th ed.). Columbus: Merrill. |
| At risk | Students who are considered to have a greater than usual chance of developing a disability | Heward, W. L. (2000). *Exceptional Children: An Introduction to Special Education* (6th ed.). Columbus: Merrill. |

and teaching English language learners will become an increasingly important issue. In addition, regional variations in language usage, commonly known as dialects, are a complicated issue for literacy and language arts teachers (Banks, 2001; Garcia, 2002). What are the beliefs regarding teaching students who speak linguistically diverse languages and dialects? What instructional principles and strategies work for these students?

## Instructional Beliefs About Linguistic Diversity

Although the United States has a long history of non-English-speaking immigrant students attending public school, **American Standard English** has been the traditionally acceptable language of instruction in schools because it is viewed as "a vital tool for success in the United States" (Garcia, 2002, p. 218). Historically, a policy of assimilating, or Americanizing, immigrants has been at work in the United States. Initially, the practice

STANDARD
1.2

of using English was practical in nature. Most legal and business documents were written in English, so it was necessary to be able to read and write English in order to fulfill civic responsibilities, which also affected upward mobility and economic success. During the late 1800s and early 1900s, the reasons for using American English in schools shifted to issues of political power and national identity. Whereas early immigrants were primarily from northern and western Europe, the influx of immigrants from southern and eastern Europe between 1890 and 1900 created feelings of unrest, fear, and even distrust in the longer-settled population. As a result, the Nationality Act of 1906 required that immigrants speak English as a prerequisite for naturalization (Banks, 2001).

Although some private schools conducted instruction in students' native languages in the 1800s, the "melting pot" notion, wherein minority students would become more like the majority, served as the metaphor that guided the role of language instruction during much of the twentieth century. English-only laws were enacted across the country and remained in effect until the civil rights movement of the 1960s (Banks, 2001).

During the 1960s and 1970s, as a result of equal opportunity initiatives, viewpoints regarding language instruction shifted. Bilingual education acts were passed in support of financial assistance to meet the special needs of students who did not come from homes in which English was the first language. In 1973 the Comprehensive Bilingual Education Amendment Act recognized that children learn through their culture and language, and that many children come from cultural backgrounds in which the heritage and language differ from that of English-speaking people. Hence, although not mandated, special language programs were offered in order to ensure equal learning opportunities for all.

Beginning in the 1980s, two political viewpoints emerged that continue to place discussions about language acquisition and culture at a crossroads. The *English-only* viewpoint is based on the notion that Standard English should be the official language of the United States government and that the English language fosters U.S. unity. The *English-plus* viewpoint advocates linguistic pluralism and encourages proficiency in more than one language. Educational programs that develop cultural awareness, sensitivity, and linguistic diversity are supported (Banks, 2001). It is generally recognized that Standard English needs to be taught in the schools for personal, social, economic, and global communication reasons. Current research, however, suggests that teachers need to promote language learning in the student's native language *first* and include cultural awareness and sensitivity toward all languages in the classroom (Banks, 2001; Diaz, 2001; Garcia, 2002).

More recently, as a result of the No Child Left Behind Act (NCLB) in 2001, the stakes were raised for English language learners. In fact, by the year 2014, *all* children are expected to be proficient in English (Hadaway & Young, 2006). In order to address this expectation, as difficult as it might be to achieve, The Teachers of English Speakers of Other Languages (TESOL, 2006) revised standards for English language learners that address:

- Proficiency standards for communication within the school setting including language arts, mathematics, science, and social studies
- Grade-level clusters that reflect educational settings in the United States including preK through grade 12
- Curriculum, instructional, and assessment standards that focus on listening, speaking, reading, and writing
- Five levels of language proficiency beginning with students who have no knowledge of the English language and progressing toward language proficiency that is fluent and spontaneous

Issues regarding the disparity in status between Standard English and various dialects have caused additional heated debates among the educational community. "A dialect is a regional variation of language characterized by distinct grammar, vocabulary, and pronunciation" (Garcia, 2002, p. 218). In particular, educational concerns regarding Ebonics and teaching African American students whose home dialect differs from that of the school have been raised. Debates and congressional hearings resulted in the affirmation that teachers of African American students must respect the language of the home (Ebonics), but that they must also be taught Standard English (Banks, 2001; Garcia, 2002; Lazar, 2004). In the next sections, we address instructional principles and strategies that support learners from these diverse language backgrounds.

## Instructional Principles for Students Speaking Diverse Languages and Dialects

Language is largely cultural in nature, and "language, identity, culture and education are inextricably intertwined" (Banks, 2001, p. 290). Although more research is needed, current studies suggest that when students maintain a strong identification with their culture and native language, they are more likely to succeed academically and they have more positive self-concepts about their ability to learn (Banks, 2001; Diaz, 2001; Garcia, 2002; Garcia, 2000; Hadaway & Young, 2006). Based on current research, the International Reading Association recommends that reading instruction be conducted in a student's native language (2001).

Although the ideal development of second-language literacy would have each nonnative speaker receiving instructional support in the home language while learning to master English, the reality is often quite different. But that does not mean that the regular classroom teacher cannot offer the ELL student rich and meaningful language-based literacy experiences. *Many of the principles that guide language and literacy learning in a first language should guide literacy learning in a second language.*

The following second-language acquisition principles for classroom practice relate to alphabetic (e.g., Spanish and German) as well as nonalphabetic (e.g., Chinese and Japanese) languages (Littlewood, 1984; Moll, 1989; Vygotsky, 1978):

- The social context for learning a second language must be a setting in which students feel accepted and comfortable.
- Students in small groups and pairs have natural opportunities for meaning making and authentic communication.
- Students need time to listen and process without the pressure of oral and written production. They are often rehearsing and creating systems while silent.

In addition, teachers need to understand that English language learners face unique challenges such as limited background knowledge and vocabulary constraints, and they are often unfamiliar with the text structures found in academic content books (Mora, 2006).

We all speak a **dialect** of English, although it is much easier for us to see our own speech as natural and the speech of everyone else as the dialect. Variations in languages also include dialectical differences. It is recommended that instruction in English include information about and respect for dialect diversity (Christian, 1997).

Although there is no easy fix or solution to bridging the gap between what research suggests and instructional practices in today's classrooms, Banks (2001) offers several benchmarks for schools that foster knowledge and respect for diverse languages, dialects, and cultures; these are adapted in the following list:

- Policies should clearly encourage mastery of the English language, proficiency in native languages, and sensitivity and respect for all languages.
- Teachers need to examine their own biases toward diverse languages and dialects and should view differences as strengths.
- Students from diverse language backgrounds should not be placed in segregated pull-out programs; however, when there are large numbers of non-English-speaking students, bilingual teachers ought to be employed.

STANDARD
2.2

- The curriculum should include materials that reflect linguistic diversity.
- All elementary, middle, and high schools should implement second-language pro-grams for *all* students if students are truly to become citizens of a global village.

## Instructional Strategies for Students Speaking Diverse Languages

As we have previously emphasized, learning a second language should not mean losing a first language (Cummins, 1989; Young & Hadaway, 2006). Fitzgerald and Graves (2004) suggest four basic principles for teaching ELL students.

- It is important to realize the benefits of bilingualism and the cognitive abilities that students bring to the classroom when they speak a language other than English.
- Teachers need to be sensitive to the language similarities and differences that bilingual students bring to the classroom, and they need to appreciate the challenges that students face when learning a second language.
- It is critical that teachers realize and build upon the rich cultural heritage that ELL students bring to the classroom.
- Teachers need to appreciate that ELL students tend to experience emotional feelings as they learn English, and they need to be sensitive to negative emotions regarding self-concept that might not appear evident on the surface.

It is helpful for teachers to have a framework of the levels of language development for English language learners. Mora (2006) suggests a four-by-four model of language arts instruction that focuses on listening, speaking, reading, and writing at four levels of English proficiency. Table 3.2 is an adaptation of the four-by-four model and includes instructional strategies for each level.

Supporting students' first languages and offering them resources to help them develop proficiency with written language is possible even without special or bilingual language classes. In addition, many activities that teachers may already use in their reading

Many principles that guide language and literacy learning in a first language can guide literacy in a second language.

# Table 3.2  ELL Developmental Language Levels and Instructional Principles and Strategies

| LISTENING | SPEAKING | READING | WRITING |
|---|---|---|---|
| **Level 1 learners are beginners. They try to grasp the meanings of words and connect them to ideas. They begin to communicate in sentences but may answer questions with only one word.** | | | |
| During read-alouds, focus on individual words in descriptive sentences. | Provide many opportunities to converse socially, allowing for inaccurate speech, but modeling Standard English. | Model concepts of print including "talk" about how books work.<br><br>Use environmental print in the student's first language and compare to English. | Develop written summaries of stories read aloud. Use the cloze technique orally to have students state words discussed in the original stories. |
| **Level 2 learners can understand simple, concrete sentences. They begin to decode words and develop the ability to read high-utility words. Following a structured framework, the learners can write simple sentences and narratives.** | | | |
| Develop phonemic awareness using songs, rhymes, and word pairs.<br><br>Have students respond to oral directions. | Scaffold vocabulary development with graphic organizers.<br><br>Elaborate on vocabulary learning in conversations about content words.<br><br>Have students retell stories and/or role-play them in small groups. | Use explicit instruction and guided reading with leveled-reading materials.<br><br>Use repeated readings.<br><br>Continue to use read-alouds of quality multicultural literature. | Use sentence transformation activities such as changing statements to questions.<br><br>Use bookmaking activities such as alphabet books and short stories. |
| **Level 3 learners have a good grasp on basic communications skills, although grammar and syntax may be incorrect. They are progressing as readers but need extensive content vocabulary to enhance subject learning.** | | | |
| Continue opportunities for learning vocabulary through discussions that focus on content words.<br><br>Encourage talk about text ideas and how they relate to background experiences. | Have students construct sentences using content vocabulary and gradually summaries.<br><br>Teachers should begin to correct speech miscues. | Continue to use leveled-reading materials and guided reading. Provide many opportunities for independent reading.<br><br>Explicit instruction in content reading should include knowledge of text structures and identifying main ideas and details. | Instruction should include composition writing. Activities should also include writing for different purposes such as letter writing. |
| **Level 4 learners have increased in fluency and can read most class assignments. They still need help with abstract concepts and writing skills.** | | | |
| Teach students how to take notes based on lectures and teacher talk. Show them how to outline and summarize based on listening to others. | Provide opportunities for oral reports. Interviews with others can be conducted.<br><br>Allow for opportunities to orally explain more complex content ideas. | In addition to continued guided reading, introduce more complex comprehension skills such as comparing and contrasting information. Develop concepts such as plot, character study, and setting.<br><br>Help students use more complex graphic organizers to understand text. | Provide students with simple research projects in which they have to gather and summarize information. |

*Source:* Adapted from "Differentiating Instruction for English Learners: The Four-by-Four Model," by J. K. Mora, in T. A. Young and N. L. Hadaway (Eds.), *Supporting the Literacy Development of English Learners: Increasing Success in All Classrooms* (Newark, DE: International Reading Association, 2006), pp. 24–40; and "No Half Measures: Reading Instruction for Young Second-Language Learners," by K. Lenters, 2004/2005, *The Reading Teacher, 58,* pp. 328–336. Reprinted with permission of the International Reading Association (www.reading.org).

classrooms to teach literacy to native speakers are especially useful for second-language learners. Freeman and Freeman (1993), Barone (1996), and Schmidt (1998c) offer realistic suggestions for supporting the first language of ELL learners:

- Include environmental print from the child's first language in the classroom. Label objects in the first language and in English so that everyone is learning a second language.
- Make sure that the classroom and school libraries have books in languages other than English as well as books written in English representing the cultures of the children.
- Encourage children to bring in artifacts, music, dance, and food from their cultures.
- Help children publish and share their writing in their first language.
- Enlist the help of bilingual aides—other students, parents, teacher aides, or community volunteers.
- Use commercial or student-produced videos and computer software to support language learning and improve self-esteem.
- Help ELL students find support on the Internet. There are web sites, open 24 hours a day, in which students can meet others speaking their first language. They can engage in peer discussions as well as share ideas about learning English.
- Connect with the families. Welcome them into the classroom to observe and to share their language and culture. Even though their English may be limited, they often enjoy teaching the numbers, days of the week, greetings, and other common expressions.

**SHELTERED ENGLISH ADAPTATIONS** ◆ Garcia (2002), and Brown and Kysilka (2002) suggest techniques teachers can use in mainstreamed classrooms that are adaptations of strategies used in *sheltered English settings*, those in which the teacher is not proficient in the student's language and the student is not proficient in the teacher's language. Non-verbal communication is maximized. The following adaptations are recommended:

- Give students time to express what they know by drawing pictures, pointing, or manipulating objects.
- Demonstrate concepts with body actions. Make use of all the senses, including sounds and smells.
- Give students more wait time. They may need more processing time to answer questions or discuss topics.
- Keep language simple; rephrase information using body actions and objects.
- Adapt materials by adding pictures, diagrams, charts, and graphic organizers.

**INSTRUCTIONAL CONVERSATIONS** ◆ Instructional conversations are another effective way to engage students in diverse language classrooms. During **instructional conversations,** teachers facilitate students' prior knowledge and experience about a topic, build on the student's background, engage in extensive discussion, and guide understanding. Teachers also scaffold learning rather than expect correct "yes" or "no" answers (Garcia, 2002). Diaz (2001) elaborates further on modifications of classroom discourse that teachers can use. For example, by allowing students to respond to more divergent, high-order, and affective questions, teachers provide students with opportunities to express reactions to content on a personal level. By minimizing teacher-talk, teachers can encourage students to role-play, carry out small activity-oriented tasks, or use dramatic presentations to express understanding. In Box 3.2 you can read how Joanna, a second-grade teacher, uses the language-experience approach to teach her ELL students.

**RESPONSE PROTOCOL** ◆ Teachers often try to engage English language learners in talking by asking questions; sometimes the responses are one word, simple phrases, or just body-language responses such as nodding the head. In order to encourage productive talk in the classroom that fosters ELLs' social as well as academic language development, Mohr and Mohr (2007) suggest how teachers can elaborate on student language using **response protocol,** which is "designed to help teachers better their understanding of

BOX **3.2**

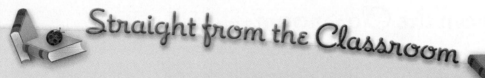

# Straight from the Classroom

## The Language-Experience Approach in a Second-Grade Multicultural Classroom

### JOANNA NEWTON

*Joanna Newton is a second-grade Title I teacher at Groveton Elementary School in Fairfax County, Virginia. In addition, she has worked as a Peace Corps volunteer in an Armenian Village School and has used the language-experience approach with elementary school students in this country as a strategy for teaching children to read using authentic language.*

Last year, my class of 20 students included children from Pakistan, El Salvador, Peru, Bolivia, Guatemala, Cambodia, and Ghana. These students were either immigrants themselves or the children of recent immigrants. Most of them had received or were receiving ESOL (English for Speakers of Other Languages) services.

Because my students are both multicultural and multilingual, I seek ways to develop their unique voices as writers and readers, regardless of their current level of English proficiency. The language-experience approach (LEA) fits these needs very well. It has become a regular component of my daily Writing Workshop. Through the regular use of LEA my students are able to take ownership of their writing, truly seeing themselves as "real" writers and readers.

I reserve one hour of the daily Language Arts block for Writing Workshop. I launch Writing Workshop with a 10–15 minute minilesson or focus lesson. The remaining 45 minutes are dedicated to individual student writing and conferences. I model the writing process for my students at least 3 days a week in a minilesson. Using LEA, the students write class stories based on shared experiences. I set aside the remaining 2 days for focus lessons about vocabulary or grammar. What follows is a description of an LEA story written by the whole class. It was about a field trip the class took to Huntley Meadows Nature Conservatory.

### Sample Lesson: Our Trip to Huntley Meadows Nature Conservatory

#### PART 1

*Brainstorming (10 minutes):* I began by telling students that today we were going to write a class story. I let the students guide the lesson by asking them where they thought we should begin. They responded by explaining that we should brainstorm. As they called out ideas for the story, popcorn-style, I recorded them on the overhead. Next, the class voted on the potential topics. This day they voted to write about our recent field trip to Huntley Meadows Nature Conservatory.

#### PART 2

*Prewrite (15 minutes):* Now that we had a topic, the second day began by asking the students to generate ideas for our story. They volunteered ideas about what we saw at Huntley Meadows, who came with us, and what we learned. As students discussed which ideas should come in the beginning, middle, and end, I recorded their thoughts on a "web" transparency. When the students had decided which ideas to use, we were ready to begin drafting the story.

#### PART 3

*First Draft (15 minutes):* Using the web as a guide, students began day 3 by discussing and then generating sentences for the draft. They decided to begin the story by describing how we got to Huntley Meadows. Several students offered specific suggestions: "We walked to Huntley Meadows," "The walk was cold and long," and "We heard leaves rustling and trees blowing." The class picked which sentences they liked best, often combining elements of various sentences. Students voted on which sentences to include. Finally, I recorded their sentences on chart paper. We continued this process over the next few days until the first draft was complete. We ended each session by choral or echo reading what we had written so far.

#### PART 4

*Revising (10 minutes):* Revising begins by listening closely to an oral reading of the draft. To build fluency, students choral read the story back to me.

As we read, I remind students to think about which areas need to be improved. They decided that the Huntley Meadows story needed more details about a blue heron they had seen on the trip. As a class they brainstormed ways to improve that section of the story. They finally decided that they should add sentences describing the blue heron in flight. They generated a variety of sentences, finally voting on and selecting "The blue heron tucks its neck in when it flies. It flies very fast and stays low near the ground." Using a caret, I inserted the sentence in the appropriate section of the story. The students continued to revise the story until they were satisfied with the content.

#### PART 5

*Editing (10 minutes):* Editing begins with a fresh reading of the revised draft. After choral reading the text, the students noticed mechanical errors, such as misspelled words and incorrect punctuation. They took turns correcting errors with different colored markers. We continued with this over the next several days until students were pleased with the story.

*(Continued)*

# Straight from the Classroom *(Continued)*

PART 6

*Publishing (10 minutes):* Finally, I read the completed story to the class. The students then choral read the text. The students gave a "thumbs up" to express their satisfaction with the story. They decided that the text was ready to publish, so I typed it in the same format as their final published stories.

PART 7

*Final Published Story (10–15 minutes):* I shared the final published story with students in a class read-aloud. We added it to the Publishers' Corner, an area of the classroom in which we display the students' written work.

### REFLECTIVE INQUIRY

◆ How does Joanna help her students see themselves as "real" writers and readers?

◆ What are some class rules that you might develop prior to engaging your students in LEA?

---

students' language development and broaden their repertoire for meeting the needs of this special population" (p. 444). The design provides a framework for teacher responses to English language learners' responses to teacher questions. See Table 3.3 for a practical synthesis of response protocol based on the types of responses English language learners typically use in the classroom.

**READING AND WRITING PRACTICES** ◆ Farnan, Flood, and Lapp (1994) suggest six research-based reading and writing practices for enhancing the comprehension of all students, including linguistically diverse learners. Below we share modified versions of these strategies:

**1.** *Use reading as preparation for writing.* Allow students time to reread favorite passages and take note of the sound of the language, including syntax and vocabulary. By reading predictable books, students can use language patterns to create books of their own. The use of story frames can also provide students with a predictable structure for writing. In addition, providing students with multiple texts that provide background knowledge about topics before they write and allowing time for students to keep logs of what they read can be useful tools for enhancing comprehension.

**2.** *Use writing as preparation for reading.* Encourage students to compose "quickwrites" on sticky notes prior to reading. These are simple notes in which the student jots down prior knowledge. This strategy helps teachers identify students' misconceptions before they read as well as understand personal attitudes and dispositions toward topics.

**3.** *Use webbing and mapping.* By scaffolding webbing strategies with small groups, teachers provide students with opportunities to learn about the prior knowledge and experiences of others in the group. Teachers can help students make connections and compare and contrast experiences in order to foster comprehension before reading.

**4.** *Use summaries.* Summary writing can help students sift through important information and select related details. By modeling summary writing or collaboratively writing summaries with students, teachers can assist students in understanding complex information. Providing students with summaries of content before they read can also enhance comprehension for students with diverse language needs.

**5.** *Use authentic messages.* Primary teachers often model writing through a strategy called "morning message." Middle school teachers can adapt this technique to meet the needs of students with diverse languages by modeling the conventions of writing. As students dictate a sequence of events that are important to them, the teacher writes the sequence and discusses concepts such as writing left to right, punctuation, and capitalization. For example, a student might describe holiday celebrations, sporting events, or family traditions. Talking about an important event that is meaningful and observing as the teacher transcribes the event can help linguistically diverse students understand how language works.

## Table 3.3 Response Protocol: Recommended Elaborations to English Language Learners' Responses

| STUDENT QUESTIONS | RESPONSE PROTOCOL |
| --- | --- |
| *When a student gives a correct response to what I ask, what should I say?* | "You're right! Can you tell me more?"<br>"Yes, that's good. What else do you know about that?" |
| *When a student's response is partially correct, what should I say?* | "Good answer! Can you tell me something else about it?"<br>"Yes, I agree with _____. Can you tell me more?" |
| *When a student responds in another language, what should I say?* | "I think I know what you said. Can you say that in English?"<br>"That sounds interesting. How can we say that in English?" |
| *When a student responds to a question by asking another question, what should I say?* | "I am glad you asked that question. Let's see how we can all answer it."<br>"Questions are good to ask. They help us understand. It is good to ask questions." |
| *When a student responds incorrectly or with a confusing response, what should I say?* | "Help me understand what you mean. Tell me again."<br>"Do you think _____ or _____ ?" (Give right answer as a choice) |
| *When a student does not respond, what should I say?* | "I think you know something about this, and I would like to hear what you have to say."<br>"Can you show us what you think? Can you draw a picture of what you are thinking?" |

*Source:* Adapted from "Extending English-Language Learners' Classroom Interactions Using the Response Protocol," by K. A. J. Mohr and E. S. Mohr, 2007, *The Reading Teacher, 60,* pp. 440–450.

**6.** *Use dialogue journals.* These are much like conversations written down. Students, regardless of their levels of proficiency, can be encouraged to write down thoughts and questions about what they are reading. The teacher responds personally to the student by addressing the questions or elaborating on thoughts in caring ways by writing to the student in a conversational tone. Dialogue journals are an effective way to personalize instruction.

**CONTENT AREA PRACTICES** ◆ It is well documented that English language learners take longer to learn academic language than social communication—approximately 5 to 7 years for children between the ages of 8 and 11 (Hadaway & Young, 2006). Pilgreen (2006, pp. 41–60) suggests specific ideas for developing English language learners' academic language in content area classrooms:

STANDARD 2.2

- Speak clearly, slowly, and use fewer idioms.
- Explicitly teach terminology associated with content area books, such as table of contents, glossary, index, illustrations, graphs, charts, title page, headings, and subtopics.
- Explicitly teach the differences between paragraphs, passages, and excerpts. These are particularly confusing terms, yet they are often used in reading assessments.
- Use icons or illustrations to capture the question types. For example, a *who* question might be labeled with a person; a *when* question might be depicted by a clock; a *why* question might be identified by a question mark.
- Model "think-alouds" that visualize information through graphic organizers.
- Teach students how to scan for important information. Help them understand how italics and bold type are used in the text.

**THEMATIC TEACHING** ◆ English language learners learn academic language when it is taught in meaningful contexts. Freeman and Freeman (2006) suggest why teaching thematically makes sense. Students learn important content in a variety of ways, including oral reports, a wide range of literature, resources using various media, and learning activities that are authentic; they learn content vocabulary in a natural context. In addition, since the vocabulary is used over and over in different subject areas, the repeated contexts foster learning in meaningful ways that make sense. Thematic teaching also provides multiple opportunities for differentiated instruction and small group work. The following suggestions will help teachers begin to organize thematic content, some of which are adaptations of Freeman and Freeman (pp. 61–78).

- Select a broad theme—a universal topic—that will be culturally relevant to the English language learners and formulate "big questions" that will relate to all students.
- Use the content standards for each subject area as guidelines for activities. Focus on what the students should be able to do. Use action words such as *analyze, problem solve, critically interpret,* or *construct organizers.*
- Gather a variety of resources making sure that some are directly related to the culture(s) of the English language learners.
- Think about cooperative learning activities and differentiated instruction with respect to your class. Would some students work well if they were all from first languages that are not English? Would partnerships that pair student abilities work?

Finally, to help students learn the English language, systematic coordination among content area teachers and the ELL teacher is vital. Teachers need to share what they are teaching and how they are teaching. In some ELL programs, students meet with the ELL teacher outside of the classroom several days a week. In other programs, the ELL teacher co-teaches with content area teachers in the classroom. In any program, the ELL teacher needs to be actively involved in team planning sessions so that there is congruency in the program.

## Dialects and Reading Strategies

Language variations and associated values affect the instructional job of literacy teachers. For instance, African American language, or Ebonics, is the dialect of a U.S. community, and to be effective, teachers need to understand it (Locke, 1989). Its rhythm, rate, phonology, syntax, morphology, semantics, lexicon, and stress, along with distinctive nonverbal communication, make it an artistic and verbally agile language (Dillard, 1983). For a time it was thought that beginning readers who spoke a variation of "standard edited English" or "standard American English," the dialect found in textbooks, would read poorly because the language was different from their own. However, this idea is unfounded. When teachers draw on a child's background knowledge, gather culturally relevant materials, effectively monitor oral reading, use language experiences, and bring the study of different language patterns into the classroom, all children can develop reading, writing, listening, and speaking skills with a similar degree of success.

**BACKGROUND KNOWLEDGE AND MOTIVATION** ◆ Connecting the known to the new has long been considered a way to motivate and focus students, as well as a means of evaluating the existence of background knowledge. When a teacher draws on a child's prior experiences and helps the child connect those to new vocabulary and story concepts, this provides a basis for making meaning. Children need to see the relevance of a story to their own lives. Classrooms with culturally relevant materials accomplish this task easily.

**CULTURALLY RELEVANT MATERIALS AND MOTIVATION** ◆ When children see books and materials with characters that look and sound like themselves, their lives are validated. The stories they read connect to their own experiences, so new vocabulary and concepts are more easily learned. Furthermore, other children in the classroom gain an understanding of diverse ethnic and cultural backgrounds as they are exposed to multicultural literature.

**DIALECTICAL MISCUES** ◆ When reading aloud, children often substitute one word for another. Such errors, or miscues, can help teachers understand how—and how successfully—a child is constructing meaning from a text. Language choices are not random; miscues help a teacher decide which cueing system a reader is using to comprehend the text. In oral reading, when a child substitutes words from her or his speaking dialect for the word printed on the page (for example, reading *he don't* for *he doesn't*), the miscue probably shows that the reader is reading the text for meaning. Such a substitution would be impossible if the reader had not comprehended the text.

As more research on reading is done in the classroom, we learn that reading revolves around the experiences that the reader brings to the text to make sense of it. Reading is only partly about the marks on the page. This in turn is changing the way we think about dialects and decoding and about how reading teachers should address dialectical differences. Teachers must of course help their students learn letter–sound correspondences in beginning reading, but they must also help students grow in their understanding that writing is not just speech written down. In fact, writing is like another dialect of English.

**USING LANGUAGE EXPERIENCE** ◆ Helping beginning readers discover the connection between spoken and written language is one of the most important aspects of teaching beginning readers. For beginning readers, and especially students who ordinarily use linguistic variations from school language, the language-experience approach (LEA) is a good way to help make the connection between speech and writing concrete. Most important, LEA gives students the kind of reading material they can most easily read—predictable, meaningful, and contextually complete—because they dictate or write it.

LEA begins with ample time for *discussion* of whatever topic interests the students. Rigg (1989) suggests stories that have interest for all students, even students with limited proficiency in English. Discussions leading to stories about pets, recipes, interviews with the class VIP-for-a-day, retellings of a story that has been read aloud, stories patterned after other stories, advice to students in next year's class, and a newcomer's reaction to life in the United States are all popular with children.

The next step, *dictating*, involves the teacher (or a student acting as a peer scribe) writing down the exact words dictated by class members. The scribe rereads each sentence, repeating it to help students remember what they had to say and to help beginning readers read back what is written. While the scribe writes down exactly what the children say, it is important to use conventional spelling and not try to reproduce phonetically what children say. Rigg (1989) points out that the focus is on students' ideas and not on adult grammatical forms. In fact, she notes that copies of LEA dictations help provide running records of student progress in mastering standard forms of English.

Students can revise the LEA text after rereading, either in groups, individually, or as a class with the author's permission. Then the text can be prominently displayed or copies can be made for individuals so that the students can use it for rereading or illustrating or as a story starter. In Box 3.2, as you recall, second-grade teacher Joanna uses LEA to engage her multilingual students in writing a story based on a field trip. Whether stories or experiences are the stimulus for LEA, the strategy is a compelling one that helps students make sense of language as they communicate experiences that are written down.

# Cultural Diversity in Literacy Classrooms

Closely related to language and linguistic diversity is **cultural diversity.** In fact, it "is believed if students were distributed evenly across the nation's classrooms, every class of 30 students would include about 10 students from multicultural groups. Of the 10, about 6 would be from language minority families" (Obiakor,

**BUILDING TEACHING SKILLS: ARTIFACTS**

Go to the Homework and Exercises section in Chapter 3 of MyEducationLab to complete the exercise to consider how you could incorporate this artifact, "Mural," into your instructional approach.

2007, p. 53). Because native speakers learn language in social settings, they also learn their culture's norms for language use. Different cultures have different rules that are culturally defined and culturally specific. When a student's norms differ from the teacher's expectations, communication is often hindered. Purpose, context, and background experiences all affect how we make sense of language.

Because rules for using language are so culturally specific, it is easy for teachers not to recognize that language rules are indeed in effect for speakers of other dialects or speakers with different cultural norms for communicating. While teaching the norms of school language, it is important for teachers to understand the manner in which the students from diverse cultures in their classrooms use language at home and in social settings. Moreover, teachers need to be aware of instructional principles and strategies for addressing the literacy needs of students from diverse cultures. What are the contemporary beliefs about cultural diversity and engaging students in literacy learning? What pedagogical principles does research suggest, and which instructional strategies work for students from diverse cultures?

## Instructional Beliefs About Cultural Diversity

Our heightened understanding and beliefs about the nature of literacy as shaped by cultural and societal influences have influenced the way school programs have attempted to transform the curriculum. Diaz (2001) describes these perspectives by categorizing and characterizing them under the following approaches:

- In the **contributions approach** teachers typically include culturally specific celebrations and holidays in the curriculum, such as Martin Luther King Day.
- The **additive approach** is a thematic approach. Teachers might integrate into the curriculum a unit that addresses multicultural issues; otherwise, the curriculum remains relatively the same.
- In the **transformative approach** teachers attempt to help students understand diverse ethnic and cultural perspectives by providing them with opportunities to read about concepts and events, make judgments about them, think critically, and generate their own conclusions and opinions.
- As an extension to the transformative approach, the **decision-making and social-action approach** provides students with opportunities to undertake activities and projects related to the cultural issues they have read about and analyzed. Projects that involve social action and civic duties are encouraged.

Diaz suggests, and we concur, that teachers need to go beyond limiting the content of literacy lessons to celebrations or thematic units. Teachers of the twenty-first century need to provide students with authentic literacy and learning experiences that will provide them with the cross-cultural knowledge and skills they will need as future adults in a nation that has become increasingly diverse. In Box 3.3, one teacher shares the way in which her beliefs about teaching diverse learners evolved.

## Instructional Principles for Students from Diverse Cultures

The U.S. Department of Education supports several guiding principles for schools regarding culturally and linguistically diverse students (Garcia, 2002). These principles include:

- Establishing high expectations for culturally and linguistically diverse students
- Instructing students with challenging content material that reflects a range of language proficiency levels
- Using assessment tools that take into account the languages and backgrounds from which diverse students come

## BOX **3.3**

# Viewpoint

### Teaching Diverse Learners
Patricia Schmidt

*Patricia Ruggiano Schmidt is a pro-*
*fessor of literacy at Le Moyne College*
*in Syracuse, New York. She works with*
*urban schools preparing teachers with the ABC's*
*of Cultural Understanding and Communication.*

As a reading teacher for 18 years in a suburban middle school in upstate New York, grades 5–8, I worked with students who had been diagnosed with difficulties in reading, writing, listening, and speaking. Each year I was also assigned the one or two new students from places such as Taiwan, Russia, Israel, Detroit, or Appalachia. Similar to other European American teachers in this suburban setting, I believed in the assimilationist perspective. I thought that students from ethnic or cultural minority backgrounds needed to fit into the mainstream to be successful academically and socially. Therefore, my task was to help them learn Standard English as quickly as possible. Some students did. They also made friends, followed peer dress codes, and were involved in school activities. They began to look and act exactly like their classmates. However, other students, who maintained their cultural identities, took longer to speak and read Standard English. They were often isolated both in and out of the classroom. Their families noticed the difficulties and enlisted my assistance.

During the school year, home visits and conferences revealed unfamiliar languages and dialects and diverse cultural perspectives. I began to understand their struggles in making new community connections. I realized that our school was ignoring the rich resources that the new families offered. Reading and study led me to the realization that the additive perspective (Cummins, 1986), which encourages the inclusion of differing languages and cultures in the classroom, could be the approach to guide connections between home and school. Those connections could help the children maintain their own cultural identities as well as see the relevance of the school culture. In addition, students in the mainstream who are unfamiliar with diversity would be gaining from the different people and cultures. So what does this experience mean for our children and schools?

Diversity in our nation's schools is inevitable due to shifting world populations. Also, because the global economy affects all of us, our children will probably work in places very different from their home communities. Consequently, our present and future teachers must be prepared to work effectively with

PATRICIA R. SCHMIDT
*LeMoyne College,*
*Syracuse, NY*

linguistic, cultural, and academic diversity. Since most teachers will have grown up in middle-class European American suburbia and have had few opportunities to develop relationships with different groups, they may unconsciously rely on media stereotypes. Differences in the classroom may be viewed as problematic rather than opportunities for children to explore physical, linguistic, cultural, and academic differences and learn to appreciate individual talents and multiple perspectives. Therefore, the classroom as social context can begin to prepare children for an appreciation of differences that gives them social and economic advantages. But how do we do this?

A major means is through effective connections between home and school. Families who are actively involved in the classroom and school community feel comfortable and needed. They see themselves as contributors to their children's education. The task for teachers then is to reach out to families who are culturally and linguistically different from the school and to families who fear and dislike the school because of their own emotional and academic failures. Teachers who realize that families are the children's first teachers and who value the family's knowledge and contributions to the child's literacy development soon begin to communicate in positive ways. Therefore, I think that a teacher's ability to communicate and connect with families and communities from underrepresented groups of people will lead to closing the academic gap.

Another key factor relates to the relevance of materials and activities for diverse learners. When children see people like themselves pictured in the resources they are using and can connect an activity with their own life experiences, they tend to stay focused on learning. Drawing on home and community literacy activities and materials as well as children and young adult literature related to diverse groups can be the means for connecting home and school for meaningful literacy development. Furthermore, children from the European American culture are enriched when they learn about diversity through literature and materials introduced and studied in their classrooms.

In addition, since immigrant students undergo a range of adjustments including mixed emotions, excitement, fear, or conflict (Hadaway & Young, 2006), it is recommended that teachers first focus on what the students can do, make sure to pronounce their names correctly, and arrange to take them on a tour of the school (Hayes, 2007b). Moreover, according to Ovando, Collier, and Combs (2003), as cited in Hadaway and Young (2006, pp. 9–10), there are several background factors that teachers of immigrants should consider, including the country of origin, extent of ties to the country of origin, reasons for immigration, amount and quality of schooling in the native language, and length of residence in the United States.

The importance of learning about the cultures of ELL students and developing communications with the families is critical. Lynch (2004) recommends that teachers read about the culture through books and the Internet, learn about the arts associated with the culture, hold discussions with other members of the culture to grasp information about perceptions and beliefs, get involved with community events that are held by the immigrants, and perhaps even learn the language of the culture.

Moreover, teachers of students from diverse cultures should plan a curriculum that supports the cultural diversity represented in their classrooms, use cooperative learning strategies that foster cross-cultural understanding, and establish collaborative relationships with the home. It is also important that teachers develop a network of support from state and regional organizations that provide a wide variety of instructional resources for teachers of diverse learners (Davidman & Davidman, 2001).

## Instructional Strategies for Culturally Diverse Students

Teachers need to be aware of their personal teaching styles and may need to make adjustments in their teaching methods and classroom organization to accommodate differences among students. Teachers also need to be cognizant of the cultural differences represented in their classrooms. They need to respect the diverse cultures and include them in the curriculum.

In the chapters that follow, we suggest more specific literacy strategies for teaching English language learners, including word identification, vocabulary, comprehension, writing, and content area reading instruction. In this section, we share ways to engage teachers in knowing their culturally diverse students, ways to help culturally diverse students understand the *process* of American schooling, and ways to foster *all* students' understanding of cultural diversity.

**CONSIDER YOURSELF AND YOUR OWN BELIEFS AND EXPERIENCES WITH OTHER CULTURES** ◆ It is important that teachers of students from cultures different from their own examine their own views of differing cultural perspectives (Lynch, 2004). The following suggestions might serve as a checklist for teachers:

- Bullet ideas that you have gleaned about teaching students that reflect your beliefs for all students. For example, what thoughts do you have about student assessment for all learners? What do you think about homework? What about home–school connections for all learners?
- Self-evaluate your knowledge about the cultural groups that might be included in your classroom. Would you rate yourself as knowledgeable about the culture(s)? Very knowledgeable? Somewhat knowledgeable? Lacking basic knowledge? If the latter is true, how might you proactively prepare yourself for teaching in a classroom that is composed of multiple cultures? Make a checklist for yourself.
- Do you have any biases that you need to consider as a teacher of students from diverse backgrounds? What are your thoughts about students who come to your class without proficient English-speaking skills? What are your expectations for those students? Are you knowledgeable about useful strategies for engaging students from diverse cultures to learn?

In essence, it is important for teachers of ELLs to consider their own beliefs and experiences with different cultures. Self-evaluation is a valuable tool for all teachers.

**DETERMINING CULTURAL EXPECTATIONS** ◆ How can a teacher decide if cultural misunderstandings are interfering with learning in the classroom? Three things to look for are lessons that continually go awry, an extended lack of student progress, or a lack of student involvement.

Teachers can observe the interactions of students as they work and play together, read about cultural differences as well as cultural similarities, and maintain communication with parents and family in order to determine appropriate classroom changes (Fitzgerald, 1993).

An awareness of cultural expectations and individual learning styles can help teachers engage students from diverse backgrounds. This is particularly important because "students from home cultures dissimilar to the school's are often at a distinct disadvantage, coming into classrooms with quite different understandings of school success, literacy, appropriate interaction between student and teacher and so on" (Pransky & Bailey, 2002–2003, p. 373). Diaz (2001) cautions teachers against stereotyping and labeling cultures. Lynch (2006) suggests that teachers consider "value sets" that are common across cultures as a way to think about cultural diversity. Figure 3.1 illustrates value-based cultural continua based on Lynch's work. These characteristics serve as broad guidelines; teachers need to understand that there is a wide range of learning styles in all cultures.

**VALIDATING EACH CHILD'S EXPERIENCE** ◆ Because we use our previous knowledge of the world to help us construct the meaning of our reading and writing, it is only sensible that students with different experiences will have different readings of books and texts. Our cultural schemata, the beliefs we hold about how the world is organized, influence comprehension. Background knowledge that may be common for and familiar to a

## 𝒥igure 3.1   Values, Beliefs, and Behavior Continua Across Cultures

|--------------------------- [continuum] ---------------------------|

| | | | |
|---|---|---|---|
| **Family** | Extended with many kinship relationships | -------------------- | Small unit with limited reliance on other family members |
| **Dependence** | Interdependence—contributions to the family are important | -------------------- | Independence—individuality and expression of self are valued |
| **Nurturing Young Children** | Close proximity to the caregivers is important | -------------------- | Early independence is encouraged |
| **Time** | Time is given depending on the circumstances | -------------------- | Time is measured and expected in a more precise manner (clock, calendar) |
| **Tradition** | Respect for elderly, traditions, and rituals is important—wisdom of ancestors is key | -------------------- | Emphasis is on youth, the future, and new technologies |
| **Ownership** | Little priority is given to individual ownership—emphasis is on the family or community | -------------------- | Emphasis is specific—"mine," "yours," "someone else's" |
| **Rights and Responsibilities** | Roles are differentiated and expected—for example, gender roles | -------------------- | Equality is expected across genders and other characteristics—for example, job equality |

*Source:* Adapted from "Developing Cross-Cultural Competence," by E. W. Lynch, in E. W. Lynch and M. J. Hanson (Eds.), *Developing Cross-Cultural Competence: A Guide for Working with Children and Their Families* (Baltimore: Paul H. Brooks, 2004), pp. 41–77.

suburban American child may be unknown and confusing to a child from an inner-city or a rural farm area and even more confusing to a child who recently arrived in the United States.

Helping students build background knowledge before reading remains an important task for teachers in classrooms with students with culturally diverse experiences. However, cultural groups are difficult to define (Yokota, 1993). Asian students will have varying experiences and languages, depending on their home country and their social class and geographic region within that country. Hispanics in the United States have vastly divergent backgrounds, ranging from Mexican American and Puerto Rican to Chilean and Peruvian. Students from the former Soviet Union will never say they come "from Russia" if in fact they grew up in one of the other republics, such as Ukraine.

In short, our nation is composed of widely diverse groups of people from around the world, and each group has contributed to the greatness of the nation. Therefore, teaching an appreciation of diversity in rural, urban, and suburban settings is relevant, natural, and appropriate. A model for classrooms is presented in the Research-Based Practices featured in Box 3.4.

**FOSTERING ETHNIC, NATIONAL, AND GLOBAL IDENTIFICATION** ◆ Teachers need to help all students develop ethnic, national, and global identification (Banks, 2001). For students from diverse cultures, ethnic identification means providing them with opportunities to develop positive self-images of themselves and their rich cultural heritage. Planning for home–school collaborations in which parents share customs, traditions, holidays, and special events is an important component of the multicultural classroom. Teachers can help students develop a sense of pride in family heritage by inviting family members as guest speakers, encouraging family demonstrations of traditional customs, and including activities that involve ethnic foods, clothing, and music.

Teachers also need to help students develop a sense of national identification. Schools should foster a commitment to democratic ideals such as equality, human dignity, freedom, and justice through activities in which the students, for example, become involved in community service projects. When teachers encourage students to read about local issues and problems and design service activities that address those issues, they are helping students develop a sense of civic responsibility (Banks, 2001).

Global identification is also important, and teachers need to help students develop a sense of world cooperation among nations. Banks (2001) suggests that students must first develop a sense of ethnic identification, followed by national identification. Only when students have developed these can they truly understand their role in the world community.

**COLLABORATIVE COMMUNITIES** ◆ Effective teachers of culturally diverse students use collaborative learning opportunities to enhance student learning. Cross-cultural interactions occur more frequently when students work together on instructional activities (Garcia, 2002). In addition, home–school collaborations are vital. Bertha Perez (2001) describes a project called Community Connections in which a group of primarily Mexican American fourth and fifth graders, their teachers, and the parents collaborated on an inquiry project. After selecting topics of interest to the students and parents based on the community, the group brainstormed questions to investigate and sources of information they wanted to explore. Parents became experts and shared information, parent and child reports were shared in Spanish and English, and technology was used for multimedia presentations. The collaborative effort was based on shared responsibility for determining goals, gathering resources, planning activities, and building interdependence.

Edwards and Danridge (2001) explain that "schools must develop creative strategies that are culturally sensitive to parents" (p. 270). They suggest initiatives that build relationships with parents, such as:

- Inviting parents to structured activities such as book reading
- Visiting parents at home and showing respect for the family

BOX **3.4**

*Research-Based Practices*

## The ABCs of Cultural Understanding and Communication

The model known as the ABCs of Cultural Understanding and Communication was created to help current and future teachers develop culturally responsive pedagogy through literacy activities. When teachers adapt the model in their own classrooms, their students also begin to understand and appreciate differences among classmates. Emphasis is on differences because differences have traditionally been the sources of human conflict. The following is a brief explanation of the model with ideas for classroom practice:

- *Autobiographies* are written in detail, including key life events related to education, family, religious tradition, recreation, victories, and defeats.
- *Biographies* of culturally different people are written from in-depth unstructured interviews that include key life events.
- *Cross-cultural analyses* of similarities and differences related to the life stories are listed in chart format.
- *Cultural analyses* of differences are examined with explanations of personal discomfort and admiration.
- *Communication* plans for literacy development and home–school connections are designed with modifications for classroom adaptation.

### Classroom Practice

The teacher participates in all of the following activities in order to build classroom community.

#### AUTOBIOGRAPHY

- Students bring in family pictures and special family objects to share.
- Students write interview questions and interview family members.
- One student each day brings in a bag of favorite things to share.
- Students draw self-portraits and family portraits using crayons or paints.
- Students write their life stories.
- Students create timelines of their life stories showing significant events.

#### BIOGRAPHY

- The class learns about interviewing and how to question.
- Students in pairs interview each other and write each other's life stories.
- Students in pairs introduce each other after listening to life stories.
- The whole class interviews the "student of the day" and completes a language-experience story.
- Each class member draws a picture of the "student of the day" doing his or her favorite activity and writes a sentence or two. The sheets are compiled for a book, and a cover is created. The "student of the day" takes home the special book at the end of the day.

#### COMPARE AND CONTRAST SIMILARITIES AND DIFFERENCES

- Create Venn diagrams showing similarities and differences.
- Study physical similarities and differences from self-portraits, photographs, and other artifacts.
- Write lists of similarities and differences and discuss them.

#### CULTURAL ANALYSIS OF DIFFERENCES

- Talk about the differences and why differences are important.
- Talk about why we like or don't like some differences.
- Talk about why some differences scare us.

#### CONNECT HOME AND SCHOOL FOR COMMUNICATION

- Invite family members to come into the class and share food, games, language, customs, and/or home artifacts.
- Invite family members to tell a story, sing a song, and/or teach a dance.
- Invite family members to talk about their lives and work.
- Invite family members to help with all of the ABCs activities.

*Source:* "The ABCs of Cultural Understanding and Communication," by P. R. Schmidt, 1998, *Equity and Excellence in Education* (www.informaworld.com), *31*(2), pp. 28–32. Reprinted by permission of Taylor & Francis Ltd., www.tandf.co.uk/journals.

- Establishing partnerships with parents by means of community members such as local business owners
- Supporting parents' ownership of their children's schooling by making connections between home and school literacy practices

**TECHNOLOGY-ENHANCED INSTRUCTION** ◆ With increased attention to the multiple ways that technology changes as well as enhances literacy learning, using technologically mediated instruction with English language learners has drawn considerable attention. Cummins, Brown, and Sayers (2007) suggest that technological innovations can enhance "curiosity, imagination, and social commitment while also promoting academic achievement . . . foster[ing] identity development, and encourage[ing] critical awareness" (p. 114). Moreover, Butler-Pascoe and Wiburg (2003) identify the following characteristics of technology as valuable for English language learners.

- Technology can provide communicative competence and foster the development of a community of learners for ELLs through multiple opportunities to collaborate with authentic audiences.
- Technology can provide comprehensible input for ELLs through schema-building, scaffolding, text re-presentation, and visuals.
- Technology can foster problem solving and inquiry for ELLs by providing contextual environments that prompt critical thinking.
- Technology can promote the development of English language skills by focusing on listening and speaking programs.
- Technology can meet the affective needs of ELLs by providing them with comfortable learning environments in which they are motivated and take risks when trying new literacy building tasks.
- Technology can foster an understanding of all cultures through multiple resources.

Box 3.5 offers some technology-based approaches for English language learners that can enhance or be used as alternatives to traditional instructional practices.

**IMAGE MAKING** ◆ Based on the notion that visual images evoke knowledge, Julia Marshall (2001) suggests "art practice" strategies—or **image making**—for middle school students that incorporate observational and critical thinking skills. "In art practice, what is observed or what has been experienced is transformed into images" (p. 88). Although valuable for all students, artistic representation can be a particularly useful way for teachers to assist students from diverse cultural backgrounds. Marshall describes an "art practice" strategy titled "Writing Our Own Histories: The History Book Project" (p. 93). The teacher provides the students with old history books that can be cut apart. The purpose of the project is to have the students rewrite the history book (or a section of the book) from their points of view. Students examine the photographs, illustrations, maps, timelines, and so forth, and cut and paste them to form collage pages. As they create the collages, students mount photographs of themselves at key points. The visual images represent the students' interpretation of history from their cultural perspectives. Students can interview parents and relatives as they create their collages and develop other artistic representations of history. Presentations of the projects are a visual way for students to express themselves and their relationships to historical events.

**CHOOSING QUALITY MULTICULTURAL LITERATURE** ◆ Teachers who use multicultural literature in the classroom help students recognize the unique contributions of each culture and the similarities of the human experience across cultures. At the same time, they help nonmainstream cultures appreciate and value their heritage and give all students the benefit of understanding ways of knowing about the world that are different from their own. Asking several questions can help teachers choose those books that will be most useful to them in their classrooms (Yokota, 1993):

- *Is this book good literature?* Is the plot strong? Is characterization true to experience? Are setting, theme, and style well developed?
- *Is this book culturally accurate?* Will it help readers gain a true sense of the culture?
- *Is the book rich in cultural details?* Do details that give readers insight into the nuances of daily life enhance the story? Or is the culture overgeneralized?

BOX **3.5**

*New Literacies*

## ENHANCING INSTRUCTION WITH TECHNOLOGY

*Numerous characteristics of technology-based enhancements can assist English language learners. The following chart identifies several technologies that can be incorporated with more traditional classroom practices based on the work of Butler-*

*Pascoe and Wiburg (2003). This synthesis provides teachers with new ways to think about technology and the possibilities for literacy learning and English language learners.*

| TRADITIONAL APPROACHES TO ELL ENGAGEMENT | NEW LITERACY TECHNOLOGICAL APPROACHES FOR ENGLISH LANGUAGE LEARNERS |
| --- | --- |
| Teacher modeling and scaffolding strategies | *Hyperstudio presentations* by peers can model strategies |
| Teacher offers opportunities for students to share background information about their cultures | Students can develop *media presentations* that reflect their culture; family tree and mapping programs can also be used |
| Teacher uses pictures to associate language and concepts | *Multimedia and video clips* can be used to develop vocabulary and clarify new content |
| Teacher attempts to develop self-esteem by providing opportunities to talk about characteristics of their culture with pride—including invitations for family members to share. | Opportunities are available for students to develop *electronic portfolios* that feature themselves and can foster self-identity |
| Teachers attempt to connect students with leveled books that match the levels of proficiency for the ELL students | *Software* is available that includes leveled word games, authoring programs, and language development activities |
| Teachers use collaborative learning strategies such as buddy projects | *Internet collaboratives* of global reach can enhance cooperative learning and communication among all cultures |
| Opportunities for small group discussions foster social and content learning | *E-mail collaboratives and electronic bulletin boards* offer opportunities to elaborate on social communication and subject learning |

We do not suggest that technology-enhanced learning opportunities should replace traditional classroom teaching practices for teachers of English language learners; however, the technological opportunities are endless, worthwhile, and have the potential for creating motivating educational experiences for our ever-growing multicultural population.

---

- *Are dialogue and relationships culturally authentic?* For example, *Pacific Crossing*, about Mexican American students who go to Japan as exchange students, deals with both cultures authentically.
- *Are cultural issues presented comprehensively?* Do they have enough depth and realism for readers to get a true sense of how culture affects the lives of people?
- *Are minorities relevant?* Are members of a minority present for a reason, or could the story be told as easily about any cultural group? Token involvement of minority characters gives little sense of their unique, culturally rooted experience.

Choosing books that reflect the insider's perspective not only helps students from nonmainstream cultures read about and validate their own experiences, but also helps children understand diverse experiences of groups other than their own. Box 3.6 on page 81 tells how one teacher chooses books for her sixth graders. See Appendix F for a list of multicultural books.

By using multicultural literature in the classroom, teachers help nonmainstream students appreciate and value their heritage.

# Academic and Cognitive Diversity in Literacy Classrooms

## BUILDING TEACHING SKILLS: READING

Go to the Homework and Exercises section in Chapter 3 of MyEducationLab to read the article "The Way We Learn" and build a deeper understanding of how to accommodate student differences.

As human beings, we make sense of our experiences by putting them into categories and giving the categories labels. Although this ability to categorize and label is essential to help us sort through the amount of information we accumulate, it's of little use as we attempt to describe the diversity of experience and ability we face in our students. Labels can never fully represent the range of experiences that students bring to the task of learning to become literate.

Nonetheless, especially in programs funded by the federal government, in most school districts labeling becomes necessary for inclusion in the program. Identifying students who may need different or more instruction is a sticky problem. For example, standardized tests do not give teachers useful guidance as to what the instructional needs of their students might be. Occasionally, a district may focus on a curriculum solely designed to raise test scores, leading to instruction focusing on basic skills that do not translate well into reading as a meaning-based activity (Strickland & Ascher, 1992). Legitimate ways of knowing are often not measured by standardized tests; gifted students and linguistically and culturally diverse students often do not test as well as their actual ability would suggest (Tuttle, 1989). Moreover, standardized tests do not always measure what students can and cannot do (Calkins, Montgomery, & Santman, 1998).

Reading failure is an emotional issue. Among students, parents, and educators alike, the belief that reading is the key to academic as well as personal success is strong. Research indicates that students who experience early reading difficulty maintain or increase below-level performance (Stanovich, 1986). The prestige and power associated with cultural and societal definitions of literacy add further to the sense of the importance of helping students become literate. However, certain categories can be used to describe learners and their needs that will help us plan the classroom activities that can help all of our students

BOX **3.6**

## Straight from the Classroom

## Kelly Carpenter's Sixth-Grade Class and Multicultural Literature

Kelly Carpenter, a sixth-grade teacher in a suburban setting, adapted the ABCs of Cultural Understanding and Communication for student research about ancestors (Schmidt, 1998a). Her students interviewed family members about customs and countries of origin. The writing and sharing of family histories in class caught students' interest in their own stories and others' stories and assisted in the building of classroom community and home–school connections. The students also began discovering literature related to their ancestry, along with other multicultural literature found in the classroom. They read in interest and ability groups, wrote analyses of books, and shared their ideas in small groups. The following format was used for written and oral discussions.

### Cultural Analysis of Literature

*Directions:* Please answer each question on your own after reading the book in a group.

1. What is the title of the book? Who are its illustrator and author?
2. What is the book about? Give a brief summary.
3. Choose a word that is new or different in the book and define it.
4. What is your favorite part of the book and why?
5. What is your least favorite part of the book and why?
6. What is your favorite illustration in the book and why?
7. What did you learn from the book?

8. How did the book make you feel when you were reading it?
9. Please complete your cultural analysis on the back:
   a. List the similarities between the book and your culture.
   b. List the differences between the book and your culture.
   c. Analyze the differences, both the ones that you liked and the ones that made you feel uncomfortable. Discuss these in your group.
10. See if people in your group are ready to discuss these questions. If they are, choose a place in the room to meet. If they are not, wait and select a literature response activity from the list of 25. This activity may be shared with the whole class.

Kelly found that this adaptation of the ABCs was a positive way for her class to practice reading, writing, listening, and speaking, as well as a means of developing an appreciation of diversity. "My students and I learned about each other from the beginning of the school year. I learned information not in the files, and they formed a cohesive community as they began to study cooperatively. I am also beginning to integrate reading, writing, listening, and speaking to develop an appreciation of diversity in math and science through ethnomathematics and nonfiction literature."

### REFLECTIVE INQUIRY

◆ What parts of the model would you find most beneficial for use in your classroom? Why?

---

grow as readers and writers, including those with linguistic and cultural differences, those with learning disabilities, young readers having difficulties, and gifted readers.

## Instructional Beliefs About Academic and Cognitive Diversity

Beliefs about **academic and cognitive diversity** are often grounded in definitions, categories, and labels. Beliefs about academic and cognitive diversity also often result in legislation that serves as guidelines for instructional policies.

The term *exceptional children* refers to students who "differ from the norm (either below or above) to such an extent that an individualized program of adapted specialized education is required to meet their needs" (Heward, 2000, p. 4). Categories of exceptionalities include learning disabilities, emotional and behavioral disorders, mental retardation, and intellectual gifts and talents, among others. As previously mentioned, labels have their drawbacks. Some disadvantages of labeling include the notion that labels tend to focus on what a student cannot do, they may negatively stigmatize a student and affect self-esteem, and they may lead to low expectations. Others argue that some systematic way to classify children is necessary in order to provide them with the services they need (Heward, 2000).

With respect to reading difficulties, an inclusive approach to identifying students is recommended because it challenges categorical differences and recognizes "those whose reading levels are low relative to their classmates but not relative to national norms, and those whose reading levels are discrepant from their aptitude but not low in relation to national (or even local) norms" (Snow, Burns, & Griffin, 1998, p. 95). This approach to identifying students with reading difficulties suggests that it is sometimes appropriate to use points of reference other than norms to distinguish students who are considered poor readers.

Several significant pieces of federal legislation reflect beliefs about the instruction of students with academic and cognitive differences. Public Law 94-142, the Education for All Handicapped Children Act, passed in 1975 and since amended, is based on several principles that remain in effect today (Heward, 2000, pp. 17–18):

- *Nondiscriminatory identification and evaluation.* Testing and evaluation procedures must not discriminate on the basis of race, culture, or native language.
- *Free, appropriate public education (FAPE).* All children with disabilities are entitled to a free, appropriate education and must have an individualized education program (IEP) that reflects their needs.
- *Least restrictive environment (LRE).* All children with disabilities must be educated with children without disabilities to the maximum extent appropriate. This mandate presumes inclusion in the regular classroom.
- *Parent and student participation and shared decision making.* Schools must collaborate with parents and students with disabilities in the design and implementation of special education.

Since 1975 the law has been restructured. IDEA 2004 added, among others, the following procedures for identifying students with specific learning disabilities:

- The states *must not require* that the criteria for determining a specific learning disability include a severe discrepancy between intellectual ability and achievement.
- The states *may* use alternative research-based methods to determine whether a student has a specific learning disability.
- The states *must* allow the use of a child's response to scientifically research-based intervention when identifying specific learning disabilities.
- With respect to the language arts, the criteria include failure of the child to adequately achieve in any one of the following areas: oral expression, listening comprehension, written expression, basic reading skills, fluency, or reading comprehension when provided with appropriate instruction based on state standards.

With respect to the academic and cognitive diversity among linguistically and culturally diverse students, issues of dialect among diverse languages and definitions of cultural diversity tend to complicate matters for teachers. Although diverse dialects are recognized as legitimate language systems, teachers struggle with issues regarding Standard English. A major concern among educators is that there is a disproportionate number of students of color and from various ethnic backgrounds in special education programs that service students with disabilities (Banks, 2001; Garcia, 2002; Heward, 2000; Hunt & Marshall, 1999). IDEA 2004 specifies that the state must follow guidelines that are designed "to prevent the inappropriate overidentification of disproportionate representations by race and ethnicity of children as children with disabilities" (U.S. Department of Education, 2007, p. 1).

Exceptional students by definition also include those identified as gifted or talented, although they are not included in the IDEA legislation. Giftedness is defined in a variety of ways. Gardner (1993) defines giftedness as abundant talent in any of seven intelligences. Sternberg's theory includes analytic, creative, and practical giftedness (Hunt & Marshall, 1999). Just as the number of ethnic and minority students in special education programs is disproportionately high, ethnic and minority students are not adequately represented in gifted or talented programs. In the next section, we address major instructional principles for accommodating academic and cognitive diversity.

# Instructional Principles for Academic and Cognitive Diversity

In the highly publicized National Reading Panel report (2000), the essential components of an effective literacy program include instruction in phonemic awareness, phonics, vocabulary, comprehension, and fluency. Needless to say, we agree that these essentials are critical. In addition, we recognize other vital components that are important for all learners, including those with diverse literacy needs. Rasinski and Padak (2004) suggest useful guidelines that capture our beliefs for what literacy learning for students with diverse cognitive and academic abilities should include:

- Students need to be engaged with authentic texts. Teachers need to engage students that are struggling or are exceptional in other ways with authentic literature. That means avoiding worksheets that are not meaningful; rather, foster a love for reading by immersing children in the "real stuff" of life—good books, engaging poetry, funny stories, and such.
- Students with diverse abilities need to see reading as purposeful; they need to see reading as "real" in their lives. They need to make connections to what they are learning and how these skills will help them later on.
- Students who differ in their reading abilities need experiences with literacy tasks that are highly engaging and that are focused on their interests as learners. Motivation to read is critical, whether it be for struggling readers or gifted readers. Students need reasons to read that tap what they want to know and purposeful lessons that will get them where they want to go.
- Students who struggle need teachers who can guide them toward success. They need teachers who can help them develop positive self-concepts about their abilities and who appreciate and commend them for the smallest of achievements.
- Teachers of students with a variety of abilities need to be focused. They need to assess students daily through observation and regular informal assessments, with specific instructional purposes as the goal. That means teachers need to be "kid watchers" when it comes to instruction. They need to ask questions. What are my students' strengths? Where are they struggling? How come Joey can't do this? How could Andrea help Joey?
- Effective teachers involve parents. Since parents are critical stakeholders in what goes on in school with and for their children, they need to be informed and invited to be involved.

**INCLUSION** ◆ Another principle of instruction for students with diverse academic and cognitive needs is the concept of **inclusion.** In the past, students with special education needs due to low academic performance or ability were mainstreamed into regular education classes in which they could succeed with little or no help from the teacher. In a sense, these students were considered "guests" in the classroom. Their primary instruction took place outside the regular education classroom. The concept of inclusion, however, means that children with special needs are included in the regular classroom and receive assistance from the regular education teacher as well as the special education teacher. In addition, special education students in regular education settings have opportunities to learn from their peers and to develop friendships and social skills. This allows students with special needs to experience instruction that focuses on their strengths and to have more opportunities to set higher goals for themselves (Friend & Bursuck, 2002; Scala, 2001).

For students from diverse linguistic and cultural backgrounds who experience difficulties with reading, the same principle of inclusion applies. As noted previously in this chapter, students of diverse linguistic and cultural backgrounds comprise a disproportionately high percentage of students in special education programs. Teachers need to understand that students from diverse backgrounds will vary in their competency levels, their background knowledge, and their linguistic abilities. Cultural and linguistic diversity should not be used as a benchmark for determining difficulty in learning to read or for placing students in special education programs (Banks, 2001; Diaz, 2001).

**CURRICULUM COMPACTING** ◆ What about gifted students? They, too, constitute a diverse group of students. Although there is some debate regarding the ability grouping of gifted students, the National Association for Gifted Children affirms the value of grouping gifted students in programs that include advanced instruction that challenges their capabilities. There is a variety of alternative ways to accommodate gifted students. In order to provide more time for gifted students to engage in more challenging content, for example, one principle of instruction is **curriculum compacting,** in which the curriculum is compressed. Teachers can also accommodate gifted students through an enriched curriculum with thoughtful and innovative methods including technology applications. In addition, teachers can provide gifted students with alternative internships and mentor programs outside the classroom (Heward, 2000).

**STANDARDS 5.2, 5.3, 5.4**

**LITERACY COACHES** ◆ Literacy coaching dates back to the 1920s and there is a resurgence of the concept today in response to standards and the goal of academic achievement for all students (Hall, 2004). According to the International Reading Association (2004), a primary goal of coaching reading is to provide long-term professional development for teachers that ultimately results in improved reading achievement. With this goal in mind, teachers of academically and cognitively diverse students ought to consider using literacy coaches in their classrooms. Ideal characteristics of literacy coaches include:

- Strong understanding of the reading process
- Excellence in teaching reading
- Exemplary communication skills with peers
- Skill in literacy assessment and instructional practices

In essence, literacy coaches need to be experts in a variety of areas (International Reading Association, 2004; Puig & Froelich, 2007). When a literacy coach is available in a school, school system, or district, we suggest that teachers of struggling readers inquire about including them in the teaching process. Box 3.7 considers the questions you might ask of a literacy coach.

---

**BOX 3.7**

## Viewpoint ᵗʰᵉ Literacy Coach

### Important Questions to Ask

Billings Middle School has recently adopted literacy coaching as a new strategy to address young adolescent struggling readers in their rural school district. The population consists of students who primarily come from farming homes and the parents, who are dedicated agricultural workers, do not have a lot of time to devote to school involvement.

The teachers have participated in several school-sponsored professional development days; the workshops were to serve as springboards for discussing how to address the needs of their middle school students who are not passing proficiency tests. According to the teachers, the majority of the students at Billings Middle School are not motivated to learn. They are not concerned about grades and they typically do not aspire to read anything other than popular preteen publications.

As a prospective literacy coach, Mr. James, a veteran social studies teacher at Billings and a recently licensed literacy specialist, was asked by the administration to work with the teachers on

the new idea of "literacy coaching" at the school. In considering the assignment, Mr. James asked the administration the following questions regarding their commitment to literacy coaching:

- How much of my time would you allow me to devote to my own professional development as a literacy coach? Would I be permitted to attend reading conferences associated with effective ways to coach?
- How much time would I be allocated each week to work with individual teachers in their classrooms? What roles would you expect of me in working with teachers? Would I serve as a mentor? Would I be expected to model strategies?
- How about time with struggling students? Would I be allotted time for tutoring or working with students that are in need of intensive instruction?

These are questions that, needless to say, complicate the potential roles of literacy coaches. What other questions might *you* have?

## Instructional Strategies for Students with Diverse Academic and Cognitive Abilities

Instructional strategies that require students to be actively involved in constructing meaning, using all the cueing systems of written language, are especially important for struggling readers. On the other hand, although gifted readers do not automatically learn without instruction, they learn quickly and need to be sufficiently challenged beyond reading instruction planned for average readers. With appropriate and innovative modifications, the strategies discussed earlier in this chapter as well as in other chapters will benefit both readers who have difficulty, including those with linguistic and cultural differences, as well as gifted readers. Next, we discuss additional topics and program considerations regarding academic and cognitive diversity.

**INQUIRY LEARNING** ◆ **Inquiry learning,** a classroom approach for teaching math and science, has helped students with special needs in literacy learning. Inquiry learning and teaching is based on the constructivist approach (Confrey, 1990; Fosnot, 1996; Piaget, 1970), which perceives learning as a meaning-making process. Children experiment, solve problems, and discover how the world functions. They are encouraged to become more active classroom participants as they connect with their own environment and the studies at hand and formulate high-level questions. Box 3.8 describes a framework for helping students form questions in inquiry learning.

For academically and cognitively gifted students, inquiry learning can be enhanced immensely by using the Internet and computer software. As students brainstorm what they know and want to learn, they can explore virtual reality and informational web sites, communicate electronically with experts, and use sophisticated computer software that helps them express and demonstrate their curricular interests and goals (Heward, 2000).

TECHNOLOGY

---

**BOX 3.8**

### Research-Based Practices        KWLQ

At the heart of inquiry learning is questioning, but student ability to ask questions about content is often based on prior knowledge. Furthermore, students with special needs may have difficulty asking questions. To help them with their questioning, a framework was developed using Ogle's (1986) KWL and an additional Q. Based on previous personal and school experiences and connected to new experiences, students in kindergarten, second grade, and fifth grade were encouraged to question and discover through the four steps of KWLQ (Schmidt, 1999):

1. The students recorded their prior knowledge about a particular subject under *K*. This was completed in pairs with individual charts or on a large class chart.
2. The students formulated, recorded, and reported questions under *W* in the same manner. The teachers also modeled the different ways to ask questions.

3. The children searched for answers through reading, interviews, field trips, videotapes, the Internet, and first-hand experiences. They recorded and reported their answers under *L*. The teacher anticipated specific answers based on the units of study; the students responded not only with those answers but also with information beyond what the curriculum required.
4. The children noted more questions for further study under *Q*. At the end of the unit, the unanswered questions from *Q* became a focus for those students who continued to be interested in finding answers and reporting them to the class.

In conclusion, KWLQ provided a framework for question formulation and practice for literacy learning as the children naturally connected reading, writing, listening, and speaking for inquiry learning.

---

*Source:* Adapted from "KWLQ: Inquiry and Literacy Learning in Science," by P. R. Schmidt, 1999, *The Reading Teacher, 52,* pp. 789–792.

Athena, for example, is a gifted student who lives in an affluent neighborhood. She is concerned about poverty as a social issue. Although she knows a lot about poverty because her mother is the director of a social service agency in a large urban city, Athena wants to know how she can help underprivileged peers in her local community. She has developed an electronic survey for middle school students that addresses questions that she would like to answer about her peers in adjacent schools. Athena's teachers are encouraging her to write a newsletter for publication on the school's web site that will foster a service-learning community project.

**DIFFERENTIATED INSTRUCTION** ◆ A presumption of **differentiated instruction** is that "different learners have differing needs. Therefore, the teacher proactively plans a variety of ways to 'get at' and express learning . . . based on his knowledge of varied learner needs" (Tomlinson, 2001, pp. 3–4). In addition, differentiated instruction is based on assessing student needs, implementing multiple approaches to learning, and blending whole class, small group, and individual instruction. Teachers can differentiate based on students' levels of readiness for a topic, student abilities, and students' interests (Tomlinson, 2001). In Box 3.9 we share an adaptation of how one teacher implemented differentiated instruction in her classroom.

**NEW LITERACIES** ◆ Whereas differentiated instruction refers to an instructional concept that provides students with alternative ways to express their abilities based on teacher

---

## BOX 3.9

### Straight from the Classroom

## How Mrs. R. Uses Differentiated Instruction

*Mrs. R. is a third-grade teacher who plans to extend her lesson on biographies using two learning centers. This strategy helps her focus on the differing abilities of her students because she develops her centers based on student assessments. Once she designs her learning centers, however, she ensures that students have choices in the activities they will select, as well as the choice to work individually, with a partner, or with a small group. Below you will see how Mrs. R. organizes differentiated learning experiences in these centers.*

### CENTER ONE

- Students select a person they have learned about and construct a time line of the person's life that is annotated and reflects a theme in the person's life.
- Students then choose to either (1) write an essay that explains why they selected the time line events of that person; (2) draw a storyboard that reflects the events; or (3) dramatize one of the events during sharing time.

### CENTER TWO

- Students first select a biography of someone about whom they have read and brainstorm the youthful experiences of that person.
- Next, they select a story about a fictional character about whom they have read and think about the youthful experiences of that character.

- The next step is to write about some early background experiences they have had (or their classmates have had).
- Next, the students compare and contrast the three "characters."
- Finally, the students select a way to represent the common themes that they learned about growing up. They can (1) design thematic trees, (2) create a matrix, or (3) conduct a conversation with another classmate.

Mrs. R. assigns centers to the students based on ability and interest levels. Beyond the assigned centers, however, the students have choices.

### REFLECTIVE INQUIRY

◆ What choices might Mrs. R. also have given her students?

*Source:* Adapted from *How to Differentiate Instruction in Mixed-Ability Classrooms* (2nd ed.), by C. A. Tomlinson (Alexandria, VA: Association for Supervision and Curriculum Development, 2001).

assessments of students' performance, new literacies, sometimes referred to as **multi-literacies,** refers to fluid representations of knowing beyond traditional linear text. Examples include visual representations with artistic interpretations (e.g., drama, painting, photography) and multiple technological representations of text (Anstey & Bull, 2006; International Reading Association, 2000b; Kist, 2005). We feature new literacies throughout the text as a way to view literacy beyond traditional text-based literacy learning. Without a doubt the new literacies, as they are construed during the twenty-first century, will open endless opportunities for students with diverse cognitive and academic abilities to express their understanding of concepts required by state standards. Consider the following example of how one middle school student uses artistic representation to express his appreciation of connections between art and music.

> Jimmy, a musically and artistically gifted eighth grader who also has a talent for writing, was interested in the relationship between album and CD cover art and the music the art represented. He photographed album and CD covers, examined styles of artistic representation on the Internet, and read about relationships between art and music. In his thesis paper, he wrote about one album, "The highs and lows seem to balance out like a bird's wings as it soars through the air."

**RESPONSE TO INTERVENTION (RTI)** ◆ As mentioned earlier, IDEA 2004 specifies that states must allow alternative methods of identifying children with learning disabilities. Currently, **response to intervention** (RTI) is the latest method that seeks to provide children with early intervention. Although questions remain regarding how RTI will play out, the purposes seem to be legitimate: "to provide struggling students with early, effective instruction and to provide a valid means of assessing learner needs" (Fuchs & Fuchs, 2006, p. 95). RTI is based on a tiered model, ranging from two to four tiers. In a three-tiered model, each child assessed at Tier 1 for being "at risk" is provided with scientifically based instruction in the regular classroom. After a period of instruction, the children are reassessed in terms of their response. Children not meeting a criteria for growth move to Tier 2, in which they receive more intensive work. Limited progress in Tier 2 qualifies the student(s) for possible placement in special education (Klinger & Edwards, 2006).

RTI raises many questions as to which assessments will be used, how long intervention will take place before reassessing, which qualifications should be required of teachers, and whether children might fail to respond because of the teacher's lack of expertise. Needless to say, although RTI holds much promise for assisting struggling readers, more information and research are needed to evaluate long-term effectiveness. Also, considering the surge of interest in literacy coaches, RTI may play a role in how literacy coaching is implemented in schools (Gersten & Dimino, 2006).

## Programs and Strategies for Struggling Readers Who Are Academically and Cognitively Diverse

There are countless instructional programs and strategies for struggling K–12 readers, many of which, since NCLB, claim to be evidence-based. Although scientifically based research is critical to informing teachers about what works, to date, the evidence has not been conclusive enough to give specific prescriptions for specific problems or to say which program is best for any particular reading problem. On the other hand, there should not be such a list of informed research programs and strategies that correlate with specific reading difficulties because the learning process is quite varied for individuals with different learning styles. Moreover, teachers vary in their teaching styles. So what are classroom teachers, literacy coaches, and those responsible for RTI supposed to do? As a starting point, we suggest that teachers ask themselves the following questions:

- How will I identify my struggling readers? Will I request referrals from the previous year's teachers? Will I use standardized assessment scores? Will I assume that a student who was in an intervention program as "at risk" is still "at risk"? What will *that* really tell me about this student? Will the information I have be specific enough to work with the student on weaknesses? Or should I design a more informal assessment that captures my students' needs? If I am a social studies teacher, how will I determine those students who might struggle with my textbook?

- Has our school system "bought into" a particular intervention program? If so, who made the decision and on what was the decision based? Did the decision makers consider the price of the program as a key point? Was the decision to purchase the program based on reported scientifically based results? How informed were the decision makers about the nature of "scientifically based" programs? Is the program "scripted"? If so, why was it selected? Was the population of our school and the expertise that would be needed to carry out the program considered? If so, how? Are there any political or business ties to the program that would benefit a constituency?

- What support systems does our school have in place to guide me in helping struggling students? Do we have a "literacy coaching program" in place? Are there reading specialists to support classroom teachers? If so, *how* do they support teachers? If I am a first-grade teacher, where do I receive support for the students that I perceive to be struggling readers? If I am a science teacher, what do I do with students who cannot read my textbook?

In essence, it is critical that all teachers at all grade levels involve themselves in serious conversations about how to address students who are academically and cognitively challenged and the programs and strategies that are or might be implemented in classrooms. Moreover, the questions listed can serve as a starting point for discussions by preservice teachers, continuing education and graduate-level students, and teachers in professional development programs. In subsequent chapters, we more explicitly address strategies that are effective for students with diverse learning needs, strategies that teachers can consider as part of these conversations.

# WHAT ABOUT STRUGGLING READERS AND *Their Diverse Academic and Cognitive Needs?*

STANDARD
3.2

It is important that teachers use fair assessments to evaluate students' academic and cognitive abilities. Students from diverse linguistic and cultural backgrounds are often considered struggling readers even though they may have adequate cognitive and academic abilities. Assessments should be multidimensional and unbiased.

Regardless of students' linguistic and cultural backgrounds, it is important that teachers look closely at the strengths and weaknesses of struggling readers and develop curricular goals that address those strengths and weaknesses. We believe that teachers need to look beyond specific programs as a "cure" for students who have reading difficulties. Instead, teachers must be responsive to students' ethnicity, learning preferences, home environments, interests, and aptitudes.

Responsive teachers are nurturing, caring, and sensitive to the difficulties that struggling readers encounter with print. They engage struggling readers in meaningful literacy experiences in which they can succeed. Moreover, responsive teachers foster positive self-esteem and hold high expectations for struggling readers' abilities to achieve.

# WHAT ABOUT STANDARDS, ASSESSMENT, AND Diversity?

Standards-based education and high-stakes assessment are realities for all of today's students, including culturally and linguistically diverse learners. Proficiency assessments, based on statewide content standards, must be in compliance with provisions of the No Child Left Behind Act (NCLB). NCLB requires that all students, including English language learners, be held accountable for achievement in a standards-based curriculum based on statewide assessments regardless of language proficiency.

NCLB exerts enormous pressure on states and school districts to meet the academic and linguistic needs of second-language learners. The goals of NCLB in relation to statewide proficiency assessments are to ensure that limited–English proficient and immigrant students meet state content standards, attain English proficiency, and achieve high levels of academic competence in English.

Ironically, the lack of appropriate, valid, and reliable assessments for culturally and linguistically diverse students has been a major educational issue for more than 2 decades. Critics contend that assessments have been culturally insensitive and have overlooked the cultural traditions of underrepresented groups. As a result, test scores may not reflect student achievement or ability level because cultural traditions are not considered in testing (Cummins, Brown, & Sayers, 2007; Lapp, Fisher, Flood, & Cabello, 2001; Lipsky & Gartner, 1997; Valdes & Figueroa, 1994). On the other hand, under the proposed reauthorization of NCLB, Education Secretary Spellings has called for improved assessments for English language learners (2007). Will NCLB make a difference in the academic success and English-language proficiency of limited–English proficient and immigrant students? Only time will tell.

## Summary

Understanding and accepting children's differences have been a common thread throughout this chapter. Diversity among learners is a fact of life in classrooms. Ignoring this creates unnecessary difficulties and frustrations for both students and teachers. Embracing it leads to effective reading instruction. Three types of learner diversity were explored: linguistic, cultural, and academic and cognitive.

*Linguistic diversity* in the classroom may be the result of a variety of factors. Dialects differ in phonology, syntax, and lexicon. Rather than viewing linguistic diversity as a disadvantage or barrier, teachers and students must understand and value linguistic diversity. Children should have many natural opportunities to use language so that they can experiment with language and discover their options as language users. Teachers must recognize that children may read in their own dialect patterns, but these dialect miscues seldom interfere with the child's quest for meaning. Instruction for linguistically diverse learners should capitalize on children's strengths in comprehension and expression. Our goals for children should center on language growth and flexibility, not change.

Many of the same principles that guide language and literacy learning in a first language can guide literacy learning in a second language.

*Cultural diversity* is closely related to linguistic diversity. Teachers need to help children acquire the norms for communication in the language of the school. They need to make adjustments in teaching strategies to accommodate difference, turning cultural misunderstandings into student involvement.

Children with learning disabilities, young readers having difficulties, and gifted readers also benefit from instructional adaptations that address *academic or cognitive diversity*. Teachers often need to provide extra instruction in order to actively involve struggling and gifted readers in constructing meaning.

Teachers who adapt instruction effectively use their understanding of children's needs and their beliefs about reading to make instructional decisions. They reach out to the families of their students in order to connect home and school for literacy instruction. They recognize that whatever adaptations are made for a child's special needs, meaning must be at the heart of reading instruction.

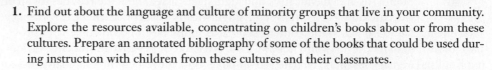

## Teacher Action Research

**STANDARD 5.1**

1. Find out about the language and culture of minority groups that live in your community. Explore the resources available, concentrating on children's books about or from these cultures. Prepare an annotated bibliography of some of the books that could be used during instruction with children from these cultures and their classmates.

2. Experience a modified version of the ABCs of Cultural Understanding and Communication. Sit down with someone from a different culture than yours. The older person spends 4 or 5 minutes sharing earliest memories of family, education, celebrations, food, fun, victories, traumatic events, loves, honors, disappointments, and so on. Next, the younger person does the same. Then, together, make a list of your similarities and differences. Afterward, describe and reflect on this experience in a paragraph or two.

3. Research book lists and annotated bibliographies for books that would be appropriate for readers with special needs, who read English as a second language, or who wish to learn about other cultures. Some journal sources include *Booklist*, *Language Arts*, and *The Reading Teacher*. Read one (or more) of the recommended books with a student. Reflect on the student's response to the books. How does reading these books differ from reading other children's literature?

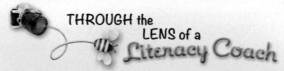

**THROUGH the LENS of a Literacy Coach**

**STANDARD 5.3**

4. Make arrangements to visit a language arts class containing at least several ELL students in which the teacher will be conducting a minilesson addressing a particular language arts standard. Prior to visiting the classroom, discuss with the teacher the standard and/or indicator that will be taught. After observing the lesson, write reflections that address the following issues:

- What was the organizational strategy that the teacher used with the ELL students? Was it a whole class, small group, paired, or individualized lesson? What do you think the teacher did well to organize the instruction? Is there anything from your observation that suggests ways the teacher might reorganize the lesson?
- How did the ELL students react to the lesson? Were they engaged? Did they seem to understand the lesson? Were they successful? If so, how do you know? If not, what suggestions do you have to engage the students?
- How might you change the lesson based on your beliefs about instructing ELL students? How would you guide the teacher if your beliefs about instruction differ from the teacher's instructional planning and instruction?

## Related Web Sites

*CAST: Center for Applied Technology*

**www.cast.org**

This primary resource focuses on universal design for learning (UDL), a concept that supports teaching diverse learners.

*Council for Exceptional Children*

**www.cec.sped.org**

The Council for Exceptional Children is an international professional organization dedicated to individuals with exceptionalities or disabilities, including the gifted.

*Destination ImagiNation*

**www.destinationimagination.org**

This is an online creative problem-solving program for students of all ages. The students work as teams to expand on knowledge and skills learned in the classroom. This program is particularly useful for gifted students.

*International Reading Association Position Paper*

**www.reading.org/resources/issues/positions_minorities.html**

IRA provides teachers with their position statement on minorities and their overrepresentation in special education programs.

*IRA Literacy Links: Readers with Special Needs*

**www.reading.org/resources/community/links_lit_special.html**

This special section of the International Reading Association web site provides a wide variety of resources for teachers who work with special needs students.

*National Association for Multicultural Education*

**www.nameorg.org**

This professional organization site contains many links to multicultural resources, information, and lesson plans.

*Reading Online*

**www.readingonline.org/newliteracies/lit_index.asp?**
**HREF=wattspailliotet1/tour.html**

IRA provides teachers with resource articles about the new literacies and invites educators to join in the discussion.

*Second-Language Literacy Instruction: A Position Statement*
*of the International Reading Association*

**www.reading.org/positions/second_language.html**

The IRA recommends that reading instruction take place in the child's home language.

Now go to the Vacca et al. *Reading and Learning to Read*, Seventh Edition, MyEducationLab course at **www.myeducationlab.com** to

- Take a pretest to assess your initial comprehension of the chapter content
- Study chapter content with your individualized study plan
- Take a posttest to assess your understanding of chapter content
- Engage in multimedia exercises to help you build a deeper and more applied understanding of chapter content

# CHAPTER 4

# Early Literacy: From Birth to School

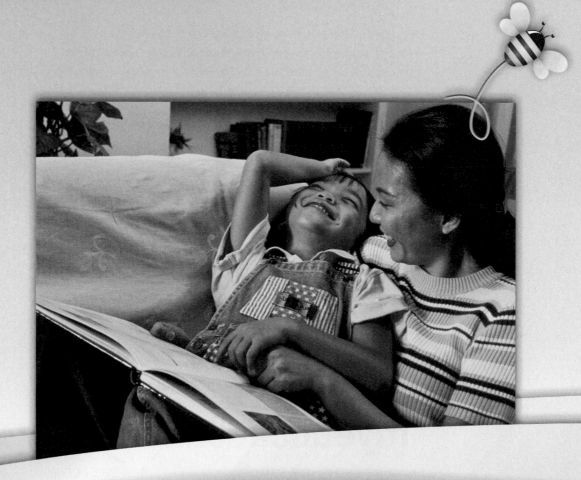

Standards found in this chapter:
- 1.1
- 1.2
- 1.3
- 2.2
- 4.1
- 4.2
- 4.3
- 4.4

## In this chapter,
### YOU WILL DISCOVER:

- The continuum of children's literacy development as they progress through various phases of learning to read and write
- How reading and writing develop in home environments that support literacy learning
- The importance of developmentally appropriate practices
- How to create literate environments
- Developmentally appropriate literacy practices emphasizing play, language experiences, and reading to children

## Key Terms

developmentally appropriate
  practice
dramatic play
environmental print
family literacy
invented spelling
language-experience activities
literacy development
literacy play center
literate environment
pretend play
scribbling
shared reading

## Concept Map

### EARLY LITERACY: FROM BIRTH TO SCHOOL

**CHILDREN'S DEVELOPMENT IN EARLY READING AND WRITING**

| How Reading Develops | How Writing Develops |
|---|---|
| Family Interactions | Developmental Stages |
| Literate Environments | Invented Spelling |

**DEVELOPMENTALLY APPROPRIATE PRACTICES FOR BEGINNERS**

| Literate Learning Environments | Literacy-Related Play Centers |
|---|---|
| Reading to Children | Language Experiences |

*B*eginnings are important. Literacy beginnings, as crucial as they are to children's development as readers and writers, often take diverse paths. For example, when Hannah was born, her mother, a reading teacher, knew she needed to read to her right from the start. In fact, even before she was born her room was decorated with a Beatrix Potter theme featuring large wall panels depicting pages from Potter's storybooks. Two bookcases were filled with all kinds of books. Hannah was read to daily by both parents from the start and always loved books. In fact, as a toddler they were her favorite toys. She could sit and look through a pile of books for about 45 minutes before she was mobile. She would open each book, turn the pages, point to things, and say a few words before putting it down. When her sister came along 3 years later, Hannah played a significant role in her sister's literacy development. She delighted in "reading" her animal books to her new sister, Emma ("Emma, the donkey says, 'Hee-Haw, Hee-Haw'"), guiding her tiny hand to touch and feel pages of her books, and chanting nursery rhymes to her. Love and respect for books bloomed naturally for Hannah and Emma in a family environment that supported and nurtured literacy learning. Books and writing tools were a big part of their lives. They attended story hour at a young age and spent time in the children's section of the library, always checking out books at the end of the visit. Reading aloud was a routine, everyday activity in their home (Lenhart & Roskos, 2003).

Both Hannah and Emma, as you have probably surmised, are in the process of becoming quite literate today. They are part of a family that values reading and communicates strong feelings and attitudes about literacy on a daily basis. The family's own interest in reading, manifested by a willingness to spend time talking, reading, and writing with the girls, provides the supportive natural learning environment they need in order to grow as readers.

Irma, by way of contrast, is a child who lives in a housing project in East Los Angeles with her mother and four younger siblings. Her mother can't read. Neither she nor her brothers and sisters have ever heard a nursery rhyme or story. Irma is trapped in a cycle of illiteracy that is passed from one generation to another: "Irma had never had a chance even to hold books before entering school" (Rosow, 1992, p. 525).

Now during the first week of the first grade, Irma checked out two library books. But what was she expected to do with the books? Where were the models of literate activity in her life? For one reason or another, the books disappeared once she brought them home. The school sent a note to the home, pinned to Irma's shirt, requesting the return of the books, lest Irma's family pay a fine and she lose her library privileges: "But the note to the nonreading mom, who herself had never had library privileges, failed to recover the books or collect the fines, so Irma spent her first year in school without books. She had no one to read to her, and she had no hope of reading to herself" (Rosow, 1992, p. 525). As bleak as the prospects for Irma's literacy development may seem, Irma's story could be different. To realize the promise of literacy in Irma's life, appropriate school experiences could very well bring the intergenerational cycle of illiteracy to an end.

The stories of Irma, Hannah, and Emma—young children from culturally diverse family backgrounds—underscore the importance of understanding the needs of all children and the conditions underlying their literate development. If we are going to make a difference in children's **literacy development,** we must be aware of the learning environment of the home, respect the diverse cultural milieus from which children learn to use language, and develop strategies to build on family strengths. Irma, Hannah, and Emma will not bring the same kinds of knowledge, values, attitudes, and strategies for literacy learning to school. Yet their school experiences will play a pivotal role in realizing their full potential as literacy learners.

This chapter is about literacy beginnings. It is forged on the dynamic and powerful connections between children's oral language and written language development. As you study the chapter overview, keep in mind several main ideas about learning to read and write in early childhood. First, there is a continuum of children's development in early reading and writing. Young children develop as early readers and writers from birth as they progress from awareness and exploration in their preschool years to independent and productive reading and writing by the end of the third grade. Second, early readers and writers develop literacy skills through developmentally appropriate practice as they participate in purposeful and meaningful activities. And third, speaking, listening, viewing, writing, and reading are interrelated, mutually supportive activities. Language experiences provide the foundation for learning to read and write.

In this chapter, we tackle important issues related to the early literacy learning of children before they enter school and the implications of such learning for beginning instruction. What do teachers, families, and caregivers need to know about young children's knowledge of and experiences with literacy? How can teachers, families, and caregivers make the child's first encounter with formal reading and writing instruction smooth and developmentally sound? In addition, in this chapter and the next we integrate a framework that emphasizes five essential learning practices and effective strategies that promote research-based literacy practices: a supportive learning environment; literacy-related play; reading aloud to children; singing, rhyming, and word play; and the developmental writing process (Neuman & Roskos, 1998).

# Children's Development in Early Reading and Writing

For decades, research has shown that children begin their journey as readers and writers early in life. From birth through preschool, young children begin to acquire basic understandings about reading and writing and their functions through home experiences with print. Children continue their literacy development as they enter school through a variety of learning experiences that allow them to experiment with language and develop early reading and writing skills in kindergarten and first grade. Learning to read and write, based on developmentally appropriate practice, takes on a more formal nature throughout the primary grades as teachers balance systematic instruction in the alphabetic code with many opportunities for fluency development and meaningful reading and writing (Snow, Burns, & Griffin, 1998). From the time children enter third grade, literacy instruction emphasizes the development and use of strategies to become independent and productive readers and writers.

The much heralded position statement on young children's development in early reading and writing, jointly adopted by the International Reading Association (IRA) and the National Association for the Education of Young Children (NAEYC) in 1998, proposed a continuum of children's development in early reading and writing to account for literacy learning from birth through the primary grades. Figure 4.1 on page 96 illustrates the phases of children's development on the reading–writing continuum as suggested in the joint position statement by IRA and NAEYC. As you study the figure, keep in mind that children at any grade level will function at a variety of phases along the reading–writing continuum.

## Phases of Literacy Development

As indicated in Figure 4.1, the continuum of children's literacy development encompasses a sequence of distinct phases.

**1.** *Awareness and exploration phase.* The awareness and exploration phase begins at birth and progresses through a child's preschool years. Children explore their environment and build the foundations for learning to read and write. The awareness and

**HOMEWORK EXERCISE: VIDEO**

Go to the Homework and Exercises section in Chapter 4 of MyEducationLab to view the video entitled "Early Development" and consider the different signs of development children demonstrate and their needs at these different stages.

STANDARD 1.1

STANDARD 1.3

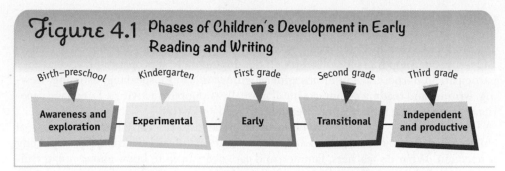

**Figure 4.1** Phases of Children's Development in Early Reading and Writing

Source: Adapted from *Learning to Read and Write: Developmentally Appropriate Practices for Young Children*, A Joint Position Statement of the International Reading Association and the National Association for the Education of Young Children, adopted 1998. Copyright 1998 by the International Reading Association. Reprinted with permission of the International Reading Association (www.reading.org).

exploration phase of literacy development marks the time when children become curious about print and print-related activities. For example, they enjoy listening to and talking about stories and understand that print carries a message. In addition, young children demonstrate *logographic knowledge* by identifying labels, signs, cereal boxes, and other types of environmental print. They also begin to *pretend-read* during their preschool years and engage in paper-and-pencil activities that include various forms of scribbling and written expression. Another literacy accomplishment in this phase occurs when young children begin to identify some letters and letter–sound relationships and write letters or approximations of letters to represent written language.

**2.** *Experimental reading and writing phase.* Early awareness and exploration lead children to experiment with oral and written language. Children enter the experimental phase of the reading–writing continuum right around the time they enter kindergarten. This phase reflects their understanding of basic concepts of print, such as left-to-right, top-to-bottom orientation. Young children enjoy being read to and begin to engage in sustained reading and writing activities. They also continue to recognize letters and letter–sound relationships, become familiar with rhyming, and begin to write letters of the alphabet and high-frequency words.

**3.** *Early reading and writing phase.* The early phase of children's development usually occurs in first grade when instruction becomes more formal. Children begin to read simple stories and can write about topics about which they have much prior knowledge and strong feelings. They can read and retell familiar stories and begin to develop strategies, such as predicting, for comprehension. They are beginning to develop accurate word identification skills through their increasing knowledge of letter–sound patterns. In addition, children's ability to read with fluency becomes more evident, as does their ability to recognize an increasing number of words on sight. Moreover, their writing shows awareness of punctuation and capitalization knowledge as they continue to engage in writing about topics that are personally meaningful to them.

**4.** *Transitional reading and writing phase.* By second grade, students begin to make the transition from early reading and writing to more complex literacy tasks. They are reading with greater fluency and using cognitive and metacognitive strategies more efficiently when comprehending and composing. During the transitional phase, children demonstrate an ever-increasing facility with reading and writing in all facets of activity, including use of word identification strategies, sight-word recognition, reading fluency, sustained silent reading, conventional spelling, and proofreading what they have written.

**5.** *Independent and productive phase.* As children progress from the transitional phase, they engage in a lifelong process of becoming independent and productive readers and writers. The third grade marks the beginning of their journey into independent and productive learning as they use reading and writing in increasingly more sophisticated ways to suit a variety of purposes and audiences. From this point on in their development as readers and writers, children extend and refine their literacy skills and strategies.

Appendix C provides a list of reading and writing accomplishments that successful literacy learners are likely to achieve from kindergarten through third grade. The accomplishments were compiled by the Committee on the Prevention of Reading Difficulties in Young Children as part of an analysis and synthesis of research on children's early reading acquisition commissioned by the National Research Council (Snow et al., 1998). The list of reading and writing accomplishments is not designed to be exhaustive or comprehensive but highlights children's typical achievements related to reading and writing revealed through several decades of research.

The set of reading and writing accomplishments in Appendix C provides, at best, a summary sketch of young children's literacy development and should not be interpreted rigidly. Teachers must take into account enormous individual differences in children's literacy development as they enter school. According to the IRA/NAEYC joint statement on children's early literacy development:

> Experienced teachers throughout the U.S. report that the children they teach today are more diverse in their backgrounds, experiences, and abilities than were those they taught in the past. Kindergarten classes now include children who have been in group settings for 3 or 4 years as well as children who are participating for the first time in an organized early childhood program. Classes include both children with identified disabilities and children with exceptional abilities, children who are already independent readers and children who are just beginning to acquire some basic literacy knowledge and skills. Children in the group may speak different languages at varying levels of proficiency. Because of these individual and experiential variations, it is common to find within a kindergarten classroom a 5-year range in children's literacy-related skills and functioning (Riley, 1996). What this means is that some kindergartners may have the skills characteristic of the typical 3-year-old, while others might be functioning at the level of the typical 8-year-old. (pp. 4–5)

What children's literacy development makes clear is that the foundations for reading and writing begin at home and that schools build on these foundations to develop skillful and strategic readers and writers. In this chapter and the next, we will examine closely the beginnings of reading and writing in the awareness and exploration, experimental, and early phases of literacy development. The remaining chapters of this book explore the roles that teachers and texts play in children's literacy development as they progress from early and transitional reading and writing to independent and productive reading and writing.

With this in mind, let's take a closer look at how reading and writing develop in the context of family interactions and home experiences. Family members and caregivers influence the oral and written language development of young children and provide the context in which they learn to read and write (Neuman, Caperelli, & Kee, 1998; Paratore & Jordan, 2007; Roberts, Jurgens, & Burchinal, 2005; Taylor, 1983; Taylor & Dorsey-Gaines, 1989).

## How Reading Develops

Most children enter school with expectations that they're "gonna learn how to read." It doesn't matter to Michael, a 5-year-old, that he can already read many signs—for example, "Stop" and "Zoo"—that have a great deal of meaning to him. It also doesn't matter that Michael "knows" most of the alphabet by name and often "reads along" by reciting favorite passages from bedtime stories that his mother and father read to him. Nor does it matter that Michael's mother still smiles over his behavior at around age 2 when he first recognized a McDonald's billboard from the backseat of the family car. Michael "oohed" and "aahed" and chanted, "Stop! Stop! Hungry, Mommy."

Michael doesn't grasp the significance of these events because he is on the threshold of starting school. Nor does his mother recognize the importance of these abilities. Despite Michael's observable reading and readinglike behaviors at home, there remains a trace of uncertainty on his mother's part. Although the groundwork has been laid for Michael to continue to grow as a reader, his mother expresses some concern as to whether he will achieve success in learning to read. She is sure that he will but adds, "We'll wait and see."

Does Michael's mother need to assume a "wait and see" attitude? A child such as hers grows up immersed in a print-oriented world. Children see written language all around them—in books, supermarkets, department stores, fast-food restaurants, and on television, signs, and a variety of printed materials from video games to labels on household products. **Environmental print** is everywhere. When aren't children confronted with written language in some form in their immediate environment? The child may also see parents, brothers, sisters, and others using written language to some degree—whether to read recipes, follow directions, do homework, solve problems, acquire information, or enjoy a story. The plethora of print that confronts young children on a daily basis plays a subtle but important role in their desire to understand written language and use it for personal and social means.

Today's preschooler acquires much more intuitive and conscious knowledge about print and its uses than most adults would imagine. As early as 1958, James Hymes observed that reading "sells itself" to the young child because written language is "in the limelight" constantly. Everyday living "beats the drums" for reading with a bombardment of print that no formal program of instruction could ever match.

Although this may be the case, informal "teachable moments" await children in a print-rich world. Parents (and teachers) should make a *conscious* effort, whenever appropriate, to create awareness of print in meaningful and functional ways. By way of illustration, 4-year-old Kesia's parents seize whatever opportunity is available to demonstrate the purposeful nature of print. Whenever they go to a restaurant, for example, they encourage Kesia to "read" the menu and to select the foods she prefers. Although Kesia may not be able to read most of the words on the menu, she pretend-reads. Her parents support her use of print by showing her the menu, by engaging in dialogue with her over possible food choices, and by pointing to the printed words as they read the menu with her.

This example, simple and straightforward as it may appear, illustrates the subtle but powerful role that parents play in literacy learning. The parent's role (and the teacher's) is to lead, model, and facilitate literacy learning by being supportive, by socializing children in the uses of written language, by engaging them in conversation about written language, and by encouraging and accepting children's constructions of meaning through written language.

**THE IMPORTANCE OF FAMILY INTERACTIONS** ◆ Michael and Kesia already know a lot about written language and have had some valuable early literacy experiences. They are learning to read informally through family interactions. During early childhood, the immediate context of the family has the greatest influence on the child (Kostelnik, Soderman, & Whiren, 2004). More than likely, Michael and Kesia will continue their growth as literacy learners and should experience success in school. As teachers we have much to gain from the study of **family literacy.**

Most parents play an important role in the oral language development of their children. Learning to read begins through interaction with parents and other significant members of a family. It is through everyday experiences filled with talking, reading, and writing that children gain the oral language they need to be strong readers and learners (Roskos, Tabors, & Lenhart, 2004). In Figure 4.2 Bennett-Armistead, Duke, and Moses (2005) outline suggestions for promoting oral language development every day.

Studies of early readers indicate that learning to read is strongly associated with positive home environments (Neuman & Roskos, 1993; Strickland & Morrow, 1990; Teale, 1978). Early readers have access to a variety of easy reading materials in the home, and they can also use the local library. Moreover, early readers are attracted to reading *anything* that

## Figure 4.2   Promoting Oral Language Development Every Day

- Talk whenever and wherever you can. Seize every moment to engage children in conversation.
- Get close to children to engage them with what you say.
- Really listen by giving your *full* attention. Look them in the eye and get down on their level.
- Respond to and expand on what children say.
- Ask open-ended questions to solicit more complex answers than simply "yes" or "no."
- Tell everyday stories about what happened at work, at home, funny things about growing up, and so on.
- Tell children *what* they need to do and then explain *why* they should do it.
- Sing songs and read nursery rhymes.
- Use rich vocabulary (judiciously) to expose children to new words.
- Provide prompts that promote oral language such as puppets or microphones.
- Encourage back-and-forth discourse and turn-taking.

*Source: Literacy and the Youngest Learner,* by V. Bennett-Armistead, N. Duke, and A. Moses (New York: Scholastic, 2005).

interests them in their immediate everyday print environment, from labels on cans and cereal boxes, to TV listings, to cookbooks, telephone directories, and bus timetables.

Although books, billboards, and package labels are all potential sources for reading in a young child's home environment, children must learn how print functions in their lives. In this respect, reading aloud to children is one of the most important contributing factors in the learning environment of early readers. Early readers' homes are frequently characterized by one or more parents and older siblings who read regularly.

As a result, children learn about reading by observing the significant people in their lives modeling reading behaviors naturally—for real purposes—in a variety of ways. Vukelich and Christie (2004) explain that "Children begin learning about reading and writing at a very early age by observing and interacting with adults and other children as they use literacy in everyday activities such as writing shopping lists and special literacy-focused routines such as storybook reading" (p. 5). They might see, for example, a parent reading a recipe while cooking or baking, studying a map on the family's vacation, singing from a hymnal at church, or reading the assembly instructions for a new bike. Some children will rivet their attention on the television screen as words flash before them during a commercial. Others quickly become aware that newspapers and magazines impart information about events occurring locally and in the world. Others realize that books may be read to learn and to entertain. Indeed, reading is part of their environment. Children need to become aware of the many purposes for reading and become involved in different kinds of reading activity frequently.

The quality of interaction that the child has with family members—whether they are parents, grandparents, aunts, uncles, or siblings—plays heavily in reading development. In fact, Lenhart and Roskos (2003) found that when siblings engage in literacy together, both benefit from the interaction. Often, however, assistance in learning to read is not consciously given. Instead, significant others, such as parents, read to children repeatedly (by reading certain stories again

Early readers thrive in environments where parents hold a high regard for reading.

and again) and *answer questions that children ask about reading.* There is no better way to help the child make the connection that print is meaningful than to respond to the question, "What does this say?" as the child points to a printed page. In Box 4.1, Research-Based Practices, Neuman, Roskos, Wright, and Lenhart (2007) outline five scientifically proven ways to encourage literacy in the home.

**THE IMPORTANCE OF LITERATE ENVIRONMENTS** ◆ As you might surmise, a **literate environment** for young children is one that fosters interest in and curiosity about written language and supports children's efforts to become readers and writers. Learning, not instruction, is the dominant force in a child's literacy development. Early readers thrive in environments in which parents and other significant persons hold a high regard for reading. Vukelich and Christie (2004) outline four home factors important to a good start in reading and writing:

STANDARDS
4.2, 4.3, 4.4

1. *Access to print and books.* Literacy learning is facilitated when books are available and there are opportunities to see a great deal of print.

2. *Adult demonstrations of literacy behavior.* Children begin to learn about the practical uses of written language and understand why reading and writing activities are worth doing when they see family members use print for various purposes.

3. *Supportive adults.* Early readers tend to have parents or other caregivers who are very supportive of their early attempts at literacy and are willing to respond to children's questions about print.

4. *Storybook reading.* Reading to children is positively related to outcomes such as language growth, early literacy, and later reading achievement.

---

BOX **4.1**

## Research-Based Practices    The Five Essentials for Families

These five essentials are scientifically based and will help motivate your child to become a better reader. Keep in mind that these essentials can happen throughout the day while waiting for the doctor, riding a bus, or grocery shopping. Opportunities abound for parents to engage their young children in meaningful activities.

- *Talking.* Talking plays a critical role in language development. Parents can help by engaging their child in conversations throughout the day, and encouraging and responding to questions. The more words the child knows prior to kindergarten, the more likely he or she will become a capable reader.
- *Singing.* Singing activities strengthen your child's ability to hear and pay attention to the sounds and rhythms of speech. Nursery rhymes, silly songs, and chants are all great ways to play and sing with language, and they can be done anywhere. This skill reinforces concepts of words

and helps your child hear differences and similarities in how words sound.

- *Playing.* Play allows children to expand and refine their ability to use objects to represent experiences in imaginary worlds and helps children develop a sense of narrative. As you play with your child, introduce new words related to the play to expand his or her vocabulary.
- *Reading.* Reading and telling stories are important because they have a beginning, middle, and end and "are the gateway to the world of the written word" (p. 185). Stories also prepare children for listening habits they will need to learn to read. Read and tell stories with your child often. Have fun making up silly stories based on common experiences.
- *Writing.* Writing is important because it helps children connect what they hear in words with the symbols that represent them. Provide paper, crayons, or markers for your child and encourage her or him to write and draw.

*Source:* Adapted from *Nurturing Knowledge: Building a Foundation for School Success by Linking Early Literacy to Math, Science, Art, and Social Studies,* by S. Neuman, K. Roskos, T. Wright, and L. Lenhart (New York: Scholastic, 2007).

Within a literate environment, there is also a preoccupation with scribbling, drawing, and writing—so much so that Durkin (1966) characterized children who learn to read naturally as "paper-and-pencil kids."

Early readers spend significant amounts of time expressing themselves through scribble writing, drawing, copying words, and inventing spellings for words. Writing is an important though often underestimated factor in learning to read. Materials that encourage and facilitate writing should be readily accessible to young children. Crayons, markers, pencils, pens, paper, postcards, stationery, and chalkboards invite self-expression and should be kept in reach of children. Parent–child activities, such as the following, extend children's interest in and knowledge about written language by providing opportunities to observe, as well as participate in, meaningful, functional writing activities.

- Parents should encourage their children to help write the family shopping list.
- Parents and children may communicate with one another through written messages, such as writing notes. A bulletin board or a chalkboard provides a designated location for writing and receiving notes.
- Parents should create occasions to write, such as writing a Christmas list or a letter to Santa. In the same vein, they should encourage children to correspond in writing or by e-mail with a responsive pen pal, perhaps a "best friend" or a relative living in another area who's about the same age. Writing invitations for a birthday party or a sleepover or writing the instructions to give to the person who will temporarily care for a pet provide meaningful writing occasions.

## How Writing Develops

Some young children are prolific with pencil and paper. Others are just as handy with crayon, ink marker, or paintbrush. Sometimes a convenient wall or refrigerator door substitutes nicely for paper. Still others take to the computer keyboard. The common denominator for "paper-and-pencil kids" is a strong desire and a need for self-expression and communication.

The noted Russian psychologist Lev Vygotsky (1962) suggests that an infant's gestures are the first visible signs of writing: "Gestures are writing in air, and written signs frequently are simply gestures that have been fixed." As Calkins (1983) explains:

> The urge to write begins when a baby, lying in her crib, moves her arms and we draw close to the crib, our faces lighting into smiles. "She's waving at us," we say. Because we attach meaning to what could be called meaningless gestures, the gestures assume meaning. Babies learn the power of their gestures by our response to them. (p. 35)

As infants learn about the power of signs and symbols, there is, in Vygotsky's words, "a fundamental assist to cognitive growth."

Klein (1985) distinguishes between the terms *writing* and *written expression*. Written expression comes earlier than writing. Scribbles and drawings are examples of written expressions *if* they have symbolic meaning to the child. The difference, then, is in the child's ability to produce units of written language—that is, letters, words, and sentences. For Klein a working definition of writing should include written expression: Writing is the "ability to employ pen or pencil and paper to express ideas symbolically so that the representations on the paper reflect meaning and content capable of being communicated to another by the producer" (pp. 3–4). How youngsters move from various representations of written expression to units of written language is a natural and important evolution.

**BUILDING TEACHING SKILLS: ARTIFACT**

Go to the Homework and Exercises section in Chapter 4 of MyEducationLab to examine the basic scribbles of a preschooler and complete the exercise.

Young children learn writing through exploration. As Clay (1988) observes, most 5-year-olds "have definite ideas about the forms and uses of writing gained from their preschool experience: exploring with a pencil, pretending to write, inventing messages, copying an important word like one's name, and writing labels, messages, or special words in favorite story books" (p. 20). The key to early writing development is found not in a child's motor development or intelligence but in the *opportunities* the child has to explore print. According to Clay, new discoveries about writing emerge at every encounter a child has with paper and pencil: Young children write "all over the paper in peculiar ways, turning letters around and upside down and letting the print drift over into drawing and coloring from time to time. We should be relaxed about this exploration of spaces and how print can be fitted into them" (p. 20). What can be learned from observing how young writers progress in their development?

**THE IMPORTANCE OF SCRIBBLING** ◆ **Scribbling** is one of the primary forms of written expression. In many respects, scribbling is the fountainhead for writing and occurs from the moment a child grasps and manipulates a writing tool. Children take their scribbles seriously, if Linda Lamme's (1984) quotation from a scribbler is any indication: "Dat's not a scrwibble. It says, 'What's for dinner, Mom?'" (p. 37). Lamme has described the progression of scribbling in children's writing development in her excellent handbook for parents.

**Early Scribbling**   Early or uncontrolled scribbling is characterized by children making random marks on paper. Evidence of early scribbling can be gathered for most youngsters before their first birthday. Very young children who scribble soon learn that whatever it is that is in their hands, it can make marks. Early scribblings, according to Lamme, compare with babbling in oral language development. In Figure 4.3, Taylor, at 21 months, is constantly preoccupied with her scribbles and often talks spontaneously as she expresses herself with paper and pencil. She tells her mother as she scribbles that she likes to make lots of "tapes" and points to a "face" in the upper right-hand corner of the scribble in Figure 4.3.

Because early scribbles are not usually representational (i.e., they do not convey meaning), parents and teachers should suppress the urge to ask a child, "What is this?"

*Figure 4.3* Taylor's Scribbling

Instead, encourage a child to make markings on paper without pressure to finish a piece of work or tell what it's about, unless the child is eager to talk about it.

**Controlled Scribbling**    Movement away from early scrawls becomes evident in children's scribbles as they begin to make systematic, repeated marks such as circles, vertical lines, dots, and squares.

Controlled scribbling occurs in children's written work between the ages of 3 and 6. The marks are often characterized as *scribble writing* in the sense that the scribbles are linear in form and shape and bear a strong resemblance to the handwriting of the child's culture, as Harste, Woodward, and Burke (1984) demonstrated. When they asked three 4-year-olds from different countries to "write everything you can write," the children produced print that reflected their native languages—English, Arabic, and Hebrew (see Figure 4.4). These writing samples show that young children have more knowledge about print than some adults might realize.

According to Harste and his collaborators, Dawn's controlled scribbles look undeniably like English. When Najeeba finished her writing, she said, "Here, but you can't read it because it is in Arabic." Najeeba went on to point out that in Arabic one uses "a lot more dots" than in English. Dalia is an Israeli child whose whole writing bears the look of Hebrew. Kindergarten and first-grade children build on their knowledge of written language by participating in planned and spontaneous writing activity. In doing so, they acquire knowledge about reading *by* writing.

In the remainder of this chapter and in Chapter 5, we show how beginners can explore the natural relationship between writing and reading through language experiences and independent writing.

Scribble writing stands in contrast to *scribble drawing*, which is more pictographic in expression. Children use drawing as a means of written expression. According to Klein (1985), "Drawing is possibly the most important single activity that assists both writing development and handwriting. It is critical to the child's evolving sense of symbol, and it directly assists

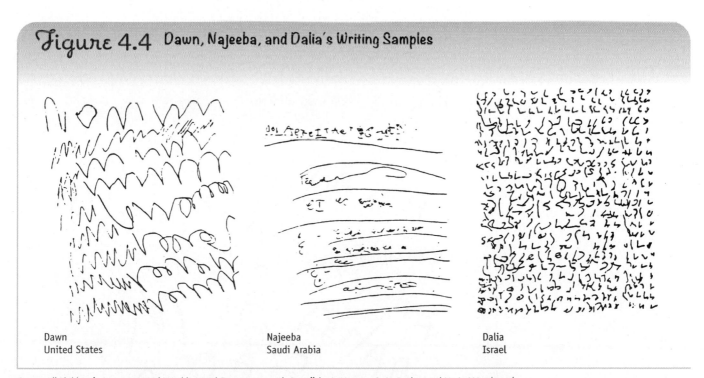

**Figure 4.4**    Dawn, Najeeba, and Dalia's Writing Samples

Dawn
United States

Najeeba
Saudi Arabia

Dalia
Israel

*Source:* "Children's Language and World: Initial Encounters with Print" by J. Harste, C. L. Burke, and V. A. Woodward, in *Reader Meets Author/Bridging the Gap: A Psycholinguistic and Sociolinguistic Perspective*, edited by J. A. Langer and M. T. Smith-Burke. Copyright © 1982 by the International Reading Association. Reprinted with permission of the International Reading Association (www.reading.org).

muscle and eye-hand coordination development" (p. 40). Children between the ages of 4 and 6 use drawings or pictographs as a form of written expression in their work.

Before the age of 4 most children don't know the difference between writing and drawing. But soon they show signs of understanding that these are two different ways to represent ideas. When children figure this out, they begin to make great strides toward understanding the symbolic nature of writing. They start to understand that there are connections between letters and meaning and are soon on their way to making the transition from drawing writing to symbolic writing. They redefine what they think writing is and start to use letters and combinations of letters and letterlike forms to communicate ideas. Usually this begins with their name, a word that fascinates and intrigues them.

**Name Scribbling**    Name scribbling is an extension of scribble writing. Scribbles become representational to the child writer: The scribbles mean something. At this point, parents or teachers should begin to model writing and write with children. This is where the language-experience activities described in Chapter 2 play an important role in the writer's development. Make cards, lists, or signs with child writers; label things. Have children dictate stories as you write them as well as encourage independent writing.

When children differentiate between drawing and scribbling as means of written expression, they begin to make great strides in their knowledge of print. Name scribbling underscores this differentiation and results in the formation of valuable concepts about written language—namely, that markings or symbols represent units of language such as letters and words, which in turn represent things and objects that can be communicated by messages.

Sam, almost 4 years old, engaged in the name scribbling shown in Figure 4.5. Her writing represents a dinner order in a restaurant. What do you notice about Sam's writing? When Sam's mother asked her to read the message aloud, she approximated a speech-to-print match. That is, she matched her spoken words to the letters and marks on the paper. This is what she read:

> You want some turkey,
> some mashed potatoes
> and some beans.
> And you want some milk.

**Figure 4.5**  Sam's Scribbling

What does Sam's written expression tell us about her development? She has clearly figured out the letters of her name but notice how some of the other letters she uses are letterlike forms. She knew that she needed to use letters to write the order down because she has seen this done in restaurants, so she uses the letters in her name to accomplish the task. Sam is aware of the message-sending function of writing. She has developed a "message concept." Through her many encounters with print in her environment Sam has also developed alphabet-letter awareness. She knows, too, some of the conventions of writing peculiar to the English language. Writing, for example, moves from left to right, then back to the left at the end of a line and from top to bottom on a page. Also, the space between some strings of letters might reveal an awareness of word forms, that words are composed of letters and are separated from one another by boundaries or white spaces.

As Sam continues to grow as a writer, her writing will become increasingly more sophisticated. She will develop a concept of word and a knowledge of letter–sound correspondence. We are confident that Sam will soon be writing words and sentences with the aid of invented spellings. Spelling invention will give way to convention as she gains greater knowledge and control of letter–sound relationships. Other writing conventions, such as punctuation and capitalization, will also evolve with continued writing experiences in an environment that encourages growth and supports Sam's literacy development. How parents and teachers view the conventions of writing, particularly invented spellings, in beginning situations is crucial to writing development.

**THE IMPORTANCE OF INVENTED SPELLING** ◆ **Invented spelling,** or temporary spelling, is a name given to children's written words before they have learned the rules of spelling. Most children don't begin school having mastered letter–sound correspondence. Yet children come to school with varying degrees of knowledge about the structure of written language because of their early explorations with reading and writing. Through their use of invented spellings, children expect their writing to make sense and have meaning.

Take the case of Paul Bissex, an early reader and writer, whose mother documented his literacy development by keeping a detailed diary of his progress (Bissex, 1980). At age 4, Paul clearly recognized the connection between writing and reading. For example, when he read his writing, complete with invented spellings, he explained: "Once you know how to spell something, you know how to read it" (p. 1). As Bissex observes, Paul developed multiple strategies because of his use of invented spellings: "Paul seemed to be asking himself not only 'What does this word *sound* like?' and 'What does this word *look* like?' but 'What does it mean?'" (p. 102).

Invented spellings signal to parents and teachers that children are beginning to analyze speech sounds in print. By first grade, for example, most children know something about letters. They may know the names and shapes of some letters. Others may be making associations between sounds and letters. The more that children explore letter–sound associations in their writing, the more progress they make toward conventional spelling.

**ADVANTAGES OF INVENTED SPELLING** ◆ The gradual sophistication in children's invented spellings should be celebrated by teachers and parents as a display of intelligence and emerging competence with written language. When "correct spelling" isn't an obstacle in the path of young writers, they are free to get their ideas down on paper. Invented spellings help children place ideas before notions of correctness. Every primary teacher knows the interruptions that can occur in class when youngsters constantly ask for the correct spelling of practically every word they don't know. What we sometimes fail to recognize, however, is that young children probably seek correct spellings because they perceive that the teacher values accuracy in their writing. When children are bound by notions of correctness, writing becomes a laborious undertaking rather than a meaning-making act. A supportive learning environment, however, encourages beginners to try to spell words as best they can during writing and to experiment with written language without the restrictions imposed by demands for accuracy and correction.

Sowers (1982) lists the advantages of not placing a premium on accuracy:

1. Children build independence because they don't have to ask for every word they don't know.
2. By emphasizing ideas rather than correctness, children become fluent in their writing. They can elaborate and play on paper without interruptions.
3. Children move efficiently through the stages of spelling development when they have opportunities to apply strategies about sound–symbol correspondences at their own pace and level of sophistication.
4. Children develop control and responsibility for their writing by taking risks and trying out the "rules" that they are forming about spelling. As Sowers noted, "The worst outcome of an unsuccessful invention is that communication stops temporarily." But if the invention succeeds, so does the child: "Real rewards await the child who writes fearlessly about a FROSHUS DOBRMAN PENSR instead of a BAD DOG" (p. 48).

The whole idea behind encouraging spelling invention is to build on the emerging competence of the beginner. As children put their ideas ahead of concerns for correct spelling, they will develop confidence in their ability to write; they will recognize the value of taking risks.

Knowing how reading and writing develop allows the teacher to plan instruction that is developmentally appropriate. The IRA/NAEYC joint position statement on learning to read and write contends that developmentally appropriate practices should be challenging but achievable with sufficient teacher support. Because ideal conditions for literacy development may not exist for all children, what do some of the insights from learning to read and write suggest for developmentally appropriate practices in kindergarten and first grade?

# Developmentally Appropriate Practices

The idea of **developmentally appropriate practice** suggests that the curriculum match or be geared to children's developing abilities (Bredekamp, 1987; Schickedanz, 1998). Kostelnik and colleagues expand the definition to include *age appropriate*, *individually appropriate*, and *socially and culturally appropriate* (2004). From a literacy development perspective, a child's first contact with a language arts curriculum in school should match his or her level of emergent literacy.

Effective teachers of literacy know how to plan developmentally appropriate experiences and how to rally instruction around children's diversity. Individual differences, however, need not suggest a unique program of instruction for each child. Individualizing a literacy program is as much a state of mind as it is a fixed or prescriptive approach to instruction. How teachers go about individualizing says more about their beliefs on reading and learning to read than it does about any specific method.

Individualized instruction is sometimes narrowly translated to mean "learning small things in small steps," wherein each child completes an individualized program "except for some differences in pacing" (Moffett, 1975). A teacher's responsibility, first and foremost, is to establish a classroom environment in which individual learning takes place during literacy instruction. Holdaway (1979) argued that it is impossible to determine the right level, content, pace, and style of learning for each child, each day. But teachers can set the conditions for developmentally appropriate learning by creating literate environments and giving enough instructional support to each child to help each child learn to read and write successfully, and coaches can help guide them. See Box 4.2 to read about coaching early childhood teachers.

BOX **4.2**

# Viewpoint

## the Literacy Coach

### Coaching Teachers and Caregivers of Young Children

*An excerpt from a conversation with Melissa, an early childhood coach.*

Q: Would you say coaching preschool teachers is the same as coaching elementary teachers?

MELISSA: Yes. Coaching teachers of preschoolers is the same as coaching any teacher. It is a reflective process of looking at strategies that teachers use based on knowledge of content, standards, and pedagogy. It was interesting that when I first coached preK they thought teaching preK was different until we examined the same principles and strategies of vocabulary development, comprehension (through oral readings), oral language, higher-level thinking skills, and so on. Once we did this they began to understand that coaching applied to them as well.

Q: Could you give an example of what coaching might look like with early childhood teachers?

MELISSA: I didn't coach in one school or district but coached regionally with teacher leaders across our state. I met with them once a month for inservice days. During these days we built knowledge of coaching strategies, read articles, viewed online video cases, practiced techniques such as questioning skills or modeling lessons, and created monthly action plans.

Q: How did the teacher leaders use this information with other teachers?

MELISSA: The teacher leaders then went back to their agencies and conducted training sessions, visited classrooms, modeled lessons, shared articles, and did informal assessments and other requirements.

## Creating Literate Learning Environments

Instruction for beginners should not be a carbon copy of practices that are appropriate for older children. Instead, the beginner needs supportive, meaningful situations in learning to read. In this respect, there is much to be learned from the behavior of parents of preschool readers.

A teacher of beginners should consider organizing literacy instruction around the natural methods of parents whose children learned to read before school entry. A literate classroom environment for reading places less attention on instructional methods and more emphasis on individual attention and a warm, accepting relationship between child and teacher. A literacy learning environment in school establishes ideal conditions for learning to read in much the same way that the home environment of the child establishes ideal conditions for learning to speak.

STANDARD 4.1

In a classroom environment that promotes literacy development, children feel free to take risks because errors are expected and accepted. Risk-taking is an important factor in literacy learning. Beginners should feel free to ask questions with the expectation that interested adults will listen and respond constructively.

Holdaway (1982) describes some of the characteristics of a natural, or home-centered, language-learning environment that operates efficiently in a preschooler's mastery of oral language.

1. Young children are allowed to develop in their own way and at their own rate using language functionally to meet their needs.
2. Parents are positive and rewarding in their reception of most responses that children attempt. In learning oral language, children have a built-in support system provided by their parents that does not stress criticism or correction but allows for trial and approximations.
3. Parents demonstrate tremendous faith and patience.
4. Parents do not create competitive situations in which children learn language. Parents may compare a child's performance with what he or she did yesterday or a week ago, but rarely do they make close comparisons of their child's performance with another child.

5. Children learn in meaningful situations that support the language being learned.
6. Children have models to emulate. Because the language-learning process is innately rewarding, they spend much of their time voluntarily practicing.

It is evident from the case studies cited earlier in this chapter that many of the conditions necessary for language learning were operating in the lives of early readers. Teachers of reading beginners must approximate these ideal conditions in their classrooms. Consider, then, establishing some of the hallmarks of a home-centered environment for learning to read.

Not only is a literate classroom environment home-centered, but it is also playful. A play-centered environment allows young children in day care or kindergarten classrooms to develop a "feel" for literacy as they experiment with written language.

## Designing Literacy-Related Play Centers

**Literacy play centers** in preschool and kindergarten provide an environment where children may play with print on their own terms. Play provides a natural context for beginners to experiment with literacy. Play centers promote literacy by giving children opportunities to observe one another using literacy for real reasons (Neuman & Roskos, 1997; Morrow, 1990; Schickedanz, 1986).

Roskos (1986, 1988) closely observed eight children, aged 4 and 5, for 6 months during free-play situations to analyze the kinds of reading and writing activities they engaged in naturally during play. She was amazed to discover the quantity and quality of early literate activity in pretend-play situations.

As a result of her study, Roskos (1986) makes three recommendations for teachers in day-care, preschool, and kindergarten settings:

1. Create and frequently use play centers that facilitate sustained **pretend play** and prompt experimentation with reading and writing. In addition to the traditional housekeeping and block areas, teachers should consider developing play centers such as the office, the travel agency, the store, the bank, or the play school that stimulate young children to explore the routines, functions, and features of literacy.
2. Ask young children to share their pretend-play stories, which can then be recorded on chart paper and used for extended language-experience activities. From play accounts like these, teaching points about story sense, print forms, directionality, and sight vocabulary can easily be inserted.
3. Begin to observe more closely the literacy at work in the pretend play of youngsters. These observations tell us much about the young child's literacy stance and may guide us in our instructional efforts to connect what is known about written language to the unknown. Scribbled recipes from the housekeeping area, stories created at the sand table, and book handling in the play school are literacy signals that should not be ignored.

In the Research-Based Practices featured in Box 4.3, examine several factors to be considered when designing literacy play centers.

Teachers often assume the role of participant in a play episode, but their main responsibility is to facilitate literacy development, which may involve appropriately intervening to create opportunities to include children in literacy-related activities during play. This may entail suggesting the need for making a list, recording an appointment, requesting a telephone number, checking food labels, or reading a bedtime story. Johnson, Christie, and Wardle (2005) describe four important roles that teachers can assume in children's play that are critical to children's learning:

*Onlooker role.* The teacher is physically present near the play setting but does not enter into it. The teacher may, however, encourage children's play through nods, smiles and suggestions or give suggestions to encourage play.

**HOMEWORK EXERCISE: VIDEO**

Go to the Homework and Exercises section in Chapter 4 of MyEducationLab to view the video entitled "Using Centers" and consider how you would design literacy play centers in your classroom.

BOX **4.3**

## *Research-Based Practices*

### Literacy Play Centers

Consider the following when designing literacy play centers.

- *Setting.* Literacy play centers are usually designed around places and contexts that are familiar to young children—for example, a doctor's or dentist's office, the post office, or a bank. The setting should be general enough so that children create their own stories and themes as they engage in play talk and action.
- *Location of Centers in the Classroom.* Literacy play centers are located in a designated area of the classroom, labeled accordingly at children's eye level. Neuman and Roskos (1997) illustrate several classroom play settings they have studied in their research.

- *Props in a Play Center.* Furnish a play center with real props found in the environment. The props may be used for dramatic effect *(dramatic props)* or for literacy-related activity *(literacy props).* For example, dramatic props in a doctor's office play setting may include a doctor's kit (with stethoscope, light, tongue depressor, etc.), a nurse's hat, a blanket for the examining table, and dolls as patients. Literacy props may include patient charts, prescription pads, sign-in sheets, magazines in the waiting room, bill forms, and checkbooks. The appropriateness of props in a play center depends on their authenticity, use, and safety. Any literacy-related item found in the "real world" may become part of a center. Neuman and Roskos (1990) list the types of props that may be used in several different literacy play settings.

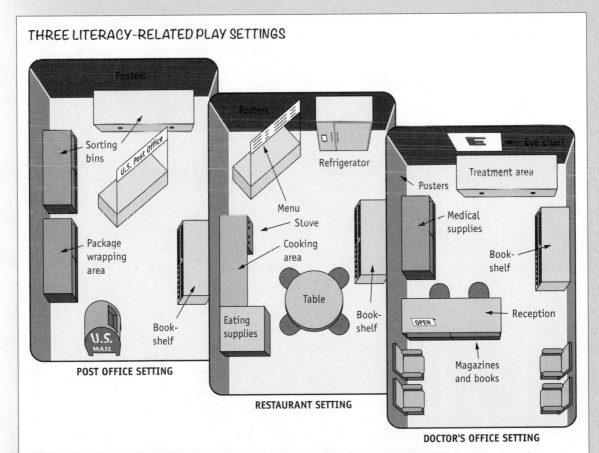

**THREE LITERACY-RELATED PLAY SETTINGS**

Posters
Sorting bins
U.S. Post Office
Package wrapping area
U.S. MAIL
Book-shelf
**POST OFFICE SETTING**

Posters
Refrigerator
Menu
Stove
Cooking area
Table
Eating supplies
Book-shelf
**RESTAURANT SETTING**

Eye chart
Treatment area
Posters
Medical supplies
Book-shelf
OPEN
Reception
Magazines and books
**DOCTOR'S OFFICE SETTING**

*Source:* "Literacy Knowledge in Practice: Contexts of Participation for Young Writers and Readers," by S. B. Neuman and K. A. Roskos, *Reading Research Quarterly, 32*(1), p. 16. Copyright © 1997 by the International Reading Association. Reprinted with permission of the International Reading Association (www.reading.org).

*(Continued)*

# Research-Based Practices (Continued)

## Types of Props Found in Literacy Play Centers

### KITCHEN CENTER

Books to read to dolls or stuffed animals

Telephone books

A telephone (preferably a real one)

Emergency number decals on or near telephone

Cookbooks

Blank recipe cards

Small plaques or decorative magnets

Personal stationery

Food coupons

Grocery store ads

Play money containers

Empty grocery containers

Small message board or chalkboard

Calendars of various types

Notepads of assorted sizes

Pens, pencils, markers

Large plastic clips

### OFFICE CENTER

Calendars of various types

Appointment book

Message pads

Signs (e.g., open/closed)

Books, pamphlets, markers

Magazines

File folders

Racks for filing papers

In/out trays

Index cards

Business cards

Assorted forms

Play money and checklike pieces of paper

Ledger sheets

Computer

Clipboards

Post-it notes and address labels

Note cards

Large and small plastic clips

Pens, pencils, markers

Trays for holding items

### POST OFFICE CENTER

Envelopes of various sizes

Assorted forms

Stationery

Pens, pencils, markers

Stickers, stars, stamps, stamp pads

Post office mailbox

Tote bag for mail

Computer address labels

Large and small plastic cups

Calendars of various types

Small drawer trays

Posters and signs about mailing procedures

### LIBRARY CENTER

Library book return cards

Stamps for marking books

A wide variety of children's books

Bookmarks

Pens, pencils, markers

Paper of assorted sizes

A sign-in/sign-out sheet

Stickers

ABC index cards

A telephone

Telephone books

Calendars of various types

Posters for children's books

File folders

*Sources:* Based on "Play, Print, and Purpose: Enriching Play Environments for Literacy Development," by S. B. Neuman and K. A. Roskos, 1990, *The Reading Teacher, 44*, pp. 214–221; and "Literacy Knowledge in Practice: Contexts of Participation for Young Writers and Readers," by S. B. Neuman and K. A. Roskos, 1997, *Reading Research Quarterly, 32*, pp. 10–32.

*Stage manager role.* The stage manager role extends the onlooker role. The teacher doesn't enter the play, but might make suggestions to extend the play or respond to requests for prompts.

*Co-player role.* The teacher becomes directly involved in the play as a participant. The goal is to model and extend language for the children, therefore supporting their literacy-related play. The teacher is a peer, not an adult with adult status or logic.

*Leader role.* The teacher is very directive in this role and models specific behaviors of play to be adapted by the children. The goal is to introduce a new play theme, explain roles and possible scripts, and introduce props and print into the setting. The teacher vacillates between participant and director.

Neuman, Roskos, Wright, and Lenhart (2007) suggest teachers remain flexible and be prepared to switch roles often, sometimes even within a single play period. Notice how a kindergarten teacher, Ms. Green, serves as both a play leader and co-player in these two timely literacy routines:

Four children are busily working in the housekeeping area when the teacher walks by.

| | |
|---|---|
| *Ms. Green:* | Mmmm! It smells wonderful in here. What are you cooking? |
| *Lonnie:* | I'm making applesauce. |
| *Tim:* | Well, I'm making some pizza. |
| *Ms. Green:* | Applesauce and pizza will make a terrific lunch! |
| *Karen:* | Yeah! Let's have pizza and applesauce for lunch. Pizza is my favorite. |
| *Ms. Green:* | Even the baby can eat applesauce. He can't chew pizza yet because he doesn't have teeth, but he can eat applesauce. |
| *Karen:* | Oh, no! The baby is crying again. That baby is crying too much! |
| *Ms. Green:* | I will help you take care of the baby while you fix lunch. Let's see. I think that he would like to hear a story. *(She selects a small board book from the bookshelf in the housekeeping center and sits down to read to the "baby.")* Yes, the baby should enjoy this book. This is a story that my children liked to hear when they were babies *(She holds the doll and reads the book. Several children come over to watch as she reads to the baby.)* |
| *Emily:* | OK, lunch is ready. Do you want some lunch, Ms. Green? |
| *Ms. Green:* | I would love to have lunch with you. I like pizza and applesauce. *(Everyone pretends to eat.)* |
| *Tim:* | Well, how do you like my pizza, Ms. Green? |
| *Lonnie:* | How's my applesauce? |
| *Ms. Green:* | Everything is delicious. Will you both share your recipes for pizza and applesauce with me? |
| *Tim and Lonnie:* | Sure! |

The teacher then provides paper for Tim, Lonnie, and the other children to write their recipes. The children's writings used a combination of scribbles, letters, and invented spellings.

Teachers may also wish to extend and elaborate on a play episode by inviting children to think about and discuss what they did during play. Pictures, three-dimensional materials, and written work (involving children's scribbles or invented spellings) may provide a basis for children to recall what they did and what they liked about the play episode.

In a post office center, a kindergarten teacher, Mrs. Chones, provided additional experiences and activities designed to extend children's prior knowledge of the responsibilities of postal workers and the process of transporting mail. She began by guiding a discussion to determine what the children already knew about the post office, what they needed or wanted to know, and any misconceptions they may have had. The children's responses were recorded on chart paper and were posted on the wall near the post office center. As a follow-up to the discussion, the teacher showed the children an interesting, current, age-appropriate video about the post office. A brief discussion followed to determine if the video provided answers to any of the questions or clarified any misconceptions.

In addition, the children were taken on a field trip to the local post office. The remaining unanswered questions from the wall charts were transferred to smaller strips of paper for the children to carry with them to the post office. The children drew pictures to accompany their questions and to serve as visual aids to help them remember what questions they wanted to ask. A postal worker served as a tour guide and patiently answered the children's questions, impromptu and planned. When the children returned to their classroom, they helped the teacher revise the wall charts based on the knowledge gained from the field trip.

As a result, the play episodes that occur in the post office center are likely to be more involved and sophisticated because the teacher provided relevant experiences designed to extend the children's knowledge and to stimulate their interest. At times, the teacher guided the children's play in the post office center by acting as a participant. For example, she mailed a package, she bought stamps and requested a receipt, and she asked for help in locating an address for a letter she was sending.

A home-centered, play-centered environment extends children's literacy learning in developmentally appropriate, creative ways. A language-centered environment provides language experiences that are crucial to a beginner's growth as a literacy learner.

## Exploring Print Through Language Experiences

Young children need to have the time and space to explore language in order to clarify its uses and gain facility in its production and reception. Children who experience language and its intricacies take giant steps on the road to becoming literate.

It is no coincidence that many preschool readers are also early writers. They have a strong desire to express themselves in symbolic terms through drawing, scribbling, copying, and, ultimately, producing their own written language. Exploring written language with paper and pencil helps children form the expectation that print is meaningful. Box 4.4 discusses how you can expand writing experiences to the Internet as well.

**TALKING, CREATING, SINGING, AND DANCING** ◆ The main feature of a language-experience approach is that it embraces the natural language of children and uses their background experiences as the basis for learning to read. This makes it a useful approach for meeting the needs of English language learners (ELLs).

**Language-experience activities** in beginning reading instruction permit young children to share and discuss experiences; listen to and tell stories; dictate words, sentences, and stories; and write independently. The teacher can revolve language experiences around speaking, listening, visual expression, singing, movement, and rhythmic activities.

Use conversation to encourage individual or group language-experience stories or independent writing. A language-experience story is a story that is told by the child and written down by the teacher for instructional purposes.

1. Talk about everyday sights and occurrences.
2. Provide problem-solving tasks (e.g., making a milkshake) or highly motivating situations (e.g., making peanut butter and jelly sandwiches) to elicit oral language.
3. Tell stories through pictures. Wordless picture books are particularly useful for stimulating language development through storytelling and creative writing.
4. Discuss enjoyable occasions (e.g., birthdays, holidays, special events such as the World Series, the class picnic).
5. Use visual experiences to stimulate conversation (e.g., television, book illustrations, artwork). Visual expression through art activity, in particular, provides exciting opportunities for language experiences.

## BOX 4.4

# New Literacies

## USING WIKIS EFFECTIVELY IN EARLY LITERACY

Jeremy Brueck and Kimberly Hartman Brueck

*Curriculum and technology specialists Jeremy Brueck and Kimberly Hartman Brueck of Akron, Ohio, continue their discussion on the use of technology in the classroom to encourage reading and writing. Here they discuss using wikis in the early literacy classroom.*

The advent of the read-write Web has had a profound effect on the way we teach students to read and write. Many new Web 2.0 technologies are available to teachers that engage students in the reading and writing process. As educators, we should strive to find ways to integrate these new literacies into our existing English language arts curriculum.

One of the first ways we introduced wikis into the early childhood classroom was through the creation of a class book. Kindergarten and first-grade teachers frequently create classroom books that are often modeled after a read-aloud story. In the traditional activity, each student contributes a page for the book from a template and illustrates it. The teacher then collects the pages and "publishes" the book so that each student can take the class book home to share with his or her parents. Activities like this present teachers with a perfect area to incorporate new literacies in their classrooms and a wiki works exceptionally well.

The teacher begins by establishing the wiki space for which a variety of free resources are available (see list at the end of this article). Once the online space is established, the teacher adds a hyperlinked page for each student to the wiki homepage. These pages can easily be created from a template on most wiki sites. To complete the activity, the student composes text on the corresponding wiki page and submits his work. The teacher might even include original illustrations on the wiki by scanning student artwork and inserting the scanned image as a .jpg or .gif file in the wiki page. We've seen some teachers show their young students how to do this themselves. A link to the class wiki, or "book," can be shared with parents via e-mail, a note home, or class newsletter.

A wiki is a great way to update the writing process and make it considerably more collaborative for all involved. We always tell apprehensive teachers that the writing process hasn't changed . . . but the paper has. That is one worry that a lot of teachers have when incorporating new literacies: that the process of reading or writing will somehow be altered. Even though students *write* in hypertext, they are still expected to compose, edit, and revise their work. And once we show teachers the power of the wiki, its *history* page, most teachers are eager to incorporate it into their classroom.

As the practice of using classroom wikis becomes more comfortable for students and teachers, we often see the writing process spread to the other content areas. Instead of writing a classic report on animals, for example, our third-grade teachers develop the writing process through a wiki about animals that lives and grows online. Initially, each student creates his or her own page to answer a few basic questions, but as the year progresses, students learn to insert pictures and links to more information.

By the end of the year, the wiki can grow into an online text about animals that first- and second-grade students are able to read in their classrooms. By organizing text, illustrations, and links on the wiki, younger students receive the scaffolding they need to be successful using developmentally appropriate multimedia resources to support their own learning.

One important thing for teachers to keep in mind when using wikis in the classroom is student confidentiality. Since the content is online, student names and pictures should never appear in wiki entries. Instead, we work with teachers to help them develop a student code that identifies the author of a post or comment. That way, students can post journals, reflections, dialogue, or group author with other students and the teacher in a safe, supportive, and—to the outside world—anonymous but productive learning environment.

WIKI RESOURCES
- http://pbwiki.com/edu.html
- www.wikispaces.com/site/for/teachers
- www.seedwiki.com
- www.editme.com
- www.wetpaint.com

Use art as a vehicle for personal expression. Artistic expression represents a powerful force in children's lives. Through various forms of aesthetic and manipulative activity, children learn that there are many ways to express what they are thinking or feeling. What children draw, paint, or sculpt today can be the basis for what they talk or write about tomorrow and then what they eventually read.

Every classroom for young children should provide enough space to work on and display art projects. Art materials should include crayons, colored chalk, clay, paints, felt-tip pens, scissors, paste and glue, paper, newsprint (unprinted newspaper), and an assortment of junk (e.g., straws, wire, boxes, soap bars, toothpicks, Styrofoam, pipe cleaners, and anything else that might lend itself to manipulative activity).

Singing, dancing, and other rhythmic activities are valuable means of expression in their own right. Such activities can also be linked easily and naturally to reading and writing instruction. For example, you can do any or all of the following:

1. Encourage readalongs as children sing familiar and favorite songs. Project song lyrics on a screen. As children sing, the teacher directs their attention to the lyrics, moving a hand across the print, left to right, top to bottom, pointing under each word, and synchronizing the movement with the music.

2. Create new lyrics for familiar songs that have a highly repetitive pattern. In one kindergarten class, the children changed "Old MacDonald Had a Farm" to "Old MacDonald Had an Amusement Park." Imagine the new lyrics that were contributed by the children!

3. Create dances that tell a story. Songs such as "The Eensy Weensy Spider" can be used to encourage movement and interpretation through dance.

4. Improvise movement stories inspired by poems and familiar stories. As you read with the students, include movement as a way to further express and interpret the reading material. Children make fine choreographers, creating spontaneous movement sequences for "The Gingerbread Man," "Peter Cottontail," and other action stories.

**ROLE PLAYING AND DRAMA** ◆ Young children delight in pretending. Role playing and dramatic activities in a beginning reading program not only stimulate the imagination but also provide many opportunities to use language inventively and spontaneously.

Role playing affords children the chance to approach ordinary or unusual events and situations from different perspectives and points of view. Children begin to recognize that there are different levels and uses of language appropriate for different situations. Role playing can be easily adapted to stimulate writing and to enhance reading comprehension throughout the elementary grades.

The objective of drama in the classroom is self-expression. Children "play along" in structured and unstructured situations. **Dramatic play** activities require very little planning and involve unstructured, spontaneous expression such as pretending to be a leaf falling from a tree or an astronaut going to Mars. *Creative drama* is more structured in that children often have definite parts to play as they act out a favorite story or event. Props, costumes, and scenery may be called for. A third kind of dramatic activity, *pantomime*, involves wordless communication in which children use their bodies to translate reality and convey meaning.

The teacher should have a dress-up area for dramatic activities. Because drama is so unlike traditional classroom activities, the teacher's approach, much like a parent's, is one of continuous encouragement and facilitation. Consider some of these language experiences.

1. Use children's literature for drama. Folktales such as *Little Red Riding Hood* or *Henny Penny* provide simple plot structures and clearly defined characters. Action-filled poems can be valuable for pantomime and movement activities.

2. Engage children in problem situations as a start for spontaneous dramatic activity. Rose (1982) suggested the following problems:
   • You have been called at school to go home immediately.
   • You are waiting in line at McDonald's or Burger King and are very hungry. On two occasions, people get ahead of you. What do you do the third time it happens?
   • You have just broken your mother's pearl necklace, and the pearls are scattered on the floor. You are picking them up when your mother enters the room.
   • You run into the police station to report that your bicycle has been stolen. The police seem to doubt your story.

STANDARD
4.3

In addition to language experiences, one of the most important developmentally appropriate practices for beginners, as well as children throughout the grades, is to read aloud from storybooks. The IRA/NAEYC joint position statement on early reading and

Incorporating creativity in classroom instruction enhances students' self-expression and encourages spontaneity.

writing underscores the importance of reading to children: "The single most important activity for building understandings and skills for reading success appears to be reading aloud to children" (Bus, Van Ijzendoorn, & Pellegrini, 1995; Wells, 1993).

## Reading to Children

There is no better way to create a love for books in both primary and middle school children than by reading aloud. Reading to children sparks their imagination and gives them a sense of wonder. Reading to children will help them appreciate the gift of literature, develop and enrich their own language, and build implicit concepts about reading and writing.

Reading to children helps them learn to read in subtle but important ways. It is through reading that children develop a schema or a sense for stories. In Chapter 10, we discuss the role of *story structure* in learning to read and how children can use their schema for stories to comprehend material. A story schema is developed early in the lives of children who have been read to frequently. Moreover, reading to children provides models for writing as they develop a sense of plot, characterization, mood, and theme.

Cramer (1975, pp. 461–462) provides timeless guidelines for reading to children:

MIDDLE GRADES

STANDARD
4.4

1. Plan each day's reading selection in advance. You might reserve at least one day a week for special selections—poetry, surprise readings, or readings designed to mesh with other daily or weekly classroom activities.
2. Select reading material best suited for the children being read to. Keep in mind age and interest levels.
3. Interpret the mood, tone, and action of the passage being read. Don't be afraid to be dramatic. Inhibition, shyness, or fear of making a fool of oneself often prevents teachers from entering into the drama of a story.
4. Differentiate the reading-to-children time from the directed reading-and-listening-activity time. It is neither necessary nor desirable to make the reading-to-children time into a structured lesson. The primary objective is enjoyment.

5. When reading a narrative that will be continued the next day, stop at a point that is likely to invite anticipation for the next episode. Judicious use of this device can have a positive effect on attendance and sustained high-interest level in the selection being read.

Reading activities may be planned to focus on children's authors and illustrators. Children may learn about the authors and illustrators by reading or listening to their stories, by corresponding with them, by creating stories in their style, or by comparing and contrasting the stories.

Jim Trelease's *Read-Aloud Handbook* (6th ed., 2006) is a valuable resource for parents and teachers who want to make reading to children a regular routine. Trelease not only provides the dos and don'ts of reading aloud but also includes annotated references of read-aloud books that can be used to make reading come alive for children of all ages.

Reading to children is an important way of sharing books. The act of sharing books with children provides valuable stimulation for relating speech to print. Almost all of the early readers in various studies came from book-oriented homes. Reading to and with children captures their fascination with print. They progress from sheer delight in the human experience of story sharing, to recognition that the pictures in books "tell a story," to the awareness that the black squiggly marks (not the pictures on a page) have a direct association with spoken language.

Books may be shared in a variety of contexts. Young children will hear good children's literature during a library story hour. Excellent literature is also available to children through book and CD combinations that are sold in bookstores or may be borrowed from a public library, and the computer has great potential for engaging young children in early reading experiences.

**SHARING BOOKS** ◆ The bedtime story, and the intimacy that surrounds it, is one of the most important ways that parents can share the joy of reading with their children. **Shared reading** is a teaching strategy that incorporates the intimate effects of sharing books with children (Holdaway, 1979) and is an important component of a balanced literacy program. The idea behind shared reading is to use a "big book" or other enlarged text to share a story with a group of children or the whole class. In Chapter 5, we provide an extensive discussion on the use of big books in primary classrooms.

The big book allows all the children in the class or in a small group to participate actively in the reading of the story. Because the print and illustrations are large enough for all the children to see, the teacher captures their attention immediately and focuses instruction around key goals. For example, the teacher should read the story aloud often enough so that children learn it by heart. The story then becomes the basis for discussion and language-related activities (i.e., story dramatization) as well as teaching children about directionality and other print-related concepts.

In shared reading, the teacher and a class of beginners partake in the reading and rereading of favorite stories, songs, poems, and rhymes. Butler (1988) recommends the use of shared reading as a way of creating opportunities for children to learn what a book is, what an "expert" reader does with a book as it is read, and what makes a story a story. Taberski (2000) claims that the use of shared reading in her classroom "offers numerous opportunities to show children what reading is all about" (p. 91). The Research-Based Practices featured in Box 4.5 outlines the steps of shared reading.

**REPEATING THE READING OF FAVORITE STORIES** ◆ Repetition of favorite stories and eventually "memory reading" play a crucial role in the child's understanding that print is supposed to sound like language. The phenomenon of memory reading involves recalling and rehearsing favorite segments of stories by heart. Young children learn to use a variety of strategies to achieve some sense of independence over their favorite stories. As part of sharing books and reading aloud, the teacher should be ready and willing to read and reread favorite books and to invite children to participate as much as possible. The language patterns of the books should be predictable, melodic, and rhythmic. We will have more to say on predictable materials and book choices for young children in Chapter 8.

BOX **4.5**

## Research-Based Practices     Shared Reading

Consider the following steps when sharing books with early readers and writers.

### INTRODUCE, TALK ABOUT, AND READ A NEW STORY

- Show children the cover of the book and invite discussion of the illustration. Ask, "What does the illustration on the cover remind you of?" "What do you think this story will be about?"
- Tell children the title of the story. Invite further predictions as to the story's content.
- Read the story dramatically. Once children have experienced the joy of hearing the story, invite conversation: "What did you enjoy about the story?" "Were the characters like you?" It is better not to overdo the discussion with lots of questions. Accept the children's personal reactions and responses, and support their efforts to express their enjoyment of the story and to talk about the meaning that it had for them.
- Encourage children to retell the story in their own words. Allow them to use picture clues, and assist them as needed.
- Reread the story, inviting children to participate in some way by focusing on repetitive elements, or chants, and having them join in with you. Keep the emphasis on meaning and enjoyment.

### REREAD FAMILIAR STORIES

- Once the children have become familiar with several stories, ask them to choose a favorite to be reread.
- Strive for the children's increased participation by creating *readalong* situations.

- Create *book experiences* to build children's book knowledge. For example, as you read, point to the words in the text and demonstrate skills such as page turning and directionality (e.g., left to right, top to bottom).
- Teach children about *book conventions* (e.g., front and back cover, title and author page, pictures to support the story).
- Make children aware of *written language conventions* (e.g., words, pages, spaces between words, the use of capital letters in proper names or at the beginning of a sentence, punctuation marks, quotation marks to indicate dialogue between characters). We will examine the development of written language and book conventions in more depth in Chapter 5.

### DEVELOP READING SKILLS AND STRATEGIES

- As children progress in the sharing and rereading of favorite stories, teach them literacy skills and strategies (e.g., recognizing letter–sound relationships in words, using context to identify words, building a sight-word vocabulary, developing oral reading fluency, comprehending meaning). These strategies and others will be examined in subsequent chapters.

### ENCOURAGE INDEPENDENT READING

- Develop a classroom library of books that have been shared and reread many times.
- Encourage students to read favorite books on their own and with others.

*Source:* Based on *The Foundations of Literacy*, by D. Holdaway (Portsmouth, NH: Heinemann, 1979).

Two additional suggestions should be considered. First, create a listening library for the classroom by recording stories on audiotapes or CD-ROM for children to listen to as they follow the story in the book. Second, children will enjoy repeating and retelling favorite stories by using a flannel board or puppets or through creative play and dramatics.

Some adults are quick to point out that children who memorize stories are just pretending to read, just "going through the motions." Pretending, however, shouldn't be discouraged. In fact, imitation establishes good models. The readinglike behaviors associated with an imitative stage in reading provide children with important early book experiences. Just consider some of the print concepts they learn: Books have pages, the pages can be turned, books have a right and wrong way up, the pictures help tell a story, and books are a source of enjoyment and pleasure.

**PROVIDING ASSISTANCE AS NEEDED** ◆ Parents of early readers answer questions when their children ask for assistance. The parent usually follows the child's lead, not vice versa. Children choose their own activities and materials, and when questions arise, a parent or more capable reader is there to help.

Read how Ben and Matt interact with each other just before bedtime. The brothers share the same bedroom and often read bedtime stories together. Ben is 8 and Matt is 5.

*Ben:* Matt, pick out a story. *(Matt proceeds to do so while Ben plays with the dog.)*
*Matt:* Ben, can I read the big words?
*Ben:* *(points to the book)* Are these the big words?
*Matt:* Yeah, those words.
*Ben:* Why don't I read the black words and you read the red ones? OK?
*Matt:* *(points to book)* You mean these?
*Ben:* Yeah.
*Matt:* But I don't know all the words.
*Ben:* Well, I'll just help ya—OK?
*Matt:* OK, I'll try. *(Matt sighs and the story begins.)* Will you help me with that? *(Matt points to a word on the page.)*
*Ben:* Scissors.
*Matt:* Scissors.
*Ben:* Yeah, good. That's right. *(The story continues until Matt reads the word* fish *for* goldfish.*)*
*Ben:* No. What kind of fish?
*Matt:* Goldfish?
*Ben:* Yeah, good. *(Ben points to a picture of the goldfish. After a while, Ben gets tired of giving Matt hints about the words.)*
*Ben:* Can I read the rest?
*Matt:* Yeah, but I want to read the last page.
*Ben:* OK. *(Ben reads the book until the last page.)* Are you goin' to read this?
*Matt:* Yeah. *(Matt attempts the last page and does fairly well with Ben's occasional assistance.)*
*Ben:* Good, Matt! You're learnin' to read real well.

Matt has acquired knowledge of written language and has developed concepts of reading by being immersed in stories from a very early age. He is learning how to read by reading with help from Ben and his parents and on his own. Matt seeks assistance when he needs it and doesn't recognize such help as corrective or critical.

We have scratched the surface in presenting some of the implications of early reading for beginning instruction. We will continue the discussion in the next chapter.

## WHAT ABOUT STRUGGLING READERS AND *Early Literacy?*

We began this chapter by stating, "Beginnings are important." In fact, good beginnings are *crucial* to children's development as writers and readers. What occurs in the life of a child prior to schooling makes a great deal of difference. Children, particularly those from very different socioeconomic backgrounds, have diverse experiences with literacy prior to schooling; some come to school ready to read, whereas others have had little exposure to print.

The family plays a critical role because the foundations of literacy are built in the home. Through interactions with their world and the people in it, children learn the many purposes for reading and writing by becoming involved in these activities on a daily basis. Children thrive in environments in which parents and significant others hold reading and writing in high regard. Getting this message to parents and caregivers of young children is vital. Whereas parents need to foster literacy experiences in the home, caregivers need to create a homelike environment that will foster a social context for reading with peers.

But what about homes where there are no models of literate activity for young children? Family literacy programs, which are based on the belief that improving the basic literacy skills of adults will foster learning and literacy among children, show promise for breaking the cycle of intergenerational illiteracy. The Barbara Bush Foundation for Family Literacy has been a major contributor to programs that support families and has published materials for parents and literacy providers. Family literacy programs offer opportunity, aid, and hope for many families, and work toward our goal of assuring that every child has a good beginning.

# WHAT ABOUT STANDARDS, ASSESSMENT, AND *Early Literacy?*

The foundation for reading success is forged long before a child begins kindergarten. In response to concern about the quality and content of preschool programs, some states have included essential preschool concepts and skills in their state educational standards. The state of Ohio, for example, has developed early learning content standards for the English language arts. The standards are research-based indicators of what preschool children should know and be able to do prior to beginning their formal schooling. Ohio's early learning content standards seek to promote high expectations for all students—including English language learners—in the areas of language, reading, and writing. The early learning content standards are aligned to the English language arts standards established for K–12 students and are applicable for a variety of preschool settings including nursery school and family care environments.

At the federal level, in addition to previously established Title I and Head Start programs, the No Child Left Behind Act includes an Early Reading First program. The Early Reading First program seeks to create early childhood centers that will prepare children—especially those from low-income families—to begin formal schooling with the necessary language, cognitive, and early reading skills. The goals of the Early Reading First Program include

- To support local efforts to enhance the early language, literacy, and prereading development of preschool-age children through the use of research-based reading strategies
- To provide preschool-age children with high-quality language and literature-rich environments
- To demonstrate language and literacy activities that support the age-appropriate development of oral language, phonological awareness, print awareness, and alphabetic knowledge
- To use screening assessments to effectively identify preschool-age children who may be at risk for reading failure
- For more information on Early Reading First visit www.ed.gov/programs/earlyreading/index.html.

# Summary

In this chapter, we dealt with the developmental aspects of literacy learning in relation to children's early reading and writing. We inquired into the nature of beginning reading instruction by looking at preschoolers' knowledge of and experiences with print. Children progress through various phases in literacy development in early reading and writing from birth through the primary grades.

Early in life, some children use what they have learned and experienced daily to build positive associations with books. Through such natural activities as the bedtime story and other types of storybook interaction, children develop a "set for literacy." Preschoolers are immersed in a world of meaningful print; they exhibit early reading behaviors well before they enter a classroom. What kinds of experiences, then, are needed to get the kindergarten child off to a good start?

Beginning readers benefit from developmentally appropriate practices that are home-centered, play-centered, and language-centered. *Home-centered* refers to supportive situations in which a warm, accepting, and patient relationship develops between teacher and child. Reading to children, sharing books, and assisting with reading are among the activities that can be easily transferred from the parent to the teacher. *Play-centered* refers to activities that allow children to explore literacy in spontaneous play contexts. Literacy play centers are powerful contexts for helping children experiment with literacy. *Language-centered* refers to experiences in which children explore spontaneous activities. Speaking, visual expression, singing, movement and rhythmic activities, role playing, and drama are all instructional devices for teachers who want to approximate ideal conditions for learning to read in their classrooms.

## Teacher Action Research

 1. Locate a kindergarten or preschool classroom that has a play-centered environment in which children can develop a "feel" for literacy as they experiment with written language. Collect data describing how children experiment with literacy in a natural context. How do play centers promote literacy? As children engage in pretend play, what do they do that will assist in their literacy development? Tape-record or take notes of conferences that occur, interview children, collect anecdotes of interactions among the children, and compile all the information into a case study of one or more children's literacy learning.

2. Reflect on the literate environment that you experienced personally as a child or that a child you know well experienced. Use the following questions to guide your retrospective inquiry:

   a. Were stories read or told?
   b. How much time was spent listening to stories?
   c. Describe an instructional situation and the child's responses.
   d. Was the child given encouragement and support, perhaps a hug or an accepting word, in the learning situation?
   e. How much time was spent doing worksheets?
   f. Was time spent scribbling, drawing, or writing? Describe the nature of the child's participation.

   What conclusions can be drawn from your personal reflection?

 3. Analyze the invented spellings of preschoolers from writing samples you have collected or from those provided by your instructor. What does the analysis of spelling tell you about each child's knowledge of words and of letter–sound relationships? How would you design age-appropriate writing experiences to help the children continue to grow and develop as writers?

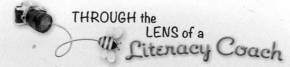

THROUGH the LENS of a Literacy Coach

4. Visit an early childhood agency. What types of new literacies do you notice teachers and children using? What new literacies are appropriate for children of this age? If there is little use of multimodal literacy, what suggestions do you have for introducing them into this context?

## Related Web Sites

*The Barbara Bush Foundation for Family Literacy*

**www.barbarabushfoundation.com**

The online home of former first lady Barbara Bush's Foundation for Family Literacy has a wealth of resources for family literacy.

*Dad's Playbook: Coaching Kids to Read*

**www.nifl.gov/partnershipforreading/publications/pdf/Dads_Playbook.pdf**

Dad's Playbook stresses the important role fathers can play in helping children learn to read. This online publication also teaches dads about the five skills children need to be readers by third grade and helps dads incorporate reading into everyday activities.

*The National Institute for Literacy*

**www.nifl.gov/nifl/publications.html**

The National Institute for Literacy develops resources for families and educators of learners across the lifespan to strengthen the teaching and learning of reading. Of special interest is the *Shining Stars* series, created to help parents get their child ready to read.

*Scholastic Publishing*

**www.scholastic.com/families/index.htm**

Tips and fun activities for nurturing children's literacy development are available for parents on this web site.

*University of Connecticut*

**www.literacy.uconn.edu/earlit.htm**

Here you will find a variety of links to activities, strategies, and instructional tips related to early literacy. It also provides links to early literacy web sites for young children.

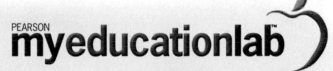

PEARSON
**myeducationlab**

Now go to the Vacca et al. *Reading and Learning to Read*, Seventh Edition, MyEducationLab course at **www.myeducationlab.com** to

- Take a pretest to assess your initial comprehension of the chapter content
- Study chapter content with your individualized study plan
- Take a posttest to assess your understanding of chapter content
- Engage in multimedia exercises to help you build a deeper and more applied understanding of chapter content

CHAPTER 5

# Inviting Beginners into the Literacy Club

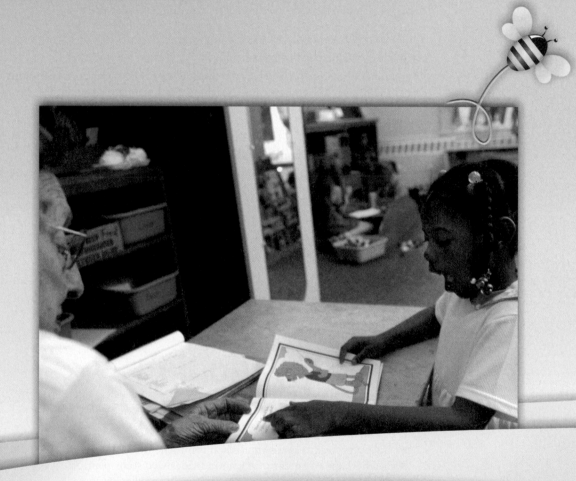

Standards found in this chapter:
- 1.1
- 1.2
- 1.3
- 1.4
- 2.2
- 2.3
- 3.1
- 3.2
- 3.3
- 4.1
- 4.2
- 4.3

## In this chapter,
### YOU WILL DISCOVER:

- The rationale for an emergent reading program
- The importance of storybooks in the lives of early readers and writers
- How to develop and assess linguistic knowledge, concepts of print, and literacy-related knowledge and skills
- How to develop phonemic awareness and alphabet knowledge

## Concept Map

### INVITING BEGINNERS INTO THE LITERACY CLUB

**LITERACY LEARNING THROUGH STORYBOOKS**

| Big Books | Interactive Reading and Writing | Electronic Books |

**LEARNING ABOUT THE RELATIONSHIP BETWEEN SPEECH AND PRINT**

| Use of Written Language | Language-Experience Stories |

**LEARNING ABOUT FEATURES OF WRITTEN LANGUAGE**

| Linguistic Awareness | Concepts About Print |

Observing Children's Emerging Literacy

**LEARNING ABOUT LETTERS AND SOUNDS**

| Phonemic Awareness | Letter Recognition |

ourtney's parents always read to her when she was little, so by the time she entered kindergarten, she was ready to approach books in a new way. On the first day of kindergarten, Mr. Young read Michael Rosen's *We're Going on a Bear Hunt* to the class, but this was no ordinary read-aloud. *We're Going on a Bear Hunt* is a fun, interactive story of a group of people swish-swashing through tall grass, splash-sploshing through a river, stumbling and tripping through a dark forest, and tiptoeing through a narrow cave in search of a big, scary bear. With Mr. Young's direction, the excited kindergartners participated in the story by performing various actions and sounds to mimic the events on the journey. They rubbed their hands together to make a swishing sound as they felt their way through the grass, and they tapped their feet on the ground to tread carefully through the cave. When they met the bear at the end of the story they covered their faces, cried out in glee, and frantically stamped their feet on the floor as they retraced their route back to their safe and warm beds. At the end of the day, Mr. Young gave each student a copy of the book to take home to read with their parents.

When Courtney got home that afternoon, armed with her own copy of the book, she told her parents all about the story Mr. Young read to the class. When her dad read the book aloud, Courtney showed them the movements. She was so excited about reading that her parents decided to follow Mr. Young's example and make reading a little bit more enjoyable for their daughter. That night, when Courtney's mother read *Clifford the Big Red Dog* to her, she made sure to point out places where Courtney could bark and thump her "tail" on the bed.

Through the social interactions that occur in the classroom, Mr. Young invites all of his students into the **literacy club** on the first day of school. In this club, nobody pays dues and nobody's excluded from joining. Mr. Young recognizes that when young children identify themselves as part of a community of readers and writers and are accepted as such, they will build on the literacy knowledge they bring to school. Confidence with print breeds competence.

The literacy club consists of the group of readers and writers with whom a child interacts (Smith, 1985). If children are to understand reading and writing and what these literacy processes are for, they must become members of the literacy club. The only requirement for membership is a mutual acknowledgment of acceptance into a group of people who use reading and writing in meaningful and purposeful ways. In other words, children must perceive themselves as readers and writers and in turn be perceived by others as readers and writers. The preceding vignette about Courtney suggests the importance of membership in the literacy club. Emergent literacy programs provide children with invitations to join the literacy club by building on and extending their knowledge and awareness of language and literacy.

## Emergent Literacy Programs for Beginners

**E**mergent literacy, as we began to develop it in Chapter 4, is a concept that supports learning to read in a positive home environment where children are in the process of becoming literate from birth. Emergent literacy assumes children are always becoming readers and writers and that they are born ready to learn about literacy and continue to grow in their understandings throughout their life

(Bennett-Armistead, Duke, & Moses, 2005). According to this social constructivist view, literacy acquisition has much in common with oral language development. The acquisition of reading should be as natural as oral language development, given ideal learning conditions. What happens in the classroom influences children's emerging literacy skills and concepts of reading, as well as their motivation to read. Children need good role models, invitations to learn, and support in their development toward skilled reading and writing. With a lot of opportunities to engage in meaningful literacy activities, large amounts of interaction with adults and peers, and some incidental instruction, children become conventional readers and writers. Beginning instruction, then, should serve to extend literacy development in early childhood.

Three questions underlie instruction and assessment in an emergent literacy program: (1) What does a child already know about print? (2) What reading behaviors and interests does a child already exhibit? and (3) What does a child need to learn? Answers to these questions will demonstrate that beginning instruction for 5- and 6-year-olds is not a period in which children progress from nonreading to reading behavior. When planning beginning instructional experiences for 5- and 6-year-olds, a basic principle of emergent literacy should guide your actions: Rather than thinking about getting children ready for reading, consider what must be done to get literacy instruction ready for children.

The old notion of **reading readiness** evolved from the belief that readiness is largely the result of maturation, to the present-day concept that children benefit from instructional experiences before engaging in reading. Although early proponents of reading readiness contended that children must reach a certain level of physical, mental, and emotional maturity to profit from teaching, there has been a dramatic shift from a maturational perspective to an instructional emphasis.

From the 1930s, readiness has implied that there is a best time to benefit from reading instruction. The idea of a best time often translated into one-dimensional indicators of reading readiness such as a child's mental maturity as reflected by a score on an intelligence test. The importance of mental age, for example, was supported by the views of Morphett and Washburne (1931). For many years, a 6.5 mental age became the benchmark for deciding matters of reading instruction. Even today, there are remnants of the best-time-for-teaching-reading theory; we still award children performance scores on a reading readiness test. But reliance on a single readiness test score, or for that matter mental age, tends to minimize the differences that children bring to reading instruction and negates a developmental view of learning to read.

Teale and Sulzby (1986) contend that reading readiness, as institutionalized by schools, curricula, and publishers of tests and instructional programs, is no longer an appropriate way to conceptualize instruction for beginners. In its place, they suggest emergent literacy as a developmentally appropriate view on which to build literacy curricula, instructional practice, and assessment for beginners. Table 5.1 compares readiness and emergent literacy along several dimensions.

If beginners are going to make a smooth transition from emergent to fluent literacy, they must feel from the outset that they belong to a classroom community of readers and writers. The challenge of working with beginners lies in scaffolding learning and weaving together experiences that build on children's knowledge of language and their previous interactions with texts. Working with beginners requires knowing about the book experiences they have had, their desire to read, and their awareness of concepts related to print. Because young children come to school with diverse literacy backgrounds, their acquaintance with texts will vary dramatically. Some will have little or no prior knowledge or experience with books and little interest in learning to read. Others will have rich experiences and considerable desire to extend what they already know about print. Many will fall somewhere between the two extremes. Invitations into the literacy club build on the instructional implications of literacy learning in early childhood.

**Table 5.1** Comparison of Emergent Literacy and Reading Readiness

|  | EMERGENT LITERACY | READING READINESS |
|---|---|---|
| **Theoretical Perspective** | Children are in the process of becoming literate from birth and are capable of learning what it means to be a user of written language before entering school. | Children must master a set of basic skills before they can learn to read. Learning to read is an outcome of school-based instruction. |
| **Acquisition of Literacy Skills and Strategies** | Children learn to use written language and develop as readers and writers through active engagement with their world. Literacy develops in real-life settings in purposeful ways. | Children learn to read by mastering skills arranged and sequenced in a hierarchy according to their level of difficulty. |
| **Relationship of Reading to Writing** | Children progress as readers and writers. Reading and writing (as well as speaking and listening) are interrelated and develop concurrently. | Children learn to read first. The skills of reading must be developed before introducing written composition. |
| **Functional-Formal Learning** | Children learn informally through interactions with and modeling from literate significant others and explorations with written language. | Children learn through formal teaching and monitoring (i.e., periodic assessment) of skills. |
| **Individual Development** | Children learn to be literate in different ways and at different rates of development. | Children progress as readers by moving through a scope and sequence of skills. |

# Learning Literacy Through Storybooks

**STANDARD 2.3**

Storybooks unlock the mysteries of reading, rivet children's attention to print, and provide models of writing that build on and extend the young child's concepts of texts and how they work. In Chapter 4, we explored the value of reading storybooks aloud, repeatedly reading familiar stories, and sharing reading experiences around the use of **big books**—enlarged versions of children's storybooks. As Figure 5.1 illustrates, a literature-rich curriculum for young children will offer numerous opportunities to interact with storybooks. Literacy lessons immerse children in **storybook experiences.** These experiences aren't mutually exclusive, but as the illustration in Figure 5.1 suggests, they are interlocking and connected. All are designed to further children's explorations with texts and to develop concepts related to print as well as strategies to construct meaning. The construction of meaning, or comprehension, is always the goal and therefore should be emphasized.

Immersing beginners in storybook literacy experiences, which include read-alouds and readalongs, **interactive reading** and **writing,** rereadings of favorite texts, and independent reading and writing, helps accomplish a variety of instructional goals:

- To motivate beginners to want to read and write
- To interest beginners in listening to, reading, and writing stories, with emphasis on predicting, sharing, and extending personal meanings
- To help beginners understand what reading and writing are all about
- To encourage beginners to respond to stories by drawing, writing, and dramatizing their explorations of texts
- To invite beginners to construct meaning through the use of picture cues and storybook illustrations
- To help beginners gain familiarity with "book language" and the meaning of terms that figure in literacy instruction

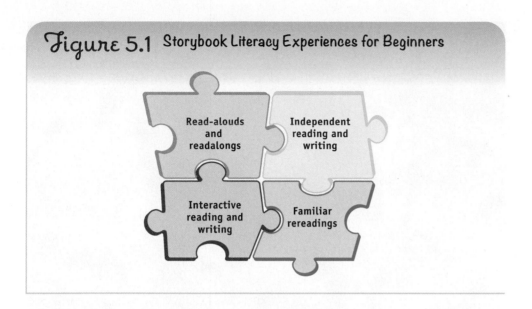

Figure 5.1   Storybook Literacy Experiences for Beginners

- To teach beginners about directionality—the left-to-right, top-to-bottom orientation of written language
- To teach beginners the meaning of *word* and the function of space in establishing boundaries between words
- To teach beginners alphabetic principles of written language
- To teach beginners to predict words that "must come next" in a sentence
- To teach beginners to recognize words that they are interested in learning or that occur frequently in meaningful contexts

These goals are not sequential in the sense that one must be accomplished before another is attempted. In classrooms where storybook experiences are an integral part of the school day, several or more may be accomplished over time in combination or simultaneously. The translation of these goals into classroom activities and experiences lies in having a developmental perspective of beginning reading. Big books provide a developmentally appropriate context for interactive reading and writing experiences.

## Big Books in U.S. Classrooms

Big books are one of the easiest and most effective ways to get beginners involved in the exploration of texts. The use of big books as an instructional resource began in the late 1960s in New Zealand, when teachers began to make their own big books from heavy brown butcher paper. Teacher-made big books retold nursery rhymes, poems, and popular stories such as "The Gingerbread Man." The critical feature common to these big books was that the stories and poems provided beginners with strong rhythms and predictable patterns of language. Roskos, Tabors, and Lenhart (2004) have this to say about big books in the early childhood classroom:

> In the early childhood setting, a big book or other enlarged text is used to share a story with the whole class or a small group of children. The big book allows all the children to participate actively in the reading of the story. If there are English-language learners in the class, keep in mind that a shorter reading session or one that is tailored specifically for them may work best. (p. 56)

The predictability of the plot and language of big books makes them easy to understand and remember. For example, after two or three readings, most 5- and 6-year-olds easily memorize Mem Fox's *Hattie and the Fox* or Bill Martin Jr.'s *Brown Bear, Brown Bear,*

**HOMEWORK EXERCISES: VIDEO**

Go to the Homework and Exercises section in Chapter 5 of MyEducationLab to watch the video "Beginning Reading" and see how two teachers develop reading readiness in their students.

DIVERSITY ELL

The use of big books for instruction encourages children's participation in the shared reading experience and connects them with the joy of literature.

*What Do You See?* Big books such as these, with their simple, repetitive refrains, colorful illustrations, and cumulative plot endings, allow children to make predictions and participate immediately in shared reading experiences.

New Zealand researchers, spearheaded by the pioneering work of Don Holdaway, observed and documented the influence of big-book teaching on children's literacy development and their social interactions in the classroom (Holdaway, 1979). Children learn to read naturally in the company of other children and the teacher. Joy Cowley's amazingly popular *Mrs. Wishy-Washy* is used today in classrooms for beginners throughout the world. According to Cowley (1991), the popularity of her big books is in the inherent appeal they have for children: "It is important to me . . . that the big books I write relate directly to the child's world and not to an adult view of what the world is or should be" (p. 19). (See her Viewpoint featured in Box 5.1.) Today's big books not only capture the child's view of the world but also range in content from traditional tales, to books of poems, to informational books in different content areas.

In addition to the pleasure and enjoyment that children get when they participate in shared readings and rereadings of big books, big-book formats are versatile in helping to achieve all of the instructional goals for beginners. The chart in Figure 5.2 on pages 130–131 suggests some of the activities that teachers and children engage in when they use big books.

In Chapter 2, we mentioned that electronic books support children's literacy development by providing activities such as interactive story writing, reading aloud text that is highlighted, and playing word identification and vocabulary games on virtually any subject. These highly motivating and interactive features make electronic books an ideal choice for emergent readers. Today, many web sites offer storybooks online. See Figure 5.3 on page 132 for sample web sites.

Teachers of young children can use talking books to support their traditional print-based literacy program. With the assistance of a parent, volunteer, or more capable peer, Labbo (2000) suggests that there are many ways emergent readers can interact with talking books in developmentally appropriate ways:

1. Listen to the story first.
2. Read along with the story.

BOX **5.1**

# Viewpoint

**Big Books**
Joy Cowley

Big book reading is a big plus for all children. It puts children in a no-risk situation where they can read with a group at their own skill level. Children who lack confidence in reading will especially benefit from big book reading. Their reading is reinforced by their peers, and they can enjoy the pleasure of stories within a group until they are ready to attempt the stories on their own.

Enthusiasm is the key emotion associated with big book reading. A confident, enthusiastic teacher will readily communicate those feelings to his or her students. Usually I introduce a big book by reading the story a couple of times to the class and inviting discussion. Then the students and I can read the book together. Big books invite student participation, not just in reading but in using a pointer for following along, turning pages, and so on. Children may extend the large group experience by reading to each other in smaller groups, reading individually, dramatizing the text, making recordings complete with sound effects, and writing their own books using a similar theme or pattern.

Whatever the follow-up or innovation, it is important to remember that reading and writing are activities we do to share ourselves with others. Big books are especially good tools for sharing. It's for that reason, I think, that teachers around the world are having such success in using big books to bring literature into the lives of children.

*Source:* "Joy of Big Books," by J. Cowley, October 1991, *Instructor,* p. 19. Copyright © 1991 by Scholastic, Inc. Reprinted by permission of Scholastic, Inc.

3. Echo-read the story.
4. Read it first, then listen.
5. Partner-read in digital reader's theater.
6. Look for familiar letters or words.
7. Select words with same sounds.
8. Select rhyming words.
9. Read along with a book copy.
10. Tell how events from one screen relate to previous screens.
11. Tell how special effects fit the story.
12. Tell about similar stories.

## Interactive Reading and Writing

When the teacher and children engage in interactive reading and writing experiences, they demonstrate that literacy learning is social and collaborative. In interactive reading, they collaborate to construct meaning and enjoy a story. In the process, children develop strategies and concepts related to print. In interactive writing, the teacher and students create a text together. The texts that are created—lists, letters, labels, story retellings, alternative texts of stories that have been shared, and language-experience stories— demonstrate some of the important uses of written language and show children what reading is all about.

## *Figure* 5.2  Big-Book Activities Before, During, and After Reading

| WHAT THE TEACHER DOES | WHAT THE CHILD DOES | OBJECTIVE |
|---|---|---|
| *Before Reading* | | |
| Stimulates discussion about relevant content and concepts in text. | Talks and listens to others talk about relevant content and concepts. | To focus listening and speaking on vocabulary and ideas about to be met in print. To activate background knowledge related to text. |
| Reads aloud title and author; uses words *title* and *author* and briefly explains what they mean. | Notes what the words on the book cover represent. | To build vocabulary and concepts: title, author, authorship. |
| Asks children what they think story might be about, based on title, cover. Or thinks aloud about what she or he thinks this story might be about. | Uses clues from title and cover together with background knowledge to formulate predictions about the story. Or observes teacher model the above. | To use clues from text and background knowledge to make inferences and formulate predictions. |
| Shows pleasure and interest in anticipation of the reading. | Observes as teacher models personal interest and eagerness toward the reading. | To build positive attitudes toward books and reading. |
| *During Reading (Teacher Reads Aloud)* | | |
| Gives lively reading. Displays interest and delight in language and story line. | Observes teacher evoke meaningful language from print. | To understand that print carries meaning. |
| Tracks print with hand or pointer. | Follows movement of hand or pointer. | To match speech to print. To learn directionality: left to right. |
| Thinks aloud about her or his understanding of certain aspects of the story (self-query, making predictions, drawing conclusions, etc.). | Observes as teacher monitors her or his own understandings. | To develop an understanding of the reading process as thinking with text. |
| Hesitates at predictable parts in the text. Allows children to fill in possible words or phrases. | Fills in likely words for a given slot. | To use semantic and syntactic clues to determine what makes sense. |
| At appropriate parts in a story, queries children about what might happen next. | Makes predictions about what might happen next in the story. | To use story line to predict possible events and outcomes. |
| *After Reading* | | |
| Guides discussion about key ideas in the text. Helps children relate key concepts. | Participates in discussion of important ideas in the text. | To reflect on the reading: to apply and personalize key ideas in text. |
| Asks children to recall important or favorite parts. Finds corresponding part of the text (perhaps with help of children) and rereads. | Recalls and describes specific events and parts of text. | To use print to support and confirm discussion. |
| Guides group rereading of all or specific parts of text for errorless repetition and reinforcement. | Joins in the reading in parts he or she feels confident about. | To develop fluency and confidence through group reading. |

*(Continued)*

## Figure 5.2 *(Continued)*

| WHAT THE TEACHER DOES | WHAT THE CHILD DOES | OBJECTIVE |
|---|---|---|
| Uses cloze activities (flaps to cover words) to involve children in meaningful (contextually plausible) offerings. Discusses response with children. | Fills in possible words for a given slot. | To use semantic and syntactic clues to determine which words fit in a slot and why. |
| *After Reading, for Repeated Readings Only* | | |
| Focuses children's attention on distinctive features and patterns in the text: repeated words, repeated word beginnings (letters, consonant clusters), punctuation marks, etc. Uses letter names and correct terminology to discuss these features. Extends discussion to developmentally appropriate level. | Notes distinctive features and patterns pointed out by teacher and attempts to find others on her or his own. | To analyze a known text for distinctive features and patterns. To develop an understanding of the elements of decoding within a meaningful context. |
| Makes books and charts available for independent reading. | Selects books and charts for independent reading and reads them at own pace. | To increase confidence and understanding of the reading process by practicing it independently. |

*Source: Language, Literacy, and the Child,* 1st ed., by L. Galda, B. Cullinan, and D. Strickland, pp. 102–103. Copyright © 1993. Reprinted with permission of Wadsworth, a division of Thomson Learning: www.thomsonrights.com. Fax 800-730-2215.

Interactive reading and writing, as you might surmise, are reciprocal processes. What children read together is the basis for what they will write together; and in turn, what they write together is the basis for what they will read together. And what they read and write together often is the springboard for independent reading and writing.

**INTERACTIVE READING** ◆ Interactive reading, as the name suggests, encourages children to interact verbally with the story being read, the teacher, and other children. Interactive reading has many of the same features of the shared reading described in Chapter 4. The difference between the two practices lies in the instructional tone and emphasis of interactive reading. Whereas the primary goal of the shared reading experience is to create an intimate context for reading much like that surrounding the bedtime story, interactive reading events engage students not only in the enjoyment of a story but also in the development of skills and strategies. During shared reading, the teacher begins with a straight-through reading of a big book as children listen to the story. Through a series of repeated readings, the literacy event becomes more instructional as the teacher interacts with children to explore reading processes and construct meaning. During interactive reading, by contrast, the teacher poses questions throughout the read-aloud using either a big book or a regular-size picture book.

When working with beginners in preschool, kindergarten, and first grade, shared reading makes good sense. However, as children begin to make the transition into more skillful and strategic reading, primary grade teachers devote considerable time to interactive read-alouds. Figure 5.2 provides an excellent sequence of instructional procedures to engage children in interactive reading. Opitz (1999) tells us we need to be mindful to include books for beginning readers that represent their cultural heritage, as well as provide children with opportunities to learn about similarities and differences among people. By doing so, we provide the necessary support while personalizing the experience for children of diverse backgrounds.

## Figure 5.3   Sources of Online Storybooks

*Starfall*

**www.starfall.com**

This exceptional resource contains a series of multimedia, interactive talking storybooks that teach early decoding skills.

*Children's Storybooks Online*

**www.magickeys.com/books**

This web site offers free storybooks for children to read online. Stories are available for young children, older children, and young adults.

*International Children's Digital Library*

**www.icdlbooks.org**

The books shown on this web site can be searched by age level, length of text, or subject. Also presents web site in a variety of languages to assist English language learners. Books and web site content can be presented in the chosen language.

*Chateau Meddybemps*

**www.meddybemps.com**

This web site presents stories that can be read or listened to online. Also includes parent and teacher guides.

*ABC Teach*

**www.abcteach.com**

This web site has a variety of online books that can be printed for use in the classroom or read online. It presents the books in levels, such as early childhood and middle school.

Barrentine (1996) provides the following suggestions for planning an interactive read-aloud:

- Select high-interest picture books with rich language, well-developed plots and characters, and multiple layers of meaning. Great stories will engage students in numerous opportunities for learning.

- Read the book several times to yourself before reading aloud to children. Think about the story's structure (e.g., the setting, the sequence of events leading to plot conflict and resolution), characters, images, illustrations, point of view, themes, and the author's use of language.

- Identify instructional goals for the interactive reading, including the reading strategies that might be developed.

- Decide on points in the story where you might pause to ask children to make predictions. Also anticipate where you may need to build children's background knowledge so that they will understand concepts with which they may not be familiar. For example, Barrentine describes how a teacher invited her students to make predictions before the reading of *Blueberries for Sal* by Robert McCloskey. The teacher, Mrs. Herbert, displayed the illustrated endpaper of the book and asked the children to make predictions about the setting of the story and the characters.

> Teacher:   Let's preview the pictures here. Who do you think this might be? *(She displays the endpaper and points to Sal's mother, who is in the kitchen pouring blueberries into a canning jar.)*

| | |
|---|---|
| *Student 1:* | They're gonna make berry pie! |
| *Student 2:* | The mama. |
| *Teacher:* | And who might this be? |
| *Student 3:* | The—the—Sal! |
| *Teacher:* | Very good. Do you think they live in the city or the country? |
| *Students:* | *(overlapping comments)* Country. City. They might be both. |
| *Teacher:* | Country? What makes you think they live in the country? |
| *Student:* | 'Cause there's a lot of trees. |
| *Teacher:* | A lot of trees. OK. Do you see any big, tall buildings and skyscrapers like we've talked about in our social studies book? |
| *Students:* | No. |
| *Student:* | They live in the country. |
| *Student:* | They live in the forest. |
| *Teacher:* | Here's the title page, *Blueberries for Sal*. This is by Robert McCloskey. He's written some other stories that we have read. Raise your hand if you've heard *Make Way for Ducklings*. |

● Plan how and when you will ask questions during the interactive reading, but be prepared to relinquish your plans in order to be responsive to children's needs. Take your lead from children's responses, and tailor questions to the dialogue that develops through the interaction.

● Plan follow-up activities that help children extend the shared meaning constructed during the interactive reading.

**INTERACTIVE WRITING** ◆ Interactive writing provides many opportunities for explicit instruction in which teachers demonstrate early writing strategies (Clay, 1985). Taberski (2000) refers to this type of writing as "shared writing," and says that through this activity she and her students work out the conventions of print, spelling, and grammar. Following steps associated with the language-experience approach, the teacher becomes a scribe for a text dictated by the children and shares the pen with them, creating text together. The focus, first and foremost, is always on composing the text. The teacher, as well as the children who volunteer, will often read, then reread, the text for emphasis and make additions and changes to clarify meaning. Within this meaningful, collaborative context, opportunities abound to demonstrate early writing strategies such as word-by-word matching, left-to-right directionality, use of space to create boundaries between words, and other print conventions. As children gain experience with the conventions of print, the teacher uses shared writing activities to focus on spelling patterns and word analysis.

Let's take a look at how interactive reading and writing play out in Stephanie Hawking's first-grade class (Hawking, 1989). Stephanie and the children have been sharing Jack Kent's story *The Fat Cat*. After the third rereading, she and the children decided to write an alternative text to the story, which they titled "The Fat Cat at Big Boy." The inspiration for the alternative story was the Big Boy restaurant, which is located near the school.

The children wondered what would happen if the Fat Cat ever prowled for food at the Big Boy. So their first interactive writing experience involved brainstorming a list of what the Fat Cat would eat at Big Boy. One student, Miranda, suggested that the Fat Cat could eat men. Stephanie invited her to write the word *men* on a list, saying, "You know how to write *ten*. Can you use *ten* to help you write *men?*" (Hawking, 1989, p. 7). Miranda first practiced on the blackboard and then wrote *men* on a chart titled "Big Boy." The class worked on the chart for several days, and when it was finished, the children taped it to the wall to use as a resource.

Stephanie and the children then began writing the alternative text together. Talk, as you might predict, was crucial to the success of the story. As Stephanie explains, "The talk surrounding shared writing is a rich source of information. . . . As the children discuss

**HOMEWORK EXERCISE: VIDEO**

Go to the Homework and Exercises section in Chapter 5 of MyEducationLab to view the video "An Interactive Writing Activity" about the relationship between interactive reading and interactive writing.

what to write and how it should be written, the teacher finds out more about their developing concepts of story and their understanding of the writing process" (Hawking, 1989, p. 7). The class began by talking about how to begin the story. Everyone agreed that it should begin with the words "once upon a time" because it was going to be a "fake" story. Stephanie used this "teachable moment" to underscore the connection the children made between their story and the fairy tale genre. She told them that another name for a particular kind of fake story is a folktale.

As the text began to develop, Stephanie wrote on the chart as children dictated, but she also invited the children to add to the story by volunteering to write parts. Stephanie observed what the children who volunteered knew about the mechanics and conventions of writing and listened to their comments and suggestions as other children added to the text. When she served as a scribe for the children, she was able to focus their attention on the use of quotation marks for portions of the text that contained dialogue. As the class finished each page of the chart, the children would tape it to the wall so that they could refer to it whenever necessary to check on continuity of story line. At other times, they would search for the spelling of a word they knew had already been written on a previous page.

"The Fat Cat at Big Boy" was eventually made into a class big book. The children illustrated the story with drawings, decided on the sequencing of pages, and assembled the entire big-book text, rereading each page several times. Stephanie served as proofreader for the final copy—the public copy—of the big book by changing children's invented spellings to conventional forms.

Alternative texts such as "The Fat Cat at Big Boy" are popular forms of interactive writing in Stephanie's class. Some of the children were so excited about the project that they wanted to write Fat Cat stories on their own. And they did. What began as interactive reading of a popular storybook for young children turned into independent reading and writing.

# Learning About the Relationships Between Speech and Print

Children must be able to figure out what spoken language and written language have in common. Without learning the relationship between speech and print, the beginner will never make sense of reading or achieve independence in it. Earlier we suggested that reading often to children, repeating favorite bedtime stories, and providing opportunities to draw, scribble, and interact with print in their immediate environment are some of the ways that children naturally learn to make sense out of reading and its uses. Nevertheless, many 5-year-olds enter school with only vague notions of the purpose and nature of reading. They are not yet aware that what is said can be written, that written language is made up of words and sentences, or that reading involves directionality, attending to the spacing between words, punctuation cues, and other conventions of print. There are several ways of going about this important instructional task.

## Understanding the Uses of Written Language

From the beginning of their school experience, children must learn that the value of reading or writing lies in its uses as a tool for communicating, understanding, and enjoying. A 5-year-old or a 75-year-old should engage in reading and writing for real reasons and in real situations. Effective teachers make their own opportunities and should consider teaching about the uses of written language when any interesting or natural occasion arises in the classroom.

The teacher and children are gathered around the guinea pig cage discussing their new pet. The teacher is explaining the food guinea pigs eat and is showing the children the food they will be feeding the pet. One of the children remembers that the class goldfish died because too much food was put in the bowl. The teacher suggests that the class make a sign to put on the package telling the right amount of food and a chart to put near the cage to be checked on the day he is fed. She discusses the reasons these written records will help. (Taylor & Vawter, 1978, p. 942)

Situations such as the guinea pig scenario evolve naturally in the classroom. Nevertheless, seizing the opportunity to help children recognize the value of reading and writing requires a certain amount of awareness and commitment. For example, Taylor and Vawter (1978) illustrate how two teachers approach an everyday event differently. As children prepare for a field trip to a farm, one kindergarten teacher passes out name tags routinely and without explanation. Another teacher, however, poses a problem to be solved by the children: "If the farmer wants to ask one of us a question, how can we help him know our names?" Through give-and-take discussion, the children offer solutions that range from "tell him" to "I don't know" to "wear our names." As the discussion progresses, the teacher passes out the name tags and suggests that names are written so that someone can read them and that writing a name helps identify someone.

In Chapter 1, we outlined the **uses of oral language.** These language functions can and should be adapted to print at the beginning of instruction in order to help children become aware of the purposes of written language. Many of the activities outlined here build word awareness. Therefore, beginners should be introduced to some of the more obvious uses of print.

In general, the classroom should reflect a living example of written language put to purposeful ends. The classroom environment should be filled with print to suit specific instructional goals. Print should be evident everywhere in the form of labels for classroom objects, simple messages, rules, directions, and locations where a specific activity takes place, such as a story-reading area or an art center. Specifically, consider these uses of written language.

STANDARD
4.3

**PERPETUATING USES** ◆ Show children how to bridge the gap between time and space through print, or *perpetuate*. To do this, keep records and charts of a daily activity. For example, develop a weekly weather chart with the days of the week at the top and slots for inserting descriptive word cards under each day. The children can then use words to describe the day's weather.

| MONDAY | TUESDAY | WEDNESDAY | THURSDAY | FRIDAY |
|--------|---------|-----------|----------|--------|
| awful | foggy | sunny | ——— | ——— |
| rainy | cloudy | clear | ——— | ——— |
| sticky | dark | dry | ——— | ——— |

Post the names of room helpers for each week. Each morning, make a point of going to the chart and having the children identify who will help the teacher for the day.

Vote or poll children on various classroom events or activities and tally the results. For example, Shelley Adams polls her class daily on a "Question of the Day" generated by a student, such as "What is your favorite ice cream?" She then allows children to take turns giving an oral response while she tallies the results for all to see. Often she creates a simple graph with the results for discussion of which response is most or least common or other analysis. For example, if the numbers are close, she asks them to predict whether the count will be the same or not.

| Chocolate | IIII |
|---|---|
| Vanilla | III |
| Cookie dough | IIIII |
| Cake batter | IIIIIII |

Use children as messengers to deliver notes to other teachers or to parents. Explain the purpose of the note and why it was written. Or display notes from the principal congratulating children for work well done. Also post thank-you notes, letters, the school lunch menu for each day, and many other forms of communication.

Finally, keep a classroom scrapbook, beginning from the first day of school and including important events throughout the year. Use a digital camera and record the importance of each event.

**REGULATORY, AUTHORITATIVE-CONTRACTUAL USES** ◆ Show children how print can be used to control and direct behavior and to establish rules and agreements. For example, list classroom rules and use print to give directions such as lining up for the bus or going to the library. Establish official written contracts with children for various classroom activities (e.g., cleaning up after art activities, taking milk count for the week).

To use print to give directions, a teacher can make recipe charts for cooking projects that may include pictures and words explaining what to do. Pictures can depict ingredients such as flour, sugar, or eggs (cut from a magazine advertisement) or processes (e.g., a sketch of eggs being broken). In addition, children can follow directions with clue cards that use pictures and simple words, or they can play scavenger hunt using simple messages to direct the hunt.

**INSTRUMENTAL USES** ◆ Children should learn that print can be used to express personal needs. Teachers and children can list materials needed to participate in various activities:

| Art | Music | Building |
|-----|-------|----------|
| clay | bells | wood |
| scissors | shakers | glue |
| paint | piano | cardboard |
| brushes | CD player | blocks |

| Planting | Field Trip | Sleepover |
|----------|------------|-----------|
| seeds | lunch | toothbrush |
| water | boots | PJs |
| pots | warm clothes | pillow |
| tools | $2.50 | teddy bear |

The teacher can write gift lists or birthday wishes dictated by the children. Signs can be used to invite children to participate in various activities:

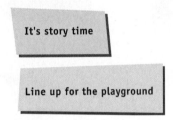

**DIVERSION USES** ◆ Demonstrate the value of print as a tool for enjoyment, or *diversion*. Read aloud to children on a daily basis. Also consider storytelling. (We will explain a variety of reading-aloud and storytelling procedures and activities in Chapter 12.) In particular, introduce children to humorous and nonsensical literature. Consider such classics as Dr. Seuss's *Cat in the Hat*, Mayer's *Billygoofang*, Pincus's *Tell Me a Mitzi*, and Krauss's *Backward Day*. Read to children those that you especially enjoy.

Tell puns, jokes, riddles, brainteasers, and the like. For example, ask children, "What's white and can be poured in a glass?" and record the responses. Or consider posting a riddle or joke on a section of the bulletin board, with the answer or punch line written on the inside flap.

STANDARD
4.3

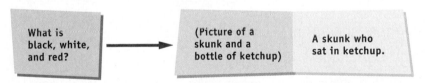

Use simple language patterns to introduce children to rhythms of language. Later in the year, use patterned stories and poems to model language patterns in writing. These patterned stories are highly predictable, enjoyable, and repetitious enough that children are naturally attracted to them. Bill Martin's *Instant Readers* or Dr. Seuss's materials develop children's sensitivity to hearing language.

As the year progressed in one kindergarten class, children were creating their own writing by dictating familiar patterns to the teacher.

> One bear, two bear.
> White bear, brown bear.
>
> This one has a big red nose.
> This one has big fat toes.

**PERSONAL USES** ◆ Children need to learn that written language can be used to express individuality, pride, and awareness of self—a *personal* use of language. Develop a "this is

As young children experiment with writing, either in attempts to write or by drawing pictures, they discover how to use writing as a form of communication and to express themselves.

me" book for each child. The book might be bound or created on the computer, and contain the child's drawings or photos and descriptions of self and family. The first page might begin "This is me," and include a self-portrait drawn by the child or a photo of the child. Other pages might include "This is my family." "This is my pet." "My favorite game is _____." "My favorite book is _____." "I like _____." "I want to be _____." "My best friend is _____."

In a similar vein, have the students make "me" cards that tell the names of pets, favorite toys, books, colors, television programs, or movies. Names of places of interest, places recently visited, or exciting places to explore in the community can also be included.

## Connecting Speech and Print Through Language Experience

There is no more appropriate way to help children understand what reading is all about than to show them how language is transcribed into print. A language-experience story is just what it implies—an account that is told aloud by a child and printed by another person. In the beginning of instruction, there are numerous ways to involve children in producing experience stories. For example, many of the suggestions for teaching about the uses of written language can serve to stimulate the child's dictation or, for that matter, a group-dictated story. Not only does an experience story vividly show the relationship between speech and print, but it also introduces children to the thrill of personal authorship. This can be especially true for children from diverse linguistic backgrounds because teachers who subscribe to the language-experience approach (see Chapter 2) support children working with their *own* language.

The value of language experience lies in the physical ease by which text is produced *to achieve reading instructional goals*. When a child dictates, the physical burden of writing is removed. This often results in more of a child's ideas being put in print than would otherwise be possible in beginning situations. In Chapter 11, we advocate regular, ongoing writing activity from the first day that children enter school. Dictated language-experience stories should be phased out as children's independent writing fluency increases.

When children have opportunities to converse naturally and spontaneously, their language is likely to be colorful and expressive, to have an almost poetic quality. For example, the following language-experience story was based on a conversation among a group of 5-year-olds as they experienced the visit of a pet mouse. It was recorded verbatim by Mrs. Ruttan, their kindergarten teacher.

> This mouse is soft.
> Soft as a baby sister?
> Soft as a little tiny ball?
> She's so small somebody could step on her.
>
> I'm afraid to hold her.
> I'll touch her and pet her,
> But I'm afraid to hold her.
> Does her tail tickle?
> Does it really?
> Are you scared of a mouse?
> No. But they tickle, you know.
>
> Feels like a pillow in my hand.
> Feels like I could sleep on her.
> Feels like a feather.
>
> I just love mouses.
> I wish we had our very own mouse.
> I held her for just a minute.
> Her claws tickled me.
> She was soft though.
> I told you I liked mouses.

Study another language-experience story based on a conversation that a group of children had about a new baby guinea pig in Mrs. Ruttan's class.

> We have a baby guinea pig.
> Her name is Nothing.
> She's not much of anything at all.
> She doesn't even weigh a pound.
>
> She wants to hide from us.
> Maybe she's scared.
> Why should she be scared?
> This is the first time she saw us.
> I think she's scared of us.
>
> Maybe she's just not used to us.
> Maybe she's just playing hide-and-go-seek.
> Maybe she's got to take lessons about knowing about people.

Much can be learned about what young children think and know and how they feel through language-experience-based instruction. An emergent literacy curriculum becomes more relevant, meaningful, and appropriate when it is based on children's own language, existing knowledge, and interests.

**STEPS TO FOLLOW IN PRODUCING LANGUAGE-EXPERIENCE STORIES** ◆ A child can dictate a complete story, or several children can collaborate on an account by contributing individual sentences. In either case, the first step is to provide a stimulus (e.g., a classroom guinea pig, photo, concrete objects, an actual experience a child has had) that will lead to dictation. Whatever the stimulus, it should be unusual and interesting enough for children to want to talk about it and to remember it 2 or 3 days later when the dictation is reread.

As children dictate, it's important to keep their spoken language intact. Therefore, write down exactly what is said regardless of grammatical errors and incomplete sentences. By capturing language just as it is spoken, the teacher preserves its integrity and ensures the child's total familiarity with the print to be read.

Once the story is written down, the teacher should read it aloud several times, carefully but steadily moving left to right, top to bottom, and pointing to each word or line as it is read and then sweeping to the next line. After that, the account should be read in unison, with the teacher continuing to model left-to-right, top-to-bottom orientation to print.

A dictated story need not be long. It can represent free-flowing language or controlled responses elicited by guiding questions. Suppose students are conversing about their summer activities. The teacher might say, "Let's tell each other what we did on our summer vacations." Jim begins, "I went fishing for the first time." As he says this, Mrs. Phillips, the kindergarten teacher, writes this verbatim on a large sheet of paper. The other children contribute to the story, with Mrs. Phillips writing out each contribution, beginning with the child's first name. The account was dictated as follows:

> Jim said, "I went fishing for the first time."
> Dory said, "We went to my grandma and grandpa's in Florida."
> Tony said, "I didn't do nothing but swim."
> Sheila said, "My family and me fished too."
> Michele said, "I went to Sea World."

If using the digital-language-experience approach (D-LEA), the process is similar. The teacher takes a digital photograph of the child engaged in an activity and then children compose a story about the experience using the photos as prompts. The teacher then types the story in and reads it back to the children (or uses a computer voice synthesizer) and revisions are made. Box 5.2 discusses another alternative LEA approach using podcasts.

**THE VALUE OF LANGUAGE EXPERIENCE** ◆ Examine what can be accomplished when young children engage in the writing of language-experience stories (Durkin, 1980):

- It can motivate children to want to read.
- It personalizes instruction.
- It demonstrates the connection between spoken and written language.
- It demonstrates the left-to-right, top-to-bottom orientation of written English.
- It demonstrates that the end of the line does not always mean the end of a thought.
- It demonstrates the value of written language for preserving information, ideas, and feelings.
- It teaches the meaning of *word* and the function of space in establishing word boundaries.
- It teaches the function of capitalization and punctuation.

In Mrs. Phillips's case, the story was read three times as the children watched her move left to right, top to bottom. Next, they read the story aloud two more times as she continued to model left-to-right orientation. She then had each child read his or her contribution, directing the children to "read it the way you said it." As a child read, she moved her hand along the bottom of each line, coordinating with the child's voice and reading in unison with each child.

Mrs. Phillips wanted to build confidence among her readers as she unobtrusively provided them with valuable learning opportunities. In addition to a "reading experience," she also spent time engaging the children in building the concept of *word.* First, she read the entire story in a natural speaking voice, pointing to each word as it was being read. By suggesting to the children that they read their individualized contributions, she reinforced

BOX **5.2**

*New Literacies*

## PODCASTS IN THE CLASSROOM

Today, everywhere you look people walk around with earphones coming out of their ears. Ask them "Who's on your playlist?" and they instantly reel off a long list of musicians, some of whom you may even have heard of. The iPod has become such a staple of children and adults everywhere that, in just a few years, an entire cottage industry has developed around the iPod and other MP3 digital recorders and players, including cars with built-in "docking stations," houses and businesses wired with MP3 connections, and numerous accessories. While many teachers and school administrators have had to restrict the use of MP3 players in school, more and more schools are also recognizing the teaching potential of the little gadgets.

One such school, Jamestown Elementary School in Arlington, Virginia, has received a great deal of publicity in recent years for their creative use of the technology. Teachers and children at Jamestown Elementary are taking LEA to the next level by producing podcasts of their experiences. Podcasts are brief radio shows that are simply audio files that can be downloaded and listened to on a portable MP3 player or on your personal computer.

At Jamestown Elementary, and a growing number of schools across the country, teachers work with the students to create podcasts of their poetry, reports, interviews, discussions on classroom topics, and more. The podcasts can be used to store information for later review, as an alternative platform for a classroom presentation, or to share with parents. Because podcasts involve various skills such as writing, editing, oral presentation, and technical work, they address different learning styles of students. One of the greatest benefits of podcasts in the schools is the level of excitement it creates among students (Long, 2007). The trendy technology and the potential to reach a wide audience serve as a great motivation for students (Shen, 2005). As stated by Tim Tyson, principal at Mabry Middle School, Cobb County, Georgia, "If kids don't learn the way we teach, maybe we should teach the way they learn" (Klein, 2006). To see how Jamestown Elementary and other schools are using podcasts, check out these web sites:

- http://web.mac.com/jamestownelementary/Jamestown 2007/Welcome.html
- www.murrieta.k12.ca.us/tovashal/bcoley/coleycast/index .htm (the official web site of Room 34 at Tovashal Elementary School, Murrieta, California)

- www.mpsomaha.org/willow/radio/index.html (Willowdale Elementary School, Omaha, Nebraska)
- www.leslienettling.com/NettlingNewscasts.htm (Carlisle Intermediate School, Carlisle, Ohio)
- www.cbsd.org/millcreek/jaffe/podcast/index.html (Mill Creek Elementary School, Warrington, Pennsylvania)
- www.ahisd.net/campuses/cambridge/radio/radio.htm (Cambridge Elementary School, San Antonio, Texas)

*Source:* Jamestown Elementary School, Arlington, Virginia.

word understanding. Mrs. Phillips also asked the children questions such as "Which word appears the most?" and discussed how space separates one word from another. Finally, Mrs. Phillips asked the children to draw an illustration for the sentence or part that each contributed to the account. These illustrations were pasted around the chart as they were completed, and the chart was posted on a bulletin board for other class members to read.

# Learning About Features of Written Language

Children's understanding of the relationship between speech and print is a vital first step in learning to read. They become aware of what reading is all about by recognizing the functionality of reading—that the purpose of reading, in its broadest sense, is to communicate ideas. A second step, or stage, is to become aware of the technical features of reading (Downing, 1979). These technical features (printed letters, words, sentences, syllables, sounds, punctuation marks, etc.) make up children's "technical vocabulary" for reading, or, according to Reid (1966), the language available to children "to talk and think about the activity of reading itself" (p. 57). To understand the technical features of reading, children must develop **linguistic awareness.**

**HOMEWORK EXERCISE: VIDEO**

Go to the Homework and Exercises section in Chapter 5 of MyEducationLab to watch the video "Connecting Speech and Print" to learn how to help early readers connect speech with print.

STANDARDS
1.1, 1.3

## Linguistic Awareness

Children of 5 and 6 may not be aware that words are language units. Spoken language, after all, is a steady stream of sounds that flow one into the other. Words and other print conventions (e.g., punctuation marks) were created to better represent spoken language in print and thus facilitate the reading of written language. For the 5-year-old, the six-word written message *Did you visit the fire station?* sounds like one big word—*Didjavisitthefirestation?* Even more difficult concepts for young children to learn are that spoken words are made up of smaller sounds (phonemes), that written words are made up of letters, and that in a written word, there is a close approximation between letters and sounds.

If children are to succeed in reading, they must acquire linguistic awareness and understand the language of reading instruction. They must learn the technical terms and labels that are needed to talk and think about reading and to carry out instructional tasks. What, for example, is the child's concept of "reading"? Of a "word"? Of a "sound"? Does the child confuse "writing" with "drawing" and "letter" with "number" when given a set of directions? Without an awareness of these terms, cognitive confusion in the classroom mounts quickly for the child (Downing, 1979). The teacher's job is to make explicit what each child knows implicitly about written language.

The technical features of written language are learned gradually by children and are best taught through real reading and readinglike activities and through discussions designed to build concepts and to untangle the confusion that children may have. Within the context of shared-book experiences, language-experience stories, and writing activities, children will develop linguistic sophistication with the technical features of print. These vehicles for instruction not only provide teachers with diagnostic information about children's print awareness but also form the basis for explicit instruction and discussion.

Agnew (1982) shows how to use language-experience stories to assess young children's emerging print awareness. The various procedures and tasks she proposed can be easily adapted to big-book and language-experience stories.

### PROCEDURES

1. Obtain a short story dictated by the child.
2. Print three or four nouns or verbs from the story on index cards.
3. Print two sentences from the story on separate pieces of paper.
4. Have available a supply of separate letters made from wood, felt, cardboard, or other materials.

5. Ask the child to complete any or all of the tasks outlined below. Record responses and impressions on the evaluation form.
6. Results should be viewed as tentative hypotheses about the child's print awareness. You'll want to validate results through classroom observation.

TASKS

1. Ask the child to point to any word on the chart story, then to "cup" his or her hands around or circle the word. (The child does not have to say the word but only show that he or she knows where the word begins and ends.) Ask the child to repeat the task with three or four other words.
2. Ask the child to match an individual word card with the same word in the story. (The child does not have to say the word; he or she simply needs to make a visual match.) If the word occurs more than once in the story, ask the child to locate the word in another place in the story. Repeat the task with several other word cards.
3. Ask the child to match a sentence with its counterpart from the story. (The child does not have to read the sentence.) Repeat the task with the other sentence.
4. Show the child an individual word card and provide him or her with the individual letters necessary to spell the word. Ask the child to build the word he or she sees on the card, using the separate letters. Ask the child for the names of the letters he or she is using. Probe the child about his or her understanding of the difference between letters and words. Repeat the exercise with two or three other word cards.
5. Ask the child to point to any letters he or she can name in the story. (Note whether the child points to letters rather than words.)

## The Concepts About Print Test

As part of a research study to investigate young children's acquisition of concepts about print, Marie Clay (1979a) developed the Concepts About Print Test. She examined not only what knowledge of print children possessed but also how their understanding of print changed. The underlying question that guided the study asked, "To what degree do young children possess reading-related concepts and linguistic abilities considered to be essential in learning to read?"

STANDARDS
3.1, 3.2, 3.3

The Concepts About Print Test is individually administered to a child. The teacher usually engages the child in a conversation and asks the child if he or she will help in the reading of a story. The teacher then proceeds to assess the child's concepts of print as they read the book together. For example, the teacher might say, "I'm going to read a story to you. Can you show me the front of the book so that I can get started?" or, once the book is opened, "Where should I start reading?" The child's responses reveal the knowledge of print he or she possesses. Table 5.2 lists the types of reading-related and linguistics concepts teachers should follow as they assess print concepts. Full instructions for the administration of the Concept About Print Test may be found in many places online or in Clay's book *The Early Detection of Reading Difficulties* (3rd ed., 1992).

## Observing Children's Emerging Literacy Accomplishments

Teachers can use **observation** to assess children's emerging literacy accomplishments. A wealth of information can be garnered from daily classroom interactions. Many of the instructional activities suggested in this book will reveal important information to help you make instructional decisions. For example, as you interact with children, ask yourself these questions (McDonnell & Osburn, 1978):

1. *Do children attend to the visual aspects of print?* If I am reading a story, can the child tell me where to start and where to go next? Is the child able to point to words as I read

## Table 5.2   Reading-Related and Linguistic Concepts Assessed in Marie Clay's Concepts About Print Test

| PRINT CONCEPT | CHILD'S TASK |
| --- | --- |
| Front of book | Identifies the front of the book |
| Difference between a picture and a page of print | Identifies a page of text (and not the picture on the opposite page) as the place to begin reading |
| Left-to-right directionality | Identifies the direction of reading as a left-to-right process |
| Return sweep | Identifies the return sweep as the appropriate reading behavior at the end of a line |
| Word pointing | Points out words as a teacher reads a line of print slowly |
| Beginning and end | Identifies the first and last parts of a story, page, line, or word |
| Bottom of a picture | Identifies the bottom of a picture that is inverted (upside down) on a page |
| Inverted page of print | Identifies the appropriate place to begin, left-to-right direction, and return sweep |
| Line order | Identifies line sequence as the correct answer when asked, "What's wrong with this?" (The teacher reads a printed sentence in which the line sequence is jumbled.) *Example:* and began to swim. I jumped into the water |
| Left page begins a text | Identifies the left page as place to begin reading when two pages of text are side by side |
| Word order | Identifies word order as the correct answer when asked, "What's wrong with this?" (The teacher reads a printed sentence in which the word order is distorted.) *Example:* I looked and looked I but could not find the cat. |
| Letter order | Identifies that the letters in simple words are not sequenced properly when the teacher reads, as if correct, a text in which the letters of the words are out of order *Example:* The dgo chased teh cat thsi way and thta way. The cta ran pu a tree. |

them, thereby demonstrating knowledge of directional patterns of print? Does the child understand the concepts of words and letters? Can he or she circle a word and letter in the book? To ensure that the child is not just a good guesser, this ability should be demonstrated several times.

**2.** *Do children use their intuitive knowledge of language?* Can the child look at a picture book and invent a story to go with the pictures? Does the invented story, when the teacher begins to write it down, indicate the child is using a more formalized language that approximates the language used in books (i.e., book-talk) rather than an informal conversational style? Does the child recognize that the print and the pictures are related? Can the child "read the words" of a memorized text such as a nursery rhyme, even though the spoken words are not completely accurate matches for the print? Is this recall stimulated or changed by the pictures?

**3.** *Are children beginning to show signs of integrating visual and language cues?* Are they beginning to read single sentences word by word, pointing to each word with a finger while reading? Can the child use all the cues available to a reader: the predictability of language, word order, a beginning sound, and an appropriateness to context while reading? Does he or she stop and correct, without prompting, when a visual–vocal mismatch occurs?

**4.** *Does the child expect meaning from print?* Does he or she demonstrate that a message is expected by relating a sensible story?

You can also adapt Clay's Concepts About Print Test to observe young children's emerging literacy concepts. Gray-Schlegel and King (1998), for example, developed a set of questions based on Clay's work to improve preservice teachers' understanding of beginners' emerging print-related concepts. The Emergent Literacy Observation (see the Research-Based Practices featured in Box 5.3) allows teachers to use storybooks as an assessment tool to interview and observe a child's concepts about print. The questions for the Emergent Literacy Observation can be adapted to any small book that has both print and pictures. Use the questions to think about why a child responded to each question in the manner that he or she did. Many of the preservice teachers in Gray-Schlegel and King's classes believed that their views on young children and emergent literacy changed as a result of using the Emergent Literacy Observation.

Read-alouds are the perfect place to teach children about the features of written language. Teachers can do this as they read stories, poems, and other texts aloud to children. For example, by pointing to the words while reading a big book, children learn important print concepts such as left-to-right directionality, where reading begins, return sweep, and that print is what is read, not pictures. Teachers can also show children the functions of navigational sections of a book, such as an index or table of contents, by thinking aloud: "I want to see if this zoo book has anything about gorillas in it so I am going to look in the index. Here we go. It says gorillas are on page 18." The assessments presented in this section can also be used as a guide for teaching features of written language.

BOX **5.3**

## Research-Based Practices

### Emergent Literacy Observation Questions

Use the following interview questions to observe a young child demonstrating knowledge of print. Consider tape-recording the interview. Reflect on the child's response to each question. What are the child's literacy accomplishments? What does the child need to learn?

1. Holding the book by its spine and letting it hang downward, hand it to the child and ask: *Show me the front of the book. Turn to the page where I should start reading.*

2. Once you've turned to the first page of the story, ask: *Where should I begin to read? Please show me with your finger. And then which way should I go? Show me what I should read when I come to the end of the line.* (Make sure you ask this question on a page with more than one line of print.)

3. Read the next few pages aloud and ask no questions. Note the child's attentiveness and interest.

4. Turn the page and ask (there must be an accompanying picture): *What do you think this page will be about?*

5. Read another page or two. Then ask: *Can you show me a word? Can you show me another word?*

6. Frame a line of print with your fingers and ask: *How many words are between my fingers?*

7. As you are reading another page, leave out a word in one of the sentences. Be sure to choose a sentence that provides lots of clues for the missing word. Ask: *What do you think is the missing word?* (You might want to do this a second time with a different sentence to make sure of the results.)

8. Finish reading the story. Note any spontaneous remarks the child might say at the end of or anywhere during the story.

9. After the story is read, ask: *What would be a good title (name) for this story?* (Important: Don't tell the child the book's title at the beginning of this exercise!)

10. General observations: *Did the child appear eager to read with you? Was his or her interest sustained throughout the story? Did he or she make comments about the story as it was being read? Did he or she ask questions, comment on the illustrations, make predictions, etc.?*

*Source:* "Introducing Concepts About Print to the Preservice Teacher: A Hands-On Experience," by M. A. Gray-Schlegel and Y. King, Fall 1998, *California Reader*, p. 18. Reprinted by permission of the authors.

# Learning About Letters and Sounds

Language-experience stories help children discover that the string of sounds in spoken language can be broken down into units of print made up of words and sentences. But children must also learn that a word can be separated into sounds and that the segmented or separated sounds can be represented by letters. Such learning involves the beginnings of *phonics,* a topic discussed in depth in Chapter 7. The smallest sound unit that is identifiable in spoken language is known as a *phone.* Although phones describe all the possible separate speech sounds in language, they are not necessarily represented by the letters of the alphabet. *Phonemes* are the minimal sound units that can be represented in written language. The *alphabetic principle* suggests that letters in the alphabet map to phonemes. Hence the term *phonics* is used to refer to the child's identification of words by their sounds. This process involves the association of speech sounds with letters. In the beginning of reading instruction, key questions that need to be asked are "Is the child able to hear sounds in a word?" and "Is the child able to recognize letters as representing units of sound?"

One of the first indications that children can analyze speech sounds and use knowledge about letters is when they invent their own spellings during writing. As discussed in Chapter 4, invented spellings are a sure sign that children are beginning to be conscious of sounds in words.

Table 5.3 records invented spellings from several samples of writing from three kindergartners, Monica, Tesscha, and James. Their spellings reflect varying levels of sophistication in hearing sounds in words and in corresponding letters to those sounds. Gentry and Henderson (1980) contend that Monica demonstrates the most phonemic awareness and James the least. **Phonemic awareness** refers to an insight about oral language and the ability to segment and manipulate the sounds of speech and is one of the five essential components of reading according to the National Institute of Child Health and Human Development's National Reading Panel (2000). A perusal of Monica's list of words indicates that she has learned to distinguish sounds in sequence and can correspond letters directly to the surface sounds that she hears. Tesscha has also developed an awareness of sounds and letters, though not to the same extent as Monica. James is the least ready of the three to benefit from letter–sound instruction. For James (and other 5- and 6-year-old children at a similar level of development), analyzing sounds in words and attaching letters to those sounds is beyond present conceptual reach. Making initial reading tasks too abstract or removed from what James already knows about print will not help him progress in reading.

STANDARD
1.4

## Table 5.3　Spellings by Three Kindergartners

| WORD | MONICA'S SPELLING | TESSCHA'S SPELLING | JAMES'S SPELLING |
|------|-------------------|--------------------|------------------|
| monster | monstr | mtr | aml |
| united | unintid | nnt | em3321 |
| dressing | dresing | jrasm | 8emaaps |
| bottom | bodm | bodm | 19nhm |
| hiked | hikt | hot | sanh |
| human | humin | hmn | menena |

Children can easily become confused when taught to identify sounds in words or correspond letters to sounds if they have not yet developed a concept of what a word is. Likewise, the level of abstraction in recognizing a word is too difficult for children if they have yet to make any global connection that speech is related to print. This doesn't mean that program goals for learning about letters and sounds are not worthwhile. However, learning letter–sound relationships must be put into perspective and taught to beginners in meaningful contexts and as the need or opportunity arises.

## Recognizing Letters

Letter recognition has been a well-established predictor of first-grade success in reading (Durrell, 1958). However, studies by Ohnmacht (1969) and Samuels (1972) show that teaching children to master the recognition of letters does not necessarily help them become better readers by the end of the first grade. Therefore, teachers of beginning reading should not assume that the relationship between letter naming and reading success is *causal*. The ability to recognize letters and to succeed in reading probably results from a more common underlying ability. Venezky (1978) contends that letter recognition scores on a reading readiness test can be interpreted as a sign of general intelligence or positive home experiences and a child's early exposure to print.

Today's 5-year-old undoubtedly brings more letter knowledge to beginning reading instruction than the 5-year-old of a half-century ago. Television plays a big part in this phenomenon. Children's programs such as *Sesame Street* are largely responsible for increasing children's letter awareness.

Kindergarten and first-grade teachers should capitalize on children's knowledge of letters in a variety of ways. Plan instruction in letter recognition around daily classroom routines and activities. Also help children discriminate small but significant differences among letters, not necessarily in isolated activity, but in meaningful written language contexts. Traditionally, visual perception tasks have involved letter identification and discrimination. Although these tasks are more justifiable than discrimination activities involving geometric shapes, the teacher should move quickly to letter recognition and discrimination within words and sentences. Consider the following instructional activities:

STANDARD
2.2

- *Discuss letters in the context of a language-experience story or key words that children recognize instantly because they are personal and meaningful.* (See Chapter 7 for a discussion of key word instruction.) For example, ask children to find at least one other child in the room whose first name begins with the same letter. If a child can't find a match, ask the class to brainstorm some names that begin with the same letter as the child's name. Write the names on the board for discussion and analysis.
- *Use alphabet books.* Every kindergarten and first-grade class should have a collection of alphabet books. Ask children to find the page that a certain letter is on. Compare and contrast the illustrations of the letter in the different books. The children can illustrate their own rendition of the letter, and over time the class can develop its own alphabet book. Some good alphabet books that can be used in class include

  *A Was Once an Apple Pie* by Edward Lear (2001, Orchard Books)

  *Alligator Arrived with Apples* by Crescent Dragonwagon (1992, Aladdin)

  *The Absolutely Awful Alphabet* by Mordicai Gerstein (2001, Voyager Books)

  *The Turn-Around, Upside-Down Alphabet Book* by Lisa Campbell Ernst (2004, Simon & Schuster Children's Publishing)

- *Target a letter for discussion.* Have children search for the letter on labels of cans and other commercial products (e.g., Special K), in magazines, newspapers, and other sources of print. Children can make a letter collage by cutting the letters they find and arranging and pasting them onto a big letter poster that the teacher has made from construction paper.

- *Tie letter recognition to writing.* Begin with each child's name. Encourage children to write their names by tracing copies of the letters or writing independently. Ask children to count the number of letters in their names, to examine their names for repeating letters, and so on.
- *Create letters through art activities.* Art plays a very important part in the child's school experience by giving children the opportunity to learn that there are many ways to express their thoughts, feelings, and points of view. Art also heightens children's awareness of their physical environment, involving them through the manipulation of different materials and the development of visual and sensory capacities. For this reason, one small but significant form of expression might be to create letters through drawing, finger painting, sculpting, and making collages such as the letter poster previously described.

Learning single alphabet letters contributes greatly to learning to read, although it is not sufficient by itself. Often some teachers may be tempted to have children memorize single alphabet letters through the use of *flash cards*. Schickedanz (1998), however, recommends avoiding flash cards for teaching young children letter naming and recognition because the practice is devoid of a meaningful context. As she puts it:

> In meaningful activities, children are able to see and appreciate a connection between what they are learning and some application of it—some reason for its importance or usefulness. If children are exposed to letters and their names through the use of flashcards . . . the purpose of alphabet letters is not obvious. But if children are exposed to letters and letter names in looking at their own names, classroom signs, or titles of storybooks, the purpose of letters is obvious. (p. 23)

To illustrate her point, Schickedanz provides several best-practice instructional scenarios for teaching alphabet letter naming and recognition. Study these Research-Based Practices scenarios featured in Box 5.4.

## Developing Phonemic Awareness

Phonemic awareness is the ability to hear and manipulate sounds in spoken words, the understanding that spoken words consist of a sequence of speech sounds, and an awareness of individual sounds (phonemes). Beginning readers must become aware that a word is made up of a series of sounds. Phonemic awareness is important because it plays a causal role in learning to read, primes the reader for print, and helps make sense of phonics instruction. Yopp (1992) explains that young children typically lack phonemic awareness, the understanding that speech is composed of a series of individual sounds: "Cat . . . is simply a cat, a furry animal that purrs. Young children are unaware that the spoken utterance *cat* is a word that is made up of a series of sounds, or phonemes, /k/, /a/, and /t/" (p. 696). The lack of phonemic awareness contributes to children's inability to identify unknown words. If beginners are to benefit from phonics instruction, they must first develop an ability to manipulate sounds in words.

Based on their research analysis, the authors of the International Reading Association's position statement, *Phonemic Awareness and the Teaching of Reading*, emphasize the importance of phonemic awareness in learning to read and spell (Cunningham, Cunningham, Hoffman, & Yopp, 1998). Research on early reading acquisition clearly demonstrates that phonemic awareness is a powerful predictor of young children's later reading development (Ehri, Nunes, Willows, Schuster, Yaghoub-Zadeh, & Shanahan, 2001; Juel, 1988).

Why is phonemic awareness such an important ability in learning to read and spell? The orthographic system of the English language is based on the alphabetic principle, so children must have an understanding of how spoken language maps to written language. Phonemic awareness helps a child grasp this understanding. Without phonemic awareness,

**BUILDING TEACHING SKILLS: CASE STUDY**

Go to the Homework and Exercises section in Chapter 5 of MyEducationLab to work through a case study about phonemic awareness and to develop a strategy you could use to help the student in the case achieve his goals.

STANDARD 1.4

BOX **5.4**

*Research-Based Practices*

## Instructional Scenarios for Teaching Alphabet Letters

1. Building a model of a trolley station in the block area, a child asks a teacher how to spell the words *Outbound Green Line*. The teacher dictates *O* and *U*, but vocalizes the *T* and *B* phonemes, leaving the letter selection to the child. Soon, the child asks the teacher to take over the writing, explaining, "It's too much." But the child remains involved, dictating *G, R, E,* and *N,* for *green* and *L, I,* and *N,* for *line,* as the teacher sounds out the words and writes the letters. As the teacher forms *G,* she says, "A line right here makes this letter *G,* not *C.*"

2. When Samantha writes her name on the picture she has drawn, she asks if her *S* looks how "it is supposed to." The teacher explains that it is backward. The teacher writes a correctly oriented *S* on another piece of paper, as Samantha watches. Soon, Samantha writes her name again. But despite having studied the teacher's *S* before starting, she writes her *S* backward once more. She shakes her head no and asks the teacher to help. This time the teacher proceeds differently: "Put your marker right here" (pointing to a spot). "Now, move your marker that way" (pointing again). "Now change directions . . ." (moving Samantha's hand in the new direction). "Keep gooooing . . . Stop!" The teacher takes Samantha's hand to guide it in the other direction.

3. A child is playing with alphabet-matching material at a puzzle table. He matches loose letter tiles to letters printed on a background board and then does it again. As the child matches the letter tiles for the third time, a teacher stops by and comments, "That's the other *K.* There's the *T.* Mmm, yes, *N* goes right there."

4. All but six children have been dismissed from music time to go with a teacher to the bathroom and then to snack.

To avoid a long wait in the bathroom area, a second teacher keeps a small group to play an alphabet-matching game. First the teacher draws a long vertical line on her paper. One child guesses that the teacher was thinking of *T.* Another guesses *L.* A third guesses *M.* The teacher confirms that she might be thinking of any of these letters. Next, the teacher draws a short horizontal line to the right of the vertical line, at the top. "I was right, *L,*" one child exclaims. The teacher says that it will be necessary to rotate the paper (she rotates it 180 degrees), and then turns the paper over and traces the faint outline showing through from the other side. "*L* is a good guess, but not the letter in my mind."

The child who suggested earlier that the teacher was thinking of *T* continues to maintain that this letter is in the teacher's mind. Another child thinks it could be *E* or *F.* For the next clue, the teacher starts in the middle of the long, vertical line, and draws a short line to the right. "*F!*" the children shout. The teacher confirms that this is the letter of which she has been thinking.

5. The children sing the song "Willoughby Wallaby Woo" during music time, and then make up some verses using names of children in the class.

6. A child uses a teacher-made manipulative. Pictures of flowers children have seen on walks and in classroom bouquets donated by parents who have home gardens are mounted on the background board. Velcro-backed name tiles (such as tulips, daffodils, or lilies of the valley) are in a small dish. The child says the name of a flower to himself and then searches for the tile bearing this name. As the child searches the tiles, he can be heard saying "*t,*" "*d,*" or "*l.*"

*Source:* "What Is Developmentally Appropriate Practice in Early Literacy? Considering the Alphabet," by J. A. Schickedanz, in *Children Achieving: Best Practices in Early Literacy,* edited by S. B. Neuman and K. A. Roskos, pp. 20–37. Copyright © 1998 by the International Reading Association. Reprinted with permission of the International Reading Association (www.reading.org).

a child might be able to learn letter–sound relationships by rote but will not understand how to use and coordinate letter–sound knowledge to read or spell new words. As a result, phonemic awareness plays a critical role in the development of skills required in the manipulation of phonemes—namely, phonics and spelling skills (Griffith & Olson, 1992).

Several kinds of tasks are involved in phonemic awareness. Children should be able to perform these tasks as a precursor to phonics and spelling instruction.

- *Phoneme isolation.* Children recognize individual sounds in a word. For example, the first sound in *dog* is /d/. This is a simple task of phonemic awareness.
- *Phoneme identity.* This is the recognition of the same sounds in different words, such as *six, sun,* and *sat.* The first sound /s/ is the same.

- *Phoneme categorization.* This task requires children to recognize a word in a set that doesn't fit or has an odd sound. A teacher might ask, "What word doesn't sound like the others—*dot, big, doll?*"
- *Rhyming.* Tasks that require children to rhyme words or to recognize rhymes are probably the easiest phonemic awareness tasks for them to perform.
- *Blending.* A more difficult task involving phonemic awareness requires children to blend a series of orally presented sounds to form a word; for example, given the separate sounds /k/, /a/, /t/, the child says *cat.*
- *Segmenting beginning and ending sounds in words.* Children who have developed the capacity to hear sounds in words are able to perform phonemic awareness tasks that require them to isolate and identify the sound at the beginning or end of a word. A teacher might ask, "What sound do you hear at the beginning of the word *pig?*" or "What sound do you hear at the end of the word *hit?*"
- *Segmenting separate sounds in a word.* This is the most difficult of the phonemic awareness tasks. Children who can segment separate sounds in a word are considered to be phonemically aware.
- *Phoneme deletion, addition, and substitution.* These phoneme manipulation tasks require children to take away or add something to make new words. For example, *stack* without the /s/ is *tack.* If you have *rain* and add a /t/ to it you have *train.* These types of activities all require children to manipulate sounds in spoken words.

Findings from the National Reading Panel (2000) advise us that blending and segmenting are probably the most useful phonemic awareness activities and that children only need a few minutes of phonemic awareness instruction daily.

When children develop phonemic awareness, they recognize that words can rhyme, can begin or end with the same sound or different sounds, and are composed of phonemes that can be separated or blended in different ways to form words. Most children develop phonemic awareness by the middle of the first grade. Because phonemic awareness appears to develop naturally in young children, some people might question whether it needs to be taught or emphasized in early reading. The IRA position statement, however, makes clear that

> insofar as it is natural for parents to read to their children and engage them with print and language, then phonemic awareness may develop naturally in some children. But if we accept that these kinds of interactions are not the norm, then we have a great deal of work to do in encouraging parents to engage their young children with print. (Cunningham et al., 1998)

Not only do parents have an important role to play in children's phonemic awareness, but so do teachers. Kindergarten and early first grade are the most appropriate times to plan activities that will develop children's ability to manipulate sounds in words. How can phonemic awareness be taught? The Viewpoint featured in Box 5.5 from IRA's position statement on phonemic awareness is a response to that question.

**DEVELOPING PHONEMIC AWARENESS IN CHILDREN** ◆ Instruction has its greatest impact on phonemic awareness when teachers balance a high level of interaction with print and explicit instruction in various tasks related to manipulating sounds in words. Consider the following practices in the development of a child's phonemic awareness.

**Play with Language Through Read-Alouds**   Use read-aloud books, nursery rhymes, riddles, songs, and poems that play with language and manipulate sounds in natural and spontaneous ways. Choose language-rich literature that is appropriate for young children and deals playfully with speech sounds through the use of rhyme, alliteration, assonance, and other forms of phoneme manipulation. In doing so, draw children's attention to the sounds of spoken language and examine language use.

BOX **5.5**

*Viewpoint*

How Should Phonemic Awareness Be Taught?

The answer to this question has both theoretical and practical implications. Theorists interested in determining the causal contribution of phonemic awareness to learning to read have conducted experimental studies in which some students are explicitly taught phonemic awareness and some are not. Many of the early studies in this genre focused on treatments that emphasize oral language work only. The findings from these studies suggest phonemic awareness can be taught successfully.

More recently, there have been studies of phonemic awareness training that combine and contrast purely oral language approaches to the nurturing of phonemic awareness abilities, with approaches that include interaction with print during the training. These studies suggest that programs that encourage high levels of student engagement and interaction with print (for example, through read-alouds, shared reading, and invented spelling) yield as much growth in phonemic

awareness abilities as programs that offer only a focus on oral language teaching. These studies also suggest that the greatest impact on phonemic awareness is achieved when there is both interaction with print and explicit attention to phonemic awareness abilities. In other words, interaction with print combined with explicit attention to sound structure in spoken words is the best vehicle toward growth.

Some research suggests that student engagement in writing activities that encourage invented spelling of words can promote the development of phonemic awareness. These findings also are consistent with continuing research into the sources of influence on phonemic awareness abilities before students enter school. It is clear that high levels of phonemic awareness among very young children are related to home experiences that are filled with interactions with print (such as being read to at home, playing letter games and language play, and having early writing experiences).

*Source: Phonemic Awareness and the Teaching of Reading: A Position Statement from the Board of Directors of the International Reading Association,* prepared by J. Cunningham, P. M. Cunningham, J. V. Hoffman, and H. K. Yopp, adopted April 1998. Copyright 1998 by the International Reading Association. Reprinted with permission of the International Reading Association (www.reading.org).

Playing with sounds through interactive reading experiences integrates phonemic awareness instruction within the context of enjoying stories, nursery rhymes, songs, poems, or riddles. You can create numerous opportunities for children to develop phonemic awareness through the questions you pose to draw children's attention to the sounds in words. For example, ask questions such as "Did you notice how those words rhymed?" "Which words start alike?" and "What sound do you hear at the beginning of all these words?" In addition, extend interactive read-alouds by creating alternative versions of the story or additional verses while maintaining the same language patterns. Some books appropriate for read-alouds in the classroom to develop phonemic awareness might include *Silly Sally* by Audrey Wood (1992, Harcourt Children's Books), *Is Your Mama a Llama?* by Deborah Guarino (1991, Perfection Learning Prebound), *Down by the Bay* by Nadine Bernard Westcott (1998, Crown Books for Young Readers), and *Four Fur Feet* by Margaret Wise Brown (1996, Hyperion). Appendix E also contains an annotated list of read-aloud books that can be used to develop children's phonemic awareness.

**Create Games and Gamelike Activities to Reinforce and Extend Children's Awareness of Sounds in Words** As children develop a familiarity with the concept of rhyme, make or purchase games that use rhyming words. For example, make a bingo-style board on which children cover pictures that rhyme with those drawn from a bag or a box. Other phonemic awareness activities might include these:

- Clapping the number of syllables heard in a name or a word. To begin, say the name or word and then repeat it in unison with the children as they clap with you.
- Play guessing games or use riddles to help children become sensitive to the sounds in words. For example, "What am I thinking of?" is a guessing game that helps

children blend spoken sounds to form a word (Yopp, 1995). Here's how it works: First, choose a category from which you will select words. Then, in a deliberate, segmented fashion, say each sound of the word and ask children, "What am I thinking of?" For example, given the category "sea animals," a teacher might say the following sounds: /k/, /r/, /a/, /b/.

- Play with tongue twisters to build awareness of the sounds in beginning letters. Have children say tongue twisters as quickly, and as slowly, as they can. Once children can recite tongue twisters from memory, write them on poster boards. Direct children's attention to the beginning sounds.
- Have children line up for lunchtime or recess by the beginning sound in their names. For example, say, "Anyone whose name begins with /b/, please line up." This activity involves *sound matching*. Sound-matching activities can be adapted in numerous ways. For example, ask children to decide which of several words begins with a given sound, or to generate a word beginning with a particular sound. Yopp (1992) recommends giving children a series of pictures of familiar animals or objects (e.g., snake, dog, cat, bird) and asking them to select the one that begins with the /s/ sound. Also, to the tune of "Jimmy Crack Corn and I Don't Care," have children generate words that begin with a particular sound by singing,

> Who has a /d/ word to share with us?
> Who has a /d/ word to share with us?
> Who has a /d/ word to share with us?
> It must start with the /d/ sound.

As the class sings together, call on individual children to volunteer words that begin with the /d/ sound. Then incorporate the words that have been contributed by the children into the song (e.g.: "*Dog* is a word that starts with /d/. *Dog* is a word that starts with /d/. *Dog* is a word that starts with /d/. *Dog* starts with the /d/ sound."). Make sure throughout the activity that the children sing the phoneme sound, not the letter name.

- In addition to sound matching, Yopp (1992) presents several other useful phonemic awareness activities that involve *sound isolation*, *blending*, *segmentation*, *sound addition*, and *sound substitution*.

**Engage Children in Numerous Occasions to Write**   Provide children with many opportunities to experiment with language through writing. Daily writing experiences may be beneficial for children who lack phonemic awareness (Klesius & Griffith, 1998). The more children write, the better they become at hearing sounds in words as they attempt to invent spelling. As they become more adept at segmenting sounds in words, encourage children to approximate spelling based on the way words sound. Teacher–child interactions should provide as much instructional support as the child needs to approximate the spelling of a word.

Notice how Mrs. Nicholas scaffolds instruction for a first grader who asks for help as she attempts to spell *hospital* in the story that she is writing (Cramer, 1978, p. 132).

| | |
|---|---|
| *Jenny:* | Mrs. Nicholas, how do you spell *hospital?* |
| *Mrs. Nicholas:* | Spell it as best you can, Jenny. |
| *Jenny:* | I don't know how to spell it. |
| *Mrs. Nicholas:* | I know you don't know how to spell it, honey. I just want you to write as much of the word as you can. |
| *Jenny:* | I don't know any of it. |
| *Mrs. Nicholas:* | Yes, you do, Jenny. How do you think *hospital* starts? (*Mrs. Nicholas pronounced hospital distinctly with a slight emphasis on the first sound, but she deliberately avoided grossly distorting the pronunciation.*) |
| *Jenny:* | (*very tentatively*) h–s. |

| *Mrs. Nicholas:* | Good! Write the *hs*. What do you hear next in *hospital? (Again Mrs. Nicholas pronounced* hospital *distinctly, this time with a slight emphasis on the second part.)* |
|---|---|
| *Jenny:* | *(still tentatively)* p-t. |
| *Mrs. Nicholas:* | Yes! Write the *pt*. Now, what's the last sound you hear in *hospital? (While pronouncing* hospital *for the last time, Mrs. Nicholas emphasized the last part without exaggerating it unduly.)* |
| *Jenny:* | *(with some assurance)* l. |
| *Mrs. Nicholas:* | Excellent, Jenny, *h-s-p-t-l* is a fine way to spell *hospital*. There is another way to spell *hospital*, but for now I want you to spell words you don't know just as we did this one. |

Because Mrs. Nicholas was willing to accept invented spellings in a beginning situation, Jenny benefited. Not only did she have an opportunity to map spoken language onto written language, but Jenny also had the opportunity to test the rules that govern English spelling in an accepting environment.

**Teach Children to Segment Sounds in Words Through Explicit Instruction**    Individual children who may be having trouble segmenting sounds in words may benefit most from explicit instruction. Clay (1985) recommends the use of Elkonin boxes (named after a Russian psychologist) as a **phonemic segmentation** strategy. Elkonin boxes are widely used today and are often called "sound boxes." Because they help fix phoneme–grapheme correspondences in children's minds, Elkonin boxes support children's spelling, reading, and writing development (Moats, 2006). The following procedures can be incorporated into individual or small group instruction once the children are identified as ready for training in phonemic segmentation. To benefit from such instruction, children must have developed strong concepts of print as "talk written down" as well as a concept of "word." Because the initial stages of training in segmenting a word into sounds is totally aural, children need not be aware of letters to profit from this type of instruction. Eventually, children learn to attach letters to sounds that are separated.

1. *Give the child a picture of a familiar object.* A rectangle is divided into squares according to the number of sounds in the name of the object. Remember that a square is required for every sound in a word, not necessarily every letter. For example, if the picture were of a boat, there would be three squares for three sounds:

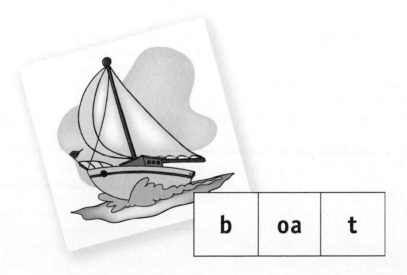

2. *Next say the word slowly and deliberately, allowing the child to hear the sounds that can be naturally segmented.* Research has shown that it is easier to hear syllables than individual phonemes in a word (Liberman, Shankweiler, Fisher, & Carter, 1974).

3. *Now ask the child to repeat the word, modeling the way you have said it.*

4. *Continue to model.* As you segment the word into sounds, show the child how to place counters in each square according to the sounds heard sequentially in the word. For example, with the word *boat*, as the teacher articulates each sound, a counter is placed in a square:

5. *Walk the child through the procedure by attempting it together several times.*

6. *Show another picture and then the word.* Ask the child to pronounce the word and separate the sounds by placing the counters in the squares. The teacher may have to continue modeling until the child catches on to the task.

7. *Phase out the picture stimulus and the use of counters and squares.* Eventually, the child is asked to analyze words aurally without teacher assistance.

In time, the teacher should combine phonemic segmentation with letter association. As the child pronounces a word, letters and letter patterns can be used instead of counters in the squares. The child can be asked, "What letters do you think go in each of the squares?" At first, the letters can be written in for the child. Clay (1985) suggests that the teacher accept any correct letter–sound relationship the child gives and write it in the correct position as the child watches. She also recommends that the teacher prompt the child with questions such as "What do you hear in the beginning?" "In the middle?" "At the end?" and "What else do you hear?"

Hearing sounds in words is no easy reading task for 5- and 6-year-olds. As we suggested earlier, helping children sound out words may be premature if they are not yet phonemically aware. That is why it is important to assess children's ability to manipulate sounds in words.

**ASSESSING PHONEMIC AWARENESS** ◆ Teachers can assess children's phonemic awareness through ongoing instruction as they engage in various activities. Observing children perform phonemic awareness tasks is an informal means of assessment that will help you plan and adapt instruction according to children's needs. Formal measures of phonemic awareness create a testlike environment but provide useful indicators of children's capacity to manipulate sounds in words. For example, the Yopp–Singer Test of Phoneme Segmentation in Figure 5.4 measures a child's ability to separately articulate the sounds of a spoken word in order. Validation studies of the Yopp–Singer Test show not only that it is a valid and reliable measure of phonemic awareness ability but also that it can be used to identify children who are likely to experience difficulty in reading and spelling (Yopp, 1995).

To administer the Yopp–Singer Test, orally present the set of target words one at a time, and ask a child to respond by segmenting each target word into its separate sounds. For example, you say the word *red* and the child responds /r/, /e/, /d/; say the word *fish* and the child says /f/, /i/, /sh/. As the child progresses through the 22-item test, it is appropriate to provide feedback. If the child responds correctly, nod approval or say, "Good job; that's right." If a child gives an incorrect answer, provide the correct response and then continue down the list. To see an online video demonstration of the Yopp–Singer Test, go to http://teams.lacoe.edu/reading/assessments/assessments.html.

You can determine a child's score on the Yopp–Singer Test by counting the number of items correctly segmented into all constituent phonemes. Although no partial credit

## Figure 5.4 A Test for Assessing Phonemic Awareness in Young Children

Name: ____________________ Date: ____________________

Score (number correct): ______________________________

Directions: Today we're going to play a word game. I'm going to say a word and I want you to break the word apart. You are going to tell me each sound in the word in order. For example, if I say "old," you should say "/o/-/l/-/d/." *(Administrator: Be sure to say the sounds, not the letters, in the word.)* Let's try a few together.

Practice items: *(Assist the child in segmenting these items as necessary.)*

ride, go, man

Test items: *(Circle those items that the student correctly segments; incorrect responses may be recorded on the blank line following the item.)*

| | | | |
|---|---|---|---|
| 1. dog | __________ | 12. lay | __________ |
| 2. keep | __________ | 13. race | __________ |
| 3. fine | __________ | 14. zoo | __________ |
| 4. no | __________ | 15. three | __________ |
| 5. she | __________ | 16. job | __________ |
| 6. wave | __________ | 17. in | __________ |
| 7. grew | __________ | 18. ice | __________ |
| 8. that | __________ | 19. at | __________ |
| 9. red | __________ | 20. top | __________ |
| 10. me | __________ | 21. by | __________ |
| 11. sat | __________ | 22. do | __________ |

*Source:* "A Test for Assessing Phonemic Awareness in Young Children," by H. K. Yopp, *The Reading Teacher, 49*(1), p. 22. Copyright © 1995 by the International Reading Association. Reprinted with permission of the International Reading Association (www.reading.org).

is given, a child's incorrect responses should be noted on the blank line following the item. These incorrect responses provide much insight into the child's developing awareness of sounds in words. As you score each test item, note that consonant and vowel *digraphs* are counted as a single phoneme (e.g., /sh/ in *she;* /th/ in *three;* /oo/ in *zoo;* /oi/ in *boy;* a more detailed explanation of digraphs and other phonics elements is given in Chapter 7).

Expect wide variation in young children's performance on the Yopp–Singer Test. Yopp (1995) reports that second-semester kindergarten students drawn from the public schools in a West Coast city in the United States obtained scores ranging from 0 to 22 correct responses on the test items. Guidelines for evaluating a child's performance include the following:

- Correct responses for *all* or *nearly all* of the items indicate that a child is phonemically aware.
- Correct responses for *some* of the items (about 12 correct responses, with a standard deviation of 7.66) indicate that a child displays emerging phonemic awareness.
- Correct responses for *few* items or *none at all* indicate that a child lacks phonemic awareness.

The Yopp–Singer Test allows teachers to identify children who are likely to experience difficulty learning to read and spell and give them instructional support using practices described earlier. In Chapter 7 examine how children use their knowledge of sounds in words to engage in code instruction as they develop word identification skills and strategies.

## WHAT ABOUT STRUGGLING READERS AND the Literacy Club?

In this chapter, as well as in Chapter 4, we emphasized that authentic beginnings are important for emerging readers, and we highlighted the important role the family plays in the early literacy development of all children. Additionally, we recognized that children come to school with varying experiences with print and stories. Some children, for example, come from home environments in which English is not the primary language; some may come from homes in which interactions with print are not evident; and some may not come from environments in which they are exposed to the joys of reading. A variety of factors such as these can place children at high risk for struggling with reading because they do not bring a schema for literacy learning that recognizes reading as an emergent, developing process. We encourage teachers to be keenly aware of the backgrounds of their students. Teachers need to provide children who do not come from home environments that foster literacy, or who come from homes in which there are language differences, with tangible and real experiences with print. While immersing children in reading through read-alouds and talk about books is essential for all beginning readers, it is crucial for those who do not have a sense about what reading is, do not have a sense of what a story is, or are not proficient in the English language. We addressed language differences in more depth in Chapter 3.

It is also important to note that when beginning readers struggle, some teachers attempt to approach the problem with skill-and-drill activities in the hopes of finding a "quick fix" strategy that will "cure" a child of deficits in learning to read. Although we do advocate explicit instruction, we caution teachers against reliance on drill-oriented programs. If our role as teachers is to invite children into literacy learning, we need to engage all children, including those who struggle, with a consistent balance of meaningful literacy experiences. Children who may be at risk for a variety of reasons need to know that they belong to the literacy club from the very beginning. Children deserve teachers who recognize that all children are capable of learning to read and that all children do belong to the literacy club.

## WHAT ABOUT STANDARDS, ASSESSMENT, AND the Literacy Club?

Ample opportunities to practice reading help children to become effective readers. Adequate access to reading materials is critical for accomplishing this goal. When young children are provided with both the time to engage in self-selected reading and the necessary resources, such as children's literature, their reading achievement and attitude toward reading improve (Fielding, Wilson, & Anderson, 1986; McQuillan, 1998).

Key professional organizations—such as the International Reading Association and the National Association for the Education of Young Children—which make recommendations on standards and policies, emphasize the need to provide young readers with access to books and print materials. The International Reading Association (2000b, para. 11) suggests that teachers, librarians, and school administrators

- Request an appropriate number of books for classrooms, school libraries, and public libraries
- Inform parents and policymakers of the importance of access to books
- Remind state and local policymakers of the need to allot funding for books

In the NAEYC report *Promoting Early Childhood Literacy: Highlights of State Efforts*, Kinch and Azer (2002) note that, although one-third of all states provides reading resources to early literacy program, additional funding is needed to make effective programs accessible to a wider range of children and families. Examples of the materials and services provided by some states to early childhood centers and family child care settings include

- Children's literature books
- Comprehensive reading kits
- Resource centers that provide children's books, reading kits, and teachers' guides to educators
- Mobile vans that travel to rural areas to supply literacy resources to teachers and families
- Literacy-oriented educational software
- Professional development opportunities that suggest instructional strategies to teachers of infants, toddlers, and preschoolers
- Hotlines for teachers and families that offer ideas for enhancing the literacy development of young children

These resources are just some of the ways in which young readers can be encouraged to join the literacy club.

## Summary

In this chapter, we explored the difference between reading readiness and emergent literacy as platforms on which to begin instruction. If reading is viewed developmentally, teachers will make use of children's preschool experiences with and knowledge of print to get beginners started in reading and writing. The principle behind instruction is to teach for literate behavior. In other words, beginning reading and writing should center on readinglike situations rather than on activities that are unrelated to having children interact with printed language.

Three strands of instruction characterize beginning reading. First, children should participate in storybook literacy experiences as well as learn what reading is all about. We showed how to use stories and incorporate language functions into instructional practices. Through these activities, children learn that the string of sounds in spoken language can be broken down into units of print made up of words and sentences. Moreover, they should be getting instruction in which they learn that a word can be separated into sounds and that these separated sounds can be represented by letters. Finally, a third phase should center on the language of instruction. Children must learn the terms and labels that are needed to talk about reading and carry out reading tasks.

We emphasized informal assessment because it provides daily judgments of children's preparedness and progress in beginning reading situations. Assessment through teaching and observation yields valuable information about a child's abilities, as well as about the teaching methods that seem to be easiest and of greatest interest to individual children. Formal measures such as the Concepts About Print Test and the Yopp–Singer Test of Phoneme Segmentation are also valuable tools for assessment in early reading.

## Teacher Action Research

1. Suppose you were planning to conduct an interview with a young child to determine the child's concepts about print. What questions would you develop to tap the child's knowledge about books and print? Develop a set of questions to use both before and during reading. Compare your questions with those of several of your classmates.

2. Roberto is an active kindergartner who loves to be on the move, playing with games, building blocks, and Lego blocks. He will sit to hear a good book, but when asked to follow along, he doesn't know where to begin. Sometimes he points to the top right side of the page and sometimes to the middle of the page. In collaboration with a fellow class member, design several classroom experiences with print from which Roberto may benefit.

3. An editorial in your local newspaper advocates a strong phonics program beginning in kindergarten. Write a letter to the editor in which you explain the importance of developing children's concepts about print and phonemic awareness before teaching phonics. Use language that parents in the community will understand.

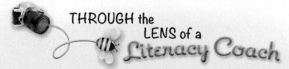

THROUGH the LENS of a Literacy Coach

4. Coaching has become popular in schools to provide professional development and support to improve the instructional skills of teachers. Imagine you are a literacy coach working in a kindergarten classroom. How would you know if the teacher is inviting beginners into the literacy club? What evidence would you need? Compare your list with your classmates or colleagues.

## Related Web Sites

*Blank Elkonin Boxes*

**http://bogglesworldesl.com/elkonin_boxes.htm**

The Elkonin boxes on this site are downloadable so teachers can print them off individually and laminate them for classroom use.

*Harlan Community School District*

**www.harlan.k12.ia.us**

New Park Elementary School in the Harlan School District has a number of resources available to primary grade teachers. Of special interest is the First Grade Big Books page that features online games and activities that coordinate with well-known stories.

*National Institute for Literacy*

**www.nifl.gov/partnershipforreading/questions/questions_about.html**

NIFL provides definitions, teaching practices, and assessment options on the five reading essentials: phonemic awareness, phonics, fluency, vocabulary, and comprehension.

*Reading Rockets*

**www.readingrockets.org/teaching/reading101/writing**

This site offers reading strategies, lessons, and activities designed to help young children learn how to read and write. Resources assist parents, teachers, and other educators in working with struggling readers and writers who require additional help in reading fundamentals and comprehension skills development.

*Resources, Lesson Plans, and Activities for Kindergartens*

**www.kn.pacbell.com/wired/fil/pages/listkindersu.html#cat1**

This site has a wealth of Web resources, lesson plans, and listservs created especially for the kindergarten teacher.

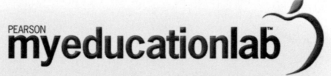

Now go to the Vacca et al. *Reading and Learning to Read*, Seventh Edition, MyEducationLab course at **www.myeducationlab.com** to

- Take a pretest to assess your initial comprehension of the chapter content
- Study chapter content with your individualized study plan
- Take a posttest to assess your understanding of chapter content
- Engage in multimedia exercises to help you build a deeper and more applied understanding of chapter content

CHAPTER **6**

# Assessing Reading Performance

Standards found in this chapter:
- ▶ **3.1**
- ▶ **3.2**
- ▶ **3.3**
- ▶ **3.4**
- ▶ **5.2**

## In this chapter,
### YOU WILL DISCOVER:

- The reasons to use authentic assessments in making decisions about instruction
- Purposes for formal, standardized assessments
- Purposes for informal, alternative assessments
- Techniques for using miscue analysis, running records, kidwatching, anecdotal notes, checklists, and interviews
- Essential elements for implementing portfolio assessment

## Concept Map

### ASSESSING READING PERFORMANCE

**MULTIPLE INDICATORS TO BUILD A CORROBORATIVE FRAMEWORK FOR DECISION MAKING**

| Trends | Formal Assessment |
|---|---|
| High-Stakes Testing | Standardized Tests |
| Authentic Assessment | Criterion-Referenced Tests |

| Informal Assessment | Portfolio Assessment |
|---|---|
| Informal Reading Inventories | Elements |
| Running Records | Implementation |
| Kidwatching | |

**Assessment Today and Tomorrow**

It was springtime, and Sue Latham smiled as she looked through a folder with assessment information on John, a "low" reader in her third-grade classroom. How her assessment of him had changed from early fall to now! She noted that on a *formal,* standardized reading test, given in October, John had scored in the 32nd percentile, which meant that he was below average in comparison to other third graders. Although she did not think this score was particularly useful to her in deciding how to work with John, Mrs. Latham knew that her principal examined these scores. She also noted that on a more *informal* assessment related to his attitude toward reading, John viewed himself positively. He also did well on a section from another informal reading assessment in which he picked questions from a list that he thought would help a person understand the important ideas about a selection. This reminded her of yesterday's social studies lesson on explorers. John and other students had raised some insightful questions as the class previewed the chapter and created a class list of questions that might be answered as they worked on the chapter.

At the start of the school year, Mrs. Latham had decided to work with John in a second-grade basal reader along with four other students. Initially, her decision was based on a conversation with John's second-grade teacher and her review of the *skill mastery tests* administered as part of the basal reader program. One of these tests assessed students' ability to associate the hard and soft sounds of the letter *g.* John didn't reach mastery of this particular skill. In other words, he didn't score correctly on 80 percent of the items related to the skill objective; in fact, he answered only six out of ten items correctly. This puzzled Mrs. Latham because just the day before, John had shared a part of a book he was reading about a visit to the zoo, which included seeing *g*iraffes and petting *g*oats. John didn't experience difficulty reading passages containing words with soft and hard *g* sounds. Later in October, she had a *miscue analysis* compiled from a *running record* of John's oral reading during small group instruction. She had noted no difficulties in his reading of either soft or hard sounds.

Mrs. Latham decided back then to capitalize on John's strength of raising questions about material read both in his reading group and in social studies and science units. She decided *not* to use additional instructional time working on the soft and hard sounds of *g,* even though he had not achieved mastery for this objective on the basal reader test. In fact, in November she thought that John was functioning well enough in the second-grade basal reader to reassign him to the third-grade reader. The bottom line is that Mrs. Latham considered information from informal and formal tests *and* her observations of John in actual reading situations. She then made decisions based on *multiple data sources.* Corroborating her instructional decisions was John's *portfolio* of work in progress: some stories and poems he was working on in response to their literature theme unit on tall tales and his personal reading list for sustained silent reading. By using examples of John's actual reading and actual writing, Sue Latham had made an *authentic assessment* of John's *performance in literacy*—a reason to smile.

We know that good teachers have a comprehensive reading program that is guided by the assessment process. Through the use of formal and informal assessments, teachers learn about their students and the impact of the instructional program. Assessment, therefore, is an integral part of teaching and learning.

As depicted in the chapter overview, we support making instructional decisions using multiple ways to assess authentically the *processes* students are engaged in as they read and learn. Formative assessment *and* teaching allow teachers to gather information in order to make inferences about a student's reading ability and performance. Tests provide one perspective for becoming knowledgeable about a student's performance; actual teaching situations provide another perspective; and portfolios of student work provide still another.

# Toward a Corroborative Framework for Decision Making

The process Sue Latham used to develop an authentic assessment of John is another example of how teachers screen and filter information about students' performance through their concepts and beliefs about reading and learning to read. Mrs. Latham holds an interactive view of the reading process. She believes that reading acquisition involves coordinating and integrating many skills during actual reading situations. A child learns to read the way Mrs. Latham first learned to use a stick shift in a car with manual transmission. What she needed to learn was how to coordinate the use of the clutch pedal, gas pedal, brake, and stick in shifting from gear to gear. A beginner may practice pushing the clutch pedal in and out in isolated drill or simulate shifting from gear to gear. However, actually experiencing stick-shifting in traffic makes the difference in learning how to coordinate and integrate the skills.

And so it is with John in his learning to become a fluent reader. When contrasting his performance on the test with his performance in a real reading situation, Mrs. Latham chose to weigh the information from the teaching situation more heavily than the score on the test. Because her students keep portfolios of their work in reading and writing, they too understand their progress in literacy and are learning to evaluate their own strengths and weaknesses in various reading and writing tasks. Portfolios also helped Mrs. Latham plan the kinds of instruction that would move her students toward more mature reading and writing. The student portfolios, works in progress in literacy, are a record of the process of learning in reading and writing for each student. They contain valuable data about growth and progress in literacy performance, and where weaknesses exist, they are useful in planning the instructional next step. Portfolios have become an important aspect of authentic assessment of literacy performance.

Casey Stengel, manager of the New York Yankees in the 1950s and later of the New York Mets, was as renowned for his wonderful use of language as he was for winning baseball games. On one occasion after losing a hard-fought game, Stengel was quoted as saying, "You can know the score of the game and not know the real score." The real score involves understanding and appreciating the dynamics of what happens on the playing field during the game regardless of the outcome.

The real score in reading involves understanding and appreciating *how* children interact with print in authentic reading situations and *why*. "To be authentic, the texts the students read need to relate to things that are interesting and real—that are meaningful for the student" (Farr & Tone, 1998, p. 19).

We advocate using *multiple indicators* of student performance for assessment. The International Reading Association (1999b) also recommends the use of multiple assessment indicators because of the complex nature of literacy and its acquisition. Any single indicator—whether it involves commercially prepared or teacher-made tests or observation—provides a perspective, one means of attesting to the accuracy of the score or phenomenon under examination. Multiple indicators, however, build a *corroborative framework* that strengthens decision making. As teachers we must constantly make decisions. Multiple indicators of reading strengthen our decision making as information from one data source builds on or contrasts with information from other data sources. The result is a rich knowledge base for understanding how and why students perform in reading.

Because reading takes place in the mind, the process is not directly observable and therefore not directly measurable. Yet one of the important functions of reading assessments, whether formal or informal, should be to help teachers understand a human process that is essentially hidden from direct examination. What are the latest trends that assist in this assessment process? To what extent do standardized, criteria-referenced, informal, or teacher-made tests play a constructive role in the classroom?

How do teachers keep a running record of performance-based assessments in their classrooms? Finally, how can the process of portfolio assessment involve parents, teachers, students, and administrators in communication about the growth students are making in reading, writing, and language?

# Trends in Assessment

Discontent among the public and within the field of education over the state of assessment has reached a fever pitch. On the one hand, the public wants assurances that students will leave school well prepared to enter the workforce or embark on postsecondary education. On the other, educators are calling for better, more authentic assessment practices that reunite goals for learning with classroom instruction and assessment. These trends are nearly opposites. As Tierney (1998) explains it, there are two different orientations; one focuses on "something you *do to* students," and the other focuses on "something you *do with* them or help them *do for themselves*" (p. 378). Assessment, therefore, needs to provide information for public accountability as well as instructional decision making (International Reading Association, 2000a).

## High-Stakes Testing

In today's standards-based education system, there is a reliance on high-stakes testing. State legislators across the country and the federal government have enacted laws such as the NCLB Act (No Child Left Behind, 2002) requiring students to pass high-stakes tests. The premise of **high-stakes testing** is that consequences good or bad, such as promotion or retention decisions, are linked to a performance on a test. Referred to as proficiency tests in the 1990s, high-stakes tests are now known as achievement and graduation tests. High-stakes testing is intended to provide the public with a guarantee that students can perform at a level necessary to function in society and in the workforce. Of course, there are no guarantees in life itself, let alone on any test, especially a test based on a one-time performance. Nevertheless, this trend is increasing. Johnston and Costello (2005) report that "The United States has currently reached the highest volume of testing and the highest stakes testing in its history" (p. 265). The International Reading Association opposes high-stakes testing and high-stakes decisions based on single test scores. As recommended in the position statement *High-Stakes Assessments in Reading* (1999a) assessments should be relied on to improve instruction and benefit the students and not to punish schools or students.

Compounding this demand for more standardized testing is the problem that the tests themselves are not adequate, given what we now know about literacy. For example, we know that "any student's performance in reading or writing will vary considerably from task to task and from time to time" (MacGinitie, 1993, p. 557).

Literacy assessment for English language learners is often seen as inequitable (Garcia & Beltran, 2003; Jimenez, 2004). Garcia and Beltran (2003) explain that the problem for English language learners with most standardized assessments is that the assessments compare the development of content for English language learners with the same standards as native English speakers. Standardized assessments also typically assess one's English ability rather than ability to utilize the various skills and strategies needed to create meaning. Therefore the result is that English language learners score below grade level. A more appropriate means of assessment, such as the supplemental use of authentic assessments and adjusting assessments to the student's English proficiency, will provide a more complete perspective of an English language learner's abilities.

DIVERSITY
ELL

STANDARD
3.2

What are some of the effects of this trend toward standard setting and high-stakes testing? Reliance on high-stakes assessment (in which students, teachers, and school districts are held accountable on the basis of their performance) eliminates the opportunity to track a student's progress in literacy as an individual. Instead, comparisons are made between groups of students, schools, and even school districts based on sets of state and national *standards* for performance in subject areas. In numerous states, newspapers are publishing "report cards" for school districts, then ranking them according to scores attained by their pupils on achievement tests, with special attention to the overall percentage passing. This in turn spawns the practice of "rewarding" districts that have higher rates of passing with awards and increased financial subsidies and "punishing" districts that have lower rates of passing with sanctions and decreased subsidies.

High-stakes testing also intrudes into classroom life. Teachers are questioning their professional beliefs and abilities as well as instructional creativity when faced with the pressures of high-stakes testing (Bomer, 2005). The time spent preparing students to take these tests has actually replaced time that would normally be spent on teaching and learning activities. Likewise, the content of the curriculum itself is being examined for its "fit" with the content of the exams. School district personnel are at work trying to align the various subject matter curricula with the areas assessed by the standardized tests. Is this the best and most efficient way for teachers and administrators to spend their time and use their talent? And is this reallocation of classroom time in the best interests of students and their learning?

Perhaps an even better question to consider is what kinds of assessment are most useful for providing students with the best possible instruction. If, for instance, high-stakes test scores were no longer an issue, what kinds of assessments would be effective and efficient? According to Leslie and Jett-Simpson (1997), our "new technology of assessment must be an efficient use of teachers' time. Efficiency means that you get a lot of information from the time invested" (pp. 8–9). For countless teachers, the answers to these and similar questions are not found in their districts' report cards; they are unfolding as teachers become more involved in the assessment process.

## Authentic Assessment

The second major trend in assessment is a movement in which teachers are exercising their empowerment as they recapture the vital role they know well—making and sharing decisions about instruction and assessment. Teachers "are being asked to become involved in the design—as well as in the administration—of the assessment procedures . . . to document growth in reading and writing with authentic reading and writing tasks" (Leslie & Jett-Simpson, 1997, p. 9). What do we mean by *authentic?* Several criteria connote **authentic assessment,** as described by Farr and Tone (1998, pp. 18–19): Students are doing reading and writing tasks that look like real-life tasks, and students are primarily in control of the reading or writing task. These two criteria then lead to a third: Students develop ownership, engage thoughtfully, and learn to assess themselves.

Today's teachers want to know more about factors that contribute to their students' literacy achievement (products) and about how the students themselves think about their reading and writing (process). Some teachers strive for more authenticity in *performance-based assessment* by "requiring knowledge and problem-solving abilities" representative of real-world purposes (Leslie &

Authentic assessment of literacy—determining what exactly students can and can't do in real-life reading and writing—is one of the major trends in assessment.

**STANDARD**
**3.2**

Jett-Simpson, 1997, p. 4). This can be seen in Box 6.1, in which Mandy Capel, a kindergarten teacher, assesses in-depth knowledge of story **retelling**. As noted in the sample rubric (Figure 6.1), Mandy goes beyond assessing the simple sequence of the story to include understanding of the story and characterization.

Teachers have many expectations for assessment. Information gathered should be useful in planning classroom instruction and guiding students to become reflective in order to help them assess their own strengths and weaknesses. Such assessment becomes **formative assessment** when the information gathered is used to adapt instruction to meet students' needs (Black, Harrison, Lee, Marshall, & Wiliam, 2004). It especially helps to identify the specific learning needs of all readers, including those who have difficulties with English. Formative assessment involves noticing details of literate behavior, interpreting student's understanding and perspective, and knowing what the reader knows (Johnson & Costello, 2005). Learning about students' development of new literacies is also an outcome of formative assessment. (See Box 6.2.)

Additionally, formative assessment helps readers to think about their own learning and use **self-assessment** strategies. Chappuis (2005) believes students learn to answer such questions as "Where am I going?" "Where am I now?" and "How can I close the gap?" (pp. 40–42). These questions lay the foundation for students to identify their strengths and weaknesses and help to provide a plan for intervention. Having students take an active role in the assessment process broadens the view of literacy development.

Finally assessment information should permit clear description of a student's literacy growth and achievement for communication with parents and administrators. In the Straight from the Classroom in Box 6.3 on page 168, third-grade teacher Shawn Jividen tells how she came to take the leadership in changing the way students' literacy development was communicated to parents in her district's report cards.

As teachers learn more about the developmental nature of reading and writing acquisition, they are likely to want more tools that authentically assess. They will seek ways to collect performance samples (both informally and formally produced), observation techniques, anecdotal records, checklists, interviews, conferences and conversations with

**HOMEWORK EXERCISE: VIDEO**

Go to the Homework and Exercises section in Chapter 6 of MyEducationLab to view the video "Performance Assessment" about using authentic assessment in the classroom effectively.

**STANDARD**
**3.1**

---

BOX **6.1**

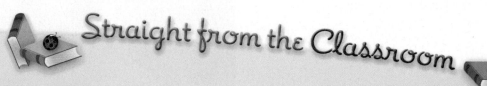

*Straight from the Classroom*

## Narrative Retelling Rubric

### MANDY CAPEL

Narrative retelling encourages young children to think about stories and begin reasoning skills. Young children quickly learn how to retell an interesting story. Initially, children begin retelling a story by telling the audience about their favorite elements of the story. Following the event of retelling favorite parts, children gradually move from discussing preferences to discussing identifiable and integral parts of the story. Although many models of retelling include a beginning, middle, and end component of discussion, few models assess a deeper understanding of the story, requiring students to think about feelings of the characters and provide an effective oral delivery when retelling story elements. Some models use graphic organizers to aid comprehension or use reflection strategies during reading to help combat any comprehension breakdowns. In my classroom, I have favored using all of those strategies in conjunction with a retelling rubric [Figure 6.1] that was initially created for my kindergarten classroom. This rubric is a way to

assess the reader's understanding of a story beyond simply listing basic components. As a replacement for granting number scores on the rubric, I found that highlighting the rubric is a more effective way to gauge the level of performance a student shows in regards to retelling narrative stories. This example rubric of retelling can also span a range of grades and texts. Materials required are:

- Books that correctly match the interests of the students
- Fiction stories that have well-informed narrative structure

#### REFLECTIVE INQUIRY

◆ Why does Mandy Capel use narrative retelling with her students?

◆ How does Mandy use the rubric to assess her students' progress?

## Figure 6.1  Retelling Rubric

| STORY ELEMENTS | ESTABLISHED | DEVELOPING | EMERGING |
|---|---|---|---|
| Characters | • Delivers enough information about characters so that nonreaders have an understanding of the story<br>• Begins to describe relationships between the characters | • Names the characters but does not deliver information about their traits and challenges | • Seems to confuse or create new characters<br>• Requires questions or prompts |
| Sequence (B,M,E) | • Uses flow map<br>• Accurately retells B,M,E in own words and in sequence | • Limited use of flow map<br>• Tells B,M,E in some details but parts are missing<br>• May be out of sequence | • Includes some inaccuracies and/or gives off-topic information<br>• Has trouble creating flow maps<br>• Requires questions or prompts |
| Setting | • Helps nonreaders visualize where the story took place<br>• Uses descriptive words | • Gives some details about where the story took place but does not use many descriptive words | • Does not use descriptive words<br>• Lists inaccurate places for setting<br>• Requires questions or prompts |
| Challenge | • Describes the story challenge and gives examples of how the challenge can be solved<br>• Discusses character feelings associated with the story challenge | • Includes parts of the story challenge but some details are missing<br>• Does not discuss the emotion behind the challenge | • Does not recognize the challenge in the story<br>• Requires questions or prompts |
| Solution | • Accurately describes what character(s) did to solve the challenge | • Provides minor inaccuracies to how character(s) solved the challenge | • Does not recognize the solution in the story<br>• Requires questions or prompts |
| Presentation | • Good usage of expression, fluency in sentence structure, and acceptance of feedback from others<br>• Used gestures and excitement when retelling story<br>• Makes connections to life experiences | • Exhibited some form of expression<br>• Had some difficulty delivering information with fluency<br>• Did not completely answer questions or respond to feedback from others | • Expression needs improvement<br>• Still needs to work on sentence structure development<br>• Did not respond to audience questions or feedback |

## BOX 6.2

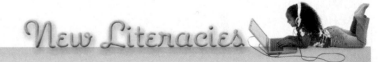

New Literacies

## ASSESSMENT AND NEW LITERACIES

Assessment is multidimensional and multifaceted in order to assess the wide variety of literacy skills readers possess. As discussed earlier, high-stakes assessment is based on a static definition of literacy that does not include new literacies. Assessment needs to be dynamic and formative to assess all skills and strategies that students utilize in order to construct meaning. New literacy assessment needs to go beyond assessing individual work. It needs to include how students learn new literacies, how students learn new literacies from others, and how they collaborate with each other in order to construct meaning. Using formative, authentic assessments while students are engaged in technology-based reading and writing tasks is essential in the assessment of new literacies.

BOX **6.3**

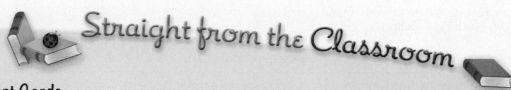

## *Straight from the Classroom*

### Report Cards

#### SHAWN JIVIDEN

*Shawn Jividen and the other six third-grade teachers in a suburban and rural district primary school had been unhappy for some time with the requirement that all third-grade children were to receive a reading grade of A through F and a score from a standardized test such as the proficiency test.*

Parents wanted to know just what "on grade level" meant for their child. After voicing our displeasure to the principal for over a year, we pursued the idea that there must be something we could do. Finally, she said that if we could all agree on a way to explain to parents exactly how their child is achieving *and developing* in reading, she would be willing to consider replacing the test score. Since I was the "lucky one" taking a graduate course that semester on curriculum evaluation, the principal asked if I would coordinate the effort—an idea immediately seconded by my colleagues!

In no time at all, my steering committee, consisting of all third-grade teachers in the building, met and came up with some basic questions to work from and decided to plunge right into a pilot project. Essentially, we all helped gather information to find out (1) what methods were currently being used by classroom teachers to evaluate children's progress, (2) how teachers collaborated to meet the needs of their students, and (3) which performance areas the teachers felt were appropriate indicators of success in literacy for our third graders. After we finished interviewing teachers and members of the school's curriculum committee, we developed a draft checklist of criteria. These became the focus of a brief survey that we then distributed to teachers, administrators, and some parents. Once the results were analyzed, we agreed on the final checklist, which included "Writes complete sentences," "Exhibits awareness of word meanings and spelling patterns," "Recognizes and self-corrects errors," and nine other items. We assessed each student for each item by marking either a *P*, for *progressing successfully*, or an *E*, for *experiencing difficulty;* comments could be written at the bottom.

When the other teachers heard about our success in developing this checklist, they decided to adopt it (with modifications) as a possible replacement for the standardized test tool for the following year. We know our checklist is far from perfect, but we believe we've improved communication about assessment of our students in a couple of concrete ways. For one, the checklist will accompany each individual child, so the new teacher will have familiar criteria on the child's strengths and weaknesses in reading. For another, parents will receive a copy with their student's report card.

STANDARD
3.4

Not only am I relieved that the pilot was successful for personal reasons, but it's been a professionally rewarding experience too. Watching the enthusiasm of my fellow teachers grow, after their initial skepticism, is an unexpected plus after 20 years of teaching—not to mention that our grade level can now use the monies that were to be spent on standardized tests for activities and reading materials for the children!

#### REFLECTIVE INQUIRY

◆ Why was a checklist developed? What would you have developed? Explain.

◆ How has communication about student assessment been imporoved?

◆ What assessments would you use to show reading growth and development? Explain.

**HOMEWORK EXERCISE: VIDEO**

Go to the Homework and Exercises section in Chapter 6 of MyEducationLab to view the video "Standardized Tests" and consider the pros and cons of formal assessment.

students, writing folders, and portfolios. Although teachers will continue to be required to administer standardized tests and assign letter grades, they can confidently rely on their professional beliefs and abilities to meet their students' literacy needs.

## *Formal Assessment*

Pressures for accountability have led many school districts and states to use formal reading tests as a means of assessment. Formal tests may be norm-referenced or criterion-referenced. Many of the recent standardized tests give *both* norm-referenced and criterion-referenced results of students' performance. Norm-referenced test results, in particular, appear to meet stakeholders' needs for making comparisons.

## Standardized Tests

**Standardized reading tests** are machine-scored instruments that sample reading performance during a single administration. Standardized test scores are useful in making comparisons among individuals or groups at the local, state, or national level. A *norm-referenced test* is constructed by administering it to large numbers of students in order to develop **norms.** It's inefficient and difficult, if not impossible, to test every student in an entire population. Norms therefore represent average scores of a sampling of students selected for testing according to factors such as age, sex, race, grade, or socioeconomic status. Once norm scores are established, they become the basis for comparing the performance of individuals or groups to the performance of those who were in the norming sample. These comparisons allow you to determine whether a child or group is making "normal" progress or performing in "normal" ways.

Normal progress or performance, of course, depends on the *representativeness* of the norming sample. Therefore, the norms of a test should reflect the characteristics of the population. Moreover, it's important to make sure that the norming sample used in devising the tests resembles the group of students tested. Some norm-referenced tests provide separate norms for specific kinds of populations (e.g., urban students). The technical manual for the test should contain information about the norming process, including a description of the norming group.

In developing norm-referenced tests, the scores in the norming sample are distributed along a *normal,* or *bell-shaped, curve.* That is to say, scores cluster symmetrically about the *mean,* the average of all scores. In Figure 6.2, notice that the majority of the scores (about 68 percent) are concentrated within *one standard deviation* above or below the mean. The standard deviation is an important measure because it represents the variability or dispersion of scores from the mean. The standard deviation, roughly speaking, can help you interpret a child's performance. You can judge how well a child performed on a test by examining a score in relation to the standard deviation. A score that falls more than one standard deviation below the mean on a reading test would probably be a cause for concern. Recognize, however, that standardized tests aren't error-free: There are measurement problems with any test. Some tests are better than others in helping

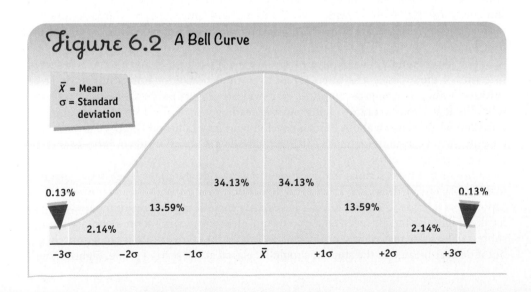

**Figure 6.2**  A Bell Curve

$\bar{X}$ = Mean
$\sigma$ = Standard deviation

0.13%    2.14%    13.59%    34.13%    34.13%    13.59%    2.14%    0.13%

$-3\sigma$    $-2\sigma$    $-1\sigma$    $\bar{X}$    $+1\sigma$    $+2\sigma$    $+3\sigma$

teachers interpret performance. The more *valid* and *reliable* the reading test, the more likely it is to measure what it says it does.

**Reliability** refers to the stability of the test. Does the test measure an ability consistently over time or consistently across equivalent forms? The reliability of a test is expressed as a correlation coefficient. Reliability coefficients can be found in examiner's manuals and are expressed in numerical form with a maximum possible value of +1.0. A reliability coefficient of +1.0 means that students' scores were ranked exactly the same on a test given on two different occasions or on two equivalent forms. If students were to take a test on Monday and then take an equivalent form of the same test on Thursday, their scores would be about the same on both tests, if the test were indeed reliable. A test consumer should examine reliability coefficients given in the examiner's manual. A reliability coefficient of +0.85 or better is considered good; a reliability coefficient below +0.70 suggests that the test lacks consistency.

A statistic tied to the idea of reliability is the *standard error of measurement*. The standard error of measurement represents the range within which a subject's *true score* will likely fall. A true score is the score a test taker would have obtained if the test were free of error. Suppose the standard error of measurement was 0.8 for a reading test. If a student achieved a score of 4.0 on the test, his or her true score would fall somewhere between 3.2 and 4.8. Rather than assume that a score received by a student is precisely accurate, the teacher should identify the standard error of measurement in the test manual and interpret each score as falling within a range.

**Validity** is probably the most important characteristic of a test. It refers to how well a test measures what it is designed to measure. A test developer will validate a test for general use along several fronts. First, the test should have *construct validity*. To establish construct validity, the test developer must show the relationship between a theoretical construct such as *reading* and the test that proposes to measure the construct. Second, the test should have *content validity*. Content validity reflects how well the test represents the domain or content area being examined. Are there sufficient test items? Are the test items appropriate? Third, the test should have *predictive validity*. In other words, it should accurately predict future performance. For test developers predictive validity is most important in order to predict reading outcomes.

**TYPES OF TEST SCORES** ◆ To make interpretations properly, you need to be aware of differences in the types of scores reported on a test. The *raw*, or *obtained*, *score* reflects the total number of correct items on a test. Raw scores are converted to other kinds of scores so that comparisons among individuals or groups can be made. A raw score, for example, may be converted into a *grade equivalency score*. This type of conversion provides information about reading performance as it relates to students at various grade levels. A grade equivalency score of 4.6 is read as "fourth grade, sixth month in school." Therefore, a student whose raw score is transformed into a grade equivalency of 4.6 is supposedly performing at a level that is average for students who have completed six months of the fourth grade.

The idea behind a grade equivalency score is not flawless. When a score is reported in terms of grade level, it is often prone to misinterpretation. For example, don't be swayed by the erroneous assumption that reading growth progresses throughout the school year at a constant rate—that growth in reading is constant from month to month. Based on what is known about human development generally and language growth specifically, such an assumption makes little sense when applied to a human process as complex as learning to read.

One of the most serious misinterpretations of a grade equivalency score involves making placement decisions. Even though a child's performance on a test or subtest is reported as a grade level, this doesn't necessarily suggest placement in materials at that level. Suppose a student received a grade equivalency score of 2.8 on a comprehension subtest. The score may represent information about the student's ability to comprehend, but it doesn't mean that the student should be placed at the second grade, eighth month of basal reading or library materials. First, the standard error of the test indicates that there is a range within which 2.8 falls. Second, the test's norms were in all likelihood not standardized against the content and level of difficulty of the basal reading curriculum in a particular school or library of books. In the early 1980s the International Reading Association cautioned teachers on the misuse of grade equivalents and advocated the abandonment of grade-equivalent scores for reporting students' performance. In place of grade-level scores, the use of *percentile scores* and *standard scores* such as *stanines* provides a more appropriate vehicle for reporting test performance.

*Percentiles* refer to scores in terms of the percentage of a group the student has scored above. If several second graders scored in the 68th percentile of a test, they scored as well as or better than 68 percent of the second graders in the norming population. Whereas grade equivalency scores are normed by testing children at various grade levels, percentile norms are developed by examining performance only within a single grade level. Therefore, percentile scores provide information that helps teachers interpret relative performance within a grade level only. For this reason, percentiles are easily interpretable.

*Stanine* is one of several types of standard score. A standard score is a raw score that has been converted to a common standard to permit comparison. Because standard scores have the same mean and standard deviation, they allow teachers to make direct comparisons of student performance across tests and subtests. Specifically, *stanine* refers to a *standard nine*-point scale. When stanines are used to report results, the distribution of scores on a test is divided into nine parts. Therefore, each stanine represents a single digit with a numerical value of 1 to 9. A stanine of 5 is the midpoint of the scale and represents average performance. Stanines 6, 7, 8, and 9 indicate increasingly better performance; stanines 4, 3, 2, and 1 represent decreasing performance.

**TYPES OF TESTS** ◆ Different norm-referenced tests have different purposes. Two broad types of tests are frequently used in schools. An assessment that is based on a **survey test** represents a measure of general performance only. It does not yield precise information about an individual's reading abilities. Survey tests are often used at the beginning of the school year as screening tests to identify children who may be having difficulties in broad areas of instruction. A survey test may be given to groups or individuals.

A standardized **diagnostic test,** by contrast, is a type of formal assessment intended to provide more detailed information about individual students' strengths and weaknesses. The results of a diagnostic test are often used to profile a student's strengths and weaknesses of reading performance. Some diagnostic tests are individual; others are designed for group administration.

Most diagnostic tests are founded on a bottom-up, subskills view of reading. Therefore, diagnostic tests are characterized by a battery of subtests that uses large numbers of items to measure specific skills in areas such as phonics, structural analysis, word knowledge, and comprehension.

The concern today is with the type of information provided by the test: What is it for? How useful is it for instructional purposes? In what ways does it apply to culturally diverse populations? Until teachers can readily answer these questions to their own satisfaction, controversy will continue to surround the use of standardized achievement tests in U.S. education. The uses and misuses of standardized tests for reading, writing, and language assessment continue to spur debate.

**USES OF STANDARDIZED TEST RESULTS** ◆ Critics of formal testing tend to argue against the uses to which the standardized test information is put. As noted earlier, scores from formal testing shouldn't be used as the *only* source of information considered in making instructional decisions. Other inappropriate uses of standardized test scores are in the evaluation of teachers, programs, and the distribution of resources.

Some critics call into question whether there is any worth at all to formal testing. For example, Goodman (1975) argued that such tests are mainly measures of intelligence and don't actually assess reading. He contended that the reading measured on reading tests isn't the same as most real-world kinds of reading. Seldom in real life would someone read a short passage and then be required to answer a series of questions about it. Test makers in the 1990s attempted to make improvements such as increasing the length of passages and using formats other than multiple-choice questions.

Most test developers assert that their tests can provide accurate and reliable information about groups of 25 or more. From this perspective, scores can show public accountability by reporting schoolwide trends and differences among groups within a school. Standardized test results can also be used to get an idea of how students in a school compare to other students across the country or indicate if a school as a whole is increasing or decreasing in general reading achievement. What large-scale single-test batteries cannot do, despite the claims of some test designers, is recommend appropriate instructional or curriculum objectives for schools, classrooms, or students.

In the meantime, state-by-state comparisons of student achievement in reading and other subject areas, using norm-referenced test scores, are widespread. The National Assessment of Educational Progress (NAEP) periodically makes available to the public data on large-scale reading and writing performance. On what is sometimes called the "nation's report card," NAEP compares several age groups over time and by geographic and other factors. It's important to keep in mind, however, that even though NAEP data make front-page news, it's not appropriate to report large-scale assessment results for individual pupils, classes, or schools (International Reading Association, 1999a).

Criterion-referenced testing is another kind of testing conducted in schools, and the assumptions underlying it are different from those of norm-referenced testing. Rather than comparing a student's test performance to that of a norming sample, performance on a criterion-referenced test hinges on mastery of specific reading skills. Let's examine criterion-referenced assessment and how test information is used in classroom decision making.

STANDARDS
3.2, 3.4

## Criterion-Referenced Tests

**Criterion-referenced tests** have been used in formal situations for districtwide purposes, in classroom situations, and more recently in statewide testing. The major premise behind criterion-referenced testing is that the mastery of reading skills should be assessed in relation to specific instructional objectives. Test performance is measured against a criterion, or acceptable score, for each of the objectives. Suppose, for example, that there are ten test items for each skill objective. Eight to ten correct items on the test would suggest a level of mastery as specified by the objective. A score of six or seven correct items would signal that additional practice and review of the skill under examination are needed. Fewer than six correct items could mean that a student is deficient in the skill and needs extensive reteaching to achieve mastery.

Performance on a criterion-referenced test, unlike a norm-referenced situation, is judged by what a student can or cannot do with regard to the skill objectives of the test. The test taker isn't compared to anyone else. The rationale for assessment, then, is that it will indicate strengths and weaknesses in specific skill areas. Whereas norm-referenced test scores are used to screen students and to make general grouping decisions, results from a criterion-referenced assessment are used to make instructional decisions about reading skills development. This same feature is viewed as a restriction by some teachers who want to plan individual instruction on variables other than test-identified weaknesses.

The reliability and validity of criterion-referenced tests have been called into question (Pearson & Johnson, 1978). It has been argued that test makers have tended not to establish statistical reliability and validity for criterion-referenced tests as they do for norm-referenced tests. As a result, users of criterion-referenced tests need to be aware of some of the important issues of reliability and validity surrounding the use of such tests.

Criterion-referenced tests often measure students' performance on a large number of objectives. Because the number of objectives tested is large, the number of items

STANDARD
3.2

testing each objective may be as low as four or five. Such a practice leads to questions of how *reliable* the measurement of each skill can be with such a small number of items. It's possible that students who perform poorly on a criterion-referenced test won't perform poorly in another situation that assesses the same skill. For example, will a child who cannot count syllables in a word be unable to break down similar words into pronounceable parts when reading orally? Will a child who cannot answer inferential questions as directed on a test be unable to make inferences from a story in an oral retelling?

Test makers assume that mastery of specific skills leads to better reading ability. This is at best a tenuous assumption. A teacher must ask, "Do test items really measure what they are supposed to measure?" Smith and Johnson (1980) pointed out the problem in this respect.

> Test purchasers rightly assume that the tests provided for measuring attainment of objectives are valid indices of the skills at issue. However, if a test uses a paper-and-pencil task, then it ought, at the very least, to validate those measures by administering group and individual tests to a small sample of students. We are not convinced that identifying the initial consonant *f* from the distractor set *f, t, v, r* when given an oral stimulus is the same as saying /f/ when seeing *f*, or reading sentences which contain words starting with *f*. (p. 169)

Smith and Johnson's point is well taken, as is their concern for questions related to the concept of mastery. What does mastery performance mean on a criterion-referenced test? For example, are comprehension skills ever mastered? As Smith and Johnson (1980) asserted, "We hope that no child could 'test out of' main ideas, or sequence . . . for if conceptual difficulty of words or contextual relationships were increased, the same child could fail to show mastery" (p. 170). Comprehension is an ongoing, developing process, as we have maintained throughout this book. To test for mastery of a comprehension skill would provide a teacher with misleading information at best.

Criterion-referenced tests are similar to standardized diagnostic tests in the sense that both attempt to identify strengths and weaknesses in specific skill areas. They share many of the shortcomings of norm-referenced testing and raise new objections among educators (Farr & Tone, 1998). The teacher must recognize that a criterion-referenced test provides only one perspective for understanding children's reading performance. Other indicators of reading should be weighed carefully when teachers plan instruction.

# Informal Assessment

Informal measures of reading such as *reading inventories*, *miscue analyses*, and *running records* yield useful information about student performance that can be used to inform and guide instruction. As the name implies, an **informal assessment** doesn't compare the performance of a tested group or individual to a normative population. Instead, informal assessments may be given throughout the school year to individuals or groups for specific instructional purposes.

Informal reading assessments gauge performance in relation to the student's success on a particular reading task or a set of reading tasks. In this respect, they are similar to criterion-referenced measures. One of the best uses of informal assessments is to evaluate how students interact with print in oral and silent reading situations. We will explore how these measures can be used to inform decision making and strengthen inferences about students' reading behavior and performance.

## Informal Reading Inventories

The **informal reading inventory (IRI)** is an individually administered reading test. It usually consists of a series of graded word lists, graded reading passages, and comprehension questions. The passages are used to assess how students interact with print orally and silently. According to the standards set for reading professionals by the International Reading Association (1998), classroom teachers across all grade levels and special education teachers should have a basic understanding of multiple forms of assessment, including formal and informal reading inventories.

The information gathered from an IRI should allow teachers to pair students with appropriate instruction materials with some degree of confidence. Moreover, an analysis of oral reading miscues helps to determine the *cueing systems* that students tend to rely on when reading. In short, IRI information can lead to instructional planning that will increase students' effectiveness with print.

IRIs are commercially available, although teachers can easily construct one. Selections from a basal reading series may be used to make an IRI. When making and using an IRI, at least three steps are necessary:

1. Duplicate 100- to 200-word passages from basal stories. Select a passage for each grade level from the basal series, preprimer through grade 8. Passages should be chosen from the middle of each basal textbook to ensure representativeness.

2. Develop at least five comprehension questions for each passage. Be certain that different types of questions (based on question-and-answer relationships, discussed in Chapter 10) are created for each graded passage. Avoid the following pitfalls:

   Questions that can be answered without reading the passage (except for on-your-own questions)

   Questions that require yes or no answers

   Questions that are long and complicated

   Questions that overload memory by requiring the reader to reconstruct lists (e.g., "Name four things that happened . . .")

3. Create an environment conducive to assessment. Explain to the student before testing why you are giving the assessment. In doing so, attempt to take the mystery out of what can be a worrisome situation for the student.

**ADMINISTERING AN IRI** ◆ Commercially published IRIs have graded word lists that can be used for several purposes: (1) to help determine a starting point for reading the graded passages, (2) to get an indication of the student's sight-word proficiency (e.g., the ability to recognize words rapidly), and (3) to get an indication of the student's knowledge of letter–sound relationships in order to attack unfamiliar words.

When giving the IRI, the teacher may simply estimate placement in the graded passages instead of using word lists. Select a passage (narrative and/or expository) from the inventory that you believe the student can read easily and comprehend fully, for example, a passage two grade levels below the student's present grade. If the passage turns out to be more difficult than anticipated, ask the student to read another one at a lower level. However, if the student reads the passage without difficulty, progress to higher-grade-level passages until the reading task becomes too difficult.

Oral reading is usually followed by silent reading. In both oral and silent reading situations, the student responds to comprehension questions. However, an excellent variation is first to require students to retell everything they recall from the reading. Note the information given and then follow up with aided-recall questions such as the following:

What else can you tell me about _____ and _____?

What happened after _____ and _____?

Where did _____ and _____ take place?

How did _____ and _____ happen?

Why do you think _____ and _____ happened?

What do you think the author might have been trying to say in this story?

Do not hurry through a retelling. When asking a question to aid recall, give the student time to think and respond.

**RECORDING ORAL READING ERRORS** ◆ During the oral reading of the passage, the teacher notes reading errors such as mispronunciations, omissions, and substitutions. As the student reads, the teacher also notes how fluent the reading is. Does the student read in a slow, halting, word-by-word fashion? Or does the student read rapidly and smoothly? Errors are recorded by marking deviations from the text on a copy of the passages read by the student. A *deviation* is any discrepancy between what the student says and the words on the page.

The following coding system can be used to mark oral reading errors:

1. *Omissions.* An omission error occurs when the reader omits a unit of written language, that is, a word, several words, parts of words, or one or more sentences. Circle the omitted unit of language.

   *Example*    Erin was (still) at school. She never played (after school.)

2. *Substitutions.* A substitution error is noted when a real word (or words) is substituted for the word in the text. Draw a line through the text word and write the substituted word above it.

   *Example*    The ~~lion~~ ^monkey^ looked lonely.

3. *Mispronunciation.* A mispronunciation miscue is one in which the word is pronounced incorrectly. Follow the same procedure as for a substitution error, writing the phonetic spelling above the word in the text.

   *Example*    Because he was a ^frag^ frog, we called him Hoppy.

4. *Insertion.* The insertion miscue results when a word (or words) is inserted in the passage. Use a caret (^) to show where the word was inserted, and write the word.

   *Example*    She ^quickly^ ran away.

5. *Repetition.* In repetition, a word or phrase is repeated. Treat the repetition of more than one word as a single unit, counting it as one miscue. Underline the portion of text that is repeated.

   *Example*    <u>This is a</u> tale about a man who is blind.

6. *Reversal.* The reversal error occurs when the order of a word (or words) in the text is transposed. Use a transposition symbol (a curved mark) over and under the letters or words transposed.

   *Examples*    He went no his trip
                 "See you later," (Sue said.)

7. *Pronunciation.* A word (or words) is pronounced for the reader. Place the letter *P* over the word pronounced.

   *Example*    This was a ^P^ startling development in his life.

In addition to marking errors, you should also code the reader's attempts to correct any errors made during oral reading. Self-correction attempts result in repetitions, which may have one of three outcomes:

1. *Successful correction.* The reader successfully corrects the error. Correct miscues are coded in the following manner:

   *Example*    I did not know where why I was going.

2. *Unsuccessful correction.* The reader attempts to correct an error but is unsuccessful. Unsuccessful correction attempts are coded in the following manner:

   *Example*    He felt compelled to leave.    1. complied    2. completed

3. *Abandoned correct form.* The student reads the text word (or words) correctly but then decides to abandon the correct form for a different response. Code this behavior in the following manner:

   *Example*    Chris wondered if the tracks were made by a bear.    wandered

Familiarity with a coding system is important in marking oral errors. To ensure accurate coding, tape-record the student's reading. You can then replay the student's reading to check whether all errors are recorded accurately. Moreover, tape-recording will help in analyzing the student's responses to comprehension questions or a retelling of the material.

**DETERMINING READING LEVELS** ◆ The following reading levels can be determined for individual students by administering an IRI.

*Independent level:* The level at which the student reads fluently with excellent comprehension. The independent level has also been called the *recreational reading level* because not only will students be able to function on their own, but they also often have high interest in the material.

*Instructional level:* The level at which the student can make progress in reading with instructional guidance. This level has been referred to as the *teaching level* because the material to be read must be challenging but not too difficult.

*Frustration level:* The level at which the student is unable to pronounce many of the words or is unable to comprehend the material satisfactorily. This is the lowest level of reading at which the reader is able to understand. The material is too difficult to provide a basis for growth.

*Listening capacity level:* The level at which the students can understand material that is read aloud. This level is also known as the *potential level* because if students were able to read fluently, they would not have a problem with comprehension.

The criteria used to determine reading levels have differed slightly among reading experts who have published IRIs. However, the most recommended over the years have been the Betts criteria, named for Emmett Betts (1946), the "father" of the IRI. Betts recommended that when students are reading instructional-level materials, the percentage of unknown words is estimated to be in the range of 1–5 percent.

In making decisions about a student's reading level, teachers should be cognizant of two powerful correlates that determine whether children will find material difficult. First, there is a strong relationship between a student's interest in a topic and reading comprehension. Second, a strong case has been built throughout this book for the relationship between background knowledge and reading comprehension. If students do

poorly on a particular passage because they have limited knowledge or schemata for its content, it's easy to err by underestimating reading level.

The point to remember is that reading levels are not chiseled in stone. Levels do fluctuate from material to material depending on a child's schemata and interest in the passage content. The placement information that an IRI yields gives an approximate figure, an indication. Placement decisions should rest on corroborative judgment, with IRI results an important source of information but not the sole determinant.

## Analyzing Oral Reading Miscues

Oral reading errors are also called miscues. The terms *error* and *miscue* essentially describe the same phenomenon—a deviation or difference between what a reader says and the word on the page. During the 1970s, the Goodmans and others popularized the term *miscue* to replace the term *error*. A miscue provides a piece of evidence in an elaborate puzzle; it helps reinforce a positive view of error in the reading process for teachers and students alike. Differences between what the reader says and what is printed on the page are not the result of random errors. Instead, these differences are "cued" by the thoughts and language of the reader, who is attempting to construct what the author is saying.

Miscues can be analyzed *quantitatively* or *qualitatively*. A quantitative analysis involves counting the number of errors; it pivots around a search for *deficits* in a student's ability to read accurately. A quantitative analysis is used, for example, to determine the reading levels previously discussed. In addition, a tallying of different types of errors has traditionally been a strategy for evaluating the strengths and weaknesses of a child's ability to analyze words. For example, does the reader consistently mispronounce the beginnings of words? An analysis based on this question helps pinpoint specific difficulties. Does the reader consistently have trouble with single consonants? Consonant clusters?

In a quantitative analysis, each miscue carries equal weight, regardless of the contribution it makes to a child's understanding of the material read. A qualitative miscue analysis, by contrast, offers a radically different perspective for exploring the strengths of students' reading skills. A qualitative miscue analysis is a tool for assessing what children do when they read. It is not based on deficits related to word identification but rather on the *differences* between the miscues and the words on the page. Therefore, some miscues are more significant than others.

A miscue is significant if it affects meaning—if it doesn't make sense within the context of the sentence or passage in which it occurs. Johns (1985, p. 17) explained that miscues are generally significant in the following instances:

- When the meaning of the sentence or passages is significantly changed or altered and the student does not correct the miscue
- When a nonword is used in place of the word in the passage
- When only a partial word is substituted for the word or phrase in the passage
- When a word is pronounced for the student

Miscues are generally *not* significant in these circumstances:

- When the meaning of the sentence or passage undergoes no change or only minimal change
- When they are self-corrected by the student
- When they are acceptable in the student's dialect (e.g., "goed" home for "went" home; "idear" for "idea")
- When they are later read correctly in the same passage

We agree with Johns that only significant miscues should be counted in determining reading levels according to the Betts criteria. He recommended subtracting the total of all dialect miscues, all corrected miscues, and all miscues that do not change meaning from the total number of recorded miscues.

**Miscue analysis** can be applied to graded passages from an IRI or to the oral reading of a single passage that presents the student with an extended and intensive reading experience. In the case of the latter, select a story or informational text that is at or just above the student's instructional level. The material must be challenging but not frustrating.

Through miscue analysis, teachers can determine the extent to which the reader uses and coordinates graphic–sound, syntactic, and semantic information from the text. To analyze miscues, you should ask at least four crucial questions (Goodman & Burke, 1972).

1. *Does the miscue change the meaning?* If it doesn't, then it's *semantically acceptable* within the context of the sentence or passage. Here are some examples of semantically acceptable miscues:

   I want to bring him home. [back, inserted]

   Marcus went to the store. [shop, over store]

   His feet are firmly planted on the ground. [to, over on]

   Mother works on Wall Street. [Mom, over Mother]

   These are examples of semantically unacceptable miscues:

   Jacob went to camp for the first time. [court, over camp]

   The mountain loomed in the foreground. [leaped, over loomed]

   The summer had been a dry one. [quiet, over dry]

2. *Does the miscue sound like language?* If it does, then it's *syntactically acceptable* within the context of a sentence or passage. Miscues are syntactically acceptable if they sound like language and serve as the same parts of speech as the text words. The above examples of semantically acceptable miscues also happen to be syntactically acceptable. Here are two examples of syntactically unacceptable miscues.

   Maria reached for the book. [carefully, over reached]

   I have a good idea. [to, over a]

3. *Do the miscue and the text word look and sound alike?* Substitution and mispronunciation miscues should be analyzed to determine how similar they are in approximating the graphic and pronunciation features of the text words. High graphic–sound *similarity* results when two of the three parts (beginning, middle, and end) of a word are similar, as in this miscue:

   He was getting old. [going, over getting]

   Scooter ran after the cat. [run, over ran]

4. *Was an attempt made to correct the miscue?* Self-corrections are revealing because they demonstrate that the reader is attending to meaning and is aware that the initial miscuing did not make sense.

## Figure 6.3  Qualitative Miscue Analysis Summary Sheet

| Text | Miscue | Semantically Acceptable | Syntactically Acceptable | Self-Corrections | Beginning | Middle | Ending | Graphic–Sound Summary |
|---|---|---|---|---|---|---|---|---|
| work | walk | no | yes | | ✓ | | ✓ | high |
| learn | lean | | | yes | | | | |
| must | mostly | | | yes | | | | |
| the | these | yes | yes | | ✓ | ✓ | | high |
| away | always | | | yes | | | | |
| that | | yes | yes | | | | | |
| lost | loose | no | yes | | ✓ | | | some |
| or | and | no | yes | | | | | none |
| these | | yes | yes | | ✓ | ✓ | ✓ | XXX |
| trained | trying | no | yes | | ✓ | | | some |
| kinds | kind | yes | yes | | ✓ | ✓ | | high |
| earn | learn | no | yes | no | | ✓ | ✓ | high |
| helpers | helps | yes | yes | | ✓ | ✓ | | high |
| one other | another | yes | yes | | | ✓ | ✓ | |
| work | working | yes | yes | | ✓ | ✓ | | high |
| dog's | dog | yes | yes | | ✓ | ✓ | | high |
| learn | leave | | | yes | | | | |
| with | and | no | no | | | | | none |
| sled | sleep | no | yes | | ✓ | | | some |
| does not | doesn't | yes | yes | | | | | |

Percentage of semantically acceptable miscues = 53 percent
Percentage of syntactically acceptable miscues = 88 percent
Percentage of successful self-corrections = 80 percent
Percentage of miscues with high graphic–sound similarity = 58 percent
Percentage of miscues with some graphic–sound similarity = 25 percent

A profile can be developed for each reader by using the summary sheet in Figure 6.3. Study the following passage, which has been coded, and then examine how each miscue was analyzed on the summary sheet.

Sheepdogs ~~work~~ [walk] hard on a farm. They must ~~learn~~ ©[lean] to take the sheep from place to place. They ©[mostly] must see that the sheep do not run ~~away~~ ©[always]. And they ~~must~~ [mostly] see ⟨that⟩ the sheep do not get ~~lost or~~ [loose and] killed.

~~Something~~ trying works UC learn
Sometimes (these) dogs are ~~trained~~ to do other kind⟨s⟩ of farm work. They ⟨l⟩earn the

helps
right to be called good ~~helpers~~, too.

another working ~~coat~~
Can you think of ~~one other~~ kind of ~~work~~ dog? He does not need a coat or strong legs

doesn't leave          and sleep
like the sheepdo(g's). He does not learn to work ~~with~~ a sled in the deep, cold snow. He

doesn't leave
~~does not~~ learn to be a farm worker.

To determine the percentage of semantically acceptable miscues, count the number of yes responses in the column. Then count the number of miscues analyzed. (Do not tally successful self-corrections.) Divide the number of semantically acceptable miscues by the number of miscues analyzed and then multiply by 100.

To determine the percentage of syntactically acceptable miscues, proceed by counting the number of yes responses in the column. Divide that number by the number of miscues analyzed (less self-corrections) and then multiply by 100.

To determine the percentage of successful self-corrections, tally the number of yes responses in the column and divide the number by the number of self-correction attempts and then multiply by 100.

To determine the percentage of higher or some graphic–sound similarity, analyze mispronunciations and substitutions only. Divide the total of high-similarity words by the number of words analyzed and then multiply by 100. Follow the same procedure to determine whether some similarity exists between the miscues and text words.

A final piece of quantitative information to be tabulated is an estimate of the extent to which the reader reads for meaning. This is calculated by determining the number of miscues that were semantically acceptable or that made sense in the selection *and* the number of successful corrections. Divide this number by the total number of miscues. This percentage gives you an estimate of the extent to which the reader reads for meaning. When referring to Figure 6.4, this percentage also becomes a quick measure of the reader's effectiveness in using reading strategies.

Inferences can be drawn about oral reading behavior once the miscues are charted and the information summarized. Although the reader of the passage miscued frequently, his strengths are apparent: He reads for meaning. More than half of the miscues were semantically acceptable. When attempting to self-correct, the reader was successful most of the time. Over 60 percent of his miscues were semantically acceptable or were

## *Figure* 6.4   The Effectiveness of Using Reading Strategies

| EFFECTIVENESS OF USING READING STRATEGIES | MISCUES THAT DID NOT CHANGE THE MEANING OF THE PASSAGE AND MISCUES THAT WERE SUCCESSFULLY SELF-CORRECTED |
| --- | --- |
| Highly effective | 60 to 100 percent |
| Moderately effective | 40 to 79 percent |
| Somewhat effective | 15 to 45 percent |
| Ineffective | No more than 14 percent |

successfully self-corrected; most of his miscues sounded like language. Moreover, the great majority of his substitution and mispronunciation miscues reflected knowledge of graphic–sound relationships.

Seven significant miscues were made on the passage (which was slightly over 100 words long). This indicates that the material bordered on frustration and is probably not appropriate for instruction. However, the reader has demonstrated strategies that get at meaning.

Miscue analysis is time consuming. However, when you want to know more about a student's processing of print, miscue analysis is very useful. McKenna and Picard (2006/2007) believe that although miscue analysis is beneficial, it does not give a complete perspective of word identification skills and strategies. They believe that miscue analysis is best utilized for determining students' reading levels, for determining inadequate decoding, and determining use of contextual clues. Other word identification skills and strategies such as analogies, sight recognition, and structural analysis should be assessed in different ways.

In order to understand English language learners' miscues it is essential for teachers to recognize that their miscues in English generally do not reflect their native language. Rather the miscues are associated with the fact that English language learners have not mastered the English language (Weaver, 2002). Weaver continues to emphasize that these miscues typically demonstrate language growth. Therefore there needs to be appropriate assessment and analysis of English language learners' reading.

Throughout this chapter, reliance on *multiple indicators* has been emphasized. This is especially important when determining a child's progress in becoming literate. Assessments need to show a student's growth rather than simply to compare a student to other students of similar age. In addition to the IRI, running records help teachers keep track of students' progress.

## Running Records

Keeping track of students' growth in reading, their use of cueing systems of language—semantics, syntax, and graphophonemics—can help teachers understand the process that goes on in readers' minds. When readers try to construct meaning as they read aloud, teachers can begin to see the relationship between the miscues readers make and comprehension. This in turn influences the teacher's instructional decision-making process.

A **running record**, originally developed by Marie Clay (1985), is an assessment system for determining students' development of oral reading fluency and word identification skills and strategies. Running records are used by teachers to guide a student's approach to learning when needed at frequent intervals, but not daily (Clay, 2001). With running records, the teacher calculates the percentage of words the student reads correctly and then analyzes the miscues for instructional purposes. The various types of decisions Clay recommends are to (1) evaluate material difficulty, (2) group students, (3) monitor individual progress of students, and (4) observe the particular difficulties of struggling readers.

**ADMINISTERING A RUNNING RECORD** ◆ A running record can be completed with only a blank sheet of paper, making it especially good for collecting data about a student's oral reading during regular classroom activities. When administering a running record, the following guidelines are recommended by Clay:

1. Sit next to the student to view the student's text (it is preferable to use text materials that are part of the everyday program) and the reader's observable reading behaviors.
2. Record everything the student says and does on a blank sheet of paper (in place of a blank sheet of paper, you can use a duplicate copy of the pages the student will read).

3. Make a record of the student reading three book selections (a sample reading of 100 to 200 words from each text is recommended, as is choosing readings from one easy, one instructional, and one difficult text).

4. Mark a check for each word the student says correctly, matching the number of checks on a line of the paper with the number of words in a line of the text being read.

5. Record every error (substitution, insertion, omission, repetition, mispronunciation, and prompt) and self-correction. Deviations from print are marked in much the same way as in other miscue analysis procedures. Sample coded running record passages in Figure 6.5 display a coding system for marking oral reading errors.

6. Record all observable behaviors.

Teachers of beginning readers (who read aloud more often, read slowly, and read shorter, less complicated texts) often prefer to take a running record because it does not require special preparation or disrupt the flow of the classroom lesson. As students read

## Figure 6.5  A Sample Coded Running Record

| Text | Coding |
|------|--------|
| **Omission:**<br><br>"See me jump rope," said Shelby. | ☑☑☑ — rope ☑☑ |
| **Insertion:**<br><br>"Look at my car," said Antonio. | ☑☑☑ new ☑☑☑ |
| **Substitution:**<br><br>Ernest climbed onto the train. | ☑☑ into/onto ☑☑ |
| **Pronunciation:**<br><br>Krystyna went to the alligator farm. | ☑☑☑☑ al- al-/alligator P ☑ |
| **Mispronunciation:**<br><br>The bell rang and Jamal came running. | ☑☑ ringed/rang ☑☑☑☑ |
| **Self-Correction:**<br><br>"Vanessa, what do you want to eat?" | ☑☑☑☑ want SC/what ☑☑ |
| **Correct Work:**<br><br>"I want to go home," said Devin. | ☑☑☑☑☑☑ |

STANDARD
5.2

faster and read more complicated texts, however, running records become more difficult to take. Nevertheless, no matter what the level, running records can be a natural part of the classroom when teachers practice with the procedures in order to become comfortable with the process. Suggestions from other teachers and working with a literacy coach will assist the teacher in becoming proficient with running records.

ANALYZING RUNNING RECORDS ◆ In order to determine appropriate material connections and instructional decisions from running records, Clay (1985) recommends that the teacher calculate the words read correctly, analyze the student's errors, and identify patterns of errors. Clay (2005) also recommends that the teacher give close attention to self-corrections. To determine the percentage of words read correctly, the total number of errors is divided by the total number of words in the selection. Then multiply this total by 100 in order to convert to a percentage. Finally, subtract the percentage from 100 to obtain the percentage correct. As shown in Figure 6.6, if the student reads 95 percent or more of the words correctly, the reading material is considered easy or at the student's independent reading level. If the reader reads 90 to 94 percent of the words correctly, the material is at his or her instructional level. Finally, the reading material is considered difficult or at the student's frustration level if fewer than 90 percent of the words are read correctly.

| *Figure 6.6* | Reading Levels Determined by Running Records |
|---|---|
| **READING LEVEL** | **PERCENTAGE CORRECT** |
| Independent | 95 to 100 percent |
| Instructional | 90 to 94 percent |
| Frustration | Below 90 percent |

Running records provide insights into students' strengths and weaknesses by allowing teachers to analyze patterns of miscues. This information provides the teacher with an understanding of the cueing systems the reader relies on. Analyzing oral reading miscues and patterns helps teachers determine the extent to which the reader uses and coordinates graphophonemic, syntactic, and semantic information from the text. To assist in this analysis process, as suggested with informal reading inventories, it is important to ask the crucial questions recommended by Clay (2005): Did the meaning or the messages of the text influence the error? Did the structure (syntax) of the sentence influence the number of error responses? Did visual information from the print influence any part of the error—letter, cluster, or word? (p. 69). Clay also recommends that the teacher scan the response record to answer two additional questions: Did the child's oral language produce the error with little influence from the print? Was the child getting phonemic information from the printed letters? (p. 70). Asking these questions will help the teacher get a more holistic view of the reading process.

It is important for the teacher to consider the pattern of responses in order to analyze errors and self-corrections. Categorizing this information based on the cueing systems helps the teacher to identify a student's specific strengths and needs. Figure 6.7 is a sample running record sheet completed with a second grader reading a passage from *Days with Frog and Toad* by Arnold Lobel (1979). The teacher, Stacy Bricker, generated this summary sheet to help categorize and analyze the data. As shown in the summary sheet, Miss Bricker totaled the miscues for each line and

Students need feedback on their efforts in order to learn how to self-assess their reading progress.

# Figure 6.7 Sample Running Record Sheet

**Student Name:** Tameko          **Age:** 8

**Grade:** 2          **Text:** Days with Frog and Toad

**Teacher:** Miss Bricker          **Date:** November 10, 2008

**Level:** *Independent*     (*Instructional*)     *Frustration*

| Page | | Total | S | M | G | SC |
|------|---|-------|---|---|---|----|
| 4 | Today ✓ ✓ / Toad | 1 | | | 1 | |
| | That ✓ ✓ / Drat | 1 | | | 1 | |
| | ✓ ✓ ✓ ✓ | | | | | |
| | ✓ ✓ ✓ ✓ ✓ | | | | | |
| | ✓ ✓  throw ✓ ✓ / through | 1 | | | 1 | |
| | ✓ ✓ ✓ | | | | | |
| | ✓ ✓ ✓ ✓ ✓ | | | | | |
| | ✓ ✓ ✓ ✓ (used picture clue) | | | | | |
| | ✓ ✓ ✓ | | | | | |
| 5 | ✓ ✓ ✓ ✓ torn SC / tomorrow | | | | | 1 |
| | ✓ ✓ | | | | | |
| | ✓ ✓ ✓ ✓ ✓ | | | | | |
| 6 | ✓ ✓ ✓ ✓ | | | | | |
| | ✓ ✓ ✓ (used intonation) | | | | | |
| | ✓ ✓ ✓ coat / jacket | 1 | | 1 | | |
| | ✓ standing / lying ✓ ✓ ✓ | 1 | 1 | | | |
| | ✓ ✓ ✓ | | | | | |
| | ✓ uncle / under ✓ ✓ | 1 | | | 1 | |
| | ✓ ✓ ✓ | | | | | |
| | ✓ ✓ ✓ ✓ plates / dishes | 1 | | 1 | | |
| | ✓ ✓ | | | | | |

then categorized the miscue as syntactic (S), semantic (M), or graphophonemic (G), and also determined the number of self-corrections. As shown in the analysis of the student sample (Figure 6.8), Tameko's teacher determined that he had difficulty with identifying unknown words and with oral reading fluency. Miss Bricker also noted that Tameko read with hesitation and did not rely on a specific word identification strategy when he came to an unknown word. Miss Bricker used this information in addition to other assessment indicators for instructional intervention and material placement. She decided to work with Tameko on word identification skills such as context clues and decoding, and placed him with reading material at approximately the second-grade level.

The approximate reading level suggested by an informal reading inventory and running records, along with other information on how a reader uses the cueing systems of language to construct meaning, can help teachers understand a student's progress in becoming literate.

## Figure 6.8    Analysis of Sample Running Record Sheet

### Analysis

Total number of words in passage: _____87_____

Total number of miscues in passage: _____7_____

Accuracy Rate 92 percent (instructional level)

Number of syntactic miscues: _____1_____

Examples:

standing
———————
lying

Miscue fits grammatically in the sentence.

Number of semantic miscues: _____2_____

Examples:

coat          plate
————        ————
jacket        dishes

Miscue fits the meaning in the passage.

Number of graphophonemic miscues: _____4_____

Example:

Today      That      throw      uncle
————      ————      ————      ————
Toad       Drat      through    under

Attention to graphic cues.

Number of self-corrections: _____1_____

The student read the text with some hesitation and had some general overall understanding of the passage. When trying to pronounce unknown words, the student had limited word identification skills. Therefore, specific instructional activities to develop word identification skills and strategies (context clues, decoding skills) are needed.

Keeping a running record need not become an overwhelming task. A folder for each child or a notebook with a page for each child that contains a collection of information about his or her literacy learning helps teachers organize the information they collect for assessment. Assessment folders or notebooks could also contain information from informal reading tests, miscue analyses, and observational data. Because it is difficult to remember classroom events, we recommend writing down anecdotal records or using a checklist to record important incidents.

The assessment folder that teachers keep for their own use or to share with parents or students is one type of portfolio. As the interest in developing authentic assessment to match our understanding of the constructive nature of the reading process grows, portfolios have emerged as important avenues of assessment.

## Portfolio Assessment

Through the process of portfolio assessment, teachers seem to have discovered a way to connect instruction and assessment by involving students in reflecting on and making decisions about their work. **Portfolios** are collections that "document the literary development of a student" and include "evidence of student work in various stages" (Noden & Vacca, 1994, p. 292). **Digital portfolios** are multimedia collections of student work stored and reviewed in digital format (Niguidula, 2005, p. 44). The evidence that goes into student portfolios is collaboratively chosen by teachers and students and is more likely to represent a process or activity than a product.

The items in a portfolio are selected with care. As teachers and students reflect on work samples, they choose those that show merit as examples of significant growth, effort, and achievement, especially those representing clear learning goals. Looking through portfolios, one sees a fairly complete picture of children as learners. Portfolios contain work samples that cross many curriculum areas and take many forms, from essays, letters, stories, poems, and anecdotal records to photographs, videos, cassette tapes, and CD-ROMs. Technology such as videotapes or digital audio or video on computers provides parents and teachers samples of the reading skills and strategies the reader relies on. It is best with technology and other portfolio content to include samples from different times of the academic year to document literacy growth over time.

Portfolios serve many purposes and vary accordingly, but their underlying value is a commitment to students' assessment of their own understanding and personal development. Above all, portfolio assessment is a powerful concept that helps teachers and students alike work toward four important goals: taking risks, taking responsibility for learning, making decisions about how and what to learn, and feeling in control using the language arts to learn (Glazer & Brown, 1993, p. 165).

### Essential Elements of Portfolios

Although portfolios differ from each other as literacy profiles of individual learners in different classrooms, they are more authentic than traditional, formal assessment procedures. To varying degrees, they measure the process of the construction of meaning. What makes a portfolio authentic? Michele McCombs, a first-grade teacher, said without hesitation, "It's child-created! The items in the portfolio are unique to each student. Emphasis is placed on making careful choices so that students' learning strengths, styles, and personalities are evident within the collection of items." She then went on to tell the following story to illustrate just what *child-created* means in her class:

Last January we were studying the Arctic; the children each selected an animal they were interested in learning about. I provided them with a list of ideas to help them explore their topic. Students used books, CD-ROM encyclopedias, and the Internet to find specific information about their animal. Each child planned a presentation for the class in which they included information about the animal's size, enemies, food, and additional interesting information. They could choose a format that would best suit their own learning style and preference; they could write a poem, story, or song, create a model, draw a picture, make a costume, create a fact sheet, or come up with their own idea. The children worked on their projects at school and at home. Parents were encouraged to provide guidance, without taking over the project. The results were wonderful! There were models of papier-mâché, Lego blocks, and watercolored panels. One student, Michael, our resident computer expert, created a Web page! His web site [see Figure 6.9] not only told information about killer whales but also displayed pictures of the whales he had colored and scanned himself.

On completion of their study, Michele took pictures of the children's work for their portfolios, along with any work samples that would fit. She is adamant that the real success of the Arctic unit was not the learning about animals but the exploration of ideas and the variety of approaches the children used as they fell in love with learning itself.

Portfolio assessment doesn't mandate or prescribe that portfolios all contain the same elements; that would be contrary to the thoughtful collaboration that is central to this process and makes it so appealing. The following elements are associated with portfolios:

- Varied types of work, often completed over time
- Written and artistic responses to reading
- Writing in several genres
- Teacher-assigned and student-generated work
- An introduction, summary, or self-reflection by the student about the nature of the piece or what it demonstrates about his or her literacy
- Collaborative decision making between teacher and student on work assigned and chosen
- Work in progress, documenting changes and growth in literacy
- Best work, selected for showcasing based on input from teachers and peer conferencing during times set aside to discuss what students are doing and planning, writing and reading and thinking
- Notes in a reading log or response journal
- List of books read, updated regularly
- Work utilizing new literacies
- Students' self-reflections

According to Kieffer and Morrison (1994), portfolios express multiple voices—reflections from students, peers, the community, parents, and other teachers. Moreover, they are multiple stories of what individuals can do, both within the language arts of reading, writing, listening, and speaking and across the curriculum. They document change and help communicate assessment information to parents, school officials, and the public. Ultimately, a portfolio "represents a creation of self . . . ; its contents, like items in a scrapbook, are tangible pieces of the story. Everything is connected" (p. 417).

## Implementing Portfolios in the Classroom

Getting started in the implementation of the portfolio assessment process, whether in grade 1 or grade 7, calls for certain decisions and logical steps. Here are a few suggestions:

- Introduce the notion of portfolios, the concept itself, and the connection with instructional activities. Show some examples from other occupations and fields; show sample items that might be found in portfolios.
- Explain your model for assessment: What is the purpose of the portfolio? Is there more than one purpose? Why are we going to use them? Who are we going to show them to?

**HOMEWORK EXERCISE: VIDEO**

Go to the Homework and Exercises section in Chapter 6 of MyEducationLab to watch the video "Portfolios and Self-Assessment" and learn how you might facilitate portfolio assessment in your classroom.

# Figure 6.9   Michael's Web Page

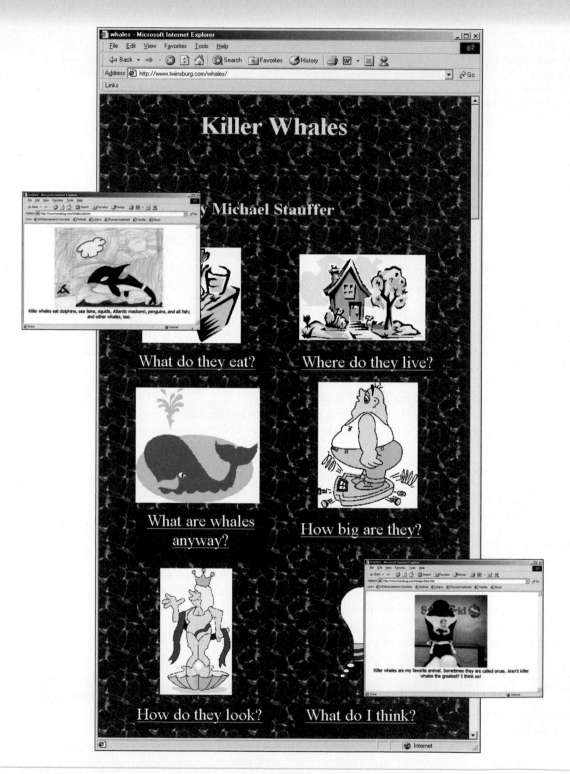

*Source:* www.twinsburg.com/whales. Reprinted by permission of Maureen Stauffer.

- Decide what types of items will be included and how they will be selected for inclusion. Who gets to choose? Approximately how large will the portfolio become, and what size will it be? What format will it take? Will different designs be permitted (or even encouraged)? What is the time frame—start date and end date?
- Consider in advance appropriate ways to communicate clear explanations of portfolios to your colleagues, your principal, your students' parents, and possibly others in your school district or community.
- Develop an array of possible contributions that are most appropriate for your class, the range of students, the language arts, or a reading or writing emphasis: writing samples, videos, conference notes, tests, quizzes, self-evaluations (see Figure 6.10), peer evaluations, daily work samples, personal progress sheets, writing conference logs (see Figure 6.11 on page 190), semantic maps, inventories (see Figure 6.12 on page 191), journal entries, observation information, interviews, and so on.

When Michele McCombs, who has been doing portfolio assessment for about eight years, gets ready to implement the process with a new group of first graders in the fall, she follows the procedures she describes in the Straight from the Classroom in Box 6.4 on page 192. Keep in mind that Michele has made numerous adjustments over the years; she suggests talking to teachers who already do this and starting out slowly with one or two new ideas a semester.

As teachers take a more direct, hands-on approach to assessment, they should try to match their beliefs about literacy and instructional practice with the assessment tools they implement. Therefore, teachers who are intent on using portfolio assessment and want to increase the likelihood for success may find certain things particularly useful to do with their students. When trying to keep writing projects challenging, even when

### Figure 6.10  Fifth-Grade Internet Inquiry Project: Rubric for Self-Evaluation

Name: _____

*Directions:* Evaluate your group's performance in each of the following categories. Be honest. Please also make comments about parts of this project you found successful and parts you found unsuccessful.

| CONTENT | POINTS POSSIBLE | POINTS EARNED | COMMENTS |
|---|---|---|---|
| Selection of topic | 5 | | |
| Evidence of planning | 10 | | |
| Bibliography of print resources (minimum of 3 per person) | 15 | | |
| Critical evaluation of web sites | 10 | | |
| Web sites (minimum of 5): usefulness, appropriateness | 20 | | |
| Web site summaries | 30 | | |
| Quality of writing | 10 | | |
| Total | 100 | | |

# Figure 6.11  Writing Conference Log

## WRITING CONFERENCE LOG FOR:  Megan O.

| Date: | Title: | Focus of Conference: | Genre: |
|---|---|---|---|
| 1-15-08 | Plot Comparison for Story of Three Whales & Humphrey the Lost Whale | Compare/contrast | fiction  (nonfiction) |

**Progress observations:**

Strengths
1) was able to correctly compare/contrast stories
2) able to complete the sentences

Spelling development: *Examples of spelling*

thay   ✓
traped   } transitional
banged
lived   } conventional

Areas to work on
1) more details for the story endings

*Developmental stage*
* work on double consonants
* able to add "ed" endings

---

| Date: | Title: | Focus of Conference: | Genre: |
|---|---|---|---|
| 1-20-08 | Double-Entry Journal for Whales Song | reflection/sharing ideas | (fiction)  nonfiction |

**Progress observations:**

Strengths
1) Megan easily identified passages she liked!
2) She picked meaningful passages

*Do more double entries! Megan would benefit!!!*

Spelling development: *Examples of spelling*
deskripting
used, good, words

Areas to work on
1) identifying more reasons for her choices, connecting to personal life (possibly)
2) risk-taking

*Developmental stage*
transitional
conventional

---

| Date: | Title: | Focus of Conference: | Genre: |
|---|---|---|---|
| Jan. 08 | Whales |  | fiction  (nonfiction) |

**Progress observations:**

Strengths
1) many details
2) topic sentence
3) lists mammal traits
4) good closing sentence

Spelling development: *Examples of spelling*
bowhead, whale
fafit (favorite)
diffrint (different)
boty (body)
tempcer (temperature)
mammel

Areas to work on
commas — for lists

*Developmental stage*
conventional

transitional

**Figure 6.12** Learning Participation Inventory

## LEARNING PARTICIPATION INVENTORY

**Name:** Megan O.

Observations for work completed Jan. '08

| | Often | Occasionally | Seldom |
|---|---|---|---|
| **1. Shows enthusiasm for learning**<br>Yes! | ☑ | ☐ | ☐ |
| **2. Raises questions**<br>*This would be a great area to work on with her. | ☐ | ☑ | ☐ |
| **3. Listens attentively during discussions**<br>Seems to listen well, but sometimes turns away. | ☐ | ☑ | ☐ |
| **4. Shares ideas**<br>Megan is reserved. She sometimes hesitates to share her ideas. | ☐ | ☑ | ☐ |
| **5. Responds thoughtfully to the ideas of others**<br>She enjoys knowing what the teacher thinks and responds well. | ☑ | ☐ | ☐ |
| **6. Participates in projects enthusiastically**<br>She is a hard worker, especially with books and topics she enjoys, such as whales. | ☑ | ☐ | ☐ |

### Observations

All lessons were completed in a one-on-one tutoring session. The student and teacher know each other very well since they have worked together twice a week for two school years.

students can't always choose their own topics, Herrington (1997) recommends that teachers do the following:

- Offer guidance
- Coach and consult
- Be responsive and constructive
- Be respectful and instructive
- Help focus
- Point to what is well-done
- Resist taking over the project

For teachers who are trying to enhance student involvement, the practice of regular conferencing allows students to share their insights (Noden and Vacca, 1994). To help

## BOX **6.4**

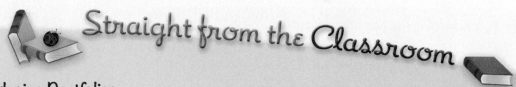

### Introducing Portfolios

### MICHELE MCCOMBS

*First-grade teacher Michele McCombs has been using portfolios in literacy instruction throughout her career.*

odeling is central to everything I teach! When I introduce portfolios to my students, I start by sharing my own portfolio—the one I created when I applied for my teaching position. In it are samples of lessons and units, copies of my transcripts, and photographs of my students engaged in learning. I explain why I put mine together and then let the students look through it.

After I've shared my own portfolio, I tell the kids that they will be creating their own. They excitedly ask questions like "Will mine be in a three-ring binder too? Will mine have pictures? Will I get to keep it?"

In the past, I've used hanging file folders to store work, pictures, and other materials because the children have easy access to them and seem to feel comfortable adding work. I'm constantly saying things like, "Wow—great work; that would be great in your portfolio." I often hear the kids tell each other the very same thing! In fact, we talk all the time about *why* we do *what* we do.

At the end of the year, the children take their portfolios home. I attach a letter to the front stating how proud the children and I are of their work.

Much of what goes into the portfolios is writing samples. I meet with each child in my classroom for an individual or small group conference once every 6 days (with 24 kids, I meet with 4 a day). During conference times, we discuss a piece of writing the child is currently working on. I make notes in a writing conference log, which I keep in a three-ring binder and then transfer to the child's portfolio. The 4 children I'm conferencing with each day and I sit on the rug so that I can easily see what else is happening; after the conference time, the 4 children share their writing with the whole class. Then the others

make comments and suggestions about the writing. These observations are added to the conference log. Finally, I collect the notebooks from the small group I worked with and write personal notes, telling the children my thoughts about their writing. Sometimes I make a recommendation, but I *always* keep the comments encouraging and supportive.

I use the writing conference log and the learning participation inventory for multiple purposes. With the writing log, I'm able to chart the progress of my students all year long. I see their strengths and areas to work on; I see which spelling stage they're at and am able to plan minilessons designed around areas of need—using capitals or punctuation, adding details, or spelling conventions, for example. Mainly, the logs help the children and me see that learning to write is a *process.* Learning participation inventories can be used across the curriculum, with small groups or whole classes. They give me comparative data on student progress in the specific learning behaviors observed and are useful for sharing with parents at conference time. They are also well-suited for students in self-evaluation. When we look back through our observations in the logs and inventories, we realize how much they have grown as writers and learners!

### REFLECTIVE INQUIRY

◆ Why does Michele McCombs begin by sharing her own portfolio with her first graders?

◆ In what ways does she connect teaching and assessment in her classroom?

◆ How does her attitude toward portfolios help communication with students, parents, and others?

students benefit from reflective, individualized conferences, Noden and Vacca recommend that teachers do the following:

- Exercise professional judgment on how best to respond
- Invite students to share how they think and how they feel
- Build on what students have done
- Listen carefully to students' perception of their achievements
- Limit the number of goals set mutually by teacher and students
- Concentrate on the strategies and process rather than the product

The bottom line is that when a student's work is judged by the standards of growth and positive change and when students play a role in the assessment of their own literacy processes and products, the teacher's role is apt to change. This role of facilitator is one of the many roles a teacher must take on in the assessment process. Another important role is that of "kidwatcher."

## Kidwatching While Teaching

Observing how students interact with print during the instructional process is what "kidwatching" is all about. The term **kidwatching** has been coined to dramatize the powerful role of observation in helping children grow and develop as language users. Yetta Goodman (1978) maintained that teachers screen their observations of children through their concepts and beliefs about reading and language learning.

In many classrooms, kidwatching is an ongoing, purposeful activity. Because language learning is complex, it's impossible to observe everything that happens in the classroom. It is especially difficult to document slow growth of young readers; also, assessment is complicated by the introduction of new kinds of learning or when complex activities are being learned (Clay, 2005). Systematic observation is a way to document the development progress of all readers. The first essential step in observing children's reading and language use is therefore to decide what to look for in advance. Clearly, teachers need to watch for signs that signify growth in reading behavior. For example, probably the clearest indicator of word identification difficulties is failure to self-correct. Consequently, this is a behavior that the teacher as an expert process evaluator would take note of as students read orally.

Because it is unobtrusive and does not interfere with ongoing activities, kidwatching enables teachers to catch students in the act, so to speak, of literate behaviors. But knowing what it is that we see and what it means in terms of our students' progress takes practice and good judgment. As Rhodes and Shanklin (1993) note, good anecdotal records and observations depend on teachers who "must understand the developmental nature of reading and writing, the processes of reading and writing, and how both might vary in different literacy contexts" (p. 28).

Dolores Fisette (1993) describes the informal reading conference as the ideal place to kidwatch. While her students choose a book and read it to her and then translate the story into their own words, she notes which reading behaviors and strategies each student evidences, as well as how completely a student has comprehended the story as evidenced in the retelling. The teacher is able to answer, What do students know how to do well? What do they need to learn or to practice?

**ANECDOTAL NOTES** ◆ Teachers write short **anecdotal notes** that capture the gist of an incident that reveals something the teacher considers significant to understanding a child's literacy learning. Anecdotal notes are intended to safeguard against the limitations of memory. Record observations in a journal, on charts, or on index cards. Post-it notes and other small pieces of paper that are easily carried about and transferred to a student's folder are perfect for writing on-the-spot anecdotal records. These jottings become "field notes" and will aid the teacher in classifying information, inferring behavior, and making predictions about individual students or instructional strategies and procedures.

It isn't necessary or even realistic to record anecdotal information every day for each student, especially in classes with 25 or 30 children. However, over a period of time, focused observations of individual children will accumulate into a revealing and informative record of literacy and language learning.

Charts are particularly useful for keeping anecdotal records. Charts can be devised to record observations in instructional situations that are ongoing: participation in reading and writing activities, small and large group discussions, book sharing, silent and oral reading. For example, the chart in Figure 6.13 on page 194 was developed to record observations of students' participation in journal-writing sessions.

In addition, charts can be used to record certain behaviors across instructional activities. A good strategy for developing a permanent record for each child in class is to cut

*Figure* 6.13    Observational Chart for Journal Writing

Mrs. Carter

Grade: __2__

Time Period: __March 27—April 2__

| Name: | Date: | Writing Strategies: | Date: | Writing Strategies: |
|-------|-------|---------------------|-------|---------------------|
| George | 3/27 | Frequently asks for assistance with spelling. | 4/2 | Appears to be writing more independently but still worries about correct spelling of words. |
| Alejandro | 3/27 | Revising draft of April Fool's story; has lots of ideas. | 3/29 | Writes fluently; ready to publish. |
| La Shawna | 3/28 | Copied a recipe from a cookbook. | 4/2 | Wrote first original story; was very anxious to have story read; wanted to begin another story. |
| Maxine | 3/29 | Draws pictures to rehearse before writing; concentrates on handwriting and neatness. | 4/1 | Wrote a riddle; wants to share it with class. |

observations apart from the individual charts and then glue each student's notes into a permanent growth record. With improved technology, some data management systems afford teachers the opportunity to use handheld computers to chart kidwatching as it occurs. The information documented can be used during conferences with students or with parents.

Some teachers find that writing anecdotal information can be unwieldy and time-consuming, especially if they are observing students over long stretches of time. An alternative to ongoing anecdotal notes is the use of checklists.

CHECKLISTS ◆ Using a **checklist** is somewhat different from natural, open-ended observation. A checklist consists of categories that have been presented for specific diagnostic purposes.

Checklists vary in scope and purpose; they can be relatively short and open-ended or longer and more detailed. To be useful, checklists should guide teachers to consider and notice what students can do in terms of their reading and writing strategies. The DR–TA checklist in Figure 6.14 can reveal how a group of students interacts with a text. Collaboratively designed checklists serve the added purpose of helping teachers develop and refine their beliefs about what constitutes important literacy performance.

## Figure 6.14 Directed Reading–Thinking Activity Checklist

**Teacher:** Mr. Niece **Grade:** 5

**Time Period:** Fourth Period **Group:** Niece's Nikes

| Reading Behavior During DR–TA | Student Name | | | | | |
|---|---|---|---|---|---|---|
| ***Reading Title of a Selection*** | Eduardo | Miguel | JoAnne | Sophia | Rich | Emma |
| 1. Participates in predicting/is cooperative. | ☑ | ☑ | ☐ | ☐ | ☑ | ☑ |
| 2. Makes some predictions with coaxing. | ☑ | ☑ | ☐ | ☐ | ☐ | ☐ |
| 3. Initiates own predictions eagerly after prompting with title. | ☑ | ☐ | ☐ | ☐ | ☐ | ☐ |
| 4. Low risk taking/reluctant. | ☐ | ☑ | ☐ | ☑ | ☐ | ☐ |
| 5. Predictions are numerous. | ☐ | ☐ | ☑ | ☐ | ☐ | ☐ |
| ***After Reading Sections of a Selection*** | | | | | | |
| 1. Retelling is accurate. | ☑ | ☐ | ☑ | ☐ | ☑ | ☐ |
| 2. Retelling is adequate. | ☐ | ☑ | ☐ | ☐ | ☐ | ☑ |
| 3. Retelling is minimal. | ☐ | ☐ | ☐ | ☑ | ☐ | ☐ |
| 4. Confirms or refutes past predictions. | ☑ | ☐ | ☑ | ☐ | ☐ | ☑ |

When Mrs. Cartwright began using an open-ended checklist designed to show evidence of creative thinking and leadership skills on the part of her second graders, she noticed an unanticipated benefit. "It was easy for me to overlook quiet students who were more peer-centered or who kept to themselves but out of trouble. But if I didn't have an annotation for a particular student for a few days, I had to stop and ask myself why. What did I need to do to make sure that all of my students were included in activities? I'm more aware of who I watch and why I watch them."

**INTERVIEWING** ◆ Through **interviewing,** the teacher can discover what children are thinking and feeling. Periodic student interviews can lead to a better understanding of (1) reading interests and attitudes, (2) how students perceive their strengths and weaknesses, and (3) how they perceive processes related to language learning.

Cecile Kraus (1983) studied the perceptions of first graders toward reading. She found not only that 6- and 7-year-olds could verbalize their personal constructs of reading but also that their perceptions reflected the way in which they interacted with print. Here are some of the questions that Kraus asked the students in individual interviews:

- Suppose someone from another planet happened to land on earth, saw you reading, and said to you, "What are you doing?" You would probably answer, "I'm reading." Then that person might ask, "What is reading?" How would you answer?
- What would you do to teach someone to read?
- Who is the best reader you know? What makes that person the best reader?

- How did you learn to read?
- What did your teacher do to help you learn?
- If you are reading all by yourself and you come to a word you don't know, what do you do? Why? What do you do if that doesn't help? Why?
- What should the teacher do when a person is reading out loud and says a word that is not the same as the word in the story?
- Is it important for the teacher to teach you the new words before you read a story? Why or why not? *(If a conditional answer is given:)* When would it be important?

Interviews provide a rich source of information. When coupled with observations made during teaching, interviews strengthen data from formal and informal tests of student performance. Moreover, interviews may reveal information that will not be provided by other means of assessment.

## Assessment Today and Tomorrow

As we have discussed, the assessment of literacy is a complex process. "Not only is literacy complex and social but also the literate demands of the world keep changing with exponential acceleration" (Johnston & Costello, 2005, p. 257).

With the demands of accountability, standards, instructional decision making, and new literacies the assessment process needs to be flexible. Multiple assessments can help provide a broader perspective of literacy development.

Alignment of assessments with standards has been and continues to influence assessment utilization. When aligning the assessment it is important that each assessment is linked to a specific objective or purpose. However, aligning assessments with state standards does not mean creating assessments that mimic the content and format of the annual test. An alignment that is too close gives the state tests more focus and narrows the curriculum (Herman & Baker, 2005). Rather, assessments that look at standards and test formats holistically measure student learning more accurately and provide the appropriate information needed for instructional decision making.

If literacy assessment is to guide reading and writing instruction then the assessment utilized needs to reflect the process of literacy learning. Teachers must also be cognizant of societal demands and the requirements of accountability. Most important, assessment practices need to reflect the values and beliefs of the teachers as well as focus on the needs of the learners.

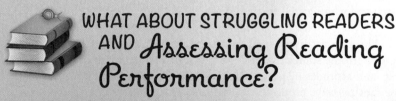

## WHAT ABOUT STRUGGLING READERS AND Assessing Reading Performance?

As teachers take a more direct, hands-on approach to assessment, they should try to match their beliefs about literacy and instructional practice with the assessments they plan to implement. This information becomes the foundation for instructional decision making for all readers, including those who struggle with reading.

The assessment process needs to focus on documenting individual student growth over time rather than on comparing students with one another. It also must take into consideration learning styles, prior experiences and background knowledge, cognitive abilities, interests, attitudes, and language proficiencies. Teachers need to stay focused on individual children, the complex nature of reading, and reading development (Valencia & Buly, 2004).

More formal means of assessment provide limited information about individual readers, particularly those who struggle with reading. Therefore, authentic assessment tools such as kidwatching, interviewing, recording anecdotal notes, and taking running records are needed to provide insightful information that teachers can use to make decisions about students' literacy programs. Relying on these multiple indicators in the natural context of the classroom helps reduce the anxiety that struggling readers may face with reading in contrived situations.

Developing portfolios as a natural part of the classroom environment also helps teachers focus on documenting individual student growth. A portfolio contains work samples crossing many curriculum areas as well as new literacies for the teacher and student to reflect on. It is important that teachers of struggling readers help their students reflect on work samples that exemplify significant growth, effort, or achievement. This process helps develop readers' ability to self-assess in order to monitor and regulate their own reading development.

## WHAT ABOUT STANDARDS, ASSESSMENT, AND *Reading Performance?*

Assessing students is a process of gathering and using multiple sources of relevant information for instructional purposes. Two major approaches to assessment prevail in education today: a formal, high-stakes one and an informal, authentic one. Pressure from policymakers and other constituencies has resulted in the adoption of curriculum standards specifying goals and objectives in subject areas and grade levels in most states. Hence student performance on state-mandated tests must also be considered by teachers who need to make instructional decisions based on their students' content literacy skills, concepts, and performance.

An informal, authentic approach is often more practical in collecting and organizing the many kinds of information that can inform decisions, including students' prior knowledge and students' use of reading strategies and other communication strategies.

## Summary

Reading is a process that takes place inside the mind; it isn't directly observable or measurable through any one instrument or procedure. To make an authentic assessment of a human process that's essentially hidden from direct examination, teachers need to base decisions about instruction on multiple indicators of reading performance. Observation and interview, informal reading inventories, miscue analysis, standardized norm-referenced tests, criterion-referenced tests, and running records and portfolio collections all contribute to teachers' understanding.

Trends in reading assessment are almost at cross-purposes with one another. Very different perspectives are held by educators who support standard setting and high-stakes testing and those who promote authentic, performance-based assessment.

The uses of formal types of assessment were considered for both norm-referenced and criterion-referenced tests. We examined how to interpret test scores and provided information about validity and reliability of standardized tests. We then explored informal assessment, beginning with informal reading inventories. For example, informal reading inventories can be useful in matching children with appropriate materials and in determining how children interact with print in oral and silent reading situations.

Oral miscue analysis provides insight into the reading strategies children use to make sense out of text. We examined examples of miscue analysis, which can be applied to any oral reading situation and therefore may be used in conjunction with informal reading inventories.

Portfolio assessment has grown in importance; it is influencing the way teachers and students think about and assess the work of students engaged in reading and language arts activities. A way to overcome, or deemphasize, the pressure for comparative scores and grades, portfolio assessment helps demonstrate growth in students' reading performance for parents and students. Numerous illustrations of actual teacher-developed suggestions for implementation, along with samples of assessment procedures that involve both teacher and student input, were offered. With its focus on self-reflection, portfolio assessment often incorporates observation, or kidwatching. This permits teachers to become more aware of students' individual behaviors as they engage in reading and learning activities within the context of the classroom community. Anecdotal notes, checklists, and interviews are some of the techniques that help broaden and deepen our understanding of what children do when they read and why.

## Teacher Action Research

1. Look at whole class data that have been gathered relating to standards and literacy development. What patterns of student learning did you notice? What additional information do you need? Create instructional lessons based on the data. Be sure to be able to defend the decisions you made.

2. Do a miscue analysis with a primary or middle school student to find out more about the student's processing of print. Or ask a classmate to read a passage and purposely make miscues; tape-record the reading. Then follow the procedures in this chapter for conducting miscue analysis to determine the percentage of semantically acceptable miscues, and so forth. Analyze to what extent the reader was able to use and coordinate grapho-phonemic, semantic, and syntactic information from the text.

3. Collaborating with a partner, develop a method of portfolio assessment that you believe would serve to show students' growth in literacy. What would be the essential elements of all of the portfolios? What elements would you leave open to student selection? Design a cover sheet to help organize and explain the portfolio's contents. Determine the criteria for evaluating the contents of the portfolio.

THROUGH the LENS of a Literacy Coach

4. Observe a reading teacher teaching the same students over a two week period of time. Document the instructional and assessment strategies utilized. What was the teacher doing well? What evidence do you see that assessment influenced instructional practices? How might you guide the teacher to improve his or her skills?

## Related Web Sites

*International Reading Association: Focus on Reading Assessment*
**www.reading.org/resources/issues/focus_assessment.html**
IRA provides links to various resources related to assessment such as recommended readings, position statements, resolutions, and meetings and events.

*National Assessment for Educational Progress: The Nation's Report Card*

**www.nces.ed.gov/nationsreportcard**

The National Assessment of Educational Progress (NAEP) provides information on continuing student assessment in various subject areas (reading, math, science, writing, U.S. history, civics, geography, and the arts).

*National Center for Education Statistics*

**www.nces.ed.gov**

The National Center for Education Statistics is a federal agency responsible for collecting and analyzing data related to education in the United States and in other nations.

*Practical Assessment, Research & Evaluation (PARE)*

**www.pareonline.net**

PARE is an online journal that provides access to peer-reviewed articles related to research and practices in education.

*Richer Picture—A Digital Portfolio of Student Achievement*

**www.richerpicture.com**

This site provides information about digital portfolios, links to various samples, and provides information about professional development.

*The Tuning Protocol: A Process for Reflection on Teacher and Student Work*

**www.essentialschools.org/cs/resources/view/ces_res/54**

The Coalition of Essential Schools describes a seven-step process for assessing student work.

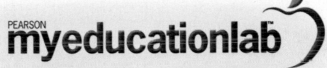

Now go to the Vacca et al. *Reading and Learning to Read,* Seventh Edition, MyEducationLab course at **www.myeducationlab.com** to

- Take a pretest to assess your initial comprehension of the chapter content
- Study chapter content with your individualized study plan
- Take a posttest to assess your understanding of chapter content
- Engage in multimedia exercises to help you build a deeper and more applied understanding of chapter content

CHAPTER 7

# Word Identification

Standards found in this chapter: ▶ 1.3
▶ 1.4
▶ 2.1
▶ 2.2
▶ 2.3

## In this chapter,
### YOU WILL DISCOVER:

- Phases of word identification
- Guidelines and strategies for teaching phonics
- Strategies for teaching words in context
- Strategies for teaching structural analysis
- Strategies for teaching rapid recognition of words
- Guidelines for balancing word identification instruction

## Concept Map

### WORD IDENTIFICATION

DEFINING WORD IDENTIFICATION AND PHASES OF DEVELOPMENT

APPROACHES, GUIDELINES, AND STRATEGIES FOR PHONICS

Consonant-, Analogy-, and Spelling-Based Strategies

USING MEANING TO IDENTIFY WORDS

Teaching Context  Cross-Checking  Self-Monitoring

USING STRUCTURAL ANALYSIS TO IDENTIFY WORDS

Strategies for Teaching Structural Analysis

TEACHING RAPID RECOGNITION OF WORDS

Strategies for Teaching Function and Key Words

BALANCING WORD IDENTIFICATION INSTRUCTION

At age 3 Jimmy, one of our children, commented while driving through the mountains of Pennsylvania on a trip to his grandparents' home, "So, where is the *pencil* in Pennsylvania?" Another time, when knocked over by a wave in the ocean (visiting his other grandparents on the East Coast), he stormed out of the water and exclaimed in somewhat childhood moodiness, "I don't like that *sexy* ocean!" Still another time, when Jimmy was running around in circles in the living room, his mother asked, "What are you doing, Jimmy?" "I'm catching pneumonia!" he earnestly replied. Hence, a young child's observations of oral language.

Jimmy also had a keen sense of the *visual* components of language. At age 3, he was adept at completing a puzzle of the United States and could name each state while working with a plastic template. When walking him in a stroller through the mall one day, he seemed to be intrigued by the "map" of the mall and wanted to know "What is Utah doing in Sears?" The shape of Utah actually resembled the shape on the mall map of the Sears store. Interesting observation. Still another time, when visiting a restaurant in southern Ohio, a sign on the building captured Jimmy's interest as a 3-year-old. Jimmy wanted to know what "OHIO" was doing in a sign that advertised "CHICKEN." (If you close the *C*s of the word *CHICKEN*, they become *O*s—hence, *OHIO*). And when asked what he was doing with pencil and paper at the dining room table, he candidly replied, "I'm doing the taxes."

These are examples of one young child's observations of the world of language and print. Not all children, however, are as observant of the purposes and components of literacy as Jimmy. Although children enter school with a broad range of literacy concepts, teachers need to have a wide repertoire of instructional strategies that teach children how to *read* print and *identify* words. Although teachers have different instructional emphases, they have the same instructional goal in mind: They want their students to achieve independence in word identification while reading. *How* teachers invest their time in helping readers identify words is an important instructional question; although there are differences in practice, it is philosophical differences that seem to predominate (Stahl, 1992; Stahl, Duffy-Hester, & Stahl, 1998).

In this chapter, we suggest strategies that reflect two broad instructional goals of word identification instruction. The first is that children should learn how to deal with unfamiliar words *rapidly* and *independently*. If children cannot quickly identify new words on their own, reading soon becomes tedious, if not overwhelming. Misty, a first grader, put it this way: "I'm in big trouble if I miss words when I'm reading." Furthermore, if word identification takes up most of the reader's energy and attention, comprehension and enjoyment will suffer (Samuels, 1994, 1996).

A second goal of instruction is that readers should develop *multiple strategies* for word identification. Readers must have an adequate sight vocabulary and know how to use phonics, the structure of words, and context clues to help them identify words.

## Defining Word Identification

Several terms have been associated with identifying words: *word attack, word analysis, word recognition,* and *decoding.* These terms are often used interchangeably. Figure 7.1 illustrates the relationship of these terms to word identification. *Word identification* means putting a name or label on words that are encountered in print. It is a comprehensive term that encompasses the use of multiple cues to identify unfamiliar words.

*Word recognition* suggests a process that involves *immediate identification.* Immediately recognized words are retrieved rapidly from *lexical memory.* Word recognition is sometimes referred to as *sight-word recognition* or *sight vocabulary.* These terms suggest a reader's ability to recognize words rapidly and automatically. In this chapter, we use *immediate word recognition* to describe rapid recognition. Keep in mind, however, that the process of immediate word recognition is far more complicated than merely recognizing words on

STANDARD
1.4

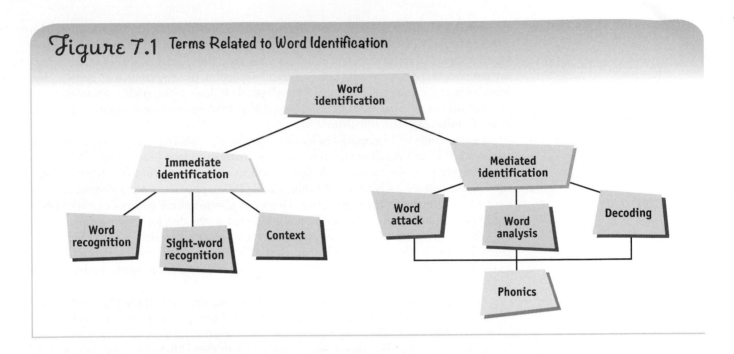

**Figure 7.1** Terms Related to Word Identification

flash cards. When a word is retrieved rapidly from memory, the process is often triggered by the application of letter–sound knowledge. Learning to read words rapidly involves making associations between particular spellings, pronunciations, and meanings by applying knowledge of letter–sound relationships (Ehri, 1995). Skilled readers use the strategy of immediate word recognition on 99 percent of the printed words they encounter. Word identification also includes strategies in which pictures and surrounding text assist the reader in recognizing words.

The terms *word attack*, *word analysis*, and *decoding* suggest the act of translating print into speech through analysis of letter–sound relationships. These terms have been used

Immediate identification of words is the result of experience with reading, seeing, discussing, using, and writing words.

frequently with what is commonly referred to as *phonics. Phonics* provides readers with a tool to "attack" the pronunciation of words that are not recognized immediately. A good way to think of phonics is that it "embraces a variety of instructional strategies for bringing attention to parts of words. The parts can be syllables, phonograms (such as *an*), other letter strings (such as *pie*), or single letters" (Beck & Juel, 1995, p. 22). Phonics, then, always involves *mediated word identification* because readers must devote conscious attention to "unlocking" the alphabetic code.

Few teachers of beginning readers would deny that phonics has an important role to play in children's development as readers and writers. Yet how best to teach children to read and write was the subject of debate and controversy throughout the twentieth century. According to the National Reading Panel (2000), phonics is one essential component of an effective reading program. However, Cunningham and Allington's (1999) argument still holds true. Phonics is not the solution to the development of skilled readers, but neither is simply *immersing* beginners in reading and writing. Study the Viewpoint featured in Box 7.1. Cunningham and Allington explain why teachers should be wary of those who advocate phonics instruction as a solution, not a means, to developing independent readers.

Teachers are in the most strategic position to make decisions about the word identification strategies children actually use to read and write well. Effective teachers ask *when, how, how much*, and *under what circumstances* word identification strategies should be taught. Understanding the phases of development that children progress through in their ability to identify words is important knowledge that teachers can use to make decisions about instruction.

# Phases of Development in Children's Ability to Identify Words

It is through frequent experiences with books and print that children develop knowledge about reading and writing prior to school. They do so at different rates, in different ways, and in different settings. When young children engage in frequent book and print experiences, the development of word knowledge may emerge during the preschool years without much, if any, formal instruction. Yet the capacity to read words cannot be left to chance or immersion in print. Teachers must build and expand on the word-reading knowledge that children bring to school.

Children progress through various developmental phases of word identification while learning to read (Ehri, 1991, 1994). In the course of their development, they first learn to identify some words purely through *visual cues*, such as distinctive graphic features *in* or *around* the words. As children continue to grow as readers, they use their developing knowledge of letter–sound relationships to identify words. The development of word learning can be divided into four phases, as illustrated in Figure 7.2 on page 206: the *prealphabetic, partial alphabetic, full alphabetic*, and *consolidated alphabetic* phases (Gaskins, Ehri, Cress, O'Hara, & Donnelly, 1997).

The *prealphabetic phase*, which has also been called the *logographic* or *visual cue* phase, occurs before the development of alphabetic knowledge. Children are able to recognize some words at sight during this phase because of distinctive visual and contextual cues in or around the recognized words. The ability to read cereal box labels, restaurant logos, and other kinds of environmental print is one of the first literacy accomplishments of a preschool child. The octagonal shape of a stop sign, for example, may prompt preschoolers to shout "stop" as their parents slow down at the sign. In addition, young children learn to attend to visual cues in words. As shown in Figure 7.2, preschoolers and kindergarten children may read the word *yellow* because they remember the two "tall posts" in the middle of the word.

**HOMEWORK EXERCISE: VIDEO**

Go to the Homework and Exercises section in Chapter 7 of MyEducationLab to watch the video "Phonics Instruction" and consider the developmental phases of word identification.

STANDARD
1.3

BOX **7.1**

# *Viewpoint*

## Why Phonics Is Not the Solution . . . But Neither Is Just Reading

Patricia M. Cunningham and Richard L. Allington

*Patricia M. Cunningham and Richard L. Allington are distinguished leaders in the field of reading. They are recognized for their research on contemporary phonics instruction and literacy policy analysis. Cunningham is a professor at Wake Forest University, and Allington is a professor at the University of Florida. Here they explain how phonics fits into the teaching of word recognition.*

At several points in American educational history, code-emphasis instruction (the phonics approach) has been touted as "the answer" to teaching all children to read. Both of us began our teaching in the 1960s, the last time phonics was offered as the answer. It wasn't the answer then and it isn't today. But once again there are claims being made for the effectiveness of phonics approaches and once again some folks are overstating and exaggerating evidence to support code-oriented materials and methods. There is a convergence of research evidence pointing to the critical role that good decoding skills play in good reading. However, there is no convergence in the research evidence indicating what types of phonics instruction, of what intensity, over what duration will produce the largest numbers of children who read well and willingly.

But this lack of evidence doesn't seem to matter to many proponents of a pro phonics agenda. Product advertisements, legislative testimonies, and various other materials have recently contained a set of strikingly similar assertions about phonics teaching and learning—assertions that are simply distortions of the research available even though often couched in terms such as "scientifically rigorous research." Here are some assertions that have appeared repeatedly and that we consider "unscientific"—assertions that cannot be drawn from the available scientific evidence.

### Unscientific Assertion #1: No One Teaches Phonics

Two recent large-scale federally funded studies provide overwhelming evidence that virtually all primary grade teachers teach phonics, usually daily. Smaller, more intensive studies of exemplary teachers point to the same conclusion but also point to an interesting phenomenon—these exemplary teachers rarely report using commercial phonics curriculum material. Instead, they teach phonics knowledge and strategies to children rather than teaching the pages in a phonics workbook.

### Unscientific Assertion #2: There Is a Phonemic Awareness Crisis

[Another] wrinkle has been added to the phonics campaign—a crisis in phonemic awareness. Oversimplifying a bit, phonemic awareness is the ability to isolate individual sounds (phonemes) in spoken words. For instance, being able to count three sounds in "cat." The evidence indicates that phonics instruction offers little benefit for children who have not developed phonemic awareness. There is compelling evidence to support the conclusion that phonemic awareness is an important understanding in learning to read an alphabetic language like English. But the evidence also indicates that most (80–85 percent) children acquire phonemic awareness by the middle of first grade. The research also indicates that 2 of those 3 or 4 children in each classroom who don't develop phonemic awareness initially can develop it within a few weeks, if offered some targeted tutorial or small group intervention. The remaining children may require a more intensive intervention.

We have learned much about the importance of children developing phonemic awareness, but the research still offers no clear basis for advocating particular instructional materials or methods. Phonemic awareness is important and it can and should be developed, but it is not "the root of all reading problems" nor will the implementation of elaborate time-consuming commercially produced phonemic awareness programs solve all our reading problems!

### Unscientific Assertion #3: Explicit, Systematic Phonics Is the Only Way to Go

There is suddenly much ado about the need to ensure that "explicit, systematic" phonics instruction is offered. Often "incidental, opportunistic" phonics instruction is contrasted negatively against the "scientific" assertions for "explicit, systematic" phonics. The problem is that the available studies of exemplary teachers portray powerful phonics instruction that is "direct and opportunistic" (and it seems systematic also). It seems obvious that well-planned instruction based on student needs would be more effective than a series of random instructional activities. But exactly what sort of "explicit, systematic" or "explicit, opportunistic" phonics instruction does the research endorse?

Simply said, there is no convergence of research on just what sort of phonics instruction should be offered. Often publishers of commercial materials seem to be suggesting that their material has been developed from some set of "scientific" principles, which suggests that there is research evidence found on just what order letters and sounds should be taught and whether the instruction should focus on synthetic or analytic approaches and so on. But there simply is no convergence of research on such points. There is no "scientifically" determined sequence of instruction and no conclusive evidence on what sorts of phonics lessons, or of what duration would most effectively develop the optimum level of decoding efficiency in children.

*(Continued)*

## Viewpoint *(Continued)*

### Unscientific Assertion #4: Decodable Texts Are Essential

Finally, the most recently touted unscientific assertion has to do with the role of, or need for, "decodable texts." Such texts are described as offering children "only words that they have been taught the phonics skills to sound out."

In fact, there is evidence that restricting beginning reading materials to any single text type will likely produce a limited set of reading strategies—though the strategies developed seem to vary by the type of text restrictions in place. There is research support for providing children with "manageable" texts—texts that they can read without too much difficulty. There is also evidence that some of the recently published reading series provide reading material that is quite difficult. But none of this suggests that a return to "Nat the Rat" is the solution.

### An Unscientific Assertion from the Last Era: Children Will Acquire Decoding Skills from Just Reading

This is the unscientific assertion most responsible for the current phonics frenzy! Both the research and our experience indicate that children need to be taught effective decoding skills and strategies. Most children don't become skillful at pronouncing unknown words just by reading. Phonics instruction is an essential part of a reading program—but it is not the reading program!

*Source: Classrooms That Work: They Can All Read and Write,* 2nd ed., by P. M. Cunningham and R. L. Allington, pp. 3–5. Published by Allyn and Bacon, Boston, MA. Copyright © 1999 by Pearson Education. Reprinted by permission of the publisher.

Children progress to the *partial alphabetic phase* when they begin to develop some knowledge about letters and detect letter–sound relationships. For example, at 4½ years old, Simon reads his name by remembering that the letter *s* looks like a snake and makes a hissing /s/ sound; and the letter *i* sounds like its name. The partial alphabetic phase emerges during kindergarten and first grade for most children, when they acquire some knowledge of letters and sounds. They remember how to read specific words by detecting

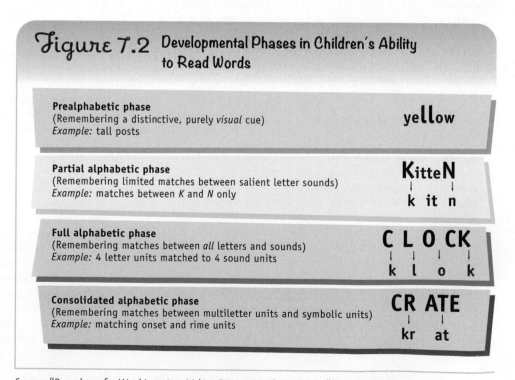

**Figure 7.2  Developmental Phases in Children's Ability to Read Words**

**Prealphabetic phase**
(Remembering a distinctive, purely *visual* cue)
*Example:* tall posts

yellow

**Partial alphabetic phase**
(Remembering limited matches between salient letter sounds)
*Example:* matches between *K* and *N* only

KitteN
k  it  n

**Full alphabetic phase**
(Remembering matches between *all* letters and sounds)
*Example:* 4 letter units matched to 4 sound units

CLOCK
k l o k

**Consolidated alphabetic phase**
(Remembering matches between multiletter units and symbolic units)
*Example:* matching onset and rime units

CR ATE
kr  at

*Source:* "Procedures for Word Learning: Making Discoveries About Words," by I. W. Gaskins, L. C. Ehri, C. Cress, C. O'Hara, and K. Donnelly, *Reading Teacher, 50,* p. 317. Copyright © 1997 by the International Reading Association. Reprinted with permission of the International Reading Association (www.reading.org).

how a few letters correspond to sounds in the word's pronunciation. As indicated in the example in Figure 7.2, a child might recognize *kitten* by remembering the letter–sound relationships between the initial *k* and final *n* letters, but not the letter–sound matches in between. Early readers who function at the partial alphabetic phase are likely to misread some words sharing the same partial letter–sound cues—for example, misreading *kitchen* as *kitten*. This is especially the case when the word is read in isolation rather than in the context of a story.

The *full alphabetic phase* emerges in children's literacy development when readers identify words by matching all of the letters and sounds. They have developed enough knowledge about letter–sound relationships to unlock the pronunciations of unknown words. As shown in Figure 7.2, readers at this phase would be able to segment the word *clock* into four letter units that match the four sounds in the pronunciation. Sounding out letters and blending them into words may be laborious and slow at the beginning of the full alphabetic stage, but as children become more accomplished at decoding unknown words, they progress to more rapid word analysis. Some children enter first grade with the capacity to analyze words fully. Others do not and will benefit from explicit, carefully planned lessons that help them make discoveries about letter–sound relationships in words (Gaskins et al., 1997).

As children become more skilled at identifying words, they rely less on individual letter–sound relationships. Instead, they use their knowledge of familiar and predictable letter patterns to speed up the process of reading words. They do so by developing the ability to analyze chunks of letters within words (Johnston, 1999; Moustafa & Maldonado-Colon, 1999). The recognition of predictable letter patterns begins to emerge in the first grade as children engage in reading and begin to recognize many words with similar spelling patterns. In the example in Figure 7.2, readers at the *consolidated alphabetic phase* would be able to segment the word *crate* into two larger letter or spelling patterns, *cr* and *ate*, and match them to larger sound units known as *onsets* (the initial consonants and consonant patterns that come at the beginning of syllables) and *rimes* (the vowel and consonants that follow them at the end of syllables). The recognition of letter patterns in the consolidated alphabetic phase eventually allows children to analyze multisyllabic words rapidly.

Although teaching children whose primary language is not English to read is a complex issue, Bear, Helman, Templeton, Invernizzi, and Johnston (2007) synthesize research by providing general instructional principles for ELLs. They suggest that word study should be explicit and systematic, yet should allow students to make connections to prior knowledge. In addition, instruction should include active engagement and focus on interaction with others. Lenters (2004/2005) recommends providing opportunities for children to demonstrate what they know in their first language and suggests that parents read to their children in first-language books.

DIVERSITY ELL

Next, we discuss the teaching of phonics in more depth. As you read about phonics instruction, however, keep in mind that phonics is only one part of a comprehensive reading program.

# Approaches and Guidelines for Teaching Phonics

Approaches to phonics instruction have been classified as traditional or contemporary (Stahl, Duffy-Hester, & Stahl, 1998). Traditional approaches reflect the type of instruction that the parents and grandparents of today's school-age children remember—often with mixed feelings. On the one hand, students from previous generations recall the drudgery and boredom associated with repetitive "skill and

Through phonics instruction, children learn to recognize words in text through letter patterns developed by using consistent letter–sound associations.

**HOMEWORK EXERCISE: VIDEO**

Go to the Homework and Exercises section in Chapter 7 of MyEducationLab to watch the video entitled "Teaching Phonics" and explore the instructional approach the teacher is using.

drill" routines, an endless stream of worksheets, and rote memorization of phonics rules. On the other hand, they recall with some pride that they learned to read because phonics taught them to "sound out" words. As Stahl and colleagues put it, traditional approaches to phonics instruction "are approaches that were in vogue during the 1960s and 1970s but seem to be returning as teachers grapple with how to teach phonics" (p. 344). Contemporary approaches to phonics instruction, however, are approaches that emerged in the 1990s. Today, teachers who hold a comprehensive literacy philosophy do not adhere to a single approach; they plan instruction using a variety of strategies and materials.

## Traditional Approaches

Traditional phonics instruction includes *analytic*, *synthetic*, and *linguistic* approaches. These approaches are favored by teachers who devote large chunks of time to *early*, *intensive*, and *systematic* instruction designed to help master the sounds of the letters. The instructional emphasis is on the teaching of isolated letter–sound correspondences separate from meaningful activities. Implicit in this "phonics first" is a bottom-up belief that children must learn letter–sound correspondences *early* in their school experiences in order to build a foundation for reading meaningful texts.

*Intensive* and *systematic* are tandem concepts often mentioned in the same breath by proponents of traditional phonics approaches. The word intensive suggests a thorough and comprehensive treatment of letter–sound correspondences. *Systematic* implies that phonics instruction should be organized sequentially and in a logical order through structured lessons. Key findings from the National Reading Panel (2000) support early, intensive, systematic phonics instruction.

**ANALYTIC PHONICS INSTRUCTION** ◆ **Analytic phonics** is defined in the *Literacy Dictionary* as a "whole-to-part approach to word study in which the student is first taught a number of sight words and then relevant phonic generalizations, which are subsequently applied to other words" (Harris & Hodges, 1995, p. 9). The sequence of instruction usually involves these steps:

1. Observe a list of known words with a common letter–sound relationship, for example, the initial consonant *t*.
2. Begin questioning about how the words look and sound the same and how they are different.
3. Elicit the common letter–sound relationship and discuss.
4. Have the learners phrase a generalization about the letter–sound relationship—for example, all the words start with the sound of the letter *t*. The sound of the letter *t* is /t/ as in *top*.

Analytic lessons in basal reading programs typically rely heavily on the use of workbooks and practice exercises. A major criticism of the analytic approach is that teachers invest too little time on the initial teaching of alphabetic relationships and students spend too much time on paper-and-pencil exercises. Oral instruction from the teacher simply serves as an introduction to worksheets rather than to help students clarify relationships and make discoveries (Durkin, 1988; Stahl et al., 1998).

**SYNTHETIC PHONICS INSTRUCTION** ◆ **Synthetic phonics** is defined in the *Literacy Dictionary* as a "part-to-whole phonics approach to reading instruction in which the student learns the sounds represented by letters and letter combinations, blends these sounds together to pronounce new words, and finally identifies which phonics generalizations apply" (Harris & Hodges, 1995, p. 250). The sequence of instruction goes something like this:

1. Teach the letter names.
2. Teach the sound or sounds each letter represents.
3. Drill on the letter–sound relationships until rapidly recognized. Discuss rules and form generalizations about relationships that usually apply to words (when vowels are short or long, for example).
4. Teach the blending of separate sounds to make a word.
5. Provide the opportunity to apply blending to unknown words.

There are similarities between analytic and synthetic phonics. Both approaches address rules, discuss isolated letter–sound relationships, break words apart, and put them back together again. In so doing, the danger of fragmenting word identification from actual text situations can be present.

**LINGUISTIC PHONICS INSTRUCTION** ◆ The *Literacy Dictionary* defines **linguistic instruction** as "a beginning reading approach based on highly regular sound–symbol patterns, temporarily substituted for the term 'phonic' early in the 1960s" (Harris & Hodges, 1995, p. 139). This approach emphasizes learning to decode words through regular letter patterns—for example: *dish, fish, wish, swish.*

Linguistic programs include stories that are written with numerous words that repeat specific letter–sound relationships, for example, "The fat cat sat on the mat" and "The car was parked at the market." Although linguistic programs are considered "traditional," a resurgence of stories that use repeated word parts has emerged; the current terminology associated with books of this type is *decodable text.* **Decodable text** contains the following features: It is text that is written with a large number of words that have phonetic similarities and there is typically a match between the text and the phonic elements that the teacher has taught (Mesmer, 2001). Although the value of using decodable text is a debated topic because the stories can often be boring, one of its purposes "is to assist beginning readers in applying phonics instruction during text reading" (Mesmer, p. 454).

Teachers who engage children in the analysis of words must be well versed and knowledgeable in the content and language of phonics. In Figure 7.3 on pages 210–212, we highlight some of the basic terms associated with phonics instruction.

## Contemporary Approaches

Contemporary approaches to phonics instruction do not emphasize an overreliance on worksheets, skill-and-drill activities, rules, or rote memorization. Instead, contemporary approaches are rooted in constructivist principles of learning and the fact that children can learn phonics through meaningful engagement with reading real texts. Compared to traditional approaches to phonics instruction during which phonics is often treated as a separate "subject," contemporary approaches integrate the learning of sound–symbol relationships within the context meaningful activities. Stahl and his colleagues (Stahl et al., 1998) observed that contemporary approaches to phonics instruction are usually components of larger reading instructional programs.

Next, we examine several approaches to teaching phonics from contemporary points of view. These perspectives are more holistic and reflect a "top-down" philosophy. By that, we mean they begin with the learner, what the learner knows, and what teachers need to teach based on that knowledge.

## Figure 7.3   A Primer on the Content and Language of Phonics

**Consonants.**   *Consonants* are all the sounds represented by letters of the alphabet except *a, e, i, o, u*. Consonants conform fairly closely to *one-to-one correspondence*—for each letter there is one sound. This property of consonants makes them of great value to the reader when attempting to sound out an unknown word. There are some consonant anomalies:

The letter *y* is a consonant only at the beginning of a syllable, as in *yet*.

The letter *w* is sometimes a vowel, as in *flew*.

Sometimes consonants have no sound, as in *know*.

The letters *c* and *g* each have two sounds, called hard and soft sounds:

Hard *c*: *cat, coaster, catatonic* (*c* sounds like /k/)
Soft *c*: *city, receive, cite* (*c* sounds like /s/)

Hard *g*: *give, gallop, garbage* (*g* sounds like /g/)
Soft *g*: *giraffe, ginger, gym* (*g* sounds like /j/)

**Consonant Blends.**   *Consonant blends* are two or three consonants grouped together, but each consonant retains its original sound. There are several major groups of blends:

*l* blends:   *bl   cl   fl   gl   pl   sl*

*r* blends:   *br   cr   dr   fr   gr   pr   tr*

*s* blends:   *sc   sk   sm   sn   sp   st   sw*

three-letter blends:   *scr   spr   str*

**Consonant Digraphs.**   When two or more consonants are combined to produce a new sound, the letter cluster is called a *consonant digraph*. The most common consonant digraphs are these:

| | |
|---|---|
| *ch* as in *chin* | *ph* as in *phone* |
| *sh* as in *shell* | *gh* as in *ghost* |
| *th* as in *think* | *-nk* as in *tank* |
| *wh* as in *whistle* | *-ng* as in *tang* |

**Vowels.**   *Vowels* are all the sounds represented by the letters *a, e, i, o, u*. The letter *y* serves as a vowel when it is not the initial sound of a word. Sometimes *w* functions as a vowel, usually when it follows another vowel. There is *rarely a one-to-one correspondence* between a letter representing a vowel and the sound of the vowel. Vowel sounds are influenced heavily by their location in a word and by the letters accompanying them. Several major types of vowel phonemes are worth knowing about.

A *long vowel* sound is a speech sound similar to the letter name of the vowel. A *macron* (ˉ) is sometimes used to indicate that a vowel is long. *Short vowel* sounds are speech sounds also represented by vowel letters. Short sounds are denoted by a *breve* (˘). An example of the long and short sound of each vowel letter follows:

| Short Vowel Sound | Long Vowel Sound |
|---|---|
| /ă/ as in *Pat* | /ā/ as in *lake* |
| /ĕ/ as in *bed* | /ē/ as in *be* |
| /ĭ/ as in *pit* | /ī/ as in *ice* |
| /ŏ/ as in *hot* | /ō/ as in *go* |
| /ŭ/ as in *hug* | /ū/ as in *use* |

Often when a vowel letter initiates a word, the short sound will be used, for example: *at, effort, interest, optimist,* and *uncle*.

**Vowel Digraphs.**   *Vowel digraphs* are two vowels that are adjacent to one another. The first vowel is usually long and the second is silent. Vowel digraphs include *oa, ee, ea, ai,* and *ay*, as in *boat, beet, beat, bait,* and *bay*. There are notable exceptions: *oo* as in *look, ew* as in *flew, ea* as in *read*.

*(Continued)*

# Figure 7.3 *(Continued)*

**Vowel Diphthongs.**   *Vowel diphthongs* are sounds that consist of a blend of two separate vowel sounds. These are /oi/ as in *oil,* /oy/ as in *toy,* /au/ as in *taught,* /aw/ as in *saw,* /ou/ as in *out,* and /ow/ as in *how.* Generally children do not need to be taught these formally.

**Consonant-Influenced Vowels.**   The letter *a* has a special sound when followed by an *l,* as in *Albert* or *tallow.* R-controlled vowels occur when any vowel letter is followed by an *r: star, her, fir, for,* and *purr.* The power of *r* over vowel sounds is perhaps the most beneficial to point out to children, although in the process of forming their own generalizations about short and long vowel sounds children have probably incorporated *r*-controlled notions (Heilman, Blair, & Rupley, 1986).

**Phonograms.**   *Phonograms* (also called *rimes*) are letter patterns that help form word families or rhyming words. Letter clusters such as *ad, at, ack, ag, an, ap, ash, ed, et, ess, en, ine,* and *ike* can be used to develop families of words; for example, the *ad* family: *bad, dad, sad, fad,* and so on. Phonograms may be one of the most useful letter patterns to teach because they encourage children to map speech sounds onto larger chunks of letters.

**Syllables.**   A *syllable* is a vowel or a cluster of letters containing a vowel and pronounced as a unit. Phonograms, for example, are syllables. The composition of the syllable signals the most probable vowel sound. Examine the following patterns:

| | | |
|---|---|---|
| Long vowels | CV | *be* |
| | CV*e* | *like* |
| | | *rote* |
| | CVVC | *paid* |
| | | *boat* |
| Short vowels | VC or CVC | *it* |
| | | *hot* |
| *R*-controlled | V*r* | *art* |
| | CV*r* | *car, her* |
| Digraph/diphthong variations | VV | *saw, book* |
| | | *boil, out* |

These patterns underlie the formation of syllables. The number of syllables in a word is equal to the number of vowel sounds. For example, the word *disagreement* has four vowel sounds and thus four syllables. The word *hat* has one vowel sound and thus one syllable.

There are three primary syllabication patterns that signal how to break down a word into syllabic units.

- *VCCV.* When there are two consonants between two vowels, the word is usually divided between the consonants: *hap-pen, mar-ket, es-cape.* However, we do not split consonant digraphs such as *sh* or *th* or *ng,* as in *sing-er, fa-ther.* There is a variation of this pattern— the VCC*le* pattern. A word with this pattern is still divided between the consonants: *sad-dle, bot-tle, rat-tle, pud-dle.*

- *VCV pattern 1.* When one consonant is between two vowels, the division is before the consonant: *re-view, o-pen, be-gin.* Again there is a slight variation with the VC*le* pattern, but still divide before the consonant: *peo-ple, ta-ble, cra-dle.*

- *VCV pattern 2.* If using VCV pattern 1 does not result in a familiar word, divide after the consonant, as in *sal-ad* or *pan-el.*

Although there is no one particular phonics sequence or program that is better than another (Cunningham, 2005), Bear, Helman, Templeton, Invernizzi, and Johnston (2007)

*(Continued)*

## Figure 7.3 *(Continued)*

suggest that early English learners begin with initial and final consonant sounds and short and long vowels by picture sorting, followed by blends, word families, and digraphs. In addition, they recommend:

- Talking with students as they perform activities such as drawing, painting, and playing with blocks

- Reading to students and talking about words and pictures

- Reading with students chorally, using repeated readings, and dictation activities

**ANALOGY-BASED INSTRUCTION** ◆ In **analogy-based instruction,** sometimes referred to as analogic phonics, children are taught to "use their knowledge of letters representing onsets and rimes in words they already know how to pronounce, rather than their knowledge of letter–phoneme correspondences to pronounce unfamiliar words" (Moustafa, 1997, p. 48). Underscoring analogy-based instruction is the notion that children learn to read words in context better than out of context and that "chunking words" by letter patterns is what good readers do (Cunningham, 2000; Goswami, 1986; Moustafa, 1997). Research suggests that we use letter patterns to read, rather than looking at individual letters and blending them (Cunningham, 2005).

Analogic phonics instruction is favored by teachers who believe that children need to actively engage in word study to make words, learn spelling patterns, and draw analogies between known and unknown word parts. See Box 7.2 for a Step-by-Step Lesson on how teach an analogic phonics lesson.

**SPELLING-BASED INSTRUCTION** ◆ **Spelling-based instruction** focuses on teaching students strategies for studying words they read and write. It is based on the premise that word study is developmental and that students need to be working with words that represent their levels of development. In other words, some students are ready for more difficult words than other students; therefore, it is important to first determine the level of development for which the student is reading. Although qualitative inventories and programs are available for assessing spelling levels, ongoing observations of students' writing and invented spelling can help teachers determine where students fall on a developmental continuum (Bear, Invernizzi, Templeton, & Johnston, 2008). Bear and colleagues' characteristics of each developmental stage of spelling along with *approximate* age and grade levels are summarized in Table 7.1.

STANDARD
1.3

BOX **7.2**    STEP-BY-STEP *Lesson*

### Analogy-Based Phonics Lesson

1. Decide on the letter pattern(s) that you are going to teach. For example, *-an* and *-at.*
2. Select literature that includes examples of the letter pattern. For example, *Angus the Cat* contains words with the letter patterns *-an* and *-at.*
3. Read the story aloud for enjoyment and discuss the story line.
4. Introduce the letter patterns and reread the story as children listen for words that contain those patterns.

5. Reread the story a third time. During this reading, pause as each word that contains the pattern is read and record the words on a chart or word wall.
6. Continue instruction by providing opportunities for the students to write the words, use them in sentences, complete cloze passages, and engage in sorting activities.
7. Provide other books that contain the letter patterns and encourage the children to partner read, silent read, or read the books in small groups.

## Table 7.1  Developmental Stages of Word Learning and Spelling

| STAGE | AGE/GRADE LEVEL | CHARACTERISTICS |
|---|---|---|
| Emergent | Ages 1–7<br>preK–mid 1 | Pretend reading<br>Memory reading<br>Identifying words through shapes and environmental print |
| Letter Name—Alphabetic | Ages 4–9<br>Grades K–early 3 | Learn most beginning and ending consonants<br>Understand directionality<br>Begin to know digraphs, blends, and word families<br>Have a growing sight vocabulary |
| Within Word | Ages 6–12<br>Grades 1–mid 4 | Can read most one-syllable words<br>Can use some vowel patterns including long vowels<br>Learn r-controlled vowels<br>Continue to develop sight vocabulary |
| Syllables and Affixes | Ages 8–18<br>Grades 3–8 | Learn structural analysis—prefixes, suffixes, root words<br>Learn vowel patterns in multisyllabic words<br>Learn inflected endings |
| Derivational | Ages 10+<br>Grades 5–12 | Understand alternative consonant and vowels sounds (e.g., chef, character, cherry)<br>Learn and understand Greek and Latin prefixes, suffixes, and roots<br>Learn advanced word study |

*Source:* Adapted from *Words Their Way: Word Study for Phonics, Vocabulary, and Spelling Instruction,* by D. R. Bear, M. Invernizzi, S. Templeton, and F. Johnston (Upper Saddle River, NJ: Prentice Hall, 2008).

Bear and Templeton (1998) identify three important research-based practices based on a developmental spelling approach to word study. These practices are synthesized in Box 7.3 on page 214.

**EMBEDDED PHONICS INSTRUCTION** ◆ **Embedded phonics instruction** is often associated with holistic, meaning-centered teaching. In literature-based instruction, for example, students learn phonics skills in the context of stories that make sense.

> Children begin with the use of whole texts involving shared literacy activities with an adult and move to the identification of phrases and words and the examination of word parts. Emphasis on meaning is maintained even as children examine word parts, because the purpose is help them see the patterns in the language so they can apply the knowledge to new situations. (Strickland, 1998, p. 50)

Although the National Reading Panel (2000) criticized embedded phonics, claiming that it is not systematic and intensive enough, Cunningham and Cunningham (2002) aptly point out that children need to be cognizant of what they are learning and teaching must be multifaceted. In addition, the National Reading Panel recognized that phonics instruction is only one component of an effective reading program.

**GUIDELINES FOR CONTEMPORARY PHONICS INSTRUCTION** ◆ Here are some guidelines for contemporary phonics instruction that work both in classrooms where the basal reader is the core text and in classrooms where reading instruction centers on literature-based programs.

**1.** Phonics instruction needs to build on a foundation of phonemic awareness and knowledge of the way language works. Young children differ in their phonemic awareness

BOX **7.3**

## Research-Based Practices
### Instructional Implications for a Developmental Spelling Model for Teaching Word Study

*First,* consider grouping students for instruction. By observing children's spelling skills during free writing, teachers can learn much about the developmental levels of their students by observing how they write and how they use invented spelling. Although informal spelling assessments are available, ongoing informal assessment can be just as valuable. Grouping students at similar levels of development can have significant instructional benefits.

*Second,* examine the patterns of spelling that students know and build upon that knowledge. Do not assume that "thematic" words are based on patterns that fit the developmental stage in which your students need to develop their skills. By "thematic" words, we mean words that are inter-

esting, but not necessarily based on spelling patterns. For example, as Bear and Templeton (1998) point out, "while many first graders can learn to read words such as *ocean* and *plankton* as part of a thematic unit focusing on oceans, their ability to remember the spelling of those words is very limited" (p. 230).

*Third,* guide students toward discovering how words are put together. Do not emphasize the memorization of spelling rules. Spelling rules are often best learned after students discover them on their own; it is often more useful for children to discover spelling generalizations on their own. Teachers need to be flexible—teaching spelling rules does not guarantee a transfer to reading and writing.

*Source:* Based on "Explorations in Developmental Spelling: Foundations for Learning and Teaching Phonics, Spelling, and Vocabulary," by D. R. Bear and S. Templeton, 1998, *The Reading Teacher, 52,* pp. 222–242.

of sounds in spoken words. Once children are able to segment sounds, they also need to be shown the blending process. As you may recall, blending means joining together the sounds represented by letters and letter clusters in a word. Essentially, the reader links the sound sequence with the letter sequence. Whenever possible, children should practice segmenting and blending unfamiliar words that are *encountered in meaningful print context.*

In addition to differing in phonemic awareness, children also come to phonics instruction with varying degrees of generalizations about the way the written language works. Their generalizations constitute a particular level of linguistic awareness. Informally, teachers may engage young children in experiences concerning the notions of word, letter, and alphabet through such activities as asking the children to cut the words apart and having them sort the words and letters.

STANDARD
2.3

**2.** Phonics instruction needs to be integrated into a total reading program. At least half of the time devoted to the teaching of reading, and probably more, should be spent on the actual reading of stories, poems, plays, and trade books. Furthermore, no more than 25 percent of the time, and possibly less, should be spent on phonics instruction and practice (Stahl, 1992).

It is important to show children how to use phonics in the actual reading of texts. Unfortunately, too many phonics programs are not related to the actual reading children are asked to do. Children seem to learn letter-pattern knowledge best if they observe a pattern appearing in many different words, rather than in repetitions of the same word. Trachtenburg (1990) provides a list (see Appendix D) of trade books with a high percentage of common letter–sound relationships.

**3.** Phonics instruction needs to focus on reading print rather than on learning rules. As noted earlier, skilled readers do not refer to phonics rules but see words in terms of patterns of letters. Adams (1990) points out that they recognize new words by comparing them to words and patterns they already know. For example, when Stahl (1992) asked skilled readers to pronounce *minatory*, most people said the first syllable was /min/ as in *minute* or *miniature*, comparing it to a pattern in a word they already know how to pronounce. Phonics instruction should help children do this. Teachers need to first draw their attention to the order of letters in words and then encourage them to examine common patterns in words, through sounding out words and showing similarities between words.

Vowel letter–sound associations are often taught with phonics rules. Adams (1990), however, points out that vowel letter–sound correspondences are more stable when one looks at rimes than when letters are looked at in isolation. Children generally find it easier to learn to read words by using rhyming phonograms, and research on the relative ease with which children learn differing kinds of phonograms has reinforced this insight (Adams, 1990; Clymer, 1963; Cunningham, 2005).

**4.** Phonics instruction needs to include the teaching of onsets and rimes. Instead of teaching phonics rules, teach children to use onsets and rimes. An **onset,** or the part of the syllable before the vowel, is a consonant or consonant blend or digraph; a **rime** is the part from the vowel onward. As we noted earlier, consonant letter–sound associations are fairly consistent. In addition, **phonograms** or rimes have been found to be generalizable. One study found that of the 286 phonograms that appear in primary grade texts, 95 percent were pronounced the same in every word in which they were found (Durrell, 1963). In addition, these 272 stable phonograms are contained in 1437 of the words commonly found in the speaking vocabularies of primary-age children (Murphy, 1957). According to Wylie and Durrell (1970), nearly 500 primary-grade words can be derived from only 37 consistent rimes. Fry (1998) provides a useful resource for teachers of the 38 most common phonograms.

**5.** Phonics instruction needs to include spelling-based strategies. When children are encouraged to write and to use invented spellings, they use their knowledge of letter–sound relationships. Writing with invented spelling improves children's awareness of phonemes, an important precursor to learning to decode words. When word study reflects spelling-based strategies, it is a powerful way to teach phonics (Bear, Invernizzi, Templeton, & Johnston, 2008).

Bear and colleagues (2007) recommend that teachers recognize the following principles for English language learners:

- Students may not initially know some English sounds because they do not exist in their first language and, therefore, they may have difficulty enunciating them.
- Teachers should not expect ELLs to pronounce new sounds perfectly; however, they should be able to distinguish between sounds that exhibit large contrasting differences (for example, /v/ from /b/).
- Before working with print, ELL students will benefit from working with sound sorting activities that use pictures. Pictures can be sorted by initial consonant sounds, final consonant sounds, digraphs, blends, and vowel sounds. Clip art can be used to make cards for the students to sort. For example, students can learn to distinguish the sounds of /t/ and /h/ with the following pictures for /t/: *top, tire, towel,* and the following pictures for /h/: *heart, horse, hat.*

## Strategies for Teaching Phonics

The five guidelines just given are broad statements of principle by which teachers can become actively involved in the teaching of phonics based on contemporary approaches to instruction. These principles are grounded in research related to the phonics children use to identify words. Contemporary phonics

**BUILDING TEACHING SKILLS: CASE STUDY**

Go to the Homework and Exercises section in Chapter 7 of MyEducationLab to work through a case study on "Fluency and Word Identification" and build an understanding of strategies you could employ to help students become fluent readers.

approaches support children's ability to identify words through explicit strategy-based instruction and integrated learning during reading and writing activities. Throughout this section, we draw heavily on the strategies and activities described in what we believe to be several of the best resources for contemporary phonics instruction: *Phonics They Use: Words in Reading and Writing* (Cunningham, 2005), *Word Identification Strategies: Phonics from a New Perspective* (Fox, 2004), *Words Their Way: Word Study for Phonics, Vocabulary, and Spelling Instruction* (Bear et al., 2008), and *From Phonics to Fluency: Effective Teaching of Decoding and Reading Fluency in the Elementary School* (Rasinski & Padak, 2001).

## Consonant-Based Strategies

In Chapter 5, we emphasized the importance of letter recognition. Recognizing and naming letters is one of the important accomplishments of early readers because it sets the stage for beginners to become involved in more sophisticated manipulations of letters and sounds. Consonant letters represent all of the individual phonemes associated with letters of the alphabet except for the vowels *a, e, i, o,* and *u.* Because consonants generally have one sound for each letter, they lend themselves well to instructional strategies that allow children to make discoveries about words. Fry (2004) provides teachers with useful tables that indicate the frequencies of consonants (and vowels). His work is based on a reanalysis of an early large-scale study that examined over 17,000 vocabulary words and the frequencies of phoneme–grapheme correspondences (Hanna, Hanna, Hodges, & Rudorf, 1966). Once children have developed a good grasp of consonant letter–sound relationships, they can engage in activities that will help them recognize consonant digraphs and blends. Consider the following consonant-based phonics instruction strategies and activities.

STANDARD
2.2

**LETTER ACTIONS** ◆ Physical actions can be used to help children learn the consonants (Cunningham, 1995, 2005). Children who are kinesthetic learners benefit particularly from this technique. Simply choose your favorite action for each of the letters. On a large card, print the letter on one side and write the action on the reverse. For young children, a simple drawing of the action can be used in place of the word. When choosing the actions, make sure that each one can only represent one letter. For example, you wouldn't want to choose giggle for *g* and laugh for *l*—this might confuse the children. Introduce new letters as they are mastered. A simple activity is to mix the letter cards up and show them for 5 to 10 seconds at a time. After the letter is shown, the children can act out the letter until you put the card down. You can increase the speed with which new letters are revealed as time goes on. Another variation is to pass out the letter cards to the students. They can act out a letter for the others to identify. A third activity is to have one child pick a card from the pile, begin acting it out, and then invite his or her classmates to do the same. The leader then picks another card and changes activities. Here is a list of actions for each consonant:

*B:*  bend, bounce, bob

*C:*  catch, call, comb

*D:*  dance, duck, dive

*F:*  fall, file, fix

*G:*  gallop, gasp

*H:*  hop, hide, hit, holler

*J:*  jump, juggle, jog

*K:*  kick, kiss

*L:*  laugh, lick, lunge

M:  march, mix, munch

N:  nap, nod

P:  punch, push, paint

R:  run, rest, rip

S:  salute, sit, sing

T:  tiptoe, talk, tickle, tap

V:  vacuum, vanish

W:  wiggle, walk, wave

Y:  yawn, yell

Z:  zip, zigzag

**FAVORITE FOODS** ◆ Cunningham (1995, 2005) incorporates children's association with favorite foods to suggest another strategy for developing knowledge about consonant letters and sounds. The strategy calls for you to select favorite or unique foods, one food per letter. Prepare the food and share it as a class. Pictures of each food can be posted with each letter in the classroom. Children will easily be able to recall a letter when they look for things they have eaten. Help children make the connection between the consonant letter that begins each food and the initial sound they hear when they say the name of the food.

B:  bananas, bagel

C:  cake, cookies, carrots, candy, celery

D:  donuts, dill (pickle)

F:  fish, fettuccine

G:  goulash, gingerbread

H:  hamburgers, ham, hummus, hotdogs

J:  jelly beans, Jell-O, jelly, juice

K:  Kool-Aid, Kisses (Hershey's), kidney beans, kabobs

L:  lettuce, lemonade, lasagna, lemons, limes

M:  macaroni, meatballs, milk, mushrooms

N:  noodles, nuts

P:  potatoes, pancakes, pizza, pumpkin pie

R:  radishes, raisins, rice

S:  soup, salad, sandwich

T:  toast, tea, tomatoes, turkey

V:  vegetables, V-8 juice, vanilla, vinegar

W:  watermelon, walnuts, water, waffles

Y:  yogurt, yams

Z:  zucchini bread, zucchini

Students can keep a cookbook with the recipes they prepare during the year. Copies of the recipe books can be sent home with the children.

**CONSONANT SUBSTITUTION** ◆ As students develop consonant letter–sound knowledge, you can use numerous activities to assist them with learning to read words that rhyme or belong to the same *word family*. These activities involve consonant substitution. The Step-by-Step Lesson featured in Box 7.4 outlines a basic procedure for consonant substitution.

BOX **7.4**

## STEP-BY-STEP *Lesson*

### Consonant Substitution

The consonant substitution strategy actively involves students in learning words that rhyme or belong to the same word family. The basic steps for consonant substitution are as follows:

1. Target a rime for instructional emphasis, for example, *at*.
2. Develop a set of word cards that include the *at* rime.
3. Ask students to identify the first word in the set, for example, *bat*. If the students do not know the word, tell them. Then have them read the word after you. Place the word in a pocket folder or on the bulletin board so that it is visible to the students.
4. Show students the next word, *cat*. Invite them to read the word, and if they don't know it, tell them. Place the word in the pocket folder next to the first word. Help students detect letter differences between the first two words and discuss how the pronunciation of each word changes when the consonant letter is substituted.
5. Repeat the activity with the remaining word cards, and provide assistance as needed as you engage in discussion.

*Source:* Based on *Words Their Way: Word Study for Phonics, Vocabulary, and Spelling Instruction,* 2nd ed., by D. R. Bear, M. Invernizzi, S. Templeton, and F. Johnston (Upper Saddle River, NJ: Prentice Hall, 2000).

**FLIP BOOKS** ◆ Another strategy is to create flip books (see Figure 7.4). Flip books are made from sentence strips, which are ideal for creating small booklets for word study. One large sentence strip is used for writing the rime (on the right side of the strip). Strips that are half the size of the larger one are cut for the onsets. Consonants, consonant blends, and consonant digraphs are written on these smaller cards and then stapled or attached with binding to the longer card. Students flip through the booklet, reading each word. *Man* is changed to *can* or *ran* with the flip of the page.

**MAKING WORDS** ◆ Flip books make students aware of their word-making capability when they substitute different consonants at the beginning of a rime. To engage children in the process of making words, consider these steps (Cunningham, 2005):

1. Decide on the rime that you wish students to practice, and develop a rime card for each of the students.

**all**

2. Develop a set of consonant letter cards for each student that can be used to make words with the rime that has been targeted for practice.

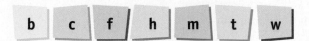

3. Direct students to use the letter cards to make the first word, *ball*.
4. Invite students to now change the word to make *call*.
5. Repeat the activity until all of the words have been made.

In addition to letter and rime cards, students could use letter tiles to make words. Decide on the rime you would like students to study. Select the letter tiles for the rime and a number of consonants on additional tiles. Have the students construct the words

## *Figure 7.4*  Flip Book

*Source: Words Their Way: Word Study for Phonics, Vocabulary, and Spelling Instruction,* by D. R. Bear, M. Invernezzi, S. Templeton, and F. Johnston (Upper Saddle River, NJ: Prentice Hall, 1996), p. 177. Reprinted by permission of Pearson Education, Inc., Upper Saddle River, NJ.

on their desks or a carpet square. Also use slate squares or mini-chalkboards for consonant substitution. Students write the rime and then change the initial consonant to make words.

Other variations are possible: Use magnetic letters on a filing cabinet, cookie sheet, or chalkboard to make words. Consider spreading shaving cream on a table or on each student's desk. Have the children write a word from the rime in the cream. With each new word, just wipe away the beginning letter and replace it with a different consonant. Fill a cookie sheet with sand or Jell-O mix. Students write the words in the medium, changing only the beginning of the word. To erase the entire word, simply tap the sides of the tray lightly. This activity works well as a learning center. Remember to have a list of the rimes on hand for the children to refer to.

Finally, create pocket holders for cards. Large tagboard can be folded to hold letter cards in a bottom pocket. The sides can be folded in to create a trifold effect (see Figure 7.5 on page 220). The teacher can call out a specific three-letter word to be formed. Students slip the letter cards into the appropriate pockets. When the words are formed, the teacher calls out "show me." Students turn their pocket folders around for the teacher to check. The following short-vowel rimes are ideal for this activity:

*an  ap  ar  ab  ad  ag  am  at*
*ed  en  et*
*id  in  ig  im  ip  it*
*ob  od  op  og  ot  ow*
*ub  ug  um  un  ut*

**MAKING AND WRITING WORDS** ◆ Rasinski (Rasinski & Padak, 2001) suggests a variation of making words (Cunningham, 1995) in which students use a form sheet to write words (see Figure 7.6 on page 221). In boxes at the top of the sheet, the students are directed to write a list of specified vowels in one box and consonants in the second box. The teacher dictates words that use the specified letters, and the students draw on the boxes at the top of the page to write the words in additional boxes listed on the form. For

### Figure 7.5  Pocket Holder

*Source: Words Their Way: Word Study for Phonics, Vocabulary, and Spelling Instruction,* by D. R. Bear, M. Invernezzi, S. Templeton, and F. Johnston (Upper Saddle River, NJ: Prentice Hall, 1996), p. 182. Reprinted by permission of Pearson Education, Inc., Upper Saddle River, NJ.

example, the vowels *a* and *i* might be listed in the vowel box, and the letters, *s, t, n,* and *b* in the consonant box. The teacher would dictate the following words: *an, in, as, it, sat, sit, bit, ban, tan, tab,* and *tin,* and the students would write them. The last dictated word uses all or most of the letters; *stain,* for example, could be written using the preceding letters. More advanced variations and word parts can add to the complexity of the word activity for older students. Blends, digraphs, prefixes, suffixes, and rimes, for example, can be used.

**CUBE WORDS** ◆ Consonant substitution activities can also be developed using letter cubes (see Figure 7.7 on page 222). Students roll the cubes, using four to six cubes, depending on their ability level. Words are formed with the letters that are rolled. Words are recorded on a sheet of paper that is divided into columns marked with the numbers 1 through 5. Words with one letter are recorded in the first column, words with two letters in the second, and so on. Students can work independently or in pairs. Students who work in pairs may take turns rolling the cubes, forming the words, and writing the words in the appropriate columns. A sand clock or egg timer may be used. When time is up, students review the words and count up the total number of letters used as the score (Bear, Invernizzi, Templeton, & Johnston, 2008).

Once the children have a strong understanding of consonants, they are ready to begin work with consonant digraphs and blends. Many of the same activities done with consonants can be adapted for the digraphs and blends.

**DIGRAPH AND BLEND ACTIONS AND FOOD ASSOCIATIONS** ◆ Association with actions can readily be done with digraphs and blends. The digraphs or blends are written on large cards, and the actions are written or illustrated on the reverse side. When the cards are shown, the children do the corresponding action. Students may take turns or may act out the digraphs or blends all together. Pictures of the foods can also be placed on large cards. Each food can be prepared and shared. The recipes can be added to the class cookbook.

## *Figure 7.6*  Form Sheet for Writing Words

| Vowels | Consonants |
|--------|------------|
|        |            |

| | | |
|---|---|---|
| 1 | 6 | 11 |
| 2 | 7 | 12 |
| 3 | 8 | 13 |
| 4 | 9 | 14 |
| 5 | 10 | 15 |

### Transfer

| | | |
|---|---|---|
| T-1 | T-2 | T-3 |
|     |     |     |

*Source: From Phonics to Fluency: Effective Teaching of Decoding and Reading Fluency in the Elementary School,* by T. V. Rasinskia and N. D. Padak, p. 87. Published by Allyn & Bacon, Boston, MA. Copyright © 2001 by Pearson Education. Reprinted by permission of the publisher.

**Figure 7.7** Letter Cubes

*Source: Words Their Way: Word Study for Phonics, Vocabulary, and Spelling Instruction,* by D. R. Bear, M. Invernezzi, S. Templeton, and F. Johnston (Upper Saddle River, NJ: Prentice Hall, 1996), p. 188. Reprinted by permission of Pearson Education, Inc., Upper Saddle River, NJ.

Here is a list of actions, adapted by Rasinski and Padak (2001) from Cunningham (1987), for digraphs and blends:

| | | | |
|---|---|---|---|
| *ch:* | cheer | *gr:* | grab |
| *sh:* | shiver, shout | *pl:* | plant |
| *th:* | think | *pr:* | pray |
| *wh:* | whistle | *sw:* | swallow |
| *br:* | breathe | *sk:* | skate, skip |
| *bl:* | blow, blink | *sl:* | sleep, slide |
| *cr:* | crawl, cry | *sm:* | smile |
| *cl:* | climb | *sp:* | spin |
| *dr:* | drive | *st:* | stand still, stop |
| *fl:* | fly | *tr:* | track, trip |
| *fr:* | frown | *tw:* | twist |
| *gl:* | glare, glue | | |

The following foods can be used to enhance the teaching of digraphs and blends:

| | | | |
|---|---|---|---|
| *ch:* | chips | *gr:* | graham crackers |
| *sh:* | sherbert | *pl:* | plums |
| *th:* | three-bean salad | *pr:* | prunes |
| *wh:* | white/wheat bread | *sl:* | sloppy joes |
| *bl:* | blueberries | *sp:* | spaghetti |
| *cr:* | cranberries | *str:* | strawberries |

**DIGRAPH TONGUE TWISTERS** ◆ Cunningham (1995) recommends that you create consonant digraph tongue twisters for word learning. The tongue twisters can be written on large chart paper or on sentence strips for easy reference. Children enjoy hearing and reciting the silly sayings such as the examples given here. Be sure to explain the meanings of any difficult words. As part of the activity, have students illustrate the tongue twisters and write sentences to match. Also, have them underline the digraphs at the beginnings of the words on both the large chart paper and on their individual copies.

### Examples of Tongue Twisters

Charles cheerfully chose cherry cheesecake.

Shy Shelly shall shake shells.

Theodore throws thistles through three thickets.

## Analogy-Based Strategies

One of the ways that readers identify unknown words is to read them *by analogy*, or to compare the patterns to known words (Goswami & Bryant, 1990). An analogy-based strategy is based on the premise that words with similar onset and rime patterns also have similar pronunciations. For example, if a reader knew the word *cat*, she would be able to separate it into the *c* onset and *at* rime. Furthermore, the reader would also identify other *c* words such as *cap*, *call*, and *cut*, as well as other *at* words such as *sat*, *hat*, and *rat*.

STANDARD 2.2

Justin, a first grader, was reading the following poem that the teacher and students constructed during an interactive writing lesson.

> In winter it's so nice,
> To slip and slide on the ice,
> Slip-sliding once,
> Slip-sliding twice,
> On ice that's white as rice.

His class had written the poem in their poetry notebooks and recited it each morning as a part of their morning poetry time. Justin was reading through his poems during quiet reading time and was slowly pointing to the words as he read. Each time he came to a word with the *ice* rime, he paused as if deep in thought. His teacher, who was close by, made these observations. "Justin was experiencing an 'aha' moment. He was piecing together what we had been talking about in class. He was making connections between the rhyming words and their letter patterns. It was almost as if I could see his mind separating the onsets and rimes and joining them back together. Justin would pause and say 'n-ice,' 'r-ice,' and 'tw-ice.' Later that day he came upon the word *mice* in a story he was reading. Immediately, he said, 'Look, this is another *ice* word.' He turned to the poem in his poetry notebook and carefully wrote the word *mice* at the bottom."

Each time that Justin pronounced the *ice* words, he left the rime intact. He automatically saw the letters *i-c-e* as a unit. He discovered that it was easier to pronounce the entire rime than to pronounce each sound separately. Because the pronunciations of onsets and rimes are consistent from word to word, it is wise to teach them in these forms.

Rimes are so numerous that teachers will need to select the most frequent patterns their students will encounter. The following list of 38 phonograms, compiled by Fry (1998), provides teachers with a useful resource of high frequency rimes:

| | | | | | | | |
|---|---|---|---|---|---|---|---|
| *ay* | *ag* | *ot* | *ain* | *op* | *ow* | *ob* | *im* |
| *ill* | *ack* | *ing* | *eed* | *in* | *ew* | *ock* | *uck* |
| *ip* | *ank* | *ap* | *y* | *an* | *ore* | *ake* | *um* |
| *at* | *ick* | *unk* | *out* | *est* | *ed* | *ine* | |
| *am* | *ell* | *ail* | *ug* | *ink* | *ab* | *ight* | |

## Figure 7.8  Examples of Onsets and Rimes in Single-Syllable and Multisyllable Words

**Single-Syllable Words**

| onset | + | rime | = | word |
|-------|---|------|---|------|
| l | + | ive | = | live |
| d | + | ark | = | dark |
|  |  | and | = | and |

**Multisyllable Words**

| onset | + | rime | + | onset | + | rime | + | onset | + | rime | = | word |
|-------|---|------|---|-------|---|------|---|-------|---|------|---|------|
| gr | + | and | + | f | + | a | + | th | + | er | = | grandfather |
| f | + | or |  |  | + | est |  |  |  |  | = | forest |
| g | + | ar | + | d | + | en |  |  |  |  | = | garden |
| b | + | e | + | y | + | ond |  |  |  |  | = | beyond |
| m | + | ead | + |  | + | ow |  |  |  |  | = | meadow |

All syllables have a rime. Whereas single-syllable words have only one rime and one onset, multisyllable words have any number of onset and rime combinations. Some words such as *at* and *it* have only a rime. To determine the onsets and rimes within a word, simply break the word apart into syllables. The number of syllables will be equal to the number of vowel sounds heard during the pronunciation of the word. For example, the word *finish* has one onset, *f*, and two rimes, *in* and *ish*. Examples of single and multisyllable words are shown in Figure 7.8.

**THE ANALOGY STRATEGY** ◆ When students have difficulty identifying particular words, analogies can be made with familiar onsets and rimes. Emily, a third grader, was reading a passage from the story *Peter and the Wolf*. She had difficulty with the word *meadow* in the following sentence: "Around Peter's house was a garden and beyond the garden was a meadow." When the word *meadow* is analyzed closely, it can be divided as *m* (onset), *ead* (rime), *ow* (rime). Emily's teacher was quick to see that she was having difficulty with the word and provided her with assistance in this manner:

1. The teacher first covered up the *ow* rime at the end of the word.
2. The teacher asked Emily to think of other words that have the *ead* rime.
3. Emily supplied the words *lead* and *head*.
4. The teacher then asked her to think how *m-ead* would be pronounced.
5. Emily blended the onset and rime together to get /med/.
6. The teacher then had Emily predict what the word could be based on the beginning of the word and the context of the sentence.
7. Emily correctly stated the word *meadow* and then confirmed that it would make sense in the context of the story.

**RIMES IN NURSERY RHYMES** ◆ Nursery rhymes are ideal for onsets and rimes. Poems and rhymes can be printed on large chart paper and posted in the classroom. Particular attention can be paid to the rime and onset patterns. Students can circle or highlight the letter patterns with colorful markers. When the poems are hung in the classroom, the children will easily be able to see the onsets and rimes from a distance. Box 7.5 outlines Rasinski and Padak's (2001) 5-day sequence of activities in which teachers use poetry to introduce two rimes a week. Duthie and Zimet (1992) offer teachers a useful list of poetry anthologies. In addition to poetry, lyrics can be used to teach onsets and rimes. Jacobi-Karna (1995) provides a list of children's books with musical possibilities.

BOX **7.5**

## Research-Based Practices

### Five-Day Sequence for Teaching Word Families

**DAY 1**

- Introduce a high-frequency rime and brainstorm words that contain the same rime and list them on chart paper. The students should practice reading and spelling the words.
- Use repeated readings of poems that have been written on chart paper that include the rime. Choral reading, paired reading, and independent reading should take place throughout the day.
- Give the students copies of the poems to read and practice at home.
- Give the students a list of the words containing the rime; they should write their own poems using the words and share them with classmates and family members.

**DAY 2**

- The students should copy their poems on chart paper and they should be hung around the room.

- Students read the poems from the previous day and the newly created poems on chart paper in a variety of ways: chorally, with a partner, individually. The student created poems can be reproduced and distributed for practice.

**DAY 3**

- Repeat Day 1 with another high-frequency rime. Review of the previous day's poems can also take place.

**DAY 4**

- Repeat Day 2 with the new rime.

**DAY 5**

- Provide the students with lists of words from all of the poetry. They should practice reading them, spelling them, and comparing and contrasting them.
- All of the poetry should be reread in a variety of ways.
- Copies of each poem can be practiced at home.

*Source:* Based on *From Phonics to Fluency: Effective Teaching of Decoding and Reading Fluency in the Elementary School,* by T. V. Rasinski and N. D. Padak, pp. 50–56 (Boston: Allyn & Bacon, 2001).

**MAKING AND WRITING WORDS USING LETTER PATTERNS** ◆ Rasinski (Rasinksi & Padak, 2001) recommends a strategy for older students in which the teacher selects a multisyllabic word that contains several onsets and rimes. Using a form sheet with boxes that contain the onsets and rimes, the students are directed to write words using the patterns. Additional words are recorded in a transfer section on the form sheet. Word sorts and card games can also be played by cutting the boxes apart. For example, beginning with the word *cabinet*, the following onsets would be recorded in boxes at the top of a form sheet: *c, b, t;* the following rimes would also be recorded: *ab, in, et.* Other onsets and rimes would be added, such as *l, r, s* and *ay, ake.* Using the preceding letter combinations, some words that can be made include: *cab, tab, set, bet, let, tin, tray, clay, rake, bake, slab, intake, baker,* and *cabin.* Words could be sorted according to long and short vowel sounds, action words, nouns, and so forth. This activity provides students with practice in using word patterns to decode longer words.

MIDDLE GRADES

**HINK PINKS** ◆ As students begin to explore rimes, they will soon discover creative combinations called "hink pinks" (Cunningham, 1995; Fox, 2004). *Sad dad, bee tree,* and *flat mat* are a few examples of hink pinks. As students encounter these colorful and often unconventional combinations, they can keep a record of them. Lists of hink pinks can be added to personal dictionaries or journals. Favorite examples can be illustrated for a class book or made into pictures for display in the classroom. One variation is to have students write the rimes on sentence strips and then illustrate them on a separate piece of paper. The illustrations and sentence strips can be mixed up and then put back together again. Pictures can be displayed on the bulletin board. Small hooks or thumbtacks could be placed under each picture. The sentence strips could then be matched with the pictures. Definitions can be written for each hink pink. For example, "an unhappy father" would be a *sad dad*, and an "overweight feline" would be a *fat cat*. The rhyming words and their definitions could also be mixed and matched. Hink pinks will not only help students think about rimes and word definitions but also engage them in mind-stretching activities.

## Spelling-Based Strategies

*Spelling-based* strategies for word identification were pioneered by Henderson (1990) and his research associates. These strategies are designed to engage children in word study (Bear et al., 2008). Through the use of *word bank*, *word wall*, and *word sorting* strategies, children examine words and word patterns.

**WORD BANKS** ◆ **Word banks** are boxes or collections of word cards that individual students are studying. Word banks are a natural extension of the language-experience approach in which students learn to read words from dictated stories. Students make word cards from the words in their language-experience stories and study them. A quick way of helping students begin a word bank without using dictation is to have them read a selection that is fairly easy for them. The students underline words they could not immediately recognize, words they cannot figure out, as well as words they consciously used context or mediated strategies to figure out. The students then write each of these words on cards. Words for word banks can also be gleaned from basal readers, trade books, signs, labels, and other print with which the children are involved. Words in the word banks can then be used in word sorting activities, as we will describe shortly.

**WORD WALLS** ◆ Another way to study words and word patterns is through **word walls.** A word wall may be started when students notice words that rhyme but are not spelled with the same letter patterns. For example, in Susan Valenti's second-grade classroom, the students participated in a shared-book experience as the teacher read Shel Silverstein's "Enter This Deserted House." In this poem, the poet rhymes the words *do, too, blue,* and *few* as he creates for readers young and old the eerie feeling of entering a deserted house.

As Susan read the poem, the students noticed that *do, too, blue,* and *few* all rhymed but were not spelled with the same letter pattern. So Susan and her class started a word wall for this sound. The word wall was constructed on a sheet of shelf paper hung on the wall. Students were asked to find words for each of the spellings of the sound /oo/. The following are some of the words they found:

| *do* | *too* | *blue* | *few* |
|------|-------|--------|-------|
| to | tool | clue | dew |
| | fool | sue | |

Word walls may be adapted for a variety of word study purposes at different grade levels. Kindergarten classrooms, for example, often begin word walls by listing the letters of the alphabet in large, bright letters. **High-frequency words,** words that occur repeatedly in text, are added to the wall underneath the letters of the alphabet. Tonya, a kindergarten teacher, uses poetry to highlight specific words for the wall. Each week Tonya introduces a poem, chant, or rhyme. She selects three focus words from the poem to add to the wall. When her students learned the nursery rhyme "Jack and Jill," they focused on the words *pail, water,* and *Jack.* The words were written on colored construction paper and cut out along letter boundaries. Illustrations were added as an aid to word identification. The words were stapled underneath the beginning letter, where they served as a reference for the children's reading and writing all year long. Primary grade word walls may also include words that are high-frequency sight words, that follow a specific rime or phonogram pattern, or that are commonly used in the children's writing.

Intermediate and middle-level teachers often target homophones, compound words, or commonly misspelled words for students to reference. Words that are part of a theme or topic may also be emphasized for word study on a classroom word wall. A sixth-grade

class studying the Civil War included words such as *slavery, Confederate, secede, union, soldier,* and *battlefield* on the word wall.

Word walls may be permanent or temporary. They may stay up for the entire school year or only for a particular unit of study. They can be written on sentence strips, word cards, poster board, or chart paper. Charts are ideal for classrooms with limited space. They may be displayed when needed and then stored away when not in use. The charts can be put back on display for review or comparisons with other word study charts.

Portable word walls can be made with file folders. Manila folders can be divided into categories according to alphabet, letter patterns, rimes, themes, and so on. Students can copy words onto the folder for personal reference at home or school. This technique may be especially helpful for intermediate grades in which students are in different classrooms each day. In addition, word walls can be individually created by ELL students as they develop their personal study of words.

**WORD SORTING** ◆ Word sorting activities are another way to engage students in studying words. When sorting words, students look for similarities in words, including letter pattern similarities.

There are two kinds of word sorts: open and closed. In both, children are guided toward *discovering* similarities in words, rather than *being told* how they are alike.

For open word sorts, the following steps are suggested:

1. Each child in a small group has a word bank. Sorting activities can be done with children seated on the floor or at a table.
2. The children are asked to go through their word banks and group some words that go together in some way.
3. After grouping words, each child tells what words he or she has grouped. Then another student "reads his or her mind" by telling how the group of words is alike.
4. In open word sorts, there is no one correct answer. Students just have to be able to explain why they grouped words as they did. For example, Jill grouped *top, tickle, to,* and *terrible* because they all begin with the letter *t*. John sorted *tomato, potato, tomorrow,* and *butterfly* because they all have three syllables. Sue sorted *mother, father, sister,* and *brother* because they are all family members. Helen classified *pretty, ugly, green,* and *fat* together because they all describe something. Notice that students can sort words by attributes concerning letter–sound relationships, the meanings of the words, or their functions in sentences.

In closed word sorts, the students try to group words according to a specific attribute the teacher has in mind. There is a correct way to sort the words in closed sorts. The students figure out what that correct way is.

The ability to generalize from the known to the unknown is a fundamental aspect of all word analysis. The closed word sort is an excellent way to get students to think about letter patterns in words. As students are learning the consonants and consonant blends, they can sort pictures of objects beginning with those consonants and consonant blends.

Students can also group words by letter patterns. By having students sort words into groups of those with the same letter patterns, you are teaching the process of looking for letter patterns; you are not just teaching individual letter patterns. The purpose in having students sort words by letter patterns is to encourage them to look for graphic similarities in words. Students can also be given word cards with letter patterns that are not similar, or a harder task is to have students sort word cards with letter patterns that are somewhat similar.

**HAVE-A-GO** ◆ The Have-a-Go strategy originated in Australia and was made popular in the United States by Regie Routman (1991). The strategy involves the use of a Have-a-Go sheet to record words from children's daily writing that are particularly challenging

## Figure 7.9  Have-a-Go Sheet

| Word | Attempt 1 | Attempt 2 | Correct Spelling |
|------|-----------|-----------|------------------|
|      |           |           |                  |
|      |           |           |                  |
|      |           |           |                  |
|      |           |           |                  |
|      |           |           |                  |
|      |           |           |                  |

to spell. Students choose misspelled words from their work and then "have a go" at the standard spelling.

Here's how the strategy works: The students write the words they think they misspelled in the first column of the Have-a-Go sheet (see Figure 7.9). Then they attempt to improve on the spelling in the second and third columns as they meet with the teacher for additional instruction. Each of the students schedules time to meet in conference with the teacher to discuss these misspellings.

Alyson Meyer's use of the Have-a-Go strategy is explained in the Straight from the Classroom featured in Box 7.6.

# Using Meaning and Letter–Sound Information to Identify Words

Some preschool children develop an expectation that print should make sense. They have heard stories frequently read to them and are immersed in a language-rich environment. These young children rely heavily on pictures or other aspects of the immediate situation in deciding what printed words say.

As children develop as readers, they learn to use with greater sophistication various kinds of *meaning and letter–sound information from the text itself*. When readers use information surrounding unknown words as an aid to word identification, they are using context or context clues. Although the issue of reliance on context for word identification has been the focus of debate among reading researchers, there is agreement that skilled readers understand that reading must make sense (Juel & Minden-Cupp, 2000; Snow, Burns, & Griffin, 1998).

## Strategies for Teaching Context

Readers use meaning clues to identify words they have heard but may not have experienced visually in print. When readers can combine meaning clues with phonic information, they have developed a powerful tool for word identification. The following activities help show readers how to use the *context* of a sentence or passage.

**HOMEWORK EXERCISE: VIDEO**

Go to the Homework and Exercises section in Chapter 7 of MyEducationLab to watch the video entitled "Word Analysis Strategy" and explore strategies you can use to teach context.

STANDARD
2.2

BOX **7.6**

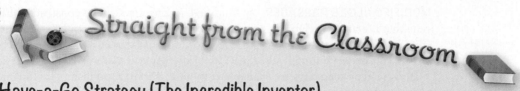

Straight from the Classroom

## The Have-a-Go Strategy (The Incredible Inventor)

Alyson Meyer uses the Have-a-Go technique with her third graders. Although she calls it an "Incredible Inventor" sheet, the idea behind it is the same. She changed the name of Have-a-Go because children were not familiar with the Australian expression.

Alyson's students keep their Incredible Inventor sheet in their writing folder, where it can be readily accessed during personal writing time and writing conferences (see accompanying figure). Students add words that they had trouble spelling to the first column of their Incredible Inventor sheet during the first draft of their writing.

After writing, the students meet in conference with Alyson. They bring their writing journals and Incredible Inventor sheets to the conference. One aspect of writing conference time is discussing the words on the Incredible Inventor sheets. Some children may have four or five words to discuss with her; others may have twice that many. Alyson will guide the students toward standard spellings of the words with comments such as "You're missing a letter here. What do you think it might be?" or "Think about how to spell the word _____. Part of this word is the same." She never just gives the students the correct answer but instead leads them to a better understanding of word and letter patterns. If a student is at a dead end, she leads them by writing three possible spellings of a word and then gives them the chance to select the word that looks correct.

During one writing conference, a student had misspelled the word *skate*, writing *skait* instead. Alyson guided the con-

ference by saying, "I see that you used a common word pattern for the long *a* sound, but that's not the right pattern for this word. Think of another spelling pattern for long *a*." The student then suggested both the *ay* and *a*–silent *e* patterns. The student experimented with both combinations in the "first attempt" and "second attempt" columns of the Incredible Inventor sheet and decided that the *a*–silent *e* pattern was the correct one for this particular word. The fourth column is reserved for the conventional spelling of the word.

After the writing conference, students then correct their own writing, using what they learned during conference time. Alyson knows that her students learn best when they are given the opportunity to experiment with letter and word patterns and when they are challenged to discover spelling conventions. The Have-a-Go strategy provides a framework to experiment with and explore words so that students can gain a deeper understanding of the English language and its conventions.

### REFLECTIVE INQUIRY

- After the students have recorded the correct spelling for words on the Incredible Inventor worksheet, how might they store the words for review at a later time?
- How would you assess the students' spelling progress using this strategy?

| Word | Attempt 1 | Attempt 2 | Correct Spelling |
|---|---|---|---|
| Squorrl | Squrorl  *i* | Squrriol  *Squirrel* | Squirrel ☺ |
| Champatison | Campatison  *tion* | *competition* Campation | competition |
| Srink | Shrink ☺ | | Shrink |
| algaba | alg*e*bra | algebra ☺ | algebra |
| wagen | wagen | wag*o*n | wagon |
| Scopian | Scorpion ☺ | | Scorpion |
| mountian | mantion | mountain ☺ | mountain |
| | | | |
| | | | |

**MODIFIED CLOZE PASSAGES** ◆ Modified *cloze passages* can be constructed from materials that are at first relatively easy to read. The material used can be stories and poems from basal readers, language-experience stories, other student-written products, or subject matter texts. Gradually, the difficulty of the reading material can be increased. Note that cloze-type materials are available commercially from publishing companies. However, teachers often produce the most effective cloze passages because they are in the best position to gear the material to the needs of their students.

Cloze activities can contain as little as 1 deletion in a sentence or up to 20 deletions in a passage. There are different deletion systems: selective word deletion, systematic word deletion, and partial word deletion. The kind of deletion system used determines what aspects of the passage are focused on as students complete the cloze passages and discuss their responses.

Using *selective word deletion*, important nouns, verbs, adjectives, and adverbs can be left out. These words carry the meaning of the context of what the author is saying. When selected nouns, verbs, adjectives, and adverbs are deleted, the focus is on meaningful information from the passage.

In *systematic word deletion*, every *n*th word in a passage is deleted—for example, every fifth, tenth, or twentieth word. When such a cloze deletion system is used as a teaching device, many function words will be deleted. Consider the following examples: "Bill went _____ the hill." Did Bill go up, down, or around the hill? The students must deduce appropriate words from the context of the rest of the passage.

In *partial word deletion*, every *n*th word or selected word is partially deleted. Three types of partial deletions can be used: (1) Initial consonants, initial consonant blends, digraphs, or initial vowels are given, and all other letters are deleted. (2) The letters mentioned in option 1 plus terminal consonants or terminal consonant digraphs are given, and all other letters are deleted. (3) Consonants are given and vowels are deleted.

Cloze passages in which only the initial letters are given help children understand that initial letters serve to reduce the number of meaningful substitutions available. The discussion of this type of cloze would include how useful the content plus some graphic information can be.

**CLOZE WITH CHOICES GIVEN** ◆ If students find it difficult to complete cloze activities, giving choices for the deleted words makes the task easier. Here are some different procedures to use in devising the choices for the cloze blanks.

1. The incorrect item, or *foil*, can be a different part of speech as well as different graphically.

   The doctor was _____ that the patient got better so quickly.
   MONKEY / AMAZED

2. The foil can be graphically similar to the correct item but a different part of speech.

   The doctor was _____ that the patient got better so quickly.
   AMAZON / AMAZED

3. The foil and correct answer can be graphically similar and the same part of speech.

   The doctor was _____ that the patient got better so quickly.
   AMUSED / AMAZED

4. Three choices can also be given: the correct response, a word of the same part of speech that is graphically similar, and a word of a different part of speech that is graphically similar.

   The doctor was _____ that the patient got better so quickly.
   AMAZED / AMUSED / AMAZON

A discussion of these particular cloze examples would include a discussion of why a doctor would be more likely to be amazed than amused by a patient's progress in getting well. Students would also note that "The doctor was amazon that the patient got better so quickly" makes no sense.

**GUESSING GAMES** ◆ Guessing games can be played to help students use visual and meaning clues to identify unknown words. Teachers can read riddles and have students guess solutions based on visual hints, such as beginning letters, as well as meaning hints. For example, a teacher might say, "I am thinking of a color word that begins with *r*. Apples are often this color." For older students, Hall (1995) devised a guessing game in which students work in teams to guess sentences of seven to fifteen words. A variation of the activity works like this:

1. The teacher selects sentences from stories or constructs sentences that have strong meaning clues (e.g., "This evening we played baseball, and our team lost.").
2. One key word is selected from the sentence to provide a schema (e.g., *baseball*).
3. Blank lines that represent each word in the sentence are written on the board and numbered. The key word is written in the appropriate blank.

| ___ | ___ | ___ | ___ | baseball, | ___ | ___ | ___ | ___ |
|---|---|---|---|---|---|---|---|---|
| 1 | 2 | 3 | 4 | 5 | 6 | 7 | 8 | 9 |

4. Two "free" cards are given to each of two or three teams that they can use to ask the teacher the beginning letters of two words during the game.
5. Members of each team discuss possible words and when it is a team's turn, a spokesperson calls out a number and guesses a word. If the word is correct, the team scores 2 points (e.g., if the spokesperson said that number 8 is *team*, 2 points would be scored). If the word is not correct, it is the next team's turn.
6. Teams may ask for a beginning letter of a word (e.g., What does number 9 begin with? Answer is *l*). If the team guesses the correct word after the letter is given, 1 point is scored. Free cards may also be used to ask for the second letter of a word if the first letter is already given.
7. The game continues until the sentence has been correctly identified. Points are tallied for each team.

During this game, the teacher encourages students to use graphic as well as meaning clues to guess words. The purpose of the game is to foster an awareness of graphic and meaning clues that can be used to identify unknown words.

**INFERRING WORD MEANINGS THROUGH CONTEXT CLUES** ◆ Buikema and Graves (1993) suggest a 5-day instructional strategy for older students that uses teacher modeling to unlock word meanings based on context clues. On day 1, the teacher introduces riddles as a motivating way to engage students in using context. Day 2 focuses on students' attempts to write their own riddles with discussion about riddle cues that help to infer unknown words. On day 3, the teacher presents key sentences that substitute nonsense words for unknown words. The students list words in the sentences that are clues to the meaning of the word. A four-step strategy on this day includes (1) boxing the unknown nonsense word, (2) listing words in the sentence that give clues to the unknown word, (3) jotting down thoughts about what the unknown word means, and (4) guessing the unknown word. Day 4 includes more practice examples, and day 5 includes a review session and student demonstrations of the strategy.

Strategies in which teachers use modeling to demonstrate how context clues can be used to identify words need to be planned and explicit. The Buikema and Graves (1993) strategy is an example of an effective systematic way to teach word identification using context clues.

## Cross-Checking and Self-Monitoring Strategies

*Cross-checking* and *self-monitoring* strategies help readers combine letter–sound and meaning information to make sense while reading. **Cross-checking** simply involves rereading

a sentence or two to "cross-check"—confirm, modify, or reject—probable pronunciations of unknown words encountered during reading. If the sentence makes sense, the meaning confirms the reader's cross-checking; if the sentence doesn't make sense, the reader tries again.

The cross-checking strategy takes little preparation and is very effective for teaching word identification in meaningful contexts. For example, notice how cross-checking brings together students' knowledge of digraph sounds and the use of context clues for decoding words. On large chart paper, sentence strips, or the overhead, write sentences similar to the ones given here. Cunningham (1995), a proponent of cross-checking, notes that children love to see their names used in the sentences, so make sure to include them.

Roderiquez likes to eat <u>chocolate chip</u> cookies.

Kate likes to have <u>wheat</u> bread for her sandwiches.

Zachary likes to eat <u>sherbert</u> on a hot day.

Tamika is good at <u>throwing</u> Frisbees.

Miguel <u>cheers</u> for his team to win.

Cover the underlined word in each sentence with a sticky note or index card. Have the students read the sentence and predict what words would make sense in the blank spot. Reveal just the initial digraph and have the children check their predictions, crossing out any that do not begin with the specific digraph. Record new words that make sense and begin with the digraph. Finally, uncover the word and see if any of the predictions match the original word.

Cross-checking, even at the earliest stages of development, is crucial in learning to read. When a teacher places a high premium on students' word-perfect oral reading performance, young developing readers are at risk of not developing strategies for **self-monitoring.** Such readers become dependent on the teacher or other able readers to help them when they encounter a hard word.

Another way to help children self-monitor is to discuss with them what to do when they come to unknown words. When children attempt to figure out unknown words in text, encourage them to use meaning and letter–sound information. Direct the process by fostering a search for information cues as described in the previous section. Help children monitor their searches by using a chart similar to the one in Figure 7.10. Explain the procedures listed on the chart and let children practice using them.

# Using Structural Analysis to Identify Words

**Structural analysis** involves identifying words through meaningful units such as prefixes, suffixes, and root words. The smallest meaningful unit of a word is a **morpheme.** In the word *unhappy*, there are two morphemes: *un* which means "not" and *happy* which means "joyful." Structural analysis also includes **inflected endings,** which are suffixes that change the tense or degree of a word but not its meaning. Examples of inflected endings are listed below:

| | |
|---|---|
| *ing* as in *going* | *s* as in *books* |
| *d* as in *saved* | *es* as in *dresses* |
| *ed* as in *looked* | *ly* as in *slowly* |
| *er* as in *smaller* | *est* as in *tallest* |

In addition, structural analysis includes compound words and contractions.

*Figure 7.10*  Monitoring an Unknown Word

## Strategies for Teaching Structural Analysis

When word identification strategies include teaching children how to identify prefixes, suffixes, root words, inflected endings, compound words, and contractions, children have a larger repertoire of methods to help them recognize unknown words (Bear et al., 2008; Bromley, 2007; Carlisle & Stone, 2005; Cunningham, 2005; Fox, 2004; Rasinski & Padak, 2001; Savage, 2004). The following activities will help children use structural analysis.

**WORD STUDY NOTEBOOK** ◆ Model for students how prefixes and suffixes can change the meanings of words and help determine the meanings of other words. For example, *bi + cycle* = a two-wheeler, and *tri + cycle* = a three-wheeler. As prefixes, suffixes, and root words are introduced, have students brainstorm other words that contain the same elements and add them to a word study notebook that has a section reserved for this type of word analysis. Following is a list of some of the more commonly used prefixes, suffixes, and root words and their meanings (Bromly, 2007; Savage, 2004).

**Prefixes**

| | | | |
|---|---|---|---|
| *re* | again | *anti* | against |
| *auto* | self | *com* | together, with |
| *un* | not | *dis* | apart |
| *ex* | out | *pre* | before |

**Suffixes**

| | | | |
|---|---|---|---|
| *ly* | the quality of | *less* | without |
| *ist* | one who does | *ful* | full |
| *ment* | quality or act | *ship* | ability or skill |
| *able* | capable of | *er* | more |

**Roots**

| | | | |
|---|---|---|---|
| *dict* | say | *port* | carry |
| *scrib* | write | *cred* | believe |
| *vid* | see | *spect* | look |
| *aud* | hear | *rupt* | break |

**WALL CHART CAROUSEL** ◆ Tack four sheets of chart paper on each of four walls of the classroom. In the center of each sheet of paper print a prefix large enough for everyone to see. Divide the class into small groups of four or five, provide each group with a marker, and allow one person per group to be the "recorder." Each group should stand by one of the prefix charts. At the signal "go" each group should record as many words as they can on the chart, making a web. Allow one minute. At the signal "stop," the students should rotate to the next chart and when they hear "go" they should record additional words. Continue until each group has rotated to each chart. Discussion can take place regarding the meanings of the recorded words. For the prefix *un,* for example, the following words might be recorded: *unlike, unnecessary, unlock, uncover, undo, unhappy, unsaid, untrue,* and discussion would focus on the meaning *not* for each word. As a follow-up to the activity, a guessing game can be played with each chart. Using the above words, the teacher (or a student) might say, "I spy a word that means sad, what could it be?" or "I spy a word that means not needed, what could it be?"

**COMPOUND WORD CUPS** ◆ Large Styrofoam coffee cups when stacked in sets of two are easy to twist when their lips fit together (Rasinski & Padak, 2001). On the lip of the inner cup write with indelible marker the first half of a compound word. On the lip of the outer cup write the second half of the word. For example, on the inner lip write *base* and on the outer lip write *ball.* Other words on the same set of cups might include: *bedroom, toothbrush, cupcake, doorbell, wallpaper.* A variety of activities can be played depending on how many cup sets are available. For example, if everyone in the class or group has a cup set, a variation of musical chairs can be played. Sitting in a circle, when music is played, each student passes his cup to the left. When the music stops, each person must form a compound word by twisting the cups and taking turns reading the words. In addition to playing the game, a word wall is a useful way for students to share compound words that they find in printed material during the school day.

**CONTRACTION SEARCH** ◆ To foster quick identification of contractions and word pairs that can be transformed into contractions, distribute junk mail, old newspapers, or magazines and have the students highlight all of the contractions and word pairs that can become contractions that they find. Using a section of a word study notebook, students can keep track of the contractions by recording them in two columns: One column contains a list of contractions; the other consists of the word pairs.

## Rapid Recognition of Words

There is more to rapid word identification than flashing a sight-word card and requiring an instant response. Immediate identification of words is the result of *experience with* reading, seeing, discussing, using, and writing words.

Several reasons are usually given for beginning word identification with whole words. One is that students learn to recognize words by their *configuration* (their length and general contour or shape). The configuration of a word, however, has been shown to be a low-utility cue in word identification (Marchbanks & Levin, 1965). A word's general contour loses its usefulness because many words have similar configurations.

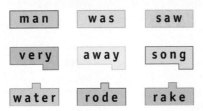

Configuration clues may be more useful for unusual-looking words. For example, we may speculate that words such as *elephant* and *McDonald's* are quickly identified by young children because of their distinctive shapes. Yet we may also argue that words such as these are identified automatically by a child because they are charged with personal meaning.

Durkin (1980) suggested whole word methodology at the outset of reading instruction on the following grounds: Whole word learning allows children to sense "real reading" quickly. It can also be of greatest interest to most children, because they are apt to be familiar with the concept of a *word* rather than linguistic concepts associated with phonics, such as *letter* or *sound*.

## High-Frequency Words

Numerous lists of high-frequency words have been compiled. Figure 7.11 on pages 236–237 contains Edward Fry's "instant words." According to Fry (1980), the first 100 instant words on his list make up half of all written material, and the 300 words make up 65 percent of all written text.

High-frequency word lists contain a large number of words that are grammatically necessary—words such as articles, conjunctions, pronouns, verbs of being, and prepositions that bind together information-bearing words. These words are called *function words*; they do much to help a sentence function, but they do not get across the meaning of a passage by themselves. Nouns, action verbs, adjectives, and adverbs are *content words*; they supply the content or information of the topic.

Compare the following paragraphs to get a better idea of how these two types of words work together in running print.

**Paragraph 1**

Once upon a _____ there was a _____ _____ _____ _____. One _____ _____ _____ an _____ in the _____. _____ _____, "An _____ _____ has a _____ of _____. I'll _____ this _____ _____ me to his _____ of _____."

**Paragraph 2**

_____ _____ _____ time _____ _____ _____ mean man named Grumble. _____ day Grumble saw _____ elf _____ _____ woods. Grumble said, "_____ elf always _____ _____ pot _____ gold. _____ make _____ elf take _____ _____ _____ pot _____ gold."

**BUILDING TEACHING SKILLS: CASE STUDY**

Go to the Homework and Exercises section in Chapter 7 of MyEducationLab to work through a case study and develop a deeper understanding of using sight words.

# Figure 7.11  The Instant Words

## First Hundred

| WORDS 1–25 | WORDS 26–50 | WORDS 51–75 | WORDS 76–100 |
|---|---|---|---|
| the | or | will | number |
| of | one | up | no |
| and | had | other | way |
| a | by | about | could |
| to | word | out | people |
| in | but | many | my |
| is | not | then | than |
| you | what | them | first |
| that | all | these | water |
| it | were | so | been |
| he | we | some | call |
| was | when | her | who |
| for | your | would | oil |
| on | can | make | now |
| are | said | like | find |
| as | there | him | long |
| with | use | into | down |
| his | an | time | day |
| they | each | has | did |
| I | which | look | get |
| at | she | two | come |
| be | do | more | made |
| this | how | write | may |
| have | their | go | part |
| from | if | see | over |

Common suffixes: *-s, -ing, -ed*

## Second Hundred

| WORDS 101–125 | WORDS 126–150 | WORDS 151–175 | WORDS 176–200 |
|---|---|---|---|
| new | great | put | kind |
| sound | where | end | hand |
| take | help | does | picture |
| only | through | another | again |
| little | much | well | change |
| work | before | large | off |
| know | line | must | play |
| place | right | big | spell |
| year | too | even | air |
| live | mean | such | away |
| me | old | because | animal |
| back | any | turn | house |
| give | same | here | point |
| most | tell | why | page |
| very | boy | ask | letter |
| after | follow | went | mother |
| thing | came | men | answer |
| our | want | read | found |
| just | show | need | study |
| name | also | land | still |
| good | around | different | learn |
| sentence | form | home | should |

*(Continued)*

# Figure 7.11 *(Continued)*

| WORDS 101–125 | WORDS 126–150 | WORDS 151–175 | WORDS 176–200 |
|---|---|---|---|
| man | three | us | America |
| think | small | move | world |
| say | set | try | high |

Common suffixes: *-s, -ing, -ed, -er, -ly, -est*

## Third Hundred

| WORDS 201–225 | WORDS 226–250 | WORDS 251–275 | WORDS 276–300 |
|---|---|---|---|
| every | left | until | idea |
| near | don't | children | enough |
| add | few | side | eat |
| food | while | feet | face |
| between | along | car | watch |
| own | might | mile | far |
| below | close | night | Indian |
| country | something | walk | real |
| plant | seem | white | almost |
| last | next | sea | let |
| school | hard | began | above |
| father | open | grow | girl |
| keep | example | took | sometimes |
| tree | begin | river | mountain |
| never | life | four | cut |
| start | always | carry | young |
| city | those | state | talk |
| earth | both | once | soon |
| eye | paper | book | list |
| light | together | hear | song |
| thought | got | stop | leave |
| head | group | without | family |
| under | often | second | body |
| story | run | late | music |
| saw | important | miss | color |

Common suffixes: *-s, -ing, -ed, -er, -ly, -est*

Source: *Elementary Reading Instruction,* by E. Fry (New York: McGraw-Hill, 1977).

When reading paragraph 1, can you tell what the paragraph is about? All of the content or information-bearing words were taken out. When reading paragraph 2, at the very least you know that the story is about a mean man named Grumble and an elf. By studying paragraph 2, you might even have figured out that Grumble wanted to take the elf's pot of gold.

In addition to what are considered traditional high-frequency function words, contemporary technology use by K–12 students demands another level of high-frequency words that teachers need to consider when teaching rapid recognition of words. See the New Literacies Box 7.7 on page 238 for a list of words that students typically need to recognize when using the computer.

## Strategies for Teaching Function Words

Function words, or high-frequency words, such as *was, there, the, has,* and *of* should be taught as sight words early in children's reading instruction. The rationale for teaching rapid recognition of these words is this: Beginning readers who can quickly and accurately

STANDARD
2.2

## BOX **7.7**

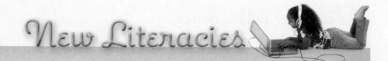

### WORDS FOR TODAY'S STUDENTS

As computer-based literacy learning continues to emerge in our ever-changing world of technological innovations, it behooves teachers to develop lessons that consider high-frequency words that students must be able to identify when navigating work on the computer. It makes sense that teachers model the words and what they "do" on the computer, as well as provide students with multiple opportunities to demonstrate their understanding of what the words mean. The following list serves as a starting point for sight-word vocabulary development that will enhance students' ability to navigate on the computer:

| | | | |
|---|---|---|---|
| enter | save | send | volume |
| file | backspace | screen | send |
| save as | view | program | print |
| cancel | edit | insert | format |
| font | tools | tab | bullet |
| layout | document | delete | home |
| scroll | play | game | shift |

identify high-frequency words will more readily read across *any line of print,* because these words make up 65 percent or more of *all* written material. Another reason children need to be taught high-frequency function words as sight words is that a large number of these words are not phonically regular. Words such as *the, one,* and *of* do not conform to predictable letter–sound associations. Consider the following strategies for teaching high-frequency words.

**LANGUAGE-EXPERIENCE STRATEGY** ◆ After providing the students with an experience, the teacher has students dictate captions describing the activities that are written on chart paper. For example, following a nature walk, Jan, a first-grade teacher, had her students dictate what they saw.

> I *saw* an oak tree.
>
> I *saw* a squirrel.
>
> I *saw* some poison ivy.

The students can read the story in unison or the teacher can provide individual copies of the captions. Students can highlight the word *saw* in this example, locate the word *saw* in books and poems, write the word *saw* in personal dictionaries, and/or add the word *saw* to a word wall. Language-experience activities provide students with a meaningful context in which to learn high-frequency words.

**WORD WALLS** ◆ Rasinski and Padak (2001) recommend introducing children to sight words using a word wall. After introducing five words per week, teachers can have the students chant the words in loud voices, soft voices, grumpy voices, and so on. The word wall becomes an instant reference for high-frequency words. Teachers can also provide students with individual word walls of sight words that are kept in pocket folders for easy reference.

**ENVIRONMENTAL PRINT** ◆ As teachers introduce high-frequency words, children can locate the words in environmental print. Teachers can provide students with junk mail, magazines, newspapers, cereal boxes, and paper place mats, for example. The students can circle words they are learning or highlight the words with markers. When environmental print sources are laminated, they can be reused with washable markers and placed in a learning center. This activity provides students with practice reading the words in a meaningful context.

**WORD GAMES** ◆ Children enjoy word games that reinforce reading high-frequency words. Adaptations of games such as bingo, Go Fish, Concentration, and Memory can serve as motivating ways to help children practice sight-word recognition. Teachers can, for example, provide students with blank bingo grids on which the children write words from a word wall. As the teacher calls words, the students use markers to identify them.

**LITERATURE AND POETRY** ◆ After introducing several sight words, teachers can provide children with a variety of books and poems. Students are encouraged to "spy" the sight words in the literature and read sentences and phrases in which the sight words are found. A word wall chart can be used to record the sentences and phrases the students "spy." Students can then highlight the words on the chart.

When teaching high-frequency words, it is important that teachers provide children with multiple opportunities to read the words in meaningful contexts. Children need to see that these words occur in print in a variety of settings.

## Teaching Key Words

One of the quickest and most interesting ways to ease children into reading is through key word teaching. **Key words** are a fundamental aspect of language-experience instruction. Key words are charged with personal meaning and feeling, for they come out of the experience and background of the child. The concept of key words emerged from the work of Sylvia Ashton-Warner (1959, 1963, 1972). Key words become the core of what might be traditionally called *sight-word development*. The emphasis in learning words is to tie instruction to meaningful activity through *seeing, discussing, using, defining, and writing* words.

Ashton-Warner (1972) suggested that each child keep a file or word bank of special personal words drawn both from personal experiences and experiences with literature. The word cards could be used in the following way. The personal word cards of a group of children are jumbled together. The children sort out their own word cards and read them to each other before placing them back into their files. Cards that are not recognized are left out and later discarded. Thus the words kept by each child retain personal meaning and use.

**GROUP ACTIVITIES WITH KEY WORDS** ◆ There are many useful strategies for key word instructional activities in small groups (Veatch, Sawicki, Elliot, Flake, & Blakey, 1979). Consider the following, all of which are excellent word learning activities for ELL students.

- *Classifying words.* Select a topic according to a classification (e.g., desserts, television characters, funny words, places, scary words). All of the children who have a dessert word, for example, would stand in one area of the room. The teacher might want to label the area with a sheet of paper marked *dessert*. Children who have words of other classifications also stand in their designated areas. (See word sorting activities in this chapter.)
- *Relating words.* If one child has the word *cake* and another the word *knife*, a child might relate the words by saying, "A knife can cut a cake." The teacher should try to get the children to relate words by asking questions such as "What can my word do to the cake?" "How can my word be used with the cake?" "Is there something that

STANDARD
2.1

my word can do with the cake?" The teacher can continue this by asking the children, "Does someone else have a word that can be used with the word *cake*?"

- *Learning a partner's words.* Each child chooses a partner, and they teach each other their own words.
- *Coauthoring.* Two or more children get together and combine their words or ideas to make longer words or stories from their original words or ideas.
- *Acting out words.* If the key word is conducive to acting out, a child could dramatize the word for the other children to guess.

**HOMEWORK EXERCISE: ARTIFACTS**

Go to the Homework and Exercises section in Chapter 7 of MyEducationLab to view one student's word list and consider what the artifact might say about how this student is learning.

# Balancing Word Identification Instruction

Learning to read cannot be limited to experiences with words alone. Throughout this chapter we have emphasized that children need to have ample experiences with books, frequent encounters with oral and printed language, and early opportunities to write. Furthermore, teaching students word recognition strategies ought to relate to their developmental needs. There is no "one-size-fits-all" approach to teaching word identification. Some kindergartners come to school reading; some middle school students are not proficient readers. Teachers need to observe how their students approach words and text and make instructional decisions based on those observations. Observe how Mrs. Bourn, the literacy coach in Box 7.8, coaches first-grade teacher Chuck to develop his own instructional skills in order to make his instruction for the children more effective.

In addition, engaging children and young adolescents with technology software and applicable web sites has the potential to enhance word identification and literacy skills. Although there is yet to be a strong research base for the effectiveness of technology applications and word recognition, we do know that many children and young adolescents are motivated by computer activities that are designed to teach reading skills (Leu, 2002b; National Institute of Child Health and Human Development, 2000).

In this chapter we have discussed the major components of teaching children how to identify words through explicit, systematic phonics instruction including onset and rime recognition; the early development of sight-word knowledge; how to use structural analysis; and instruction in how to use context clues. There are countless web sites that reinforce these skills. There are stories that teachers can download, interactive games in which students can engage in active learning, and word recognition resource materials for teachers including lessons, flash cards, worksheets, and ideas for games. Valmont (2003) provides teachers with a comprehensive and practical look at teaching literacy word recognition skills using technology. Butler-Pascoe and Wiburg (2003) provide an equally extensive perspective on using technology to teach English language learners. We invite you to view some web sites that address word study at the end of this chapter.

In addition to online resources, there is a myriad of software programs that engage students in word learning. Fox (2003) recommends that teachers and preservice teachers consider the following when selecting software for supporting learning words:

- Develop a checklist of your goals that will help you evaluate the software.
- Consider whether the software is child friendly.
- Preview the software and observe children using it.
- Consider what the parents think about the software.
- Consider whether the software is teacher friendly.

BOX 7.8

# Viewpoint

## the Literacy Coach
### Using Phonics Instruction Effectively

It is October and Chuck, a newly hired first-grade teacher, is required to use a scripted phonics program. He is frustrated because many of the first graders are not engaged during the lessons. He asked Mrs. Bourn, the literacy coach, to observe a lesson and guide him toward motivating his students to enjoy learning to read.

During the 20-minute lesson, Mrs. Bourn observed Chuck read a script that focused on the /at/ rime. Although he read the script accurately, his voice was monotone and she noticed that Chuck did not seem particularly involved with the lesson. Mrs. Bourn also observed that although the majority of the children were initially on task as Chuck prompted them to recite words such as *bat, cat, rat,* and *fat,* midway through the lesson several of the students were yawning or had their heads on their desks.

After the lesson, the following conversation took place between Mrs. Bourn and Chuck:

MRS. BOURN: Well, what did you think about the lesson, Chuck?

CHUCK: Frankly, I don't like these scripts. The children don't seem to understand the purpose of reciting them and they appear bored.

MRS. BOURN: Okay. What could we do to help them understand the purpose of the lessons? How could we make the lessons more meaningful?

CHUCK: I really don't know. We are required to read them 20 minutes a day but it seems like a waste of time since they don't "get it."

MRS. BOURN: Well, let's talk about the purpose of this particular lesson. It was to teach the /at/ rime, correct?

CHUCK: That's right.

MRS. BOURN: But you don't think the students understood the idea?

CHUCK: No, I don't think so. Maybe some of them did.

MRS. BOURN: What do you think is the purpose of teaching rimes, Chuck, in this case the /at/ rime?

CHUCK: So they can read words that have that rime.

MRS. BOURN: Okay. Maybe we could locate or write some poetry that uses the rime. Or maybe we could find a Dr. Seuss book. The idea would be to engage the children in a fun read-aloud first, then point out words that use the /at/ rime and explain to the children that grown-ups use this rime to read poetry and books. Next, it might be a good idea to explain that we are going to practice reading /at/ words so they can read the poetry or book by themselves. Following the scripted lesson, the children could practice reading copies of the poetry or selections from the book with a buddy. Do you think that would work?

CHUCK: Sure sounds like it might. I'll give it a try. Thanks, Mrs. Bourn!

What is the teacher doing well? What evidence of this would we see? How might you guide the teacher to improve his or her skills?

# WHAT ABOUT STRUGGLING READERS AND Word Identification?

Students who struggle with word identification do not read fluently; they are trapped in a world of word-by-word reading that does not make sense to them, and thus they become frustrated easily. Skilled readers, on the other hand, have quick and accurate word recognition; they phrase words correctly; and they read with expression and understanding. Although some beginning readers appear to need relatively little explicit instruction in word recognition strategies, those who struggle may need more direct instruction. What works for some children, however, does not always work for others. Additionally, direct instruction does not mean laborious drilling of sounds in isolation. Effective classroom practices for struggling beginning readers are those in which phonics instruction includes sound blending, chunking words into onsets and rimes, hands-on activities in which words are sorted using cards, writing activities, and teacher modeling in small instructional groups. Just as important, struggling readers benefit from consistent opportunities to read a wide variety of authentic texts, including literature that is carefully selected based on instructional reading level.

In addition to the explicit teaching of word identification strategies and frequent opportunities to apply those strategies to authentic texts, struggling readers need and deserve informed teachers who know how to observe the cues children use and fail to use when approaching unknown words. We recommend that teachers of struggling readers choose a small number of word recognition strategies based on the needs of the students and help the students apply *those* strategies systematically and daily in a variety of settings.

# WHAT ABOUT STANDARDS, ASSESSMENT, AND *Word Identification?*

In order to comprehend text, readers identify words rapidly, automatically, and accurately. National, state, and local standards recognize that students learn to recognize words by using a variety of strategies including phonics, sight recognition, structural analysis, and context. According to *Standards for the English Language Arts*, an International Reading Association (IRA) and National Council of Teachers of English (NCTE) (1996) document, students must apply a wide variety of word recognition strategies as they learn to read. In addition, according to the IRA's *Standards for Reading Professionals* (2003), reading teachers must be versed in a wide range of strategies for teaching word identification, including phonics.

In Ohio, Standard One of the English-language-arts standards covers phonemic awareness, word recognition, and fluency. The benchmarks (goals) associated with word identification in Ohio (Ohio Department of Education, 2001, p. 158) by the end of grade 3 are that children will be able to

- Use letter–sound correspondence knowledge and structural analysis to decode words
- Demonstrate fluent oral reading using sight words and decoding skills, varying intonation and timing as appropriate for text

In addition to the benchmarks, Standard One of Ohio's English-language-arts standards for K–3 specifies word identification indicators for each grade level. These indicators (Ohio Department of Education, 2001a) appear repetitive but actually build on each other.

### KINDERGARTEN INDICATORS

- Recognize, say, and write the common sounds of letters
- Read one-syllable and often-heard words by sight (p. 177)

### GRADE 1 INDICATORS

- Identify and say the beginning and ending sounds in words
- Demonstrate an understanding of letter–sound correspondence by saying the sounds from all letters and from a variety of letter patterns, such as consonant blends and long- and short-vowel patterns, and by matching sounds to the corresponding letters
- Decode by using letter–sound matches
- Use knowledge of word families (e.g., *-ite* or *-ate*) to sound out unfamiliar words
- Blend two to four phonemes (sounds) into words
- Add, delete, or change sounds in a given word to create new or rhyming words
- Demonstrate a growing stock of sight words (p. 181)

GRADE 2 INDICATORS

- Identify rhyming words with the same or different spelling patterns
- Read regularly spelled multisyllable words by sight
- Blend phonemes (sounds) of letters and syllables to read unknown words with one or more syllables
- Use knowledge of common word families (e.g., *-ite* or *-ate*) to sound out unfamiliar words
- Segment letters, letter blends, and syllable sounds in words
- Distinguish and identify the beginning, middle, and ending sounds in words
- Identify words as having either short- or long-vowel sounds
- Demonstrate a growing stock of sight words (p. 187)

GRADE 3 INDICATORS

- Identify rhyming words with the same or different spelling patterns
- Use letter–sound knowledge and structural analysis to decode words
- Use knowledge of common word families (e.g., *-ite* or *-ate*) and complex word families (e.g., *-ould*, *-ight*) to sound out unfamiliar words
- Demonstrate a growing stock of sight words (p. 193)

We suggest that you locate and review the ELA standards for your state at www.education-world.com/standards/state/toc/index.shtml.

Teachers need to be cautious about assessing word identification skills in isolation. For example, students who can read sight-word flash cards with accuracy may not be able to identify the same words in the context of a story. Others may not be able to identify words in a list but readily understand those same words in the context of a meaningful story. Real reading takes place within meaningful contexts, and having students read lists of words may not be an accurate assessment of word identification skills.

## Summary

The underlying premise of this chapter is that *how* teachers help children with word identification is extremely important. We looked at word identification abilities within the context of the developmental phases associated with children's ability to identify words. Rather than recommending teaching word identification through worksheets, rules, and jargon-filled instruction, this chapter presented a variety of strategies that children actually use to decode words. Instructional strategies were examined for teaching phonics, context, structural analysis, and rapid recognition of high-frequency words and key words.

When readers can combine meaning cues with phonics cues and the structure of words, they have developed a powerful tool for word identification. This is why readers must learn how to use contextual information to recognize words. Various kinds of contextual activities can be designed to help students coordinate semantic, syntactic, and phonemic information. These activities include cloze-type passages in which target words are deleted from the text. These words can be deleted selectively or systematically, depending on the teacher's purposes. Readers must also become aware that a text selection can be read and understood without every word being identified. Context-centered activities such as the reader-selected miscue strategy can help students in this respect.

## Teacher Action Research

1. Select a piece of children's literature and type 100 words from the selection. Using Fry's instant word list, highlight each word on the list that you locate in the piece of literature and calculate the percentage of words that are high frequency. Repeat the same procedure using a college textbook. What did you find?

2. Collect several samples of writing from a child in primary school. Analyze the writing to determine the child's letter–sound knowledge. Then interview the child's teacher to determine his or her perceptions of the child's strengths and gaps in phonics. Does your analysis match the teacher's perceptions? Why or why not?

3. Analyze the word identification strand of a basal reading program. How is decoding or word identification defined? What are the major components of the strand? How is phonics taught—for example, is phonics taught analytically or synthetically? What provisions are made to help children develop multiple strategies for identifying unknown words? How comprehensively is context taught and reinforced?

4. Now compare the word identification strand with a published supplementary phonics program. How are the two alike? Different? Describe the extent to which the supplementary program is compatible with the basal's word identification program.

5. What should be the role of parents in helping children identify words? Brainstorm ways in which parents can help children with word identification at home.

 6. Prepare and teach a word identification lesson to a small group of second or third graders. Make provisions in the lesson to combine phonics with context usage and application so that the focus of the lesson is not on learning rules but on reading print. Describe the reactions and interactions of the children during the lesson. How would you change the lesson if you were to work with the same group of children tomorrow? How would you extend the lesson?

7. Arrange to visit an early childhood classroom in which the teacher is teaching a phonics lesson. Observe the content of the lesson in terms of skills and materials. What materials is the teacher using that you would consider meaningful to the children? Observe the nature of the children's engagement in the lesson. Are the students interacting with enthusiasm? What strategies is the teacher implementing to foster a meaningful phonics lesson in which you observe student engagement and understanding of the phonics lesson that is being taught? What would you tell the teacher that is positive about the lesson and what suggestions would you have for the teacher based on your observations?

## Related Web Sites

*The Dolch Kit*

**www.theschoolbell.com/Links/Dolch/Dolch.html**

The Dolch Kit contains high frequency word and phrase cards, as well as games and activities for practicing sight words.

*Four Blocks Literacy Framework: Word Wall Cheers*

**www.k111.k12.il.us/lafayette/fourblocks/word_wall_chants.htm**

This site includes ideas and "cheers" for teaching spelling using word walls.

*Learn to Read*

**www.starfall.com/n/level-a/index/play.htm**

Learn to Read includes stories that focus on onsets and rimes for the primary grades.

*Multnomah County Library*

**www.multnomah.lib.or.us/lib/kids/games.html**

This library site has links to numerous games and activities about word study for all ages.

*Read Write Think—Word Build and Bank*

**www.readwritethink.org/student_mat/student_material.asp?id=3**

This site provides a wide variety of phonics activities that involve word building as well as strategies for teaching onsets and rimes, high-frequency words, and context.

*Role of Phonics in Reading Instruction*

**www.reading.org/resources/issues/positions_phonics.html**

This summary synthesizes the position statement of the International Reading Association.

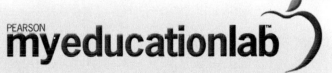

Now go to the Vacca et al. *Reading and Learning to Read*, Seventh Edition, MyEducationLab course at **www.myeducationlab.com** to

- Take a pretest to assess your initial comprehension of the chapter content
- Study chapter content with your individualized study plan
- Take a posttest to assess your understanding of chapter content
- Engage in multimedia exercises to help you build a deeper and more applied understanding of chapter content

# CHAPTER 8
# Reading Fluency

Standards found in this chapter:
- ▶ 1.4
- ▶ 2.2
- ▶ 2.3
- ▶ 3.1
- ▶ 3.2
- ▶ 4.1
- ▶ 4.4
- ▶ 5.2
- ▶ 5.3

## In this chapter,
### YOU WILL DISCOVER:

- The importance of developing fluency in young readers
- What classroom routines, strategies, and reading materials help foster fluency development during oral reading
- How to monitor oral reading fluency

## Concept Map

**READING FLUENCY**

**DEFINING ORAL READING FLUENCY**

Immediate Word Recognition    Predictability of Texts

Automaticity

**STRATEGIES FOR DEVELOPING ORAL READING FLUENCY**

Repeated Readings    Automated Reading

Performance Strategies    Involving Families

**MONITORING ORAL READING FLUENCY**

**DEVELOPING SILENT READING FLUENCY**

Sustained Silent Reading

*J*uana, a second grader, first learned to read in her native Spanish. But when her family moved to Florida recently, she had trouble reading books at school in a new language even though she knew a little English. As with many ELL students who live in homes where the family only speaks the native language, Juana also never hears or speaks fluent English. At school, Juana doesn't read aloud and always puts her head down and looks away when called on in class discussions. Juana's teacher, Mrs. Milkie, has heard her talk to friends on the playground and knows that she is intelligent. What can Mrs. Milkie do to give her student more confidence and skills in reading fluency?

After meeting with the school's literacy coach, Mrs. Milkie decided to take a multicultural approach to reading instruction. Last Tuesday, she read aloud to the class *A Bear for Miguel* by Elaine Alphin. In this book, a young El Salvadoran girl named Maria finds a very special way to help her family during troubled times. The book contains a map as well as a glossary of the Spanish words and phrases used in the story. During her read-aloud, Mrs. Milkie used a big book and modeled reading with expression, creeping along slowly during dramatic moments and raising her voice at the end of questions. This was the first time Juana heard a book read in fluent English, and she was happy to hear a story so closely related to her own culture. Next, Mrs. Milkie put the students in pairs and had them read every other page to one another; she paired Juana with a very strong reader who helped her when she struggled with words. At the end of the day, Mrs. Milkie gave Juana a tape player, a headset, and a copy of *A Bear for Miguel* on tape that she could listen to at home while she read along with the story. During class time, Mrs. Milkie continued to model fluent reading and gave Juana and the other students a lot of practice reading aloud multicultural books in pairs as well as reading chorally. Over time, Juana's fluency skills began to improve. The little girl took delight in teaching her classmates the correct pronunciations of the Spanish words used in the stories, and she became so excited about books that she began reading the stories to her family at home, teaching them fluent English as she learned it herself.

The role of practice in learning to read is extremely important. As the authors of *Becoming a Nation of Readers* (Anderson, Hiebert, Scott, & Wilkinson, 1985) suggest: "No one would expect a novice pianist to sight read a new selection every day, but that is exactly what is expected of the beginning reader" (p. 52). A budding pianist practices a piece again and again to get a feel for the composition, to develop control over it, and to become competent and confident with it.

So it is with young readers. In this chapter, we underscore the value of having readers develop fluency in oral and silent reading situations. Examine the Concept Map. It depicts the connections among key concepts related to developing fluent reading, one of the five essential components of effective reading instruction according to the National Reading Panel (2000). We begin by defining reading fluency as *reading easily and well with a sense of confidence and knowledge of what to do when things go wrong.* By examining the concepts of immediate word identification and automaticity, we see that fluent reading is far more than reading words smoothly out loud; fluency is the core of comprehension. After considering how materials influence fluency development, we describe teaching strategies and routines to teach fluency, as well as ways to monitor oral reading fluency. Included are descriptions of "best practices" that help orchestrate the teaching and training of fluency with the teaching of comprehension.

Let's begin by focusing on immediate word recognition, which allows a skilled reader to concentrate on comprehension.

STANDARD
1.4

# Defining Oral Reading Fluency

The term *fluent* is often associated with doing something easily and well. When applied to reading, **fluency,** in everyday terms, means reading easily and well. Padak and Rasinski (2008) define fluency as "the ability to read expressively and meaningfully, as well as accurately and with appropriate speed" (p. 3). With this ability comes a sense of control and confidence, and often a knowledge of what to do when the reader gets bogged down or entangled in a text. Rasinski (2004) explains that fluency has three dimensions. The first is *accuracy in word decoding;* readers must be able to sound out words (using phonics and other word decoding strategies) in text with few errors. The second dimension is *automatic processing.* This is when the reader uses as little mental effort as possible in the decoding of text, saving mental energy for comprehension. The third dimension is *prosody* or *prosodic reading.* Prosody is a linguistic concept that refers to such features in oral language as *intonation, pitch, stress, pauses,* and the *duration* placed on specific syllables. These features signal some of the meaning conveyed in oral language.

Have you ever sat in a class or been to a presentation where the speaker used few prosodic cues while speaking? Sometimes it's difficult to focus on what the person is trying to say or what the person means. In the same way, reading with expression, or using prosodic features while reading orally, has the potential of conveying more meaning than reading without expression. In addition, prosodic cues convey moods and feelings. Children generally know instantly when a parent is irritated with them. A mother's tone of voice (intonation) is usually enough to signal, "Mom is mad."

In learning to understand oral language, children rely on prosodic features. Similar conditions appear to be necessary in learning to understand written language. Schreiber (1980) found that students learned how to put words together in meaningful phrases, despite the fact that a written text provides few phrasing cues and uses few graphic signals for prosodic features in print. In classrooms we often hear teachers tell students to "read with expression." This suggestion is a hint that the reader should rely on intuitive knowledge or prosodic features in oral language, not only to help convey meaning to others but also to help the reader's own understanding of what is being read.

Effective fluency instruction has three parts: instruction, practice, and assessment. Fluency *instruction* should incorporate the teaching of basic skills such as phonemic awareness and phonics. It should also model what fluency looks and sounds like. Fluency *practice* includes the use of decodable text and other independent level texts to strengthen the sounds and spelling that are taught in the classroom. Strategies such as repeated readings, covered later in this chapter, should be utilized often.

Instruction in fluent oral reading produces readers who move from word-by-word reading to more efficient phrase reading (Chomsky, 1976; Samuels, 1979). Fluency instruction has also resulted in improved reading achievement, assessed through measures of comprehension (Dowhower, 1987). Rasinski (2003) explains that because fluent readers do not have to spend time decoding words they are able to spend time and energy on making sense of and comprehending the text.

The final component of fluency is *assessment.* Assessing fluency can be done relatively easily and requires little time, especially with today's available technology. It will be discussed later in this chapter.

## Immediate Word Identification

The term **immediate word identification** is often used to describe rapid recognition. Keep in mind, however, that the process of immediate word identification is far more complicated than recognizing words on flash cards. When a word is retrieved rapidly from long-term memory, the process is often triggered by well-developed schemata that the reader has developed for a word. In immediate word identification, semantic

**HOMEWORK EXERCISE: VIDEO**

Go to the Homework and Exercises section in Chapter 8 of MyEducationLab to read the article "Why Reading Is Not a Natural Process" and develop a deeper understanding of phonics instruction and how you can use scientific research to implement instruction.

STANDARD 1.4

STANDARD 1.4

or physical features in a word (e.g., a single letter or a letter cluster) trigger quick retrieval of that word.

Immediate word identification is the strategy used by skilled readers on 99 percent of the printed words they meet. It is also the method used by children when they identify their first words. Often one of the first words children learn to identify in print is their name. Jessica, a 4-year-old, can recognize her printed name but may not attend to each individual letter. She recognizes her name because some distinctive feature triggers rapid retrieval from long-term memory.

In Chapter 7, we looked at children acquiring phonic knowledge as one tool in identifying words. We also considered how to help children analyze syllabic or meaning-bearing units in unfamiliar words. Both phonic and structural analysis involve *mediated word identification*. Mediation implies that the reader needs more time to retrieve words from long-term memory. Readers use mediating strategies when they don't have in place a well-developed schema for a word: The schema is lacking in either semantic or physical features sufficient for rapid retrieval.

We think that experiencing problems in fluency is a major contributor when students lag behind in reading ability. This can be particularly true for students from diverse linguistic backgrounds. Rasinski and Padak (1996) studied elementary school children from a large urban district who were referred for special tutoring in reading in the Title I program. The children read passages near their grade level and were measured on word recognition, comprehension, and reading fluency. Although the students' performance tended to be below grade level on all measures, only reading fluency was drastically below grade level. Their oral reading was slow and belabored.

How do skilled readers reach the point at which they read fluently and don't have to rely on mediated word identification strategies? Researchers are finding that *repetition is extremely important in learning to recognize words*. The amount of repetition needed for beginning readers to be able to recognize words immediately has not been appreciated. Traditionally, repetition of reading texts has not been systematically included in reading instruction. Today, reading familiar text is considered a key component of a comprehensive literacy program.

As mature readers, we are able to identify immediately or sight-read thousands and thousands of words. How did we learn to identify these words? Did we use flash cards to learn each one? Did we first sound out each word letter by letter? Probably not. The effects of developing oral reading fluency in meaningful texts have been studied with impressive results (Allington, 1983; Chomsky, 1976; Dowhower, 1987; Koskinen & Blum, 1986; Samuels, 1979).

## Automaticity

Samuels (1988) argues that word recognition needs to be accurate and *automatic*. To explain the term **automaticity,** an analogy is often made to driving a car. Most of the time, a skilled driver will focus little attention or use little mental energy while driving. Skilled drivers frequently daydream or ponder happenings in their lives as they drive, yet they still manage to drive in the appropriate lane at an appropriate speed (most of the time!). They drive on automatic pilot. Nevertheless, when the need arises, a driver can swiftly focus attention on driving—for example, when a warning light goes on or when weather conditions suddenly change. In other words, most of us drive with automaticity, with little use of mental energy, but when necessary, we're able to refocus rapidly on what we're doing as drivers.

When readers are accurate but not automatic, they put considerable amounts of mental energy into identifying words as they read. When readers are both accurate and automatic, they recognize or identify words accurately, rapidly, easily, and with little mental energy. Like the skilled driver, the skilled reader can rapidly focus attention on a decoding problem but most of the time will put energy into comprehending the text.

Fluency strategies are also one way of getting rid of the "uh-ohs," which are a part of learning any new skill. When taking tennis lessons, the beginner often makes mental comments such as "Uh-oh, I need to hit in the middle of my racket" or "Oh, what a crummy backhand shot." Each hit is judged as either good or bad. Children are also prone to struggling with the "uh-ohs" when learning to read. This happens especially when they think about which words they can and cannot identify. As with the beginning tennis player, the reading beginner often gets anxious because the "uh-ohs" interfere with constructing meaning from the text. Developing automaticity is one way to give beginning readers a feel for reading without anxiety.

## Predictability of Reading Materials

For children to develop into confident, fluent readers, they need to read lots of texts that are easy for them. For first and second graders, *predictable literature* can be read with ease. Rhodes (1981) has delineated several characteristics of predictable stories. Some criteria for predictable literatures are outlined in Figure 8.1.

Predictable books have a context or setting that is familiar or predictable to most children. The pictures are supportive of the text; that is, there is a good match between the text and the illustrations. The language is natural, meaning that common language patterns are used. The story line is predictable. There is a repetitive pattern such as the mother rocking the child at night regardless of the trials during the day. There is also repetitive language in the refrains. Further contributing to the predictability of the book is the rhyme of language.

Other characteristics of predictable books delineated by Rhodes (1981) are rhyme and the use of cumulative patterns, as in *The Napping House* (Wood, 1984):

> And on that dog
> there is a cat,
> a snoozing cat
> on a dozing dog
> on a dreaming child
> on a snoring granny
> on a cozy bed
> in a napping house,
> where everyone is sleeping.

**Predictable texts** are particularly helpful in developing fluency because children can rely on these characteristics of predictability. With predictable stories, less able

---

### Figure 8.1    Characteristics of Predictable Stories

1. Is the context (setting) one that is familiar or predictable to the reader?
2. Are the pictures supportive and predictable given the text?
3. Is the language natural? That is, does the author use common language patterns?
4. Is the story line predictable after the book has been started? Are the transitions clear?
5. Does the language "flow"?
6. Does the book reflect creativity, capture an interesting thought, or communicate something worthwhile, worthy of the title "literature"?
7. Is there repetition of specific language?
8. Are there cumulative episodes in the plot?
9. Is there rhyme?

*Source:* "I Can Read! Predictable Books as Resources for Reading and Writing Instruction," by L. K. Rhodes, 1981, *The Reading Teacher, 34,* pp. 314–318.

readers can use intuitive knowledge of language and sense rather than rely on mediated techniques that draw on their mental energy. Using predictable texts, readers can develop fluency by reading them repeatedly with less and less assistance.

# Developing Oral Reading Fluency

STANDARD
2.2

Children learn to become fluent in environments that support oral reading as communication. Mindless classroom situations in which children take turns reading in "round-robin" fashion accomplishes little that is constructive. In round-robin reading, the teacher randomly calls on students to read a section of text "cold" in front of the class. When teachers utilize this traditional practice, students often do not view their role as that of tellers of a story or as communicators of information. Instead, since their role is to be word perfect, they focus on accuracy, not automaticity or comprehension. We've asked our students what they recall from their school years about reading aloud in front of peers and it always begins a rich conversation about this outdated practice. Andrew's poignant story in Box 8.1 is one of them. Although we are strong proponents of oral reading in classrooms, the emphasis during oral reading must be on communication and comprehension, not word-perfect renderings of a reading selection. We suggest that students, especially English language learners, have the opportunity to practice text silently before they read aloud. Let's take a closer look at some classroom routines and strategies that can help foster fluency during oral reading and then how parents and families can support fluency at home.

DIVERSITY
ELL

## Repeated Readings

According to the National Reading Panel (2000), **repeated readings** increase reading fluency. Rasinski (2003) informs us that, "Oral repeated readings provide additional sensory reinforcement for the reader, allowing him or her to focus on the prosodic elements of reading that are essential to phrasing. Oral readings also ensure that the student is actually reading, not skimming or scanning the text" (p. 31). Repeated readings, as defined in earlier chapters, involve simply having a child reading a short passage from a book, magazine, or newspaper more than once with differing amounts of support. Reading poetry is a natural way to develop fluency. Children of all ages enjoy and respond to the rhythm of poetry, and it can be incorporated easily into the classroom routine (Perfect, 1999). In order to read or share a poem for the class, students need to practice the poems using repeated reading, thus developing reading fluency. Box 8.2 on page 254 describes poems available online, some of which are presented with audio of poets reading their own works.

Samuels (1979) proposes the method of repeated readings as a strategy to develop rapid, fluent oral reading. Here are several steps Samuels suggests when using the method of repeated readings:

1. Students choose short selections (50 to 200 words) from stories that are difficult enough that students are not able to read them fluently.
2. Students read the passage several times silently until they are able to read it fluently.
3. The teacher can involve students in a discussion of how athletes develop athletic skills by spending considerable time practicing basic movements until they develop speed and smoothness. Repeated reading uses the same type of practice.
4. Samuels suggests that students tape-record their first oral rendition of the passage as well as their oral rendition after practice so that they can hear the difference in fluency.

HOMEWORK EXERCISE: VIDEO

Go to the Homework and Exercises section in Chapter 8 of MyEducationLab to read the article "Creating Fluent Readers" and consider strategies you could use to develop oral reading fluency.

BOX **8.1**

# *Viewpoint*

## Andrew: My Reading History

*Andrew is a middle school social studies teacher who is passionate about using reading strategies in his content area teaching. When people ask him why he cares so much about teaching students to read texts, he tells them his story.*

I remember the day and event that happened thirty years ago like it was yesterday. Part of this day feels thirty years ago for I can't recall my teacher's name, but the pain I felt is still very palpable. I was in my second-grade class and it was the first day we were put into reading groups. I sat there and waited, well aware of what it meant to be in the *yellow* group, as opposed to the "smart kids" in the *red* and *blue* groups. I remember waiting my turn and hoping for at least a shot in the *blue* or "average smart" *red* group. Then I heard her, "Andrew, go to the *yellow* group." I felt dumb. I was humiliated in front of all of my classmates. Whether or not this was effective differentiated instruction or just plain de facto sorting, I can't say, although today I tend to think it was the latter. Little did I know at the time this turned out to be a defining moment, not only in my reading history, but my life—I let the event become a self-fulfilling prophecy. Since I was put in the "slow readers" group, I felt I was no good at reading. While some students may want to strive to improve from this point and use it to motivate them, I chose the path of proving that the teachers were correct. I gave up.

From this point forward I hated to read, and there didn't seem to be any intervention at school or at home. The third- to the sixth-grade years seem to be a blur, except for incessant daydreaming. By the time of the sixth-grade class production of *Julius Caesar* I was the only child in the class without a speaking part. This stung in a way that my teacher, or others for whom learning came easy, could probably never understand. But I still remember how it felt today.

I spent the next few middle school years being embarrassed daily by my mispronouncing easy words during "popcorn" or "round-robin" reading. By this time, I had enough of trying, and I dealt with it by the only way acceptable to my peers: getting into trouble. From this point forward it was going to be fun to get bad grades in school and be a smart aleck in class. Also in middle school, the real sorting of students began. I had the same teacher for seventh, eighth, tenth, and eleventh grade. She was given the kids who were unmotivated or lacking in "college potential"—in other words, kids like me. Maybe she was given us because no one else wanted us or because the administration figured the better teachers should teach the college-bound students—I don't know. But I do know that I spent four crucial years with a teacher who expected nothing from me and I delivered exactly that. I can honestly say that outside of round-robin reading in class, I read *nothing*. To compound this, I wrote one paper in those four years and it was about the designated hitter in baseball, a two-page piece of trash with illustrations taking up most of the paper. I was exposed to no literature, other than the in-class reading that was never comprehended. My senior year I actually had a teacher who cared and expected me to learn something, but by this time I didn't see the point in it, so I slept in several days a week so I could miss her class. Needless to say, I did not attend college out of high school.

I finally did attend college after coming to the realization that I might want a future that did not consist of sanding boards on an assembly line. College was a struggle, and for four-plus years I was being self-taught on how to read for comprehension, write, and study. It took most of my undergraduate years to learn to read with comprehension, not get distracted and daydream, and then have to constantly reread the pages. I finally broke through at some point towards the end of my undergraduate studies. Now, thirty years after being put in the "slow reading" group, I devour books one after another. My comprehension is to a point that I can read a book while watching a ball game on television yet still manage to comprehend the written words.

This self-fulfilling prophecy stripped me of the enjoyment of reading for ten critical, developmental years of my life. It took six years of extreme difficulty in breaking the cycle of "slow reading" while also trying to earn a bachelor's degree so that I could become a teacher.

Today I have two young daughters of my own and I read to them all of the time. Before we read I ask them to guess what they think the story will be about, and throughout the story I often stop and have them retell me what we've read. I tell them to use the pictures and other clues in the story to help them make sense, and I tell them they should be forming pictures in their heads as they are reading.

As a teacher, I believe the experience has given me empathy for students who have the same kind of difficulties I had. I often share parts of my story with them so they know that I understand what it's like to struggle with reading. I tell them that if they find that they are daydreaming when they are reading, it doesn't mean they're dumb; it just means that they have to learn how to think with text and comprehend it. I incorporate reading strategies in my teaching, and I *never* have kids read unfamiliar text out loud in front of others. Hopefully, I can take my understanding and compassion for these students and combine it with literacy practices that will change *their* reading history.

BOX **8.2**

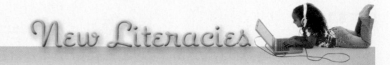

*New Literacies*

## PRACTICING FLUENCY ONLINE

The oral reading of poetry is useful in supporting fluency for students because it can be fun and unintimidating, especially for struggling readers. The Internet site www.poets.org is a rich collection of Web resources created by the Academy of American Poets for teachers seeking ways to incorporate new literacies into the classroom. The site includes more than 600 poems online, many of which have audio versions that allow students to listen to and read along with a fluent reader. Some of the poems are read by the authors themselves, who provide historical context for particular pieces. For example, in one clip, Gwendolyn Brooks explains the motivation behind her poem "We Real Cool." That backstory sets up her subsequent reading, done with a flair and cadence that reflects the mood described by the author. Therefore, in addition to offering students an opportunity to practice fluency, they can also gain a feel for the flow and rhythm of poetry.

The site also offers a calendar of poetry-related events, biographies of more than 200 poets, links to numerous poetry-related sites, and multiple search engines, as well as online discussion forums where students can communicate with others about poetry. Students can even create online notebook collections of their favorite poems.

For educators, the site contains a special section that offers tips, discussion forums, and a collection of lesson plans and activities that can be used when teaching poetry.

Lauritzen (1982) proposes modifications to the repeated-reading method that make the method easier to use with groups of children. Mrs. Leonardo, a first-grade teacher, used the repeated-reading method in this way. She began by reading aloud to her students and discussing what happened in *Love You Forever*, a predictable text written by Robert Munsch (1989) and illustrated by Sheila McGraw. It begins:

> A mother held her new baby and very slowly rocked him back and forth, back and forth. And while she held him, she sang:

> > I'll love you forever, I'll like you for always,
> > As long as I'm living my baby you'll be. . . .

However, when the baby grew and pulled all the food out of the refrigerator and took his mother's watch and flushed it down the toilet, sometimes his mother would say, "This child is driving me crazy!"

> But at night, while she rocked him, she sang:

> > I'll love you forever, I'll like you for always,
> > As long as I'm living my baby you'll be.

After this initial reading by the teacher, Mrs. Leonardo read it with the children in choral reading fashion. She and individual children next took turns reading parts of the passage, with the children reading the refrain with repetitive language: "I'll love you forever, I'll like you for always, / As long as I'm living my baby you'll be." Then Mrs. Leonardo asked the children how they thought the mother felt when she was rocking her son at night and how they could read the refrain to show that feeling. She also asked how the mother felt when she said, "This child is driving me crazy!" and how she showed this with her voice.

Finally, each child chose a passage in the book and read the passage silently and then several times orally to a partner. Some of the children also read along while listening to a tape-recorded version of the story. These activities were continued until each child was able to read the passage with accuracy and fluency.

Studies on repeated readings have fallen into two categories: *assisted* repeated readings, in which students read along with a live or taped model of the passage, and *unassisted* repeated readings, in which the child engages in independent practice (Dowhower, 1989). In both assisted and unassisted repeated readings, students reread a meaningful passage until oral production is accurate and smooth and resembles spoken language. Notice that Mrs. Leonardo used both assisted and unassisted readings to develop reading fluency, beginning initially with assisted reading. First she read the passage and the students listened and discussed the story. Then she gradually assisted students less as they continued to reread the story.

When teachers discuss the repeated-reading strategy, they frequently ask, "Don't students find repeated readings of the same story boring?" To the contrary, teachers who have used repeated readings find that young children actually delight in using the strategy. Children plead to have their favorite bedtime story read again and again. In the same vein, they get very involved in practicing a story with the goal of reading it accurately and fluently and are eager to share their story with parents and classmates.

## Paired Repeated Readings

In paired repeated readings, students select their own passage from the material with which they are currently working. The passage should be about 50 words in length. Students, grouped in pairs, should each select different passages, which makes listening more interesting and discourages direct comparison of reading proficiency. The material should be predictable and at a level where mastery is possible.

When working together, the students read their own passage silently and then decide who will be the first reader. The first reader then reads his or her passage out loud to a partner three different times. Readers may ask their partner for help with a word. After each oral reading, the reader evaluates his or her reading. A self-evaluation sheet might ask the reader, "How well did you read today?" Responses to be checked might range from fantastic, to good, to fair, to not so good. The partner listens and tells the reader how much improvement was made after each rendition of the reading; such as if the reader knew more words and read with more expression during the final reading. A listening chart can be used to help a student evaluate a partner's reading (see Figure 8.2). The partners then switch roles.

**PEER TUTORING** ◆ Another way to organize fluency practice is to use a **paired reading** strategy with peer tutoring. This is a particularly useful strategy in second and third grade, where differences between the most fluent and the least fluent readers become evident.

Topping (1989) noted that the collaborative work of children in pairs has enormous potential, but teachers must be able to organize and monitor this activity carefully. He

---

### Figure 8.2   A Listening Chart

**Reading 3**

How did your partner's reading get better?

He or she read more smoothly.                      ...............................

He or she knew more words.                         ...............................

He or she read with more expression.              ...............................

Tell your partner one thing that was better about his or her reading.

Paired reading is a useful strategy for developing reading fluency.

advocated structured pair work between children of differing ability in which a more able child (tutor) helps a less able child (tutee) in a cooperative learning environment.

Teachers often recognize the value of extra reading practice in a paired reading situation for less able children but sometimes express concern about the worth of the activity for more able students. Research reviews on the effectiveness of peer tutoring with paired reading have shown that the more able reader accelerates in reading skill at least as much as the less able reader (Sharpley & Sharpley, 1981).

For growth in fluent reading to be maximized, the teacher needs to pair students carefully. One way to do this is to match the most able tutor with the most able tutee. This procedure seems to aid in matching students with an appropriate *relative competence* to each other, which maximizes the success of using this technique. As in any collaborative learning group, do not group best friends or worst enemies. You also need to consider how to handle absences.

Here's a general plan for paired reading with peer tutoring. The tutee chooses a book that has been read to the children or used in direct instruction. The book needs to be within the tutor's readability level (i.e., 95 to 98 percent accuracy level). The tutor and the tutee discuss the book initially and throughout the reading. They read together aloud at the tutee's pace. If the tutee happens to make a word error, the tutor says the word correctly. The pair continues reading together. When the tutee wants to read alone, he or she signals nonverbally—for instance, with a tap on the knee. The tutor praises the tutee for signaling, then is silent and the tutee reads alone. The tutor resumes reading when requested by the tutee. If the tutee makes an error or does not respond in 5 seconds, they use the correction procedure just described, and then the pair continues to read together. At the conclusion, the pair discusses the story based on questions developed by the tutor before the session.

This procedure allows tutees to be supported through the text with higher readability levels than they would attain by themselves. The text level also ensures stimulation and participation for the tutor, who promotes discussion and questioning on the content of the text.

## Automated Reading

Another practice that supports children as they increase oral reading fluency is **automated reading,** or listening while reading a text. An automated reading program employs simultaneous listening and reading (SLR), a procedure suggested by Carol Chomsky (1976). In the SLR procedure, a child reads along with a tape recorder. In addition to audiotapes, SLR can be done with digital text stories and stories on CD-ROM. The steps in SLR are as follows:

1. Students listen individually to audio-recorded stories, simultaneously following along with the written text. They read and listen repeatedly to the same story until they can read the story fluently.
2. Students choose the book or a portion of the book in which they want to work. When they are making their selections, the teacher explains that they will continue listening to the same story until they are able to read it fluently by themselves. Students need to choose a book that is too hard to read right away but not out of range entirely.
3. Students are to listen to their books every day, using earphones and following along in the text as they listen. They need to listen to the entire story through at least once; then they can go back and repeat any part they choose to prepare more carefully.
4. Every 3 or 4 days, the teacher listens to the students read orally as much as they have prepared. Students are encouraged to evaluate themselves on how fluently they read the selection they have prepared.

Chomsky (1976) reported that when students first begin using this method, it may take as long as a month before they are able to read a fairly long story aloud fluently. As they become more proficient with SLR, the time can be reduced by as much as half.

When students are able to read the story fluently without the aid of the tape, they need to be given opportunities to read the story to their parents, the principal, or fellow students. Students using this strategy could not present the story without having a book to follow, so they have not really memorized the book. However, a combination of memorization and reading enables students to have an experience of successful, effective, fluent reading. These techniques are effective with students of all ages, including those in middle school.

Several schools in Madison, Wisconsin, used SLR in an automated reading program (Dowhower, 1989). Children were sent to the library to choose a book, accompanied by an audiotape, that was not too easy or too hard for them to read. The criteria for selecting tapes for the automated reading program included high interest, appropriate pacing, language patterns, clear page-turning cues, and lack of cultural biases. To monitor the difficulty level of books chosen, each child took a test by reading a list of 20 words from the story. If the child knew more than 15 words, the book was probably too easy; if 8 or fewer words, the book may have been too hard. Another way to monitor book difficulty level is for the child to read a short section orally, with a teacher, librarian, or aide keeping a running record of miscues made. Dowhower (1989) indicated that on the first reading a child should read with 85 percent accuracy or better before starting to practice; otherwise, the text is too hard.

Once a book was selected, the child then read along with the audiotape several times daily until the story could be read smoothly and expressively. When children were ready, they read the entire book (or several pages, if the book was very long) to an adult.

To provide further fluency practice, the SLR strategy can be used with computer software. Some "talking books" read the text to the child, allowing the child to slow down and speed up the reading speed, to click on text to have it reread, to click on a word to be given help, and to click on an illustration to learn additional information or activate animation.

The use of the tape recorder and automated reading has great promise for independent practice for English language learners (ELLs). Koskinen and his colleagues (1999) reported that most ELL students reported that they practiced almost daily reading with the books and tapes, and that the least proficient ELL readers were most likely to use the prerecorded materials to practice and improve their reading at home.

The SLR strategy as used in automated reading is a useful way for students to develop fluency through practice reading. It is important, however, that students be involved in experiences in which expressive oral reading is modeled and texts are discussed, in addition to having the opportunities for practice that SLR provides. With this word of caution, we turn next to two performance strategies that actively engage students in fluent and accurate oral reading.

## Choral Reading

Telling students to read with expression is not enough for many developing readers. Rather, many children need to listen to mature readers read with expression and interpret and practice different ways of orally reading selections. **Choral reading** is an enjoyable way to engage children in listening and responding to the prosodic features in oral language in order to read with expression. In essence, through the use of choral reading techniques, students consider ways to get across the author's meaning using prosodic cues such as pitch, loudness, stress, and pauses. For English language learners, choral reading provides practice in a nonthreatening atmosphere, allowing them to build meaning from text and learn more about language.

Choral reading is defined as the oral reading of poetry that makes use of various voice combinations and contrasts to create meaning or to highlight the tonal qualities of the passage. Primary children enjoy choral reading combined with puppetry. For

Choral reading can increase fluency, and children enjoy the opportunity to read and reread texts.

example, with the cumulative story *An Invitation to the Butterfly Ball* by Jane Yolen, children can use paper bag puppets representing ten different kinds of animals invited to a dance by a tiny elf. The story begins, "One little mouse in great distress looks all around for a floor-length dress," and adds two moles, three rabbits, and so on, up to ten porcupines (Walley, 1993).

In preparing for a choral reading of a text, the teacher models one way the selection can be read while the children listen. Then students identify how the teacher read the passage. Were parts read loudly or softly? What was the tempo? Did the teacher emphasize particular syllables? Was his or her voice pitched higher or lower in different parts of the passage? Students are then invited to try different ways of reading or interpreting a part, and they may want to respond to the mood or feeling that each interpretation imparts (Cooper & Gray, 1984).

Choral reading increases reading fluency (Bradley & Talgott, 1987; Chomsky, 1976; Dowhower, 1987; Samuels, 1979; Schreiber, 1980). In addition, it provides a legitimate, fun way for children to practice and reread a text that leads to a decreased number of oral reading miscues (Herman, 1985).

There are different types of choral reading: refrain, line by line, dialogue, and unison. Each type works well with different kinds of selections.

For example, Mrs. Leonardo used the refrain type of choral reading with *Love You Forever*; that is, she read the stanzas and the children chimed in on the refrain. The refrain is the easiest type of choral reading to model and learn.

Mrs. Leonardo used the line by line type of choral reading with "Five Little Chickens," an old jingle from *Sounds of a Powwow* by Bill Martin and Peggy Brogan (1970):

> Said the first little chicken with a queer little squirm,
> I wish I could find a fat little worm.
> Said the second little chicken with a queer little shrug,
> I wish I could find a fat little bug. . . .

After the five little chickens have spoken:

> Said the old mother hen from the green garden-patch,
> If you want any breakfast, just come here and scratch!

She had the whole group read the lines that began with *said* and individual children read what the little chickens and the mother hen said. The line by line format can be easily used on selections in which different characters have lines to speak. When using this type of choral reading, children learn that listening for one's cue is essential or the choral reading breaks down.

Mrs. Leonardo's children giggled when she read to them "The Deaf Woman's Courtship."

> Old woman, old woman, will you do my washing?
> Speak a little louder, sir; I'm rather hard of hearing.
> Old woman, old woman, will you do my ironing?
> Speak a little louder, sir; I'm rather hard of hearing.
> Old woman, old woman, can I come a-courting?
> Speak a little louder, sir; I think I almost heard you.
> Old woman, old woman, marry me tomorrow.
> GOODNESS GRACIOUS MERCY SAKES! NOW I REALLY HEARD YOU!

Then the class discussed and practiced a dialogue type of choral reading with the boys reading the male part and the girls reading the old woman's responses. This selection was also useful for discussing with the children when to use soft and loud voices and when to pitch their voices high or low.

A fourth type of choral reading is reading in unison, which is often used by teachers who work on oral reading fluency. Yet from a choral reading perspective, this is the most difficult because the entire group speaks all the lines and responds to the prosodic cues simultaneously. Timing, parallel inflections, and consistent voice quality are of prime importance; otherwise, there is a singsong effect. This points to the need for the teacher to model how to read a selection with expression and to discuss how to use stress, pitch, intonation, and loudness when reading in unison. Otherwise, students may get the idea that oral reading should be done in a singsong fashion.

## Reader's Theater

Another way to involve children of all ages in orally reading literature to other children is through **reader's theater.** McCaslin (1990) defines reader's theater as the oral presentation of drama, prose, or poetry by two or more readers. Reader's theater differs from orally reading a selection in that several readers take the parts of the characters in the story or play. Instead of memorizing or improvising their parts as in other types of theater productions, the players read them. Because the emphasis is on what the audience *hears* rather than sees, selection of the literature is very important. Reader's theater scripts generally contain a great deal of dialogue and are often adapted from literature. Researchers have found that the use of reader's theater significantly improves reading fluency (Martinez, Roser, & Strecker, 1998/1999). Although fluency instruction is most often emphasized in the early grades, middle and high school students also have much to gain from becoming more fluent readers. Older students can become more fluent readers through repeated reading practice, which is best accomplished through performance-based activities such as reader's theater. An example of a reader's theater script is illustrated in Figure 8.3. Be sure to include stories that reflect culturally and linguistically diverse characters.

During a reader's theater program, the members of the audience use their imagination to visualize what is going on, because movement and action are limited. Although there is no one correct arrangement of the cast in presenting reader's theater, an effective procedure is to have the student readers stand in a line facing away from the audience and then turn toward the audience when they read their part.

Reader's theater is not simply reading a selection of text over and over and then performing it for an audience. Effective teachers know that following several key features will yield much better results from this research-based instructional strategy. Notice in the following guidelines how parts are not assigned until the entire class has practiced the text:

- Introduce the piece and have the students read it through once (chorally) to become familiar with the words
- Direct students to look for places where they could "add" things like feeling, expression, pauses, and enunciation
- Ask students to model suggestions for the class for enhancing the text
- Practice the piece of text together, phrase by phrase
- Read the entire piece as a class using the suggested expression
- Stop the process when necessary to reteach, model, or discuss fluency issues
- Assign reader's theater parts to students
- Practice individual reader's theater parts
- Perform reader's theater
- Ask students to self-assess: "What did you do this time that was better?"
- Confirm their comments, offering suggestions

Props and scenery may be used but should be kept simple. As with oral reading of literature, giving an introduction and setting the mood before the presentation are important.

## Figure 8.3  A Reader's Theater Script: The Gifts of Wali Dad

**Reader Ages:** 8–13
**Characters:** 15

Narrators 1–4, Wali Dad, Merchant, Queen, King, Ministers 1 & 2, Peris 1 & 2, Servants 1–3

*Notes:* Wali Dad rhymes with "Wally Todd." *Paisa,* the smallest Indian coin, is pronounced "PAY-sa," sounding like "pace a." *Khaistan* is pronounced "KI-ston," rhyming with "iced on." *Nekabad* is pronounced "NEK-a-bod." *Peri* sounds like "Perry." *Peris* are benevolent beings akin to fairies or angels, imported into India from Persian mythology.

---

NARRATOR 1: In a mud hut far from town lived an old grass-cutter named Wali Dad.

NARRATOR 4: Every morning, Wali Dad cut and bundled tall, wild grass. Every afternoon, he sold it as fodder in the marketplace.

NARRATOR 2: Each day, he earned thirty paisa. Ten of the small coins went for food. Ten went for clothes and other needs. And ten he saved in a clay pot under his bed.

NARRATOR 3: In this manner Wali Dad lived happily for many years.

NARRATOR 1: One evening, Wali Dad dragged out the pot to see how much money it held. He was amazed to find that his coins had filled it to the brim.

WALI DAD: (to himself) What am I to do with all this money? I need nothing more than I have.

NARRATOR 4: Wali Dad thought and thought. At last he had an idea.

NARRATOR 2: The next day, Wali Dad loaded the money into a sack and carried it to a jeweler in the marketplace. He exchanged all his coins for a lovely gold bracelet.

NARRATOR 3: Then Wali Dad visited the home of a traveling merchant.

WALI DAD: Tell me, in all the world, who is the noblest lady?

MERCHANT: Without doubt, it is the young queen of Khaistan. I often visit her palace, just three days' journey to the east.

WALI DAD: Do me a kindness. The next time you pass that way, give her this little bracelet, with my compliments.

NARRATOR 1: The merchant was astonished, but he agreed to do what the ragged grass-cutter asked.

NARRATOR 4: Soon after, the merchant found himself at the palace of the queen of Khaistan. He presented the bracelet to her as a gift from Wali Dad.

QUEEN: (admiring the bracelet) How lovely! Your friend must accept a gift in return. My servants will load a camel with the finest silks.

NARRATOR 2: When the merchant arrived back home, he brought the silks to the hut of Wali Dad.

WALI DAD: Oh, no! This is worse than before! What am I to do with such finery?

MERCHANT: Perhaps you could give it to someone else.

NARRATOR 3: Wali Dad thought for a moment.

WALI DAD: Tell me, in all the world, who is the noblest man?

MERCHANT: That is simple. It is the young king of Nekabad. His palace, too, I often visit, just three days' journey to the west.

WALI DAD: Then do me another kindness. On your next trip there, give him these silks, with my compliments.

NARRATOR 1: The merchant was amused, but he agreed.

NARRATOR 4: On his next journey, he presented the silks to the king of Nekabad.

KING: A splendid gift! In return, your friend must have twelve of my finest horses.

*(Continued)*

MIDDLE GRADES

## 𝓕igure 8.3 *(Continued)*

NARRATOR 2: So the merchant brought the king's horses to Wali Dad.

WALI DAD: This grows worse and worse! What could I do with twelve horses? (thinks for a moment) I know who should have such a gift. I beg you, keep two horses for yourself, and take the rest to the queen of Khaistan!

NARRATOR 3: The merchant thought this was very funny, but he consented. On his next visit to the queen's palace, he gave her the horses.

NARRATOR 1: Now the queen was perplexed. She whispered to her prime minister,

QUEEN: Why does this Wali Dad persist in sending gifts? I have never even heard of him!

MINISTER 1: Why don't you discourage him? Send him a gift so rich, he can never hope to match it.

NARRATOR 4: So in return for the ten horses from Wali Dad, the queen sent back twenty mules loaded with silver.

NARRATOR 2: When the merchant and mules arrived back at the hut, Wali Dad groaned.

WALI DAD: What have I done to deserve this? Friend, spare an old man! Keep two mules and their silver for yourself, and take the rest to the king of Nekabad!

NARRATOR 3: The merchant was getting uneasy, but he could not refuse such a generous offer. So not long after, he found himself presenting the silver-laden mules to the king of Nekabad.

NARRATOR 1: The king, too, was perplexed and asked his prime minister for advice.

MINISTER 2: Perhaps this Wali Dad seeks to prove himself your better. Why not send him a gift he can never surpass?

NARRATOR 4: So the king sent back

NARRATOR 2: twenty camels with golden anklets,

NARRATOR 3: twenty horses with golden bridles and stirrups,

NARRATOR 1: twenty elephants with golden seats mounted on their backs,

NARRATOR 4: and twenty liveried servants to care for them all.

NARRATOR 2: When the merchant guided the servants and animals to Wali Dad's hut, the grass-cutter was beside himself.

WALI DAD: Will bad fortune never end? Please, do not stop for a minute! Keep for yourself two of each animal, and take the rest to the queen of Khaistan!

MERCHANT: (distressed) How can I go to her again?

NARRATOR 3: But Wali Dad pleaded so hard, the merchant consented to go just once more.

NARRATOR 1: This time, the queen was stunned by the magnificence of Wali Dad's gift. She turned again to her prime minister.

MINISTER 1: Clearly, the man wishes to marry you. Since his gifts are so fine, perhaps you should meet him!

NARRATOR 4: So the queen ordered a great caravan made ready, with countless horses, camels, and elephants. With the trembling merchant as guide, she and her court set out to visit the great Wali Dad.

NARRATOR 2: On the third day, the caravan made camp, and the queen sent the merchant ahead to tell Wali Dad of her coming. When Wali Dad heard the merchant's news, his head sank to his hands.

WALI DAD: (mournfully) Oh, no! Now I will be paid for all my foolishness. I have brought shame on myself, on you, and on the queen. What are we to do?

MERCHANT: I fear we can do nothing!

NARRATOR 1: The next morning, Wali Dad rose before dawn.

WALI DAD: (sadly) Good-bye, old hut. I will never see you again.

*(Continued)*

# *Figure 8.3*   *(Continued)*

NARRATOR 4: The old grass-cutter started down the road. But he had not gone far when he heard a voice.

PERI 1: (gently) Where are you going, Wali Dad?

NARRATOR 2: He turned and saw two radiant ladies.

NARRATOR 3: He knew at once they were peris from Paradise.

WALI DAD: (kneels) I am a stupid old man. Let me go my way. I cannot face my shame!

PERI 2: No shame can come to such as you. Though your clothes are poor, in your heart you are a king.

NARRATOR 1: The peri touched him on the shoulder.

NARRATOR 4: To his amazement, he saw his rags turn to fine clothes. A jeweled turban sat on his head. The rusty sickle at his waist was now a gleaming scimitar.

PERI 1: Return, Wali Dad. All is as it should be.

NARRATOR 2: Wali Dad looked behind him. Where his hut had stood, a splendid palace sparkled in the rising sun.

NARRATOR 3: In shock, he turned to the peris, but they had vanished.

NARRATOR 1: Wali Dad hurried back along the road. As he entered the palace, the guards gave a salute. Servants bowed to him, then rushed here and there, preparing for the visitors.

NARRATOR 4: Wali Dad wandered through countless rooms, gaping at riches beyond his imagining.

NARRATOR 2: Suddenly, three servants ran up.

SERVANT 1: (announcing) A caravan from the east!

SERVANT 2: No, a caravan from the west!

SERVANT 3: No, caravans from both east and west!

NARRATOR 3: The bewildered Wali Dad rushed outside to see two caravans halt before the palace. Coming from the east was a queen in a jeweled litter. Coming from the west was a king on a fine horse.

NARRATOR 1: Wali Dad hurried to the queen.

QUEEN: My dear Wali Dad, we meet at last. (looks at KING) But who is that magnificent king?

WALI DAD: I believe it is the king of Nekabad, Your Majesty. Please excuse me for a moment.

NARRATOR 4: He rushed over to the king.

KING: My dear Wali Dad, I had to meet the giver of such fine gifts. (looks at QUEEN) But who is that splendid queen?

WALI DAD: (smiling) The queen of Khaistan, Your Majesty. Please come and meet her.

NARRATOR 2: And so the king of Nekabad met the queen of Khaistan, and the two fell instantly in love.

NARRATOR 3: A few days later their marriage took place in the palace of Wali Dad. And the celebration went on for many days.

NARRATOR 1: At last Wali Dad had said good-bye to all his guests. The very next morning, he rose before dawn, crept quietly from the palace, and started down the road.

NARRATOR 4: But he had not gone far when he heard a voice.

PERI 1: Where are you going, Wali Dad?

NARRATOR 2: He turned and again saw the two peris.

WALI DAD: (kneels) Did I not tell you I am a stupid old man? I should be glad for what I have received, but—

PERI 2: Say no more. You shall have your heart's desire.

*(Continued)*

## Figure 8.3   *(Continued)*

NARRATOR 1: So Wali Dad became once more a grass-cutter,

NARRATOR 4: living happily in his hut for the rest of his days.

NARRATOR 2: And though he often thought warmly of his friends the king and queen,

NARRATOR 3: he was careful never to send them another gift.

*Source:* "The Gifts of Wali Dad: A Tale of India and Pakistan," by Aaron Shepard (New York: Atheneum, 1995). Adapted for storytelling by Aaron Shepard (2003). Reprinted by permission of the adapter (AS@aaronshep.com; www.aaronshep.com).

After students have presented several reader's theaters using teacher-made or commercially prepared scripts, students can write their own scripts, either adapting literature, poetry, plays, song lyrics, or speeches they enjoy or using stories they have written. Here's how to guide students to develop their own scripts: Once children have read a story, they transform it into a script through social negotiation. The writing of a story into a script requires much rereading as well as knowledge and interpretation of the text. Once the script is written, the children formulate, practice, and refine their interpretations. Finally, the reader's theater is presented to an audience from handheld scripts (Shanklin & Rhodes, 1989).

Choral reading and reader's theater motivate children to read the same material repeatedly to increase fluency. Many children will rehearse a part enthusiastically to present it to an audience.

## Involving Parents

The subject of reading is often perceived by parents as too complicated for them to teach their children. However, the success of a literary program, to a certain extent, depends on the literacy environment at home and involving parents as an essential part of literacy instruction (Morrow, Kuhn, & Schwanenflugel, 2007). In fact, when Don Holdaway (1979) conceived the shared book experience used in the majority of primary classrooms today, he was trying to mimic the authentic oral reading experiences of parents and children when children were read to at home.

Many teachers develop home reading programs that motivate parents to read to their children on a regular basis. Some hold evening workshops where they model simple strategies such as paired reading, choral reading, and repeated readings and then engage parents in discussions on the significance of the methods (Morrow, Kuhn, & Schwanenflugel, 2007; Rasinski & Fredericks, 1991). Others simply send home leveled classroom books and expect parents to read to or with their child daily. Although family involvement programs vary from classroom to classroom, the following guidelines should be present for a successful program (Morrow, Kuhn, & Schwanenflugel, 2007; Padak and Rasinski, 2008):

- Use proven and effective strategies to maximize the effectiveness of the time parents have to work with children.
- Make the activities easy to understand and initiate for quick results.
- Provide a forum such as a workshop for parents to report on what they are noticing.
- Use content that is nonthreatening and fun.
- Encourage parents to use expression while reading so that the text comes alive and children hear fluent reading.
- Provide materials. Some parents don't have reading materials available—don't let this cause your plan to be unsuccessful.

# Routines for Fluency Development

In Boxes 8.3 to 8.6 over the next few pages we examine four fluency routines: the **fluency development lesson (FDL)** (Box 8.3), the **oral recitation lesson** (Box 8.4), the **support reading strategy** (Box 8.5), and **cross-age reading** (Box 8.6). Each emphasizes specific aspects of fluency training and integrates the teaching of fluency with teaching other important aspects of reading such as comprehension and word recognition.

Routines such as the fluency development lesson, the oral recitation lesson, the support reading strategy, and cross-age reading are best practices that need to be included in the teaching of reading. Not only do they provide systematic fluency instruction and practice, but they also focus on comprehension. Box 8.7 on page 268 discusses how a literacy coach might help a teacher with fluency instruction.

Next the focus shifts to informal ways to assess and monitor fluency development. How does a teacher know if students are developing fluency? There are no formal tests to measure automaticity in reading.

**STANDARD 2.2**

**BUILDING TEACHING SKILLS: CASE STUDY**

Go to the Homework and Exercises section in Chapter 8 of MyEducationLab to complete the case study and to identify strategies you might use with students struggling with word identification and fluency.

# Monitoring Oral Reading Fluency

One of the best ways to begin to understand how students approach reading and ensure they are making appropriate progress is to periodically listen to them read orally and keep records of assessment. Monitoring students' progress in reading fluency will help determine the effectiveness of your instruction as well as helping

---

**BOX 8.3**

STEP-BY-STEP *Lesson*

## The Fluency Development Lesson

The fluency development lesson (FDL) was devised for primary teachers to help students increase reading fluency (Rasinski, Padak, Linek, & Sturtevant, 1994). The FDL takes about 10 to 15 minutes to complete. Each child has a copy of passages from 50 to 150 words.

### Steps in the Fluency Development Lesson

1. Read the text to the class while students follow along silently with their own copies. This step can be repeated several times.
2. Discuss the content of the text as well as the expression the teacher used while reading to the class.
3. Together, read the text chorally several times. For variety, the students can read in antiphonal and echo styles.
4. Have the class practice reading the text in pairs. Each student takes a turn reading the text to a partner three times. The partner follows along with the text, provides help when needed, and gives positive feedback.

5. Working with the entire class, have volunteers perform the text. Individuals, pairs, and groups of four perform for the class. Arrangements can be made for students to read to the principal, the secretary, the custodian, or other teachers and classes. Students should also read the text to their parents. In this way, students are given much praise for their efforts.

Rasinski and colleagues (1994) worked with primary-grade teachers in implementing FDL three to four times a week from October to June. The children in these classes experienced greater improvement in overall reading achievement, word recognition, and fluency than a comparable group of children who received a more traditional type of supplemental instruction using the same passages. The greatest gains were made by the children who were the poorest readers at the beginning of the year.

---

*Source:* Based on "Effects of Fluency Development on Urban Second Grade Readers," by T. V. Rasinski, N. D. Padak, N. L. Linek, and E. Sturtevant, 1994, *Journal of Educational Research, 87,* pp. 158–165.

BOX **8.4**

## STEP-BY-STEP *Lesson*

### The Oral Recitation Lesson

The oral recitation lesson (ORL) also provides a useful structure for working on fluency in daily reading instruction (Hoffman, 1985). ORL has two components: *direct instruction* and *student practice*.

#### Steps in the Oral Recitation Lesson

##### DIRECT INSTRUCTION COMPONENT

1. Model fluency by reading a story to the class.
2. Lead a discussion of the story, and ask students to summarize what happened. (As a variation, the children can predict what will happen as the story unfolds. Hoffman emphasizes that predictable stories should be used in the ORL.)
3. Talk with students about what expressive oral reading is like—that it is smooth, not exceedingly slow, and that it demonstrates an awareness of what punctuation marks signal.
4. Have students read in chorus and individually, beginning with small text segments and gradually increasing the length of the segment. (We suggest that choral reading techniques be used. This can show students how prosodic cues facilitate meaning for listeners.)

5. Choose individual students to select and orally read a portion of the text for their classmates. Other class members provide positive feedback to students on the aspects of expressive oral reading discussed.

##### STUDENT PRACTICE COMPONENT

Students practice orally reading the same text used in the direct instruction component. The goal is to achieve oral reading fluency. Hoffman suggests that second graders should reach the goal of reading 75 words a minute with 98 percent accuracy before moving to another story. This component takes from 10 to 15 minutes, with students doing soft or whisper reading. The teacher checks on individual mastery and maintains records of students' performance on individual stories.

Pairs of students:

1. Read a personally selected portion of the selection silently
2. Read to a partner three times
3. Self-evaluate each repetition
4. Evaluate improvement in smoothness, word accuracy, and expression

*Source:* Based on "The Oral Recitation Lesson: A Teacher's Guide," by J. V. Hoffman (Austin, TX: Academic Resource Consultants, 1985).

---

BOX **8.5**

## *Research-Based Practices*    The Support Reading Strategy

The support reading strategy was designed to integrate several aspects of fluency growth into traditional basal instruction over a 3-day period. Morris and Nelson (1992) used this strategy in a second-grade classroom with low-achieving students who had made little progress in the preceding 11 months and thus were at the initial stages of reading development. Their reading achievement increased substantially after 6 months of the support reading strategy.

The first day, the teacher reads a story to a small group of children in a fluent, expressive voice. Throughout the reading, the teacher stops and asks the children to clarify what is happening in the story and then to predict what will happen

next. The teacher and children echo-read the story, with the students reading their own books. The teacher monitors each child's reading and provides assistance where needed.

The next day, the teacher pairs the readers, and the pairs reread the story; each reader reads alternating pages. Each pair is then assigned a short segment from the story to practice reading orally with fluency.

The third day, while the class is working individually or in small groups on writing or other tasks, individual children read the story to the teacher. The teacher monitors the reading by taking a running record, a procedure for monitoring word recognition strategies (see Chapter 7).

*Source:* Based on "Supported Oral Reading with Low-Achieving Second Graders," by D. Morris and L. Nelson, 1992, *Reading Research and Instruction, 31*, pp. 49–63.

BOX **8.6**

## Research-Based Practices

## Cross-Age Reading

Labbo and Teale (1990) claimed that a significant problem with many struggling readers in middle school is a lack of fluency. Cross-age reading provides these readers with a lesson cycle that includes modeling by the teacher, discussing the text, and allowing for opportunities to practice fluency.

Cross-age reading also provides middle school youngsters with a legitimate reason for practicing for an oral reading performance. In short, cross-age reading seems to be a powerful way to provide middle school students with purposeful activities to develop reading fluency, as well as to provide younger students with valuable literary experiences.

The cross-age reading program described by Labbo and Teale (1990) has four phases: preparation, prereading collaboration, reading to kindergartners, and postreading collaboration.

### Phase 1

In the preparation phase, the older students are helped by their teacher to prepare for a storybook-sharing session in three specific ways. First, the teacher helps select appropriate books. Students can be guided to select books they personally like, that have elements in the story that the kindergarten students can identify with, and that have illustrations that complement the story.

Second, the teacher helps the students prepare by having them engage in repeated readings of the text. Students may be paired with partners who can give each other positive feedback concerning growth in fluency and expressiveness of oral reading. Students should also rehearse on their own to gain control over and confidence with a story.

Third, as part of preparation, the teacher helps the students decide how their books will be introduced, where to stop in their books to discuss the story, and what questions to ask to ensure the kindergartner's involvement in the story.

### Phase 2

The purpose of the *prereading collaboration* phase is to ensure that the students are ready to share their books orally. In a 15- to 20-minute session a few days before the actual reading to the kindergartners, the older students set personal goals concerning their reading, report on and try out their ideas for involving the kindergartners, and receive and give feedback in a positive, supportive environment.

### Phase 3

Once the readers are prepared, they are ready for *reading to kindergartners*. They go as a group with the teacher to the kindergarten classroom and read their prepared story to small groups of youngsters. This activity generally generates enthusiasm among both readers and kindergartners.

MIDDLE GRADES

### Phase 4

The *postreading collaboration* phase is an opportunity for the students to share and reflect on the quality of the storybook reading interactions. The reflective nature of these postreading discussions can also help students develop strategies to improve subsequent readings.

In an urban district in Texas, fourth graders regularly read to kindergartners and first graders in a cross-age reading program. But soon after the program began, the fourth-grade teachers realized they were not able to provide sufficient support to help their students read fluently and lead the younger children through a directed listening–thinking activity. Some children needed more encouragement to practice the book enough to become fluent themselves—particularly as teachers expected the fourth graders to be able to ask the younger children for predictions about a reading as well as answers to simple comprehension questions. To help solve the problem, fourth-grade teachers enlisted the aid of high school students. Soon the fourth graders were paired with high school buddies. Once a week, each pair met to practice fluency and to prepare ways to engage the kindergartners and first graders in making predictions at different junctures in the story.

Cross-age reading has expanded to involve having the middle school children write stories for the younger children to read and then to write stories with the younger children (Leland & Fitzpatrick, 1994). Cross-age reading and writing programs often also have both the older and younger students read the stories to their parents or some other caring adult (Fox & Wright, 1997; Leland & Fitzpatrick, 1994).

*Source:* Based on "Cross-Age Reading: A Strategy for Helping Poor Readers," by L. Labbo and W. Teale, 1990, *The Reading Teacher, 43*, pp. 362–369.

## BOX 8.7

*Viewpoint*  the *Literacy Coach*

### Coaching for Fluency

Literacy coaches are working closely with teachers to discuss fluency assessment results and identify students who need particular kinds of fluency instruction. A coach might discuss strategies for improving fluency and then possibly demonstrate one of the strategies as the teacher observes the lesson for key teaching actions and student performance. Following the lesson, the teacher and coach would debrief the lesson demonstration and coplan the next fluency lesson that the teacher would implement. This process of coplanning, observing, and then debriefing would continue one or more times as

the teacher hones the strategy and observes improvement in the student's fluency.

A reading coach may also discuss and demonstrate ways to assess fluency in the context of the instruction (e.g., records of oral reading, audiotaping students' reading and analyzing afterward, and teaching students to keep track of their own progress in words read per minute, accuracy, and use of expression). Can you think of other kinds of support a coach might provide?

**STANDARDS 5.2, 5.3**

**STANDARD 3.1**

you set instructional goals. Also, seeing their fluency growth reflected in the graphs you keep can motivate students. The quickest and most informal way to monitor a reader's fluency is simply to listen to the child read orally. By listening to phrasing, rate, and expression, teachers informally monitor which students are not fluent readers. Teachers might want to use a simple fluency rating scale, such as the one shown in Figure 8.4, for this type of monitoring.

There is another simple informal procedure a teacher can use to check students' ability to read fluently. First, the student reads orally from a passage that he or she has not previewed or practiced. After reading, the student retells everything that he or she remembers about the passage. The teacher can follow up with questions that probe comprehension if the child does not provided enough information. This informal test gives the teacher two indications of automaticity. First, does the child read with few hesitancies and with expression? Lack of expression is an indicator of a disfluent reader. The second indicator is the quality of the child's retelling of the story or the ability to answer questions about it. If the child can read orally and comprehend the text at the same time, as these tasks' conditions demand, the decoding had to be automatic (Samuels, 1988).

The rate at which one reads is related to fluency. Poor fluency is characterized by slow, word-by-word reading. Thus calculating a reading rate offers an approach to monitoring fluency for teachers who desire a more formal, quantitative approach. Probably the easiest way to formally assess fluency is to take timed samples of students' reading and

**HOMEWORK EXERCISE: CASE STUDY**

Go to the Homework and Exercises section in Chapter 8 of MyEducationLab to complete the case study and develop a deeper understanding of how you can monitor students' progress.

**STANDARD 3.2**

## *Figure* 8.4    Rating Fluency

As a child reads, listen and decide which of the descriptions below best describes his or her general fluency during reading. Chart fluency each time a child reads. In the process, you may want to take notes about what seems to influence the child's reading performance.

RATING

- Poor: Reads primarily word by word
- Fair: Reads primarily in phrases with little intonation; ignores some punctuation
- Good: Reads fluently with expression

*Source:* Adapted from *Classrooms That Work: They Can All Read and Write*, 2nd ed., by P. M. Cunningham and R. L. Allington, p. 49. Published by Allyn and Bacon, Boston, MA. Copyright © 1999 by Pearson Education. Reprinted by permission of the publisher.

## Figure 8.5 Monitoring Fluency by Calculating Reading Rates

Ask the reader to read the text in a normal manner as you time the reading. The text should be at or slightly below the level the student can read and understand with little difficulty. Keep track of when the reader has read for 1 minute. Then count the number of words read. This is the reader's rate per minute. You need several 60-second samples before you can calculate an average rating. Compare the reader's oral reading rate against the following second-semester grade-level estimates:

- Grade 1: 80 words per minute
- Grade 2: 90 words per minute
- Grade 3: 110 words per minute
- Grade 4: 140 words per minute
- Grade 5: 160 words per minute
- Grade 6: 180 words per minute

Readers who read at a rate that is consistently and substantially below the appropriate grade-level reading rate need assistance in developing reading fluency.

*Source:* Adapted from *Effective Reading Strategies: Teaching Children Who Find Reading Difficult,* 2nd ed., by T. Rasinski and N. Padak (Upper Saddle River, NJ: Merrill, 2000), p. 105.

to compare their performance (number of words read correctly per minute) with published oral reading fluency norms or standards. Rasinski and Padak (2000) suggest the fluency-monitoring procedure in Figure 8.5 to calculate reading rate.

Technology available today is making an impact on how teachers across the country assess fluency and other early literacy skills. Instead of assessing fluency with a timer and paper and pencil and then entering the data manually as described above, teachers are learning how to use handheld devices to administer assessments. With this technology, data are immediately entered and teachers are able to view the results at once in several formats (including charts and graphs) on their handheld computers. Teachers we have talked with report that once they learn how to use these new devices, they enjoy the efficiency handhelds bring to the process. They value the ease of administration and all-inclusiveness of the tool, the accuracy it provides since they don't have to worry about managing a timer while marking responses, and the easy-to-read graphics and display of data that are immediately entered into a central system.

In addition to developing oral reading fluency, students need time in class to develop fluency in silent reading, in which comprehension is the sole reason for reading. Next we concern ourselves with the silent reading program.

## Developing Silent Reading Fluency

At the beginning of this chapter, we defined fluent reading as reading easily and well with a sense of confidence and knowledge of what to do when things go wrong. Fluent readers are seasoned readers, just as some individuals are considered to be seasoned runners. A seasoned runner has knowledge of what it is like to run for long periods of time. Although seasoned runners have developed patterns of running, they choose when, where, and how far to run. They have gained much knowledge about themselves, how to assess how they feel so they do not run too far (or they run far enough), and what they can do to protect themselves from a running injury. Self-knowledge contributes to self-confidence as a runner. In short, seasoned runners have *metacognition* for running—they know about the task of running, about themselves as runners, and how to monitor themselves during running.

STANDARD
1.4

Fluent readers are seasoned readers in that they are able to sustain reading for longer periods. They know that productive silent reading means accomplishing as much silent reading as possible during a period of time. They know that to do this they must keep their mind on the ideas being expressed, responding to high-potency words and sentences and giving less attention to ideas of lesser importance. Although there are distinct patterns in their reading, they choose daily what they are going to read, for what purposes, and how long they need to read to suit those purposes. They know that on some days and with some reading materials, they probably won't be able to concentrate as well as on other days or with other materials.

Similar to seasoned runners, fluent readers develop a metacognition for reading. They know about the task of reading, about themselves as readers, and how to self-monitor their reading. Fluent readers perceive themselves as able readers. They engage in a reading task with confidence that they will succeed.

Fluent readers grow in leaps and bounds from silent reading experiences. *Sustained silent reading*, in which children read materials they choose themselves, is important to the development of reading fluency.

**BUILDING TEACHING SKILLS: LESSON PLANNING**

Go to the Homework and Exercises section in Chapter 8 of MyEducationLab to create a new lesson plan around a sustained silent reading activity.

STANDARD 4.1

## Sustained Silent Reading

As explained by Hunt (1970), **sustained silent reading (SSR)** is a structured activity in which students are given fixed time periods for reading self-selected materials silently. SSR is often creatively coined: *SQUIRT* (sustained quiet un-interrupted reading time), *DEAR* (drop everything and read), or *DIRT* (daily individualized reading time). Whatever the acronym, the intention is to provide the students with time to read books of their choice.

One of the basic guidelines of SSR is that students should be allowed to select their own books to read during the set aside time. Most teachers give students the freedom to choose a book that they think they'll enjoy. However, some teachers have students select from a predetermined reading list or a bin of books color coded to indicate reading level. "Silent" means different things to different teachers, too. Some teachers require complete silence, while others allow children to share quietly with a friend or partner up for paired reading.

A major reason why a structured reading activity such as SSR is so important is that despite teacher encouragement, many students do not choose to read on their own. SSR provides for all students the kind of reading experience in school that avid readers get on their own—the chance to read whatever they want to read without being required to answer questions or read orally. In other words, reading for the sake of reading should not be reserved for only the good readers.

STANDARD 4.4

The overall goals of SSR are (1) to produce students who choose reading *over other activities* and (2) to encourage students to read *self-selected material voluntarily* for information or pleasure. Today there is growing evidence that these goals are being met. Readence, Bean, and Baldwin (2004) report that SSR influences fluency and students' attitudes toward reading. Gardiner (2001) conducted research in English classes over a 20-year period in order to gauge the impact of SSR on high school students' achievement. He found that students who were engaged in repeated SSR earned higher grades and were more likely to read for pleasure outside of school. Likewise, international assessments of literacy development show that higher-achieving students are more likely to have positive attitudes toward reading (Shiel & Cosgrove, 2002). These students also check out more library books and engage in pleasure reading outside of school.

Even the most reluctant reader is motivated to read when a structured period of silent reading is provided Gambrell (1996). Levine (1984) found that special education high school students who read 6 to 8 years below grade level became engrossed in reading during SSR. In fact, children who say they do not like to read and who disrupt classes will read during SSR.

Learning to read independently is a major benefit. Without SSR some students may never obtain independence and self-direction in reading and in choosing what they would like to read. Students will read if they are given time to read, if they are permitted to choose their own reading selections, and if what they read does not have to be discussed, labeled, or repeated back to the teacher.

McCracken and McCracken (1978), who have contributed much to the concept of SSR, identified seven positive messages about reading that children learn by participating in SSR.

1. *Reading books is important.* Children develop a sense of what the teacher values by noting what the teacher chooses to have them do. Children who spend most of their time completing worksheets will perceive this work as important. Children who read only basal-reader-length stories will perceive reading stories five to ten pages in length as important. If teachers want their students to choose to read fully developed pieces of literature, they must provide time for children to read such materials.

2. *Reading is something anyone can do.* Because no one watches them, poor readers can make mistakes without worrying. Able readers are "relieved they do not have to prove that they are bright every time they read something" (McCracken, 1971, p. 582). When one is allowed to choose one's own material and read at one's own rate, reading is something *everyone* can do.

3. *Reading is communicating with an author.* Reading is often perceived by students as communicating with a teacher if it is done only in situations in which short snatches of material are read with reactions then elicited by the teacher. One of the most exciting reactions to SSR we have observed in students is their individual responses to an author's message.

4. *Children are capable of sustained thought.* Many teachers are concerned that students "have short attention spans" and that they "don't stick to a task for very long." Students, however, have relatively little trouble sustaining their reading for long periods of SSR. They actually look forward to the extended peacefulness.

5. *Books are meant to be read in large sections.* If basal reading is the main way students participate in reading, they often get the notion that reading involves reading three- to ten-page segments, not whole selections of literature. In SSR, students get to read larger chunks of material.

6. *Teachers believe that pupils are comprehending.* It is neither possible nor desirable for teachers to know what each student has learned and felt about every story or book read. Students take something away from every reading experience. One way teachers can show students they trust them to learn from reading is not to question them about what they read during SSR.

7. *The teacher trusts the children to decide when something is well written.* When SSR programs are functioning, students are not asked to report on what they have read. What often happens is that students will want to share spontaneously what they have read and feel is worth sharing.

Classrooms without voluntary, sustained reading often foster the idea that reading is something one does when forced and only for short periods of time. Each of these positive messages about reading is an important notion to get across if we want students to choose reading over other activities.

## Putting SSR into Action

When beginning SSR with your class, talk over with students the reasons for having it and the rules. For example, (1) everyone reads; (2) everyone is quiet; and (3) everyone stays seated (Hilbert, 1993). If they are near the end of a book, they need to have a new choice at hand. Many teachers do not require that students sit at their desks during SSR, but students must decide where to sit before SSR begins. A "Do Not Disturb" sign outside the classroom door is often helpful.

Initially, begin with short periods of SSR, perhaps 5 to 10 minutes for first and second graders and 10 to 20 minutes for third through sixth graders. Gradually extend the time to 30 to 45 minutes for the middle school students. Hilbert (1993) suggests beginning the timing when the last child has actually begun to read.

During SSR, children read books of their own choosing. At first many reluctant readers choose comics, joke books, and other short books with pictures. Often, as the year goes on, children begin selecting more challenging pieces of literature as well as nonfiction selections (Hilbert, 1993). It often takes a month of daily SSR for the more reluctant or restless reader to get into reading for a sustained period of time.

By discussing their own experiences with sustained silent reading and using questions, teachers can develop the understanding in young readers' minds that reading means getting as many big ideas out of print through sustained silent reading as they possibly can. The teacher's main role in SSR is one of modeling the importance of reading, showing students the "teacher as reader."

## WHAT ABOUT STRUGGLING READERS AND *Reading Fluency?*

Slow, inefficient reading requires students to invest large amounts of time and mental energy in the task of reading, time that could be better spent processing and comprehending text. One important way to assist struggling readers is to provide models of fluent reading so they know what a good reader sounds like. This can be accomplished through teacher read-alouds or by using books and audiotapes in a listening center. Audiotapes can be sent home with children as an effective way to practice fluency outside of school. Minilessons on the essentials of fluency prior to reading aloud will help students focus on important features of fluent reading such as attention to punctuation, appropriate phrasing, and expression.

Research has shown that fluency can be increased through repeated readings of texts. Struggling readers will benefit from repeated readings of predictable and familiar texts, choral reading, and reader's theater. Strategies such as these support struggling readers by providing them with opportunities to enhance reading fluency without risking failure. Providing safe opportunities for oral reading practice will increase fluency for struggling readers, enhancing text comprehension.

## WHAT ABOUT STANDARDS, ASSESSMENT, AND *Reading Fluency?*

Fluent readers are able to read aloud with ease, accuracy, and proper intonation and phrasing. They recognize words with a high degree of automaticity and are therefore able to focus their attention on the meaning of the text rather than on simply decoding words (Rasinski, 2003). A report of the National Reading Panel (2000) cites fluency instruction as a key, though often neglected, component of effective reading programs.

Most grade-level standards for the English language arts established by state departments of education include an explicit standard for fluency development in the elementary grades. Included among North Carolina's third-grade competency expectations, for example, is the goal of being able to read aloud a grade-appropriate text with fluency, comprehension, and expression. Similar fluency goals are included in the North Carolina standards for other elementary grade levels (North Carolina Department of Public Instruction, 2004).

At the national level, the National Assessment of Educational Progress (NAEP), a program sponsored by the U.S. Department of Education to evaluate the academic achievement of students nationwide, has included the study of oral reading fluency in its assessment of reading achievement. To assess the oral reading fluency of fourth-grade students, NAEP (NCES, 1995) used the four-level rubric summarized below:

*Level 4.* The student reads primarily in larger, meaningful phrase groups. Some deviations from the text may be present; however, these do not detract from the overall clarity of the story. The author's intended syntax is consistently communicated. Appropriate expression is used throughout the reading of the story.

*Level 3.* The student reads primarily in three- or four-word phrase groups. Some smaller word groupings may also be present. Most of the student's phrasing is appropriate and the author's syntax is preserved; however, little or no expressive interpretation is evident in the reading.

*Level 2.* The student reads in two-word phrases with some three- or four-word groupings. Some word-by-word reading may also occur. The manner in which words are grouped may make the reading sound awkward, and may inhibit the meaning of the passage from being appropriately conveyed.

*Level 1.* The student reads primarily word-by-word. Occasionally, two- or three-word phrases may occur, but these are infrequent and do not preserve meaningful expression of the story.

The NAEP assessment also considers the accuracy and rate of the student's oral reading. Accuracy is defined in terms of the number of miscues made by the reader including omitted, inserted, or substituted words. Reading rate is defined by the number of words read per minute. NAEP data suggest that students who read with greater fluency also read with greater speed than less fluent readers.

## Summary

This chapter explored how to help children develop both oral and silent reading fluency. An important goal of reading instruction, fluent reading with expression and comprehension requires practice and rereading.

We examined how automaticity in word recognition leads to the growth of competence and confidence in the developing reader. We defined and discussed repeated readings, choral reading, reader's theater, the use of technology, and routines and strategies that can be used to foster and develop fluency. Ways to involve parents and older students were suggested through paired reading and cross-age tutoring.

To provide all students with the kind of experience in school that avid readers get on their own—reading without having to respond immediately to questions—we believe in building a program of sustained silent reading (SSR). SSR is important in developing independent readers.

## Teacher Action Research

1. Either interview several elementary teachers or conduct a short survey in an elementary school about the different ways that teachers provide practice in oral reading for the purpose of developing students' reading fluency. Compile a list of the ideas in this chapter, including the oral recitation lesson (ORL), paired repeated readings, choral reading, cross-age reading, and automated reading. Based on what the teachers report, which of the ideas on your list seem to be the most popular ways of developing oral reading fluency in students? Furthermore, how does a teacher monitor for oral reading fluency? What are some of the indicators that a child is a disfluent reader? If the opportunity presents itself, observe one or two of the classrooms and describe what actual practices are used.

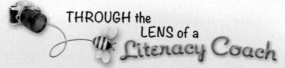

THROUGH the LENS of a Literacy Coach

2. Visit Readers Theatre Digest online (www.readerstheatredigest.com/viddown.php), a web site that provides an excellent video of a reader's theater performance of *The Three Wishes*. What features of fluency presented early in this chapter (accuracy, automaticity, and prosody), do you see in the video? If you were a literacy coach, how might you use this video to coach teachers in their use of reader's theater?

## Related Web Sites

*Aaron Shepard's Homepage*

**www.aaronshep.com**

An excellent resource for reader's theater and the possibilities it holds for enhancing fluency, this site has scripts to download as well as resources for storytelling.

*Gander Academy's Readers' Theater Page*

**www.stemnet.nf.ca/CITE/langrt.htm**

Gander Academy's Readers' Theater page has downloadable scripts, recommendations for writing your own scripts, and links to online resources.

*National Institute for Literacy*

**www.nifl.gov/partnershipforreading/publications/reading_first1fluency.html**

NIFL provides a definition of fluency and the components of fluency instruction, as well as describing how reading fluency can be developed and how to monitor student progress in fluency.

*Poetry Teachers.Com*

**www.poetryteachers.com**

The site provides ideas for poetry lessons, contests, and activities, as well as poetry plays students can perform.

*Scripts for Schools*

**www.scriptsforschools.com/1.html**

This comprehensive reader's theater resource for educators offers high-quality reader's theater scripts for elementary, middle, and high school levels. It also features a number of choral reading scripts, puppet scripts, and additional play scripts.

*StoryPlace: The Children's Digital Library*

**www.storyplace.org**

This award-winning bilingual (Spanish and English) site, sponsored by the Public Library of Charlotte and Mecklenburg Counties, North Carolina, includes a collection of online materials for elementary students including texts for reading along.

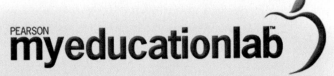

Now go to the Vacca et al. *Reading and Learning to Read*, Seventh Edition, MyEducationLab course at **www.myeducationlab.com** to

- Take a pretest to assess your initial comprehension of the chapter content
- Study chapter content with your individualized study plan
- Take a posttest to assess your understanding of chapter content
- Engage in multimedia exercises to help you build a deeper and more applied understanding of chapter content

CHAPTER **9**

# Vocabulary Knowledge and Concept Development

Standards found in this chapter:

- ▶ 1.3
- ▶ 1.4
- ▶ 2.2
- ▶ 2.3
- ▶ 4.1
- ▶ 4.2
- ▶ 5.3

## In this chapter, YOU WILL DISCOVER:

:• The relationship among students' experiences, concepts, and words
:• Principles that guide the teaching of vocabulary in elementary classrooms
:• Instructional strategies for teaching vocabulary using a variety of activities
:• Why vocabulary functions differently in literature and in content material
:• The use of the dictionary in vocabulary development

## Concept Map

### VOCABULARY KNOWLEDGE AND CONCEPT DEVELOPMENT

**THE RELATIONSHIP BETWEEN VOCABULARY AND COMPREHENSION**

| Best Practice | Experiences, Concepts, and Words |

Principles to Guide Vocabulary Instruction

**INSTRUCTIONAL STRATEGIES**

| Relating Experiences | Developing Word Meaning |

| Using Context | Classifying and Categorizing |

Developing Word Meaning Through Stories and Writing

Developing Independence in Vocabulary Learning

Maria, like so many children at the age of 4, is curious about language and undaunted in the use (and misuse) of words. In her zest to learn, Maria plays with language, often experimenting and using words spontaneously to express herself or to describe new experiences and understandings. As her language expands, so does Maria's world. Ever since developing the concept of *word,* she does not hesitate to ask, "What's that word mean?" when she hears an unfamiliar word used in conversation or in media. No one in her family blinked when Maria asked, "What is a distracter?"

Maria and her family were visiting a friend's family on the Fourth of July to enjoy an afternoon of food and an evening of fireworks. During a conversation between Maria's mother and Terry, a family friend, Maria overheard Terry using the word *distracter.* Terry was explaining that it was difficult to get anything done at work because of all the distractions and continued to explain that when she goes home there are many distractions and distracters. She talked about the difficulty of completing work around the house because of the many day-to-day distractions and referred to her two children as "distracters." Terry did not make reference to her children as "distracters" in a mean way—rather as a matter of fact.

Later that afternoon Maria's mother was sitting in a lounge chair in the backyard enjoying the picnic. Maria jumped up on her mother's lap and asked, "What is a distracter?" Her mother asked why she wanted to know and Maria said that Terry called her children "distracters." Maria's mother proceeded to explain that a distracter is someone that takes someone else away from something that they were doing. Maria, satisfied with the explanation, jumped off her mother's lap and went to play with the other children. Later that evening after the fireworks, Maria's mother was gathering up their things to get ready to go home. Her mother went to Maria who was busily playing with sparklers and said that she needed to get ready to go home because it was late. Maria without hesitation turned to her mother and said, "Mom, you are a distracter" and went back to playing with the sparklers.

It's like day and night, the difference between classrooms where children like Maria are allowed to experiment and play with words and classrooms in which the learning of words is focused on lists. Teachers in the former take advantage of children's natural spontaneity and creativity, knowing that part of the joy of teaching is the unpredictability of what children will say or do. These teachers create classroom environments in which opportunities to experiment with words abound. Every time a student makes a decision as to which word is best in a piece of writing, vocabulary learning takes place. Mark Twain said that the difference between the right word and the almost right word is the difference between lightning and the lightning bug. Children experiment with words whenever they hear unfamiliar words read aloud in literature or whenever they encounter new words while reading. They develop an ear for language and an eye for the images created by language.

Nevertheless, teachers face real problems in developing vocabulary knowledge and concepts in their classrooms every day. For as "children's vocabulary grows, their ability to comprehend what they read grows as well" (Rupley, Logan, & Nichols, 1999, p. 336). Children are likely to have trouble understanding what they read if they are not readily familiar with most words they meet in print. A foundation in oral language and concept development is essential (Blachowicz & Fisher, 2004).

Too often we assume that children will develop an understanding of words from such staple activities as discussing, defining, and writing the words in sentences. We do little else instructionally. Yet students must not only be able to define words but also experience unfamiliar words in frequent, meaningful, and varied contexts. Nagy and Scott (2000) believe that "knowing a word means being able to do things with it: to recognize it in connected speech or in print, to access its meaning, to pronounce it—and to be able to do these things within a fraction of a second" (p. 273). Therefore a major premise of this chapter is that *definitional knowledge* is necessary, but students must also develop *contextual* and *conceptual knowledge* of words to comprehend fully what they read.

STANDARD
1.4

Children experiment with words whenever they encounter new words while reading.

Defining and using words in sentences are insufficient to ensure vocabulary learning. Teaching vocabulary through the memorization of short definitions and sentences suggests a "reductionist perspective," which contradicts the understanding of the reading process (Nagy & Scott, 2004, p. 574). Students need to be involved in *constructing* meaning rather than memorizing definitions. According to Nagy and Scott (2004), a reader who knows a word can recognize it, understand it, and use that understanding in combination with other types of knowledge, to construct meaning from text. The more that students, including those from diverse backgrounds, encounter vocabulary in as many language contexts as possible, the more they will come to know and use words. "Vocabulary plays an important role in reading, in many other aspects of schooling, and in the world beyond school" (Graves & Watts-Taffe, 2002, p. 141).

Have you ever heard a student who encounters a difficult word say with confidence, "I know what that word means!"? We share a concern that there are not enough children developing the I-know-that-word attitude. This chapter will emphasize ways to increase children's sensitivity to new words and their enjoyment in word learning. What instructional opportunities can be provided to influence the depth and breadth of children's vocabulary knowledge? What are the instructional implications of vocabulary for reading comprehension? How do students develop the interest and motivation to *want* to learn new words? How can students grow in independence in vocabulary learning? To answer these questions, we must first recognize that vocabulary development is not accidental. It must be orchestrated carefully not only during reading time but throughout the entire day.

## The Relationship Between Vocabulary and Comprehension

The relationship between knowledge of word meanings and comprehension has been well documented by researchers and acknowledged by children. Many students admit that sometimes they don't understand what they're reading because

**BUILDING TEACHING SKILLS: CASE STUDY**

Go to the Homework and Exercises section in Chapter 9 of MyEducationLab to complete the case study and think about the close relationship between vocabulary and comprehension and how that will influence the strategies you use.

"the words are too hard." The seminal work of F. B. Davis (1944) and other researchers such as Thurstone (1946) and Spearitt (1972) have consistently identified vocabulary knowledge as an important factor in reading comprehension.

Various explanations are used to account for the strong relationship between vocabulary and comprehension. Anderson and Freebody (1981) proposed three hypotheses: the **aptitude hypothesis**, the **knowledge hypothesis**, and the **instrumental hypothesis**. These three hypotheses are capsulized in Figure 9.1.

All three hypotheses have merit in explaining the relationship between word knowledge and comprehension. The implications of the aptitude and knowledge hypotheses signal the importance of reading aloud to children and immersing them in written language. Wide reading experiences develop a facility with written language. Further, the instrumental hypothesis is important to us as teachers: If word meanings are taught well enough, students will find reading material easier to comprehend. Unfortunately, vocabulary instruction research has provided contradictory evidence on this effect. Nagy (1988) summarizes some of the research this way:

> Imagine an experiment with two groups of students who are about to read a selection from a textbook. One group is given typical instruction on the meaning of some difficult words from the selection; the other group receives no instruction. Both groups are given passages to read and are tested for comprehension. Do the students who received the vocabulary instruction do any better on the comprehension test? Very often they do not. (p. 1)

According to several studies, many widely used methods generally fail to increase comprehension (Mezynski, 1983; Pearson & Gallagher, 1983; Stahl & Fairbanks, 1986). Why might this be the case? One explanation may involve the very nature of practices associated with vocabulary instruction. This instruction usually involves some combination

## *Figure 9.1*  Three Hypotheses for the Strong Relationship Between Vocabulary and Comprehension

**Aptitude Hypothesis**

Both vocabulary and comprehension reflect general intellectual ability. A large vocabulary as measured by test performance is a solid indicator of verbal and mental ability. The relationship is explained this way: The more intellectually able the student, the more she or he will know the meanings of words and therefore comprehend better while reading. It is best to guard against the pessimistic attitude that only the most intelligent child profits from instruction in vocabulary. A child's environment and experiences, including those in the classroom, are crucial in learning concepts and words.

**Knowledge Hypothesis**

The knowledge hypothesis suggests that vocabulary and comprehension reflect general knowledge rather than intellectual ability. In other words, students with large vocabularies related to a given topic also have more knowledge about the topic, which in turn produces better comprehension. Closely tied to the schema view of reading, the knowledge hypothesis proposes that vocabulary words must be taught within a larger framework of concept development.

**Instrumental Hypothesis**

The instrumental hypothesis establishes a causal chain between vocabulary knowledge and comprehension. The instrumental hypothesis can be defended thus: If comprehension depends in part on the knowledge of word meanings, vocabulary instruction ought to influence comprehension.

of looking up definitions, writing them down or memorizing them, and inferring the meaning of a new word from the context. These activities do not create enough *in-depth* knowledge to increase comprehension of difficult concepts. Other studies, however, indicate that comprehension is facilitated when vocabulary is taught *in depth* before reading begins (Beck, McKeown, & Omanson, 1987; McKeown & Beck, 2004; Stahl, 1983).

We've noticed that many teachers spend instructional time introducing vocabulary words *before* students read but do not spend much time on vocabulary *after* students have read. For example, few teachers encourage children to use significant vocabulary words *after* reading texts in activities such as retelling and written, oral, artistic, and dramatic responses to what has been read. Providing young students as well as middle school students opportunities to develop vocabulary throughout the reading process is essential.

Teaching vocabulary is not a simple process of teaching words but rather a systematic process that is multifaceted and influenced by various factors (Blachowicz & Fisher, 2000). Blachowicz and Fisher (2000) believe that teaching vocabulary involves "teaching particular words to particular students for a particular purpose" (p. 517). Therefore teachers need to understand vocabulary acquisition, students' vocabulary needs and abilities, and how to facilitate vocabulary learning for each student.

In order to produce the desired rates of learning vocabulary for struggling readers and second-language learners, vocabulary development must go beyond simple instruction and natural vocabulary acquisition. Nagy and Scott (2004) stress that the students who need the most help are those whose home experiences have not given them support in vocabulary learning. They are at a disadvantage in increasing their vocabulary if they are unable to use context to access word meanings and to do the amount of contextual reading required to develop their vocabulary.

Pearson, Hiebert, and Kamil (2007) stress the importance of connecting vocabulary instruction and assessment. When assessing vocabulary it is important to assess the in-depth knowledge of vocabulary. Therefore, assessments need to be authentic, performance based, and occur in multiple contexts. For assessment and vocabulary instruction for English learners, authentic reading materials that connect to real-life experiences in various contexts and adjusted to the appropriate level of English proficiency are essential.

Words need to be taught directly and well enough to enhance comprehension. Students must have quick access to word meanings when they are reading. Quick access for all students can be achieved through a variety of strategies that make use of students' definitional, contextual, and conceptual knowledge of words.

Before examining instructional strategies, the relationships of students' experiences, concepts, and words need to be explored. What are concepts? What does it mean to know words?

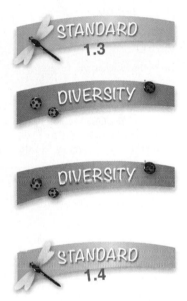

## Experiences, Concepts, and Words

One way to define **vocabulary** is to suggest that it represents the breadth and depth of all the words we know—the words we use, recognize, and respond to in meaningful acts of communication. *Breadth* involves the size and scope of our vocabulary; *depth* concerns the level of understanding that we have of words.

Vocabulary has usually been classified as having four components: *listening, speaking, reading,* and *writing.* These components are often said to develop in breadth and depth in the sequence listed. Children ages 5 and 6, for example, come to school already able to recognize and respond to thousands of spoken words. Children's first vocabulary without much question is listening vocabulary. However, as a child progresses through the school years, he or she eventually learns to identify and use as many written as spoken words. By adulthood, a person's reading vocabulary often outmatches any of the other vocabulary components.

**HOMEWORK EXERCISE: VIDEO**

Go to the Homework and Exercises section in Chapter 9 of MyEducationLab to watch the video "Teaching Vocabulary" and observe how one teacher connects concepts with new words.

An additional component of vocabulary includes new literacies. Since students need to be able to read critically and write functionally in various media, vocabulary development, regardless of the medium, is essential. A classroom that utilizes new literacies features daily work in multiple forms of representation (Kist, 2005). Understanding the various media and their key terms (e.g., digitalized, WebQuest, imaging, nonlinear, and visualization) is essential for developing new literacies.

Because of the developmental nature of vocabulary, it is more or less assumed that listening and speaking vocabularies are learned in the home, whereas reading, writing, and new literacies vocabularies fall within the domain of school. Although this assumption may generally hold, it creates an unnecessary dichotomy between inside and outside school influences. It is much safer to assume that both home and school are profoundly influential in the development of all components of vocabulary.

## Words as Labels for Concepts

Although **words** are labels for **concepts,** a single concept represents much more than the meaning of a single word. It might take thousands of words to explain a concept. However, answers to the question "What does it mean to know a word?" depend on how well we understand the relationships among words, concepts, and experiences. Understanding these relationships provides a sound rationale for teaching vocabulary within the larger framework of concept development.

Concepts are learned through our acting on and interaction with the environment. Edgar Dale (1965) reminded us how children learn concepts best: through direct, purposeful experiences. Dale's Cone of Experience in Figure 9.2 depicts the levels of abstraction from the most concrete, nonverbal experiences beginning at the base of the cone to the most abstract and removed experiences at the tip of the cone—verbal symbols. For a child who has never ridden on a roller coaster, the most intense and meaningful learning would occur during a trip to an amusement park! The relationship of experiences to concepts and words sets the stage for an important principle of vocabulary instruction: To learn new or unfamiliar words, it is necessary to have experiences from which concepts can be derived.

## Words and Concepts: A Closer Look

One way of thinking about a concept is that it is a mental image of something. By *something,* we mean anything that can be grouped together by common features or similar criteria—objects, symbols, ideas, processes, or events. In this respect, concepts are similar to schemata.

Concepts are synonymous with the formation of categories. We would be overwhelmed by the complexity of our environment if we were to respond to each object or event that we encountered as unique. So we invent categories (or form concepts) to reduce the complexity of our environment and the necessity for constant learning. Every canine need not have a different name to be known as a dog. Although dogs vary greatly, the common characteristics they share cause them to be referred to by the same general term. Thus to facilitate communication, we invent words to name concepts.

Scan a page from any dictionary and you will discover that most words are the names of concepts. The only place these words stand alone is on a dictionary page. In your mind, concepts are organized into a network of complex relationships. Suppose you were to fix your eyes on the word *baboon* as you scanned the entries in the dictionary. What picture comes to mind? Your image of *baboon* probably differs from that of another person. Your background knowledge of *baboon,* or the larger class to which it belongs known as *primates,* will very likely be different from someone else's. So will your experiences with and interests in baboons, especially if you are fond of frequenting the zoo or reading books about primate behavior. The point is that we organize background

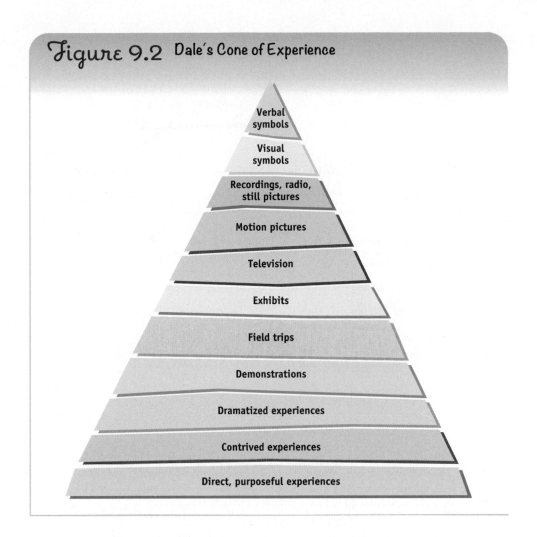

**Figure 9.2**  Dale's Cone of Experience

Verbal symbols

Visual symbols

Recordings, radio, still pictures

Motion pictures

Television

Exhibits

Field trips

Demonstrations

Dramatized experiences

Contrived experiences

Direct, purposeful experiences

knowledge and experiences into conceptual hierarchies according to class, example, and attribute relations. Let's take a closer look at these relationships.

## Class, Example, and Attribute Relationships

We stated that the concept *baboon* is part of a more inclusive class called *primates*, which in turn is a member of a larger class known as *mammals*, which in turn is a member of an even larger class of animals known as *vertebrates*. These *class relationships* are depicted in Figure 9.3 on page 284.

**Class relationships** in any conceptual network are organized in a hierarchy according to the **superordinate** and **subordinate** nature of the concepts. For example, in Figure 9.3, the superordinate concept is *animals*. There are two classes of animals, known as *vertebrates* and *invertebrates*, which are in a subordinate position in the hierarchy. However, *vertebrates* is superordinate in relation to *amphibians, mammals, birds,* and *fish*, which, of course, are types or subclasses of vertebrates. To complete the hierarchy, the concept *primates* is subordinate to *mammals* but superordinate to *baboons*.

By now you have probably recognized that for every concept there are examples of that concept. In other words, an *example* is a member of any concept under consideration. A *nonexample* is any instance that is not a member of the concept under consideration. Class example relationships are reciprocal. *Vertebrates* and *invertebrates* are examples of *animals*. *Mammals, birds, fish,* and *amphibians* are examples of *vertebrates*. A *primate* is an example of a *mammal*, and so on.

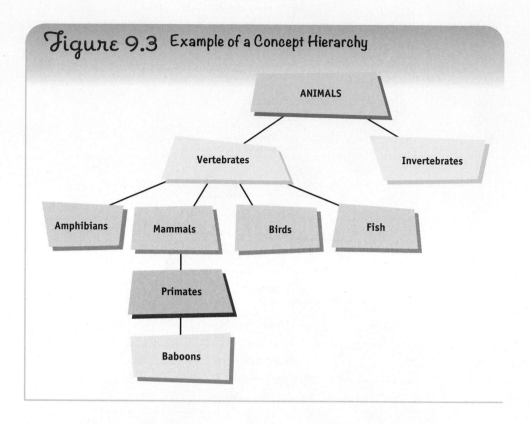

*Figure 9.3*  Example of a Concept Hierarchy

To extend this discussion, suppose we were to make *primates* our target concept. In addition to baboons, what are other examples of primates? No doubt, *apes*, *monkeys*, and *humans* come quickly to mind. These examples can be shown in relation to each other.

Note that the examples of primates given in Figure 9.4 are not exhaustive of all possible primates we could have listed. Nevertheless, we might ask, "What do baboons, apes, monkeys, and humans have in common?" Answers to this question would force us to focus on relevant *attributes*, the traits, features, properties, or characteristics that are common to every example of a particular concept. In other words, the relevant attributes of primates refer to the characteristics that determine whether baboons, monkeys, apes, and humans belong to the particular class of mammals called *primates*.

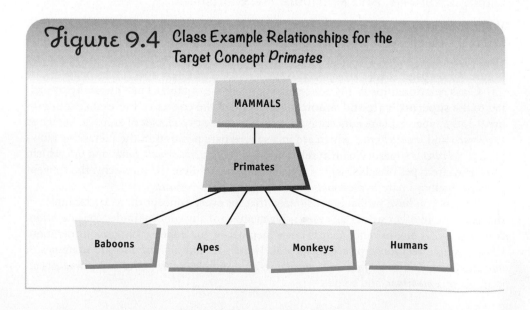

*Figure 9.4*  Class Example Relationships for the Target Concept *Primates*

All primates, from baboons to human beings, have certain physical and social characteristics, but not every primate shares each of these features. Nearly every example of a primate can grasp objects with its hands and/or feet. Vision is a primate's most important sense. Most species of primates live in groups, but some live alone. A social group is often considerable in size and highly organized. Primates have the capacity to communicate with one another by means of signals based on scent, touch, vision, and sound. And, of course, primate infants depend to a large extent on their mothers.

This discussion began when we asked you to form a mental image of *baboon*. The clarity with which you were able to picture a baboon in your mind depended, as you may have surmised, on how familiar you were with the characteristics of primates in general and baboons specifically. Baboons, apes, monkeys, and humans share common characteristics, but they also differ.

In what ways are baboons similar to other primates? How are baboons different? These are important questions in clarifying your concept of *baboon*

As children progress through their school years, they learn to identify and use as many written as spoken words.

and sorting out the relationships that exist among the various examples. Concept learning involves a search for attributes that can be used to distinguish examples from one another and to differentiate examples from nonexamples.

To promote students' conceptual understanding of key vocabulary, Simpson (1987) calls for an instructionally useful answer to the question "What does it mean to know a word?" Suppose that a concept to be developed in a third-grade social studies unit was *wigwam*. Students would need to be able to generate the information that wigwam was a shelter or home for Native Americans and that it was not as sturdy as a house. They could relate the wigwam to a tent they may have used on a camping trip or a scout outing, while noting that wigwams were made of lightweight wooden poles covered by layers of bark or reed mats. But suppose the concept in a science unit was a more abstract one such as *energy*. In this case, students would need to be able to generate the information that they needed energy to play and work but that they did not need much energy to sleep or to watch television. As the concept *energy* was explored further, students would realize that our bodies need food to produce energy, just as cars and airplanes need fuel to keep running. Students could even come up with the notion that nuclear reactors split atoms to produce electrical energy, which lights their houses and runs their television sets and video games.

Through such understandings, children gain depth in their word learning. Next, before we examine teaching strategies, let's look at some guidelines for establishing vocabulary programs throughout the primary and middle grades.

# Principles to Guide Vocabulary Instruction

In this section, we consider six principles to guide the teaching of vocabulary in elementary classrooms. They evolve from common sense, authoritative opinion, and research and theory on the relationship between vocabulary knowledge and reading comprehension.

## Principle I: Select Words That Children Will Encounter While Reading Literature and Content Material

**HOMEWORK EXERCISE: VIDEO**

Go to the Homework and Exercises section in Chapter 9 of MyEducationLab to watch the video "Introducing Words to Young Readers" and think about ways in which you can introduce words to young readers.

Readers can tolerate not knowing some words while reading; they can still comprehend the text selection. So vocabulary instruction that introduces a smattering of new words prior to a reading selection will boost comprehension. However, when vocabulary learning is centered on acquiring a large percentage of words appearing in actual selections that will be read in class, comprehension is likely to be enhanced significantly (McKeown & Beck, 2004; Stahl, 1983). Which words are the best choices for vocabulary instruction? Which aren't?

Words shouldn't be chosen for instructional emphasis just because they are big or obscure. Teaching archaic or difficult words just because they are unusual is not a legitimate reason for instruction. A reader learns to use monitoring strategies to overcome such obstacles. Nor should difficult words be chosen in expository and narrative texts if they do not relate to the central meaning of the passage or important concepts in it. McKeown and Beck (2004) suggest choosing words that students will read most often and that are useful to them. Maps or organizers of the reading material can be used to help identify the words for study. This is true for literature as well as for content area vocabulary instruction. For example, for the book *The Paperbag Princess*, by Robert N. Munsch (1980), one teacher chose the vocabulary from a map she constructed (see Figure 9.5).

Consider the following additional ways to choose words for instructional emphasis.

**KEY WORDS** ◆ Key words come directly from basal, literature, or content text selections. These words convey major ideas and concepts related to the passage content and are essential for understanding to take place. Key words need to be taught, *and taught well*, because they present definite obstacles to comprehension that cannot be overlooked by the reader.

**USEFUL WORDS** ◆ Useful words are relevant. Children encounter useful words repeatedly in a variety of contexts. In some cases, a child may be familiar with useful words, having learned them in earlier stories or units or in previous years. However, it cannot be assumed that these words are old friends; they may be mere acquaintances.

---

### Figure 9.5    Map for *The Paperbag Princess*

Characters:
1. Elizabeth: a princess with expensive clothes
2. Ronald: a prince
3. dragon: dragon smashed castle, burned Elizabeth's clothes, and carried off Ronald

Problem:
Elizabeth wanted Ronald back.

Resolution:
Elizabeth outwitted dragon by telling him he was the "fiercest" dragon and got Ronald back. Ronald told her to "come back when dressed like a real princess." Elizabeth told Ronald he looked like a prince but he was a bum.

Big Ideas:
* Sometimes using your brains wins out over physical strength.
* At times what you do is more important than what you wear.

**INTERESTING WORDS** ◆ Interesting words tickle the imagination and create enthusiasm, excitement, and interest in the study of words. Words that have unique origins, tell intriguing stories, or have intense personal meaning for students make good candidates for instruction. Children can get hooked on words through the study of interesting words.

**VOCABULARY-BUILDING WORDS** ◆ Classroom instruction should include words that lend themselves readily to vocabulary-building skills. **Vocabulary-building skills** allow children to seek clues to word meanings on their own. Words should be selected for instruction that will show students how to inquire into the meaning of unknown words—through structural analysis (i.e., drawing attention to word parts) or context analysis (Vacca & Vacca, 2005).

Choosing the appropriate words for English learners is important. Freeman and Freeman (2004) explain the need to teach explicitly content-specific vocabulary (key words) and general academic vocabulary (useful words). Although content-specific or key words are typically taught more often, developing general academic or useful words is just as essential, especially for English language learners.

## Principle 2: Teach Words in Relation to Other Words

Vocabulary words are often crucially tied to basic concepts. Children, as we have contended earlier, develop definitional knowledge when they are able to relate new words to known words. When words are taught in relation to other words, students are actively drawn into the learning process. They must use background knowledge and experiences to detect similarities and differences. When words are taught within the context of concept development, children develop a greater sensitivity to shades of meaning in communication. Rather than learning words randomly, students, especially linguistically and culturally diverse students, should deal with words that are related semantically and belong to categories.

Henry (1974) outlined four basic cognitive operations associated with learning concepts and words. The first involves the act of *joining*, or "bringing together." Comparing, classifying, and generalizing are possible through the act of joining. Asking children to explain how words are related or having them sort through word cards to put words into groups involves the act of joining.

The act of *excluding* is another conceptual operation worth considering when teaching words in relation to other words. Children must discriminate, negate, or reject items because they do not belong in a conceptual category. When a child must decide which word does not belong in a set of words, the process involves exclusion. In this case, the child would search through his or her background knowledge to distinguish examples from nonexamples or relevant attributes from irrelevant attributes. So when a child is asked to decide which word does not belong in the list *flower, music, perfume, skunk*, on what set of criteria is a decision made? One immediate response may have been that music doesn't belong since it has little to do with the concept of smell.

A third conceptual activity or operation involves the act of *selecting*. Students learn to make choices and to explain why they made their choices based on what they have experienced, know, or understand. Synonyms, antonyms, and multiple-meaning words lend themselves well to the act of selecting. For example, select the *best* word from the choices given in the following sentence:

Tyrone's quiet behavior was mistaken for _____.

SHYNESS / MODESTY / TERROR

Any of the choices might be acceptable. Yet the value of the activity is in providing a rationale for your choice by judging the worth of several potentially correct answers.

A fourth aspect of thinking conceptually involves the act of *implying*. Is a child able to make decisions based on if-then, cause-and-effect relationships among concepts and words? Dupuis and Snyder (1983) contend that the most common form of vocabulary exercise using implication is the analogy. They believe that the act of completing an analogy is such a complex activity that it actually requires the use of joining, excluding, and selecting processes.

## Principle 3: Teach Students to Relate Words to Their Background Knowledge

Judith Thelen (1986) likened children's schemata of differing subjects to having file folders inside the brain. Let's suppose a math text reads, "A negative number is on the left of a number line." If Joe has a well-developed file folder for some schema for *number line*, this explanation of a negative number will be useful to Joe. But suppose Shantell has heard of *number line* but has an underdeveloped file folder for the concept. In that case, the sentence defining negative numbers will have little meaning for Shantell.

Pearson (1984) admonished educators by saying that we have asked the wrong question in teaching vocabulary. Instead of asking, "How can I get this word into the students' heads?" we should be asking, "What is it that students already know about that they can use as an anchor point, as a way of accessing this new concept?" If we ask the latter question, we will always be directing our vocabulary instructions to the file folder issue—where does this word fit? Following Pearson's line of thinking, Joe and Shantell's teacher could help each of them think, "How can I use what I know about a number line to learn what a negative number is?" In Shantell's case, the teacher needs to show her a number line and have her work with it to develop her notions of the concept. Teaching students to relate words to their background knowledge is important for all students, especially for English learners.

## Principle 4: Teach Words in Prereading Activities to Activate Knowledge and Use Them in Postreading Discussion, Response, and Retelling

Through **prereading activities,** vocabulary words can be focused on *before* students read to help activate background knowledge in activities involving predicting. For example, Ms. Vizquel, a second-grade teacher, used vocabulary words she had chosen from *The Paperbag Princess* in a technique called Connect Two (Blachowicz, 1986). Her students predicted ways in which the terms would be connected in the story (see Figure 9.6). Then since the words she chose reflected the story line, her students used them quite naturally when responding *after* reading. Here is a retelling given by Omar, a second grader:

> Elizabeth was a princess who wore *expensive* clothes and was going to marry a prince named Ronald. A dragon *smashed* her castle and took Ronald. Elizabeth told the dragon, "Aren't you the *fiercest* dragon in the world?" and "Can't you burn up ten forests?" and stuff like that. The dragon did this stuff and got so tired he went to sleep so Elizabeth got Ronald. Then Ronald told her, "Come back when you look like a real princess." Elizabeth told him he looked like a prince but he was a *bum*.

In this way, Omar was able to integrate the words *expensive, smash, fiercest,* and *bum* as he retold the story. He related vocabulary to text.

Prereading and postreading vocabulary activities that connect vocabulary words to content are more desirable than isolated vocabulary exercises, especially for English language learners. Freeman and Freeman (2003) emphasize that English language learners have more difficulty applying knowledge that they've gained through isolated drill. Therefore, they suggest that teachers rely more on reading-related vocabulary activities to help the English learners make connections to text.

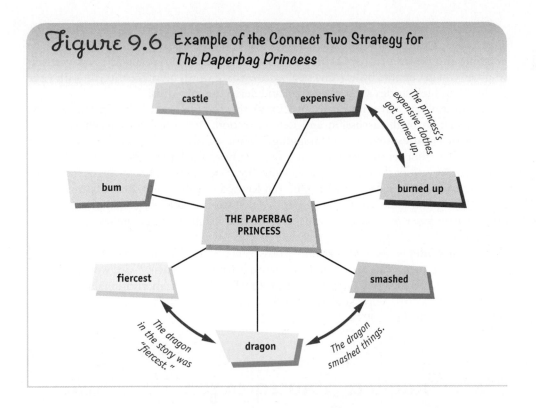

**Figure 9.6** Example of the Connect Two Strategy for *The Paperbag Princess*

## Principle 5: Teach Words Systematically and in Depth

As discussed earlier in the chapter, vocabulary knowledge is applied knowledge. Knowing and teaching a word in depth means going beyond having students parrot back a definition. It means more than having students do something with a definition such as finding an antonym, fitting the word into a sentence blank, or classifying the word with other words. All these are excellent activities and do need to be a part of a systematic vocabulary program. However, researchers are finding that for students to process vocabulary *in depth*, they must *generate a novel product using the term:* They could restate the definition in their own words, compare the definition to their own experiences with the concept, or make up a sentence that clearly demonstrates the word's meaning. These novel products can be written. But, in fact, class discussion leads students to process words deeply by drawing connections between new and known information (Stahl, 1986).

By teaching systematically, we mean following a vocabulary program that includes 10 to 12 conceptually related words that are taught and reinforced over an extended period of time. Networks of meanings of these words, as well as links to students' experiences, are established. Students are engaged in words by hearing them, saying them, manipulating them, and playing with them (Blachowicz & Fisher, 2004, 2005). In addition, for English language learners a systematic vocabulary program by Hickman, Pollard-Durodola, and Vaughn (2004) consists of daily read-aloud sessions. This 5-day program encourages the English learners to preview the story and vocabulary, participate in guided discussions, reread passages, and extend their vocabulary knowledge.

## Principle 6: Awaken Interest in and Enthusiasm for Words

Too often in elementary classrooms, vocabulary learning is one of the dullest activities of the school day. Children tend to associate vocabulary instruction with dictionary drill: looking up words, writing out definitions, and putting words in sentences. Though these activities have some merit, they quickly become routine. Students need to know *why*, *when*, and *how* to use dictionaries. Dictionary usage is discussed later in the chapter.

**BUILDING TEACHING SKILLS: CASE STUDY**

Go to the Homework and Exercises section in Chapter 9 of MyEducationLab to complete the case study and think about what strategies you would implement to help a student struggling with vocabulary and concept development.

Nothing can replace the excitement about words that a good teacher can generate. The teacher's attitude toward vocabulary instruction can be contagious. What you do to illustrate the power of words is vital in improving children's vocabulary. Ask yourself whether you get excited by learning new words. Share words of interest to you with your students, and tell stories about the origin and derivation of words.

Help students play with words, as Cindy's third-grade teacher did. In one activity, her teacher, through discussion and demonstration, developed for the children the concept of facial expression, or "mugging." With a Polaroid camera, she took "mug shots" of her students and placed them prominently on the bulletin board. The children learned to "mug" for the camera by acting out "mug" words (e.g., happy mugs, sad mugs, angry mugs). The very last mug the children learned was the smug smile of satisfaction, or the "smug mug." Cindy's teacher explained that when a child knew something that no other person knew or took great pride in an accomplishment, he or she was to flash the "smug mug."

When students see that learning words can be fun they become interested and curious about them. This results in the desire to learn more. Playing with words utilizing various forms of media is important (see Box 9.1). Besides being motivational to students, playing with words helps students develop an understanding of how words work (Blachowicz & Fisher, 2004).

## Best Practice: Strategies for Vocabulary and Concept Development

Vocabulary instruction should not be neglected in the primary and middle school classrooms. Teachers in most grades worry that they "don't have the time to spend on vocabulary instruction." Direct vocabulary instruction need not take more than 20 minutes a day. Moreover, opportunities for incidental instruction and reinforcement arise in content area instruction throughout the school day.

**BOX 9.1**

*New Literacies*

### THE MOTIVATION OF TECHNOLOGY

What makes new literacies so beneficial for students is the motivational power technology has for students. Students spend more time on tasks and are willing to practice reading and writing activities when they occur online. Students read widely and are exposed to a variety of perspectives and vocabulary. Vocabulary building online helps to connect concepts to printed words, develops word recognition, and enhances word usage. Various Internet sites serve as powerful tools to support and stimulate vocabulary development, including:

*Wacky Web Tales*
**www.eduplace.com/tales**
Students use their vocabulary knowledge to create stories. The vocabulary used must associate to the different parts of speech.

*A Word a Day*
**http://wordsmith.org/awad/about.html**
Students share words, word play, and literature with a community of readers who enjoy learning new vocabulary.

*Words@Random*
**www.randomhouse.com/words**
Students have the opportunity to learn new words and usage of the dictionary, as well as engage in a series of puzzles and games.

The teacher plays an important role in ensuring proper Internet usage and vocabulary development. Setting bookmarks and establishing computer usage schedules are two key supports needed to guide students' online vocabulary development as well as valuing new literacies.

Best practice in vocabulary instruction begins with the teacher's commitment to teach words well. So start slowly and gradually build an instructional program over several years. We have already recommended that words be selected for emphasis that come from the actual materials children read during the year—basal and literature selections as well as content area text selections. For best practice, the program should evolve from the instructional implications of the knowledge, instrumental, and aptitude hypotheses discussed earlier. Therefore, consider a three-component approach to classroom vocabulary instruction as illustrated in the Research-Based Practices featured in Box 9.2.

## Relating Experiences to Vocabulary Learning

Dale's Cone of Experience (Figure 9.2 on page 283) is a good place to begin when planning and selecting vocabulary strategies that are experience based. The more direct, firsthand experiences students have, the better.

But different levels of vicarious experience can also establish bases for vocabulary learning. Vicarious experiences, though secondhand, are valuable in their own right.

STANDARD
2.2

---

BOX **9.2**

**Research-Based Practices**

### A Three-Component Approach to Classroom Vocabulary Instruction

Instructional strategies are not unique to any one component illustrated. In fact, strategies for teaching vocabulary should cut across components. Therefore, select strategies based on planning decisions that include provisions for a variety of activities, the types of information you wish to convey about words, and ways to link concepts to the children's experiences.

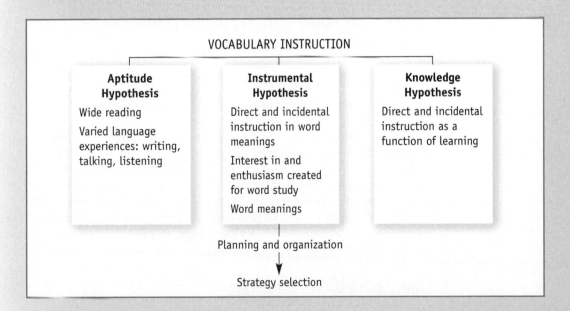

VOCABULARY INSTRUCTION

| **Aptitude Hypothesis** | **Instrumental Hypothesis** | **Knowledge Hypothesis** |
|---|---|---|
| Wide reading | Direct and incidental instruction in word meanings | Direct and incidental instruction as a function of learning |
| Varied language experiences: writing, talking, listening | Interest in and enthusiasm created for word study | |
| | Word meanings | |

Planning and organization

Strategy selection

*Source:* Adapted from "Vocabulary Knowledge," by R. C. Anderson and P. Freebody, in *Comprehension and Teaching: Research Perspectives,* edited by J. T. Guthrie (Newark, DE: International Reading Association, 1981).

Dale's Cone of Experience indicates possibilities for planning experiences that are vicarious: demonstrations, simulations, dramatization, visual and audio media, reading to children, and reading on one's own.

The use of technology also provides opportunities for the students to see, hear, and use words. These experiences provide for in-depth vocabulary development. Through the use of various vocabulary development software (drill and practice, tutorial, and learning games), Internet sites, and talking books, students learn to use words, understand concepts, and appreciate how words are related to the content being studied. The National Reading Panel (2000) recognizes the potential of computer usage and encourages teachers to rely on computers as a valuable instructional tool for vocabulary development.

Next we will consider how wide reading is useful for growth in vocabulary learning and how to help students use context to extend this growth.

## Using Context for Vocabulary Growth

Teachers and experts know that in addition to defining new terms, students need some examples of the concept; that is, students need to hear the new words used in different contexts. Hearing a dictionary definition is not enough to learn a new word.

Defining a word and using the word in a sentence or a context is a common and useful practice. In studying sound, a third-grade class learned that the definition of *vibrate* was "to move rapidly back and forth." They also discussed different contexts for *vibrate*—how a violin string vibrates and how blowing into a bottle or a flute makes the air vibrate. Even though we know that using context while reading is an important avenue for vocabulary growth, we agree with Nagy (1988) that when teaching *new* meanings, context alone is not effective. We know that the context provided in most texts tells us something about the word's meaning, but seldom does any single context give complete information (Deighton, 1970; Shatz & Baldwin, 1986). Nevertheless, we suggest that *the instructional goal should be to teach students to use context to gain information about the meanings of new terms.* For example, Judy led a group of first graders in reading a book about the skylab. First, when she asked the children what they thought a skylab was, Jan said, "A lab in the sky, of course." Judy wrote this on the board. As Jan and the first graders read the book together, they made a list of what a skylab is:

> It is a space station.
>
> A rocket takes a skylab into space.
>
> A skylab goes around the earth.
>
> Astronauts stay on a skylab.
>
> A skylab has big solar collectors. Solar collectors change sunlight into electricity.

Helping students learn to use context to gain information about words new to them is particularly important for struggling readers of any age. In addition, young students as well as middle school students need to know that they must accept partial word knowledge, some degree of uncertainty, and occasionally misleading contexts as they meet new words in their independent reading (Beck, McKeown, & McCaslin, 1983).

We will examine ways to help children grow in independence by using different contexts to extend their vocabulary knowledge. But first we look at more direct instructional strategies to develop word meanings.

## Developing Word Meanings

**Definitional knowledge,** or the ability to relate new words to known words, can be built through synonyms, antonyms, and multiple-meaning words.

**Synonyms** are words that are similar in meaning to other words. **Antonyms** are words that are opposite in meaning to other words. Synonyms and antonyms are useful ways of having children define and understand word meanings. Antonyms in particular can demonstrate whether children really comprehend the meanings of new words. Moreover, words that have multiple meanings tend to confuse students, especially when they are reading and encounter the uncommon meaning of a word used in a passage.

**SYNONYMS** ◆ Synonym instruction has value when a child has knowledge of a concept but is unfamiliar with its label—the new word to be learned. In such cases, the focus of instruction is to help the student associate new words with more familiar ones. This particular strategy is a good example of the cognitive principle of bridging the gap between the new and the known.

For example, a fifth-grade teacher provided a synonym match for words that children were studying in a unit on ecology. Here are several of the matching items:

MIDDLE GRADES

| Column A: New Words | Column B: Words That You Already Know |
|---|---|
| cultivate | change |
| erode | surroundings |
| environment | wearing away |
| modify | work |

The students were directed to match the words from column B with the words from column A. A discussion followed, with students giving reasons for their matchups. The discussion led to further clarification of each new term and the realization, as one child put it, that "some words just look hard but really aren't."

In another synonym-related activity, students were given overworked or unimaginative words in sentences or paragraphs, and asked to supply alternative words that would make each sentence or the paragraph more descriptive and interesting. Words such as *nice*, *great*, and *neat* are good candidates for this type of activity.

> Our trip to the zoo was *neat*. The entire family had a *swell* time. Dad thought that seeing the monkeys on Monkey Island was *fun*. So did I. But Mom *said*, "The monkeys were OK, but I liked the reptiles even more." The snakes were *terrific*. We all had a *great* time at the zoo.

This activity, and adaptations of it, can be used as a springboard for students to analyze a piece of their own writing, looking for overworked words and substituting more interesting and precise words.

Many word processing programs now have a built-in thesaurus. Children can be shown how to use the thesaurus to help find "just the right word" for what they want to say. Teachers can also use the thesaurus to develop exercises in which students must decide which synonyms would fit best in specific contexts, such as the following:

> Which synonym would you most likely find in a funeral announcement or an obituary?
>
> dead        departed        extinct

Exercises such as this one are a part of vocabulary instruction that promotes deep and fluent word knowledge.

**ANTONYMS** ◆ In addition to matching activities (in which students associate the target words with words that are opposite in meaning) and selecting activities (in which students select the best choice for an antonym from several listed), consider strategies that challenge students to work with antonyms in various print contexts.

For example, ask children to change the meanings of advertisements: "Change the ad! *Don't* sell the merchandise!" Children can ruin a good advertisement by changing the underlined words to words that mean the opposite. The following are examples of the antonym advertisement activity:

Today through Tuesday!

Save now on this <u>top-quality</u> bedding.

The <u>bigger</u> the size, the <u>more</u> you save.

<u>GREAT</u> truckload sale!

Just take your purchase to the checkout, and the cashiers will <u>deduct</u> 30% from the ticketed price.

Similar activities can be developed for a target word in a sentence or several new vocabulary words in a paragraph. You may devise an activity in which children work with sentence pairs. In the first sentence, the target word is underlined. In the second sentence, a child must fill in the blank space with an antonym for the target word.

1. The ship sank to the <u>bottom</u> of the ocean.
   The climbers reached the _____ of the mountain.
2. The <u>joyful</u> family reunion never had a dull moment.
   The funeral was the most _____ occasion I had ever experienced.

Sentence pairs will generate variations of antonyms. Therefore children should be asked to defend their choices. In the first pair of sentences, *top*, *peak*, and *highest point* are acceptable antonyms for *bottom*. *Sad*, *solemn*, and *depressing* are all possible antonyms for *joyful*.

**WORDS WITH MULTIPLE MEANINGS** ◆ **Multiple-meaning words** give students opportunities to see how words operate in context.

The *hall* was so long that it seemed endless.

The concert took place in a large *hall*.

The Football *Hall* of Fame is located in Canton, Ohio.

In content area textbooks, children frequently run across common words that have different meanings (e.g., *mean*, *table*, *force*, *bank*, *spring*). These can lead to confusion and miscomprehension. A strategy for dealing with multiple-meaning words involves prediction and verification (Vacca & Vacca, 2005).

1. Select multiple-meaning words from a text assignment. List them on the board.
2. Have students predict the meanings of these words and write them on a sheet of paper next to each term.
3. Assign the reading selection, noting the numbers of the pages where students can find each word in the text reading.
4. Ask students to verify their original predicted meanings. If they wish to change any of their predictions, they can revise the meanings based on how each word was used in the selection.

## Classifying and Categorizing Words

When children manipulate words in relation to other words, they are engaging in critical thinking. Vocabulary strategies and activities should give students the experience of *thinking about*, *thinking through*, and *thinking with* vocabulary. Working with relationships among words provides this opportunity.

Through the aid of **categorization** and classification strategies, students recognize that they can group words that label ideas, events, or objects. Such strategies involve the processes of joining, excluding, selecting, and implying. Children will learn to study words critically and form generalizations about the shared or common features of concepts. Word sorts, categorization, semantic mapping, analogies, paired-word sentence generation, and collaborative learning exercises are all activities that help students, including those from diverse backgrounds, conceptualize as well as learn and reinforce word meanings.

**WORD SORTS** ◆ The process of sorting words is integrally involved in concept formation. A **word sort** is a simple yet valuable activity to initiate. Individually or in small groups, children sort through vocabulary terms that are written on cards or listed on an exercise sheet. The object of word sorting is to group words into different categories by looking for shared features among their meanings. The strategies can be used effectively at any grade level.

As discussed in Chapter 7, there are two types of word sorts: the *open sort* and the *closed sort*. In the *closed sort*, students know in advance what the main categories are. In other words, they must select and classify words according to the features they have in common with a category. The closed sort reinforces and extends the ability to classify words. The *open sort* stimulates inductive thinking. No category or grouping is known in advance of sorting, and students must search for meanings and discover relationships among words.

Fifth-grade students participating in a unit on the newspaper discovered the many functions of a newspaper: to inform and interpret, influence, serve, and entertain. A closed-sort task that children participated in involved the completion of the following worksheet in small groups:

*Directions:* In your groups, place the topics below under the proper headings. You may use a topic more than once. Base your decisions on class discussions and what is found in today's newspaper.

| | |
|---|---|
| the largest picture on page A-1 | the Market at a Glance column (business) |
| Weather Watch | the Transitions column (sports) |
| News Watch | the Bridge column |
| the first full-page ad | the classified index |
| the first Focal Point story | display advertising |
| legal notices | death notices |
| the first letter to the editor | the headline on page A-1 |
| Dear Abby | the crossword puzzle |
| the astrology column | |

| Informs or Interprets | Influences | Serves | Entertains |
|---|---|---|---|
| | | | |

Ms. Prince modified word sorts when she introduced a science unit on fish. She had her third graders work in groups to brainstorm and list everything they could think of relating to the word *fish*. Their list included:

| | | |
|---|---|---|
| good to eat | fun to catch | slippery |
| pretty | water | bugs |
| fins | tail | shiny |

While the students were still in groups, she then asked them to come up with one or more categories or groups that two of the words could go into. The students came up with the following categories:

Fins and tail are *parts of a fish's body*.

Pretty, slippery, and shiny describe *how fish look*.

Good to eat and fun to catch tell about *things people like to do with fish*.

After the children had read the chapter on fish, Ms. Prince asked them to find words from the chapter that could go in the category or group that describes parts of a fish's body. The students very quickly added *scales* and *gills* to this category. In this way, Ms. Prince involved students in an open sort before reading and a closed sort (using a category identified by the children) after reading the text.

An excellent use of open sorting is to coordinate it with word banks. Word banks, closely associated with the language-experience approach, are collections of cards bearing words that a student does not recognize immediately. (Word banks were discussed in Chapter 7.)

**CATEGORIZATION** ◆ Vocabulary activities involving categorization help students form relationships among words in much the same manner as open and closed sorts. The difference, however, lies in the amount of assistance a child is given. For example, a teacher may give students two to six words per grouping and ask them to do something with the sets of words. Different formats may be used to "do something" with the word sets. Consider giving the children sets of words and asking them to circle the word in each set that includes the meaning of the others. This exercise requires them to perceive common attributes or examples in relation to a more inclusive concept and to distinguish superordinate from subordinate terms. Children are involved in the cognitive process of joining.

*Directions:* Circle the word in each group that includes the meaning of the others in the group.

| | | |
|---|---|---|
| generals | ocean | spicy |
| troops | lake | sour |
| armies | water | taste |
| warriors | bay | salty |

Other categorization exercises may direct students to cross out the word that does not belong in each set. This format forces students to manipulate words that convey the meanings of common items. In these activities, children learn to exclude words that are not conceptually related to other words.

*Directions:* Cross out the word in each group that doesn't belong.

| | | |
|---|---|---|
| meat | earth | judgment |
| butter | ground | treasure |
| oatmeal | stable | cash |
| fish oil | soil | price |

The younger the children are, the more manipulative and directed the categorization activity might be. Word cards may be used instead of worksheets. Working with sets of cards, a teacher may place one set at a time on a worktable and call on a child to remove the card that doesn't belong. The other children around the table must then attempt to explain the child's choice. Manipulative activities that require cutting, pasting, or drawing also work well.

CONCEPT CIRCLES ◆ A versatile activity appropriate for students at a wide range of grade levels, **concept circles** provide still another format and opportunity to study words critically and to relate words conceptually to one another. A concept circle simply involves putting words or phrases in the sections of a circle and then directing students to describe or name the concept relationship among the sections. In the example in Figure 9.7, Diane Burke asked her seventh graders, after they had read about climate, to determine the main idea of the concept circle.

Alternatively, you might invite students to shade in the section of a concept circle containing a word or phrase that *does not relate* to the other words or phrases in the circle's sections and then identify the concept they have in common. See Figure 9.8 for an example of a concept circle that Debbie Schmidt's eighth graders were asked to do in groups of three during their history lesson on Roosevelt's New Deal.

Other modifications include leaving one or more sections of the circle empty, inviting students to fill in the empty sections with a word or two relating in some way to the terms in the other sections. Students must then justify their choices by identifying the larger concept depicted by the circle.

Although these activities are similar to categorization exercises, students may respond more positively to the visual aspect of the sections in a circle than to category sorting because the circles seem less like tests.

SEMANTIC MAPPING ◆ **Semantic mapping,** or webbing, is a strategy that shows readers and writers how to organize important information. Semantic mapping can also revolve around vocabulary learning by providing a visual display of how words are related to other words. Earlier in this chapter, semantic mapping was used to make distinctions among class, example, and attribute relations. Similarly, students can use semantic mapping to cluster words belonging to categories and to distinguish relationships. According to Smith and Johnson (1980), the procedures for semantic mapping can be varied to suit different purposes.

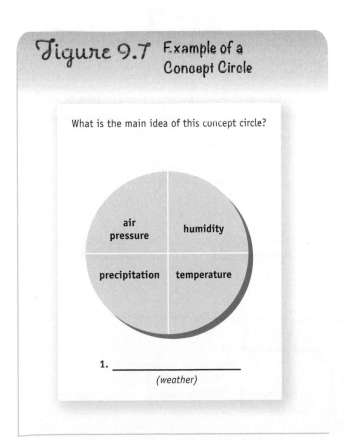

**Figure 9.7** Example of a Concept Circle

What is the main idea of this concept circle?

air pressure | humidity
precipitation | temperature

1. _____
   (weather)

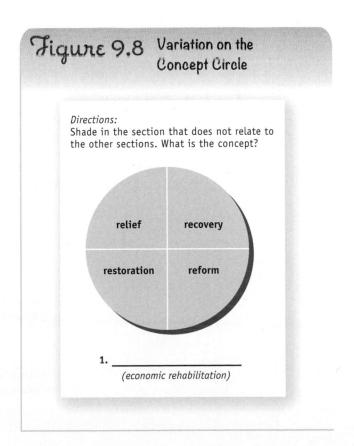

**Figure 9.8** Variation on the Concept Circle

Directions:
Shade in the section that does not relate to the other sections. What is the concept?

relief | recovery
restoration | reform

1. _____
   (economic rehabilitation)

The first step in the semantic mapping of vocabulary is for the teacher to select a word central to a story or from any other source of classroom interest or activity and then write this word on the board. From this point, the procedures can vary, depending on the objective of the lesson. For example, the teacher can ask the students to think of as many words as they can that are in some way related to the word and jot them down. As students share the words they have written with the class, the words are grouped into categories on the board around the central concept. The students can suggest names for the categories and discuss the category labels, relating their experiences to the words on the board.

Semantic maps can be elaborately developed or kept relatively simple, depending on the sophistication of the class and grade level. In Figure 9.9, a group of beginning readers developed a concept of the five senses through a mapping strategy.

The teacher began the map by writing the target concept, *five senses*, in the middle of the board. She then presented the class with a familiar situation: "How often have you known that your sister was making a snack even before you got to the kitchen to see or taste it?" The children responded by saying they could smell food cooking or hear a

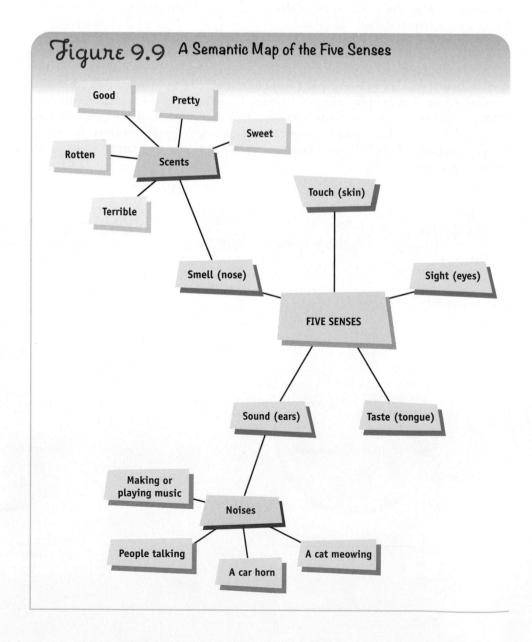

**Figure 9.9** A Semantic Map of the Five Senses

sibling preparing the snack. The teacher praised the student responses and continued, "You were using your senses of smell and sound to know that a snack was being fixed." She then wrote *smell* and *sound* on the board and connected the words to the central concept.

The children's attention was then directed to the bulletin board display of five children, each employing one of the senses. Through a series of questions, the class gradually developed the remainder of the semantic map. For example, when the concept of smell was being developed, the teacher noted, "We call a smell 'scent,'" and connected *scent* to *smell* on the map. She then asked, "How do you think flowers smell?" "What words can you tell me to determine different types of smells?" As the students volunteered words, the teacher placed them on the map. When the teacher asked, "When you think of sound, what's the first thing that comes to your mind?" the children quickly said "noises." The teacher connected *noises* to *sounds*. Further discussion focused on types of noises, both pleasant and unpleasant.

**ANALOGIES** ◆ An **analogy** is a comparison of two similar relationships. On one side of the analogy, the words are related in some way; on the other side, the words are related in the same way. Analogies probably should be taught to students beginning in the intermediate grades. If they are not familiar with the format of an analogy, they may have trouble reading it successfully. Therefore, give several short demonstrations in which you model the process involved in completing an analogy. The Step-by-Step Lesson in Box 9.3 provides an outline for using analogies. In Figure 9.10 on page 300, we illustrate some of the types of word relationships from which many analogies can be developed.

MIDDLE GRADES

**PAIRED-WORD SENTENCE GENERATION** ◆ Students often need many exposures to new and conceptually difficult words in order to begin using these words in their speaking and writing vocabularies (Duin & Graves, 1987). After students have classified and categorized words through word sorts or other strategies, **paired-word sentence generation** can spur them into using these words in their speaking and writing.

---

**BOX 9.3**  STEP-BY-STEP *Lesson*

## Teaching Analogies

Ignoffo (1980) explained the value of analogies this way: "Analogies are practical because they carry an implied context with them. To work the analogy, the learner is forced to attempt various . . . procedures that involve articulation, problem solving, and thinking" (p. 520). Consider the following steps when teaching vocabulary using analogies.

1. Begin by asking students to explain the relationship that exists between two words. For example, write on the board a simple class example relationship:

   apple    fruit

2. Ask students, "What is the relationship between the two words?" Explanations may vary greatly, but arrive at the notion that an apple is a type of fruit.

3. Explain that an analogy is a comparison of two similar sets of relationships. Write on the board:

   <u>Apple</u> is to <u>fruit</u> as <u>carrot</u> is to _____.

4. Suggest to students, "If an apple is a type of fruit, then a carrot must be a type of _____." Discuss the children's predictions, and provide additional examples.

5. Note that an analogy has its own symbols:

   apple:fruit::carrot: _____

6. Point out that the symbol : means *is to* and :: means *as*. Walk students through an oral reading of several analogies, saying, "An analogy reads like this." (The class reads the analogy in unison following the teacher's lead.)

7. Provide simple analogies at first and gradually increase the complexity of the relationships.

8. Develop analogies from vocabulary used in stories, content area texts, or topics of interest in the classroom.

## 𝒥igure 9.10   Using Word Relationships to Form Analogies

*Directions:*  Study each type of relationship, and for each example given, complete the analogy. Then compare your responses with a classmate or colleague.

1. Purpose relationship
   Teeth:chew::pen: _____
   Chair:sit::knife: _____

2. Part-to-whole relationship
   Antler:deer::tusk: _____
   Cat:feline::dog: _____

3. Synonym relationship
   Small:tiny::create: _____
   Copy:imitate::large: _____

4. Antonym relationship
   Black:white::day: _____
   High:low::morning: _____

5. Place relationship
   Book:bookcase::car: _____
   Flowers:vase::clothes: _____

6. Attribute relationship
   Rare:whale::common: _____
   Detective:clue::scientist: _____

7. Cause-and-effect relationship
   Furnace:heat::freezer: _____
   Seed:tree::egg: _____

Simpson (1987) described paired-word sentence generation as a task that could be used to *test* students' understanding of difficult concepts. We have taken her notion of paired-word sentence generation and developed it into a teaching strategy. In using this strategy, the teacher gives the students two related words. The goal of the strategy is to generate *one* sentence that correctly demonstrates an understanding of the words *and* their relationship to each other. However, several steps in the process help elementary students reach this goal. We will describe these steps by illustrating how Mr. Fratello used the strategy with his fifth-grade class as they worked with the concepts *reptile* and *cold-blooded*. First, Mr. Fratello had each student write sentences with the terms *reptile* and *cold-blooded* in them. The class came up with sentences such as these:

Reptiles are cold-blooded.

Snakes, lizards, and turtles are reptiles.

*Cold-blooded* means that when the air is warm, their bodies are warm, and when the air is cold, their bodies are cold.

Mr. Fratello then led the class in a sentence-combining activity to write a sentence that would give the reader information about what *reptiles* are and what *cold-blooded* means, as well as how the two concepts are related to each other. The class came up with sentences such as these:

Reptiles, like snakes, lizards, and turtles, are cold-blooded because they are cold when the air is cold and warm when the air is warm.

Snakes, lizards, and turtles are reptiles that are cold-blooded, which means they are warm when the air is warm and cold when the air is cold.

Mr. Fratello asked his fifth graders to generate paired-word sentences throughout the school year. They first worked as a whole class and later worked in groups of four made up of both high and low achievers. Finally, they worked alone, devising their own sentences.

In addition to being considered a classifying and categorizing strategy, as described in the previous illustration, paired-word sentence generation is also considered an instructional strategy for developing word meanings through stories and writing.

## Developing Word Meanings Through Stories and Writing

Vocabulary functions differently in literature and in content material. First of all, when reading literature, knowing the meaning of a *new* word may not be necessary for understanding the gist of the story. In contrast, content area vocabulary often represents major concepts that are essential for comprehension and learning. For example, children who cannot give a definition of *stamen* after reading about the parts of a flower have not grasped important content. But children can understand a story about a band even if they glean from context only that a *tambourine* is a musical instrument but don't know what exactly it is like. Second, vocabulary in literature often involves simply learning a new label for a concept already possessed, such as learning that *desolate* means "very sad." In content areas, often the purpose of the text is to teach the concepts, as in the example of the second-grade science material labeling the parts of the flower, whereas this is not generally true in stories. Finally, in content texts, vocabulary terms often have a high degree of semantic relatedness—as the terms *nectar, pollen, anther, stamen, stigma,* and *style* do. This is less likely to be true of vocabulary terms selected from literature (Armbruster & Nagy, 1992).

Yet, as mapping the story *The Paperbag Princess* illustrates, story grammar can be used to develop word meanings. The following two strategies, semantic analysis to writing and predictogram, draw on insights from story grammar.

STANDARD
2.2

**SEMANTIC ANALYSIS TO WRITING** ◆ Because authors develop a theme through a series of related incidents, Beyersdorfer and Schauer (1989) reasoned that stories provide a situational context that could be used for rich development of word meanings. When using this strategy, the teacher narrows the selection of words to those semantically related to the theme. Students then develop definitions based on personal schemata for the theme.

In using *semantic analysis to writing:*

1. The teacher identifies the theme and composes a question involving critical thinking related to the theme.
2. The teacher selects words used by the author or consults a thesaurus to find about five words, both synonyms and antonyms, relating to the theme (words that are too closely synonymous are discarded).
3. The teacher constructs a **think sheet** (see Figure 9.11 on page 302) for discussion purposes as well as for writing.

## *Figure 9.11*  Think Sheet for Extended Definition of Self-Reliance

**QUESTIONS YOU WILL RESPOND TO IN AN ESSAY:**

Was Meg in *A Wrinkle in Time* self-reliant? If so, how? What did she do that showed self-reliance? If not, what did she do that was not self-reliant? Further, did she change during the story?

What is self-reliance? _____

_____

***Directions:***

1. As a class, we will define the terms. Write down definitions as we do this.

2. To this list add two words (numbers 6 and 7) suggested during brainstorming. Consult your dictionary and record a definition.

3. Decide which of the seven words contribute an essential characteristic to your definition of *self-reliance*.

4. Find evidence from the story that proves that Meg did or did not demonstrate the characteristics. Give the page number and a phrase description of the event.

5. Using the order of importance, rank the essential characteristics.

6. Write an essay. Define *self-reliance* and support the definition with evidence from *A Wrinkle in Time*.

| TERM—DEFINITION | ESSENTIAL—YES/NO | ILLUSTRATION—STORY, PAGE NUMBER |
|---|---|---|
| 1. Self-confidence | | |
| 2. Certainty | | |
| 3. Trust in oneself | | |
| 4. Independence | | |
| 5. Conviction | | |
| 6. Courage | | |
| 7. Determination | | |

MIDDLE GRADES

Mr. Bradford, a sixth-grade teacher who was piloting a literature-based reading program, decided to involve his students in semantic analysis to writing with the thought-provoking book *A Wrinkle in Time*, by Madeleine L'Engle. In this story, Meg Murry, along with her precocious brother Charles Wallace and their friend Calvin O'Keefe, hope to rescue her father from a mysterious fate. The children travel through time to the planet Camazotz with the assistance of Mrs. Whatsit, Mrs. Who, and Mrs. Which. There they confront IT, the planet's intimidating force for conformity. Meg and friends find her father, but Charles Wallace gets swallowed up in IT. Meg's father cannot rescue Charles Wallace because he has been away from him so long that the familiar ties are too weak: Meg has to go back to IT and rescue Charles Wallace.

Although many themes can be derived from this book, Mr. Bradford chose to use *self-reliance* in semantic analysis to writing because Meg, the main character, changed in terms of self-reliance through the many incidents in the book. Mr. Bradford found that the dictionary definition of *self-reliance* was "sure of oneself and one's ability; needing, wishing for, and getting no help from others."

Mr. Bradford then devised the questions "Was Meg in *A Wrinkle in Time* self-reliant?" "If so, how?" "What did she do that showed self-reliance?" "If not, what did she do that was not self-reliant?"

To make the think sheet, Mr. Bradford used a thesaurus and chose the following words and phrases:

self-confidence

certainty

trust in oneself

independence

conviction

Because he knew that the book would prove quite difficult for some of the readers in the class, Mr. Bradford read the book orally to the class over a two-week period. He knew that some of these same readers would write interesting essays on self-reliance. Each day as he read the chapters, students wrote in a response journal (response journals will be described in Chapter 11), and the class had lively discussions comparing their responses.

Students were now prepared for Mr. Bradford to involve them in the semantic analysis to writing strategy. As a result of class brainstorming and discussion, the terms *courage* and *determination* were added to the think sheet. Small group work then began in earnest to find incidents that showed that Meg was or was not self-reliant.

Next the class had an animated debate about whether Meg was or was not self-reliant, citing evidence for both positions. Many felt that Meg was not self-reliant and supported this with the incident when Meg finds her father and becomes disillusioned when her father is not able to get her brother, Charles Wallace, away from IT. Students who felt Meg became self-reliant cited the fact that Meg finally mustered the courage to attempt to save Charles Wallace from IT. Thus two different initial statements and story frames were formulated to help students begin writing their first drafts, after they had worked in pairs to rank the importance of their supporting evidence.

I think Meg in *A Wrinkle in Time* _____

self-reliant. I think this because _____. Further, _____.

In addition, _____

_____

    In conclusion, _____

_____

_____.

Mr. Bradford took home many stimulating essays to read after his students had eagerly read them to each other. Many students later chose their self-reliant essay from all those accumulated in their writing folder to revise and edit.

**PREDICTOGRAM** ◆ Story elements—including the setting, the incidents in the plot, characterization, the character's problem or goal, how the problem or goal is resolved, and the theme or larger issue to which the problem or goal relates—can be used to develop students' meaning vocabulary with the **predictogram** strategy.

In planning for predictogram, teachers choose words from a story that they feel will be challenging to the students. The words and their meanings are discussed in class, and students relate their personal associations with the words. Finally, students work in groups to predict how they think the author might use each term in the story. Would the author use it to tell about the setting? The characters? The problem or goal or trouble the characters have? Would the author use the word to tell about how the problem or trouble was solved? Students then read to discover how the author did use the terms.

Mrs. Nowak, a third-grade teacher in the same school as Mr. Bradford, was also beginning to use a literature-based program with the basal reading program she had used for five years. She was planning for a group of students to read *Crow Boy*, by Taro Yashima. The words she thought would be challenging included *forlorn, interesting, trudging, admired, announced, imagine, graduation, attendance, charcoal,* and *rejected.* To get students thinking about the problems in the story, she asked them to freewrite about their thoughts on the idea that "sometimes kids tease a classmate who is shy or different." The students shared their freewrites. Then Mrs. Nowak told them what was happening at the beginning of the story. She led them in a discussion concerning how the meanings of the terms related to personal experiences and predicting which of the words the author would use for each story element.

Figure 9.12 shows how the group completed the predictogram for *Crow Boy.* The students then read the story, looking to see how the author actually used the challenging vocabulary terms. Next we suggest ways to help children gain control over their own vocabulary learning.

## Developing Independence in Vocabulary Learning

There is no question that wide reading and thus learning the meaning of words from context is an important way for people to extend their vocabularies. "Anyone interested in increasing students' vocabularies should see that they read as much and as widely as

---

### Figure 9.12  Predictogram for *Crow Boy* by Taro Yashima

*Directions:* Discuss with members of your group how you think Taro Yashima would use the vocabulary words below. Would he use them to describe the characters? Or the problem or goal of the character? Or the solution to the problem? Place each word in the appropriate square. Be prepared to tell why you think so.

| Vocabulary words: | forlorn | imagine |
| | interesting | graduation |
| | trudging | attendance |
| | admired | charcoal |
| | announced | rejected |

| *Setting*<br>where the story took place | charcoal<br>interesting |
| --- | --- |
| *Characters*<br>the people in the story | forlorn<br>imagine<br>trudging |
| *Problem or goal*<br>main character | rejected |
| *Solution to problem or attainment*<br>*of goal* | graduation<br>attendance<br>announced<br>admired |

possible" (Graves & Watts-Taffe, 2002, p. 143). Fielding, Wilson, and Anderson (1986) found that the amount of free reading was the best predictor of vocabulary growth between grades 2 and 5. Nagy (1988) theorized that after third grade, for children who do read a reasonable amount, reading may be the single largest source of vocabulary growth.

In order to continue to develop student independence, teachers should next teach dictionary usage and the strategies of self-selection and word knowledge rating. The dictionary is an important tool for independent readers. Using a dictionary to effectively obtain information is a complex task and requires teaching students proper usage. Self-selection and word knowledge rating are two strategies that aid students in monitoring their own growth in vocabulary knowledge as they use context in reading and listening. The *self-selection* strategy helps students of all ages and abilities become sensitized to the many words they read and hear in school and at home that they can add to their meaning vocabulary. *Word knowledge rating* helps children develop an awareness of the extent to which they know the words they come across as they read and interact with others.

**DICTIONARY USAGE** ◆ Interpreting definitions of words from a dictionary involves more that just choosing a synonym or the first definition from the word entry. It requires connecting word usage with context. Nagy and Scott (2004) believe that a real weakness of dictionary usage and definitions is that the definition may not provide needed information related to context. Many times children are looking up words in isolation from a list and do not look at the context and may choose a definition that may or may not relate to text. The use of the dictionary should not be a primary activity to develop vocabulary; rather, it should be used as a reference tool to verify the meanings of words to ensure that the meanings are syntactically and semantically suitable. Therefore, teachers need to look at dictionary usage and the role it plays in their classrooms.

A few activities that utilize the dictionary as a verification tool are contextual search and word part connections. With **contextual search,** the teacher assigns a few words to each student. Each student is responsible for reading each word in three different contexts. It is recommended that the text in which the word was originally located is used as well as using the Internet. The student records the contextual usage from all three examples. The student predicts the meaning of the word from the information gathered and verifies the predictions with the dictionary. The definition is then shared with the class and the student explains why he or she came up with the definition that was decided on. Breaking up a word into word parts in **word part connections** is another dictionary-related activity. Students are encouraged to analyze the unknown word and identify various word parts. Based on word parts such as root, prefix, or suffix, the student is to deduce the meaning of the word. The dictionary is used to verify the meaning of the word and/or word part. The vocabulary word is then read in context to ensure that the meaning is correct. If not, the dictionary may be used again to help the student determine the correct meaning of the word. The student should be prepared to explain the reasoning behind his or her definition. With contextual search and word part connections, using the dictionary to verify word meaning is key. Other instructional vocabulary activities discussed in the chapter when paired with the dictionary can be used to enhance word meaning.

**SELF-SELECTION STRATEGY** ◆ Words for the **self-selection strategy** can be drawn from basal readers, literature, content area instruction, or incidental learning experiences. As the name implies, children select the words to be studied. In describing how to use this strategy, Haggard (1986) explained that the first step is to ask students to bring to class one word they believe the class should learn; the teacher also chooses a word. These words are then written on the board and students give the definitions they gleaned from the context in which they found the word. Class members add any information they can to each definition. The students and teacher consult pertinent references such as

dictionaries (texts and CD-ROMs), glossaries, thesauri, dictionary Internet sites, and textbooks to add to definitions that are incomplete or unclear.

At this point, students can explain why they think a word is important to learn. Through this discussion, students narrow the list, agreeing to exclude terms that many already know or are not useful enough. The agreed-on terms and their definitions are recorded in vocabulary journals that are kept throughout the year. Students may also enter into their own vocabulary journal personal words that they chose but that were not chosen by the group. The class list of words is then used in activities such as word sorts, analogies, synonym matching, or any of the other activities that have been described. The class-selected words also become part of end-of-unit tests. By using this strategy, students become aware of many striking words that they see and hear in their daily lives.

**WORD KNOWLEDGE RATING** ◆ **Word knowledge rating** is a way to get children to analyze how well they know vocabulary words. Words chosen by the teacher or by the students in the self-selection strategy are written on a worksheet or on the board. We suggest students rate words using Dale's (1965) continuum to explain the degrees of word cognition.

> I've never seen the word.
>
> I've heard of it, but I don't know what it means.
>
> I recognize it in context. It has something to do with _____.
>
> I know the word in one or several of its meanings.

After students have rated themselves on their knowledge of the words, the teacher should lead them in a discussion using questions such as "Which are the hardest words?" "Which do you think most of us don't know?" "Which are the easiest?" "Which do you think most of us know?" (Blachowicz, 1986). The exchange could also involve consideration of the question "Which terms are synonyms for concepts we already know, and which are somewhat or totally new concepts to us?"

Through such discussions, students will begin to make judgments concerning the depth of their knowledge of vocabulary terms they have encountered, as well as the amount of effort needed to add the term to their meaning vocabulary.

# WHAT ABOUT STRUGGLING READERS AND *Vocabulary Knowledge?*

Children learn many new words each year. Extensive reading and writing opportunities contribute to this development, but children learn most of their vocabulary from explicit instruction. Natural vocabulary acquisition is not efficient enough to produce the rate of vocabulary development needed, especially for struggling readers.

In order to narrow the gap in vocabulary development between struggling and more able readers, teachers should consider the following recommendations to guide the teaching of vocabulary for struggling readers:

- Rely on direct instruction using semantic-based techniques.
- Use teaching strategies that encourage active learning.
- Provide multiple exposures to vocabulary through multiple kinds of texts.
- Personalize word learning.
- Teach a core vocabulary in order to facilitate learning from context.
- Incorporate computer-assisted instruction with stories that highlight words and provide contextual definitions.
- Develop independent vocabulary skills and strategies.
- Teach how to use textbooks, the dictionary, the Internet, and other references.

Teaching vocabulary is not a simple process; it requires teachers to be knowledgeable about what they want students to know and what the students already know. It is important that teachers provide explicit and direct vocabulary instruction for all students, especially struggling readers, so that students can develop independence in word learning.

## WHAT ABOUT STANDARDS, ASSESSMENT, AND Vocabulary Knowledge?

The development of vocabulary knowledge and concepts is essential for students to comprehend and critically think about texts across the curriculum. Although most state and national content standards in the various academic disciplines do not explicitly state a standard for vocabulary learning, it is more broadly implied in content standards that relate to comprehension, interpretation, inquiry, and critical thinking. Some state proficiency assessments may not have direct measures of word meaning related to specific disciplines, but they generally do have reading and language arts assessments.

Informal, authentic assessments are an important aspect of literacy instruction. Blachowicz and Fisher (1996), for example, recommend Knowledge Rating as a self-assessment/instructional strategy before students read a chapter or book. The steps in Knowledge Rating include the following:

1. Develop a Knowledge Rating sheet to survey students' prior knowledge of vocabulary they will encounter in the text assignment.
2. Invite students to evaluate their level of understanding of key words on the Knowledge Rating sheet.
3. Engage in follow-up discussion, asking the class to consider questions such as "Which are the hardest words? Which do you think most of the class doesn't know? Which words do most of us know?" Encourage the students to share what they know about the words and to make predictions about their meanings.
4. Use the self-assessment to establish purposes for reading. Ask, "What do you think this book is going to be about?"
5. As the students read the text, refer to the words on the Knowledge Rating sheet as they are used in text. Have the students compare their initial word meaning predictions with what they are learning as they read.

## Summary

Vocabulary instruction is one facet of reading instruction about which there is minimal controversy. Educators agree that it is possible to extend students' knowledge of word meanings, and it is important to do so because of the relationship between this knowledge and reading comprehension. This chapter explored that relationship and then delved into the instructional opportunities teachers can provide to expand children's vocabulary knowledge and to develop their interest and motivation to *want* to learn words and to monitor their own vocabulary learning.

Six guidelines for establishing vocabulary programs throughout the elementary grades were presented. For best practice, a three-component approach to classroom instruction was suggested, with numerous strategies for vocabulary and concept development that capitalize on students' natural spontaneity, using direct instruction and cooperative learning groups as well as reinforcement activities. These strategies can be adapted for teaching vocabulary through basal readers, literature, or content area instruction, providing a natural framework for concept development at all ages, including students from diverse backgrounds.

## Teacher Action Research

1. Choose any grade level and plan a vocabulary lesson. Teach it to a small group of your classmates or children. The lesson should emphasize one of the following strategies discussed in the chapter: (a) relating experiences to vocabulary learning; (b) developing word meanings using synonyms, antonyms, or multiple-meaning words; and (c) classifying and categorizing words. In what ways did the strategy selected work well with the students?

STANDARD 5.3

2. Observe a classroom teacher during reading and language arts instruction for several consecutive days. Record the time spent on vocabulary instruction. Look for vocabulary instruction that reflects the aptitude and knowledge hypotheses as well as the instrumental hypothesis. How much time is devoted to vocabulary learning in each category? What kinds of activities have been incorporated into the instruction? What conclusions do you draw from your observations? What implications can you make for further instruction?

3. Modify a vocabulary instructional strategy discussed in the chapter in order to pair it with dictionary usage. What specific dictionary activities would you implement in your class to ensure syntactic and semantic accuracy?

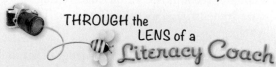

### THROUGH the LENS of a Literacy Coach

4. Take the opportunity to watch vocabulary development in either a content discipline or language arts class. What do you see the teacher doing well? What evidence of this would we see? How might you guide the teacher to improve his or her skills?

## Related Web Sites

*Discovery School's Puzzlemaker*

**www.puzzlemaker.com**

Puzzlemaker is a puzzle generation tool for creating and printing customized word searches and crossword puzzles using your own word lists.

*Fake Out*

**www.eduplace.com/fakeout**

Fake Out is a definition guessing game for primary and middle school students. Participants choose words from various grade-level lists in order to guess the definition.

*Internet Oxford English Dictionary*

**www.oed.com**

This site is the online version of the *Oxford English Dictionary*.

*New York Times Crossword Puzzle*

**www.nytimes.com/learning/teachers/xwords/index.html**

These crossword puzzles from the *New York Times* can be worked online or can be printed.

*Ohio ESL*

**www.ohiou.edu/esl/english/vocabulary.html**

Ohio ESL provides information and activities for English language learners to build vocabulary skills and strategies, with such major areas on the site as vocabulary activities, idioms, vocabulary study, references, and vocabulary for special purposes.

*Vocabulary University*

**www.vocabulary.com**

This site links to various vocabulary learning activities for three levels ranging from high elementary through high school, including interactive vocabulary puzzle, synonym and antonym encounters, and word finds.

*Word Central*

**www.wordcentral.com**

Merriam-Webster provides a variety of dictionary-related links. Students have access to a student dictionary, a Daily Buzzard game, poetry building using parts of speech, and a build-your-own-dictionary tool.

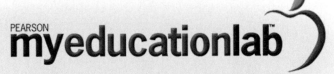

Now go to the Vacca et al. *Reading and Learning to Read*, Seventh Edition, MyEducationLab course at **www.myeducationlab.com** to

- Take a pretest to assess your initial comprehension of the chapter content
- Study chapter content with your individualized study plan
- Take a posttest to assess your understanding of chapter content
- Engage in multimedia exercises to help you build a deeper and more applied understanding of chapter content

# CHAPTER 10

# Reading Comprehension

Standards found in this chapter:

- 1.3
- 2.1
- 2.2
- 2.3
- 4.1
- 4.2
- 4.3
- 5.3

## In this chapter,
### YOU WILL DISCOVER:

- Explicit instructional strategies to model and guide the development of comprehension skills and strategies
- The importance of story structure as an aid to comprehension
- Instructional strategies to scaffold readers' awareness of story structure
- Instructional strategies to guide readers' interactions with texts
- Web-based considerations and reading comprehension

## Concept Map

### READING COMPREHENSION

**SCAFFOLDING READERS' DEVELOPMENT OF SKILLS AND STRATEGIES**

QARs | Reciprocal Questions

Reciprocal Teaching | Think–Alouds

QtA

**DEVELOPING READERS' AWARENESS OF STORY STRUCTURE**

Story Elements | Building Schema

**GUIDING INTERACTIONS WITH TEXTS**

DR–TA | Discussion Webs

Story Impressions | KWL

**READING COMPREHENSION AND THE WEB**

**S**econd graders have just finished silently reading an article about spiders. Mrs. Bonomo, the second-grade teacher, divides the students into small groups and instructs them to discuss what they learned and record the information on their individual KWL charts. Prior to reading, the second graders shared what they already thought they knew about spiders and recorded the facts in the K, What I Know, column of the charts. In their small groups, the students also recorded questions that they hoped would be answered by reading the article about spiders. Each child had different questions that were listed in the W, What I Want to Know, column. Now it is time for the students to share what they learned in the L column of the charts. Read one small group discussion to see how Mrs. Bonomo assists the second graders in the process of sharing information.

*Mrs. Bonomo:* Let's begin by reviewing what we thought we knew about spiders.

*Alex:* We knew that spiders make webs.

*Tommy:* And we also wrote that they use their webs to catch food.

*Alex:* They use them like traps.

*Mrs. Bonomo:* Okay! Did we have any questions about spiders' webs?

*Christina:* Yes! I wanted to know how long it takes for a spider to make a web!

*Mrs. Bonomo:* Did anyone find the answer to Christina's question?

*Christina:* I found the answer to my question, Mrs. Bonomo!

*Mrs. Bonomo:* How long does it take, Christina?

*Christina:* It takes about an hour!

*Alex:* I found that out, too. It says it right here. (Alex points to the page where the answer is found).

Exemplary teachers engage children in explicit strategy instruction through the use of well-planned lessons or *minilessons*. Minilessons allow teachers to take the mystery out of comprehension and learning by sharing insights and knowledge students might otherwise never encounter. Explicit strategy lessons create a framework that provides the instructional support students need to become aware of, use, and develop control over comprehension skills and strategies. Striking a balance between strategy instruction and readers' actual interactions with texts is the key to comprehension development. In addition, informal, opportunistic occasions to *make explicit* a strategy for constructing meaning contribute to children's comprehension development. Exemplary literacy teachers take advantage of these spontaneous, often unplanned opportunities throughout the day to *embed* the teaching of skills and strategies within the context of meaningful reading, writing, and discussion activities.

As the chapter overview suggests, you will explore three dimensions of reading comprehension instruction: (1) how to scaffold students' development and use of comprehension strategies through explicit instructional techniques; (2) how to develop students' awareness of *story structure*, the underlying organization of stories, to facilitate comprehension of narrative texts; and (3) how to guide students' interactions with texts as they read. In Chapter 14, we will continue to examine comprehension strategies within the context of content area learning.

As you study the various instructional ideas in this chapter, think about reading comprehension as a dialogue between the author of the text and the reader. Authors use written language to communicate their ideas or tell a good story to someone else—an audience of readers. Readers use *cognitive* and *metacognitive strategies* to engage their minds in the dialogue so that they can understand, respond to, question, and even challenge the author's ideas. Students are in a strategic position to comprehend whenever they use their prior knowledge to construct meaning. Prior knowledge is the sum total

STANDARDS
1.3, 4.2

of the student's world. It represents the experiences, conceptual understandings, attitudes, values, skills, and strategies that students put into play to comprehend what they are reading. Given the multicultural nature of today's school population, it is particularly important that teachers honor the diverse backgrounds from which their students come as they help students construct meaning from the texts they are reading. Today's teachers are challenged with the task of helping students from a wide variety of ethnic backgrounds and cultures identify with literature that reflects those backgrounds.

In this chapter, you will learn how to create strategy lessons that scaffold students' ability to construct meaning and "take on" the author. You will learn how to demonstrate to students the importance of prediction making, raising questions, questioning the author, and other strategies that connect their world to the world of texts and new ideas.

DIVERSITY

STANDARD
2.2

# Scaffolding the Development and Use of Comprehension Strategies

As mentioned earlier, the National Reading Panel (2000) identified reading comprehension as one of the five essential components of an effective reading program. In order to develop students' comprehension abilities, teachers need to consider multiple levels of reading instruction including decoding skills, vocabulary development, and context clues, as well as more specific comprehension strategy instruction based on what we know skilled readers do when they read (Pressley, 2000). Good readers use an array of strategies in order to comprehend. They make connections as they read; they visualize, infer, and synthesize information; and they ask questions as they read. Teachers need to explicitly teach and demonstrate these strategies so that students know how to construct meaning before, during, and after reading.

As we mentioned in an earlier chapter, when teachers explicitly teach strategies with the purpose of eventually fostering independent use of those strategies, teachers are scaffolding instruction. With respect to teaching comprehension, **scaffolded instruction** means that teachers model strategies step-by-step and explicitly demonstrate the processes of thinking before, during, and after one reads. Next, teachers provide the students with guided practice in the strategies, followed by independent practice and application. See Box 10.1 for an example of scaffolded instruction.

**HOMEWORK EXERCISE: VIDEO**

Go to the Homework and Exercises section in Chapter 10 of MyEducationLab to watch the video "Defining Comprehension" to develop a deeper understanding of the concept of comprehension and its role in learning.

## Active Comprehension and Asking Questions

A common comprehension strategy is to have children answer questions about what is read. Traditionally such questions have been organized into three categories:

- **Literal questions.** Students answer by using information explicitly stated in the text.
- **Inferential questions.** Students answer by using their background knowledge along with information from the text.
- **Evaluative questions.** Students answer with judgments they make about what they read.

Figure 10.1 on page 314 provides examples of each type of question.

When children are engaged in a process of generating questions and making connections throughout reading, they are involved in **active comprehension.** According to Singer (1978), teachers encourage active comprehension when they *ask questions that elicit questions in return.* A first-grade teacher, for example, might focus attention on a picture or an illustration from a story or a book. Instead of asking, "What is the picture about?"

## BOX 10.1    STEP-BY-STEP Lesson

### Scaffolded Instruction

When teachers scaffold instruction they demonstrate, guide, and provide students with independent practice in comprehension strategies. In the following example, the teacher is scaffolding instruction in how to make predictions as they read.

1. The teacher explicitly describes the strategy.

   "Good readers predict what the text will be about and as they read they think about what will happen next."

2. The teacher models the strategy.

   "I am going to predict what this story is about by looking at the pictures first. I see pictures with a lot of snow and I see a car on the side of the road. I think the story will be about a snowstorm and the car is stuck."

   "Now I am going to read a couple of pages and stop to think if my prediction was right. Next, I will read a couple more pages and predict what might happen next."

3. The teacher guides the students in using the strategy.

   "What do you predict will happen in the story when you look at the other pictures?"
   "What do you predict after you silently read the next couple of pages?"
   "Let's talk about your predictions after you read."

4. The teacher provides the students with independent use of the strategy.

   "Today we are going to begin a new story. As you read the story, be sure to make predictions every couple of pages and read to see if your predictions were right."

*Source:* Based on "Scaffolding Students' Comprehension of Text," by K. F. Clark and M. F. Graves, 2005, *The Reading Teacher, 58*, pp. 570–580.

the teacher poses a question that elicits questions in response: "What would you like to know about the picture?" or "What does this picture remind you of?" In return, students might generate questions that focus on the details, main idea, or inferences from the illustration.

Not only do questions stimulate interest and arouse curiosity, but they also draw students into the story. In the process, students' reading comprehension will be more goal-directed. That is, they will read to satisfy purposes that *they*, not the teacher, have established. When selecting literature for active comprehension, it is important that teachers select stories that foster questions and understandings that reflect the diverse nature of their classrooms. In classrooms of mixed ethnic backgrounds, for example, teachers need to provide students with opportunities to respond to literature that reflects their culture.

DIVERSITY

STANDARD
2.3

### Figure 10.1    Types of Questions

*A woman walked into a university cafeteria. She was wearing high heels, a navy blue suit, and she was carrying a briefcase. The woman was also wearing a gold band on the fourth finger of her left hand. The woman placed her briefcase on a table and went to the counter to order a cheeseburger, french fries, and a milkshake. When the woman returned to the table, she opened her briefcase and took out a stack of papers and a red pen. There was also a picture drawn in crayon inside the briefcase.*

| | |
|---|---|
| *Literal questions:* | What was the woman wearing? Where was the woman? |
| *Inferential questions:* | What was the woman going to do with the papers and red pen? What was the woman's occupation? |
| *Evaluative questions:* | Was the woman eating a healthy meal? If the woman was going to grade papers, should she be using a red pen? |

Nolte and Singer (1985) explain that teachers can show students how to generate their own questions for a story by adhering to a "phase-in, phase-out" strategy. "Phase-in, phase-out" simply means that you gradually shift the burden of responsibility for question asking from your shoulders to those of your students. A good deal of this strategy involves modeling question-asking behavior and making students aware of the value of questions before, during, and after reading. The plan in Box 10.2 will ensure a smooth transition from teacher-directed questions to student-generated questions.

There are a variety of ways to encourage students to ask questions. Teachers, however, should be clear on the purpose of generating questions. In the past, teachers typically asked questions after the text was read; this often led struggling readers to feel that the purpose for reading was to answer questions that would be posed by the teacher. Teachers tended to view this as an assessment process. Did the students understand the text or not? Modeling question asking *while reading* and encouraging students to ask *their own questions* fosters ownership in the reading process. Highlighting sections of copied text, recording questions on sticky notes, developing question maps, and coding questions are several strategies that can be effectively used with all students (Harvey & Goudvis, 2000; Keene & Zimmerman, 1997). Harvey and Goudvis suggest that students can code their questions in the following manner:

| | |
|---|---|
| A | means that the question is answered in the text |
| BK | means it is answered from background knowledge |
| I | means it is inferred |
| D | refers to questions that can be answered by further discussion |
| RS | requires further research for an answer |
| Huh? or C | signals confusion |

For example, while independently reading *The Best Christmas Pageant Ever*, a fourth grader in Ms. Mayer's class might have placed a sticky note labeled "Huh?" next to the word *toolbox* if it was not clear what a *toolbox* was. Another student might have placed a "D" next to the text that states, "The Herdmans were absolutely the worst kids in the history of the world," in hopes of generating a discussion about behaviors that

---

## BOX 10.2 · STEP-BY-STEP *Lesson*

### Teaching Question Generation

1. Discuss the importance of asking questions as you direct students' story comprehension.
2. Model the types of questions that can be asked about central story content, including the setting, main characters, problem or goal, and obstacles encountered while attempting to resolve the problem or achieve the goal.
3. As you work through the story, ask questions that require questions in response (e.g., "What would you like to know about the setting of the story? The main character?" "What would you like to know about what happened next?"). Spend several class periods guiding question generation in this manner.
4. Divide the class into small groups of four to six children. Have one student in each group play the role of the teacher by eliciting questions from the other members. Circulate around the room to facilitate the process. Spend several class periods in small group question generation. Allow several minutes toward the end of each class period for debriefing with students (e.g., "How did the questioning go?" "Were there any problems?" "Why does question asking make a story easier to read?").
5. Have students work in pairs, asking each other questions as they read.
6. Have students work on their own to generate questions. Discuss the questions they raise as a whole group.

*Source:* Based on "Active Comprehension: Teaching a Process of Reading Comprehension and Its Effects on Reading Achievement," by R. Y. Nolte and H. Singer, 1985, *The Reading Teacher, 39*, pp. 24–28.

characterize people as "bad." As Harvey and Goudvis suggest, helping students ask questions as they read is an important skill that enhances reading comprehension.

A technological way to encourage questions is through e-mail. In one study, McKeon (1999) found that 9- and 10-year-olds could effectively use e-mail to ask questions about stories they were reading with preservice teacher partners. The fourth graders were partners with education students for a fourteen-week semester and they e-mailed weekly. After getting to know each other socially, the dialogue turned to electronic conversations about a book that the teacher had selected based on a social studies theme. Initially, the preservice teachers asked the students questions about the literature; eventually, the fourth graders were encouraged to ask questions of their own. The lowest-level readers in this study did in fact ask the most questions.

Regardless of the approach used to develop students' ability to ask questions as they read, it is important that teachers model questions of their own. This is a crucial instructional component of enhancing the active comprehension of all readers. In addition, it is critical that teachers of English language learners select literature that is culturally relevant to the students. If learning to comprehend stories is to occur through the social interaction that "asking questions" demands, teachers need to be cognizant of the background knowledge of culturally diverse students. Drucker (2003) makes a case in point regarding this issue. If the students are reading a story about a birthday party, for example, can we assume that children from other cultures have the same schema for what a birthday party is? Hence, teachers of ELL students need to carefully select literature in which the students will have adequate prior knowledge that enables them to ask questions as they read. Keeping this in mind, we now address additional strategies that involve students thinking and questioning as they read.

## Reciprocal Questioning (ReQuest)

Reciprocal questioning, also known as **ReQuest,** encourages students to ask their own questions about the material being read (Manzo, 1969; Vacca & Vacca, 2002). Box 10.3 synthesizes the steps for implementing ReQuest. Figure 10.2 provides question prompts to use with ReQuest.

---

**BOX 10.3**

### Implementing Reciprocal Questioning (ReQuest)

When teachers model the importance of asking questions as they read, they foster reading comprehension. By using scaffolding as students learn to construct questions, teachers assist students in thinking critically and taking ownership of their understanding of what they are reading. The following guidelines serve as steps to consider when using reciprocal questioning as a reading comprehension–teaching strategy. They are adapted from the original strategy developed by Manzo (1969).

1. Introduce students to the idea of asking questions as they read. Model the process by reading aloud and developing your own questions about the text.
2. Provide reading material to the students. Have them read a short segment or paragraph. Model questions you have

about the text and provide time for the students to answer the questions.
3. Continue with the next segment of the text. Now it's time for the students to ask you the questions.
4. Continue with steps 2 and 3 by taking turns asking questions. Be sure to model questions that go beyond literal information. Encourage questions that include critical thinking such as "What do you think the author means by this?"
5. At a suitable point in the text, when students have had enough time to process information about the selected text, encourage predictions and allow the students to read the rest of the selection independently.
6. Facilitate discussion and additional questions after reading the remaining text.

## Figure 10.2   Question Prompts for ReQuest

What does _____ remind you of?

Do you know someone like the character _____?

Do you agree with what _____ did in the story?

What do you think will happen next in the story?

Why do you think the author chose _____ as the setting?

Can you think of a different way to describe the action in this part of the story?

What do you picture in your mind when you read this part of the story?

The ReQuest procedure also works well in groups when you alternate the role of student questioner after each question. By doing so, you will probably involve more students in the activity. Also, once students understand the steps and are aware of how to play ReQuest, you may also try forming ReQuest teams. A ReQuest team made up of three or four students challenges another ReQuest team.

Whenever students are asked to generate questions, some will not know how to do so. Others will ask only literal questions because they don't know how to ask any others; they don't know how to ask questions that will stimulate inferential or evaluative levels of thinking. One way to deal with these situations is to provide a model that students will learn from. Your role as a questioner should not be underestimated. Over time you will notice the difference in the ability of students to pose questions and in the quality of questions asked.

Notice how in a third-grade class the teacher used her children's penchant for asking detailed questions to an advantage. ReQuest was being played from a social studies text-book, and the text under consideration consisted of two pages, one explaining map symbols and the other a map of the city of Burlington to practice reading the symbols or key. The children sensed that it would be difficult for the teacher to recall every detail relating to the map of Burlington. So they zeroed in, hoping to stump the teacher with precise questions. Notice how the teacher (*T*) uses the occasion to make students (*S*) aware of how to interact with the text.

S:   Where is the lake in Burlington?

T:   Oh-oh. I'm not sure I studied the map well enough. Let me think. *(closes eyes)* I'm making a picture in my head of that map. I can almost picture that lake. I think it's in the northeast corner of Burlington.

S:   You're right.

T:   I'm glad I made that mental picture as I was reading.

S:   Where are the railroad tracks in Burlington?

T:   I'm not sure. My mental picture is pretty good, but I don't have every single detail.

S:   Close to City Hall.

S:   Where is the hospital?

T:   *(closes eyes)* Near the center of town.

Questioning continued in this manner with the teacher knowing some of the answers and the students informing her of others. At the conclusion of the lesson, the teacher summarized this way: "Who would have ever thought you'd get so many questions from two short pages of social studies? I'm glad you asked all those. I sure learned a lot about reading maps! When we do ReQuest, I do two things that might help you, too. First, if there's a chart, picture, or map, I try to take a photograph of it in my head. Then if you ask me questions about it, I can bring it up in my memory. Also, as I'm reading, I ask myself questions that I think you might ask me. Then I'm ready for them! This is a good thing to do anytime you're reading. Stop, ask yourself questions, and answer them. That helps you understand and remember what you have read."

## Question–Answer Relationships (QARs)

When asking questions, special attention should be given to the most likely source of information the reader needs to answer the question. Certain questions can be thought of as *textually explicit* because they promote recall or recognition of *information actually stated in the text*. Other questions are *textually implicit* because they provoke thinking. Readers must search for text relationships and think about the information presented. If students are to integrate ideas within a text, textually implicit questions are likely to be the most useful. Finally, some questions usually place the reader's knowledge of the world at the center of the questioning activity. Such questions are *schema-based*. Because students' schemata will vary depending on the nature of their diverse backgrounds, teachers must be knowledgeable about the various cultures from which the students come. And because students must rely on their own resources as well as the text to solve problems, discover new insights, or evaluate the significance of what was read, teachers should include reading material that reflects the students' backgrounds.

**Question–answer relationships (QARs),** as proposed by Raphael (1986), help learners know what information sources are available for seeking answers to different types of text questions. Through this strategy, readers become more sensitive to the different mental operations and text demands required by different questions. As a result, teachers and students become cognizant of the three-way relationships that exist among the question, the text to which it refers, and the background knowledge and information at the reader's disposal. QARs enhance children's ability to answer comprehension questions by teaching them how to find information they need to answer questions. Explicit instruction will make students sensitive to two information sources where answers can be found.

The first information source is the *text*. Some answers to questions can be found *right there* in the text. Other answers found in the text, however, demand a *think-and-search* strategy in which students *search* the text for information and *think* about the relationships that exist among the bits of information found. For example, if the question about a house is "What color is the house?" and the text reads "The old house was white," the answer to the question is *right there* because it is directly stated. On the other hand, if the question about the house is "What characteristics of the house indicate that it is haunted?" the answer would involve *thinking and searching* for clues that the author gives about the house being haunted. Such clues might include "the house is spooky," "the residents claimed to feel the presence of ghosts," or "weird sounds could be heard at midnight."

The second information source is the *reader*. Some questions signal to the reader "I am on my own." Other questions may signal "It's up to the author and me." In either case, the text may help, but answers must come from inside the reader's mind. A question such as "How would you feel about being in a haunted house?" might elicit the response, "I would be scared. I was in a spooky house on Halloween once and it was creepy." This answer would be "On My Own" because it reflects personal prior knowledge. The use of Right There, Think and Search, Author and You, and On My Own are mnemonics to help readers recognize question–answer relationships. A chart such as the one in Figure 10.3 can be used to make readers aware of QARs. The Research-Based Practices steps featured in Box 10.4 on page 320 will assist students in their understanding and use of QARs.

## *Figure 10.3*  Introducing Question–Answer Relationships

### Where Are Answers to Questions Found?

**In the Text:**

Right There

The answer is in the text. The words used in the question and the words used for the answer can usually be found in the same sentence.

Think and Search

The answer is in the text, but the words used in the question and those used for the answer are not in the same sentence. You need to think about different parts of the text and how ideas can be put together before you can answer the question.

**or**

**In My Head:**

On My Own

The text got you thinking, but the answer is inside your head. The author can't help you much. So think about the question, and use what you know already to answer it.

Author and You

The answer is not in the text. You need to think about what you know, what the author says, and how they fit together.

## Questioning the Author (QtA)

**Questioning the author (QtA)** is another instructional strategy that models for students the importance of asking questions while reading. Beck, McKeown, Hamilton, and Kucan (1997) devised the QtA strategy to demonstrate the kinds of questions students need to ask in order to think more deeply and construct meaning about segments of text

STANDARD
2.2

BOX **10.4**

### Research-Based Practices

## Steps in the Development of Students' Understanding of QARs

The QAR instructional strategy enhances students' ability to answer comprehension questions. Raphael (1982, 1986) recommends the following steps for developing students' understanding of QARs:

#### DAY 1

- Introduce the concept of QARs by showing students the chart in Figure 10.3 or an overhead transparency containing a description of the basic question–answer relationships. The chart should be positioned in a prominent place in the classroom so that students may refer to it whenever the need arises.
- Begin QAR instruction by assigning students three short passages (no more than two to five sentences in length). Follow each reading with one question from each of the QAR categories on the chart.
- Then discuss the differences between a Right There question and answer, a Think and Search question and answer, an Author and You question and answer, and an On My Own question and answer. Explanations should be clear and complete.
- Reinforce the discussion by assigning several more short passages and asking a question for each. Students will soon begin to catch on to the differences among the QAR categories.

#### DAY 2

- Continue practicing with short passages, using one question for each QAR category per passage. First, give students a passage to read with questions *and* answers *and* identified QARs. Why do the questions and answers represent one QAR and not another?
- Second, give students a passage with questions and answers; this time they have to identify the QAR for each.
- Finally, give students passages, decide together which strategy to use, and have them write their responses.

#### DAY 3

- Conduct a brief review. Then assign a longer passage (75 to 200 words) with up to five questions (at least one each from the QAR categories).
- Have students work in groups to decide the QAR category for each question and the answers for each.
- Next, assign a second passage, comparable in length, with five questions for students to work on individually. Discuss responses either in small groups or with the whole class.

#### DAY 4

- Apply the QAR strategy to actual reading situations. For each question asked, students decide on the appropriate QAR strategy and write out their answers. Here is an example:

What is Jack's problem?

_____ Right There

_____ Think and Search

_____ Author and You

_____ On My Own

Answer:

(Discussion follows.)

- Once students are sensitive to different information sources for different types of questions and know how to use these sources to respond to questions, variations can be made in the QAR strategy. For example, during a discussion, consider prefacing a question by saying, "This question is *right there* in the text" or "You'll have to *think and search* the text to answer" or "You're *on your own* with this one." Make sure that you pause several seconds or more for "think time."

*Source:* Based on "Teaching Question–Answer Relationships Revisited," by T. E. Raphael, 1986, *The Reading Teacher, 39,* pp. 516–522.

as they read. The strategy is based on the notion that successful readers act on the author's message. If what they are reading doesn't make sense to them, successful readers raise questions about what the author says and means. QtA shows students how to read text closely as if the author were there to be challenged and questioned.

QtA places value on the quality and depth of students' responses to the author's intent. It is important that students keep their minds active while reading as they engage in a dialogue with an author. A successful reader monitors whether the author is making sense by asking questions such as "What is the author trying to say here?" "What does

**BOX 10.5** STEP-BY-STEP *Lesson*

## Implementing the Questioning the Author (QtA) Strategy: An Adaptation

1. Select a story or subject matter text in which you can identify conflict or problems that raise potential questions.
2. Read the text closely and identify the major themes and passages where questions may arise.
3. Segment the text so that the students stop reading at a critical point.
4. Construct questions that prompt the students to think about what the author suggests by rereading the text. The questions should encourage students to verify how the author is getting the point across.
5. Continue with thoughtful queries that encourage the students to question the author.

*Source:* Based on strategy in *Questioning the Author: An Approach for Enhancing Student Engagement with Text,* by I. L. Beck, M. G. McKeown, R. L. Hamilton, and L. Kucan (Newark, DE: International Reading Association, 1997).

the author mean?" "So what? What is the significance of the author's message?" "Does this make sense with what the author told us before?" "Does the author explain this clearly?" These questions, according to Beck et al. (1997), are posed by the teacher to help students "take on" the author and understand that text material needs to be challenged. Through QtA, students learn that authors are fallible and may not always express ideas in the easiest way for readers to understand. QtA builds metacognitive knowledge by making students aware of an important principle related to reading comprehension: *Not comprehending what the author is trying to say is not always the fault of the reader.* As a result, students come to view their roles as readers as "grappling with text" as they seek to make sense of the author's intent.

Box 10.5 outlines the steps for planning QtA lessons for narrative or informational texts.

When using QtA to comprehend stories, pose *narrative queries.* Through the use of narrative queries, students become familiar with an author's writing style as they strive to understand character, plot, and underlying story meaning. The following queries help students think about story characters: "How do things look for this character now?" "Given what the author has already told us about this character, what do you think the author is up to?" Understanding the story plot can be accomplished with queries such as these: "How has the author let you know that something has changed?" "How has the author settled this for us?" The thoughtful use of queries is vital for classroom discussion. As students actively explore and clarify meaning, guide the discussion as you progress from one text segment to the next.

## Reciprocal Teaching

**Reciprocal teaching,** as devised by Palincsar and Brown (1984), depends on the teacher's ability to model how an expert reader uses four comprehension activities to understand a text selection: (1) raising questions about a text segment, (2) predicting what the segment is about, (3) summarizing the important points, and (4) clarifying difficult vocabulary and concepts.

In reciprocal teaching, the teacher begins the lesson by modeling each of the four comprehension activities while leading a discussion of the text. During this phase of the lesson, the quality of the dialogue between teacher and students depends on how explicit the teacher is in demonstrating each of the comprehension activities.

After observing the teacher, students are invited to share or add to what the teacher has stated and then to teach the remaining sections of the text selection. For example,

STANDARD 2.2

In reciprocal teaching, a student assumes the role of the teacher and models one or more comprehension activities from a text.

a student assumes the role of the teacher and proceeds to model one or more of the comprehension activities on the next segment of text. If the student runs into trouble with any of the activities, the teacher recenters the lesson to provide support by adjusting the demands of the task. Gradually, the teacher withdraws support and the student continues teaching the lesson. In the Step-by-Step Lesson featured in Box 10.6, Herrmann (1988) provides an excellent model of a reciprocal teaching lesson.

Reciprocal teaching helps students think more strategically about reading. Our experience with the procedure suggests that it is a complicated strategy; teachers will need to work with it several times before they feel accomplished with its implementation. Oczkus (2003) suggests using large comprehension charts that visually organize each step. After modeling your responses and writing on the chart, the children add their contributions on sticky notes. The notes then become the focus of discussion and the basis for the reciprocal teaching lesson.

## Think-Alouds

A **think-aloud** is a strategy in which students talk about their thoughts while reading aloud (Davey, 1983). When teachers model what they are thinking as they read, they can help students develop visual images and link new information to what they already know. Think-alouds provide a window to view what is going on in the minds of the students as they read.

To conduct a think-aloud, the teacher should select a passage that elicits ambiguity, difficult vocabulary, or contradictions. As the teacher reads aloud, the students follow along silently and listen as the teacher describes what he or she is thinking. After modeling, the students are encouraged to describe their thoughts. Examine Box 10.7 on page 324 to see how Beth uses a think-aloud to encourage visual imagery and discussion in a story. Students can also work with partners to share their thinking. When students come from diverse backgrounds, pairing students with similar or different backgrounds can be an effective way to activate schemata. In the New Literacies Box 10.8 on page 325 see

## BOX 10.6   STEP-BY-STEP *Lesson*

### Model of a Reciprocal Teaching Lesson

1. Read the text title and have the students tell what they expect or would like to learn from the selection. Summarize the group's predictions and, if appropriate, add a few of your own. Note how the lesson begins in the following lesson excerpt:

   T: What's the title of our new passage?
   S: "The Miracle of Butterflies."
   T: Right. What's the miracle of butterflies? In your own words, what would you predict this will be about?
   S: How butterflies fly?
   T: Oh, that's a good prediction!
   S: What they do.
   S: What season they come out, like summer.
   T: Okay. Those are excellent predictions. Let's begin.

2. Read a small portion of the text aloud, paragraph by paragraph.

3. Ask a question about the content. Invite the group to answer the question. Invite individuals to share additional questions generated while they read the selection.

   T: My question is: What have the people of Butterfly City, U.S.A., done to protect the butterflies?
   S: They made a law making it illegal.
   T: To do what?
   S: To kill butterflies.
   T: Exactly. Does anyone else have a question?

4. Summarize what has been read by identifying the gist of the segment and explain how you arrived at this summary. Invite the group to comment on the summary. Note how the teacher summarized in the following lesson excerpt:

   T: My summary is that this is about the migration of monarch butterflies. I thought of that summary because the authors introduced the story with a good topic sentence. That was a good clue. Do you have anything that should be added to my summary?

5. Lead a discussion to clarify any words or ideas that are unclear or confusing.

   T: Let me ask you something here. Is there an unclear meaning in this paragraph?
   S: Yes. Where it says "scrawls in wavy light."
   T: Now, does the sun ever write a message in the sky?
   S: No.
   T: No. What is the author doing here?
   S: Making up the whole thing in his mind.
   T: All right. It doesn't really happen but the author is using this expression to say that the sun sends us a message and that it can be used as an energy source. But certainly you will never look at the sky and see a message written by the sun.

*Source:* "Two Approaches for Helping Poor Readers Become More Strategic," by B. A. Herrmann, *The Reading Teacher, 42*, p. 27. Copyright © 1988 by the International Reading Association. Reprinted with permission of the International Reading Association (www.reading.org).

**HOMEWORK EXERCISE: VIDEO**

Go to the Homework and Exercises section in Chapter 10 of MyEducationLab to watch the video "Think Aloud Strategy" and consider how you would apply the think-aloud strategy in your classroom.

how think-alouds can be used to demonstrate the process of reading and comprehending online text containing hypertext.

In summary, strategy instruction lets children in on the secrets of reading comprehension. What they discover through explicit instructional techniques like reciprocal teaching and QtA is that meaning doesn't lie hidden in text like buried treasure, waiting for readers to dig it out. On the contrary, readers must actively engage in reading to construct meaning. Reading comprehension is triggered by the knowledge that readers bring to print. Through explicit strategy instruction, teachers provide all students, including those from diverse backgrounds, with opportunities to make connections between what they are reading and their prior experiences. Culturally and linguistically diverse students especially benefit from instructional strategy demonstrations when they are modeled in small groups. In fact, the most effective programs for English language learners are those that include collaborative, interactive learning, such as those discussed in this chapter (Sturtevant, 2001). In addition, middle school students who are exposed to increasingly difficult reading material need explicit strategy instruction in comprehension in all of their classes (Moore, Bean, Birdyshaw, & Rycik, 1999). In the next section, we pay attention to the underlying elements that make up the structure of well-told stories.

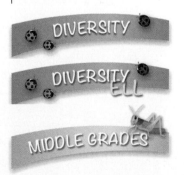

BOX 10.7

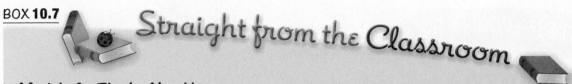

# Straight from the Classroom

## Model of a Think-Aloud Lesson

BETH: Today we are going to read a story about an unusual house that is unique. Our story doesn't have any pictures, so we are going to try to form pictures in our heads as we read about this house. When I think of an unusual house, I think of one that might be haunted and look spooky. (The teacher reads aloud the beginning of the story.)

BETH: The story says, "The house was in Texas and it was unique because it had a purple roof that almost touched the sky and a front door that opened upside down like a toaster oven." Hmmm. I have a different picture in my head now. I don't know if this house is haunted because when I think of a haunted house it doesn't have a purple roof. I see a house that is probably unique because it is different than usual houses. What do you see in your head that makes this house unique?

CARLOS: I see a big tall roof on the house and the front door is weird because it is not like the doors you seen in America. In my country our houses don't even have doors. The houses in my country are mud huts.

BETH: I like what you said, Carlos. Let's talk more about what you said. Can you tell us about the picture in your head about the house in the story? What is weird about the front door?

CARLOS: It's like it opens upside down like the garages in America! Front doors don't open like that.

BETH: I guess the author is trying to tell us that this house is unique because it is not what we usually see.

EMILY: I think that Carlos's house is unique then, because the houses in his country don't even have doors and our houses do. I've never seen a house without a door.

BETH: I haven't seen a house without a door either, Emily, except in pictures. So, yes, for me, too, Carlos's house is unique. What else is unique about the house in the story?

JOE: It has a roof that is way too big to be real in this country. Our houses don't reach the sky, except maybe castles, but I don't think they do either.

BETH: Good ideas, everyone! Let's see what else the author tells us about this house that could be unique and let's try to make pictures in our heads as I read the story to you. (Story reading continues along with think-aloud discussion.)

### REFLECTIVE INQUIRY

- How does Beth encourage her students to visualize as they read?
- How can you encourage beginning readers to make pictures in their minds as they read?
- What can you do if students don't understand how to visualize what they read?

# Developing Readers' Awareness of Story Structure

Although including informational text in the teaching of reading is an important component of an effective literacy program (Kletzien & Dreher, 2004), stories are basic to any school's reading curriculum. Because stories are central to children's reading development, much time and effort have been spent attempting to understand how stories are comprehended. A child's knowledge of stories begins to develop at an early age. Children hear and tell simple stories and then read and view them in both home and school experiences, and children learn implicitly that well-told stories are predictable. There is an underlying structure that all simple stories appear to have in common. As children develop a **story schema,** they begin to sense what comes next.

A simple story actually isn't as simple as it might appear on the surface. The underlying structure of a story can be quite complex. Attempts have been made to identify the basic elements that make up a well-developed story (Mandler & Johnson, 1977; Stein & Glenn, 1979; Thorndyke, 1977). These efforts have led to the development of several variations of **story grammar.** Just as sentence grammar provides a way of describing how a sentence is put together, story grammar helps specify the basic parts of a story and how

BOX **10.8**

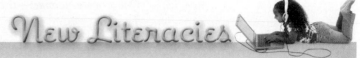

*New Literacies*

## "THINKING ALOUD" WITH HYPERTEXT

Traditional think-alouds are used with print-based linear text. Kymes (2005), however, suggests how the strategy can be useful for modeling the processes that occur when one reads online. She proposes that teachers demonstrate and scaffold specific navigational strategies when reading in a nonlinear hypertext environment by verbalizing the process—hence, "thinking aloud." Gradually, the students can work with partners to practice "thinking aloud" as they read online material containing hypertext. Below are examples of online think-alouds based on specific questions:

- What is the purpose of my online search? The teacher talks through her reasoning behind clicking on each link and explains how her decision is driven by her purpose.
- How will I skim, scan, and read online selectively? The teacher demonstrates how this can take place by highlighting important main ideas; cutting and pasting ideas; and bulleting ideas. The process does not include reading all of the text, but selectively reading based on the purpose.
- How does the online information relate to my prior knowledge and what information is brand new to me? Using the cursor, the teacher talks through the process while highlighting sections of the text. New information can be categorized by bulleting ideas. The ideas should also relate to the purpose for reading the text.

- What new words am I discovering as I read? As the teacher comes across new words, she clicks on any hyperlinks that further define the word and explains what she is doing.
- What information should I cut and paste or print so that I can reread it later? The teacher "thinks aloud" as she explains why certain information might be useful to have for further study.
- What are the main ideas that the author(s) is trying to convey? The teacher clarifies ideas by using the cursor and considers whether the author can or should be contacted for additional information.
- How can I be sure the source is accurate? The teacher models how to determine the credibility of the work.
- How can I use this online information? The teacher demonstrates how to summarize the ideas for a paper, a poster, a discussion, an application, or a debate.

Kymes (2005) recommends that teachers model one strategy at a time with extended practice, rather than attempting to scaffold each strategy simultaneously. Using think-alouds with online texts will help students begin to understand the process and why they are doing it, rather than struggling through the massive information that digital text has to offer.

*Source:* "Teaching Online Comprehension Strategies Using Think-Alouds," by A. Kymes, 2005, *Journal of Adolescent & Adult Literacy, 18,* pp. 492–500. Copyright © 2005 by the International Reading Association. Reprinted with permission of the International Reading Association (www.reading.org).

they tie together to form a well-constructed story. What do most well-developed stories have in common? Although individual story grammars may differ somewhat, most people would agree that a story's structure centers on *setting* and *plot*.

## Elements in a Story

The setting of a story introduces the main character (sometimes called the *protagonist*) and situates the characters in a time and place. The plot of a story is made up of one or more *episodes*. A simple story has a single episode. More complex stories may have two or several episodes, as well as different settings. Each episode is made up of a chain of events. Although the labeling of these events differs from story to story, the following elements are generally included:

> *A beginning or initiating event*—either an idea or an action that sets further events into motion
>
> *Internal response (followed by a goal or problem)*—the character's inner reaction to the initiating event, in which the character sets a goal or attempts to solve a problem
>
> *Attempts*—the character's efforts to achieve the goal or alleviate the problem; several attempts may be evident in an episode

*One or more outcomes*—the success or failure of the character's attempts

*Resolution*—the long-range consequence that evolves from the character's success or failure to achieve the goal or resolve the problem

*A reaction*—an idea, emotion, or further event that expresses a character's feelings about success or failure in reaching a goal or resolving a problem or that relates the events in the story to some broader set of concerns

The events in the story form a causal chain. Each event leads to the next one as the main character moves toward reaching a goal or resolving a problem.

Keeping the elements of story grammar in mind, read the story "People of the Third Planet" in Figure 10.4 and then analyze its structure. To help you map the story's structure, use the chart in Figure 10.5 on page 329. In the spaces provided on the chart, write what you believe to be the major story parts, including the setting and chain of events.

After you have completed the chart, compare your mapping of the story elements with those of other members of your class. Although there will undoubtedly be some differences in the way the story elements are interpreted, there will probably be a fair amount of similarity among ideas of what constitutes the elements of story grammar in "People of the Third Planet."

Knowing the underlying elements of a story benefits both teacher and students. You can use story organization to plan instruction more effectively and to anticipate the problems students might have in following a specific story's action, especially if it lacks one or more story elements. Students can build and use the story schema to make better sense of what they read. The closer the match between the reader's story schema and the organization of a particular story, the greater the comprehension is likely to be. This is why a *story map* is an important planning tool in the hands of teachers.

## Mapping a Story for Instructional Purposes

**HOMEWORK EXERCISE: VIDEO**

Go to the Homework and Exercises section in Chapter 10 of MyEducationLab to watch the video "Mapping" and consider how mapping can help students understand story structure.

An analysis of a story's organizational elements strengthens instructional decisions. Beck, McKeown, McCaslin, and Burket (1979) recommend creating a **story map** as a way of identifying major structural elements, both explicit and implicit, underlying a story to be taught in class. A chart such as the one in Figure 10.5 helps you map the relationships that exist among the major events in a story. Once these relationships are established, they form the basis for developing a line of questions that will help students grasp the story parts under discussion. According to Beck and her associates, students should thoroughly understand the general framework of the story before broader, evaluative questions can be considered.

The following generic questions are easily applied to specific stories. As you examine these questions, consider how you would adapt them to "People of the Third Planet."

**Setting:**
Where did the story take place? When did the story take place? Who is the main character? What is _____ like? What is _____'s problem? What did _____ need? Why is _____ in trouble?

**Internal Response and Goal/Problem:**
What does _____ decide to do? What does _____ have to attempt to do?

**Attempts and Outcomes:**
What did _____ do about _____? What happened to _____? What will _____ do now? How did it turn out?

# Figure 10.4   People of the Third Planet

The silver flying saucer came down silently and landed in a parking lot in a small town on Earth. It was one o'clock in the morning, and the streets were dark.

Slowly a section of the saucer slid open. Two creatures from another world stepped out. For a moment they thought no one was near. Then they noticed a line of figures standing before them.

One creature whispered to the other, "Over there I see some people of the Third Planet. But they do not come forward to greet us. Perhaps this is not the time to tell the people of the Third Planet about our world."

The other creature shook his head. "No, our orders are clear. Now is the time. We must approach these Earth people and arrange a meeting with their leader."

He stepped forward and began to speak. "People of the Third Planet—or Earth, as you call it. We greet you in peace. We are messengers from a world that is millions of years older than your own. We wish to establish a peaceful link between our two worlds and exchange ideas with you. We would like to speak to someone of importance on your planet. Please direct us to such a person." No one in the line of figures moved. They did not even seem interested in the space creature's words.

After several seconds the creature stepped back and whispered to his friend, "These Earth people act as if they do not understand what I am saying. How can that be? We monitored their radio signals and listened to them speak. I am sure we are using their language correctly."

"Stay calm," said the other creature. "I will speak to them."

He raised his voice and said, "Earth friends! Perhaps you are frightened by our sudden appearance. Or perhaps you do not fully understand our message. I assure you that it is of the greatest importance. It is necessary that we speak to the leader of the Third Planet. Please tell us where we may find this person."

The figures remained absolutely still.

"We will not harm any of you," the space creature went on. "We only wish to talk with your leader. But—if you do not cooperate—we will be forced to take one of you with us for questioning."

Not one figure moved or said a word.

The creature from the saucer began to get angry. He clenched his fists and whispered to his friend, "Apparently these Earth people will not tell us anything. Let us take one aboard. We will force the Earth person to speak."

He shouted at the figures standing before him, "You have left us no choice! We will have to use force."

He was amazed that even these words had no effect. The figures did not turn and run. They did not move at all.

In a fury he raced up to the first figure in line and said, "You are my prisoner. March forward to the saucer!"

Nothing happened.

Then he hit the figure hard, but still the figure did not move.

"It is no use," he said. "I cannot force this Earth person to walk. It is as if the Earth person has roots that go deep into the ground."

"Use your ray gun!" his friend yelled. "Cut the Earth person away from the Earth that these people love so much."

There was a single flash of fire from the space creature's gun. The Earth person fell noisily to the ground.

Even then none of the other figures moved.

This was more than the space creatures could believe.

"People of the Third Planet!" the first creature said. "We greeted you in peace, and you did not answer us. We captured one of your people, and you did not stop us. You are strange people with no feelings for anyone. Farewell, people of the Third Planet. Farewell."

The two creatures put the captured figure into their saucer and then climbed in themselves. With a sudden flash of light the flying saucer took off from Earth.

*(Continued)*

## *Figure* 10.4   *(Continued)*

A police car was coming down the street just as the saucer flashed up into the sky. "What was that?" one of the police officers asked.

"Looked like an explosion in the parking lot," his partner said. "Better see what happened."

The car raced toward the lot and screeched to a stop. The driver jumped out and flashed his light and found the officer down on one knee, pointing to a metal base that was still hot to the touch.

"Something sliced off this thing," the police officer said. "Did a neat job of cutting too. But what for? They could only get away with a few pennies. Why would anyone want to steal a parking meter?"

*Source:* Adapted from *People of the Third Planet,* by Dale Crail. Copyright © 1968 by Scholastic, Inc. Reprinted by permission of Scholastic, Inc.

**Resolution:**
How did _____ solve the problem? How did _____ achieve the goal? What would you do to solve _____'s problem?

**Reaction:**
How did _____ feel about the problem? Why did _____ do _____?
How did _____ feel at the end?

When students have responded to questions related to the story line, engage them in discussion centered on other important aspects of the story, such as its theme, character development, and the reader's personal response to the story.

**Theme:**
What is the moral of the story? What did you learn from the story? What is the major point of the story? What does this story say about _____? Why do you think the author wanted to write this story?

**Characters:**
Why do you think _____ did that? What do you like about _____? Dislike?
Does _____ remind you of anyone else you know?

**Personal Response:**
Is there anything you would have changed in the story? How did the story make you feel? Happy? Sad? Angry? Bewildered? Was there anything about the story that didn't make sense?

For English language learners, Fitzgerald and Graves (2004) recommend a visual aid that resembles a "yellow brick road" to foster understanding the sequence of a story map. The activity resembles a game board in which each "brick" is numbered and corresponds to questions that identify the sequential organization of the story. It is suggested that ELL students can work in pairs to write answers to the questions and share in small groups.

Not only is story mapping useful for planning questions, but it also provides you with information about "break points" during reading. A break point occurs whenever students are asked to stop an in-class reading to discuss story content. When and where to stop reading, as we will explain later in this chapter, is one of the most important decisions you can make when guiding reading.

## *Figure* 10.5   Mapping Story Structure

| Chain of Events | |
|---|---|
| Time and place: | Character(s): |

| Chain of Events | |
|---|---|
| The beginning event that initiates the action | |
| Internal response and goal/problem | |
| Attempt(s) and outcome(s) | |
| Resolution | |
| Reaction | |

## Building a Schema for Stories

We don't advocate teaching story elements for the sake of teaching story elements. Such practice can turn out to be counterproductive. However, making children aware of the predictability of a well-developed story is appropriate, especially if the children don't appear to use a story schema during reading. You can put story structure to good use in the classroom when students have access to reading materials that are written around recognizable story structures. Moreover, avoid using narrative selections that masquerade as stories. These so-called stories go nowhere; they're incomplete and severely lacking in one or more story parts.

There are many resources available to teachers for locating quality children's literature for teaching comprehension. For example, the International Reading Association

STANDARDS
2.3, 4.2

As students engage in discussions about story elements, they should be encouraged to express their opinions and react personally to the content of the story.

provides book reviews through its journals and annual publication *Children's Choices*, and Carol Hurst's web site at www.carolhurst.com is another excellent resource for children's literature. Gunning (2000) includes an annotated listing of easy books for struggling readers. In Chapter 12, we discuss guidelines for selecting literature; Appendix F includes recommended books for multicultural reading experiences.

The following activities and suggestions will help students build a sense of story and reinforce their awareness of story structure.

**READ, TELL, AND PERFORM STORIES IN CLASS** ◆ There is no better substitute for building experience with stories or extending students' knowledge of how stories are put together than to read, tell, and perform stories in class on a regular basis. These types of experiences with stories are as paramount in the middle grades as they are in the beginning grades. For beginning English language learners, drama can help with understanding new ideas as they watch students enact story parts (Fitzgerald & Graves, 2004). In addition, tableau and pantomime are activities in which students can create scenes from stories as an expression of comprehension (Cornett, 2006).

**DON'T TEACH THE LANGUAGE OF STORY GRAMMAR AS AN END IN ITSELF** ◆ Although children need to be aware of the language of instruction, avoid teaching jargon for the sake of learning technical terms. Children develop a story schema gradually and implicitly, mainly through direct experience and interaction with stories. However, when teaching story parts explicitly to children, use language that is simple and familiar. For example, instead of asking a child to identify the "initiating event" in the story, you may want to phrase the question in more familiar language such as, "What happened in the beginning of the story to get things started?"

Build on children's concepts of *problem* and *trouble*. You might ask, "What does trouble mean? Have you ever been in trouble with a parent or a friend? What kind of trouble happens in stories you have read? How did [the main character] get into trouble? How did [the main character] get out of trouble?"

**SHOW RELATIONSHIPS AMONG STORY PARTS** ◆ Flowcharts reflect best practices for mapping relationships that exist among events in the story. Flowcharts give children a visual image of how stories are organized. Gordon and Braun (1983) suggest giving students copies of a diagram without the story information. As information is discussed relating to the story parts depicted on the flowchart, students can write what is being said on their own copies.

Pearson (1982) claims that children as young as 8 years old are successful, with much teacher modeling, at representing a story on a flowchart. Flowcharting can take many different forms, including the one illustrated in Figure 10.6 on page 332. Study the generic flowchart and how a second-grade teacher adapted that format to develop a story map based on students' suggestions during discussion.

The value of flowcharting lies in the discussions that take place before, during, and after the activity. Discussions should revolve around the relationships of one event to another. The goal behind a discussion is to make students consciously aware that events in a story form a causal chain. With much teacher-led discussion, modeling, and guided practice, many students beginning in the second or third grade will grasp how to map story parts and make flowcharts on their own. Once this is the case, have students share their products with one another. Rather than emphasize accuracy during sharing sessions, ask for reasons and rationales. Encourage speculation and risk-taking. Also, allow students the opportunity to revise or alter their individual efforts based on the discussion.

**REINFORCE STORY KNOWLEDGE THROUGH INSTRUCTIONAL ACTIVITIES** ◆ Children's understanding of story structure can be extended through varied instructional tasks. Whaley (1981) suggests two activities: **macrocloze stories** and **scrambled stories.** Other activities involve the use of **story frames** and **circular story maps.**

**Macrocloze Stories**    A macrocloze story is based on the same principle that operates for a cloze passage. A teacher constructs cloze material by deleting single words from a passage. Children are then given copies of the cloze passage and are required to supply the missing words. When constructing a macrocloze story, instead of omitting single words, delete one or more parts from the story—for example, a sentence, several sentences, or an entire paragraph. Reproduce copies of the story with rules indicating where the text deletions have been made. Students should then read the story and discuss the missing information orally or in writing.

**Scrambled Stories**    A second instructional task involves scrambled stories. As the name implies, a story is separated into its parts and jumbled. Students must then read the scrambled story and reorder it. Try your hand at reordering the story events in Figure 10.7 on page 333 from Aesop's fable "The Crow and the Pitcher." Decide which story event comes first, second, third, and so on. Compare your reordering with others in your class.

**Story Frames**    Story frames present a third way of heightening an awareness of stories. Fowler (1982) showed that story frames may be particularly appropriate in the primary grades or in situations in which students are at risk in their development as readers. A story frame provides the student with a skeletal paragraph: a sequence of spaces tied together with transition words and connectors that signal a line of thought. Fowler identified five story frames, each with a different emphasis: *plot summary, setting, character analysis, character comparison,* and the story's *problem.*

In Figure 10.8 on page 334, examine how two third graders completed a frame for the story "Owl at Home." The frame centers on the story's problem. The children bring differing abilities to the task, yet both capture the central focus of the story. As students become familiar with using story frames, you may want to involve them simply in writing summary paragraphs that focus on different elements of the story.

## Figure 10.6    Generic Flowchart for Mapping a Story and a Classroom Example of the Format

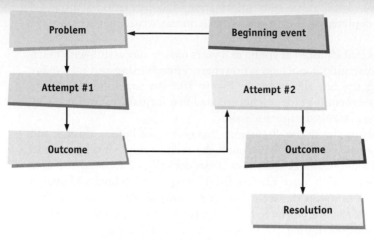

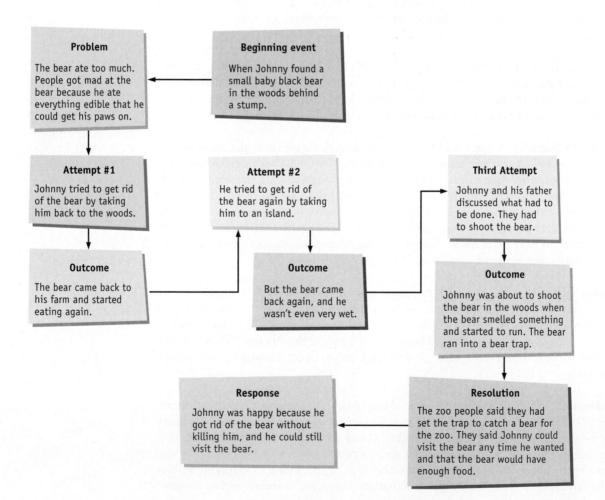

## Figure 10.7    Scrambled Story from Aesop's Fable "The Crow and the Pitcher"

By using this method, the water gradually reached the top, and the crow was able to drink it with ease.

The crow hoped that the pitcher was filled with water.

A crow was ready to die from thirst when he spotted a pitcher.

Little by little does the trick.

So the crow gathered up some pebbles and began to drop them into the pitcher one by one.

He tried to overturn the pitcher, but it was too heavy.

Much to his dismay, the crow found only a little drop of water at the bottom, which he was unable to reach.

**Circular Story Map**    A circular story map uses pictures to depict the sequence of events leading to the problem in the story. This strategy is useful for students whose strengths include visual representation. Using Latino literature, Smolen and Ortiz-Castro (2000) describe how individual figure drawings that represent the major story events can be glued in a circle on poster board to represent the story sequence. Refer to Figure 10.9 on page 335 for an example of a circular story map based on the picture book *The Always Prayer Shawl* (Oberman, 1994). In this story, a young Jewish boy in Czarist Russia, Adam, moves to the United States during the revolution. Before Adam embarks on his journey, Adam's grandfather gives him a shawl that becomes part of a powerful family tradition passed from generation to generation.

# Guiding Interactions Between Reader and Text

On the road to reading maturity, elementary and middle school readers need to become aware of and skilled at recognizing when shifts in thinking occur during reading. The shift may involve an author's transition to a new topic, changes in setting, twists in the plot, and so on. Or the author may put demands on the reader's

## Figure 10.8  Comparison of Story Frames for "Owl at Home"

**TANNER'S FRAME**

In this story the problem starts when    Owl thought the moon
was following him home.

After that,    He started walking and he said that
the moon was ~~fm~~ following him.

Next,    He was almost home and he still thougt
the moon was still following him.

Then,
he went inside his house and he got
his p.J's on.

The problem is finally solved when    Owl looks out the
window and says night to the moon and
went to bed.    The story ends    with owl
sleeping.

---

**RENEE'S FRAME**

In this story the problem starts when    everything was dark.

After that,    a tip of the moon appeared over
the seashore.

Next,    Owl watched the moon go
higher, higher.

Then,
They became good friends.

The problem is finally solved when    Owl went to bed

The story ends    good

**Figure 10.9** A Circular Story Map Based on the Picture Book *The Always Prayer Shawl* (Oberman, 1994)

Illustrations by Matthew McKeon.

ability to make inferences. For whatever reason, many youngsters run into trouble while reading because they don't know *how* or *when* to adjust their thinking as a particular reading selection demands.

Suppose you were teaching a class in which most of the students had appropriate background knowledge for the reading selection. Discussion before reading activates schemata, and students approach the selection with anticipation of what lies ahead in the material. But somewhere during reading, you sense that the readers are having trouble understanding the story. Some look confused as they read; a couple raise their hands to ask for clarification. Others just plow ahead; whether they are comprehending is anyone's guess.

Readers sometimes get lost in a welter of details or bogged down in the conceptual complexity of the selection. The prereading activity initiated at the beginning of the lesson, though necessary, wasn't sufficient to maintain readers' interactions with the text. As a result, they're able to process only bits and pieces of information but fail to grasp the author's intent and message. How can you help? Or suppose you were teaching a class in which multiple cultures and languages were represented and the students had a variety of background knowledge for the story. What would you do?

Assigning questions *after* reading may clarify some of the confusion but does little to show readers how to interact with the author's ideas *during* reading. This is why guiding reader–text interactions is an important part of comprehension instruction. In this section, we explain several instructional strategies that teachers have found useful for this purpose.

## Directed Reading–Thinking Activity

The **directed reading–thinking activity (DR–TA)** builds critical awareness of the reader's role and responsibility in interacting with the text. The DR–TA strategy involves readers in the process of predicting, verifying, judging, and extending thinking about the text material. Throughout this process, the teacher agitates thinking by posing open-ended questions. The learning environment for DR–TA lessons must be supportive and encouraging so as not to stifle or inhibit students' participation. For example, never refute the predictions that children offer. To do so is comparable to pulling the rug out from under them.

"Think time" is important in a DR–TA lesson. We suggest that you pause several seconds or more for responses after posing an open-ended question. If there is silence during this time, it may be an indication that children are thinking. So wait and see what happens.

To prepare a DR–TA for a story, analyze its structure first. Map the story as we suggested earlier. Once you have identified the important story parts, decide on logical stopping points within the story. In Figure 10.10, we indicate a general plan that may be adapted for specific stories.

Linda Fleckner, a sixth-grade teacher, used the DR–TA to guide reader–text interactions for the short story "People of the Third Planet." Earlier you were invited to map the elements of this story. Study the dialogue that occurred between Ms. Fleckner and two students at the beginning of the lesson.

> Ms. F.:     *(writes title on the board before assigning the story)* What do you think this story's about?
> Student:    It's about outer space.
> Ms. F.:     Why do you say that?
> Student:    Because it's about a planet.
> Ms. F.:     *(writes the prediction on the board)* Let's have some more predictions.
> Student:    This is about space, I think. But something happens on Earth.
> Ms. F.:     Why do you think it's about Earth?
> Student:    Earth is the third planet from the sun, right?
> Ms. F.:     *(writes the prediction on the board)*

Note that Ms. Fleckner used two open-ended questions and resisted posing additional questions to clarify students' predictions. In doing so, she set a tone of acceptance and didn't turn the question–response exchange into an interrogation session. In addition, she wrote the predictions on the board. Later, she returned to the predictions and asked students to verify their accuracy, reject them outright, or modify them in light of information gained from reading.

After five or six predictions about the title were written on the board, Ms. Fleckner assigned the first segment of text. Students read through the story's initiating event, the first eight lines from the story. Study the exchange that followed with the student who predicted that the Third Planet was Earth.

> Ms. F.:     *(points to the board)* Well, how did some of your predictions turn out?
> Student:    I was right. It's about Earth.
> Ms. F.:     You certainly were! So what do you think is going to happen now that the spaceship has landed on Earth?

## STANDARD 2.2

## HOMEWORK EXERCISE: CASE STUDY

Go to the Homework and Exercises section in Chapter 10 of MyEducationLab to read how one teacher employs the DR–TA strategy during a lesson.

## Figure 10.10    Potential Stopping Points and Open-Ended Questions in a DR–TA

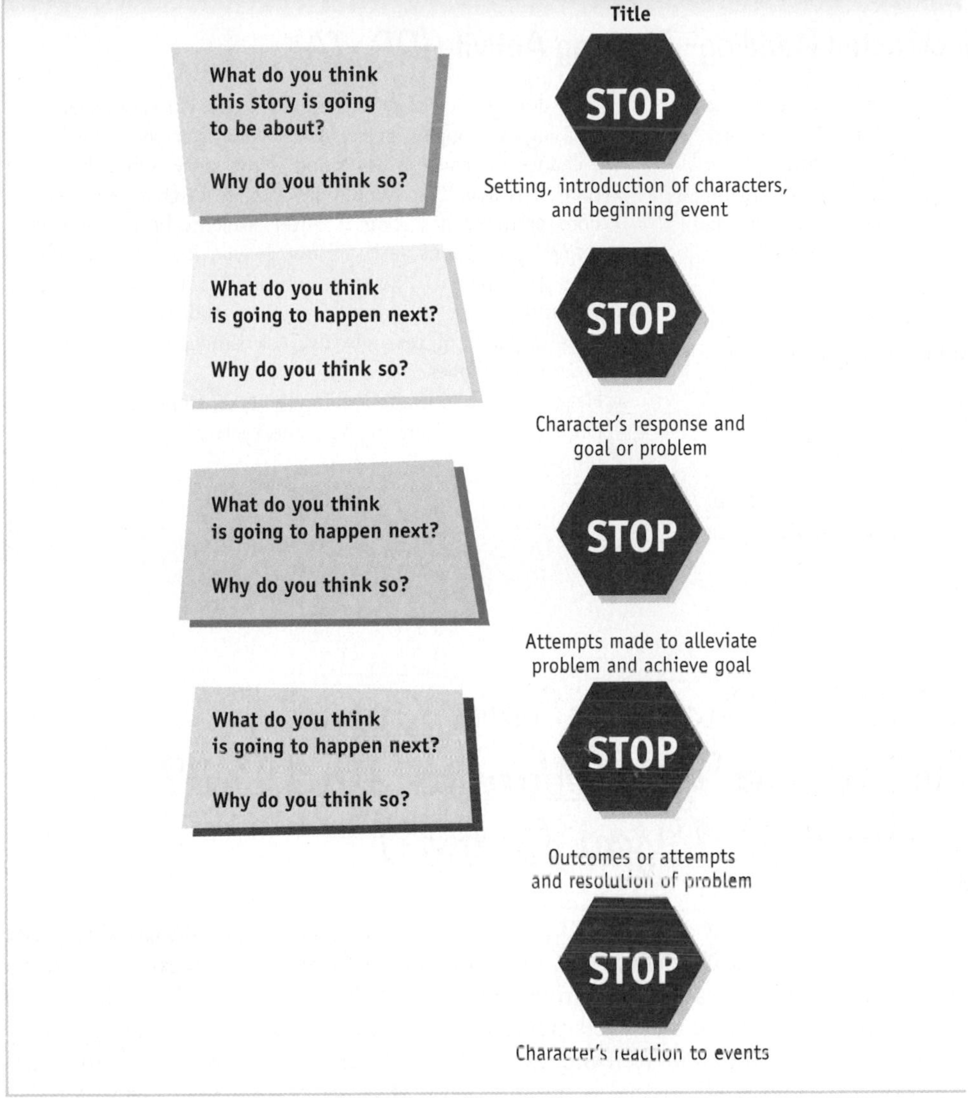

**Title**

What do you think this story is going to be about?

Why do you think so?

**STOP**

Setting, introduction of characters, and beginning event

What do you think is going to happen next?

Why do you think so?

**STOP**

Character's response and goal or problem

What do you think is going to happen next?

Why do you think so?

**STOP**

Attempts made to alleviate problem and achieve goal

What do you think is going to happen next?

Why do you think so?

**STOP**

Outcomes or attempts and resolution of problem

**STOP**

Character's reaction to events

*Student:*   War will break out. Someone's going to report the spaceship. The creatures are going to come out and capture the people.

*Ms. F.:*   Why do you say that?

*Student:*   Because that's what happens in the movies.

*Ms. F.:*   That's a possibility! *(turns her attention to the class and asks for other predictions)*

Initial predictions are often off the mark. This is to be expected as students' predictions are fueled by background knowledge and experience.

The DR–TA begins with very open-ended or divergent responses and moves toward more accurate predictions and text-based inferences as students acquire information from the reading. See the Step-by-Step Lesson featured in Box 10.9 on page 338 for general procedures in using the DR–TA strategy.

## BOX 10.9   STEP-BY-STEP *Lesson*

### Steps in the Directed Reading–Thinking Activity (DR–TA)

Two features that distinguish the DR–TA from some of the other instructional strategies for guiding reader–text interactions are (1) that the students read the same material at the same time and (2) that the teacher makes frequent use of three questions to prompt inquiry and discussion: "What do you think?" "Why do you think so?" and "Can you prove it?"

#### Steps in the DR–TA Plan

1. Choose an interesting narrative or informational text. If you choose a story, initiate the DR–TA by having students focus on the title and illustrations and ask them to predict what the selection will be about. Ask, "What do you think this story will be about?" "Why do you think so?"
2. Write students' predictions on chart paper or the chalkboard so there is a visible record to which students can refer during discussion. Then invite students to read silently to a logical stopping point. Ask, "Now that you have had a chance to read the beginning of the story, what do you think it is about?" "Would anyone like to change predictions or make new ones?" After students have made or refined predictions, ask, "How do you know? Read the lines that prove it." Redirect questions as needed.
3. When there are no more ideas, invite students to read the next segment of text silently. Ask similar questions and other related ones.
4. Have students continue reading the text, stopping at logical points, and engaging in the same cycle of questions until the story is finished.

## *KWL (What Do You Know?*
## *What Do You Want to Find Out?*
## *What Did You Learn?)*

Ogle (1986) as described **KWL** as a three-step teaching plan designed to guide and to motivate children as they read to acquire information from expository texts. The strategy helps students think about what they know or believe they know about a topic, what they need to find out by reading the text, what they learned by reading, and what they still need and want to learn about the topic from other information sources. The KWL model is outlined on a chart or teacher-made handout that children use as they proceed through the steps of the strategy (see Figure 10.11).

The first two steps in the model are prereading activities. The beginning step (K—What do you *know?*) involves brainstorming with a group of students to help them focus on their current knowledge of a topic. The teacher's questions should lead children to think about and to respond *specifically* to the topic being discussed. Teachers of students with multicultural backgrounds need to be aware of their students' cultures and schemata in order to "tap" their prior knowledge about a topic. Teachers can learn about the diverse cultural and linguistic backgrounds of their students through parent or home communication. Inviting parents to share cultural beliefs and traditions with the class can be a rewarding experience for the children and parents alike. The purpose of this brainstorming process is to activate children's prior knowledge to help them understand what they will read in the text. The children's responses are recorded on the board or on worksheets. The teacher, however, does not merely accept children's ideas or statements. As the discussion progresses, the teacher encourages children to extend their thinking by asking questions that require them to consider the source as well as the substance of their information. Children are asked to reflect on where they learned their

*Figure* 10.11   KWL Chart

| K<br>What do you <u>know</u>? | W<br>What do you <u>want</u> to find out? | L<br>What did you <u>learn</u>? |
| --- | --- | --- |
| | | |

**CATEGORIES OF INFORMATION YOU EXPECT TO USE**

A.                              E.

B.                              F.

C.                              G.

D.                              H.

information and how they might prove that what they said is accurate. Organizing children's statements into general categories of information they may come across as they read and discussing the kinds of information they are likely to find in the article provide additional structure, guidelines, and direction for children as they read.

The next step (W—What do you *want* to find out?) evolves naturally from assessing the results of the brainstorming and categorizing activities. As children identify areas of controversy and/or key categories that contain little or no information, a purpose for reading is developed. Although this step is done mainly as a group activity, each student writes the questions that he or she is most interested in learning about on the worksheet. Students' personal interests guide and motivate their reading. The length and the complexity of the material determine whether children can effectively read and derive information by reading the entire text or if the piece should be read in steps that provide opportunities for children to think, at logical intervals, about what they are reading.

During the final step of the KWL process (L—What did you *learn*?), the students record their findings on their worksheets. They have the option of writing down information either as they read or immediately after they finish reading. With teacher guidance and assistance, the students assess whether their questions and concerns were satisfactorily

## Figure 10.12  Completed KWL Chart

| K<br>What do you <u>know</u>? | W<br>What do you <u>want</u> to find out? | L<br>What did you <u>learn</u>? |
|---|---|---|
| 1. They run fast.<br>2. They eat nuts.<br>3. They dig holes.<br>4. They climb trees.<br>5. They are afraid of people.<br>6. Some are brown. | 1. Do they come out in the daytime or at night?<br>2. How old are they when they live on their own?<br>3. How long do they live?<br>4. What colors are they?<br>5. How fast can they dig?<br>6. How fast can they run?<br>7. How deep can they dig? | 1. I learned they live under rocks.<br>2. Their holes are 20 to 30 feet long.<br>3. Cats eat them.<br>4. Baby chipmunks grow up in one month.<br>5. Chipmunk is an American Indian word.<br>6. They have two pouches for storing food.<br>7. They work, play, and rest at different times during the day and night.<br>8. They have eyes on the sides of their heads.<br>9. They have sharp claws and teeth.<br>10. They are good at hiding.<br>11. They nibble on leaves. |

**CATEGORIES OF INFORMATION YOU EXPECT TO USE**

A. Where chipmunks live (homes)

B. How they look (appearance)

C. How they act (behaviors)

D. What they eat

---

answered by reading the text. When students need or want additional information about a topic, they should be guided to other sources of information. In Figure 10.12, examine the KWL chart on chipmunks that was developed by a third-grade class.

## Discussion Webs

**Discussion webs** require students to explore both sides of an issue during discussion before drawing conclusions. When classroom discussions occur, they can quickly become dominated by the teacher or a few vocal students. In an effort to move the discussion forward, the teacher may ask too many questions too quickly. Usually children are more reticent about participating or becoming involved when discussions are monopolized by teacher talk or the talk of one or two students. This can be particularly true for students from diverse linguistic and cultural backgrounds.

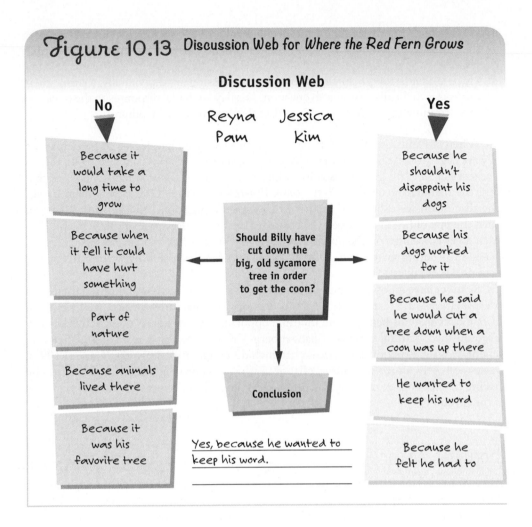

**Figure 10.13** Discussion Web for *Where the Red Fern Grows*

**Discussion Web**

| No | Reyna  Jessica | Yes |
|---|---|---|
| | Pam  Kim | |

**No**

- Because it would take a long time to grow
- Because when it fell it could have hurt something
- Part of nature
- Because animals lived there
- Because it was his favorite tree

**Should Billy have cut down the big, old sycamore tree in order to get the coon?**

**Conclusion**

Yes, because he wanted to keep his word.

**Yes**

- Because he shouldn't disappoint his dogs
- Because his dogs worked for it
- Because he said he would cut a tree down when a coon was up there
- He wanted to keep his word
- Because he felt he had to

The discussion web strategy uses a graphic aid to guide children's thinking about the ideas they want to contribute to the discussion. The graphic aid is illustrated in Figure 10.13. In the center of the web is a question. The question reflects more than one point of view. Students explore the pros and cons of the question in the No and Yes columns of the web—in pairs and then in groups of four. The main goal of the four-member group is to draw a conclusion based on the discussion of the web.

Alvermann (1991) suggests the following steps in the use of discussion webs for classroom discussions:

1. Prepare students for reading by activating prior knowledge, raising questions, and making predictions about the text.
2. Read the selection and then introduce the discussion web by having students work in pairs to generate pro and con responses to the question. The partners work on the same discussion web and take turns jotting down their reasons in the No and Yes columns. Students can use key words and phrases to express their ideas and need not fill in all of the lines. They should try to have an equal number of pro and con reasons represented on the web.
3. Combine partners into groups of four to compare responses, work toward consensus, and reach conclusions as a group. Explain to students that it is OK to disagree with another member of the group, but they should try to keep an open mind as they listen to others during the discussion. Dissenting views can be aired during the whole class discussion.

4. Give each group three minutes to decide which of the reasons given best supports the group's conclusion. Each group selects a spokesperson to report to the whole class.

5. Have students follow up the whole class discussion by individually writing their responses to the discussion web question. Display students' responses to the question in a prominent place in the room so that they can be read by others.

When students use discussion webs, there is usually a high degree of participation; they are eager to hear how other groups reach consensus and draw conclusions. In Gloria Rieckert's class, sixth graders use discussion webs to think about several dilemmas that Billy, the main character, faces in the book *Where the Red Fern Grows,* by Wilson Rawls. The discussion web shown in Figure 10.13 asks the question, "Should Billy have cut down the big, old sycamore tree in order to get the coon?" Reyna, Pam, Jessica, and Kim reach a yes consensus on the question, but Reyna still has her doubts and Jessica clearly voices a dissenting view. Each member follows up the discussion by writing his or her response to the question.

Readers have an opportunity through discussion webs to view and refine their own interpretations of a text in light of the points of view shared by others. Students from diverse backgrounds benefit from multiple opportunities to express their points of view based on their cultural heritage (Spangenberg-Urbschat & Pritchard, 1994). They also benefit from instructional practices that include cooperative learning (Garcia, 1999). Discussion webs afford students a collaborative way to enhance their comprehension by making connections to the story and listening to the connections made by other members of the group.

DIVERSITY

STANDARD
2.1

## Story Impressions

**Story impressions** is the name of a strategy that helps children anticipate what stories *could* be about. As a prereading activity, this strategy uses clue words associated with the setting, characters, and events in the story (the story impressions) to help readers write their own versions of the story prior to reading. McGinley and Denner (1987), originators of the strategy, describe it this way: "Story impressions get readers to predict the events of the story that will be read, by providing them with fragments of the actual content. After reading the set of clues, the students are asked to render them comprehensible by using them to compose a story of their own in advance of reading the actual tale" (p. 249).

Fragments from the story, in the form of clue words, enable readers to form an overall impression of how the characters and events interact in the story. The clue words are selected directly from the story and are sequenced with arrows or lines to form a descriptive chain. The chain of clue words triggers children's impressions of what the story might be about. Children then write a "story guess" that predicts the events in the story.

As McGinley and Denner (1987) explain, "The object, of course, is not for the student to guess the details or the exact relations among the events and characters of the story, but to simply compare his or her own story guess to the author's actual account" (p. 250). They suggest the following steps to introduce story impressions to the class for the first time:

1. Introduce the strategy by saying to the students, "Today we're going to make up what we think this story *could* be about."

2. Use large newsprint, a transparency, or a chalkboard to show students the story impressions (see Figure 10.14 for an example), saying, "Here are some clues about the story we're going to read." Explain that the students will use the clues to write their own version of the story and that after reading, they will compare what they wrote with the actual story.

**Figure 10.14**   Story Impressions for Chapter 9 of *Where the Red Fern Grows*

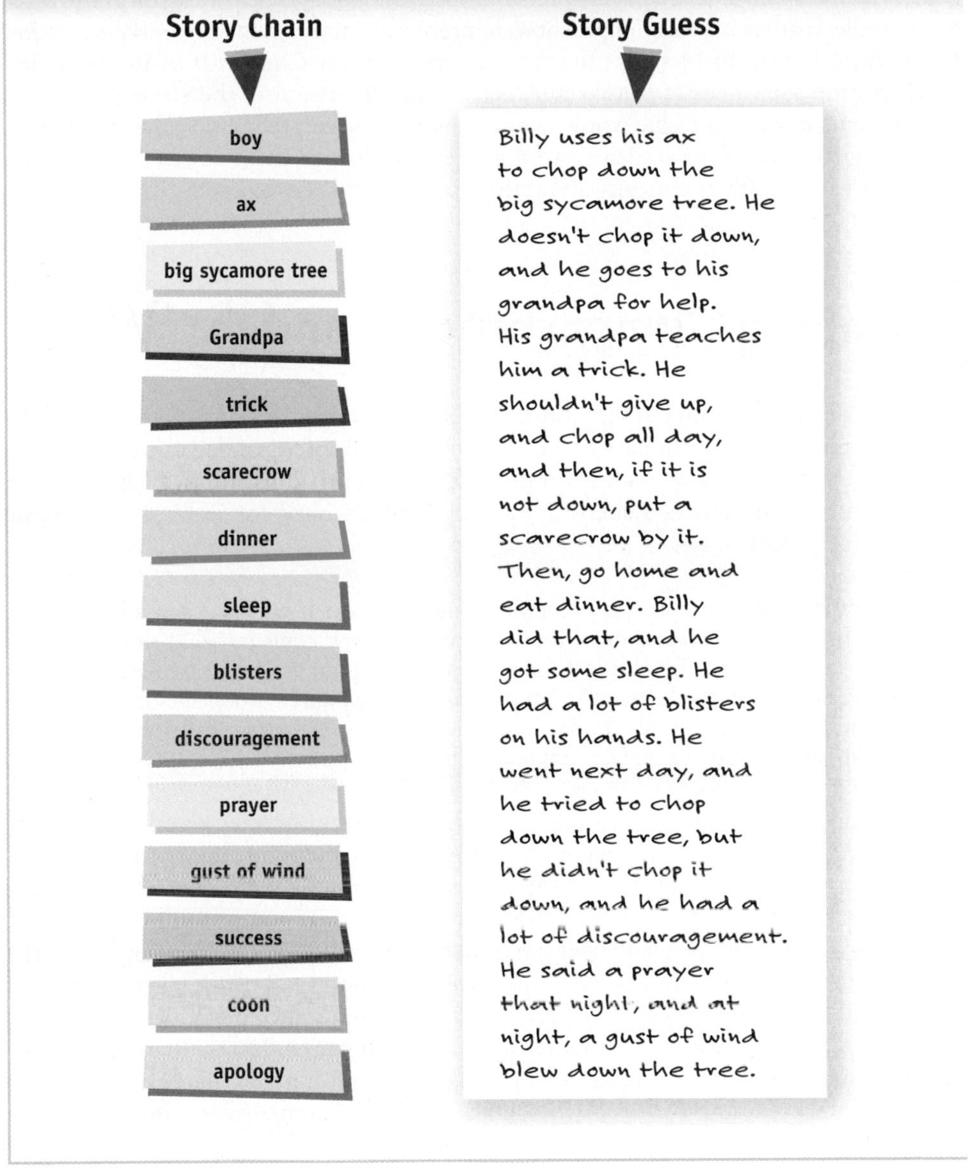

**Story Chain**

- boy
- ax
- big sycamore tree
- Grandpa
- trick
- scarecrow
- dinner
- sleep
- blisters
- discouragement
- prayer
- gust of wind
- success
- coon
- apology

**Story Guess**

Billy uses his ax to chop down the big sycamore tree. He doesn't chop it down, and he goes to his grandpa for help. His grandpa teaches him a trick. He shouldn't give up, and chop all day, and then, if it is not down, put a scarecrow by it. Then, go home and eat dinner. Billy did that, and he got some sleep. He had a lot of blisters on his hands. He went next day, and he tried to chop down the tree, but he didn't chop it down, and he had a lot of discouragement. He said a prayer that night, and at night, a gust of wind blew down the tree.

3. Read the clues together, and explain how the arrows link one clue to another in a logical order. Then brainstorm story ideas that connect all of the clues in the order in which they are presented, saying, "What do we think this story could be about?"

4. Demonstrate how to write a story guess by using the ideas generated to write a class-composed story that links all of the clues. Use newsprint, the chalkboard, or a transparency for this purpose. Read the story prediction aloud with the students.

5. Invite the students to read the actual story silently, or initiate a shared reading experience. Afterward, discuss how the class-composed version is the same and different from the author's story.

6. For subsequent stories, use story impressions to have students write individual story predictions or have them work in cooperative teams to write a group-composed story guess.

MIDDLE GRADES

Story impressions work well in primary, intermediate, and middle school classrooms. Younger readers may need more than one introductory lesson that models the strategy. With middle school readers, story impressions can easily be adapted for longer literary texts, which may involve several chapters or more. In Gloria Rieckert's sixth-grade class, for example, readers use story impressions to predict events from the novel *Where the Red Fern Grows*. Figure 10.14 shows the story impressions for Chapter 9 of the book and compares the story guesses of two students. A class discussion of the strategy revealed that students felt that the clue words made it easier to make predictions about the story. According to some of the students, story impressions helped them key in on important events and aroused their curiosity about the chapter.

## Reading Comprehension and the Web

TECHNOLOGY

We need to point out that contemporary viewpoints regarding reading comprehension and conventional text are being challenged and expanded as we learn more about the process of reading on the Internet (Coiro, 2003; Leu & Kinzer, 2000; Reinking, McKenna, Labbo, & Keiffer, 1998). Coiro, for example, raises the following questions:

> Is the comprehension process different on the Internet? If so, what new thought processes are required beyond those needed to comprehend conventional print? Are these processes extensions of traditional comprehension skills, or do Web-based learning environments demand fundamentally different skills? If comprehension is different on the Internet, what implications do these differences have for comprehension instruction, assessment, and professional development? (p. 458)

In addressing these questions, Coiro (2003) frames her queries based on the 2002 RAND Reading Study Group's report on reading comprehension and a broader understanding of text, the reading activity, the reader, and the social context in which reading occurs when the Internet is used. Regarding text, Coiro points out that electronic Web-based text is nonlinear and challenges the reader to think differently as one navigates the information. In addition, the reader is confronted with new symbols and formats, as well as interactive environments in which online dialogue can occur.

With respect to reading activities, Coiro (2003) suggests that the nature of Web-based, inquiry-based projects tends to entail high levels of thinking that leave room "for personal interpretation" (p. 461). In addition, Web searches often involve online collaborative problem-solving and decision-making skills that may not be typically encountered when reading linear text. Another factor to consider with respect to the different comprehension skills the Internet requires includes the complex nature of searching and the potential problems that can occur for some readers versus the facility it may bring for others who struggle with linear text. Earlier we discussed how think-alouds can be used to walk students through the decision-making process that hypertext demands. In addition, Ikpeze and Boyd (2007) suggest how WebQuests can facilitate learning by providing students with problem-solving tasks, resources, and opportunities to collaborate.

In summary, as you begin to think about teaching reading comprehension strategies to your students, we suggest that you also consider the broader notion of reading comprehension that Coiro (2003) suggests when using the Internet, as well as traditional strategies that could be adapted to Web-based reading. As teachers of reading, we cannot ignore the implications for instruction that reading electronic text brings with it. In Box 10.10, see how Amy coaches Judy, a third-grade teacher, as she makes her first attempt to plan for a WebQuest.

**BUILDING TEACHING SKILLS: READING**

Go to the Homework and Exercises section in Chapter 10 of MyEducationLab to read the article "The Internet Reader" and think about what reading comprehension strategies would apply to reading electronic text on the Internet.

BOX **10.10**

# Viewpoint

## the Literacy Coach

### Planning for a WebQuest Activity

*Judy, a third-grade teacher, has mentioned to Amy, a literacy coach, that she would like to use a WebQuest that she found online about* Charlotte's Web *that was designed by third-grade teachers (www2.tltc.ttu.edu/butler/Student-Webquests/fun_with_charlotte.htm). Observe the conversation in which Amy collaborates with Judy to organize the WebQuest project.*

JUDY: Thanks for agreeing to help me out, Amy. This is a wonderful WebQuest that I found, but the amount of information is overwhelming!

AMY: Let's take a look!

JUDY: (Judy brings up the site.) Here it is. Let me just surf around and show you the massive amounts of information that are here. Look at this! There are chapter summaries, crossword puzzles, word searches, rebus stories, pictures and diagrams of spiders, and even links to spiders worldwide. It's incredible, isn't it! I just don't know where to start; we could spend months on this WebQuest!

AMY: That sure is true! How about we list the skills you want the students to learn by using the WebQuest. What goals do you have, based on your curriculum and standards?

JUDY: That's a great idea. Originally, I had thought I would use the project as enrichment because we just finished reading *Charlotte's Web.* I read an article about WebQuests and the author said that students are motivated by them, so I thought I'd give it a try.

AMY: I think I read the same article. It was in the teacher's lounge, wasn't it?

JUDY: Yes, that's where I picked it up.

AMY: I agree, Judy. I remember the author making a strong case for WebQuests because children like the wide variety of activities they can complete. I also recall that the author said that they can sometimes be distracting and students can get lost in the process of searching the sites. It is easy for them to get off task.

JUDY: Right. So, I guess I need to make sure that the tasks are focused, and getting back to your comment about the standards, I think I need to take a closer look at the WebQuest and decide which standards would best be met by the activities.

AMY: Great thinking. Let's take a look at your standards and see if we can match some of the project activities with those, and then decide a way to manage it all. I think there will be a lot of decisions to make. We'll have to decide if you want the students to work individually or in groups and how you want to evaluate their work. Also, do you want to focus on a theme, such as friendship, or on a science topic, such as spiders, or both?

JUDY: Okay. Sounds like an excellent way to start. Thanks for helping me!

How is Amy, the literacy coach, initiating assistance with Judy's request for help? What characteristics of an effective literacy coach seem to be evident? If you were Judy, would you start getting organized by looking at the standards first or would you look at the web site activities and try to match them with the standards? Why? How long would you anticipate planning to use the WebQuest would take? Would it be worth the effort? Why or why not?

# WHAT ABOUT STRUGGLING READERS AND Reading Comprehension?

When students struggle with word recognition and fluency, they often struggle with reading comprehension because word inaccuracy and choppy reading can lead to misunderstanding. When students misread words, what should teachers do? Schwartz (2005) suggests teacher prompts. For example, when students incorrectly read a word or words and do not notice the mistake and continue reading, teachers can ask:

- "Were you right?"
- "Does that make sense?"
- "Does that sound right?"
- "Does that look right?"

STANDARD
1.4

When students stop reading because they don't know what to say, teachers can say:

- "What can you try?"
- "Try to think what would make sense."
- "Try to think what would sound right."
- "Try to get your mouth ready for the first sound."

It is important that teachers refrain from telling the student the word; prompting supports independence in reading.

## WHAT ABOUT STANDARDS, ASSESSMENT, AND *Reading Comprehension?*

Almost every national and state standards document—regardless of content domain or grade level—highlights the importance of comprehension, inquiry, and critical thinking. Critical thinking, interpretation, and analysis are highly valued in education in the United States. In the science standards developed by the National Science Teachers Association (NSTA), for example, science as inquiry is a critical dimension of what students should know and be able to do; the NSTA standards acknowledge that students at *every* grade level must have opportunities to engage in scientific inquiry and to think and act in ways that support inquiry. Similarly, the IRA and NCTE standards documents emphasize that students need to apply a wide variety of comprehension strategies that include (but are not limited to) interpreting, evaluating, and appreciating texts. Clearly, then, literacy standards nationally indicate that multiple levels of reading-comprehension instruction are critical at all levels of instruction.

What about assessing students and their abilities to reach these higher levels of comprehension? State proficiency assessments, according to test makers, tend to provide limited information about how students comprehend, synthesize, and critically think about what they read. If that is true, how can teachers ensure that students are learning to comprehend what they are reading beyond literal levels? How can teachers assess critical thinking skills in the classroom?

Throughout this chapter, we have shared many instructional strategies for teaching students how to comprehend and think as they are reading. We suggest that teachers can use these strategies as authentic assessment practices that have the potential for providing them with real information about how their students comprehend what they are reading. For example, teachers can make anecdotal records as students "question the author" or engage in reciprocal teaching. Teachers can also evaluate students' abilities to think as they read by providing them with graphic organizers to complete while reading. Think about alternative ways to assess student comprehension and think about the variety of ways that students can express what they have learned by reading: artistic representations, oral representations, visual representations, written representations, dramatic representations, or combinations of these activites.

Although national and state standardized tests tend to explicitly set minimum scores for specific grade levels, often standardized assessments do not tell teachers much about their students beyond overall achievement in comprehension. We believe that teacher observations regarding how students interact in meaningful ways with print can provide teachers with more specific information about how students comprehend and make sense of text.

## Summary

In this chapter, we examined three dimensions of reading comprehension instruction from an active, meaning-making stance. The first instructional dimension involves explicit instruction in the development and use of strategies for comprehending text. We explored various instructional techniques devised to build knowledge and awareness of the student's role in reading comprehension and the questioning skills needed to construct meaning: active comprehension, reciprocal questioning (ReQuest), question–answer relationships (QARs), questioning the author (QtA), reciprocal teaching, and think-alouds. These strategies model and guide students' development of comprehension strategies.

The second dimension of comprehension instruction that we examined covered techniques for building and reinforcing children's awareness of a story's underlying structure. The elements that make up a well-told story were discussed, as were activities for building and reinforcing children's sense of stories. There is, however, no better way to build experience with stories than to have children read, tell, listen to, and perform them on a regular basis.

The third dimension of comprehension instruction focused on instructional strategies to model and guide reader–text interactions. Directed reading–thinking activities (DR–TA), KWL, discussion webs, and story impressions are useful instructional frameworks for guiding readers' responses to text and developing metacognitive and cognitive thinking strategies as readers engage in a dialogue with authors. All of these strategies involve prediction making, activating prior knowledge, engaging children actively in constructing meaning, and making inferences during reading.

We concluded the chapter with a thought-provoking commentary on the changing nature of reading comprehension presented by the Internet, including a coaching scenario intended to prompt teachers to think critically about engaging students in Web-based activities.

## Teacher Action Research

1. Visit the web site for the Spartanburge County School District 3 (www.spa3.k12.sc.us/WebQuests.html) and review the material they have developed on WebQuests to help their teachers. Then select one of the WebQuests on the site and a set of language arts standards for a particular grade level from your state. Search the WebQuest and develop a matrix that matches the activities with the grade-level standards you have selected.

2. Discuss with a group of children a story they have just read, and tape-record the conversation. Analyze the discussion to see if you followed these guidelines to keep students on task: (a) Ask a preliminary question to identify a problem or issue, (b) insert a question or two as needed to clarify or redirect the discussion, and (c) pose a final question or two to tie together loose ends or establish a premise for further discussion. Also check to see if you used declarative or reflective statements, state-of-mind queries, or deliberate silence as alternatives to questions.

3. Choose a story from a basal reader and construct a story map, using a chart similar to the one suggested in the chapter. Then examine the story map to determine where to create "break points" in planning a DR–TA. Try out the DR–TA with an appropriate group of elementary school students (or your classmates) and report on the lesson.

4. Access the International Reading Association's web site at www.reading.org. Work with a partner and practice a think-aloud as you surf the site by explaining your decision-making process as you click on particular links. What did you want to learn? What did you want to learn after that?

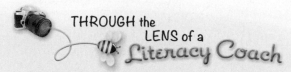

STANDARD
5.3

5. Choosing different grade levels, conduct an action research project and observe three elementary school or middle school classrooms during reading instruction time. Take notes on what the teacher does to facilitate comprehension. Also watch what students are doing when they are not working directly with the teacher: Are they completing worksheets, reading selections longer than one or two sentences or a paragraph in length, or writing about what they have read? Are they involved in other instructional activities? What types of activities and instruction discussed in this and previous chapters are the teachers incorporating? Are they effective?

## Related Web Sites

### ABC Toon Center
**www.abctooncenter.com/chaponea.htm**

This site provides stories for primary children that can be used to develop reading comprehension. Activities for following directions are also included. This site can also be viewed in Spanish, as well as other foreign languages.

### Education World Family Celebration Project
**www.education-world.com/a_tech/TM/WS_tech094-02.shtml**

Education World site provides a printable graphic organizer that can be used to help students from any culture activate prior knowledge about a family celebration. This would be useful for teachers who are interested in learning about the culturally diverse nature of the classroom.

### Interweb Schoolhouse: Web Sites for Kids
**http://home1.gte.net/sfn1/kids.htm**

Interweb Schoolhouse has appropriate nonfiction reading material for developing comprehension strategies with middle school students.

### Reading for Understanding: The Rand Report
**www.rand.org/multi/achievementforall/reading/readreport.html**

You can download the entire reading comprehension report and access additional sites on reading comprehension. Search under education publications available online.

### RHL School—Reading Comprehension
**www.rhlschool.com/reading.htm**

RHL School includes a variety of activities for teaching reading comprehension, including creative short stories with motivating questions, activities for teaching comprehension using context clues, poetry for teaching reading comprehension, and more. The activities can be downloaded in a readable font for children. Activities are appropriate for grades 2 and higher. Many would be suitable for struggling middle school readers.

### Sites for Teachers
**www.sitesforteachers.com**

Teachers can access a quick reference to numerous outstanding web sites that include lessons to download for reading comprehension instruction.

**PEARSON**
# myeducationlab

Now go to the Vacca et al. *Reading and Learning to Read*, Seventh Edition, MyEducationLab course at **www.myeducationlab.com** to

- Take a pretest to assess your initial comprehension of the chapter content
- Study chapter content with your individualized study plan
- Take a posttest to assess your understanding of chapter content
- Engage in multimedia exercises to help you build a deeper and more applied understanding of chapter content

CHAPTER **11**

# Reading–Writing Connections

Standards found in this chapter:
- ▶ 1.2
- ▶ 2.1
- ▶ 2.2
- ▶ 4.1

## In this chapter,
### YOU WILL DISCOVER:

- ❖ Relationships between reading and writing
- ❖ Conditions contributing to a classroom environment that supports reading–writing connections and alternative strategies
- ❖ How to use journals to integrate reading and writing
- ❖ How to create a predictable classroom structure for writing
- ❖ How to organize writing workshops and guide the writing process
- ❖ How to enhance reading–writing connections through technology, including integrating children's literature and technology

## Concept Map

### READING–WRITING CONNECTIONS

- RELATIONSHIPS BETWEEN READING AND WRITING
- CREATING ENVIRONMENTS FOR READING AND WRITING
- LITERACY LEARNING THROUGH STORYBOOKS
  - Journal Writing
  - E-Mail Messages
  - Alternative Strategies
- ESTABLISHING A STRUCTURE FOR WRITING
  - Writing Workshops
  - Guiding the Writing Process
- READING–WRITING–TECHNOLOGY CONNECTIONS
  - Word Processing
  - Multimedia Authoring
- Children's Books and Technology

*I*n Kay Dunlop's first-grade class, the children listen to Kay read *Happy Birthday, Martin Luther King,* a wonderfully written and illustrated book highlighting the important events of King's life. It has become routine for the students in the class, as part of their development as a community of learners, to connect talking *and writing* to what they have read or have heard read to them. *Happy Birthday, Martin Luther King* provides an occasion to connect reading and writing as they think about and reflect on King's life.

So Kay asks, "What if Martin Luther King Jr. were alive today? What would he be disappointed about?" Some of you may wonder whether first graders have the wherewithal to think about and re-spond to such an analytic and speculative question. Yet in Figure 11.1, James, one of Kay's students, grapples with the question and speculates that King would be angry if he were alive today. James doesn't let the conventions of punctuation and spelling get in his way as he writes his response to the question in his reading journal. Nor does he shy away from the use of "big" words such as *angry, violence, freedom,* and *separate* to express his feelings

and thoughts. He knows that his teacher, in this learn-ing situation, is more concerned with what's on his mind than with the surface features of his writing. This is not to say that Kay doesn't want James and his classmates to excel in all aspects of writing, including its mechanics, but she recognizes that important func-tions of writing are to make sense of experience and to think analytically.

Asking a "What if . . . ?" question prompts James's thinking about the story of Martin Luther King Jr.'s life. He uses this occasion to connect reading and writing to express his dismay at the violence that is all too real in his world. James reasons that King would not want teenagers to bring guns to school and kill people. James also uses his understanding of the life and times of King to interact personally with the concept of integration as he asserts that King "dos not wut [want] poeple seprt [separate]." James even uses a refrain from one of King's speeches, "Let freedom ring," to support his assertion that King would be angry if he were alive today. James constructs meaning as he connects reading and writing to gain perspective on his world.

**HOMEWORK EXERCISE: VIDEO**

Go to the Homework and Exercises section in Chapter 11 of MyEducationLab to watch the video "Writing and Reading," which provides an overview of strategies for making the reading and writing connection with students.

As the vignette suggests, in this chapter we show how writing helps children understand *and* be understood. Our emphasis throughout the chapter is on the strong bonds that exist between learning to write and learning to read. These connections are powerful enough to suggest that children probably learn as much about reading by writing as they learn about writing by reading.

## Relationships Between Reading and Writing

*C*ommon sense tells us that writing is intended to be read. When children are writing, they can't help but be involved in reading. Before writing, they may be collecting and connecting information from books, and during and after writing, they are revising, proofreading, and sharing their work with others. Children and young adolescents should be invited to write about what they are reading and to read about what they are writing. Therein lies the real value of *reading–writing connections.*

Writing and reading have been described as two sides of the same process (Squire, 1984). Yet in many elementary and middle schools, writing and reading are strangers to one another, isolated and taught as separate curriculum entities. In the past, reading and writing have been taught separately and sequentially. The premise underlying this

### Figure 11.1    James's Response to the Question, "If Martin Luther King Jr. were alive today, what would he be disappointed about?"

if Martin L. king wher a liv he wood be age. dcos tenagrs are doing vials and. they bring guns to. scoohl and they kill ppoepel.

But he wats Feetm! to. Reiing he dos not wut poeple Sept he wats. Feetm!

instructional path is that reading ability develops first and writing ability follows. Nevertheless, supported by new knowledge about literacy development, today's teachers recognize that when young children are engaged in writing, they are using and manipulating written language. In doing so, children develop valuable concepts about print and how messages are created.

There is compelling evidence to suggest that writing and reading abilities develop concurrently and should be nurtured together. Carol Chomsky (1970, 1979) was one of the first language researchers to advocate that children write first and read later. She contends that writing is a beneficial introduction to reading because children acquire letter and word knowledge through invented spellings. Marie Clay (1991) also supports the powerful bonds between writing and reading. She views reading and writing as complementary processes. Judith Irvin (1998) underscores the importance of making the reading and writing connection explicit for the middle school student. She points out that

STANDARD
1.2

MIDDLE GRADES

Reading and writing are related, and both are acts of making meaning for communicating.

the young adolescent is undergoing a transitional stage of language development and that language instruction needs to be integrated. In addition, Eugene Garcia (2002) contends that teachers need to understand that the reading and writing connections for students from diverse backgrounds ought to be based on the roles reading and writing play in the social lives of people of various cultures. Needless to say, literacy development demands that students engage in reading and writing concurrently for a variety of reasons.

The connections between reading and writing have been examined formally through research studies and theoretical explorations (Shanahan, 1990; Tierney & Shanahan, 1991). How are reading and writing related? The following are some of the conclusions that can be drawn about the relationships between reading and writing:

- Reading and writing processes are correlated; that is, good readers are generally good writers, and vice versa.
- Students who write well tend to read more than those who are less capable writers.
- Wide reading may be as effective in improving writing as actual practice in writing.
- Good readers and writers are likely to engage in reading and writing independently because they have healthy concepts of themselves as readers and writers.

These conclusions suggest that reading and writing are related. The two processes share many of the same characteristics: both are language and experience based, both require active involvement from language learners, and both must be viewed as acts of making meaning for communication. This is why elementary and middle school students' writing should be shared with an audience composed of readers, in *and* out of the classroom.

As much as reading and writing are similar, Shanahan (1988) warns that research suggests that the two processes may be different as well. Some good readers, for example, aren't good writers, and some good writers may indeed be poor readers. Nevertheless, if writing is to have an impact on reading, and vice versa, then instruction in writing and reading must be integrated throughout the instructional program.

Integrating writing and reading is no easy task. An occasional foray into creative writing will not appreciably affect children's writing or reading development. Where does a teacher begin? How do you get started? How do you guide children's writing day in and day out throughout the school year?

# Creating Environments for Reading and Writing

Since the mid-1970s, Donald Graves (1983, 1994) and Jane Hansen (1987) have conducted research on the writing and reading development of elementary school children. Extensive fieldwork in primary and middle school classrooms has yielded valuable insights into the influence of the learning environment on children's writing and reading. Graves and Hansen have shown that *informal* learning environments increase the volume of writing and reading elementary children do. Not only do they write and read more, but they also take greater control over and responsibility for their writing and reading. Students need much less external motivation to write and read from their teachers when they have time to read and write and have the chance to select their own writing topics or reading material.

In the primary years, children develop fluency and power in their reading and writing when they have *time* and *choice* on their side. Additionally, Tom Romano (1987) emphasizes the benefits of providing adolescents with reading and writing choices.

Children must have numerous occasions to write about things that are important to them. This is why a teacher's positive attitude toward invented spellings contributes greatly to children's writing development. Concerns for the form and mechanics of writing matter but must be viewed from a developmental perspective. It is equally important that teachers provide middle school students with opportunities to write freely in any form they choose without initial intense concern about grammar and punctuation. In order to develop their writing skills, they need the chance to develop a writing voice (Romano, 1987). The first order of business for encouraging an environment that supports writers should be the exploration of topics that matter to all writers.

Examine, for example, the following suggestions for encouraging classroom writing, and note the italics, which underscore connections between writing and reading. These suggestions are equally important for elementary and middle school students.

1. Use students' experiences, and encourage them to write about things that are relevant to their interests and needs. Students must choose topics they care about. Yet a fear teachers often harbor is that students will have nothing to say or write about if left to select their own topics. Rarely is this the case. Students want to write. But before students begin, they should have good reason to believe that they have something to say. How can you help? Guide students to choose topics they have strong feelings about; *provide opportunities for reading literature, surfing the Internet,* and brainstorming ideas before writing; show students how to plan and explore topics by using lists, jotting notes, and clustering ideas.

2. Develop sensitivity to good writing by reading poetry and literature to students. All writers need to listen to written language. *Although literature is a mirror that reflects good writing to students, the writings of other students also serve as a powerful model.* Sharing good literature and students' writing helps writers feel that they are capable of producing similar work.

3. Invent ways to value what students have written. Students need praise and feedback, the two mainstays of a built-in support system for classroom writing. *Sharing writing in progress* is an important way to ensure response, or feedback, in the classroom. *Displaying and publishing writing* is another.

Students' writing reflects the functions of written language. Like adults, they don't engage in writing for the sake of writing. Because their efforts are purposeful, their writing must result in products. Later in this chapter, we explain ways to *value students' products through publication.* Certainly one of the best ways to value writing and reading is through bookmaking. *In no way do students build a sense of authorship better than by writing and illustrating their own books.*

4. Guide the writing personally. As students are writing, you should circulate around the room to help and encourage. Conferencing then becomes the primary means by which to respond and to give feedback in the writer's environment. Teacher–student and peer conferences help create a collaborative, noncompetitive environment in which to write, *try out work in progress,* and *share what has been written with others.*

5. Write stories and poetry of your own and share them with your students. *Sharing your writing with students* or discussing problems you are having as a writer signals that writing is as much a problem-solving activity for you as it is for them. There is no better way to model writing than to let students in on the processes you use as a writer. Students need to know that writing is as exciting for you as it is for them.

6. Tie in writing with the entire curriculum. Content area activities may provide the experiences and topics that can give direction and meaning to writing. *Writing to learn will help students discover and synthesize relationships among the concepts they are studying in social studies, science, mathematics, art, music, and health. The connections between reading and writing are especially meaningful when students explore concepts through written language.*

7. Start a writing center in your classroom. A writing center is a place where young writers can go to find ideas, contemplate, or *read other students' writing.* The center should be well equipped with lined paper of various sizes and colors; lined paper with a space for a picture; drawing paper of all sizes; stationery and envelopes; tag board; index cards; a picture file; pencils, colored pencils, crayons, and markers; paper clips; white glue and paste; paper punches; *book display stands; informational texts such as magazines, dictionaries, and encyclopedias; a classroom library for students' writing;* and *an address file of book authors, sports figures, celebrities, and magazines that print students' work.* A writing center isn't a substitute for having a classroom program in which students work every day at developing the craft of writing. Instead, the center is a visible support that enhances the writing environment in your classroom.

8. Create a relaxed atmosphere. Ganske, Monroe, and Strickland (2003) point out that ELL students benefit from learning environments in which teachers provide "smiles and humor to lighten the intensity of the learning experience" (p. 122). Although students need challenging and motivating assignments, they must feel comfortable with making mistakes.

When a teacher encourages students to write, they engage in reading activities in varied and unexpected ways. An environment that connects writing and reading provides students with numerous occasions to write and read for personal and academic reasons, some of which are suggested in Figure 11.2. Examine Box 11.1 on page 358 to learn how first-grade teacher Lynn Weber engages her students in meaningful writing through pen pal correspondences.

## Connecting Reading and Writing

When journals are part of the writing environment, students use them to write about things that are important to them and that they have strong feelings about. Journals can be used to help students examine their personal lives and explore literary and informational texts. A journal brings students in touch with

**BUILDING TEACHING SKILLS: READING**

Go to the Homework and Exercises section in Chapter 11 of MyEducationLab to read the article "Teaching the Art of Writing" about combining visual images and art as a way to motivate students to write.

DIVERSITY ELL

## Figure 11.2  Occasions for Writing and Reading

- Pen pal arrangements with other classes within the building
- Pen pal and "key pal" (Internet correspondence through e-mail) arrangements with a class from another school in the same district or in classrooms around the world
- Writing stories for publication on the Internet
- Writing for a school or class newspaper
- Writing for a class, school, or electronic magazine on the Internet
- "Author of the Week" bulletin board that features a different student writer each week
- Entering writing contests in the local community or on the Internet
- Opportunities for students to read pieces of writing over the school's public address system
- Opportunities for students to read selected pieces of writing to a younger class
- Outings where students can read selected pieces of writing to children in a day-care center
- Displays of student writing in the classroom, on a classroom homepage, and in the corridors of the school
- Videotapes of students reading their writing
- Multimedia authoring presentations of students' projects
- Play festivals featuring student-authored scripts
- Student-made publicity for school events
- Student-written speeches for school assemblies and programs
- A "young author festival" to highlight student-authored books
- Student-prepared speeches in the voices of characters from stories or from social studies
- Daily journals and diaries
- Biographical sketches based on interviews or research
- Songwriting
- Reviews of movies or television programs
- Cartoon scripts

themselves as they record their thoughts and feelings, and it is a gold mine for generating ideas. All forms of written expression are welcomed in journals—doodles, comments, poems, letters, and—for the purpose of the next section—written conversations between child and teacher and child and child.

## Using Journals (and E-Mail Correspondence) for Written Conversation

If journals are to be used to generate ideas, the teacher must set aside time to read and respond to children's entries on a regular basis. It can be helpful to develop a system where you collect, read, and respond to several journals a day rather than attempting to read the journal entries of an entire class at one time. Because child and teacher enter into a personal relationship through the vehicle of journal writing, there are, as we have seen, many occasions for a dialogue in writing.

**DIALOGUE JOURNALS**  ◆  According to Gambrell (1985), the **dialogue journal** emphasizes meaning while providing natural, functional experiences in both writing and reading. Child and teacher use dialogue journals to converse in writing. A teacher's response to children's entries may include comments, questions, and invitations to children to express themselves. The Research-Based Practices featured in Box 11.2 on page 359 offers guidelines for using dialogue journals in the classroom.

BOX **11.1**

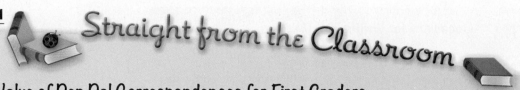

## Straight from the Classroom

## The Value of Pen Pal Correspondences for First Graders

### LYNN WEBER

*Lynn Weber teaches at Greentown Elementary School in North Canton, Ohio.*

Because I feel that writing for a real purpose is the best way for first graders to develop good writing skills, I am always looking for opportunities for my students to write in new and different situations. We make cards for many occasions, thank-you letters, lists, signs, invitations, notes to friends and family, announcements, and letters of persuasion. One of the writing activities that my students have found to be the most enjoyable, and which provided an ongoing reason to read and write, was a pen pal project between my first graders and teacher preparation students at a local university. The students were paired and exchanged biweekly letters for an entire semester.

The day my students received their first letters, they were so excited. I was surprised that they didn't open them immediately. They examined the envelopes and the way their names were written. Many were written in bright colors on interesting stationery; some had stickers or drawings on them. When they finally opened the letters, their enthusiasm exploded. They wanted to be able to read everything immediately! Some of them could read the letters quite easily and some had great difficulty. But before long, they had their heads together and students were helping each other read the treasured letters. "What does this say?" "Here's my name!" Soon they were looking for words they knew and trying to piece together the messages from their new friends. It was a very engaging day. Motivation in the classroom that day was about as high as you are ever going to find it.

I told them that I would get some special paper so they could write return letters to their pen pals, and one little person raised his hand and said, "But I want to write my letter *now!*" So the children wrote their first letters that day. We talked

about finding the pen pal's name at the end of the letter and copying it into the greeting. We worked on looking for questions in the letter. The students realized they could use some of the pen pal's words in their answers. The letters were completed and on their way in record time.

Each time we received letters, the students read eagerly for news that helped them know their pen pals better and make connections with them. "Her birthday is the same month as mine!" "My pen pal has a big dog, too!" The favorite topic was how old the pen pals were. Students who had been reluctant readers were extremely motivated to find out more about their new friend. Enthusiasm remained high for the entire semester. The day the letters arrived was always a *special* day. The project culminated with a face-to-face meeting. Addresses and phone numbers were exchanged and some of these pairs are still writing to each other.

This project was one of the most successful of my career. My students had a real reason to read and write. They were self-motivated and needed no prodding from me to read their letters or write their answers. The children's skills in both reading and writing blossomed because they really wanted to do their best. One student summed up this project: "It's the most funnest thing I ever did."

### REFLECTIVE INQUIRY

◆ What are some reading skills that Lynn Weber's students might have learned from the pen pal project?

◆ What are some writing skills that can be taught as part of a similar project?

MIDDLE GRADES

In Figure 11.3, study how second-grade teacher Sharon Piper responded to Tammy Lynn's September 20 journal entry. Mrs. Piper's dialogue with Tammy Lynn encourages a response and a continuation of the conversation through subsequent journal writing.

Dialogue journals can be especially meaningful for middle school students because they provide an authentic avenue for expressing concerns that young adolescents typically have. Stowell (2000) describes how a diverse class of seventh-grade students effectively communicated through dialogue journals with preservice teachers. She found that the middle school students benefited from the individualized nature of the project in multiple ways. They were able to write about themselves reflectively, and they corresponded about issues that were important to them, such as friendships, fears, and difficulties at home.

BOX **11.2**

## *Research-Based Practices*    Guidelines for Using Dialogue Journals

One of the most important ways to encourage reading is through an ongoing, sustained written conversation with students. Dialogue journals serve to scaffold reading–writing interactions through informal conversations. Guidelines for the use of dialogue journals include the following:

1. Use bound composition books. (Staple appropriate writing paper inside a construction paper cover. The paper should be large enough for several journal entries so children can see the developing dialogue.)
2. To motivate students, tell them journals are like letters. They will write to you and you will write back. Encourage writing about any topic of interest or concern to them.

3. For best results, write daily. Set aside a special time for writing and reading. For children in grades 1 and 2, 10 minutes might be appropriate, whereas older children may need 20 minutes.
4. Focus on communication. Do not correct entries; instead, model correct forms in your response.
5. Respond in a way that encourages written expression such as, "Tell me more about . . . ," "I'd like to know more about . . . ," "Describe . . ."
6. Dialogue journals are private. Convey to students that they belong to the two of you, but they may share their journals if they wish. Sharing should always be voluntary.

*Source:* "Dialogue Journals: Reading–Writing Interactions," by L. B. Gambrell, *The Reading Teacher, 38,* pp. 512–515. Copyright © 1985 by the International Reading Association. Reprinted with permission of the International Reading Association (www.reading.org).

**BUDDY JOURNALS** ◆ A **buddy journal** is a variation of the dialogue journal. However, instead of a teacher engaging in written conversation with a student, a buddy journal encourages dialogue between children (Bromley, 1989). Before beginning buddy journals, children should be familiar with the use of journals as a tool for writing and also be comfortable with the process of dialoguing with a teacher through the use of dialogue journals. To get buddy journals off and running, have the students form pairs. Each child may choose a buddy, or buddies may be selected randomly by drawing names from a hat. To maintain a high level of interest and novelty, children may change buddies periodically.

Buddies may converse about anything that matters to them—from sharing books they have been reading to sharing insights and problems. As Bromley (1989) advises, teachers who use buddy journals for natural writing occasions should promote student interaction, cooperation, and collaboration: "Buddy journals enhance socialization since they allow students a forum for learning about each other" (p. 128).

For example, in Megan's elementary school, the fifth-grade students participate in a family living class where they explore a variety of social, emotional, and psychological issues that, in Megan's words, "teaches us growing up." A textbook and supplementary materials, including imaginative and informational trade books, pamphlets, magazines, and newspaper articles, provide numerous reading opportunities for the students. An integral part of the class is to examine adolescent behavior and its effect on the family.

"Teenagers," Megan hears her teacher say in class discussion, "worry about a lot of things." "What things?" Megan wonders to herself, but the question is left unexplored as the discussion shifts to another subject.

When she gets home from school that day, the question of what teenagers worry about is still on Megan's mind: "I didn't have much to do and I was kinda bored, so I began to draw about what teenagers think." In her notebook, she sketches the drawing shown in Figure 11.4 on page 361 and titles it "What Most Adolescents Think."

The next day Megan brings her drawing to class and shows it to the teacher. Delighted, the teacher invites Megan to share the drawing with other class members. Later that morning, as the students write in their buddy journals, a classmate asks Megan about her drawing and why she thinks teenagers worry about such things as being normal,

## Figure 11.3   Tammy Lynn and Mrs. Piper's Dialogue Entries

mRs. piper We have
Bunkbeds and my sister
fell of and harT her head and
arm it was bresed bad but she
still vent to school and my
mom Told me if i wanted to
sleep on the Top becuse
every cuple munts my mom
puts up plain beds and
we take torns and it was
kristys torn but she fell
off

Dear Tammy Lynn,
I am sorry to hear about Kristy's fall from
the bunkbed. I hope her bruise went away
and that she is feeling better. When will
you be sleeping on the top bunk? What
will you do to not fall out of the top bed?

looking good, and fitting in. Megan responds to her writing partner with the journal entry in Figure 11.5 on page 362.

The buddy journal allows Megan to explore and clarify ideas encountered in class and in her own life experiences through informal written conversation with a classmate. It provides Megan with another tool, in addition to cartooning, for self-expression and meaning-making.

Van Sluys and Laman (2006) found that when written conversations between classmates took place immediately, much like online chats, the students wrote jokes and exaggerated stories, talked about books they were reading together, used language from comics and videos, and utilized unusual handwriting to convey messages. They concluded that the students were "learning about language inside of meaningful interactions" (p. 231).

**ELECTRONIC MAIL (E-MAIL) CONVERSATIONS** ◆ E-mail communication engages students in written conversations with others in the same learning community, at a neighboring school, or anywhere in the world. When students use e-mail, reading–writing connections are both personal and social (through **key pal correspondence**—the

## Figure 11.4 "What Most Adolescents Think" by Megan Woodrum

electronic equivalent of pen pals) and educational (through Internet projects—a collaborative approach to learning on the Internet).

Key pal correspondence creates opportunities for students to communicate with other students from around the world, learn about different cultures, ask questions, and develop literacy skills. When students communicate with key pals from other countries or communities, they have the opportunity to broaden their knowledge of diverse cultures, dispel misconceptions about cultures that differ from their own, and develop understanding and respect for differences.

Internet projects also promote global conversations and learning connections between students. According to Leu and Leu (1999), Internet projects are designed within the framework of a thematic or topical unit. To proceed with an Internet project, a teacher plans an upcoming unit and writes a description of the project. The project description is then posted in advance on a site in order to locate classrooms that may be willing to become collaborating partners in the project. Planning and posting the project 2 or 3 months in advance will help identify classroom partners and provide enough time to work out the details of the collaboration. Teachers from the collaborating classrooms communicate electronically to make arrangements and plan project-related activities for students. In addition, Charron (2007) suggests that when students communicate with children from another country, teachers need to consider the time of year and the school schedule, including vacations and whether the correspondences will occur weekly, monthly, or on some other schedule. In Chapter 14, we elaborate on alternative ways to engage students in inquiry using the Internet.

In one Internet project in northeastern Ohio, preservice teachers engaged in e-mail conversations with fourth graders (McKeon & Burkey, 1998; Vacca & Vacca, 2002). The collaborative project revolved around conversations about trade books that the preservice teachers and their fourth-grade partners were reading. The collaborative project was

STANDARD 2.2

DIVERSITY

> ## 𝒥igure 11.5   Megan's Response to Her Buddy's Question, "Why do you think teenagers worry?"
>
> Why do I think that's what adolecents think? Well, for starters, I have a sister who is 17. Exsperence, I guess. Also, we have a teacher who teaches us about growing up. And she's defently had experence! So, I guess that's that.
>
> From,
> Megan
> Woodrum
> The Artist of
> "What most Adolecents
> think."

a joint venture between university instructors and classroom teachers. Throughout the semester, the e-mail partners dialogued about the books, engaging in authentic talk. In addition, the preservice teachers incorporated instructional strategies into electronic conversations. For example, in one correspondence just prior to reading the book *A Taste of Blackberries*, a preservice teacher invited his partner to make predictions about the book:

> Just to let you know before you start reading, the book is very sad and it involves people dying. I would like you to brainstorm a little bit about the name of the book and give me some guesses of what you think the story may be about. Then we will take your guesses, and after we read the book, we can find out how close you were with some of your guesses. I am really looking forward to hearing from you.

Not only did the e-mail collaboration serve to make reading–writing connections during the literature discussions, but also the e-mail partners got to know one another socially as they shared information and asked questions about college life, hobbies, interests, and family life. The social nature of e-mail can also motivate reluctant readers, enhance self-confidence, provide students with opportunities to take ownership of their reading and writing, and help them make decisions about what they will read and write (McKeon, 2001).

## Using Journals to Explore Texts

Journals create a nonthreatening context for children to explore their reactions and responses to literary and informational texts. Readers who use journals regularly are involved actively in the process of comprehending as they record their feelings, thoughts, and reactions to various types of literature. Journals create a permanent record of what readers are feeling and learning as they interact with texts. As a result, they have also been called *logs* because they permit readers to keep a visible record of their responses to texts. Such responses often reflect thinking beyond a literal comprehension of the text and engage students in inferential and evaluative thinking.

Providing time for literature response journal writing is also an effective way to engage students from diverse backgrounds in writing. When students respond to multicultural

**STANDARD
2.1**

books that reflect the values of their cultures, for example, they have the opportunity to explore writing about what they know. When they read about the cultures of others, students gain an appreciation for values and beliefs that differ from their own. Writing about those beliefs in journals fosters reflective thinking, and entries can be used as a stimulus for discussions about diversity (Laier, Edwards, McMillon, & Turner, 2001).

Several types of journals may be used to explore texts: **double-entry journals, reading journals,** and response journals. What do these different types of journals have in common? Each integrates reading and writing through personal response, allowing readers to feel and think more deeply about the texts they are reading.

DOUBLE-ENTRY JOURNALS ◆ A double-entry journal provides students with an opportunity to identify text passages that are interesting or meaningful to them and to explore—in writing—why. As the name of the journal implies, students fold sheets of paper in half lengthwise, creating two columns for journal entries. In the left-hand column, readers select quotes from the text—perhaps a word, a phrase, a sentence or two—that they find interesting or evocative. They then copy the text verbatim and identify the page from which each text quote is taken. In instances in which the quoted passage is several sentences or a paragraph long, the student may choose to summarize rather than copy the passage verbatim.

Across from each quote, in the right-hand column, readers enter their personal responses and reactions to the text quotes. As Yopp and Yopp (1993) explain, students' responses to a text will vary widely: "Some passages may be selected because they are funny or use interesting language. Others may be selected because they touch the student's heart or remind the student of experiences in his or her own life" (p. 54).

Children as early as first grade have used double-entry journals with success, once they have developed some confidence and fluency reading simple stories (Barone, 1996). Teachers, however, must model and demonstrate how to respond to text using the two-column format. The Research-Based Practices featured in Box 11.3 provides guidelines for scaffolding the use of double-entry journals with beginners.

BOX **11.3**

## Research-Based Practices

### Guidelines for Using Double-Entry Journals with Beginners

Use double-entry journals in the context of interactive reading and writing experiences. With reading beginners, teachers sometimes follow these steps:

1. Help children interact with a text through a shared reading experience.
2. After sharing a story several times, have young readers gather around an experience chart.
3. Divide the chart paper into two columns; label the left column "What I Liked the Best" and the right column "Why I Liked It."
4. Illustrate how to use the double-entry format for response by sharing with the class a text quote or two that you like. You might say, "One of my favorite parts of the story is on page 5." Then you turn to page 5 and read it to the class. Next, copy the text quote in the left-hand column. Tell why you like the text quote—how it makes you feel

or what it reminds you of. Write your personal reaction in the right-hand column.

5. Then invite children to volunteer some of their favorite words, lines, or parts from the text. Encourage them to share their reactions. Serve as a scribe by writing their quotes and reactions on the chart paper.
6. Vary the demonstrations with subsequent interactive writing experiences; for example, ask children to volunteer to write on the chart paper.
7. Introduce the class to double-entry journals. Begin by showing students how to make their own journals using 8½-by-11-inch lined paper. Encourage children to use the double-entry journal as a follow-up to a shared reading. Share the journal entries as a group. Phase children into the use of double-entry journals for texts read independently.

*Source:* Based on *Literature-Based Reading Activities,* by R. H. Yopp and H. K. Yopp (Boston: Allyn & Bacon, 1993).

## 𝒯igure 11.6   Example of a Third Grader's Double-Entry Journal Response

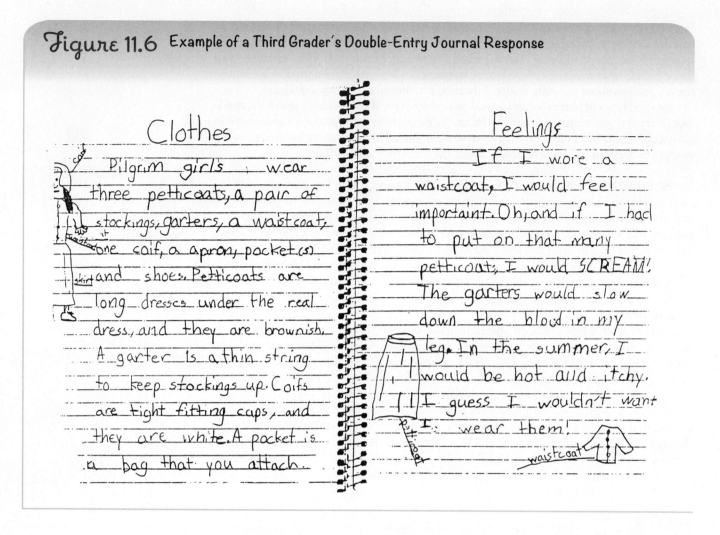

Clothes

Pilgrim girls wear three petticoats, a pair of stockings, garters, a waistcoat, one coif, a apron, pocket (s) and shoes. Petticoats are long dresses under the real dress, and they are brownish. A garter is a thin string to keep stockings up. Coifs are tight fitting caps, and they are white. A pocket is a bag that you attach.

Feelings

If I wore a waistcoat, I would feel importaint. Oh, and if I had to put on that many petticoats, I would SCREAM! The garters would slow down the blood in my leg. In the summer, I would be hot and itchy. I guess I wouldn't want I wear them!

Older children will not need as many demonstrations before they develop the knack of using double-entry journals, and the payoffs from using such journals will be readily evident in class discussions. One of the big benefits of a double-entry journal is that it encourages interactions between reader and text. Another benefit is that it makes children sensitive to the text and the effect the author's language has on them as readers. A third payoff is that students explore texts for personally relevant ideas. Examine in Figure 11.6 a third grader's journal entry as she describes and reacts to the clothes worn by Pilgrim girls in response to her teacher's read-aloud of *The Thanksgiving Story* by Alice Dalgliesh.

**READING JOURNALS** ◆ In contrast to double-entry journals, reading journals provide students with more structure and less choice in deciding what they will write about. The teacher often provides a prompt—a question, for example—to guide students' writing after a period of sustained reading. Reading journals are usually used with a common or *core* text that everyone in a class is reading or listening to.

Prompts may include generic "process" questions such as the following: What did you like? What, if anything, didn't you like? What did you think or wonder about as you were reading? What will happen next? What did you think about the story's beginning? Its ending? What did you think about the author's style? Did anything confuse you? At times, reading journals use prompts that are more content-specific, asking readers to focus on their understanding of an important concept or some relevant aspect of plot, setting, character, or theme.

**RESPONSE JOURNALS** ◆ The main difference between a reading journal and a response journal is the amount of prompting that teachers use to elicit students' reactions to a text. Response journals invite readers to respond to literary texts freely, without being prompted. Hancock (1993a) suggests an extended set of guidelines (see the Research-Based Practices in Box 11.4) for students who use response journals. These guidelines are perhaps best suited for intermediate and middle-grade students but can easily be adapted to the primary level.

Sixth-grade teacher Gloria Reichert introduces students to response journals with a letter at the beginning of the school year. In one section of the letter, she explains response journals this way:

> I'm sure you are wondering about what a response journal is. It is a place where you will be able to write about books and stories that you will be reading throughout the year in our class. The response journal will be a great way to help us explore what we are feeling and thinking about what we are reading.

BOX **11.4**

## Research-Based Practices     Guidelines for Response Journals

- *Feel free to write* your innermost feelings, opinions, thoughts, likes, and dislikes. This is your journal. Feel the freedom to express yourself and your personal responses to reading through it.
- *Take the time to write* down anything that you are thinking while you read. The journal is a way of recording those fleeting thoughts that pass through your mind as you interact with the book. Keep your journal close by and stop to write often, whenever a thought strikes you.
- *Don't worry* about the accuracy of spelling and mechanics in the journal. The content and expression of your personal thoughts should be your primary concern. The journal will not be evaluated for a grade. Relax and share.
- *Record the page number* on which you were reading when you wrote your response. Although it may seem unimportant, you might want to look back to verify your thoughts.
- *Use one side only* of your spiral notebook paper, please. Expect to read occasional, interested comments from your teacher. These comments will not be intended to judge or criticize your reactions, but will create an opportunity for us to "converse" about your thoughts.
- *Relate the book* to your own experiences and share similar moments from your life or from books you have read in the past.

- *Ask questions* while reading to help you make sense of the characters and the unraveling plot. Don't hesitate to wonder why, indicate surprise, or admit confusion. These responses often lead to an emerging understanding of the book.
- *Make predictions* about what you think will happen as the plot unfolds. Validate, invalidate, or change those predictions as you proceed in the text. Don't worry about being wrong.
- *Talk to the characters* as you begin to know them. Give them advice to help them. Put yourself in their place and share how you would act in a similar situation. Approve or disapprove of their values, actions, or behavior. Try to figure out what makes them react the way they do.
- *Praise or criticize* the book, the author, or the literary style. Your personal tastes in literature are important and need to be shared.
- *There is no limit* to the types of responses you may write. Your honesty in capturing your thoughts throughout the book is your most valuable contribution to the journal. These guidelines are meant to trigger, not limit, the kinds of things you write. Be yourself and share your personal responses to literature through your journal.

*Source:* "Exploring and Extending Personal Response Through Literature Journals," by M. R. Hancock, *The Reading Teacher, 46*(6), p. 472. Copyright © 1993 by the International Reading Association. Reprinted with permission of the International Reading Association (www.reading.org).

What will you be writing in your response journals? You can write anything you want about the book or story you are reading. You can express your thoughts, your feelings, or your reactions. How do you feel about the book? What does the book make you think about? What do you like or dislike about it? Who are the characters? Do you like them? Can you relate to their problems? What does the story mean to you?

Gloria then shows the class some different types of responses she has collected from past students who read Wilson Rawls's *Where the Red Fern Grows*. One entry she shows mixes literary commentary with personal involvement in the story:

> I thought chap. 5 was very good. I'm glad Billy got the dogs. I thought it was really, really mean that all the people were laughing at him because he was carrying the pups in the gunny sack. I mean, come on. He had nothing to carry them in, and they needed air to breathe. I can't believe a fight would actually start because it got so bad. The part where the mountain lion came, and the two pups saved Billy by howling was amazing. I thought the chapter had good action.

Another entry critiques a chapter from the perspective of someone who has had dogs as pets:

> I didn't like chapter two. How can a kid get so sick from just not having a dog. Dogs are not always perfect anyways. They wake so early in the morning by barking there head off and sometimes they run around the house making a ruckus.

Regardless of format, journal writing reflects children using language as if engaged in talk. Such writing does not place a premium on perfection or mechanics—spelling, punctuation, or grammar. Teachers encourage students to write freely in journals, placing their reactions and responses ahead of concerns for correctness.

## Alternative Strategies That Motivate Students to Write

Just as journal writing is a vehicle for developing writing fluency, alternative genres can provide students with motivating and creative ways to express themselves in writing. In the following sections we discuss ways to encourage students to gather ideas for writing; we also discuss multigenre projects, writing nonfiction, and using plot scaffolds for creative writing.

**GATHERING IDEAS** ◆ It is well recognized that students are motivated when they are given choices about what to read and write. In order to help students gather ideas that they might choose to craft as writing drafts, Olness (2005) recommends Ralph Fletcher's (1996) idea of providing students with **writing notebooks** in which they gather observations, thoughts, reactions, ideas, unusual words, pictures, and interesting facts that might later spur them to write. Unlike journals, the notebooks are meant to provide students with a place to collect thoughts for future writing. Similar to writing notebooks, Rog (2007) suggests providing children with large envelopes, "topics in your pocket," in which they jot down ideas and collect pictures or drawings about which they might like to write.

Regardless of the manner in which students gather writing ideas, teachers need to provide students with choices. As Gillespie (2005) points out, "students (prefer) to choose for themselves rather than write what I (impose) on them" (p. 680).

**MULTIGENRE PROJECTS** ◆ A **multigenre project** or paper is a collection of genres that reflects multiple responses to a book, theme, or topic (Romano, 2000). Students are given choices about which genres to use and they experiment with writing in a variety of ways.

Gillespie (2005) suggests over 50 genres, including advice columns, biographies, comic strips, death notices, greeting cards, posters, prayers, and talk show transcripts. After reading *A Single Shard* (Park, 2001), a story that takes place in a twelfth-century

Korean village and is about a homeless man and an orphan boy, one of her seventh graders chose to develop a crossword puzzle to review new vocabulary words. Another student designed a map of the locale; another wrote a letter to one of the main characters. Gillespie requires her students to develop 10 pieces and experiment with at least 7 different genres, as well as write a reflection about each piece. A final activity is to organize the project into a booklet and provide time for students to share.

**WRITING NONFICTION** ◆ Some children do not enjoy writing stories, but are motivated to write nonfiction. Although all children should experience crafting nonfiction pieces, struggling readers often enjoy writing more when they are encouraged to write expository text (Olness, 2005).

Sharing nonfiction books is a critical component to introducing children to this type of writing. Teachers can use read-alouds and point out the features of nonfiction writing and the variety of text-based characteristics such as a table of contents, index, glossary, bold print, and subheadings. Read (2005) suggests having emerging writers create informational texts in pairs because collaborative partnerships take advantage of the "social nature of learning" (p. 43). For young writers, an "all about" book can be a simple way to begin writing expository text (Olness, 2005). If the children have gathered interesting pictures in a "pocket," as suggested above, they might select a topic based on a picture of their choice. Kletzien and Dreher (2004) suggest a variety of informational or nonfiction texts that young children can write:

- *Recounts.* Children write about a personal event.
- *Reports.* Children describe something such as an animal.
- *Procedural text.* Children give directions for making something.
- *Explanatory text.* Children explain how something happens.
- *Persuasive text.* Children try to convince the reader about something.

For young adolescents, Pullman (2000) suggests that students work in pairs to develop "wanted posters" based on influential historical figures. After reading information and taking notes, the partners design a character sketch, create a nickname for the figure, write a final draft, and orally present the information learned. Baines (2000) suggests a group activity in which students develop fact sheets about a controversial topic and present the facts to different audiences. For example, a school dress-code issue might be presented to parents, peers, and a clothing store. In addition, Booth (2001) offers a variety of genres in which young adolescents can create informational text:

- Alphabet books based on new content learned
- Directories, manuals, glossaries, and definitions with new information learned
- Recipes that reflect a particular culture or historical period or instructions for creating a culturally specific item
- News flashes, reports, articles, memos, and announcements
- Maps, atlas entries, and graphic charts that capture the locale of the information

**PLOT SCAFFOLDS** ◆ A **plot scaffold** is an open-ended script in which students use their imaginations and creative writing in a playful manner (O'Day, 2006). The open-ended scripts include characters, a setting, problem, and resolution with spaces for the students to write additional descriptions and problem-solving dialogue. For example, if the script read, "The house was dark," the students might be instructed to "describe the house and why it was dark." If the script read, "Joe spoke to Teresa," the students might be instructed to "describe how Joe spoke and what he said."

Prior to working with plot scaffolds, the students are taught that story plots have more than a beginning, middle, and end; they include the answers to three questions: "What if (the problem is stated)? What is the catch (what makes the problem worse)? What then (how is the problem solved)?" (O'Day, 2006, p. 11). In addition, the teacher introduces seven elements and how to elaborate on each one:

SEVEN ELEMENTS OF PLOT

- *The hook.* To capture the interest of the audience
- *The problem.* A situation that needs to be resolved
- *Backfill.* More details about the problem
- *A complication.* Something that happens to make the problem worse
- *Action–reaction.* How the characters try to solve the problem
- *Dark moment.* The characters face the dilemma
- *Resolution.* The problem is solved

Box 11.5 synthesizes the steps for implementing plot scaffolds and Figure 11.7 provides an example of a plot scaffold.

The open-ended scripts work well for students of all writing abilities since the children can work in groups. In addition, the strategy is particularly useful for ELL students because they can share their ideas on a level at which they are comfortable (O'Day, 2006).

Although there are multitudes of ways to engage students in writing, as we emphasized earlier children need to take ownership of what they compose. Providing students with choices and scaffolding creative options are two key elements that will foster effective instruction. In the next section we discuss ways to organize writing instruction.

**BOX 11.5**   STEP-BY-STEP *Lesson*

## Plot Scaffolding

Time: Using plot scaffolds will take a week or more with sessions of about an hour each.

1. Prepare an original plot scaffold (or rewrite the plot from a story in the form of a script). In parentheses, write the directions and leave spaces for the students to write. When you write the plot scaffold, present a conflict that the students need to resolve. Activate prior knowledge by using the following prompts as they relate to the plot: "What if? What is the catch? What then?" (O'Day, 2006, p. 34). For example, if the plot is about a monster that lands in your chimney and gets stuck, you might ask:

    - What if a monster landed in your chimney?
    - What happens if there is a fire in the chimney?
    - What might you do then?

2. Distribute copies of the plot scaffold and read it aloud with the students (do not read the parenthetical instructions).

3. Assign or have the students select "parts." Allow time for the plot scaffold to be read orally several times. This will ensure that struggling readers and ELLs will have the opportunity to process the print.

4. Next, give the students the opportunity to dramatize the parts by moving around, making facial expressions as the parts are read, or by adding props.

5. Instruct the students to complete the plot scaffold by following the parenthetical instructions. They may work individually, with a partner, or in small groups.

6. Have the students rewrite the plot scaffold by adding descriptive words, stage directions, adding costume suggestions, and so on. Allow time to practice reading the revised plot scaffold aloud.

7. A final draft can be written paying careful attention to grammar and spelling.

8. If time permits, the plot scaffolds can be rewritten in story form.

*Source:* Adapted from *Setting the Stage for Creative Writing: Plot Scaffolds for Beginning and Intermediate Writers,* by S. O'Day (Newark, DE: International Reading Association, 2006).

# Figure 11.7   Sample Plot Scaffold

**A Monster in the Chimney**

**Characters:** Monster, Child 1, Child 2, Child 3

Narrator/Writer:   The scene takes place in a house. Three children are playing and they hear a sound. *(What does the house look like and where is it? What are the children playing and where? What kind of sound do they hear?)*

*[Provide Space for Writing]*

_____

_____

Child 1:   What was that? *(Give the child a name and describe how the child is talking and describe the situation.)*

_____

Child 2:   I don't know. *(Give the child a name and describe the situation.)*

_____

Child 3:   I think the sound is from over there. *(Give the child a name and describe where the child thinks the sound is coming from.)*

_____

Monster:   Help me! Help me! I'm stuck in your chimney! *(Describe the scene and the children's reaction.)*

_____

_____

Child 1:   Who are you? *(Describe the child's reaction to hearing the monster speak.)*

_____

Monster:   *(What does the monster say and how does he or she say it?)*

_____

_____

Child 2:   *(What does the child say and how does he or she say it?)*

_____

Child 3:   I'm scared. *(Describe the situation.)*

_____

Monster:   Call someone! Call someone quickly! *(Describe the situation.)*

_____

Child 1:   I'm calling the police.

Child 3:   I think we should call the fire department!

Child 2:   I think we should call 911!

Monster:   *(What does the monster say?)*

_____

Narrator/Writer:   *(What happens next? Add new characters.)*

_____

Monster:   *(What does the monster say and how does he say it?)*

_____

Child 1:   *(What does the child say?)*

_____

Child 2:   *(What does the child say?)*

_____

Child 3:   *(What does the child say?)*

_____

Narrator/Writer:   *(Describe how the problem is solved. Add your own dialogue.)*

_____

_____

# Establishing a Predictable Structure for Writing

No two writing classrooms are the same, nor should they be. Instructional routines and procedures vary from classroom to classroom. However, effective classrooms often have certain characteristics in common.

One characteristic involves continuity from day to day. It's crucial to establish a regular writing time that students will come to expect and anticipate. Try to set aside 30 to 60 minutes every day, if possible, for writing. This is not to suggest that students shouldn't be encouraged to write at other times of the day. However, it does suggest a set time for writing that will provide students with a sense of continuity and regularity. When there's a special time for writing every day, students learn to anticipate writing *when they are not writing* (during lunchtime, on the playground, or at home). Writing becomes habitual (Atwell, 1998).

In addition to journals, an integral part of the routine of classroom writing can involve the use of folders or writing portfolios. In process-centered classrooms, there is often a box of writing folders that contains the collected pieces the students have written. The pieces are chosen by the students or the teacher. They may be selections that represent the students' best work or ones that demonstrate growth in writing. The folders are often stored in a brightly decorated cardboard box or in a filing cabinet within the students' reach.

Some teachers recommend using two writing folders: a *daily folder* that contains a students' immediate work in progress and a *portfolio* for completed pieces of writing. The portfolio has at least two important purposes. First, it documents students' writing development during the school year. Students (as well as parents) can study their progress and the changes that have occurred in their writing. They enjoy reading and reviewing the topics they've written about and the types of writing they've completed. Teachers find that folders are valuable for helping students understand the writing process. Second, when students accumulate their writings, they can see the investment they have made. The folder then helps build a sense of pride, accomplishment, and ownership. It is a visible record of a student's growth as a writer (Graves, 1994). When students have access to computers and word processing software for their writing, electronic folders can be used. Students need not do all of their writing on the computers, but they can use them to select samples they would like to enhance with graphics and interesting fonts. We will discuss this further in the Reading–Writing–Technology Connections section of this chapter.

## Organizing the Writing Workshop

**STANDARD 2.2**

Many teachers think about writing time each day as a workshop; the classroom is the student writer's studio. The **writing workshop** begins by providing students with the structure they need to understand, develop, or use specific writing strategies or by giving them direction in planning their writing or in revising their drafts. The **minilesson,** as the name implies, is a brief, direct instructional exchange (usually no longer than 10 minutes) between the teacher and the writing group (which may include the whole class). The exchange isn't a substitute for individual guidance; instead, it is meant to get students started on a writing project or to address their specific problems or needs. For example, a minilesson can stimulate topic selection, brainstorm ideas and rehearse for writing, illustrate interesting versus dull writing, model literary style by reading passages from literature, illustrate good sentence and paragraph structure, teach or model strategies for revision, and teach a mechanical skill. Heffernan (2004) uses examples from children's literature that focus on social issues to develop minilessons that model quality writing.

Following the minilesson is the actual time the students spend "in process," whether they're collecting information, drafting, revising, or editing their work. For part of this time, you may find yourself working on your own writing. In addition, your role is primarily to facilitate the workshop by responding to the needs of writers as specific situations demand. Hence, this would be the time to circulate among students and conduct individual and/or group conferences about initial drafts, questions, revisions, and final products. As teachers develop minilessons that focus on the **writing process,** they need to think of the variety of genres in which students can write, ought to be allowed to write, and should be taught to write. Consider the following writing genres (Booth, 2001):

- Letters
- Memoirs and biographies
- Responses to literature
- Information organized for following instructions
- Opinions and reports on articles
- Fiction
- Nonfiction
- Research reports
- Poetry
- Scripts

One plan that teachers can follow in facilitating the writing workshop might go as follows:

### A WRITING WORKSHOP PLAN

1. Minilesson (3–10 minutes)
2. Writing process (45–120 minutes)
3. Group share session (10–15 minutes)

Ideally, the students need to have a significant amount of time to write. Teachers can certainly vary a writing workshop time frame to suit the needs of students and to accommodate different language arts schedules. For example, teachers might decide to have a group share session once a week, but for a longer period of time. Other teachers may find that they need a longer time to conduct minilessons for ELL students and/or struggling or advanced writers.

A main purpose of a **group share session** is to have writers reflect on the day's work. "Process discussions" focus on concerns implicit in the following questions:

How did your writing go today? Did you get a lot done?

Did you write better today than yesterday?

Was it hard for you to keep your mind on what you were writing?

What do you think you'll work on tomorrow?

What problems did you have today?

Calkins (1983, 1994) provided these guidelines to facilitate reading and discussion of students' drafts:

*Raising concerns:* A writer begins by explaining where he or she is in the writing process and what help he or she needs. For example, a student might say, "I'm on my third draft and I want to know if it's clear and makes sense" or "I have two beginnings and I can't decide which is best."

*Reading aloud:* Usually, the writer then reads the writing (or the pertinent section) out loud.

*Mirroring the content and focusing praise:* The writer then calls on listeners. A classmate begins by retelling what he or she has heard: "I learned that . . ." or "Your story began . . ." Sometimes a listener may begin by responding with praise or showing appreciation for the writing.

*Making suggestions:* Questions or suggestions are then offered about the concern raised by the writer. Sometimes other things will come up as well.

Besides reflecting on the day's writing, reserve the share session for celebrating finished work. Ask volunteers to share their writing with an audience. For elementary

BOX **11.6**

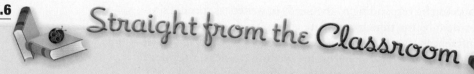

## Using Social-Issue Texts as a Springboard for a Writing Workshop

*Lee Heffernan, a third-grade teacher, uses social-issue texts, stories or passages that deal with social concerns and lend themselves to provocative discussions and powerful writing, as springboards for writing workshops. In the following lessons, see how Lee organizes her writing workshop based on the book* Crow Boy *(Yashima, 1976).*

### Lesson 1

The teacher reads aloud the story. *Crow Boy* is about a talented young boy who can imitate the sounds of crows. Unaware of his talent, the children in his school ignore Crow Boy during most of his elementary school years. In sixth grade, a teacher recognizes his unique talent which he subsequently shares at a talent show. The moral of the story is that all people are special in their own ways.

### Lesson 2

The students are randomly paired and given response sheets that serve to stimulate discussion about the book. Sample prompts might include: "Write something important about the book"; "Write something that you learned"; "Write about a connection to your own life that the book reminded you of." A sample response from one of Lee's students was "A question we have about this book is why did it take 6 years to get a good teacher?" (Heffernan, 2004, p. 28).

### Lesson 3

Triangle talk is initiated by distributing a list of typed questions from the response sheets. Working in groups of three, the students rate the questions according to value. Some questions may have obvious answers of limited value for further discussion, and some questions may lend themselves to interesting talk. Triangle talk takes about 10 to 15 minutes. Sample questions from *Crow Boy* include: "Where did the zebra grass come

from?" and "Why did people make fun of Crow Boy when he was only short?" (Heffernan, 2004, p. 30).

### Lesson 4

Following small group conversation, the whole group discusses the questions. According to Heffernan (2004), these discussions "tend to be lively and emotional" (p. 29).

### Lesson 5

Next, the class selects a picture from the book that best characterizes the conversations.

### Lesson 6

The final lesson is notebook writing. Here the students think about how the conversations and issues discussed connect to their own lives, write about them, and share through read-alouds. After working through *Crow Boy,* topics that the students wrote about included: being "teased about their names, clothing, hair, abilities in sports, and for being new at school" (p. 32).

#### REFLECTIVE INQUIRY

◆ Lee's writing workshop is considerably different from others because it focuses on a common book that addresses a social issue. What are the advantages and disadvantages of using this approach to writing?

◆ How could you incorporate a minilesson into Lee's organization for her writing workshop?

*Source:* Adapted from *Critical Literacy and Writer's Workshop: Bringing Purpose and Passion to Student Writing,* by L. Heffernan (Newark, DE: International Reading Association, 2004).

students, the author's chair is an integral part of the sharing experience. The celebration that students take part in reflects their payoff for the hard work that writers go through to craft a piece of writing to their satisfaction. Instead of using the author's chair, at the end of writing time Heffernan (2004) implements "Circle Check Out." The students sit in a circle and share "snapshots" of their writing that reflect examples of the concept taught during the minilesson. Heffernan (2004) also suggests a unique way to organize a writing workshop based on social issues that foster critical thinking. In Box 11.6 see how Heffernan (2004) implements a writing workshop based on the book *Crow Boy* (Yashima, 1976).

## Guiding Writing (and Observing Reading)

**STANDARD**
**2.2**

In a process-centered classroom, students quickly become aware that writing evolves through steps and stages. The **stages in the writing process** have been defined by different authorities in different ways. In this book, the stages are referred to as *rehearsing, drafting, revising and editing,* and *publishing.* These stages aren't neat or orderly; that is why they have been described as *recursive.*

**REHEARSING** ◆ Rehearsing is everything that writers do before the physical act of putting ideas on paper for a first draft. "Getting it out" is a useful mnemonic because it helps us remember that rehearsal means activating background knowledge and experiences, getting ideas out in the open, and making plans for approaching the task of writing.

The rehearsing stage has also been called *prewriting,* a somewhat misleading term because "getting it out" often involves writing of some kind (e.g., making lists, outlining, jotting notes, writing in a journal). Regardless of terminology, rehearsing is a time to generate ideas, stimulate thinking, make plans, and create a desire to write. In other words, rehearsing is what writers do to get energized, to explore what to say and how to say it: "What will I include?" "What is a good way to start?" "Who is my audience?" "What form should my writing take?"

There are many ways to rehearse for writing: talking, reading to gather information, brainstorming and outlining ideas, role playing, doodling, drawing, cartooning, jotting down ideas, taking notes, interviewing, and even forming mental images through visualization and graphic organizers.

**DRAFTING** ◆ "Getting it down" is an apt way to describe drafting. Once writers have rehearsed, explored, discovered, planned, and talked (and done whatever else it takes to get ideas out in the open), they are ready to draft a text with a purpose and an audience in mind. A student is reading when drafting. The writing workshop provides the in-class time for first-draft writing. As students draft, the teacher regulates and monitors the process.

Drafting is a good time to confer individually with students who may need help using what they know to tackle the writing task. The teacher can serve as a sounding board, ask probing questions if students appear to be stuck, and create opportunities for a student to read what he or she is writing. A teacher may want to ask the following questions:

How is it going?

What have you written so far?

Tell me the part that is giving you a problem. How are you thinking about handling it?

I am not clear on _____. How can you make that part clearer?

Are you leaving anything out that may be important?

What do you intend to do next?

How does the draft sound when you read it out loud?

What is the most important thing you're trying to get across?

Once completed, a first draft is just that—a writer's first crack at discovering what he or she wants to say and how he or she wants to say it.

**REVISING** ◆ Each interaction that occurs when a writer seeks a *response,* either from the teacher or from another writer in the class, constitutes a *conference.* Students have many opportunities to read their work critically during conferences. Simply stated, a conference may be held when a writer needs feedback for work in progress. The conference may last 5 seconds or 5 minutes, depending on the writer's needs. However, once a student decides to rework a first draft, conferencing becomes a prominent aspect of *revising* and *editing.*

When writers work on a second or third draft, they have made a commitment to rewrite. Rewriting helps students take another look. This is why good writing often reflects good rewriting and rereading of a piece.

To conduct a teacher–student conference, a teacher must learn to define his or her role as listener. Graves (1983) noted that when conducting a conference, the student leads and the teacher intelligently reacts.

To elicit clarification of a piece of writing, a teacher might focus the conference with a specific question or two appropriate to the writer's needs. The following general steps will help in conducting a conference.

1. The writer *reads* the draft out loud.
2. The teacher *listens* carefully for the meaning of the draft.
3. The teacher then *mirrors the content* ("Your draft is about . . ."), *focuses praise* ("The part I liked the best about your draft is . . ."), *elicits clarification* ("Which parts are giving you the most trouble?"), *makes suggestions* ("I think you should work on . . ."), and *seeks the writer's commitment* ("Now that we have talked, what will you do with the draft?").

Sandmann (2006) uses peer writing conferences as part of the revising process by implementing what she calls the **focused question card strategy.** The conferences initially focus on meaning by asking the students to think about what they want to say. Box 11.7 explains the strategy. In addition, Dix (2006) acknowledges that students tend to revise in a variety of ways. For example, one early childhood student was asked "what happens in her head" when writing, and she replied:

> Probably, either there are two . . . I think there are two sort of, like, columns in my head, and if I don't like it then I put it in one column and I say, "I don't like it" and I just put it away—forget about it. . . . Then the ones I do like, I write them down. So I think in my head first before I write it down. (Dix, 2006, p. 570)

When asked to describe the process of writing a poem, another student wrote:

> Well, just say if the thing I was writing about was trees, I just go, "What shall I write about? What color are the leaves? Or how many rings do they have to say how old they are? And what shape they are, what shape different types of trees are." (Dix, 2006, p. 571)

---

**BOX 11.7**

## Research-Based Practices

### Revising Using the Focused Question Card Strategy

1. Discuss the difference between revising questions that focus on content and editing questions that focus on mechanics such as spelling, grammar, and punctuation. A content question might be "What are my three basic points?" An editing question would be "Am I using commas correctly?"

2. Distribute small cards and have the students reread their draft and write a content revising question on the card. Students share their questions and discussion takes place as to whether the questions address content. If not, the questions are rewritten. Following this step, the students sign their cards.

3. Students choose a partner with whom to work. They are encouraged to work with someone whom they think will help them based on previous observations of their work or interests. For example, if a student is writing about animals, he might choose to work with a student who has several pets.

4. Partners sit across from each other and take turns reading the questions on their cards followed by focused listening and discussion. Next, the students take notes on their cards based on suggestions.

5. Editing conferences also take place with questions that focus on one or two issues such as punctuation or spelling. During these conferences, the students sit side by side so they can follow along as the drafts are read.

6. As students work with their partners, the teacher monitors learning and takes notes on minilessons that would be helpful.

7. Although a rubric can be used to assess the final draft, errors are not corrected. Instead, the purpose of the strategy is to help students focus on specific questions that they have about their writing.

*Source:* Based on "Nurturing Thoughtful Revision Using the Focused Question Card Strategy," by A. Sandmann, 2006, *Journal of Adolescent and Adult Literacy, 50,* pp. 20–28.

BOX **11.8**

# Viewpoint

## the Literacy Coach
### Organizing Writing Instruction

Jackie, a fourth-grade teacher, has been struggling with how to effectively provide writing instruction during her language arts class. During a 45-minute class, Jackie typically allows the students one-half hour to write as she walks around the room to monitor and assist individual students. She is frustrated, however, because this time does not seem focused. Although the students seem to be writing, Jackie does not feel that she is providing effective writing instruction. She asked Marla, her school's literacy coach, to assist her. Marla suggested that Jackie consider the following:

- First, examine the purposes for which you are having the students write. Have you discussed the audience for whom the pieces should be written?

- Do the writing assignments involve a prompt? If so, do the students know the expectations of the assignments?
- Do the assignments involve choices? Are the students permitted to write fiction or nonfiction or multigenre pieces? Poetry?
- Are the students writing in responses to pieces of literature or are the assignments to compose creative pieces?
- Have you modeled the types of writing you expect? How did you scaffold instruction?

Marla developed the following template to help Jackie organize her writing instruction constructively.

| Grade-Level Standard and Indicator | Purpose of the Writing Assignment | How Will I Scaffold Instruction? | Choices for Completing the Assignment | Conference Options | Evaluation |
|---|---|---|---|---|---|
| | | | ☐ Poetry<br>☐ Narrative<br>☐ Nonfiction<br>☐ Multigenre<br>☐ Self-selected | ☐ Teacher—small group<br>☐ Teacher—individual<br>☐ Peer partners<br>☐ Small group<br>☐ Peer sharing | ☐ Checklist<br>☐ Rubric<br>☐ Peer evaluation<br>☐ Self-reflection<br>☐ Other |
| | | | | | |

As students revise, it is useful for teachers to observe, ask questions, and note how students approach the task. This can provide teachers with useful information for minilessons to share with the rest of the class. Teachers can ask questions such as: "What goes on in your mind as your write? What pictures do you have in your head when you write?" See Box 11.8 to see how one literacy coach assists a teacher in organizing the writing process.

**EDITING** ◆ During revision, students will be messy in their writing, and they should be encouraged to be messy. They should be shown how to use carets to make insertions and be allowed to make cross-outs or to cut and paste sections of text, if necessary. The use of arrows will help students show changes in the position of words, phrases, or sentences within the text.

Once the content and organization of a draft are set, students can work individually or together to edit and proofread their texts for spelling, punctuation, capitalization, word choice, and syntax. Accuracy counts. "Polishing" or "cleaning up" a revised draft shouldn't be neglected, but students must recognize that *concern for proofreading and editing comes toward the end of the writing process.* This is particularly true for struggling writers and ELL students who need to be encouraged to take risks with the writing process (Ganske et al., 2003).

**HOMEWORK EXERCISE: VIDEO**

Go to the Homework and Exercises section in Chapter 11 of MyEducationLab to watch the video "The Writing Process: Editing," in which a teacher conferences with a student on a writing project.

DIVERSITY ELL

Students should edit for skills that are appropriate to their ability and stage of development as writers. An editing conference should provide a *focused evaluation* in which one or two skill areas are addressed. If students have edited their writing to the best of their ability, the teacher may then edit the remainder of the piece for spelling and other conventions.

PUBLISHING ◆ If writing is indeed a public act, it is meant to be shared with others. Writing is for reading, and students learn quickly to write for many different audiences. When young writers have a sense of their audience, the task of writing becomes a real effort at communication. Recall the enthusiasm that Lynn Weber's first graders had when they wrote to their preservice teacher pen pals (Box 11.1, page 358). Their sense of audience was very real. Opportunities to publish writing for a specific audience engages elementary and middle school students in exciting purposes for writing.

The pride and sense of accomplishment that come with *authorship* contribute powerfully to a writer's development. Publishing provides a strong incentive for children to keep writing and rewriting. But more than anything else, publishing in the classroom is fun. Young people take great pride in writing and illustrating their own books. Producing a book often provides the impetus for writing and justifies all the hard work that goes into the final product. Writing a book creates a meaningful context and motivates youngsters to revise and edit stories, focusing on content, organization, sentence structure, interesting words, and correct spelling. Young writers are especially inspired to write books when they are exposed to children's literature on a regular basis. They are also eager to make books when they can choose the type of book they want to write. Some possibilities for bookmaking are given in Figure 11.8.

For older students, class-produced newspapers, magazines, anthologies, and books are excellent ways to publish student writing. The students should be involved in all phases of the publication's production. We suggest that students not only participate as writers but also work in groups to assume responsibility for editing, proofreading, design, and production. Production of a class publication need not be elaborate or expensive. Photocopied or computer-generated publications have the same effect on student writers as more elaborate presentations when they see their work in print. Finally, be sure to display student writing. Establish an author's day or a reading fair in which students circulate around the room reading or listening to as many pieces as they can.

Letters, community publications, commercial magazines, and national and state contests are all vehicles for real-world publishing outside of the classroom and school. Letters, in particular, are valuable because there are so many audience possibilities.

In addition to letters, other outlets for class-related writing activity include the local newspaper, PTA bulletin, or school district newsletter. Commercial magazines and national, state, local, or school writing contests also offer opportunities for publication. Commercial magazines and writing contests, of course, are highly competitive. However, the real value of writing for commercial publication lies in the authenticity of the task and the real-world audience it provides.

Finally, students have countless opportunities to publish their writing on school and individual classroom web pages. There are a growing number of central sites on the Internet that support student publications and provide helpful hints for student writing. At the end of this chapter, we share some of these web sites.

# Reading–Writing–Technology Connections

**HOMEWORK EXERCISE: CASE STUDY**

Go to the Homework and Exercises section in Chapter 11 of MyEducationLab to watch the video "An Interactive Writing Project," in which students learn to create a graphic organizer using a software program.

Advances in technology are quickly changing how we communicate and disseminate information. Technology, integrated into the curriculum for meaningful learning, can be a powerful tool in students' literacy development. E-mail conversations, as noted earlier, hone reading and writing skills by putting students in

## 𝒥igure 11.8   Ideas for Making Books

| Type of Book | Sample | Construction |
|---|---|---|
| **Shape books**<br>Stories about animals, objects, machines, people, etc.; poems; nursery rhymes; innovations | | Make pages in the shape of your book. Bind together with staples or masking tape or lace with yarn. |
| **Ring books**<br>Group stories; word fun; poems; collection of poems | | Punch holes in pages and use notebook rings or shower curtain rings to bind together. |
| **Stapled books**<br>Individual stories; group contributions; alphabet books; word books; poems | | Pages and cover are stapled together, then bound with masking tape for added durability. |
| **Fold-out books**<br>Poems; patterns; sequences; stories | | Pages are folded accordion-style and then stapled or glued to covers. |
| **Bound cloth books**<br>Poems; collections of poems; stories that have been edited and prepared for printing | | (See extended directions on the next page.) |

(Continued)

# *Figure 11.8* *(Continued)*

## Extended Directions for Bound Cloth Books

*Supplies:* **1 piece of lightweight fabric (approximately ¹/₂ yard), several needles, white paper, dry-mount tissue, cardboard, masking tape, an iron, and an ironing area.**

1. Each child should have 6 or 7 sheets of paper. This will make a finished book with 10 to 12 pages but will not be too difficult to sew. Fold each sheet of paper in half (one by one). (Fig. 1)

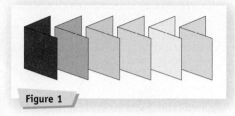

**Figure 1**

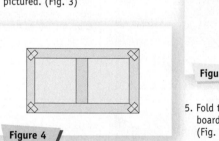

Stitches

**Figure 2**

2. Bring the sheets together and sew along the fold. *Hint:* Start on the outside of the fold so that the knot will not be seen when binding is finished. (Fig. 2)

3. Cut out the fabric to measure 12" x 15". Prepare some templates from cardboard for students to use as guides. (Fig. 3)

4. Spread out the materials as pictured. (Fig. 3)

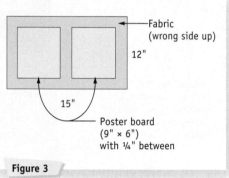

Fabric (wrong side up)

12"

15"

Poster board (9" × 6") with ¼" between

**Figure 3**

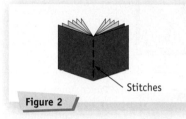

**Figure 4**

5. Fold the edges of the fabric over the two boards, and tape in place at the corners. (Fig. 4)

6. Now make a sandwich using the cover, then a piece of dry-mount tissue (8½" x 11"), then the sewn pages, and iron in place as pictured. Iron only on the endpapers since the pages can be scorched. (Fig. 5)

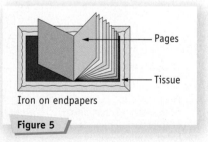

Pages

Tissue

Iron on endpapers

**Figure 5**

communication with other students and content experts throughout the world in a matter of seconds. Moreover, the digital forces of the computer have paved the way for an information age that affects the literacy learning of today's generation of students like no other generation before it. Students have instant access to **electronic texts** on the Internet or CD-ROM software. Electronic texts, which are constructed and displayed on a computer screen, are becoming an integral part of students' literacy lives in *and* out of classrooms. These texts are not fixed entities, set in print. They are fluid, interactive, and engaging.

Teachers can provide instruction in these new literacies by helping students recognize significant questions as they search for writing topics online and critically evaluate

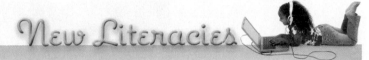

BOX **11.9**

*New Literacies*

## THE EARTH DAY GROCERIES PROJECT

In 1994 Mark Ahlness, a third-grade teacher at Arbor Heights Elementary School in Seattle, Washington, began The Earth Day Groceries Project, a community-service venture in which his students borrowed and decorated grocery bags that were returned for shoppers to use on Earth Day (Ahlness, 2005). Although the project did not use technology initially, Mark eventually used the Internet to expand the program to what it is today, an international partnership in which schools all over the world write environmental messages and decorate brown paper bags that are shared via The Earth Day Groceries Project

web site (www.earthdaybags.org). Not only do students write powerful messages, but they also read about the projects worldwide.

The project is an outstanding example of how students can connect with other communities via technology, practice environmental awareness, learn about geography as they map the locations of project participants, and experience a firsthand civics lesson. When ventures such as this one occur, students encounter "multiple aspects of literacy . . . through technology" (Kinzer, 2005, p. 65).

topic-related information (Kara-Soteriou, Zawlinski, & Henry, 2007). In addition, technology today redefines a sense of community when students communicate with others worldwide and participate in community-based projects that can be shared online (Kinzer, 2005). See the New Literacies Box 11.9 for an example of a community service learning project mediated by technology.

Supporting students' writing of electronic texts is one of the important reading–writing technology connections that can be made in the classroom. Using computers to construct electronic texts helps students examine ideas, organize and report information and inquiry findings, and communicate with others. Word processing, desktop publishing, and authoring software programs, for example, allow students to use and develop literacy skills to publish writing in creative ways and prepare multimedia reports and presentations relevant to curriculum objectives. The technology available today makes it possible for students to connect what they are reading and writing about to sound, graphics, illustrations, photographs, video, and other nonprint media in multimedia environments.

## Word Processing

**Word processing** offers much to classroom writing environments. The computer screen lends a public quality to writing that can encourage sharing and communication. It can encourage children to perceive text as flexible and malleable, and it can increase teacher involvement in writing and, paradoxically, student independence as writers.

Here are some suggestions for teaching word processing:

- *Become familiar with the program yourself first.* Use it for your own writing. While learning, you may wish to make a poster and/or a duplicated sheet of major editing commands for your students.
- *Start simple.* Teach only a few basic commands; then add more to students' repertoires as necessary.
- *Consider introducing word processing in a whole class language-experience setting.* As each command is clicked or key is pressed, discuss what it does, why it is needed, and how to do it.
- *Work intensely with a small group to develop your first "experts."* Post students' names with the instructions for using the program so that others can ask them for help.
- *Continue presenting short, direct lessons to the class followed by work on the computer in pairs.*
- *If few computers are available, rotate groups using the word processor for compositions.* Or have students write their first draft in pencil. When they are finished, they can sign

Word processing can encourage children to see text as flexible and malleable.

up for a 20- to 30-minute session at the computer. Working in pairs, one student types in his or her own composition as the other student reads it, suggesting changes along the way. The students then switch places. One teacher who had only one computer every third week had a parent volunteer type in students' work after school during the 2 weeks in which the class did not have access to the computer. In the third week, students would read and revise their work. Although these methods are compromises to an extent, students can still benefit from using the computer, especially in reviewing and revising, the final, crucial step in writing.

- *Model and follow the writing process as described in this chapter.*

Because students find themselves writing more on word processors, their work may be less organized and need more revision than paper-and-pencil writing does. Fortunately, this free, continuous writing followed by reflection and revision is one of the best ways to compose. In addition, students can store their work in the form of electronic folders or portfolios or on individual disks, which can make the revision process easier. Electronic portfolios can also store biographical information, PowerPoint presentations, research references, electronic communication, favorite web sites, and the list goes on.

Word processing software can encourage students to be active writers as they engage in rehearsing, drafting, revising, and editing. For students who have trouble with fine motor control and find writing with paper and pencil difficult, computers can make writing easier by taking away some of the physical demands of putting ideas on paper. Freed from the physical tasks associated with writing, students can expend more cognitive energy on the communication itself.

Used correctly, word processors can help students write. Words are not carved in stone; they are painted in light, permitting effortless manipulation. The more students intelligently manipulate text—the more they read their work and revise—the better writers they will become.

## Desktop Publishing and Multimedia Authoring

**Desktop publishing** and **multimedia authoring** software programs give students an authentic reason for reading and writing: publishing. These programs enhance the writing

BOX **11.10**

## *Research-Based Practices*    Guidelines for Author's Computer Chair

1. Establish a comfortable atmosphere for sharing and discussion. Explain to the students that the purpose of the author's chair is to provide feedback for each other's ideas as they work with the computer.

2. Provide minilessons that demonstrate purposeful uses of the computer such as composing, researching, using graphics, and publishing.

3. Arrange for class time on the computer and time for sharing. A sign-up schedule works well.

4. Explain that during sharing time the students can talk about work in progress, ask for feedback, talk about something they learned or an area in which they have become an expert, or share a computer activity they have completed. For example, a student who has learned how to use the spell-check function could demonstrate the process. Another student might opt to show interesting information about a topic that was found on the Internet. Someone else might share a composition that was written with a word-processing program and illustrated with a drawing program.

5. Establish typical patterns for sharing. Sharing might include stating the purpose of the showcased work, answering peer questions, showing examples, and demonstrating a strategy.

*Source:* Adapted from "Author's Computer Chair," by L. D. Labbo, 2004, *The Reading Teacher, 57,* pp. 688–691.

process and help students create stories and reports for classroom publication as part of writing workshops or thematic units of study. Software for desktop publishing typically permits students to integrate text and graphics, use different text styles, and arrange text in columns. Today many word processing programs include basic publishing features that make student authorship appealing. Multimedia authoring programs heighten even further the pride of authorship as students build stories and reports using text, colorful illustrations, sound, and animation. Labbo (2004) suggests guidelines for implementing an author's computer chair as part of the classroom writing program. The idea behind an author's computer chair is to capitalize on the social nature of the writing process and to foster discussion. In Box 11.10, we synthesize Labbo's guidelines.

When using multimedia authoring programs, it is best to begin with simple projects and presentations and gradually introduce students to more complicated uses of the software. Jane Fuller, a fifth-grade teacher, introduces students to HyperStudio, a multimedia authoring program, by showing them how to make a business card. She integrates the lesson into a review of U.S. historical figures that students study as part of a unit on the Revolutionary War. First, Jane invites the class to design "business cards" for historical figures of the 1770s. She assigns the students to research the individuals they have chosen in order to determine their particular contributions or importance to U.S. history. Once students have completed the research, they must then create a sentence or two, similar to what is found on business cards, "advertising" the historical person's talents and contributions. For example, George Washington's card might say, "A Tough Man for Tough Times" or "Leadership in Times of Danger and Discouragement." In addition to the catchy descriptions, students incorporate into the card's design basic data related to the lives of the historical figures and information concerning their accomplishments, using HyperStudio to position the information and select background choices, font, bold type, italics, and so on. Finally, the students print their cards, share, and display them.

## Children's Books and Technology

Earlier we suggested that children's literature can serve as excellent examples of quality writing to share with students. In addition, children's books can spark writing instruction during the minilesson portion of the writing workshop. Kara-Soteriou, Zawilinski, and Henry (2007) suggest a number of books and computer resources that can be adapted to lessons including the following:

- *Jazz ABZ* (Marsalis, 2005) is a poetry alphabet book that can inspire poetry writing, along with an online rhyming dictionary (www.rhymer.com) from WriteExpress.
- *A Lime, a Mime, a Pool of Slime: More About Nouns* (Cleary, 2006) uses comical cats to illustrate the differences between common and proper nouns. The Guide to Grammar and Writing web site (http://grammar.ccc.commnet.edu/grammar) can also serve as a resource for the study of nouns and other parts of speech.
- *Hey There, Stink Bug* (Bulion, 2006) is a multigenre book that includes silly poetry. It can be linked with Giggle Poetry (www.gigglepoetry.com), a web site with poetry activities and poetry performance plays.
- *Dougal the Garbage Dump Bear* (Dray, 2005), a story about a stuffed bear who makes friends with other stuffed animals in a garbage dump, offers excellent examples of character description. Character description can be elaborated on at the Read* Write*Think website (www.readwritethink.org/lessons/lesson_view.asp?id=101), which provides information on using picture books to teach characterization.
- *The Trouble with Tilly Trumble* (Manuel, 2006) shares the story of a woman who searches for old chairs to keep her company and instead finds a four-legged friend. This story is filled with descriptive text. Coupled with the web site Descriptive Writing with Virginia Hamilton (http://teacher.scholastic.com/writewit/diary/index.htm), students can learn to write descriptively.

In addition to exposing children to quality literature with which teachers can conduct minilessons during a writing workshop and elaborate further using Web-based resources, many Internet sites contain other valuable information for teachers to craft lessons about writing. For example, the Petra Project on the Eclipse web site (http://eclipse.rutgers.edu/petra/index.jsp) takes users through the stages of drafting, editing, and publishing a children's story, *Kisses from Rosa*, by Petra Mathers (1995), including copies of drafts, questions to consider, a dummy book, and visual interpretations of her illustrations. Lessons can be adapted for all ages. For older students a fascinating history of Mother Goose rhymes also can be found on the Eclipse site (http://eclipse.rutgers.edu/goose). Scriptito's Place (http://members.aol.com/vangarnews/scriptito.html), a writing resource center provided by Vangar Publishers, includes tips for creative writers, how to write and edit a story, how to gather ideas for story writing, tips on illustrating stories, how to publish them, and samples of stories written by children.

As teachers gather resources to elaborate on the teaching of writing and connect reading to writing, it makes sense to use the wide range of Web-based resources that are available for instruction. How teachers organize the information can be challenging. Create a table such as the one shown in Table 11.1 for easy reference to useful sites that you find.

## Table 11.1  Organizing Web-Based Resources

| ENGLISH/LANGUAGE ARTS STANDARD/ INDICATOR | WEB SITE | WEB ADDRESS | PURPOSE |
|---|---|---|---|
| [insert grade level standard and indicator] | Guide to Grammar and Writing | http://grammar.ccc.commnet.edu/grammar | Grammar study ideas |
| [insert grade level standard and indicator] | The Petra Project | http://eclipse.rutgers.edu/petra/index.jsp | To show the students the process of publishing a children's book |

## WHAT ABOUT STRUGGLING READERS AND *Reading–Writing Connections?*

Research shows that struggling writers very often have difficulty choosing a topic about which to write, find it hard to organize their ideas, write choppy sentences, and have trouble with grammar, spelling, and punctuation (Christenson, 2002). Whereas teachers sometimes tend to focus on the weaknesses of struggling writers, Christenson (2002) emphasizes the importance of showing writers what they can do well. Since students who struggle with the writing process frequently have low opinions of themselves as writers, it is critical to bolster their self-esteem by pointing out their strengths as well as the growth you see on a regular basis through individual and small group conferences.

Christenson (2002) also points out that writing workshops provide struggling writers with an environment that fosters growth because students have choices, they are invited to write, and they are not tied to completing worksheets that they feel are useless exercises that often focus on what they cannot do. In addition, writing workshops provide struggling writers with the chance to improve at their individual levels of ability. Conferences afford teachers distinct opportunities to offer positive feedback, as well as personalized instruction based on specific needs.

As Christenson (2002) recommends, we suggest that teachers teach writing as a process that includes brainstorming, drafting, editing, and producing final copies. When struggling writers view composing as a process, rather than a lesson to be performed, they will grow more confident in their strengths as writers.

## WHAT ABOUT STANDARDS, ASSESSMENT, AND *Reading–Writing Connections?*

National, state, and local content standards for teachers of K–12 students typically indicate that students need to be able to read and write clearly and effectively in a variety of situations. More specifically, the *National Standards for the English Language Arts* (International Reading Association and National Council of Teachers of English, 1996) specifies that students must be able to adjust their written communication skills to a wide variety of audiences, and they must know how to write for a variety of purposes. In addition, students must know the conventions of written communication, including spelling and punctuation, and they must be able to generate and synthesize ideas via the written word.

Olness (2005) recommends rubrics that rate the writer on a scale of 5 (strong) to 3 (developing) to 1 (weak). For example, when evaluating *voice*, a student whose writing is convincing, includes an appropriate tone, and demonstrates feeling would rate a 5. A student whose writing is not individualized and includes more "telling" than "feeling" would rate a 3. A rating of 1 means the reader could not tell what the writer means or cares about.

Regardless of the rubric used to evaluate student writing, teachers must ask themselves if the students are meeting the standards. Proficiency assessments, especially test situations in which students must respond to open-ended questions or write extended essays, evaluate both the content and the process by which students produce a piece of writing. Often, this type of writing assessment is evaluated using holistic scoring. In holistic scoring, a rubric is typically used to assess the quality of writing. The rubric might ask test evaluators to judge the piece of writing based on a general impression of its overall effectiveness or on an assessment of more specific skills. Although national, state, and local standards are relatively consistent with respect to overall student expectations, proficiency assessment practices vary. We certainly do not advocate practices that "teach to the test," but we do suggest that teachers inform themselves about the statewide assessment practices that are used to evaluate their students' proficiency in writing. How specifically are your students evaluated on their writing skills via your statewide tests? What are the standards? These are some questions teachers need to consider.

## Summary

Learning to write is as natural to students as learning to read. Recent research has resulted in compelling evidence that suggests that reading and writing develop concurrently. Rather than teaching reading and writing as separate curricular entities, they should be taught in tandem.

One of the keys to writing and reading connections in classrooms rests with the environment that teachers create. Natural environments for learning provide encouragement and a built-in support system, and there is tremendous, patient faith that children will develop as writers. Time for writing, response to writing, and ownership of one's own writing are the hallmarks of a natural learning environment.

Writing leads to reading. Getting started with writing instruction is challenging. Teachers must establish a routine for writing. For example, there should be time to write every day, freedom of movement in the classroom, and occasions to write.

Reading is a natural springboard into students' writing. Making the connection between children's literature and writing and informational texts in content areas and writing is important because writing is a way of comprehending. Through journals, students can respond personally to text in order to explore, clarify, and extend meaning. Writing, we believe, can help students grow in every facet of reading. Journals and writing folders should be the focal point of the classroom writing program.

Process-centered classrooms allow for great flexibility, not anarchy, and have a predictable structure. Guidelines need to be established to set clear expectations for behavior and interactions in the classroom. In process-centered classrooms, students are encouraged to choose topics that matter to them and to rehearse for writing through talking, reading, brainstorming, and other prewriting strategies. Talking and journal writing, in particular, will help students discover and select topics for writing.

Drafting, revising, and editing are commonplace occurrences in process-centered classrooms. Throughout the stages of writing, students need responses from the teacher and other students. Conferences are the vehicles by which teacher and writers respond to one another in order to try out work and get ideas on how to improve their drafts. Revising requires that the writer resee or rethink a piece. Only once the content of writing is set does editing become a major writer responsibility. Editing means preparing the writing for an audience and involves polishing the writing by attending to such matters as spelling, punctuation, and usage.

Publishing provides the payoff for the hard work that goes into the writing process. Encouraging students to value writing is crucial. Some suggestions include providing an author's chair; sponsoring class publications, bookmaking, oral presentations, and contests; and advising students about submission to magazines that publish student work, including locations on the Internet.

## Teacher Action Research

1. Select a Newbery Award–winning book from the American Library Association web site (www.ala.org/ala/alsc/awardsscholarships/literaryawds/newberymedal/newberywinners/medalwinners.htm). Analyze the book from the point of view of using it to model writing by answering the following questions:

   What selections would you use to demonstrate the author's intent to "catch the reader"?

   What selections would you use to demonstrate character description?

   How does the author set the scene?

   How would you use selections from the book to demonstrate this?

Develop a template based on the book that you selected in which you could develop minilessons based on language arts standards for a grade level that you have selected. See the sample template below:

**Book citation:**

| Language Arts Standards | Minilesson Topic | Pages from the Book | Minilesson Plan | Writing Assignment |
|---|---|---|---|---|
| | | | | |
| | | | | |

2. Interview a teacher who has a limited number of computers in his or her classroom and a teacher who uses a computer lab as the primary vehicle for using technology. Ask the teachers the following questions:

   - Do you organize the time for children to explore writing assignments on the computer? If so, how?
   - If you use the computer for writing assignments, what is the nature of the assignments? Do the students have choices or do you assign topics?
   - If your students use the computer to develop their writing skills, how do you evaluate their work?

3. Select a grade level. Using the English language arts standards for your state, design a 15-minute writing minilesson that addresses a specific expectation for the standard that you selected. Peer-teach the lesson to your classmates and gather reflections about the nature of your lesson. Ask your colleagues:

   What was the goal of my minilesson?

   Were my goals evident?

   Were you engaged during my lesson?

   How might you adapt my lesson?

   After reading your classmates' reflections, write a reflective piece that captures how your lesson might improve or change.

4. Ask a teacher if you may talk with several of her or his students individually about writing, or use your own students. Develop interview questions such as the following and record the students' responses:

   - Do you like to write? Why or why not?
   - Can you tell me about something that you have written?
   - How did you start to write it? What did you do next? How did you continue to write this piece?
   - What is the favorite part of this piece of writing that you did? Was there a part of this writing that was easy for you? Difficult?
   - Can you explain to me what you think about writing?

   After conducting several interviews, analyze the responses in terms of positive statements and negative statements. What are your conclusions about the students that you interviewed?

5. Use the same or similar questions from the previous item to interview yourself and a colleague. Compare and contrast your responses. What can you learn about yourself and your colleague as writers?

6. Think back to when you were a child and try to recall the first time you engaged in writing something. Start with your earliest memory and trace your journey as a writer up to and including the present time. Think about

| | |
|---|---|
| teachers | settings |
| assignments | grades |
| advice | topics |
| feelings | habits |
| senses | idiosyncrasies |

Let these questions guide you:

- What are some words that come to mind when you think of "writing" in relation to your school experiences?
- Who were the teachers that mattered? That didn't matter?
- Do you like to write?
- Do you, or would you, like to teach writing?
- What are your most effective characteristics as a writer? Your least effective?
- Have you ever written anything you were proud of? What is it?
- When, where, and how do you usually write?
- What is your most effective characteristic as a teacher of writing? Your least effective?
- What are some good and bad experiences you've had as a writer?

Add comments to make a portrait of yourself as a writer. Focus on what your personal journey shows you about the way writers develop—or don't develop. What does your experience show you about novice writers who are learning how to write? In what ways will your experiences influence the way you teach writing? What advice would you give to teachers of writing?

7. Locate a classroom in which process writing, including conferences, is used. Observe the interactions that occur when writers seek a response to their writing, from the teacher or other writers in the class. Do the students seem to have sufficient opportunities to read their work critically during conferences? How long do the conferences tend to last? In a week or two, collect the same type of data based on observations in another classroom either at the same or another grade level. Or revisit the same classroom each week for the same amount of time during the course of a month. Do you notice any changes in the conduct of the conferences or the interactions among the students?

8. Conduct a writing-process conference with an elementary or middle school student who has just completed a draft (use some of the suggestions in this chapter for conducting the conference). Describe what happened during the conference. What did you learn from the experience? (Tape-record, if permissible.)

9. Collect several journal entries of students at different grade levels. What do students write about? What kinds of responses do they make to literary texts? How would you plan instruction to help each student continue to grow and develop as a journal writer?

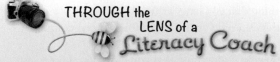

**THROUGH the LENS of a Literacy Coach**

10. Observe a teacher during a language arts lesson that involves writing. Prior to observing the lesson, ask the teacher, "What is the purpose of the writing assignment?" As you observe the lesson, consider:

Has the teacher clearly explained the purpose of the writing activity to the students?

Did the teacher scaffold the expectations of the assignment through a minilesson?

What did the teacher do to ensure that the students understood what they were supposed to do? Would you have done this differently?

What would you suggest to the teacher based on your observations of the lesson?

## Related Web Sites

*Ace Writing*

**www.geocities.com/fifth_grade_tpes**

Teachers of writing can find links for publishing student works and lesson plans for teaching a wide variety of writing strategies, including persuasive writing and creative writing.

*Cyberkids*

**www.cyberkids.com/we**

Young writers can submit their stories for publication on this Web-based magazine for children ages 7 to 12. The submission guidelines provide helpful guidance.

*MidLink Magazine*

**www.ncsu.edu/midlink**

This online magazine for students ages 8 to 18 includes many writing links and opportunities for students to publish their work.

*ReadWriteThink*

**www.readwritethink.org/lessons/lesson_view.asp?id=23**

ReadWriteThink offers many activities that expose students to a variety of rewritten fairy tales and provides formats for students to rewrite their own versions of the tales.

*Web English Teacher*

**www.webenglishteacher.com**

This site provides a wide variety of creative lessons and activities for teaching grammar and writing and is an excellent resource for middle school teachers. Click on the links for grammar, mechanics, and usage.

*Writing with Writers*

**http://teacher.scholastic.com/writewit/index.htm**

This outstanding writers' resource by Scholastic offers tips from well-known authors for writing biographies, fairy tales, folktales, mysteries, myths, news articles, poetry, and book reviews. Students can listen to authors read their works. This site also includes opportunities for students to publish their work.

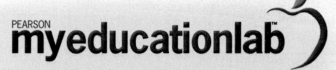

Now go to the Vacca et al. *Reading and Learning to Read*, Seventh Edition, MyEducationLab course at **www.myeducationlab.com** to

- Take a pretest to assess your initial comprehension of the chapter content
- Study chapter content with your individualized study plan
- Take a posttest to assess your understanding of chapter content
- Engage in multimedia exercises to help you build a deeper and more applied understanding of chapter content

## CHAPTER 12

# Bringing Children and Literature Together

Standards found in this chapter:
- 2.1
- 2.3
- 4.1
- 4.2
- 4.3
- 4.4
- 5.1
- 5.3

## In this chapter,
### YOU WILL DISCOVER:

- That literacy is personal and that readers benefit from a supportive environment
- What it means to bring children and books together in a literature-based program
- How to choose literature and involve children through activities
- Ways to organize classes around books and literature circles
- Major strategies for encouraging readers to respond to literature

## Concept Map

### BRINGING CHILDREN AND LITERATURE TOGETHER

**SUPPORTING A COMMUNITY OF READERS**

**Surrounding Children with Literature**

Selecting Classroom Collections of Books
Helping Children Select Books
Listening to Literature

**Organizing the Classroom as Children Respond to Literature**

Literature-Based Instruction
Encouraging Responses to Literature

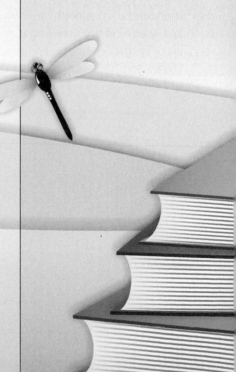

Imagine the expression on Laura Pils's face when she received a brightly colored, handmade Valentine's Day card in the shape of a heart from Michael, a friend of one of Laura's first-grade students. In purple letters, the card said, "Happy Valentine's Day. I love you, Miss Piss" (Pils, 1993).

"It's so fitting," Laura thought of Michael's card. "It is these first attempts at literacy that are so wonderful. . . . All the parts are not in place yet, but the soul is there, speaking loud and clear while trying to find its own voice" (Pils, 1993, p. 653). Laura's first-grade class in Middleton, Wisconsin, personifies the type of literate community where all of the students, including those who fall behind the others in their literacy development and are not particularly eager to learn, feel that they are valued members of the class and that they have something to offer the rest of the students. Michael is a case in point. So is Dan.

Michael is Dan's friend. Although Laura never had Michael as a student, she came to know him through Dan. Dan was one of the needier students in Laura's class and had been struggling from the beginning of the school year with reading and writing. His language skills were limited; he had difficulty expressing himself other than through crying, acting out, and sometimes getting into verbal and physical fights with his classmates.

Dan's story is not unlike that of students in other schools and in other classrooms whose path to literacy, for one reason or another, is rough and uncertain. Yet within the literacy community that is Laura's classroom, there is an air of confidence that all of the children will find their way to literate activity. "But how to reach them?" That is the challenge she faces. Twenty-five years of teaching experience with literacy beginners helps Laura realize that she must first establish a level of trust in the classroom and then find a "hook" that will connect literacy to the lives of the children. For many teachers, like Laura, literature is the hook.

Her attempts to reach Dan were eventually realized when Laura learned that his grandparents, with whom Dan spent summers near the ocean, were visiting from Connecticut. She arranged in advance for the grandparents to make a surprise visit to the classroom as "mystery readers." Throughout the year, mystery readers are invited into the classroom, unannounced to the children, to share in a surprise reading of a child's favorite book. Open invitations are extended to parents, grandparents, and older brothers and sisters to visit and read to the class. On the day that his grandparents visited the classroom, Dan "stood proudly next to his grandma and grandpa and introduced them. As they read, they stopped often and had Dan assist in the telling of the story. We took their picture with Dan and tacked it to the Mystery Reader board" (Pils, 1993, p. 652). On that eventful day, Dan took a giant step forward in his journey toward literacy; he felt, perhaps for the first time, that he had something of himself to give to the other students. Throughout the remainder of the year, he made steady progress and contributed to the community through the stories he wrote and shared with others.

Dan is now in the third grade and is still making an impact on the community of readers and writers in Miss Pils's first-grade class. He helps select books for her class: "Knowing that I like pigs, he checked out every pig book in the library. He came into the room beaming when he found a pig story that had just arrived; he was teaching me about a new book" (Pils, 1993, p. 653). And Michael, who once declared his love for Miss Pils, also helps select books for her class. Dan and Michael were even invited to participate in reading to the class books they had liked "when they were little." As Laura Pils explains, "We took their pictures and put them on the Mystery Reader board. We wrote them thank-you notes. Their teacher said they were so proud. I was proud too" (p. 653).

The story of Dan and Michael illustrates convincingly that at its best, literacy is a personal and self-engaging activity. Children who view themselves as contributing members of a classroom of readers and writers develop a sense of self-worth and commitment. Bringing children and books together in a literate community fosters the ability not only to think better but also to feel and to imagine.

Reading literature requires students to respond to books affectively as well as cognitively. Children respond emotionally to the literary text as a whole. These feelings are unique and tied to each reader's life experiences. Emphasizing personal involvement in literature develops in students an imagination, a sense of wonder, and an active participation in the literary experience. To our mind, bringing children and literature together is one of the highest acts of humanity in the classroom.

How teachers capture children's interest in books and bring them into a supportive community of readers is the subject of this chapter. Examine the concept map, which depicts connections among several key concepts related to bringing books and children together. It is important to surround children with books, including those with a multicultural perspective, in order to immerse young children, as well as middle school students, in hearing literature and to help them find books they want to read.

We also emphasize in this chapter the importance of children's responding personally to literature as a way to extend critical thinking and make connections to other readers. We look at how to organize the classroom so that children can authentically respond to books. Finally, students' freedom to choose what they read is considered in relation to different ways of organizing for instruction.

# Supporting a Community of Readers

Within the past 15 years, there has been more emphasis on literature-based instruction. Simply defined, a **literature-based reading program** may be viewed in the context of instructional practices and student activities such as independent reading, sustained reading and writing, social interactions, and read-alouds using literature, books, novels, short stories, magazines, plays, poems, and electronic books that have not been rewritten for instructional purposes.

There are long-term benefits implicit in bringing children and books together on a regular basis. First, reading expands children's experiential backgrounds. Children who have never milked a cow and been awakened by a rooster or never lived in a tenement apartment and played in the alley of a big city can expand their world through reading. Second, literature provides readers with good models of writing. These models are valuable in children's own writing development and teach the unique characteristics of written language. Third, students learn to read by reading, a theme we have repeated throughout this book. When they are encouraged to read books regularly, children are more likely to develop patience with print, and thus they gain valuable practice in reading. Fourth, when the prime purpose for reading is pleasure, children want to understand what they are reading and are likely to select books with familiar topics, themes, or characters. These natural reading situations will promote students' use of reading strategies. And fifth, wide reading provides opportunities for children to develop vocabulary knowledge. Readers learn the meaning of words by meeting them again and again in a variety of contexts.

Literature-based reading programs have the potential for success with all types of students, but particularly with struggling readers like Dan and Michael, who can easily slip through the cracks without a supportive environment for literacy development. Studies have been conducted in classrooms where literature-based programs were beginning to be used with populations that had traditionally been unsuccessful in literacy learning in school. Stewart, Paradis, Ross, and Lewis (1996) conducted research in a literature-based developmental reading program for seventh and eighth graders. They determined that the students in the literature-based program had increased their fluency and comprehension skills. Children who speak limited English have made great gains in reading when immersed in their new language (Vardell, Hadaway, & Young, 2006). Free reading of second-language texts, as reported by Krashen (2003), contribute to advanced second-language development. Finally, D'Alessandro (1990) researched emotionally disabled children and reported that gains in reading ability were significantly increased when they participated in literature-based reading programs.

Reading achievement studies of literature-based reading programs also report significant shifts in the students' attitudes toward reading. Tunnell, Calder, Justen, and Waldrop (1988), for example, found that for included children with learning disabilities in a literature-based program, "negative attitudes toward books and reading virtually disappeared as self-concept in relation to literacy rose" (p. 40). In another study, Ivey and Fisher (2006) reported that for struggling adolescents exposure to appropriate literature can help them to "stimulate their minds—make them laugh, puzzle, empathize, question, or reconsider previously held notions" (p. 17).

Providing all students with many and varied opportunities to read high-quality literature is essential. As the International Reading Association has aptly stated, "Children who read more, read better" (2002b, p. 6). Literature-based reading instruction enhances overall reading performance by developing reading skills and strategies as well as positive attitudes toward reading (Morrow & Gambrell, 2000).

Moreover, literature-based reading programs create a **community of readers.** Hepler and Hickman (1982) proposed the idea of a community of readers to characterize how students, in alliance with their friends and teacher, work together in classrooms in which school reading becomes like adult reading, where adults are motivated to read. In these classrooms, students informally and spontaneously talk over their experiences with books and recommend books to each other. In Hepler's (1982) yearlong study of a fifth- and a sixth-grade classroom, she found it common for children who discovered something of particular appeal to read that passage aloud to a friend, offer the book to a friend for approval, or simply nudge the nearest person and point out "the good part."

Hansen (1987) has expanded this idea into "a community of readers and writers." She explains that students should help each other learn, not out of a sense of duty, but because they know each other as people. Children sharing their thoughts on what they have read helps make this happen. In book-sharing talks, sometimes readers have similar thoughts about a book, but often they have unique contributions to make to the discussions. Hansen suggests, "When words, whether our own written words or our verbal responses to someone else's, give us a place in the group, print acquires a new dimension for us. Learning is usually social; we learn very little entirely on our own. Without a community, people have less desire to write or read" (p. 64). The interactions that students experience help them to learn from each other and share their confidence as readers.

Classrooms where students support each other as readers and writers do not arise spontaneously. Rather, "they are carefully structured environments that reflect a teacher's commitment to literature as a natural medium for children's reading and language learning as well as a source of fun and satisfaction" (Hickman, 1983, p. 1). Galda and Beach (2004) believe that "by creating opportunities for students to read and respond in the company of others, teachers foster their students' ability to make sense of text worlds and lived worlds" (p. 865). In a classroom with a community of readers the students' responses to literature are livelier, more positive, and their choices of books seem to be made with more care.

Hooking children on books helps them realize their literacy potential. Figure 12.1 outlines some of the hooks we explore in this chapter, all of which support a community of readers in the elementary classroom.

## Surrounding Children with Literature

One feature that sets literature-based classrooms apart from traditional classrooms is that the teachers are enthusiastic about children's literature. Teachers who make a point of talking about their own favorite books or stories or are themselves engrossed in a new book often find their students wanting to read those same books for themselves. These teachers also show personal interest in books in other ways. Some teachers share autographed copies of books from their own collections or display

## Figure 12.1   Hooking Students on Books

**Immerse Students in Literature**

- Create a classroom climate in which literature is an integral component.
- Use many genres of children's books with multicultural perspectives, including folktales, poetry, realistic fiction, historical fiction, and informational books.
- Select and organize a classroom collection of books.
- Read and tell stories. Show films and filmstrips of literature selections.
- Integrate talking books.

**Use Instructional Time to Show the Value of Reading**

- Find classroom time for students to read books of their choice.
- Model reading behavior and become a reader of children's books.
- Encourage students to respond to the aesthetic dimensions of literature.

**Help Students Find and Share Books They Want to Read**

- Help students find books of interest at the appropriate level.
- Tell or read the beginning of interesting stories.
- Develop annotated lists of books worth reading.

book-related items such as ceramic or stuffed toy characters or posters designed by a picture-book artist. No matter how the teacher's enthusiasm is expressed, it creates a setting in which children know that attention to the world of books is authentic and desirable. This is especially important for students in high-poverty areas and for English language learners, for whom there are limited print resources outside of the school.

## Selecting a Classroom Collection of Books

A major classroom characteristic that brings children and books together is many carefully selected books. These books come from different sources—the teacher's personal collection, the school library, the public library, and paperback book clubs. Although the core collection is permanent, many of the borrowed titles change frequently, so there is always something new to encourage browsing.

Another way to encourage browsing is to include a selection of talking books in the classroom collection. "Talking books are hypermedia texts with digitized pronunciations of words and larger textual units" (Leu, 2000, p. 755). These books may include features such as animated illustrations, highlighted text, and skill-development activities. Leu (2000) reports that comprehension is increased when readers are provided with talking books.

Books chosen for a classroom collection, no matter what type, should not be chosen for the sake of quantity. Rather, books should be carefully chosen for a variety of reasons, as illustrated by Hickman (1983):

> One teacher of a fourth- and fifth-grade group, for example, often includes many picture books. She chooses some like Mizumura's *If I Were a Cricket* and Foreman's *Panda's Puzzle* for the special purpose of comparing the artists' way with watercolor; others, like Wagner's *The Bunyip of Berkeley's Creek*, are chosen just because they are good stories and the teacher thinks the children will enjoy them. The teacher is sensitive to children's interests and books that will have immediate appeal; thus the presence of *Tales of a Fourth Grade Nothing* by Blume, *How to Eat Fried Worms* by Rockwell, and *The Mouse and the Motorcycle* by Cleary. The teacher also recognizes that the students need some books that

Providing a broad collection of books that appeal to all ability levels creates an environment that encourages all children to find something they can enjoy reading. It also demonstrates a teacher's own love for literacy.

will stretch their imaginations and abilities, stories of sufficient depth to bear rereading and reflection. Some of the titles chosen for this purpose are Babbitt's *Tuck Everlasting*, Cooper's *The Dark Is Rising*, and Steig's *Abel's Island*. Still others, like Konigsburg's *From the Mixed-Up Files of Mrs. Basil E. Frankweiler*, are available in multiple copies so that small groups can read and discuss them. (p. 2)

One notable feature of book selection is that each title bears some relationship to others in the collection. There may be multiple books by an author or an illustrator or several books that represent a genre such as modern fantasy. For example, a classroom that contains Rowling's *Harry Potter* books would also have *A Series of Unfortunate Events* by Lemony Snicket. Other connections may be based on a content theme such as spooky books, nature books, or survival books.

**HOMEWORK EXERCISE: CASE STUDY**

Go to the Homework and Exercises section in Chapter 12 of MyEducationLab to review the case study "Helping Children Select Books" and consider how you would assist your students in selecting literature that is relevant to their interests and reading levels.

CHOOSING CLASSROOM LITERATURE ◆ To be able to choose literature for classroom collections and to give guidance to students as they choose books to read, a teacher needs to be familiar with children's literature. Because children's literature has expanded extensively in the past 20 years, this is a formidable task.

Several strategies can be used to help choose classroom literature. Here are some tips on how to avoid being overwhelmed as you become familiar with children's literature.

1. *Read and enjoy children's books yourself.* The best way to become familiar with students' books is not to read anthologies or reviews but to read the books themselves. It is a good idea to keep a card file on the books you have read to jog your memory later. This card file can be used with children to help them in choosing books to read. It can also be used as you share your feelings about particular books with other teachers.
2. *Read children's books with a sense of involvement.* Only by reading books thoroughly can you prepare yourself to share them honestly with children.
3. *Read a variety of book types.* There are various classifications of genres or types of books. By being familiar with specific books in each of the different genres, you can be more helpful when children ask for such things as "a scary mystery" or "something true to life."

4. *Read books for a wide variety of ability levels.* Students at any grade level vary tremendously in their reading abilities and interests. For example, Haywood's *B Is for Betsy* is read avidly by some second and third graders. Other students at the same grade level will read somewhat more difficult books such as Sobol's *Encyclopedia Brown Lends a Hand* and Blume's *Tales of a Fourth Grade Nothing*. Still others may benefit from spending time with picture books such as *Where the Wild Things Are* by Sendak or *The Great Thumbprint Drawing Book* by Emberley.

5. *Share how your students respond to particular books with other teachers or other university students.* In the San Antonio, Texas, school district, a book-reporting system was developed. Anyone who read a book and used it with students filled out a review card, which included a brief summary, a rating, comments on the book's unique value, and recommendations for suggested ability levels. Teachers used these cards to help select books for their classrooms. Not unexpectedly, with this teacher-sharing system in place, the children read more, as did their teachers.

6. *Start by reading several books of good quality.* Lists for the Newbery Medal and Caldecott Medal book award winners can be found on the American Library Association's homepage (www.ala.org). As you read these and begin using them with students, you will begin to know books to which children in your class will respond favorably.

**DETERMINING GOOD LITERATURE** ◆ A teacher's first priority is to choose books that students will like and will read. It is important to take into consideration students' diverse backgrounds, academic abilities, and interests. To choose such a collection of books, teachers must be knowledgeable and enthusiastic about children's literature. Through reading children's literature and talking about books with children, teachers learn which books to use in their classrooms. A few criteria to use in building a balanced collection of books are:

1. *The collection needs to contain modern, realistic literature as well as more traditional literature.* In recent years, some critics have voiced concern about the appropriateness of realism in some children's literature. Other observers feel that realism is justified because it depicts problems children must face while growing up. Each teacher and school must decide whether to include books that deal with divorce, death, and drug use—issues that touch the lives of many of today's children. Traditional literature, which children have delighted in for many years, should also be a part of the classroom collection of books. "These books not only have artistic and literacy merit but also generate strong personal response and have universal appeal" as Livingston and Kurkjiam point out (2003, p. 96).

2. *The collection needs to contain books that realistically present different ethnic and minority groups and nontraditional families as well as mainstream Americans.* See Chapter 13 for specific criteria useful in evaluating books for stereotyping.

3. *The collection needs to contain books with different types of themes and books of varying difficulty.* Students generally choose books based on reading level, content, and style (Ivey & Fisher, 2006). For English learners book selection is more complex. Teachers need to consider language and writing complexity and use of visualization. The classroom library needs traditional literature, fantasy, poetry, historical fiction, non-fiction, and picture books. Even middle school classroom collections should have some picture books. Picture books often have a good story plot and provide a way to get less enthusiastic students into reading. A few picture books appropriate for middle school students are *Amazing Grace* by Mary Hoffman, *Baseball Saved Us* by Ken Mochizuki, and *Grandfather's Journey* by Allen Say.

4. *The collection needs to include nonfiction.* Students from all grades should have access to a wide selection of high-quality information books (Saul & Dieckman, 2005). The use of nonfiction trade books is common in middle school classrooms (Moss & Hendershot, 2002). However, this does not seem to be true in primary grades, where

fiction is dominant. Palmer & Stewart (2003) report that in spite of the increase of nonfiction being published that includes simpler concepts, various topics, and a wide range of reading levels, teachers of young children are unaware of the availability and have limited access to quality nonfiction. Therefore, primary teachers need to become more familiar with information books and select appropriate ones to include in their classroom collection.

**LITERATURE WITH MULTICULTURAL PERSPECTIVES ◆** In a multicultural society made up of diverse groups who maintain their own cultural traditions and experiences, books help us celebrate our distinctive differences and understand our common humanity. Culturally diverse books in the United States typically tell the stories of people of color—African Americans, Native Americans, Asian Americans, and Hispanic Americans. These stories are told through poems, folklore, picture books, realistic and historical fiction, biography, and nonfiction. Junko Yokota (1993) broadens the description of multicultural children's books to include literature that represents *any* distinct cultural group through authentic portrayal and rich detail. Culturally diverse books, therefore, also may represent the literature of regional white and religious groups—for example, Appalachian, Ozark, Jewish, Muslim, or Amish cultures—or the cross-cultural stories of people from other nations. What all culturally diverse books have in common is that they portray what is unique to an individual culture and universal to all cultures.

The power of multicultural literature lies in the human connections that we make. Not only do books about people of color or distinct cultural groups help us understand and appreciate differences among people, but they also show how people are connected to one another through human needs, desires, and emotions (Cullinan & Galda, 1994). At an exhibit of the Cleveland Museum of Art, "Lasting Impressions: Illustrating African American Children's Books" (featuring original drawings, prints, and collages by 15 illustrators of African American children's books), we observed a young child standing pensively in front of a drawing from Ann Grifalconi's *Kinda Blue*. The pastel painting that captured her attention depicts the wistful image of Sissy, a young black child living on a farm in Georgia who's "kinda blue" since her father's death. After viewing the illustration for a while, the child began to walk away but then pulled her parents back and said, "I want to be just like her." The emotional connection she made with Sissy is strong enough to attract her to the book *Kinda Blue*. And the parents did not have to go far to find it. The exhibition included a reading table with the books for which the illustrations were made. Children, their parents, and other viewers of the exhibition spent as much time browsing through and reading the books as they did viewing the illustrations.

**WHY MULTICULTURAL LITERATURE? ◆** There are fundamental social and educational reasons why multicultural literature should be woven into the fabric of children's home and school experiences. In the Viewpoint in Box 12.1 Peter Schneller passionately expresses the need for teachers to integrate multiple perspectives in the curriculum using multicultural literature. Violet Harris, a children's literature scholar and advocate of multicultural books in classrooms, outlines a compelling rationale for making culturally diverse books an integral part of the literacy curriculum. In an interview with Martinez and Nash, Harris (1993) gives five reasons for multicultural literature in the classroom:

1. All children, and especially children of color, need to experience multicultural books. Children receive an affirmation of themselves and their cultures when their life experiences are mirrored in books. The infusion of multicultural literature in the classroom affirms and empowers children and their cultures.

BOX **12.1**

# Viewpoint

## Literature and Multiple Perspectives

Peter L. Schneller

*To a worm in horseradish, the
whole world is horseradish.*
—Yiddish proverb

I'm afraid that most Americans are becoming comfortable in horseradish. In a world that's becoming increasingly global, we tend to immerse ourselves in the routine and familiar; whether it's horseradish or ketchup, if it's familiar, we relish it. Admit it, the American perspective is often limited—myopic and xenophobic. So here's my command to teachers: Use literature to broaden your students' perspectives.

And it's easy. There is a plethora of literature that can provide multiple perspectives for students of all ages. An excellent example is *The True Story of the 3 Little Pigs!* by Jon Scieszka and Lane Smith. It enables students to think about the standard nursery rhyme through the eyes of the wolf, who is perhaps the most maligned archetype utilized by the seemingly unbiased and always good Mother Goose. Another picture book that offers a point of view rarely imagined is *Baseball Saved Us* by Ken Mochizuki and Dom Lee. It takes readers to the Japanese internment camps in Idaho during World War II and stimulates us to envision life through the eyes of a young Japanese American who's been imprisoned unjustly, yet intermittently is freed through playing the great American pastime. For older readers there's *The Flip-Flop Girl* by Katherine Paterson. Paterson delicately permits us to walk in the shoes of Vinnie, a social outcast with complex life problems. The book dishes out generous doses of bibliotherapy; it's ideal for building a classroom

community that honors students of all backgrounds. All teachers should read and share with their students Mark Haddon's *The Curious Incident of the Dog in the Night-Time*. Haddon's point of view enlightens the reader through the inner life of an autistic child. It's also a nifty narrative filled with delightful literary intricacies.

Unless teachers integrate multiple perspectives into the curriculum, what's familiar may smother us. Gary Howard, author of *We Can't Teach What We Don't Know,* and the Respecting Ethnic and Cultural Heritage Center (REACH) (www.reachctr.org) have developed curricula for all grade levels that convey multiple perspectives as a foundation for increasing an awareness of diversity. Teachers should be obligated to examine REACH's ethnic perspectives series, which presents views of American history via American Indians, African Americans, European Americans, and Japanese Americans. It's a profound first step in developing cultural competency.

Mark Twain claims that "Travel is fatal to prejudice, bigotry, and narrow-mindedness, and many of our people need it sorely on these accounts" (1897, p. 444). Although there is no education quite like travel, books can be luxurious vehicles for vicarious sightseeing. Emily Dickinson was correct when she wrote, "There is no frigate like a book, To take us lands away. . . ." We must help our students understand the dimensions of a multicultural United States that is globally interdependent. Exposing students to multiple perspectives through good books may be the way to a better, albeit increasingly smaller, world.

2. Children perceive that members of their cultural group make contributions to the world.
3. Children derive pleasure and pride from hearing and reading stories about children like themselves and seeing illustrations of characters who look as if they stepped out of their homes or communities.
4. Multicultural literature offers hope and encouragement to children who face the types of dilemmas and experiences depicted in some of the books they read.
5. Children who read culturally diverse books encounter authors who use language in inventive and memorable ways, who create multidimensional characters, and who engender aesthetic and literary experiences that can touch the heart, mind, and soul.

DIVERSITY

Multicultural literature helps readers understand, appreciate, and celebrate the traditions and experiences that make each culture special in its own way. It opens doors to other cultures and introduces readers to ideas and insights they would otherwise not have encountered (Landt, 2006). When children read books that depict cultural differences, they not only view the world from another's perspective but also learn more about themselves.

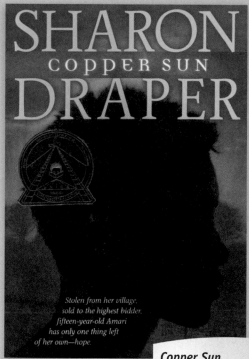

**Arrorró, Mi Niño: Latino Lullabies and Gentle Games**
Lulu Delacre (Lee & Low Books, 2004)

**Copper Sun**
Sharon Draper (Atheneum, 2006)

**Moses: When Harriet Tubman Led Her People to Freedom**
Carole Boston Weatherford
(Jump at the Sun, 2006)

**Bound**
Donna Jo Napoli (Atheneum, 2004)

**The Book Thief**
Markus Zusak (Knopf Books for Young Readers, 2006)

**Hanukkah at Valley Forge**
Stephen Krensky (Dutton Juvenile, 2006)

**José! Born to Dance**
Susanna Reich (Paula Wiseman
Books/Simon & Schuster, 2005)

**Peek! A Thai Hide and Seek**
Minfong Ho (Candlewick Press, 2004)

**CRITERIA FOR SELECTING MULTICULTURAL LITERATURE** ◆ Yokota (1993) notes that the standards for selecting quality literature in general apply to culturally diverse books as well. In addition to these criteria, she suggests that teachers select quality multicultural literature based on these considerations:

1. *Cultural accuracy.* Are issues and problems authentic and do they reflect the values and beliefs of the culture being portrayed?
2. *Richness in cultural details.* Do readers gain a sense of the culture they are reading about?
3. *Authentic dialogue and relationships.* Is the dialogue indicative of how people in the culture really speak, and are relationships portrayed honestly and realistically?
4. *In-depth treatment of cultural issues.* Are issues given a realistic portrayal and explored in depth so that readers may be able to formulate informed thoughts on them?
5. *Inclusion of members of a minority group for a purpose.* Are the lives of the characters rooted in the culture, no matter how minor their role in the story?

In addition to Yokota's questions, the following checklist is designed by Cullinan and Galda (1994) to help teachers select quality multicultural literature.

- Are characters from different cultures portrayed as individuals without stereotyping?
- Does the work qualify as good literature in its own right?
- Is the culture accurately portrayed from the point of view of someone inside the cultural group?
- Are issues presented in their true complexity as an integral part of the story—not just a focus on problems or social concerns?
- Does the dialogue maintain the natural melodies of the native language or dialect without making it difficult to read?
- Do the books show the diversity within as well as across human cultures?
- Do the illustrations contain accurate, authentic representations of people and scenes from different cultural groups?
- Do people of color lead as well as follow? Do they solve their own problems, or do they depend on white benefactors?

Appendix F contains a partial listing of children's books representative of African American, Asian American, Hispanic American, and American Indian cultures. These books and many others may easily be incorporated into a literature-based classroom.

**DESIGNING THE CLASSROOM LIBRARY** ◆ Access to books in classroom libraries impacts students' reading. Morrow (2003) reports that students will read 50 percent more books in classrooms with libraries than those who don't have such access. A wide range of books on various reading levels is essential. As a classroom collection is compiled, the science, math, art, social studies, and music curricula need to be considered. Include books on topics that will be studied in these subject areas. Again, make materials on specific topics available in a wide range of reading levels because of the different reading abilities of students in the same grade level.

As the classroom collection develops, attention must be given to the area of the classroom that houses the library. Specific physical features of classroom libraries can increase children's voluntary use of books (Fractor, Woodruff, Martinez, & Teale, 1993; Morrow, 1985; Morrow & Weinstein, 1982; Routman, 1991). The classroom library should be highly visible; this communicates that it is an important part of the classroom. Clear boundaries should set the library area apart from the rest of the classroom. The library is a quiet place for five or six children to read away from the rest of the classroom. It should afford comfortable seating—perhaps carpet pieces, beanbags, or special chairs. It should hold five or six books per child. Multiple copies of favorites are included. A variety of genres and reading levels should be available, arranged on both open shelves to display attractive covers and shelves to house many books with the spine out. Books in the library

are organized and labeled by genre, theme, topic, author, reading level, content area, or some combination of these features. Literature-oriented displays, such as flannel boards, puppets, book jackets, posters, and talking books boost interest and enthusiasm.

Once the classroom library is in place, the literature program itself needs attention. A major part of the program includes reading aloud and telling stories to children.

## Listening to Literature

According to Stewig (1980), "most elementary school teachers understand the values that accrue as a result of sharing literature with children" (p. 8). Teachers naturally seem to know that there is no better way for students to become interested in the world of books than through listening to stories and poems. In this way, children learn that literature is a source of pleasure. When they listen to literature, children—especially those from culturally and linguistically diverse backgrounds—are exposed to stories and poems they cannot, or will not, read on their own. Often, once children are excited by hearing a selection, they want to read it for themselves.

Through hearing stories and poems, students develop a positive disposition toward books. Cumulative experiences with hearing stories and poems are likely to improve reading comprehension and vocabulary development. Listening to stories and poems can also provide a basis for group discussion, which often leads to shared meanings and points of reference. Galda, Ash, and Cullinan (2000) conclude that being read aloud to helps students develop literacy and language skills and interest in reading, and provides opportunities for social interactions. For these reasons, literature listening time can be one of the most productive times in the school day. Sharing literature with students is not a "frill."

Most teachers include some time for reading aloud in their schedules. In fact, Lehman, Freeman, and Allen (1994) report that 85 percent of the teachers they researched reported reading aloud to their students at least once a day. Another study of **read-aloud** practices shows that teachers tend to read to children 10 to 20 minutes a day (Hoffman, Roser, & Battle, 1993). However, only 34 percent of the time spent on these read-alouds is related to units of study. Further, the amount of book-talk following read-alouds often lasts fewer than 5 minutes. Children rarely engage in exploring their response to literature during a read-aloud.

It is important to note that although teachers may read aloud to students to fill odd moments between a completed activity and the bell or schedule reading aloud as a calming-down activity, sharing literature is not a time filler. It is too serious and central to the reading program as a whole to be treated in an offhand way. Reading aloud needs to be incorporated into all aspects of the curriculum.

**CHOOSING LITERATURE TO READ ALOUD** ◆ What kind of thought and planning go into deciding what literature to share? Why not go to the library, pull some books from the shelf, and, when reading-aloud time arrives, pick up a book and read? In classrooms where students become enthusiastic about literature, the teachers have carefully selected which books to read. They have considered the age, background, and interests of the students. They also present different types of literature. Often books read aloud are related to each other in some way. For example, a middle school teacher read several books by Russell Freedman: *The Adventures of Marco Polo* and *Freedom Walkers: The Story of the Montgomery Bus Boycott.* Soon the students could recognize a Freedman book by his writing style.

Hickman (1983) notes the example of a fourth-grade teacher who thought her students would be excited by characters that were transformed magically from one type of being to another. She read to her students tales of magical changes such as "Beauty and the Beast" in Peace's version and Tresselt's retelling of Matsutani's story "The Crane Maiden." Her class also heard Perrault's version of the familiar "Cinderella" and a Native American myth, "The Ring in the Prairie," by Schoolcraft. Last, she read "A Stranger Came Ashore" by Hunter, a fantasy story with magical transformation that is more difficult to understand than the transformations in the preceding stories.

Another teacher might focus on books to demonstrate an assortment of character types.

In planning experiences with characterization, the teacher chooses books that present a wide variety of characters: male and female, young and old, rich and poor, real and imaginary. The books are read to children and savored. Sometimes the selections are discussed; at other times they are not. Reading occurs each day; the teacher is aware that children may be assimilating unconsciously some of the aspects of successful characterizations exemplified in what they are hearing. (Stewig, 1980, pp. 62–63)

Folktales in which the plot is generally very important can be read to illustrate simple characterization. Other authors give vivid physical descriptions. Consider this description from Judy Blume's *Are You There, God? It's Me, Margaret* (1970):

When she smiles like that she shows all her top teeth. They aren't her real teeth. It's what Grandmother calls a bridge. She can take out a whole section of four top teeth when she wants to. She used to entertain me by doing that when I was little. . . . When she smiles without her teeth in place she looks like a witch. But with them in her mouth she's very pretty. (pp. 15, 18)

Teachers can also share with students books in which authors show what the characters are like by describing what they do and how they interact with others. Even books for the very young do this. For example, in *Sam* by Ann Herbert Scott, Sam tries to interact with his mother, his brother George, his sister Marcia, and his father, all of whom are too preoccupied with their own concerns. Finally, the family responds. All the characters are developed skillfully by the author and portrayed in subtle monochromatic illustrations by Symeon Shimin. In hearing and discussing such books, children gain an awareness of how authors portray characters.

When choosing text to read aloud for English language learners it is important to choose books with topics of familiarity, simple sentence structure, and illustrations. For older readers go beyond chapter books to include nonfiction, picture books, newspapers, and magazines to accommodate interest and reading abilities.

**PREPARING TO READ ALOUD** ◆ Teachers need to prepare for story time. First, before reading a book aloud to the class, they should be familiar with the story's sequence of events, mood, subject, vocabulary, and concepts. Second, teachers must decide how to introduce the story. Should the book be discussed intermittently as it is read, or should there be discussion at the conclusion of the reading? Furthermore, what type of discussion or other type of activity will follow the reading?

**SETTING THE MOOD** ◆ Many teachers and librarians set the mood for literature-sharing time with a story hour symbol. One librarian used a small lamp—when the lamp was lit, it was time to listen. Deliberate movement toward the story-sharing corner in the classroom may set the mood for story time. Some teachers create the mood with a record or by playing a piano. As soon as the class hears a specific tune, they know that it is time to come to the story-sharing corner. Norton (1980) describes using a small painted jewelry box from Japan. As she brings out the box, Norton talks with the children about the magical stories contained in it. She opens the box slowly while the children try to catch the magic in their hands. The magic is wonderful, so they hold it carefully while they listen. When the story ends, each child carefully returns the magic to the box until the next story time. Others create bulletin board displays or spotlight web sites that connect the story to similar books, themes, and authors.

**INTRODUCING THE STORY** ◆ There are numerous ways to introduce stories. The story-sharing corner could have a chalkboard or an easel bearing a question relating to the literature to be shared or a picture of the book to focus the children's attention. Many teachers effectively introduce a story with objects. For example, a full-length coat may be used to introduce *The Chronicles of Narnia* by C. S. Lewis. A good way to introduce folktales is with artifacts from the appropriate country.

Other ways to introduce a story would be to ask a question, to tell the students why you like a particular story, or to have the students predict what will happen in the story using the title or the pictures. You might tell them something interesting about the background of the story or its author. It is advantageous to display the book, along with other books by the same author or with books on the same subject or theme. Introductions, however, should be brief and should vary from session to session.

**ACTIVITIES AFTER READING ALOUD** ◆ There are many different ways to encourage students to respond after hearing a piece of literature; the more direct ways such as literature circles, book-talks, free response, and literature journals are discussed later in this chapter. A more informal approach to reader response is simply to encourage children to react privately to what they have heard. Davis (1973) calls this the *impressional approach*. The basic idea is that children will take from an experience whatever is relevant to them; therefore, each child will benefit from the listening experience. There is no particular reason for the teacher to know precisely what each child gets from each listening experience. Therefore, teachers should strike a balance between these two approaches. Too many discussions and other follow-up activities may diminish interest; too little will diminish the impact of the literature.

**ALLOWING OTHERS TO PRESENT LITERATURE** ◆ Trelease (1989) suggested that in addition to reading literature aloud daily, a good way to promote the importance of reading aloud is to set up guest reader programs in which the principal, literacy coaches, parents, the superintendent, and local sports and news personalities read literature favorites to students. Children, too, can present literature to children. In Chapter 8, we described a cross-age tutoring program in which middle school students can be shown how to select and prepare for reading to younger children. Note that selecting the books to be read and preparing the presentation are extremely important. The reader should be guided throughout the read-aloud process.

## Storytelling

**Storytelling** is the act of telling a story orally without the use of a text. It is a natural way to present literature and oral traditions to both young and older students. There are three significant reasons for including storytelling in the curriculum:

1. *An understanding of the oral tradition in literature.* Young children in many societies have been initiated into their rich heritage through storytelling; today, few children encounter such experiences.
2. *The opportunity for the teacher to involve the children in the storytelling.* A teacher who has learned the story is free from dependence on the book and can use gestures and action to involve the students in the story.
3. *The stimulus it provides for children's storytelling.* Seeing the teacher engage in storytelling helps students understand that storytelling is a worthy activity and motivates them to tell their own stories (Stewig, 1980).

Each of these reasons is important. Students are sure to be spellbound by a well-told story. Close eye contact, the storyteller's expressions, ingenious props, and the eliciting of the children's participation contribute to the magic. Although we cannot expect everyone to acquire a high level of expertise for a large number of stories, storytelling is a skill one can master with practice, a story at a time.

**SELECTING THE STORY TO TELL** ◆ Beginning storytellers should choose selections they like and with which they feel comfortable. Simple stories are often the most effective for storytelling. Stories with which many children are familiar and can help with the dialogue are excellent choices for younger children. "The Three Bears," "The Three Little Pigs," and "The Three Billy Goats Gruff" fit in this category. Because ancient and modern fairy tales usually appeal to primary students, consider stories such as "The Elves and the Shoemaker," "Rumpelstiltskin," and "The Bremen Town Musicians." Middle school students frequently prefer adventure, so myths, legends, and epics such as "How Thor Found His Hammer," "Robin Hood," "Pecos Bill," and "Paul Bunyan" tend to be popular choices.

You might select several stories about a certain topic. For example, Norton (1980) suggests telling two stories about "forgetting": "Icarus and Daedalus," a Greek legend in which Icarus forgets that his wings are wax, and "Poor Mr. Fingle" (Gruenberg, 1948), who wanders about a hardware store for years because he forgot what he wanted to buy.

One of the purposes of storytelling is to give children an understanding of the oral tradition. Even very young children can understand that today stories are usually passed down in books, whereas many years ago they were handed down orally.

An effective way to help children gain this understanding is to tell stories that are similar in plot, such as "The Pancake" from Norse tales included in Sutherland's *Anthology of Children's Literature* (1984) and *The Bun* by Brown. Both of these stories have some kind of personified edible goodie chased by a series of animals and eaten by the most clever animal. Jane, a kindergarten teacher, read these stories to her class and then guided her students in making a chart showing how the stories were alike and different. The class then dictated a story titled "The Pizza." In the class's story, the pizza rolled and was chased by the school nurse, some first graders, and the principal. Its fate, of course, was to be gobbled by the kindergartners. Through their experiences, the kindergarten class developed a story using elements from school life, just as storytellers in the oral tradition did from their personal experiences.

**PREPARING A STORY FOR TELLING** ◆ The task of memorizing a story may seem formidable. How can teachers or children prepare for telling a story in front of others? Actually, stories do not need to be memorized. In fact, the telling is often more interesting if the story unfolds in a slightly different way each time. Refer to Box 12.2 for helpful steps in preparing to tell a story.

Once you have prepared the story, decide how to set the mood and introduce it, just as you would before reading a piece of literature. Effective storytelling does not require props, but you may want to add variety and use flannel boards and flannel board figures

**BOX 12.2    STEP-BY-STEP Lesson**

## Preparing a Story for Telling

The following steps are helpful in preparing to tell a story.

1. Read the story two or three times so that it is clear in your mind.
2. List the sequence of events in your mind or on paper, giving yourself an outline of the important happenings. Peck (1989) suggested mapping the story to show the setting, the characters, the beginning event, the problem and attempts at solving it, and the solution. This structure enables students to tell stories without stilted memorization of lines.
3. Reread the story, taking note of the events you didn't remember. Look for lines of text you do need to memorize, such as "Mirror, mirror, on the wall, who's the fairest of them all?" from "Snow White." Many folk- and fairy tales include elements like this, but such passages are not difficult to memorize.
4. Go over the events again and consider the details you want to include. Think of the meaning of the events and how to express the meaning, rather than trying to memorize the words in the story. Stewig (1980) recommends jotting down the sequence of events on note cards and reviewing the cards whenever possible. With this technique, he reports, it seldom takes longer than a few days to secure the story elements.
5. When you feel you know the story, tell the story in front of a mirror. After you have practiced it two or three times, the wording will improve, and you can try changing vocal pitch to differentiate among characters. Also, try changing your posture or hand gestures to represent different characters.

or puppets. These kinds of props work well with cumulative stories containing a few characters. Jessica, a first grader, told how her teacher had a puppet of "The Old Lady Who Swallowed a Fly" with a plastic see-through window in her stomach. As the story was told, the children delighted in seeing the different animals in the old lady's stomach and helping the teacher tell the repetitive story.

## Helping Children Select Books

One trait of independent readers is the ability to select books they can enjoy and from which they can get personally important information. In fact, Anderson, Higgins, and Wurster (1985) find that good readers know how to select literature relevant to their interest and reading level, whereas struggling readers do not. More often than not, a teacher will hear a child moan, "I can't find a book I want to read." Comments like this usually reveal that students do not feel confident about finding good books by themselves. We have alluded to ways for students to become acquainted with specific books: Teachers can tell exciting anecdotes about authors, provide previews of interesting stories, show videos about stories, suggest titles of stories that match students' interests, share leveled book listings, or compile teacher- and/or student-annotated book lists. To be able to do these things well, teachers need to be well versed in children's literature and know their students.

Beyond this, children need to be shown how to choose books. Hansen (1987) proposes that children be asked to choose and read books of three different difficulty levels. Children should have an "easy book" on hand to encourage fluent reading and the "I can read" feeling. Second, children need a "book I'm working on," in which they can make daily accomplishments by working on the hard spots. Finally, children need a "challenge book," which they can go back to repeatedly over a period of time. This helps them gain a sense of growth over a long period. By letting children know we expect them to read at all levels, children learn to judge varying levels themselves and to give honest appraisals of how well books match their reading ability.

For independent readers, book choice is related to reading purposes and intentions as they read the book. Rick may decide to read *A Wind in the Door* because he liked *A Wrinkle in Time* by the same author, Madeleine L'Engle. When he begins to read, he compares the two books. As he becomes engrossed in the book, he reads to see how the story unfolds. Children need to discuss with each other and their teacher why they chose a specific book and what they are thinking about as they read it.

The use of dialogue journals is an effective tool used by teachers to get to know how students feel about their reading and to guide students to "the right book." Jan, a fifth-grade teacher, has her students write daily in a journal. One of her students wrote, "I like it when the whole class reads together. I think it makes me want to read more." Jan responded with, "I'm glad." Another student made the following journal entry: "My favorite book was *Florence Nightingale*. I liked it because of the way she improved the hospitals and made them stay clean. Also she acted differently than any other person I've read about" (Smith, 1982, p. 360). In response to this journal entry, Jan suggested that the student read other biographies of courageous women.

Dialogue journals seem to work well at the beginning of the school year in providing a response to children concerning their thoughts and feelings about the books they are choosing and reading. Later in the year, buddy journals can be instituted, as was explained in Chapter 11. Sometimes students will begin recommending books to each other in their buddy journals. Peer recommendations make the act of choosing a book more efficient and less risky. Recommendations from friends are a good way to connect books and readers.

Smith (1982) encouraged children to ask for suggestions about which books are interesting. But each reader needs to decide if a book is too hard, too easy, or interesting enough to be read cover to cover. Of course, there are times when students need to be nudged to finish a book or to make the next "book I'm working on" a bit more challenging. In Box 12.3 on page 406, a librarian shares her perspective on how to get books into the hands of children.

MIDDLE GRADES

BOX **12.3** 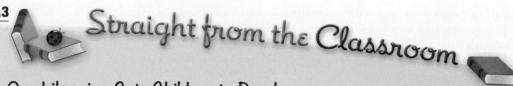 *Straight from the Classroom*

## How One Librarian Gets Children to Read

*Elizabeth Gray is a librarian in a K–2 suburban school. Classes come to Elizabeth's library for 30 minutes once a week. She and two mother volunteers work with approximately 20 children. For half the allotted time, Elizabeth either reads them a story or gives a lesson showing them how the library is organized. Then the children find a book. Some take the whole remaining time; others choose their books quickly and begin reading, perhaps with an adult to read to. Each child chooses one free-choice book and one reading book. Elizabeth thinks it important for children to find books they want to read. Here are her thoughts on how to do this.*

*How do you help children find "the right book" for them?*

The volunteer mothers and I listen to what the child is looking for. We also help the children to be independent in finding what they want in the library. Since the children are young and are new readers, I have lots of labels, both written and pictures. For example, books about animals are quite popular, so I have a picture of an animal like a zebra in front of where books about that animal are located. Often I display the covers of books, not just the spines. We have an online cataloging system. Even with kindergartners, we model how to use the online cataloging system, and by the second grade, the children are using the keyboard and using the catalog by themselves.

Sometimes children choose books that may be too hard for them. I show them the "five finger test"—they read a page, and if there are more then five words they don't recognize, they probably need an easier book. I never force a child to change books. If a child is quite interested in a book, he or she will put a lot of effort into it. I consider the taking of books to be a privilege. The children often choose fairy tales. It surprises me how much they choose nonfiction books, especially books about animals. They often choose books about weather in the news, like tornadoes and hurricanes.

*There are so many great children's books being published, plus many classics. How do you keep current?*

I constantly read reviews in such journals as the *School Library Journal* and *Horn Book*. Once a month I go to the county library. They arrange new books by the Dewey system—that is, all the science books, math books, biographies, picture books, chapter books, and fiction books are grouped together. At the beginning of the day, someone talks for about an hour on the new books that particular person thinks are extraordinary. The rest of the day, I browse through the books. After this, I decide what books to buy, considering our curriculum needs.

*Multicultural literature is much talked about in recent years. How does this trend enter into your work as a school librarian?*

I see it as quite important. I think children need to be aware of how many different people there are in the world. I focus on different cultures, and there is so much good material coming out in this area. I go to the Virginia Hamilton Conference of Multicultural Literature each year, which always spotlights three different authors. One year I heard Eloise Greenfield, an African American who writes wonderful, elevating poems and stories; Vera B. Williams, who tells stories of Jewish life in New York City; and Ashley Bryant, an African American illustrator.

*How do you work with teachers?*

I have a form teachers complete to let me know the topics they are working on. For example, one teacher wants books about the ocean. They also request sets of early readers for their classrooms.

I bring an author or an illustrator to the school for Right to Read week. The guests generally talk about how they wrote or illustrated their books. Children love this. We are fortunate that the PTA gives us money for this. This year we will have Marilyn Sadler, originally a British author who wrote the Alistar series and the Funny Bunny series.

We participate in the Buckeye Children's Award. I read the books to the children, and they vote for their favorite books. The children get quite excited to know which books win. During Black History Month, I have African American parents come to the library and share their favorite books.

### REFLECTIVE INQUIRY

◆ How can you help children find "the right book" for them?
◆ There are so many great children's books being published, plus many classics. How can you keep current?
◆ Multicultural literature is much talked about in recent years. How does this trend enter into your work as a teacher?

# Organizing for Literature-Based Instruction

Organizing patterns for literature-based instruction vary from structured whole class studies of **core books** to independent reading of self-selected books in **literature units, reading workshops,** and **literature circles.** The integration of the Internet with literature is also an organizational consideration. Just as time, response, and choice are important in writing, these factors are also critical to the success of literature-based reading programs.

## Core Books

Sometimes teachers will organize literature around the study of core books. In some schools, a set of core books forms the nucleus of the reading program at each grade level (Routman, 1991). A curriculum committee of teachers throughout the district is often assigned to develop a collection of books at each grade that is judged to be age-appropriate and of high quality.

Core books are taught within the framework of whole class study. Students have little or no choice in the selection of core books. As part of a whole class study, teachers assign various activities and use a variety of instructional strategies to support students' interactions with the texts. Many of the comprehension, vocabulary, word identification, and fluency strategies discussed in this book are easily adapted to the study of core books.

Often teachers use core books as springboards for independent reading in which children choose books with related themes and situations or decide to read other works by an author they have studied. For example, when Brenda Church taught in an inner-city fifth grade In Akron, she introduced a unit on survival by having her students do a whole class study of Jean George's *Julie of the Wolves.* As the unit evolved, the students also read novels in groups. They would select a novel from the choices that Brenda gave them from a book list.

A major problem with the core book approach is the risk of "basalizing" literature. Core books and novels should not be treated like basal textbooks, whose major purpose is to organize instruction around the teaching of reading skills. Basalization could lead to students' completing worksheets, responding to literal comprehension questions, and engaging in round-robin reading (Zarrillo, 1989).

## Literature Units

Teachers also organize instruction around literature units. Literature units, also known as **thematic** and **integrated instruction,** usually have a unifying element such as the study of a genre, an author, or a conceptual theme. With literature units, a teacher usually chooses the theme (or negotiates one with the students) and pulls together a collection of books relating to the theme; the students, however, have options as to what books to choose from the collection and what activities they might pursue. Successful literature units strike a balance between whole class, small group, and individually selected activities.

## Reading Workshops

Nancie Atwell (1998) originated the reading workshop as a way to integrate the language arts around literature. Reading workshops provide an organizational framework that allows readers to demonstrate their use of reading strategies by responding to books and sharing meaning with others. Reutzel and Cooter (1991) describe how Atwell's reading workshop, with several modifications, can work with elementary school children.

The reading workshop has several key features:

**SPARKING INTEREST** ◆ The teacher shares literature. Reutzel and Cooter (1991) provide an example of a teacher reading about vampires and ghouls from Jack Prelutsky's collection of poetry called *Nightmares: Poems to Trouble Your Sleep* while showing overhead transparencies of some of the book's spooky pen-and-ink sketches. In this way, the teacher sparks interest in various literary genres for free reading.

**MINILESSONS** ◆ The teacher takes several minutes after sharing time to demonstrate a reading strategy through explicit teaching. The focus of a minilesson is often drawn from the observed needs of students, at times discovered during individual reading conferences.

**STATUS-OF-THE-CLASS REPORT** ◆ A status-of-the-class chart helps both teacher and students monitor their responsibilities and progress in a reading workshop. The teacher briefly surveys the class to determine how each student plans to use his or her time during sustained silent reading time and/or group activity. The teacher records students' responses on a chart and, as a result, has a record of each student's commitment for the day. Once students are familiar with the status-of-the-class report, the process takes no more than 5 minutes a day to complete.

**SUSTAINED SILENT READING** ◆ During sustained silent reading, everyone, including the teacher, reads. This free-reading phase varies from classroom to classroom but accounts for a significant amount of class time as students select and read books of their own choosing. They also keep up-to-date logs recording time spent reading, titles of books read, and when they plan to have individual conferences with the teacher.

**INDIVIDUAL READING CONFERENCES** ◆ Each day, the teacher meets with one or more students for an individual reading conference. Students make appointments on a sign-up board at least one day prior to the conference. Many teachers require that each student have at least three conferences per grading period. During the reading conferences, the teacher and the student discuss the book the student is currently reading. Questions such as the following can be used to guide the conference:

> What part did you find particularly interesting? Funny? Thrilling? Why?
>
> Did anything in the book bring to mind an experience you have had? What was it?
>
> How was it similar to or different from what happened in the story?
>
> Why do you think the author wrote this book?

Individual reading conferences generally last from 5 to 8 minutes.

**GROUP SHARING TIME** ◆ At the end of a reading workshop, the class comes together for 10 minutes or so to share details about the books they are engaged in and the activities they have been working on.

Like reading workshops, literature circles involve students in extending personal responses to literature and provide another way of organizing the classroom.

## Literature Circles

Historically, teachers grouped students on the basis of measured reading ability. Recently, however, educators have questioned that practice because such grouping limits student choice, interest, and motivation. The criticism of grouping students by ability has led

**BUILDING TEACHING SKILLS: CASE STUDY**

Go to the Homework and Exercises section in Chapter 12 of MyEducationLab to read the case study "Literature Circles Open the World of Literature" to develop an understanding of how you could implement literature circles in your classroom.

practitioners to experiment with heterogeneous groups reading a common text (e.g., Atwell, 1998; Keegan & Shake, 1991) and whole class models such as the previously described use of core books. Further, teachers and researchers have been collaborating on how to work with groups of children leading their own discussions. By studying transcripts of students participating in student-led literature groups (McMahon, 1997), two such teacher-researchers, Deb and Laura, became aware that students they perceived as "average" and "weak" readers were quite articulate when orally expressing their ideas in student-led groups. At the same time, some of the "good" readers responded to their classmates in these groups in ways that were extremely text based and thus did not connect what they read to other reading or to their own or others' experiences.

Many teachers now seek to move beyond developing reading fluency and comprehension. They want to provide students with time and opportunity to use language to express ideas and explain their thinking to each other and in this way extend their thinking (Villaume, Worden, Williams, Hopkins, & Rosenblatt, 1994). They see literature circles as a way to do this for all students, including linguistically and culturally diverse learners (Samway & Whang, 1996) and learners with special needs (Gilles, 1990). Teachers who implement literature circles (also known as *literature study groups* and *book clubs*) rely on cooperative learning strategies that show students how to work together and discuss books on the basis of their personal responses to what they have read.

Daniels (1994) defines *literature circles* in this way:

> Literature circles are small, temporary discussion groups [that] have chosen to read the same story, poem, article, or book. While reading each group-determined portion of the text (either in or outside of class), each member prepares to take specific responsibilities in the upcoming discussion, and everyone comes to the group with the notes needed to help perform that job. The circles have regular meetings, with discussion roles rotating each session. When they finish a book, the circle members plan a way to share highlights of their reading with the wider community; then they trade members with other finishing groups, select more reading, and move into a new cycle. Once readers can successfully conduct their own wide-ranging, self-sustaining discussions, formal discussion roles may be dropped. (p. 13)

Gay, a third-grade teacher, organizes literature circles in her classroom. Gay introduces to the class potentially worthwhile books for discussion. If a book is fictional, she builds interest in the story by overviewing its plot, acquainting the students with characters, and reading parts of the story aloud. If the book is informational, she builds anticipation by overviewing the content, reading aloud, and showing the students illustrations from the text. The students then select the books they want to read. Teams are formed not by ability level but by choice of reading material (Vacca & Rasinski, 1992).

Thus in the ideal classroom, the size of the literature circle is determined by the number of students who freely choose a particular book. In real classrooms, some decision making and negotiation may be necessary to achieve groups of productive size. The preferred size for literature circle groups among Chicago-area teachers who worked with Harvey Daniels (1994) was four or five in the middle grades and three or four in the primary grades. This size allows for a productive mix of perspectives and roles without distractions and inefficiencies. Therefore, compromises concerning who reads which books do have to occur. If six students want to read the same book, a decision needs to be made: "Do we want two groups of three or one group of six?" If only two students are interested in a book, the teacher needs to decide if the two will generate enough insightful interactions. If not, the students should be asked to make a second choice to end up in a group of more appropriate size. The teacher may need to say things like, "OK, if you'll read *Hatchet* now and be the fourth member of this group, I'll help you get a group together for *The Phantom Tollbooth* the next cycle" (p. 60).

Jane is a fourth-grade teacher who is enthusiastic about literature circles. When it is time for literature circles, students bring three items to the group: the book their circle is reading, response journals and drawings reflecting their ideas about their reading, and completed role sheets for the roles Jane chose for the circles. Jane uses the roles delineated in Daniels's book, *Literature Circles: Voice and Choice in One Student-Centered Classroom* (1994). These roles are defined in the Research-Based Practices illustrated in Box 12.4. On this day, the roles were *discussion director, literary luminary, connector,* and *word wizard.* After a few minutes of settling and joking, the groups began working. For the next 30 minutes, these 10-year-olds conversed with each other using open-ended questions and read passages to prove points or settle disagreements. They kept one eye on the clock to make sure everyone got a fair share of talking. Some of the books discussed in these literature circles were Katherine Paterson's *Bridge to Terabithia,* Daniel Keyes's *Flowers for Algernon,* H. G. Wells's *War of the Worlds,* and Beverly Cleary's *Dear Mr. Henshaw.*

Let's explore further how a teacher can give students of all abilities the opportunity to read and discuss literature in student-led groups by looking at how to share and what to share in literature circles.

**STUDENT-LED LITERATURE CIRCLES: HOW AND WHAT TO SHARE** ◆ Teachers whose students lead their own literature circles need to explain clearly that these groups help participants explore different perspectives that each person brings to the discussion. Students are to evaluate, critique, and revise their own individual responses in light of the perspectives their peers express. To clarify how to participate in literature circles, emphasize the differences between "school talk" and "outside-school talk." Through discussion, students will conclude that in most classroom interactions, the teacher asks questions and students answer. "Outside-school talk" is characterized by talking when someone has an

---

**BOX 12.4**

## Research-Based Practices

### Roles for Literature Circles

Literature circle roles rotate every time the group meets. Two students can have the same role in a group meeting.

#### Required Roles

**DISCUSSION DIRECTOR**

Has the official responsibility to think up some good discussion questions, convene the meeting, and solicit contributions from the other members.

**LITERARY LUMINARY/PASSAGE MASTER**

Takes the readers back to memorable, important sections of the text and reads them aloud.

**CONNECTOR**

Takes everyone from the text world out into the real world, where the reader's experiences connect with the literature.

**ILLUSTRATOR**

Provides a graphic, nonlinguistic response to the text.

#### Optional Roles

**SUMMARIZER**

Gives a quick (1- or 2-minute) statement of the gist, key points, and highlights of the day's reading when the group convenes.

**VOCABULARY ENRICHER/WORD WIZARD**

Marks down puzzling, interesting, or unfamiliar words encountered while reading, looks them up in a glossary or dictionary if need be, and points them out during literature circle.

**TRAVEL TRACER**

Tracks where the action takes place in the book. (This is useful in books in which the characters move around a lot and the scene changes frequently.)

**INVESTIGATOR/RESEARCHER**

Digs up background information on any topic related to the book (e.g., geography, history, information about the author).

*Source:* Based on *Literature Circles: Voice and Choice in One Student-Centered Classroom,* by H. Daniels (York, ME: Stenhouse, 1994).

idea to share; thus sometimes there is overlapping talk. Further, it is important to note that different members of the group informally assume responsibility for maintaining the conversation. In working with a diverse group of learners, action researcher Virginia Goatley (1997) formulated the following strategies for students participating in literature circles:

HOW TO SHARE

1. Maintain conversations without long pauses.
2. Respond to questions asked by other participants.
3. Elaborate your response to include your reason for the answer.
4. Challenge others' interpretations of the story.
5. Clarify ideas, questions, answers, and responses.
6. Stay on task.
7. Include all group members in the discussion.
8. Take turns.

WHAT TO SHARE

1. Written responses that support discussion
2. Questions for clarification and interest
3. Personal responses, prior knowledge, personal experiences
4. Comprehension activities that construct meaning and support ideas
5. Interpretations beyond the literal level
6. Feelings about the text
7. Connections between books, movies, and shows
8. Evaluation of the text

These can be modeled and explored in whole class discussions while watching a videotape of a literature circle in action. Also, as children talk to each other in student-led literature circles, the teacher can walk from group to group, facilitating the use of these conversational skills. Sometimes the students' conversations will wander to topics other than the book, and at other times members will be silent and need to be encouraged to participate. The teacher joins a group just long enough to help members identify the problem and solve it. Laura and Deb found that this modeling and analysis of the litera- ture groups took up significant instructional time at the beginning of the school year; however, as students learned to assume responsibility for their own discussions, the need for modeling, discussion, and intervention diminished.

Another way to guide students to take responsibility for their own literature discussion is through the use of self-assessment (see Figure 12.2 on page 412). Students complete the form, and then the teacher helps them see how to solve their own dilemmas and what they could do the next time the group meets (McMahon, 1997).

**ADAPTING LITERATURE CIRCLES FOR THE PRIMARY GRADES** ◆ Daniels (1994) describes how Angie Bynam's 32 second graders in a Chicago housing project met regu- larly in literature circles. Angie has a large number of picture books in multiple-copy sets that she received through a grant from the *Chicago Tribune*. She displays these titles in face-up stacks. When it is literature circle time, the children browse through these books, gradually forming groups of four or five. It takes about 10 minutes for the children to look through the books, talk, and negotiate. Some children choose to reread old favor- ites; others venture into new ones. Each group then checks in at Angie's desk, where she gives role sheets to members of the group.

Within the group, children sit in a circle and take turns reading the book aloud to each other. Then they take a few moments to make some notes on their role sheet. The discussion director begins the conversation. As is true of literature circles with middle school students, the discussion is natural and spontaneous. The entire process of select- ing books, forming groups, reading, and discussing the books takes about 45 minutes.

## Figure 12.2  Self-Assessment in Literature Circles

Name: _____          Book: _____

### Looking Back and Forward

|  | Date | Date | Date | Date |
|---|---|---|---|---|
| Did I share during literature circles? |  |  |  |  |
| Were my comments relevant to the discussion? |  |  |  |  |
| Did I let others have a turn? |  |  |  |  |
| Did I listen to others? |  |  |  |  |
| Did I offer to help when it was needed? |  |  |  |  |

Important comments: (What would I do the same and different the next time?)

Daniels (1994) points out that few adults realize that children so young are capable of such child-directed activity.

Here are some guidelines that primary teachers can use to adjust literature circles to their students (Daniels, 1994, pp. 107–109):

- Primary literature circles should have a maximum of three or four participants.
- The books should be appropriate for emergent readers; that is, they should be picture books, wordless books, big books, or children-made books.
- The books are read aloud so that everyone comprehends the story.
- The children record their responses in writing with invented spellings or in drawing.
- Even with their reading logs or notes, young children may need extra help remembering what they want to share. Some teachers have their students use large sticky notes to mark their favorite parts of a book.
- Some primary teachers organize literature circles in which children read different books and meet in a literature circle to share different books.
- Primary literature circles may be organized so that children do not take different roles. In this case, all the children have the same two-part job: (1) to share something of their book using their writing and/or drawing log and bookmarks as cues and (2) to join in an open discussion.
- Primary literature circles tend to be one-meeting-per-book events owing to short books and short attention spans.
- The teacher is present during the primary literature circle, and just as with middle school students, the teacher's role is to facilitate the process, not direct it.

BOX **12.5**

*New Literacies*

## COLLABORATIVE LITERATURE PROJECT, PEER RESPONSE, AND NEW LITERACIES

New literacies provide the means and motivation for students to develop, share, discuss, and appreciate student reading and writing. A collaborative literature project can include all of these components as well as develop peer response. Collaborative literature research projects occur when two students work together to research a specific topic. One student posts the research project topic on his or her web site for accessibility of the partners and the teacher. The students then complete the research project by reading literature, researching information, and making use of hypertext documents. The use of streaming videos and graphic illustrations from the Web are also encouraged.

The students collaboratively work on the project and keep the postings up to date. The teacher provides guidance and feedback as the students proceed through the research project.

The teacher also posts reader response questions for peers to offer feedback to the collaborative research team. Peer feedback can be posted. The teacher needs to be sure that the students have been informed on appropriate feedback responses to ensure support and provide informative feedback rather than criticize and judge.

Having the literature research process include new literacies provides the researchers as well as the peers the opportunity to learn from each other and show respect for others' opinions. The structure expands from a two student research project to a more open collaborative process. All students involved learn by discussing, collaborating, connecting, reviewing, and responding. These are all essential skills needed when utilizing new literacies.

**INTEGRATION OF THE INTERNET** ◆ Teachers also organize literature around the Internet. "Today, opportunities exist for our students to travel to new places and experience richer and more powerful responses to children's literature when the Internet is thoughtfully integrated with the classroom literature program" (Leu, Castek, Henry, Coiro, & McMullan, 2004, p. 497). Lessons that rely upon the students searching specific Internet sites facilitate conceptual development. In addition, Leu et al. (2004) point out that integration of the Internet in a literature program expands response opportunities, develops new literacies related to information technologies, and provides opportunities to help students better understand cultural diversity (see Box 12.5). A few recommended Internet sites that develop these ideals are:

Book Adventure (www.bookadventure.com)

Book Raps (www.oz-teachernet.edu.au/projects/br)

Children's Literature Webguide (www.acs.ucalgary.ca/~dkbrown)

Education World (www.education-world.com)

Kids Search Tools (www.rcls.org/ksearch.htm)

Poem Hunter (www.poemhunter.com/poems)

## *Encouraging Responses to Literature*

After reading a book or seeing a movie, we may share the experience by briefly describing the plot. Most often, though, we tell how we felt and why. We point out something in the film or text and/or our personal histories that made us feel the way we did. We give examples from our lives and retell parts of the story. Yet when discussion shifts to the classroom, what usually happens? Often teachers ask questions to elicit a "right answer." Because we have often tried to evaluate what and how much

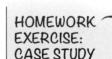

**HOMEWORK EXERCISE: CASE STUDY**

Go to the Homework and Exercises section in Chapter 12 of MyEducationLab to review the case study "Art Responses to Literature" to learn how a high school teacher combines an art response assignment with literature.

Reader response to literature is critical to developing a lifelong appreciation of the literacy experience. Students who develop an aesthetic appreciation for literature tap into their emotional reactions to the story.

students have understood about the text, teachers spend little time helping students explore, defend, or elaborate on ideas. In this section, we explore the need to lead students in classroom experiences in which they analyze their *personal* reactions to what they have read. Such action supports a **reader-response theory,** a theory that proclaims that *the reader is crucial to the construction of the literary experience.*

Louise Rosenblatt (1982) was one of the earliest proponents of a reader-response theory. She stated:

> Reading is a transaction, a two-way process, involving a reader and a text at a particular time under particular circumstances. . . . The reader, bringing past experiences of language and of the world to the task, sets up tentative notions of a subject, of some framework into which to fit the ideas as the words unfurl. If the subsequent words do not fit into the framework, it may have to be revised, thus opening up new and further possibilities for the text that follows. This implies a constant series of selections from the multiple possibilities offered by the text and their synthesis into an organized meaning. (p. 268)

Every reading event or transaction involves a reader and a text (a set of signs capable of being interpreted as verbal symbols); meaning that results from the transaction are dependent on both entities (Rosenblatt, 2004). They are not mutually exclusive. Rosenblatt took her analysis of reading one step further into implications for classroom literature discussions. In any reading event, the reader adopts one of two stances: the **efferent stance** or the **aesthetic stance.**

When a reader approaches a reading event with an efferent stance, attention is focused on accumulating what is to be carried away from the reading. Readers using this stance may be seeking information, as in a textbook; they may want directions for action, as in a driver's manual; or they may be seeking a logical conclusion, as in a political article. In an aesthetic stance, however, readers shift their attention inward to center on *what is being created during the reading.* Reading is driven by personal feelings, ideas, and attitudes that are stirred up by the text.

In most reading situations, there is both an efferent and an aesthetic response to the text. In reading a newspaper article, for example, a reader may take a predominantly efferent stance, but there may be an accompanying feeling of acceptance or doubt about the evidence cited. Although one stance usually predominates in most reading events, the text itself does not dictate a reader's stance. A text is chosen because it satisfies a reader's intended purpose. Rosenblatt's (1982) description of what happens in predominantly aesthetic reading situations holds direct implications for bringing children and literature together:

> In aesthetic reading, we respond to the very story or poem that we are evoking during the transaction with the text. In order to shape the work, we draw on our reservoir of past experience with people and the world, our past inner linkage of words and things, our past encounters with spoken or written texts. We listen to the sound of the words in the inner ear; we lend our sensations, our emotions, our sense of being alive, to the new experience which, we feel, corresponds to the text. We participate in the story, we identify with the characters, we share their conflicts and their feelings. (p. 270)

Teachers create responsive environments in their classrooms by inviting students of all abilities and from diverse backgrounds to react to literature through various symbol systems and modes of expression: art, movement, music, creative drama, talk, writing. Alternative forms of communication such as art or movement are especially appealing for students who may have difficulty expressing their feelings and thoughts in words. When children connect drawing with reading, for example, their artwork often helps them discover and shape their response to a story. Various visual arts media—pencil drawings, chalk, markers, crayons, paint, cardboard, paper construction, computer-based art, and paint programs—can be used to encourage responses to literature. In addition, students can design book jackets, mobiles, posters, comic strips, or PowerPoint presentations to capture the personal appeal or meaning that texts evoke.

Drawing, creative drama, role playing, and computer-generated projects often serve as springboards for oral and written responses. Children, especially at the primary level, gravitate naturally to drawing or dramatically performing a story before they talk or write about it.

## Sparking Discussion with Book-Talks

Whole class study of core books, reading workshops, and literature circles provide numerous opportunities for children to talk about books. Having **book-talks** is a great way to evoke children's responses to literature. The different types of discussions that evolve from student- or teacher-led small group or whole class formats lead students of all grades to acquire language skills and response strategies for the appropriate discussion genres (Galda & Beach, 2004). Utilizing the various discussion types also provides English learners the opportunity to develop language, literacy, and critical thinking skills. Here are some suggestions to spark book discussions:

1. Depending on the text, ask questions such as "Did anything especially interest you? Frighten you? Puzzle you? Seem familiar? Seem weird?" Have students tell which parts of the text caused these reactions, and have them compare these experiences to their real-life experiences (Rosenblatt, 1982).
2. Have children tell about the most memorable incident, character, or setting of the book. Then have them share with each other the specific parts of the text they recalled most clearly after hearing or reading the story (Benton, 1984).
3. Ask students to tell about the part of the story or character they remember most vividly. For example, "How did that character feel in this part of the story?" "Have you ever felt like this?" "Describe the situation you were in."
4. Read the opening of a story. Immediately afterward, tell students to jot down what was going on in their heads—pictures, memories, thoughts—during the reading. The jottings should be in a stream-of-consciousness style. Then share the responses and distinguish the common responses from the idiosyncratic ones. This shows students that reading has shared elements as well as highly individual ones and that sharing reactions is a valid way of talking about literature (Benton, 1984).
5. Ask students, "What pictures do you get in your mind of this character, setting, or event?" "If character $X$ were to come through the door now, what would he or she look like?" "If you went to the place where the story occurred (i.e., setting), what would you see?" "Why do you say so?"
6. Ask, "What do you feel about this character? This setting? This event? Why?"
7. Ask, "What opinions do you have of this character? Setting? Incident? The way the story was told? Why?"

Book-talks encourage children to go beyond a literal retelling of a story. The collaborative nature of book-talks helps students relate reading to prior knowledge, construct meaning, critique related texts, and share personal responses (Raphael, McMahon, Goatley, Boyd, Pardo, & Woodman, 1992). Book-talks can be used in concert with a free-response heuristic to help students discover and shape their responses

**HOMEWORK EXERCISE: CASE STUDY**

Go to the Homework and Exercises section in Chapter 12 of MyEducationLab to watch the video "Teaching with Literature" and consider how a teacher can use guided reading to enable various levels of readers to participate.

DIVERSITY ELL

to literature. A heuristic, by its nature, is any kind of a prompt that stimulates inquiry and speculation.

## Engaging in Free Response

**Free response** encourages active involvement in reading and an integration of students' background knowledge with the selection's meaning. This technique generates a spirited discussion going far beyond the recall of information. Inferential, evaluative, and analytic thinking are the rule when children's free responses are discussed (Santa, Dailey, & Nelson, 1985).

Free response works well with literature selections that generate diversity of opinion or emotional reactions from readers. The first time a group of students is guided through free response, they hear a portion of a narrative and then stop to respond in writing. Primary students, for example, might be given 3 minutes to respond in writing, and middle school students 5 minutes. Analyzing the structure of a particular story is useful in determining where to make the breaks for students to respond.

Mrs. Nowak used a free-response heuristic with her second-grade class for *Thomas' Snowsuit* by Robert Munsch (1985) and illustrated by Michael Martchenko. This story is a humorous treatment of power struggles between Thomas, who does not want to wear his new snowsuit, and his mother. The power struggle concerning whether he should wear his snowsuit continues with his teacher and the principal at school.

Mrs. Nowak introduced the story to her class by asking if the children could recall not wanting to wear some clothing they were supposed to wear. A lively discussion ensued. Then Mrs. Nowak asked what they thought *Thomas' Snowsuit* would be about, and the children had no difficulty predicting that Thomas didn't want to wear his snowsuit. Mrs. Nowak then began reading.

> One day Thomas' mother bought him a nice new brown snowsuit. When Thomas saw that snowsuit, he said, "That is the ugliest thing I have ever seen in my life. If you think I am going to wear that ugly snowsuit, you are crazy!"
>
> Thomas' mother said, "We will see about that."
>
> The next day, when it was time to go to school, the mother said, "Thomas, please put on your snowsuit," and Thomas said, "NNNNNO."

Mrs. Nowak stopped reading and asked her students to write down their reactions to what they had just heard. She emphasized that "any thought related to the story is correct; there are no wrong responses." After several segments of reading and responding, Mrs. Nowak led a discussion in which the children shared their free responses. When she asked their reactions to Thomas's telling his mother, "NNNNNO," Jeremy said, "He's going to get into trouble!" Sue said, "I wouldn't want to wear an old brown snowsuit, either." After each response, Mrs. Nowak probed, "Why do you think so?" Mrs. Nowak remained impartial, and the children's responses became a catalyst for discussion.

Santa and colleagues (1985) recommend that when students are freely responding independently, teachers develop with their students criteria for free response, which are then displayed in the classroom.

Things that I like or dislike about a character or event.

Questions about things I do not understand.

Comments about what I think an unfamiliar word might mean.

Events from my life that come to mind as I read.

Situations or events with which I do not agree.

Can I make predictions? What will happen next? Is the author giving me a clue here?

These heuristic situations prompt students to view reading as a problem-solving activity. As such, free response is easily incorporated into the use of reading journals that help students explore and clarify their responses to text. Various kinds of reading journals, as we explored in Chapter 11, encourage children to solve problems as they respond to meaning during reading. Response journals, in particular, invite students of all abilities and from diverse backgrounds to respond to literature freely and personally. Their responses vary from monitoring understanding to plot and character involvement to literary evaluation.

## Exploring Response Options in Literature Journals

**Literature journals** provide readers with the freedom to express their feelings and perceptions about literary texts. They help students to communicate their thoughts during and after reading as well as before discussion (Galda & Beach, 2004). The potential for students to do more than summarize the text is omnipresent when they are invited to write freely as they engage in reading. Research on the content of literature journals shows that readers often expand their ways of thinking about a text beyond retelling when they write journal entries or literary letters on a regular basis (Hancock, 1993a, 1993b; Wells, 1993).

Teachers can enhance the variety of reader responses by making children aware of the various options for responding in a literature journal. As Hancock (1993a) explains, "The classroom teacher plays a vital role in the expansion and enrichment of student response to literature. The teacher serves as a catalyst for encouraging exploration [of response options]. . . . Striving to awaken new modes of response within the reader is the responsibility of the teacher in the role of facilitator and response guide" (p. 470).

Hancock (1993b) explores the journal responses of sixth-grade students to several award-winning books: *Hatchet* by Gary Paulsen, *One-Eyed Cat* by Paula Fox, *The Great Gilly Hopkins* by Katherine Paterson, and *The Night Swimmers* by Betsy Cromer Byars. As a result of her analysis of the content of the students' literature journals, Hancock identified three categories of response: *personal meaning-making, character and plot involvement,* and *literary evaluation.* Table 12.1 on the next page outlines response options available to students in these three categories.

Options for personal meaning-making encourage students to make sense of the emerging plot and characters. Journal entries might reflect the students' attempts to monitor understanding of the story; make inferences about characters; make, validate, modify, or invalidate predictions about the plot; and express wonder or confusion by asking questions or raising uncertainties.

Options for character and plot responses engage students in character identification, character assessment, and personal involvement in the unfolding events of the story. For example, some students will identify strongly with the goals and problems associated with the main character of the story; they put themselves in the character's shoes. As a result, the reader may express a strong sense of empathy for the character's predicament. Readers will also judge the actions of characters within the framework of their own moral standards and value systems. Moreover, students' responses suggest that they become personally involved in the story, expressing satisfaction or dissatisfaction as they become caught up in the plot.

Finally, readers take on the role of literary critic as they evaluate authors or make comparisons with other books they have read.

A crucial step in becoming a catalyst for student response is to share guidelines, such as those suggested in Chapter 11, for writing in literature journals. In the guidelines, it is especially important to establish an environment for response by encouraging students to react freely and informally without fear of making mechanical writing errors. Also, suggest different response options as outlined in Table 12.1.

In addition, one of the most effective ways to extend response options is to start a dialogue with students in their journals. A teacher's comments in response to a journal

## *Table* 12.1    Response Options for Literature Journals

| RESPONSE OPTION | EXAMPLE |
| --- | --- |
| **Personal Meaning-Making** | |
| Monitoring understanding | In this story, Brian has divorced parents. (*Hatchet*) |
| | Ned's really taking the gun being put away really hard. (*One-Eyed Cat*) |
| | Oh, now I get it. The door is too heavy for the animals to open. (*Hatchet*) |
| | These past few pages show how one lie can lead to a whole series of lies. (*One-Eyed Cat*) |
| Making inferences | I think Gilly is jealous of W.E. because Trotter loves him. (*The Great Gilly Hopkins*) |
| | Brian must be very very hungry to eat a raw egg. (*Hatchet*) |
| | Ned probably doesn't mean he wants the cat to die. (*One-Eyed Cat*) |
| | Retta seems a little like Gilly Hopkins—rebellious and different. (*The Night Swimmers*) |
| Making predictions | I think the Secret was his mom's dating another man. (*Hatchet*) |
| | I was right about the Secret! (*Hatchet*) |
| | I bet Gilly's mother won't show up. (*The Great Gilly Hopkins*) |
| | I didn't think she'd steal the money. (*The Great Gilly Hopkins*) |
| Expressing wonder or confusion | I wonder if Gilly is so mean because she wasn't brought up by her own mother. (*The Great Gilly Hopkins*) |
| | The author is telling so many things . . . I got lost on p. 28. (*Hatchet*) |
| | Is that cat supposed to be playing the role of some sort of sign? (*One-Eyed Cat*) |
| | Bowlwater plant? Are these people really cheap or what? TV Ping Pong? (*The Night Swimmers*) |
| **Character and Plot Involvement** | |
| Character identification | If I were Ned, I'd want to get the thought out of my head. (*One-Eyed Cat*) |
| | Poor Gilly. I guess that's the way it is if you're a foster kid. (*The Great Gilly Hopkins*) |
| | Johnny is like my brother. Roy is like my sister. I'm like Retta, not so bossy. (*The Night Swimmers*) |
| | He shouldn't waste time waiting for the searchers; he should get food. (*Hatchet*) |
| Character assessment | Brian is stupid for ripping a $20 bill. (*Hatchet*) |
| | It's really mean of Gilly to use W.E. in a plan to run away. (*The Great Gilly Hopkins*) |
| | I don't think I like Mrs. Scallop. She is sort of mean and has crazy ideas like that Ned's mother got sick because Ned was born. (*One-Eyed Cat*) |
| | Brian is getting better and having less self-pity on himself. (*Hatchet*) |
| Story involvement | Eyes rolling back in his head until it is white showing. How gross! (*Hatchet*) |
| | The scenery sounds so pretty. (*One-Eyed Cat*) |
| | I wish Ned hadn't shot that poor cat. He did though. (*One-Eyed Cat*) |
| | I can't wait to get on with my reading. I hope Shorty asks Brendelle to marry him. (*The Night Swimmers*) |
| **Literary Evaluation** | |
| Literary criticism | These were boring pages because all they talked about were fish. (*Hatchet*) |
| | I don't think the author should have Gilly use swear words. (*The Great Gilly Hopkins*) |
| | I like this author because she has some suspense like the spy. (*The Night Swimmers*) |
| | This is fun reading this part because it's like *My Side of the Mountain*. (*Hatchet*) |

*Source:* Based on "Exploring and Extending Personal Response Through Literature Journals," by M. R. Hancock, 1993,
*The Reading Teacher, 46,* pp. 466–474.

entry will help students reexamine their responses to the text. When responding to journal entries, it is best to be nonjudgmental, encouraging, and thought-provoking. Once a supportive comment is written, the teacher may decide to direct a student toward an unexplored area of response. Hancock (1993a) describes how Michael wrote many responses (about 40 percent) relating why he did or did not like the book he was reading. He was mainly using his journal as a place to express his *literary evaluations*. Here is one such entry:

> This is getting real boring because the author is writing so much about one thing. The author keeps going back to the same thing "Mistakes" this is getting boring.

His teacher wrote back the following comments:

> I really appreciate your efforts to critique *Hatchet*. It seems that you are a bit disillusioned with some of Brian's actions. You've been attributing that dissatisfaction to the author. Have you thought of sharing your advice with Brian?
>
> Although he can't really hear you, your suggestions for plot changes may be directed to the main character as well as to the author. You may even find your involvement in the book will increase if you feel you can talk to Brian. Give this a try and see if you feel comfortable with this mode of response. (p. 472)

Interactive comments such as these help students refocus and redirect their responses to a literary text; they pave the way to personal meaning-making.

## WHAT ABOUT STRUGGLING READERS AND *Literature?*

STANDARD
4.2

Providing access to literature that relates to each individual student's interests, needs, and abilities is essential in an environment that supports a community of readers. It is also important to provide opportunities for readers to share and learn from books.

When working with readers, especially struggling readers, it is necessary to match student and text. The teacher should encourage readers to read books from a variety of genres at their independent reading level. The teacher can help the student choose these books, but, more important, it is essential to help the reader self-select the most *appropriate piece of literature*.

One technique that readers can use to facilitate this process is the five finger method. Following is the procedure for Veatch's (1968) five finger test:

1. The student chooses a book of interest and opens the book to a page with a large amount of print.
2. The student starts reading at the top of the page. Each time the student runs into a word that he or she doesn't know (pronunciation or meaning), he or she puts up a finger.
3. The student continues to read to the end of the page and puts up a finger for each unknown word.
4. In order to decide on the correct level of book to read, the number of fingers raised will determine the level: 0–1 easy, 2–5 medium difficulty, 6 or more challenging.

A good choice for the struggling reader is either an easy book or one on the medium difficulty level depending on the level of interest. Students can also self-select with the Goldilock's Rule where students ask themselves if the book is too hard, too easy, or just right (Taberski, 2000).

Once the books have been chosen and students have access to them, it is important that the teacher supports all readers, especially the struggling reader, by creating occasions to share and respond to literature. In a literacy-rich environment, time is reserved for sustained silent reading and various reading modeling opportunities (such as teacher read-aloud, peer read-aloud, buddy reading, books on tape, and talking books). Literature circles and book buddies also provide opportunities for the students to share insights. Time set aside for individual conferences also helps encourage the teacher and student to share and exchange reflections about books, authors, illustrators, and writing styles. Finally, in a literate environment, students are encouraged to respond to texts in their own way. The use of free-response journals in formats made appropriate for the individual struggling reader's abilities, such as the use of invented spelling and artwork, needs to be accepted and encouraged.

Supporting a community of readers, especially the struggling reader, is essential. Surrounding students with literature and providing opportunities for sharing and learning from literature are important in all classrooms for literacy development.

## WHAT ABOUT STANDARDS, ASSESSMENT, AND *Literature?*

The ability to read literary and information texts is an important component of all statewide proficiency assessments in reading and language arts. In addition, most proficiency assessments outside of reading are in actuality assessments of literacy. In order to respond to content-specific assessment questions, students need to be able to read and write effectively. It's not surprising, then, that the first two content standards in the *Standards for the English Language Arts* (International Reading Association and National Council of Teachers of English, 1996) have broad implications for the use of literary and informational texts in all content areas:

- Students read a wide range of print and nonprint texts to build an understanding of texts, of themselves, and of the cultures of the United States and the world; to acquire new information; to respond to the needs and demands of society and the workplace; and for personal fulfillment. Among these texts are fiction, nonfiction, classic, and contemporary works.
- Students read a wide range of literature from many periods in many genres to build an understanding of the many dimensions (e.g., philosophical, ethical, aesthetic) of human experience.

## Summary

Capturing students' interest and bringing them together in a literate community where they can be immersed in books is a top priority of most reading and language arts teachers. In this chapter, we have offered a variety of ways for teachers to bring children and literature together.

As children learn to work together in a community of readers and writers, they talk over their experiences with books and recommend books to each other. Teachers, in turn, facilitate an environment supportive of literature by carefully structuring the classroom, selecting a collection of books, and creating settings and predictable routines. Literature-based reading programs, hooking students on books, storytelling, and classroom libraries all assist children in reading more both in and out of the classroom.

Organizing for literature-based instruction revolves around (1) studies of core books (a collection at each grade level judged to be age-appropriate and of high quality), (2) literature units (around a theme), (3) reading workshops (integrating language arts and literature in responding and sharing), (4) literature circles (which may be student-led), and (5) the Internet.

We explored strategies for responding to literature, such as book-talks, conferences, and response journals, which encourage children to extend their individual thoughts and feelings about books they read through a variety of response options.

## Teacher Action Research

1. Reread the Viewpoint in Box 12.1 on page 397, Literature and Multiple Perspectives, and reflect on the author's thoughts. Discuss your reactions. How do the author's thoughts reflect your philosophy of teaching reading?

2. Interview several primary or middle school librarians or media center directors. In what ways do they use technology to support the reading development of children and assist the classroom teacher? Compile their ideas, summarizing them, and report your findings to the class.

3. Work with a group of children and guide them in dramatizing a story after they have read it or heard it read aloud. The selection could be from either a basal reader or a trade book. Videotape the dramatization and encourage students to reflect after viewing it.

4. Collaborate with a fellow student or a classroom teacher to set up a book display to interest children, including those with limited English proficiency, in reading. Decide on a theme and ways to introduce the children to books related to that theme. If possible, observe what happens in the classroom and talk with the teacher about the children's use of the display. Or compile a list of things you would expect to see and questions you would like to have the classroom teacher answer.

5. Prepare a bibliography of children's literature that would be appropriate for a particular grade level's classroom library. Use the school librarian, classroom teachers' recommendations, and bibliographies from journals such as *Language Arts*, *Journal of Adolescent and Adult Literacy*, and *The Reading Teacher* as resources. What books would be the core of the library? What books could be added over time? Include annotations that would explain why each book was chosen. For example, which books would be useful in content area instruction? Which books would help teach letter–sound correspondence?

6. Observe a content area discipline teacher teaching his or her class. How does the teacher utilize literature? What does he or she do well? What evidence of literature usage do you see that supports his or her strengths? How might a literacy coach guide the teacher to improve usage of literature?

## Related Web Sites

*ALSC: The John Newbery Medal Homepage*

**www.ala.org/alsc/newbery.html**

The John Newbery Medal is awarded annually by the Association for Library Service to Children, a division of the American Library Association.

*ALSC: The Randolph Caldecott Medal Homepage*

**www.ala.org/alsc/caldecott.html**

The Randolph Caldecott Medal is awarded annually by the Association for Library Service to Children, a division of the American Library Association.

*Carol Hurst's Children's Literature Site*

**www.carolhurst.com**

Hurst provides book reviews and various links. In addition, lesson plans and thematic units related to children's literature for all elementary grades are shared.

*The Children's Literature Web Guide*

**www.acs.ucalgary.ca/~dkbrown**

This guide links to various web sites and Internet resources related to books for children and young adults.

*Coretta Scott King Award*

**www.ala.org/ala/emiert/corettascottkingbookaward/corettascott.htm**

The Coretta Scott King Award is presented annually to an author or illustrator of African descent.

*Fables, Fairy Tales, Stories, and Nursery Rhymes*

**http://ivyjoy.com/fables**

A selection of links for fables, fairy tales, stories, and rhymes are listed by title and author.

*Multicultural Children's Literature: Creating and Applying an Evaluation Tool in Response to the Needs of Urban Educators*

**www.newhorizons.org/strategies/multicultural/higgins.htm**

This article from New Horizons for Learning provides information from a research project that evaluated multicultural children's literature. The methodology and results of the research are shared, as well as a list of quality multicultural literature.

*Notable Children's Books*

**www.ala.org/ala/alsc/awardsscholarships/childrensnotable/ notablebooklist/currentnotable.htm**

The Association for Library Service to Children identifies the best children's books of all genres and for ages birth through 14.

*Young Adult Library Services Association*

**www.ala.org/ala/yalsa/booklistsawards/booklistsbook.htm**

This site provides links and information on book lists and book awards for young adults.

# PEARSON
# myeducationlab

Now go to the Vacca et al. *Reading and Learning to Read*, Seventh Edition, MyEducationLab course at **www.myeducationlab.com** to

- Take a pretest to assess your initial comprehension of the chapter content
- Study chapter content with your individualized study plan
- Take a posttest to assess your understanding of chapter content
- Engage in multimedia exercises to help you build a deeper and more applied understanding of chapter content

## CHAPTER 13

# Basal Readers and Instructional Materials

Standards found in this chapter:
- 1.2
- 2.2
- 2.3
- 3.1
- 4.1
- 4.2
- 5.2
- 5.3

## In this chapter,
### YOU WILL DISCOVER:

- An overview of the terminology, components, and characteristics of core, or basal, reading programs
- How types of instructional decisions and reading materials relate to belief systems
- How three districts selected and implemented reading materials

## Concept Map

### BASAL READERS AND INSTRUCTIONAL MATERIALS

**BASAL READERS**

| The First Basals | Basal Characteristics |

**Making Instructional Decisions**

Modifying Lessons

**INSTRUCTIONAL MATERIALS**

| Commercially Available Materials | Electronic Materials |

Selection and Evaluation of Materials

Selection and Evaluation of Materials

*L*iz jumped at the chance to be on the selection committee. She wanted to be part of the venture because she was trying to break away from some old practices. Liz was anxious to see what the publishers were offering. "We used an evaluation form that asked questions about the program's philosophy, goals, instructional program, and so on. At first I was overwhelmed by the comprehensiveness, not just of the contents of the materials, but of the descriptions of the components! During one of our meetings we were debating whether the program was child-centered or teacher-centered, literature-based or skills-based. We all stopped and looked at each other and then answered in unison, *'Yes!'* As the laughter subsided, I remember feeling that somehow a lot of the pressure was gone. At least for me, I finally realized that I needed to rely on my beliefs as an experienced teacher. I just concentrated on how I thought my first graders and I would like and use this series. The stories were often about animals, a motivating topic for my 6- and 7-year-olds, yet there were plenty of nonfiction pieces, too. The text represented different cultures and refrained from stereotyping. The language sounded whimsical and natural to the ears of first graders. The teacher's guide looked more like a resource book with a variety of activities. It wouldn't meet the needs of all my students; fortunately, I share a planning time with the special education teacher who will help me modify some objectives. If anything, working on the committee made me realize that *I* still have to make choices and decisions about how to use the new materials in my classroom. But the colorful illustrations, bright covers, and authentic literature in our new reading series certainly make my job a lot more pleasant."

STANDARD 4.1

Basal reading programs, also known as core reading programs, are the most popular materials used for reading instruction in this country. In fact, our nation's school districts invest over a billion dollars in reading textbooks *every year* (Walsh, 2003). In their *Consumer's Guide to Evaluating a Core Reading Program Grades K–3*, Simmons and Kame'enui (2006) state that "a core reading program is the primary instructional tool that teachers use to teach children to learn to read and ensure they reach reading levels that meet or exceed grade-level standards. A core program should address the instructional needs of the majority of students. . . . Historically, core reading programs have been referred to as basal reading programs in that they serve as the 'base' for reading instruction. Adoption of a core does not imply that other materials and strategies are not used to provide a rich, comprehensive program of instruction" (p. 1).

Knowing and understanding how these sets of materials can support students' literacy development is essential for prospective and veteran teachers, given the "staying power" of core reading programs in our schools. Teachers need to assess which educational opportunities are best offered by the reading series and then look for other reading and skill activities without pressure about students' performance on state proficiency and other standardized tests. The Concept Map depicts how the key concepts connected to basal reading and instructional materials relate to each other.

Teachers, according to research by Baumann and Heubach (1996) and Mesmer (2006), are for the most part discriminating consumers who view the basal reader as just one instructional tool to be used in a variety of ways. Most teachers in today's classrooms have flexibility in selecting and using materials and in modifying ideas from the teacher's guides. To do this in an effective, efficient, and professional manner, teachers will continue to benefit from assistance in (1) judging what reading material should be assigned and when supplementary materials are needed; (2) determining which basal teacher's guide suggestions should be omitted, followed, or modified; and (3) evaluating student responses to questions (Barr & Sadow, 1989).

We devote the last section of this chapter to an analysis of instructional materials, beginning with the types of materials available. We will determine how different types of materials correspond to our belief systems. Finally, we'll look into several ways of evaluating and selecting commercial materials for classroom use.

# The First Basals

Young newspaper readers in the greater Cleveland area were treated to a historical tour of their basal reading books in a news article written especially for elementary-age students and featuring "McGuffey and His Readers." Pictures of William McGuffey, his birthplace, and his writing desk accompanied an actual page reproduction with a story about Bess and her two goats from Lesson 33 in the *McGuffey Primer*, the very first book in a series used for reading instruction.

Here's how basal readers were described in the news article so that children could understand what they are all about:

There are many different kinds of basal texts.

How and when words are introduced are carefully planned by experts.

The books come in a series.

The words and stories get longer and harder as the child moves from one level to the next.

Moreover, children were informed that McGuffey first published his series in 1836 and that the readers began with the *Primer* and ended with the *Sixth Reader*. As far as the content of the basal readers was concerned, stories were about everyday life and the rewards of good behavior. According to a study by Aaron and Anderson (1981), a remarkable number of values appearing in the readers of the early 1900s appeared in the 1970s as well. Although the stories had changed, apparently "the same virtues are there waiting to be taught" (p. 312).

Just as the young Cleveland readers found insightful differences and similarities between their reading material today and the *McGuffey Readers*, teachers also benefit from such comparisons. A page from an 1878 reader is shown in Figure 13.1 on page 428.

## Basal Programs Today

In Chapter 2 we provided a historical overview of basal reading programs. Today, published reading programs are still the most widely used materials for teaching reading in the elementary classroom in the United States. (See Figure 13.2 on pages 429–430 and Figure 13.3 on page 431 for a sample scope and sequence and table of contents for a contemporary reading program.) The latest trends have now been incorporated into most reading programs sold by various publishers. Goals emphasize the connectedness of the language arts, the importance of meaning-making, the immersion of children in literature, and the five essential components of reading as identified in the National Reading Panel Report (National Institute of Child Health and Human Development, 2000). Thinking, comprehension, and study skills are featured and are often integrated with other subjects, such as music, science, and social studies. More programs are organized thematically and contain stories by well-known children's authors and nonfiction selections.

Most reading series on the market today attempt to satisfy every consumer's appetite when it comes to reading instruction. In order to do that, publishing companies take great care to include major components. There are certain concepts and terms germane

## Figure 13.1 Page from *The Appelton Reader* (1878)

28          SECOND READER.

### LESSON XV.

| drĕss | hĕard | ŭn'-ele | her-sĕlf' |
| knĭfe | wĭshed | lăd'-der | stŏ'-rieş |
| wrŏng | stränġe | fĭn'-ġer | lŏŏk'-ing |

### WILLIE'S STORY.

One day, when Willie had been reading in his new book, his mother wished him to tell her what he had read in it, and Willie said :

"I read about a little girl who wanted to do just as she liked for one whole day.

"Her mother said she could. So the little girl cut her own bread and butter; but she let the knife slip, and cut her finger.

"Then she ate so much candy that she made herself sick. Then she put on her prettiest dress to play in the garden, and tore it.

"And then she went up a ladder, which her mother never would let her climb, and when she was up very high she heard a noise in the garden.

SECOND READER.          29

"It was the dog barking at a strange cat, mamma; and while the little girl was looking around to see what it was, she put her foot on the wrong part of the ladder.

"I mean, mamma, she only put her toe on the round; so her foot slipped, and she fell, and was almost killed.

"That was the end of her day of doing just as she liked."

*Write a sentence having in it the word* knife.
*Write a sentence having in it the word* ladder.

---

to basal reading instruction; some would say it's like a language of its own. Figure 13.4 on pages 432–433 presents key terms and definitions that should prove helpful in understanding some key concepts. The terms in Figure 13.4 may vary from series to series, but it is safe to assume that certain major components will be found in most programs, as well as new strategies that reflect changes in American culture (see Box 13.1 on page 434). A brief overview of some of the similar components that are part of almost every basal series follows:

● *Readiness program.* Big books or big storybooks are used to introduce children to shared reading and how reading works. Along with workbooks, they are used to develop basic concepts in language, letter–sound relationships, sense of context, following directions, and listening comprehension. Emergent literacy programs are often organized thematically, include a variety of support materials, and capitalize on children's curiosity about print to get them excited about reading and making predictions. Theme books, picture books, a read-aloud anthology, literature and music CDs, home and school connection sheets, picture–word cards, an assessment package, and a teacher's edition can all be part of a readiness program.

● *Beginning reading.* New basic sight words are introduced; high-frequency sight words accumulate. Children use storybooks and sometimes workbooks and eventually construct their own books as they proceed through multiple levels by the end of first grade. Vocabulary and repetition are no longer as controlled as previously; experience charts are used to help word recognition. Predictable features abound in rhyme, rhythm, and repeated patterns. Today, most feature explicit, systematic, and intensive phonics with decodable text. Little books, combining predictable elements with phonetically regular words, are often included.

## Figure 13.2  Sample Scope and Sequence Chart

### SCOPE AND SEQUENCE

#### Reading

| Concepts of Print and Print Awareness | Pre-K | K | 1 | 2 | 3 | 4 | 5 | 6 |
|---|---|---|---|---|---|---|---|---|
| Develop awareness that print represents spoken language and conveys and preserves meaning | • | • | • | | | | | |
| Recognize familiar books by their covers; hold book right side up | • | • | | | | | | |
| Identify parts of a book and their functions (front cover, title page/title, back cover, page numbers) | • | • | • | | | | | |
| Understand the concepts of letter, word, sentence, paragraph, and story | • | • | • | | | | | |
| Track print (front to back of book, top to bottom of page, left to right on line, sweep back left for next line) | • | • | • | | | | | |
| Match spoken to printed words | • | • | • | | | | | |
| Know capital and lowercase letter names and match them | • | •T | • | | | | | |
| Know the order of the alphabet | • | • | • | | | | | |
| Recognize first name in print | • | • | • | | | | | |
| Recognize the uses of capitalization and punctuation | | • | • | | | | | |
| Value print as a means of gaining information | • | • | • | | | | | |

| Phonological and Phonemic Awareness | Pre-K | K | 1 | 2 | 3 | 4 | 5 | 6 |
|---|---|---|---|---|---|---|---|---|
| **Phonological Awareness** | | | | | | | | |
| Recognize and produce rhyming words | • | • | • | | | | | |
| Track and count each word in a spoken sentence and each syllable in a spoken word | • | • | • | | | | | |
| Segment and blend syllables in spoken words | | | • | | | | | |
| Segment and blend onset and rime in one-syllable words | | • | • | | | | | |
| Recognize and produce words beginning with the same sound | • | • | • | | | | | |
| Identify beginning, middle, and/or ending sounds that are the same or different | • | • | • | | | | | |
| Understand that spoken words are made of sequences of sounds | • | • | • | | | | | |
| **Phonemic Awareness** | | | | | | | | |
| Identify the position of sounds in words | | • | • | | | | | |
| Identify and isolate initial, final, and medial sounds in spoken words | • | • | • | | | | | |
| Blend sounds orally to make words or syllables | | • | • | | | | | |
| Segment a word or syllable into sounds; count phonemes in spoken words or syllables | | • | • | | | | | |
| Manipulate sounds in words (add, delete, and/or substitute phonemes) | | • | • | | | | | |

| Phonics and Decoding | Pre-K | K | 1 | 2 | 3 | 4 | 5 | 6 |
|---|---|---|---|---|---|---|---|---|
| **Phonics** | | | | | | | | |
| Understand and apply the **alphabetic principle** that spoken words are composed of sounds that are represented by letters | • | • | • | | | | | |
| Know letter-sound relationships | | •T | •T | •T | | | | |
| Blend sounds of letters to decode | | • | •T | •T | •T | | | |
| Consonants, consonant blends, and consonant digraphs | | • | •T | •T | •T | | | |
| Short, long, and r-controlled vowels; vowel digraphs; diphthongs; common vowel patterns | | | •T | •T | •T | | | |
| Phonograms/word families | | • | • | • | • | | | |
| **Word Structure** | | | | | | | | |
| Decode words with common word parts | | • | •T | •T | •T | • | • | • |
| Base words and inflected endings | | | •T | •T | • | • | • | • |
| Contractions and compound words | | | •T | •T | •T | • | • | • |
| Suffixes and prefixes | | | •T | •T | •T | • | • | • |
| Greek and Latin roots | | | | | | • | • | • |
| Blend syllables to decode words | | | •T | •T | •T | • | • | • |
| **Decoding Strategies** | | | | | | | | |
| Blending strategy: Apply knowledge of letter-sound relationships to decode unfamiliar words | | • | • | • | • | | | |
| Apply knowledge of word structure to decode unfamiliar words | | • | • | • | • | • | • | • |
| Use context and syntax along with letter-sound relationships and word structure to decode | | • | • | • | • | • | • | • |
| Self-correct | | | • | • | • | • | • | • |

| Fluency | Pre-K | K | 1 | 2 | 3 | 4 | 5 | 6 |
|---|---|---|---|---|---|---|---|---|
| Read aloud fluently with accuracy, comprehension, appropriate pace/rate; with expression/intonation (prosody); with attention to punctuation and appropriate phrasing | | | •T | •T | •T | •T | •T | •T |
| Practice fluency in a variety of ways, including choral reading, partner/paired reading, Readers' Theater, repeated oral reading, and tape-assisted reading | | • | • | • | • | • | • | • |

**TR18**  Reading Street

• instructional opportunity    **T** tested in standardized test format

*(Continued)*

## Figure 13.2 *(Continued)*

| | Pre-K | K | 1 | 2 | 3 | 4 | 5 | 6 |
|---|---|---|---|---|---|---|---|---|
| Work toward appropriate fluency goals by the end of each grade | | | •T | •T | •T | •T | •T | •T |
| Read regularly in independent-level material | | | • | • | • | • | • | • |
| Read silently for increasing periods of time | | | • | • | • | • | • | • |
| **Vocabulary (Oral and Written)** | **Pre-K** | **K** | **1** | **2** | **3** | **4** | **5** | **6** |
| **Word Recognition** | | | | | | | | |
| Recognize regular and irregular high-frequency words | • | • | •T | •T | | | | |
| Recognize and understand selection vocabulary | | • | • | •T | • | • | • | • |
| Understand content-area vocabulary and specialized, technical, or topical words | | | • | • | • | • | • | • |
| **Word Learning Strategies** | | | | | | | | |
| Develop vocabulary through direct instruction, concrete experiences, reading, listening to text read aloud | • | • | • | • | • | • | • | • |
| Use knowledge of word structure to figure out meanings of words | | • | •T | •T | •T | •T | •T | |
| Use context clues for meanings of unfamiliar words, multiple-meaning words, homonyms, homographs | | • | •T | •T | •T | •T | •T | |
| Use grade-appropriate reference sources to learn word meanings | • | • | • | • | •T | •T | •T | •T |
| Use picture clues to help determine word meanings | • | • | • | • | • | | | |
| Use new words in a variety of contexts | • | • | • | • | • | • | • | • |
| Examine word usage and effectiveness | | • | • | • | • | • | • | • |
| Create and use graphic organizers to group, study, and retain vocabulary | | • | • | • | • | • | • | • |
| **Extend Concepts and Word Knowledge** | | | | | | | | |
| Academic language | • | • | • | • | • | • | • | • |
| Classify and categorize | • | • | • | • | • | • | • | • |
| Antonyms and synonyms | | • | •T | •T | •T | •T | •T | |
| Homographs, homonyms, and homophones | | | • | •T | •T | •T | •T | |
| Multiple-meaning words | | • | • | •T | •T | •T | •T | |
| Related words and derivations | | | | • | • | • | • | • |
| Analogies | | | | | • | | • | |
| Connotation/denotation | | | | | • | • | | • |
| Figurative language and idioms | | | • | • | • | • | • | • |
| Descriptive words (location, size, color, shape, number, ideas, feelings) | • | • | • | • | • | • | • | • |
| High-utility words (shapes, colors, question words, position/directional words, and so on) | • | • | • | • | | | | |
| Time and order words | • | • | • | • | • | • | • | |
| Transition words | | | | | • | • | • | • |
| Word origins: Etymologies/word histories; words from other languages, regions, or cultures | | | | | • | • | • | • |
| Shortened forms: abbreviations, acronyms, clipped words | | | • | • | • | • | •T | |
| **Text Comprehension** | **Pre-K** | **K** | **1** | **2** | **3** | **4** | **5** | **6** |
| **Comprehension Strategies** | | | | | | | | |
| Preview the text and formulate questions | • | • | • | • | • | • | • | • |
| Set and monitor purpose for reading and listening | • | • | • | • | • | • | • | • |
| Activate and use prior knowledge | • | • | • | • | • | • | • | • |
| Make predictions | • | • | • | • | • | • | • | • |
| Monitor comprehension and use fix-up strategies to resolve difficulties in meaning: adjust reading rate, reread and read on, seek help from reference sources and/or other people, skim and scan, summarize, use text features | | | | • | • | • | • | • |
| Create and use graphic and semantic organizers | | • | • | • | • | • | • | • |
| Answer questions (text explicit, text implicit, scriptal), including *who, what, when, where, why, what if, how* | • | • | • | • | • | • | • | • |
| Look back in text for answers | | | • | • | • | • | • | • |
| Answer test-like questions | | | • | • | • | • | • | • |
| Generate clarifying questions, including *who, what, where, when, how, why, and what if* | • | • | • | • | • | • | • | • |
| Recognize text structure: story and informational (cause/effect, chronological, compare/contrast, description, problem/solution, proposition/support) | • | • | • | • | • | • | • | • |
| Summarize text | | • | • | • | • | • | • | • |
| Recall and retell stories | • | • | • | • | • | • | • | • |
| Identify and retell important/main ideas (nonfiction) | • | • | • | • | • | • | • | • |
| Identify and retell new information | | | • | • | • | • | • | • |
| Visualize; use mental imagery | | • | • | • | • | • | • | • |
| Use strategies flexibly and in combination | | | | • | • | • | • | • |

Scope and Sequence  **TR19**

*Source: Reading Street.* Scott Foresman Reading, Teacher's Edition, Grade 5, Unit 4 (Glenview, IL: Scott Foresman), pp. TR18–TR19. Copyright 2008 by Pearson Education, Inc.

● *Strategy lessons.* Many options for strategies are suggested for individual and group lessons and activities to teach sight vocabulary, phonics, structural analysis, and use of context. Teaching vocabulary is usually directly related to the story being read; workbook pages reinforce the words, and teachers are given many alternative choices for activities before and after each story. Students are exposed to new skills, systematically and sequentially; these are often logically tied in to the literature selection and taught in a context of making meaning rather than in isolation. Teacher's manuals also offer many ways to build reading fluency, from choral reading to recording stories and poems.

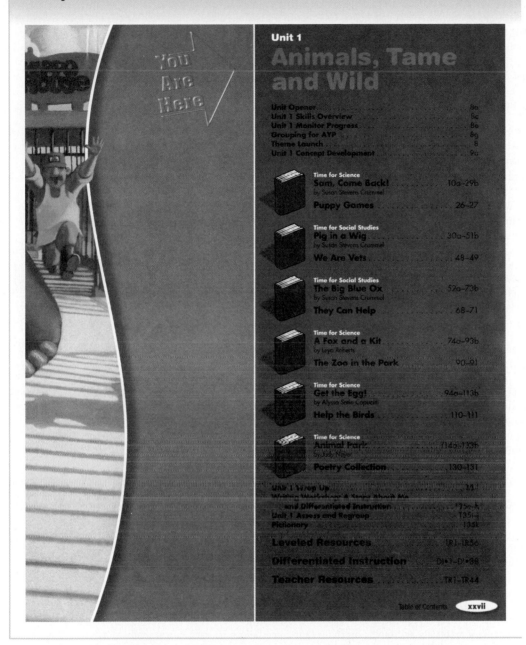

**Figure 13.3** Table of Contents

*Source: Reading Street.* Scott Foresman Reading, Teacher's Edition, Grade 1 (Glenview, IL: Scott Foresman), p. xxvii. Copyright 2008 by Pearson Education, Inc.

● *Comprehension strand.* Comprehension is stressed strongly, with prereading, during-reading, and postreading strategies and lessons. Quality literature, with considerable attention to multiculturalism, appears in largely unabridged formats. Ethnically and racially diverse pictures and stories are found in a truly comprehensive variety of literary genres, ranging from animal fantasy, science fiction, autobiography, and poetry to folktale, fable, diary, and legend. The teacher's manual suggests numerous ideas for extending children's understandings; for using a particular story in other subjects such as English, art, music, social studies, science, and math; for group and individual

## Figure 13.4    The Language of Basal Instruction

**Anthologies**

Collections of stories and poems bound together in a book are usually organized by themes that tie the content and materials together. Today's literature-based anthologies contain more predictable selections from children's literature and less controlled vocabulary, signaling a shift in focus and philosophy. Traditional components such as a teacher's guide, student texts, and practice books are still offered. Most anthologies include activities that reflect current best practice in instruction based on research about cooperative learning, the writing process, and modeling comprehension strategies.

**Controlled vocabulary**

Until the mid-1990s, when vocabulary control was being replaced by predictable texts, the number of "new" words that students encounter in each reading lesson was controlled. Publishers control vocabulary in their reading programs in three ways: (1) Many high-interest words are used first, followed by the introduction of more abstract words. (2) High-frequency words appear in the beginning, with low-frequency words gradually inserted in the text. (3) Words that follow regular spelling patterns are used first, and then words with some irregular spelling patterns are used. Words introduced in the lower-level readers are repeated often in subsequent readers.

**Criterion-referenced tests**

Informal tests devised by either the publishing company or the teacher measure individual student attainment in skills associated with phonics, vocabulary, and comprehension. The teacher sets the criterion (e.g., 8/10) for adequate performance. The purpose is to assess a reader's performance, regardless of how that performance compares to that of others taking the same test.

**Differentiating instruction**

To adapt teaching for all learners (gifted students, visual learners, English language learners, etc.), suggestions are given for tailoring instruction to individual needs.

**Extension (integrating across the curriculum)**

After the story is read and the main parts of the suggested lesson framework are completed, teachers continue or extend themes and make cross-curricular connections with projects and activities. Art, music, and writing are catalysts to extend ideas and concepts initiated during the lesson. Questioning at the interpretive and applied levels extends comprehension through group discussion.

**Informal assessment opportunities**

Suggestions are given in the teacher's manual for noticing and observing children's strengths and weaknesses as they read and write to develop a "picture" of their performance. Tips for portfolios, grading suggestions, and checklists are often provided and sometimes packaged in an assessment handbook.

**Instructional aids**

Graphics disks, CDs and DVDs, theme logs, write-in booklets, workbooks, instructional charts, hands-on manipulatives, videos, links to online resources (e.g., games, activities, and podcasts), and other prepared materials are provided at various levels to support classroom instruction.

**Levels**

Each level provides a sequential arrangement of student books (readers), teacher's editions, and ancillary materials and builds on those that come before it; each corresponds to a grade level. There may be more than one book for some grade levels, making continuous progress possible. By grade 4, most literature-based series have only one level (book) per grade.

**Reinforcement**

To ensure that skills have been learned, exercises involving similar and contrasting examples are used to reinforce the learning. This reteaching cycle includes the use of extension activities.

**Scope and sequence**

This general plan in core reading programs is for the introduction of skills in a sequential or vertical arrangement and with expanding or horizontally conceptualized reinforcement. Students move up through the levels and across within each level.

*(Continued)*

## Figure 13.4 *(Continued)*

| | |
|---|---|
| **Skill building** | Skills (e.g., basic sight vocabulary, conceptual development, listening facility, comprehension) are not presented only once. They are introduced at one level and then repeated and reinforced at subsequent levels with increasing depth. Instruction begins with simpler subskills and follows this design: introduction of a skill, reinforcement of the skill, and review of the skill. |
| **Strands** | Strands are groups of skills that are developed at increasingly higher levels throughout the program. Some popular strands of instruction are word identification, vocabulary development, comprehension, reading study skills, and fluency. |
| **Vocabulary development** | Teachers work to increase students' vocabularies. In order to develop a large number of sight words, new words are introduced, these are repeated often in the text selections, and more new words are introduced. Phonics and other word analysis skills and meaning-getting strategies using context are employed to continue vocabulary development. |

activities; and for making the connection to writing. The instructional program follows a set routine, using prompts consistently throughout the book. Questions are fewer in number, inquiring into purpose, motives, and acts of main characters. Emphasis is on critical reading through higher-level questions and encouragement for prediction making.

- *Language arts.* Creating a literary environment by integrating reading, writing, listening, and speaking at each grade level is promoted; some programs outline, in lesson format, strategies to merge the language arts. Learning centers, workshops, group discussions, cooperative learning projects, library corners, technology, and art and music centers may be set up. Writing activities are frequently mentioned throughout the teacher's manual. Journal entries, posters, charts, letters, thank-you notes, stories, group big books, and thought bubbles reinforce the focus on the connection between reading and writing. A writing assignment often accompanies a reading comprehension activity. For children who are English language learners, there are language development exercises and also suggestions for flexible grouping to assist in meeting students' individual needs.

- *Management.* Systematic instruction of reading or language arts programs provides teachers with goals and objectives along with teaching plans and assessment tools, all toward the end of documenting individual student and class progress. Their systematic organization is evident and may have special appeal for teachers who rely on the sequential path of the program.

- *Assessment.* Teachers are given numerous types of formal and informal assessment options. The newer, broader approach of ongoing assessment of student performance and attitudes toward the language arts is geared to inform teachers' instructional decision making and students' understanding of their progress toward their own goals.

## Characteristics of Basal Readers

More significant than similarities and differences among reading series are improvements in components over the past decade. Overall physical appearance, literary variety, and efforts to eliminate stereotyping and infuse diversity deserve special recognition. In general, components have become more comprehensive, thorough, or complex, depending on one's viewpoint.

BOX **13.1**

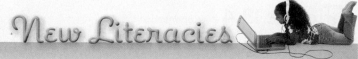

## INTEGRATING TECHNOLOGY INTO BASAL PROGRAMS

In this chapter we've discussed how basal reading programs consistently update their materials by incorporating the latest research and thinking in the field to meet classroom needs. The figure below shows a page from a fifth-grade instructor's edition from one reading program that outlines how new literacies are integrated into their instructional materials. Suggestions like these appear in every chapter throughout the instructor's edition, correlating content with pertinent activities that can be conducted in class.

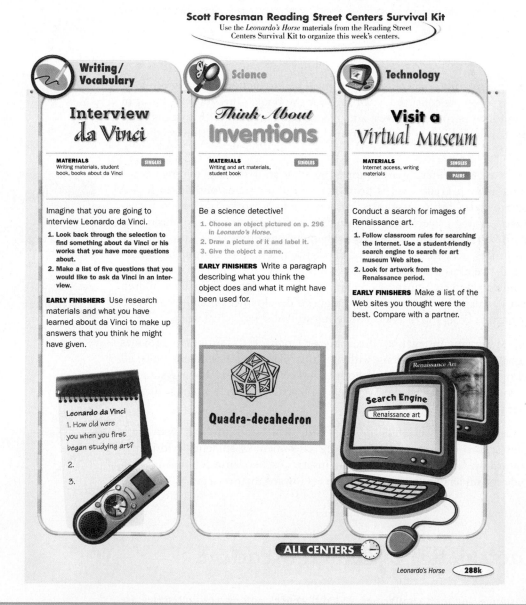

Source: *Reading Street.* Scott Foresman Reading, Teacher's Edition, Grade 5, Unit 3 (Glenview, IL: Scott Foresman), p. 288k. Copyright 2008 by Pearson Education.

## Appearance

Student books, anthologies, trade books, big books, little books, DVDs, CDs, assessment guides, spiral-bound teacher's editions with integrated and strategic lesson ideas, spelling books, practice books, and journals are just some of the physical components now available. Hardcover anthologies are coordinated in cover design, themes, and artwork with corresponding supplemental materials at each level. Appearance is surely a contributing variable when teachers consider the relative merits of a new reading series.

## Illustrations

Illustrations reveal an important growth in the quality of reading material. Today, actual illustrations from the original children's literature selection are used.

Teachers remain the most important element in terms of critically evaluating and deciding what is appropriate and valuable for their classes to read. When the experience of their culture isn't addressed in the illustrations or text of a basal series, children may not become motivated for meaningful learning. Culturally relevant teaching (Ladson-Billings, 1992) celebrates and builds on the cultural background of students as they move into literacy. Such teaching helps students examine their reading critically, helping them ask, "How does this compare to my experiences? My knowledge? My feelings?" The validity and logic of what we read in school can be assessed in terms of how it fits the values not only of our own beliefs and assumptions but also of people with different worldviews from our own.

## Stereotyping

The illustrations and content of basal readers have made great strides in guarding against stereotyping, tokenism, and lifestyle oversimplifications. Nevertheless, educators should continue to be sensitive to these issues as they evaluate and use reading materials. Some distinctions in terminology are in order.

*Stereotyping* is an oversimplified generalization about a particular group, race, or sex, with derogatory implications.

*Tokenism* is a minimal (token) effort to represent minorities, such as nonwhite characters whose faces look like white ones tinted or colored in.

*Lifestyle oversimplifications* show an unfavorable contrast between minority characters and their setting with an unstated norm of white middle-class suburbia. Typical are inappropriate settings and exaggerations of reality, such as "primitive" living.

To help both teachers and students choose books with undistorted views and non-racist histories, Slapin (1992) offered these suggestions: (1) Look at how ethnic groups are portrayed in illustrations and in picture books; (2) look for stereotypes; (3) look for loaded words; (4) look for tokenism; (5) look for distortions of history; (6) look at lifestyles; (7) look at dialogue; (8) look for standards of success; (9) look at the role of women; (10) look at the role of elders; (11) look at the authors' or illustrators' background.

## Language Style

The style of written language found in basal readers has been an interest of researchers for decades. Ruth Strickland (1962) was among the first to verify that children's command of oral language surpassed the language appearing in their basal readers. Reading and language researchers of the 1980s and 1990s continued to find out more about *basalese*, a pejorative term for the language style used in basal readers.

With the advent of the newer basal reading series described in this chapter, the style of language found throughout the anthologies reflects probably the greatest change in decades. The shift from controlled vocabulary to predictable stories and authentic literature selections can be observed in most of the major reading programs. This shift followed extensive criticism and charges that the demands of readability (controlled vocabulary and sentence length) had led to a stilted, unnatural, and bland language, referred to as *basalization* (Goodman, 1988) or *primerese* (Ammon, Simons, & Elster, 1990).

Because controlled vocabulary for beginning readers was always a hallmark of basal programs, there was concern that overreliance on pictures, dialogue, and short sentences would lead young readers to picture dependence, hindering reading acquisition (Simons & Elster, 1990). When basal readers are written to meet readability standards rather than to include authentic and meaningful language, Goodman (1988) and others argued, students are denied the opportunity to rely on what makes sense as a guide to meaningful reading. However, now that most programs have moved away from controlled vocabulary, some questions still remain about how beneficial this will really be for beginning readers.

For example, in the more traditional basal instructional program, children read from their preprimers or primers. Now that we offer children a variety of reading experiences and trade books, "the use of controlled-language texts seems well advised, especially for children who find learning to read difficult," according to Francine Johnston (1998, p. 674). This seems to go hand in hand with previously mentioned concerns that for students who are less skilled readers, the lack of controlled vocabulary may be too challenging and might make success more difficult to achieve in the newer programs. Teachers need to modify their instruction and select stories to serve the needs of their own students, encourage spontaneous conversation, and accept the children's natural language. The idea continues to be to build on children's language strengths.

## Workbooks

Workbook content has expanded somewhat in the past decades. While still providing practice in spelling, phonics, or decoding skills in the primary grades and comprehension or study skills in the intermediate grades, there are opportunities for open-ended, personal, and creative response too. Newer programs often offer a wide range of workbooks or practice books. Some include state-specific practice books that map to state standards and others include extra handbooks for English language learners. No longer must teachers merely decide how many workbook pages to assign; today's question is how to choose among and then orchestrate the multiple types of practice books suggested in the manual's lesson plan guide.

In the past, workbooks were criticized because the tasks demanded of the student required little actual reading; many asked students to focus on a single word rather than supply or compose words in open-ended responses. Mastery of the skill being practiced bore little relation to correct or incorrect responses. Often workbooks were not related to the textbook selections students were reading. Workbooks today are more aligned than ever before.

## Lesson Framework

Most basal reading programs organize instruction around some variation of the directed reading activity (DRA) first described by Betts in 1946. Although the sequence and suggested activities are relatively standard, enough variation in strategies and emphasis exists to give each publisher's version a unique feel.

The newest basal programs incorporate lessons and activities designed to promote strategic reading and to learn strategies for making informed decisions. With so many marginal notes, highlights, features, and extensions, lesson plans in a teacher's manual can be overwhelming. Although the confusing nature of so many options could be overwhelming to novice teachers, many others have become discriminating consumers who realize that they need not slavishly follow the teacher's manual. The options for teaching strategies in each basal lesson are numerous, but most are organized around three or four phases that correspond to a similar, traditional sequence. As Figure 13.5 illustrates, the new series have lesson planning guides with a sequence laid out but use different terminology.

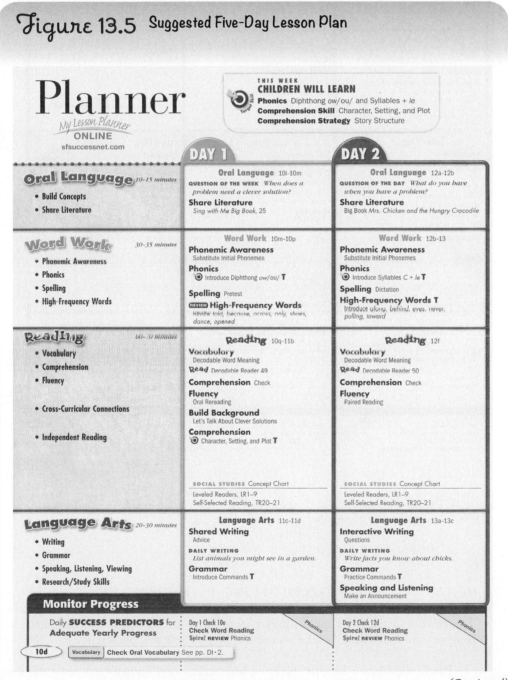

**Figure 13.5**  Suggested Five-Day Lesson Plan

*(Continued)*

## Figure 13.5 (Continued)

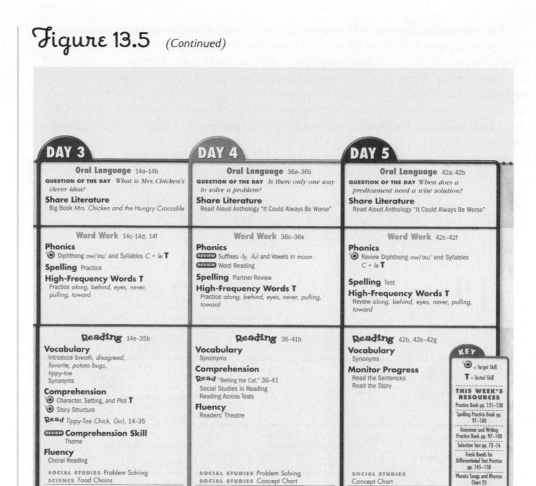

*Source: Reading Street.* Scott Foresman Reading, Teacher's Edition, Grade 1, Unit 5 (Glenview, IL: Scott Foresman), pp. 10d–10e. Copyright 2008 by Pearson Education, Inc.

**MOTIVATION AND BACKGROUND BUILDING** ◆ This aspect of the lesson involves getting ready to read. It is sometimes referred to as the prereading phase of instruction. The teacher attempts to build interest in reading, set purposes, and introduce new concepts and vocabulary. Several procedures may include the following:

1. Predicting—based on title, pictures, and background knowledge—what the story might be about
2. Teacher think-alouds to model prediction, set purposes, and share prior knowledge

3. Discussion of the pronunciation and meaning of new words; review of words previously taught
4. Location of geographic setting, if important (map and globe skills)
5. Development of time concepts
6. Review of important reading skills needed for doing the lesson

Although progress has been made, Neuman (2006) suggests that today's basals still misunderstand the importance of building background knowledge, calling it a "catastrophic misunderstanding. Instead of systematically building children's background knowledge and vocabulary, basals systematically limited the background knowledge and vocabulary covered by their texts" (p. 25).

**GUIDED READING (SILENT AND ORAL)** ◆ Depending on the grade level, the story may be read on a section-by-section basis (in the primary grades) or in its entirety. Following silent reading, children may be asked to read the story aloud or orally read specific parts to answer questions. The guided reading phase of the lesson focuses on comprehension development through questioning. Strategic reading, including explicit comprehension and vocabulary skill instruction, is explained in the teacher's guide, along with prompts such as "teachable moments" interspersed throughout the teacher's copy of the story. Teachers, as they have always done during a directed reading activity (DRA), may create their own questions. They may also omit some of the suggestions provided in the teacher's guide, gearing the lesson to the experiences and prior knowledge of their students in relation to a given story. Stopping the students' reading is helpful to articulate predictions, but when they are anxious to find out what happens and totally involved in the piece of literature, teachers should avoid interrupting the reading and let students finish the story.

**SKILL DEVELOPMENT AND PRACTICE** ◆ Skill development and practice activities center on direct instruction of reading skills, arranged according to "scope and sequence" and taught systematically. Sometimes this phase of the DRA involves oral rereading, for a specific purpose. Activities and exercises from the various practice books that accompany the basal story are intended to reinforce skills in the broad areas of word analysis and recognition, vocabulary, and study skills. They are interspersed throughout the phases of the lesson in the teacher's guide.

**FOLLOW-UP AND ENRICHMENT** ◆ There are more possibilities for enrichment and follow-up activities after the actual reading phase of a lesson than teachers will ever be able to incorporate into the curriculum. The options most favored today center on integrated curriculum, an effort to connect the language arts with other subject areas, often through themes. Integration is encouraged across all subject areas, including math, which was previously ignored. Skill development and practice activities are often interspersed with creative enrichment ideas in the teacher's guide. Here is a sample of some follow-up and enrichment activities:

- Writing activities
- Drama activities, reader's theater
- Integrated curriculum hands-on projects
- Response through personal reflection or literature circles
- Minilessons
- Podcast topics
- Additional comprehension strategy lessons and checks
- Whole class, community, or family activity
- Reading related stories or other genres
- Links to related web sites

**HOMEWORK EXERCISE: VIDEO**

Go to the Homework and Exercises section in Chapter 13 of MyEducationLab to watch the video "Guided Reading" to observe how one teacher uses a variety of techniques to guide students while they read a book.

# Making Instructional Decisions

STANDARD
2.2

STANDARDS
5.2, 5.3

The basal lesson can be a tool at our command, or it can dominate our classroom actions. Teachers who rely solely on their teacher's manual are not following best practice. They must make informed decisions about using, not using, and/or supplementing basal reading programs. Literacy coaches can be useful resources in helping teachers make instructional decisions. Teachers can work with coaches to help them modify and select lessons and materials for various kinds of learners from the plethora of materials a core reading program offers. See Box 13.2 to read about how Jane Hallisy, a coach, has supported teachers in their use of the basal.

Let's consider how two primary teachers handle their teacher's manuals. LeAnn has been teaching for 10 years. She follows the lessons in her core reading program assiduously, lesson by lesson and page by page from the teacher's manual. Her compliance, she suggests, is based on a couple of factors. The basal program, she says, was put together by experts "who know far more than I ever will about reading." But do these experts know her students as well as she does? Do they know her children's reading strategies? Their diagnostic results? LeAnn replied, "Perhaps not. But the lessons must be good or they wouldn't be in the book, and the publisher has aligned the materials with our state's standards and it says it's research-based. I like that I don't have to think about that. It saves me hours of planning time. If I follow the book I know I'm getting it all in there."

---

## BOX 13.2

# Viewpoint

### Coaching the Use of a Basal Program
Jane Hallisy

*Jane Hallisy has served as a mentor coach for four years.*

At times I have worked with teachers to help them plan the use of their core reading programs. I mainly focus on helping them understand the layout of the manual and how to differentiate for various needs. Often teachers think they need to teach everything on the page and use all of the materials, so my job was to help them sort through all of the resources available. We spend quite a bit of time discussing the many components of their district's selected reading program and what materials might work best for the different abilities in small, flexible groups. For example, I help teachers understand how to use the various leveled books to assist students with reading at their ability level. The focus skill remains the same for all groups. However, the activity or materials used are differentiated to meet the students' needs. Extra support materials assist struggling readers' instruction while advanced readers utilize materials and activities that are more challenging.

Within the core or basal teacher's manual, strategies such as Questioning the Author are presented. Sometimes we took those strategies and provided a more in-depth study of the strategy. For example, we might use the same strategy with a professional journal article. We would have teachers walk through the steps and then discuss how they could use the strategy with their students.

When presenting professional development on a particular topic such as the five essentials, we have the teachers go through their core program teacher's edition and materials, search for these components, and determine how that specific component was stressed. Then we would have them plan for the week. Using the suggestions from the manual, teachers would plan how they would explicitly teach the essentials or how they might extend the practice in it through center activities.

Finally, another big piece that was coached using the core program was classroom management. Along with the school's literacy specialists we noted observations that teachers' classroom management was weak and thus affected their ability to use flexible grouping properly. The teacher's editions often have a section on classroom management and we were able to use this portion of the program to coach teachers individually.

Using the core program when coaching teachers allows the coach and teacher an opportunity to engage in dialogue on instructional practices that include careful planning and thoughtful consideration of students' needs.

By contrast, Lori is a 12-year veteran. She has a core program adopted by her district and uses it but "reorganizes parts to fit what I think my students need." When asked whether it takes time to do this, Lori replied, "It does. But I think it's time well spent. I keep what I think is worthwhile and skip the activities that don't make sense to me. I make these decisions on the spot so they take very little time. Sometimes I create my own activities such as Venn diagrams if I think that will better target a skill or concept my students need, but I think it's worth the extra time."

More and more teachers are taking the same professional stance as Lori. The survey on basal instruction found that rather than passively following the manual, teachers actually find themselves empowered by materials that give them "instructional suggestions to draw from, adapt, or extend as they craft lessons" (Baumann & Heubach, 1996, p. 511).

As teachers reflect on why and how they use basals, they will find more opportunities to use their knowledge and skills more fully and effectively. Modifications of basal reading lessons allow teachers to rely on their own strengths as well as those of the students. After all, teachers should not have to face an "either/or" dilemma in using basals to teach reading. Rather, they need to decide where to place instructional emphasis.

It is not unusual to discover very different kinds of reading instruction going on in the same elementary school. Even when a school uses just one core reading program, instructional emphasis often varies from teacher to teacher. It is clearly impossible to teach every activity suggested in a basal reading lesson. There isn't enough time in the day; moreover, we wonder whether a teacher would need to do so to produce proficient readers. From an instructional point of view, the question is not "Am I going to do everything as suggested in the teacher's manual?" The more appropriate question was posed this way by an elementary teacher: "If I'm going to skip parts in the teacher's manual or modify the lesson, I have to have the courage to believe that what I am emphasizing is instructionally worthwhile. I ask myself, 'What do I need to change in the lesson to make it work for my students?'" In Box 13.3 on page 442, Kathy Perfect describes the role of basals and other instructional materials in her literacy program.

## Modifying Lessons

As teachers of reading become more familiar with instructional strategies in this book and others, they try them out in their classrooms. Many will use alternative strategies in conjunction with their basal anthologies. They may prefer to follow the basic lesson framework, incorporating some alternatives into this structure.

Modifying lessons personalizes reading instruction for teachers and students. The reasons behind this lesson planning are varied, but the most important one is the need to adapt in order to meet the special needs of students. The nature of students as readers, and as individuals within a social situation in which language plays a large role, causes teachers to modify instruction.

Children who are reluctant to read, who are just learning English, who are in some way gifted, or who face developmental or other challenges benefit when teachers plan lessons with them in mind. Sometimes lessons may simply be rearranged; at other times, parts might be omitted or expanded. If material seems too difficult, teachers may incorporate some content area prereading strategies suggested in Chapter 14. Using the directed reading–thinking activity (DR–TA), in conjunction with suspenseful stories, facilitates prediction making and provides an alternative lesson structure to the DRA. For more ideas and discussion about alternative instruction, see Chapter 3.

### BUILDING TEACHING SKILLS: READING

Go to the Homework and Exercises section in Chapter 13 of MyEducationLab to read the article "The Science of Reading Research" and develop an understanding of how you might use research to help you make instructional decisions.

BOX **13.3**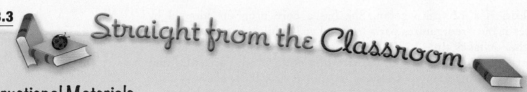

## Instructional Materials

### KATHY PERFECT

*Kathy Perfect, a fourth-grade teacher, lives in Kent, Ohio.*

I want the resources and materials I use in the classroom to reflect what I value as a literacy teacher. If my program is to be rich and multidimensional, my choices will need to include a healthy sampling of literary texts and other materials: the basal reading anthology, chapter books, picture books, poetry volumes, CDs & DVDs, informational and reference books, and books for self-selected reading.

The basal series we have, though it's only one of many resources used in my reading–writing program, takes a comprehensive approach to language arts. Each grade-level anthology has a wide array of authentic text selections to choose from according to what I think best suits our purposes, needs, and interests. The basal is useful as a place to begin as a community of readers.

I start the school year with a selection from the anthology to read or listen to on CD. Each student then chooses a page, practices it, and reads it to me in a private conference. Listening to students one on one gives me important information about them as readers: oral reading fluency, reading rate, strategies they use for miscues or unknown words, attention to conventions of print (punctuation, quotations, etc.), and expression. Since our basal text is already leveled to some degree, this first selection helps me assess my students as individual readers, as well as how they compare with their peers. This quick and informal "running record" serves also as a window into the strategies I need to focus on for minilessons and what interventions might be appropriate—and for whom. The basal, then, is a helpful part of my instructional toolbox. I use it intermittently over the school year as it fits what I need or want.

To help instill a passion for reading, there is no substitute for putting real books in the hands of my students where they can see, feel, and smell them. So after an initial selection or two from our reading anthology, we typically move into a class set of a chapter book (e.g., *Sarah, Plain and Tall; Dear Mr. Henshaw; Shiloh*). I especially love chapter books for the rich discussion they promote and the personal level of engagement that occurs. Reading a chapter book together from cover to cover is an experience that often propels students into a greater confidence in themselves as readers and thinkers, and helps them begin to gel as a "literate community."

An alternative to everyone reading together in one book is forming literature circles of only four to six students reading the same title of a chapter book. Most students appreciate being given some autonomy in choosing which book to read or group to join. Peer-led, small group discussion is at the heart of this approach, so students learn valuable lessons in social construction of meaning, group dynamics, and collaboration.

Another favorite approach, which we do several times throughout the year, is a *themed study* using a collection of various books related to a chosen topic (e.g., cowboys and the Wild West); an *author study* featuring a particular writer (e.g., Patricia Polacco); or a *genre study* that focuses on a certain type of literature (e.g., folk/fairy tales). In a themed study approach, students are able to read and sample many of the books from the collection (books that have been chosen purposefully to include varying reading levels to accommodate individual readers), and they enjoy becoming "experts" about the theme/author/genre under study. It is an approach especially conducive to both collaborative group activities and individual inquiry.

Finally, if there's one aspect of my literacy program that is sacred, it's our daily read-aloud time from a chapter book. The lights go off, the room is hushed, and together we climb into a world of magic. Together, day by day, we may fall in love; have our hearts broken; get amazed, amused, or confused; and come away being changed forever. Together we've discovered the power and joy of reading.

### REFLECTIVE INQUIRY

- How does Kathy Perfect personalize reading instruction for her students?
- How does her choice of materials reflect an informed instructional decision?

## Instructional Materials

Due to the proliferation of reading materials and the technological changes induced by computers, we cannot offer teachers a comprehensive listing of current instructional materials in reading. Such a list would be out of date before this book reached your hands. Consequently, it becomes even more essential that teachers be aware of the types of materials available and how to select and evaluate them.

It is important to consider the relationship between materials used to deliver instruction and the beliefs teachers hold about reading instruction.

BUILDING TEACHING SKILLS: LESSON PLANNING

Go to the Homework and Exercises section in Chapter 13 of MyEducationLab to create a new reading lesson plan that incorporates electronic materials.

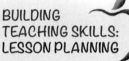

STANDARDS 2.3, 4.2

As we already know, most elementary teachers use instructional materials in addition to or in place of the basal reading program to teach reading. This willingness to broaden the materials used for instruction is a double-edged sword: There is a lot to choose from and not a lot of guidance on how to go about it. This is especially the case when it comes to electronic materials.

Table 13.1 displays three broad categories of reading materials: basic instructional programs, supplemental materials, and trade books. Core material such as a comprehensive reading or language arts program will be used by the majority of elementary children. Supplementary programs, in particular technology-based materials, will be used as enrichment for some children and a reinforcement of basic skills for others or will be fully integrated into the lesson. Unlike basic reading programs, supplementary programs are less likely to be scrutinized by selection committees. Trade books, such as library hardcover and paperback books, and sets of trade books related to literature-based programs will be selected by librarians, specialists, and classroom teachers.

Examples of the types of reading materials listed in Table 13.1 can be added as you come into contact with the materials in schools. Take a few minutes now to think of some

## Table 13.1  Types of Reading Materials

| TYPE | LABEL | PURPOSE |
| --- | --- | --- |
| Core instructional programs and materials | Basal readers and anthologies of literature from a wide range of genres | Intended to provide the majority of reading instruction to the majority of students |
| Supplementary programs | Skills kits; high-interest, low-vocabulary series; software packages; CD-ROMs, Internet usage, desktop publishing | Intended to meet special needs and enrich classroom instruction; reinforcement of skills; the needs of particular groups such as the gifted, bilingual–bicultural, and learning disabled |
| Trade books | Library books; popular fiction and nonfiction paperbacks for children and adolescents | Individual titles suited to children's interests; intended for independent reading rather than direct instruction |

in each category. Classrooms you visit will differ as to the predominant types of reading material supplied for the students. Some rooms, for example, contain almost exclusively textbooks for reading, science, social studies, mathematics, and so on. Others have hundreds of paperback books and magazines displayed in an assortment of racks. Some classrooms have sturdy cardboard kits and piles of student record books; some have computer workstations along one wall. Few classrooms have the same mix of reading materials.

Many variables could account for a teacher's decision to favor one type of reading material over another for instruction. Grade level, school district policy, influence of colleagues, curriculum objectives, and available resources are some that come to mind. Two others, the impact of technology and the teacher's belief system, are influences that need to be considered.

## Electronic Materials

Today's technology can enrich classroom reading instruction just as trade books and literature-based programs of the 1990s did. Teachers are increasingly aware of the possibilities for reading and learning with technology. As they require students to share a computer, write a blog, or join an online discussion board, teachers are encouraging social interaction. Students communicate about discoveries they're making and collaborate naturally with other students about the content and process of navigating a multimedia environment. We've come a long way from computer-aided instruction (CAI) software of the 1980s; electronic options available today make exciting opportunities for reading and language instruction. Reading, writing, and communicating on the Internet are ways to include new literacies in a purposeful way, develop students' abilities, and create incentives for improvement. However, using these new literacies also means that students need to know how to use new technologies, such as the Web, e-mail, and hyperlinks, as well as knowing the unwritten rules for participating in online discussion groups and distinguishing biased and irrelevant information from credible and relevant information.

WORLD WIDE WEB ◆ Just one decade ago the Internet was not critical to education, but today it is a normal, integral part of the learning process. Access to the Web on the Internet connects students to a vast network of computers around the world that effectively mix text, graphics, sound, and images. Students can gather information on every imaginable topic, publish their research reports, and ask questions of experts and other students. Much quicker than a library visit, information access is instantaneous, once students develop some expertise at navigating the Web. Students can take guided tours or be given "bookmarks" to take them directly to sites teachers want them to visit. A wealth of online curriculum support is also available for students to support their core reading materials. Chapter-by-chapter support such as self-tests, Internet activities, references, teaching links, and much more are all available on publisher web sites to accompany today's texts.

E-MAIL, DISCUSSION GROUPS, AND BLOGS ◆ Students on the Internet can communicate instantaneously by means of e-mail and discussion boards anywhere in the world. They can connect with others about books they are reading, share information, and ask questions about school hobbies, interests, family, and friends. Teachers often use e-mail to send and collect homework assignments, make general announcements to the class, send students links to web sites and even administer quizzes and tests. Discussion boards are increasingly being used by teachers to promote rich discussion around a topic or idea in both reading and content area classrooms. Students and teachers can also join large-scale discussion groups by subscribing to online mailing lists or a listserv. Blogs, a type of online journal, are used to encourage students to dialogue with one another. A blog is characterized by a personal style, either in the writing itself or in the selection of links passed on to the reader. Teachers looking for ways to increase reflection and discussion might implement student blogs.

WORD PROCESSORS ◆ Computers as word processors in the classroom can help develop students' writing abilities. Students can keep daily journals; write letters and thank-you notes; draft, edit, and revise their writing; and produce attractive stories and reports that others can read. With *desktop publishing* programs, which combine text and graphics in various arrangements, such as pamphlets, signs, brochures, and invitations, students can contribute their own creations to the theme or topic under study.

**SOFTWARE PROGRAMS** ◆ In addition to software accompanying comprehensive reading programs, many publishers have inundated the education market with innovative software. Some packages are highly interactive multimedia software, in which students interact with concepts, engaging in investigations using three-dimensional environments.

**ELECTRONIC BOOKS** ◆ Electronic books, unlike other educational software, contain electronic text that can be presented to readers visually, in a variety of ways. Electronic books that embed prompts, hints, model answers, and instant feedback into the text to provide individualized instruction are available. Some come equipped with adjustable font sizes and text captioning. Others include translations for ELL students. Teachers looking for ways to increase positive response in children and improve their comprehension would want to consider supplementing their reading or language arts program with these materials.

**EDUCATIONAL GAMES** ◆ The instant motivation associated with playing games continues to make them popular in some classrooms. Often used to let students practice or reinforce skills, they have grown in sophistication from cardboard flash cards and spin-the-dial to online versions with colorful graphics. Teachers use these games to assist students in practicing categorizing, reviewing vocabulary meanings, or sequencing. Students may also benefit from learning how to cooperate with one another because the competitiveness is now redirected toward the computer.

## Beliefs About Reading and Instructional Materials

How do teachers' beliefs about reading correspond to their selection and use of instructional materials for reading? There is no definitive answer to this question. Many complicating factors prevent teachers from exercising complete freedom of choice and hence prevent us from knowing why certain materials are present in any given classroom. Nevertheless, we believe it is important to consider the relationship between materials used to deliver instruction and the beliefs teachers hold about reading instruction. In other words, it makes sense to assume there is a relationship between what we do and why we do it.

Figure 13.6 on page 446 illustrates the major types of reading materials across the continuum of beliefs, from bottom-up (at the bottom) to top-down (at the top). Basal reading programs, with their multiple strands, take up the vast middle sections of the continuum. Programmed, prescriptive materials and children's literature books reside in the bottom-up and top-down sections, respectively. Supplementary materials appear in several sections, from flash cards and drill-and-practice software to journals, CD-ROMs, and electronic books.

Differences in beliefs about unit of language to be emphasized are superimposed in the next layer. Letter–sound emphasis corresponds to materials found in prescription programs with a heavy word analysis component. Whole language emphasis corresponds to materials such as library books and paperbacks without arbitrary skill divisions. This unit-of-language emphasis is illustrated further by a dotted boundary line for context. Materials involving minimal use of context are on the left, whereas materials involving maximal use of context are on the right.

A third layer that we might add is instructional strategy corresponding to these materials. We have initiated this with several basic strategies discussed in other chapters. For example, the DRA corresponds to most lessons in reading programs, while the DR–TA corresponds to many stories in anthologies and in supplementary literature. Sustained silent reading (SSR) corresponds to magazines and trade books—that is, personalized rather than prescriptive materials. What other strategies would you place in one spot or move to several points on this continuum?

Unfortunately, often by the time we step back, look at the types of instructional materials we are using, and relate them to our beliefs and priorities, the materials are already in place. How were they selected in the first place?

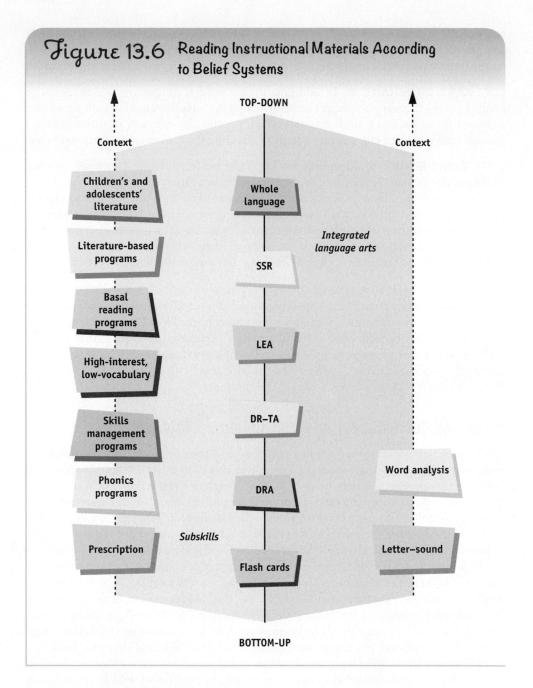

**Figure 13.6** Reading Instructional Materials According to Belief Systems

## Selecting Reading Materials

Like Liz in the chapter's opening vignette, many teachers have served on textbook selection committees. Some probing would reveal the sophistication of the process: Did the committee seek and obtain information from the various stakeholder groups such as parents, administrators, students, and other teachers? Were there presentations and question-and-answer sessions with company representatives? Was there ample time to pilot one or two of the finalists in classrooms?

Social trends such as treatment of women and minorities, return to basics, and increasing involvement of parents have varying degrees of impact on curriculum development and materials selection. Depending on the community, other issues need to be considered. Censorship is probably the most pervasive issue because it deals with people's values. Examining publications for objectionable matter is not the intended mission of most educational materials selection committees. Yet there is a fine line between examining materials for their contribution to instructional goals and banning materials for their conveyance of implicit or explicit messages to students. In Box 13.4 district leaders reflect on instructional materials.

Another issue is the increased accountability coming from both the federal and state governments to boost test scores, which has garnered media attention. Newspapers run feature articles comparing local school districts to one another based on percentages of students passing these tests. Pressure is then put on the school board and administrators of a district to improve their scores. As this filters down to the individual classroom level, teachers devote more instructional time to practicing for the test. How does this affect the use of the various types of instructional strategies and reading materials? Will teachers, for example, feel free to start additional literature circles or take that block of time to drill and practice subskills?

---

BOX **13.4**

## *Viewpoint*    A Conversation with Three District Leaders

*There is an abundance of instructional materials available to today's teacher of reading. Read what three different district leaders have to say about the materials used in their district and the rationale for selecting these materials.*

*What instructional materials are you currently using in your district to teach reading to young students, and why?*

DISTRICT 1: We use a basal reading program in grades K–6. We recently revised our reading course of study, and we needed a core reading program that closely aligns to it. Teams of teachers, principals, and curriculum consultants reviewed several different basal series using a checklist we created. The series we chose introduces concepts and skills in very systematic manner, and the philosophy of the program, in general, is closely aligned with our goals and our state's standards.

DISTRICT 2: After two years of minimal movement in our reading scores, the administration in our district convinced the board of education that we needed to adopt a new core reading series or basal. Teachers were asked to volunteer to participate on a textbook adoption committee and to ultimately vote on a core reading program. Using the *Consumer's Guide to Evaluating a Core Reading Series* (Simmons & Kame'enui, 2006) we examined six reading program series, but one series scored quite a bit higher than the others. Since the selection, we have done training with our teachers to ensure the program's successful implementation.

DISTRICT 3: Rather than one core reading program, we use a wide variety of reading materials in our reading instruction, including but not limited to leveled books from several publishers, a basal series that includes individual leveled books, trade books, sets of class books that include novels, a variety of student periodicals, students' own published books, self-selected books from classroom libraries and the school library, as well as Internet sites.

*As you reviewed core reading programs, what were you looking for? What features were most important?*

DISTRICT 1: We wanted all materials to be appropriate for the grade-level age groups and the materials had to map to our course of study which is aligned with the state standards. The illustrations and pictures needed to present a culturally diverse view for our students. This was very important to our selection teams. We want students to be placed in the position of using a variety of higher-level thinking skills. The program developers were also very cooperative in providing professional development during the initial implementation period and were available on an "on call" basis. This was important to the teachers.

DISTRICT 2: We were looking for a strong writing component, representation of authors from different cultures, as well as illustrations that are engaging and contain characters from multiple cultures. We wanted a program that had a strong scientific research base that include the five essential components (phonemic awareness, phonics, comprehension, vocabulary, and fluency) as well as writing and oral language. We also wanted something very complete and comprehensive so that teachers had a wide variety of resources available to them.

DISTRICT 3: We did not choose to implement a core reading program. We prefer our teachers to pull from a variety of sources when planning instruction.

*How closely does your district follow your core reading program?*

DISTRICT 1: Although we have adopted a core reading program, we encourage teachers to use many resources to make a complete program for students. The core program is not the sole method of instruction.

DISTRICT 2: We are strictly adhering to the program's guidelines, and our teachers are excited to be using the program. There are so many resources available.

What are the advantages and disadvantages of using a core basal program? As a beginning teacher, do you have a preference for teaching from a structured program or would you prefer to teach reading using your choice of instructional materials? Why?

Trends and issues are important as they directly or indirectly influence curriculum materials selection. We need to keep them in perspective. The next time you are asked to assist in selecting materials, here are some questions to use as criteria to guide the process:

1. Have you personally evaluated the content of the materials in terms of accuracy of content, level of presentation, and use of level of language? Have you found the materials acceptable in these areas?
2. Do the data reveal on whom the materials were field-tested? How many students were involved in the use of the materials? In what geographic location were these tests conducted? What were the results?
3. Are authors and publishers readily identifiable within the content of the material?
4. Is there an accompanying instructional guide, and, if so, are the curriculum aims, objectives, and instructional strategies presented?
5. Have these materials been used on pupils similar to the pupils in your reading programs? If so, what results were achieved using these materials?
6. Do you feel you will present these materials with honesty and objectivity?
7. Have members of your district formulated specific ways or methods for using these materials?
8. Will these materials complement the other instructional messages of your reading programs?
9. Does the content present information in a fair and nonbiased manner?
10. Are important concepts reinforced so that there is sufficient repetition of major points?

## Evaluating Reading Materials

Reading programs, the most prevalent type of instructional material, are also the most likely to be evaluated by teachers and other groups. Publishing companies have become so attuned to this process that they mount high-power, professional presentations to convince school districts to adopt their particular program. School districts have in turn developed extensive evaluation forms to keep track of and compare the programs' elements.

A thorough evaluation of a program currently in use is beneficial for assessing the instructional program in relation to the curriculum goals of the school district. Teachers who participate in answering these questions gain the professional development so often neglected when it comes to reading materials. This process should be done before deciding whether to consider new programs; it's important to have this information as baseline data.

1. What is the overall philosophy of the program? How is reading discussed in the teacher's guide?
2. What kind of learning environment does the program recommend? Is it child-centered? Teacher-centered? Literature-centered? Skills-based? Scientific?
3. Describe the emergent literacy program in detail. How does it provide for communication between school and home?
4. Describe the instructional program in detail. How are lessons structured to teach phonemic awareness, word identification, vocabulary, reading fluency, comprehension, writing?
5. Describe the literature of the program. Are the selections in unabridged form? Are different genres included? Is there a strong presence of nonfiction text? How culturally diverse is the literature?
6. How well does the program integrate across the curriculum? In what ways is assessment connected to daily instruction? What opportunities are there for connections between the various language arts?

The evaluation sheet in Figure 13.7 illustrates how major components, once examined at some length, can be rated in a kind of "executive summary." This form could apply to textbooks in other subject areas and to high school as well as elementary and middle-grade levels.

## *Figure* 13.7  Textbook Evaluation Profile Sheet

| Title of Textbook | Excellent | Good | Acceptable | Poor | Not included | Not applicable |
|---|---|---|---|---|---|---|
| 1. Authorship | | | | | | |
| 2. Research base | | | | | | |
| 3. Learner verification and revision | | | | | | |
| 4. General characteristics | | | | | | |
| 5. Physical and mechanical features | | | | | | |
| 6. Philosophy | | | | | | |
| 7. Organization of material | | | | | | |
| 8. Objectives | | | | | | |
| 9. Subject matter content | | | | | | |
| 10. Readability | | | | | | |
| 11. Teaching aids and supplementary material | | | | | | |
| 12. Teacher's edition or manual | | | | | | |
| 13. Fair and realistic treatment of people | | | | | | |
| Total number in each rating classification for all categories | | | | | | |

Checklists designed to evaluate reading materials of a supplementary nature may be criticized as rather shallow analysis. Their benefits, however, far outweigh this criticism. Checklists are relatively easy to construct; teachers are more willing to spend the short amount of time it takes to develop a list to help them examine materials. Figure 13.8 on page 450 presents a sample checklist for examining the potential effectiveness of materials; it is one informal evaluation designed by teachers of elementary reading and language. The form is brief and to the point, deals with teachers' own programmatic goals, and yields useful information. Unlike more elaborate and lengthy commercial evaluation instruments, such checklists can be employed by the people who actually select and use the materials.

With the ongoing proliferation of electronic materials and continuing efforts to develop multicultural, diverse, and authentic materials, teachers need to be more aware than ever about what they are using in instruction. Here are some questions to think about before buying additional materials: Does the material actually contain what its advertisement claims? Are the skill areas emphasized really important to literacy? Are the materials likely to hold the interest of the students in your class? Is there sufficient time devoted to reading in relation to other activities? Are thinking and metacognitive strategies included? Is writing integrated in a meaningful way?

## *Figure* 13.8   Checklist for Examining the Potential Effectiveness of Materials

| Statement | Yes | No | Unsure | Does Not Apply |
|---|---|---|---|---|
| 1. Reading materials are consistent with: | | | | |
|    a. philosophy and goals of the program | ____ | ____ | ____ | ____ |
|    b. standards | ____ | ____ | ____ | ____ |
| 2. Materials are adequate for various phases of the program: | | | | |
|    a. oral language development | ____ | ____ | ____ | ____ |
|    b. listening comprehension | ____ | ____ | ____ | ____ |
|    c. word recognition | ____ | ____ | ____ | ____ |
|    d. reading comprehension | ____ | ____ | ____ | ____ |
|    e. fluency | ____ | ____ | ____ | ____ |
|    f. study skills | ____ | ____ | ____ | ____ |
|    g. phonics | ____ | ____ | ____ | ____ |
|    h. vocabulary | ____ | ____ | ____ | ____ |
| 3. The materials are | | | | |
|    a. interesting and stimulating | ____ | ____ | ____ | ____ |
|    b. easy for children to use | ____ | ____ | ____ | ____ |
|    c. durable | ____ | ____ | ____ | ____ |
|    d. well organized | ____ | ____ | ____ | ____ |
|    e. cost-effective | ____ | ____ | ____ | ____ |
| 4. The materials accommodate the range of reading abilities. | ____ | ____ | ____ | ____ |
| 5. A variety of cultures is depicted in illustrations and text content. | ____ | ____ | ____ | ____ |
| 6. The technology integrates with the content and objectives. | ____ | ____ | ____ | ____ |
| 7. The technology is motivating and thought-provoking. | ____ | ____ | ____ | ____ |
| 8. The program is easy to operate. | ____ | ____ | ____ | ____ |
| 9. I feel adequately prepared to use all materials available. | ____ | ____ | ____ | ____ |

Teacher's Name: _____     Grade Level: _____

# WHAT ABOUT STRUGGLING READERS AND *the Basal Reader?*

Bearing in mind that basal readers are used in most elementary classrooms, it is worth our time to consider the basal reader and how it attempts to meet the needs of the child who struggles with reading. The newer basals have some advantages to offer teachers as they work with struggling readers:

- They offer flexibility for addressing a variety of instructional needs.
- Review is provided in the form of workbooks, CD-ROMs, and online materials and can be helpful if properly directed by the teacher.
- They provide a language arts framework across grade levels.
- They provide a variety of ongoing assessment options to inform instruction.

Throughout this chapter, we strongly suggested that teachers make instructional decisions based on their students' needs and then modify the lessons in the basal. Children who are struggling with reading, including those who are just learning English, will benefit when teachers plan lessons with them in mind, personalizing the lesson. Sometimes this means that lessons can simply be rearranged; other times it means omitting or expanding parts, or picking and choosing specific practice materials from the vast array of supplemental activities offered. One thing is clear: The effective teacher orchestrates the materials based on student needs. Therefore, teachers need to become familiar with instructional strategies that assist students in becoming effective readers and then use these alternative strategies in conjunction with the basal anthologies to scaffold learning for students.

DIVERSITY
ELL

# WHAT ABOUT STANDARDS, ASSESSMENT, AND *the Basal Reader?*

As the standards movement has become prevalent in education, many states have worked to align their subject area standards with assessment measures and instructional materials. Doing so allows instruction to be planned so that students can progress toward meeting desired academic outcomes (Ohio Department of Education, 2001b).

Basal readers—comprehensive reading programs that include components such as literature anthologies, decodable texts, skill-oriented workbooks, and recommended before-reading and after-reading activities—are frequently used to increase the likelihood that students will achieve required grade-level standards.

District level administrators intend that state standards and the mandated assessments that accompany them influence the reading programs and materials selected for use in school systems (Mraz, 2000). Districts adopt new reading programs or purchase supplemental materials that they believe will be aligned with their state's standards and assessment measures. For example, in recent years, state policy changes that favored explicit and direct instructional methods were implemented in Texas. Based on those changes, the basal reading programs adopted by the state have shifted from literature-based programs used in the early 1990s to programs that emphasized skill instruction and the use of controlled vocabulary (Hoffman, Sailors, & Patterson, 2002). Other states, such as Virginia, have adopted and approved for use specific basal reading programs that align with state standards and policy requirements (Virginia Department of Education, 2004).

## Summary

We examined basal, or core, reading programs and other types of instructional materials in this chapter, emphasizing the need for teachers to understand and use materials wisely. Beginning with the predominant vehicle for reading instruction in elementary classrooms, we reminisced about the origins of basals and some instructional concepts that have been associated with their use throughout the years.

Current basal programs, best described as comprehensive, have come a long way. Consequently, we investigated their concepts and defined their "language." Rather than assigning pros and cons to basal reading programs, we concentrated on the significant improvements made in several areas. Their appearance, organization, illustrations, and success in publishing authentic literature and reducing stereotyping mark genuine strides made by companies. What teachers choose to do with all the aspects of basal reading instruction is an important issue.

Teachers make decisions daily about instruction best suited to the children in their classrooms. They balance the needs of students with all the materials available, relying on their experience, knowledge, and beliefs about reading and learning to read. They may emphasize prescriptive decoding programs, or favor other strategies that may or may not be suggested in the teacher's guide. When teachers modify and adapt lessons, it's often because they need to meet the special needs of their students.

When we considered the wide assortment of instructional materials, we stressed the importance of becoming aware of what is available, especially in light of technological advances. There are current trends and issues teachers should keep in mind as they analyze the materials they are using or considering. They also need to differentiate among the types of commercial reading materials and broaden their view of supplementary materials to incorporate electronic materials. Evaluation criteria are helpful in the selection and use of instructionally worthwhile materials.

In the final analysis, as overwhelming as it might seem to deal sensibly and meaningfully with the array of materials described in this chapter, teachers do exactly that every day.

## Teacher Action Research

1. Select a teacher who uses a core reading program. Interview the teacher about his or her attitude toward basal instruction. How closely is the teacher's manual followed? How does the teacher use the basal workbooks? In what ways, if any, does the teacher deviate from the suggested steps in the manual? What reasons does the teacher give for making modifications?

2. Go to http://reading.uoregon.edu/curricula/index.php and download the *Consumer's Guide to Evaluating a Core Reading Program Grades K–3* by Simmons and Kame'enui (2006). Select a basal and evaluate it using this guide. Compare it to guides completed by other classmates who evaluated a different basal series. What are the strengths and weaknesses of each series? Could this basal be used as a core reading program or supplemental?

3. Compare some selections in a literature-based basal to the actual works of literature. What changes (if any) were made to the authors' original texts? How did that alter your responses to the stories? What instructional decisions might a teacher need to make if the literature selections in his or her basal series or electronic materials were adapted from children's literature rather than being actual whole texts?

THROUGH the LENS of a Literacy Coach

4. Consider a student in your class who struggles with reading or another who has advanced reading skills. How might you work with a literacy coach to meet the needs of either student? Prepare a list of questions you might ask a literacy coach about instructional materials and these students.

## Related Web Sites

*The Florida Center for Reading Research*
**www.fcrr.org/FCRRReports/reportslist.htm**
This site provides a lengthy look at reading programs broken down into the following categories: core reading programs, supplemental and intervention programs, technology-based programs, programs that may be implemented by tutors or mentors, intervention and remedial programs for students above third grade, prekindergarten programs, and professional development.

*Scholastic*
**www.scholastic.com**
Scholastic offers something for parents, teachers, and students. Live author interviews are available, as well as project ideas for trade books, online activities, and other trade-book-related activities.

*TIME For Kids*
**www.timeforkids.com/TFK/teachers**
TIME For Kids is a weekly classroom newsmagazine. Issues cover a wide range of real-world nonfiction topics kids love to learn about. This web site is a companion to the hard copy and the student web site www.timeforkids.com/TFK/kids.

*The University of Oregon Big Ideas in Beginning Reading*
**http://reading.uoregon.edu/curricula/index.php**
The Consumer's Guide to Evaluating a Core Reading Program is a tool to help guide an in-depth analysis of basal reading programs.

*What Works Clearinghouse*
**http://whatworks.ed.gov/Topic.asp?tid=01&ReturnPage=default.asp**
This site focuses on reading programs, products, practices, and policies for students in grades K–3 that are intended to increase skills in the areas of reading essentials.

*Yahooligans! Directory*
**http://kids.yahoo.com**
This directory connects to various online magazines for children.

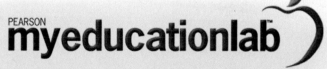

Now go to the Vacca et al. *Reading and Learning to Read*, Seventh Edition, MyEducationLab course at **www.myeducationlab.com** to

- Take a pretest to assess your initial comprehension of the chapter content
- Study chapter content with your individualized study plan
- Take a posttest to assess your understanding of chapter content
- Engage in multimedia exercises to help you build a deeper and more applied understanding of chapter content

## CHAPTER 14

# Making the Transition to Content Area Texts

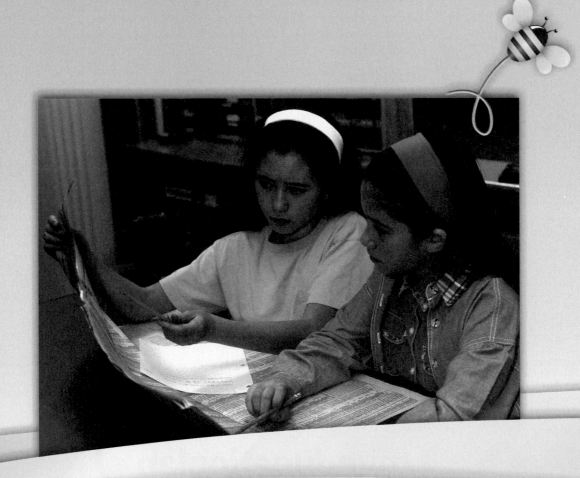

Standards found in this chapter:
- 1.4
- 2.1
- 2.2
- 2.3
- 4.2

## In this chapter,
### YOU WILL DISCOVER:

❖ Why content area textbooks are difficult for students

❖ Factors that help determine textbook difficulty

❖ How using literature and nonfiction trade books across the curriculum benefits teaching and learning

❖ How to integrate the use of textbooks, trade books, and electronic texts into units of study and inquiry-centered projects

❖ A variety of learning strategies for students to use before and during reading and writing

## Concept Map

### MAKING THE TRANSITION TO CONTENT AREA TEXTS

FACTORS THAT MAKE LEARNING FROM TEXTBOOKS DIFFICULT

Readability

USING LITERATURE, TRADE BOOKS, AND ELECTRONIC TEXTS

CONTENT AREA STRATEGIES

Extending Learning Through Reading and Writing

Idea Circles
I-Charts
Point-of-View Guides
Internet Inquiry
Curriculum-Based Reader's Theater

Before Reading

Organizers
Brainstorming
Previewing and Skimming
Anticipation Guides

*It* is mid-October and two eighth graders, Jimmy and Matt, are talking about science class as they walk home from school.

*Jimmy:* I sure don't like science class this year!

*Matt:* How come, man?

*Jimmy:* It's all about tests! Mr. Lee just keeping testing us on stuff I don't even know! He tells us to read the book but it's so boring. I just don't get it!

*Matt:* Wow! Maybe you could change teachers! I have Miss Smyth and she's great! We haven't had one single test! We do hands-on science and we work in small groups and talk about what we learned. Miss Smyth also gives us lots of choices about how we learn the stuff in the book. We can read the chapter summaries and we can look up information in the summaries on the Internet. Then we talk about it in class. It's cool!

*Jimmy:* Well, you're pretty lucky, Matt. I think it's too late to change teachers. I guess I'll have to just sweat it out.

A textbook relies heavily on an expository style of writing—description, classification, and explanation. By its very nature, a textbook is often dry and uninteresting to the novice reader. In fact, as young adolescents enter the middle school years, textbooks often become less and less appealing and more difficult for students. The curriculum, on the other hand, is often, unfortunately, driven by textbook learning at the middle school level. Note the frustrations that Jimmy expressed in the above scenario.

In addition, students from diverse ethnic, cultural, and linguistic backgrounds may find the complex content and new vocabulary in textbooks daunting. Teachers need to develop strategies for making subject area textbooks manageable for these students; otherwise they will get lost in a sea of meaningless text and quickly become frustrated.

As shown in the Concept Map, you'll explore some of the factors that make content area textbooks difficult, as well as strategies teachers can use to enhance content area teaching. Elementary teachers often view their responsibilities in a reading program primarily in terms of skill and strategy development. Their actions are motivated by the question, "How can I help children become more skillful and strategic as readers?" Their main concern, then, is the *process*, or how to guide children's reading development. Yet a concern for the *content* of the reading program should be as important as concern for the process. When children enter the middle school years, teachers are usually concerned with the content of subject matter and spend little time on instructional strategies for helping young adolescents learn how to read the content. It is crucial that content area teachers and reading teachers collaborate in teaching middle school students how to read their textbooks. It is also critical that elementary school teachers include informational text in the early years of teaching reading (Kletzien & Dreher, 2004).

The resurgence of children's literature in the 1980s and of children's nonfiction books in the 1990s and the twenty-first century underscores the importance of meaningful content and authentic texts in elementary and middle school classrooms. In addition to reading trade books in content area learning, children can use electronic texts to read extensively and think critically about content. Reading and writing with computers allows children to access and retrieve information, construct their own texts, and interact with others. In fact, computer technologies have the potential to redefine our more traditional notions of literacy. Content area reading by means of the Internet, for example, opens a world of opportunities for teachers to connect students to worldwide information about all content areas.

## Figure 14.1 Qualities of Effective Teachers

| Reading Teachers | Content Area Teachers |
| --- | --- |
| Use a variety of reading assessments that drive instruction. | Use a variety of content assessments that drive instruction. |
| Explicitly teach reading skills and reading comprehension strategies. | Explicitly teach and model how to become active readers of content area texts. |
| Provide students with opportunities to read meaningful materials that they find interesting. | Provide students a variety of interesting reading sources that teach the content. |
| Provide students with engaging literacy tasks as they are learning to read. | Provide students with a variety of engaging activities in which they are learning new content. |
| Have high expectations that all children will learn how to read. | Have high expectations that all children can learn the content of a subject. |

STANDARD
4.2

There is a growing consensus about what qualities characterize an effective teacher of reading (Blair, Rupley, & Nichols, 2007). We suggest that the same attributes distinguish successful content area teachers. In Figure 14.1 we synthesize Blair, Rupley, and Nichols's characteristics of effective reading teachers and elaborate on the qualities as they apply to content area teachers. See Box 14.1 on page 458 for an example of how one literacy leader assists content area teachers by helping them identify struggling readers and modifying instructional strategies and materials.

We next focus our attention on factors that make learning from textbooks difficult for many children. These include assumptions about vocabulary and prior knowledge, and the readability levels of content area texts.

**BUILDING TEACHING SKILLS: VIDEO**

Go to the Homework and Exercises section in Chapter 14 of MyEducationLab to watch the video "Reading a Textbook" and think about what strategies you could use to help students get the most out of their textbooks.

# Why Are Content Area Textbooks Difficult?

Content area textbooks are an integral part of schooling. In most classrooms, textbooks blend into the physical environment, much like desks, bulletin boards, chalkboards, and computers. Even a casual observer expects to see textbooks in use in the elementary classroom. Yet teachers often remark that children find textbooks difficult. When students have trouble reading texts, we are acutely aware of the mismatch between the reading abilities students bring to text material and some of the difficulties of the text. This can be particularly true for English language learners.

To compensate for this, some teachers avoid textbook assignments. Instruction revolves around lecture and other activities instead of the textbook. Some teachers abandon difficult materials, sidestepping reading altogether as a vehicle for learning.

In lieu of either abandoning difficult materials or avoiding reading altogether, we need to get answers to some very basic questions. How does the textbook meet the goals of the curriculum? Is the conceptual difficulty of the text beyond students' grasp? Does the author have a clear sense of purpose as conveyed to this audience? How well are the ideas in the text organized? With answers to these and other questions, teachers of young as well as middle school students have some basis on which to make decisions about text-related instruction, allowing them to exercise their professional judgment.

DIVERSITY
ELL

# BOX 14.1

## Viewpoint

## the Literacy Coach

### Leading Content Area Teachers Toward Excellence

*David W. Anderson is the literacy lead teacher at the Canton McKinley High School Freshman Academy in Canton, Ohio. As the literacy lead teacher, he serves on the Canton McKinley literacy team, a cadre of content area teachers whose function is to promulgate literacy-based methods across all content areas at the high school. Dr. Michelle L. Lenarz is an associate professor at Walsh University in North Canton, Ohio, where she teaches reading in the content area.*

The McKinley Freshman Academy is a ninth-grade, interdisciplinary "small school" on the Canton McKinley High School campus, an urban high school of approximately 1600 students. Mr. Anderson and Dr. Lenarz have collaborated for two years on improving fluency and comprehension levels of ninth graders using a variety of reading strategies including sustained silent reading and reader's theater. Recent implementation of Measures of Academic Progress™ (MAP) (www.nwea.org/assessments) and testing in language usage, mathematics, reading, and science at the McKinley campus has allowed Dr. Lenarz and Mr. Anderson to add Lexile™ (www.lexile.com/EntrancePageFlash.html) measurements to their assessments of students' reading ability over the course of each school year. MAP assessments are state-aligned computerized adaptive tests that accurately reflect the instructional level of each student and measure growth over time.

Through the administration of the MAP testing twice during the academic year, faculty at the McKinley Freshman Academy can identify the skills and concepts individual students have learned, diagnose instructional needs, monitor academic growth over time, make data-driven decisions at the classroom, school, and district levels, and place new students into appropriate instructional programs.

Content area teachers on three interdisciplinary teams of the McKinley Freshman Academy and Dr. Lenarz's students in reading in the content area at Walsh University administer the Quick and Easy High School Reading Assessments (www.ohioliteracyalliance.org/fluency/fluency.htm) to the ninth graders three times during the academic year and record their individual word recognition accuracy; fluency automaticity (words read correctly per minute); multidimensional fluency score comprised of expression and volume, phrasing and intonation, smoothness, and pace; and comprehension score.

Students identified by these state-aligned computerized adaptive tests and reading assessments as reading below expectation for grade level are provided with additional intervention beyond the cross-curricular literacy strategies employed by all teachers at the McKinley Freshman Academy. One of these interventions involves working with the student and his or her parent(s) to identify trade books within his or her independent reading Lexile range for use during sustained silent reading over the ensuing weeks.

Dr. Lenarz's students also practice this approach by creating a sequenced, content area reading list of increasing difficulty, as indicated by the Lexile measurement, for a struggling reader in their discipline. Starting at the independent reading level indicated by the MAP assessments, each preservice teacher selects four books, with each subsequent book on the list measuring 50 to 75 Lexile above the previous book.

The literacy cadre at the McKinley campus participates in monthly inservice presentations of high-payoff literacy strategies, and each member of the cadre works personally with a "clone"—an interested teacher who is struggling with implementation—to help integrate these strategies into regular lesson planning. Mr. Anderson is currently working with a very dedicated fifth-year science teacher. They will meet at least weekly to identify places in her lessons where she can effectively insert a high-payoff literacy strategy in place of lecture or unstructured reading. As these lessons are executed, they will track the results using Excel and add formative assessment to their meeting agenda, modifying the strategies as necessary to meet the needs of her students.

The composition of interdisciplinary teams has varied at the McKinley Freshman Academy over its eight years, but English, science, and history have always been represented on each team. This year, Mr. Anderson's team consists of English, science, history, math, Spanish, and special education. The members of Mr. Anderson's team are remarkable in their pursuit of innovation and their dedication to improving their collective pedagogy. Their focus is whole-child education with a literacy and numeracy focus. Three of their members are part of the McKinley High School Literacy Cadre, attending training provided by the KnowledgeWorks Foundation (www.kwfdn.org) six times a year. Everyone contributes to the planning and coordination of learning activities. Mr. Anderson's team also meets voluntarily with parents five evenings over the course of the school year beyond their mandated parent–teacher conferences and uses this time to develop individualized, cross-curricular reading intervention plans built around Lexile measures and fluency scores. Despite reductions in scheduled team planning time that have been imposed in the years since they started, Mr. Anderson's team continues to meet regularly, often over lunch.

## Factors in Judging the Difficulty of Textbooks

The difficulty of text material is the result of factors residing in both the reader and the text. Therefore, to judge well, you need to take into account several types of information. A primary source of information is the publisher. Consider the publisher-provided descriptions of the design, format, and organizational structure of the textbook, along with grade-level readability designations. A second source is your knowledge of students in the class. A third source is your own sense of what makes the textbook useful for learning a particular subject.

The first order of business is to define how the textbook will be used. Will it be used as the sole basis for information or as an extension of information? Will it be used in tandem with informational books and other forms of children's literature? Is it to provide guided activities?

**HOW DIFFICULT IS THE TEXT TO UNDERSTAND?** ◆ This question might be recast into a set of subsidiary questions: How likely are students to comprehend the text? How difficult are the concepts in the text? Has the author taken into consideration the prior knowledge that students bring to the text? The ability to understand the textbook, to a large extent, will be influenced by the match between what the reader already knows and the text itself. Background knowledge and logical organization of expository texts are crucial factors for comprehending new information (Beck & McKeown, 1991).

Irwin and Davis (1980) suggested that teachers analyze a text using questions such as the following:

> Are the assumptions about students' vocabulary knowledge appropriate?
>
> Are the assumptions about students' prior knowledge of this content area appropriate?
>
> Are the assumptions about students' general experiential backgrounds appropriate?
>
> Are new concepts explicitly linked to the students' prior knowledge or to their experiential backgrounds?
>
> Does the text introduce abstract concepts by accompanying them with many concrete examples?
>
> Does the text introduce new concepts one at a time with a sufficient number of examples for each one?
>
> Does the text avoid irrelevant details?

Teachers need to be aware that students from culturally, linguistically, and socially diverse backgrounds will bring a wide range of experiences to the classroom. These experiences will influence how students understand or fail to understand their textbooks. Fitzgerald and Graves (2004) elaborate on factors associated with text difficulty for English language learners (ELLs). They point out that while difficult vocabulary is relatively easy to identify, texts that contain "a lot of difficult words are likely to be harder for English-language learners" (p. 333). Although it is important that ELL students have access to text in which they will *learn* new words, when they are overloaded with new terminology, learning is impeded. Regarding vocabulary and texts, it is also important to realize that, although some English language learners have adequate conversational skills, their knowledge of academic English vocabulary is typically less developed.

In addition to vocabulary, it is important to consider the complexity of sentences, as well as the "natural-sounding" nature of the text. Long and complex sentences can make reading difficult for all readers, including English language learners. On the other hand, short choppy sentences can interfere with understanding. The length of a reading assignment is another factor to consider in terms of readability for ELL students, as well as how clearly examples are elaborated upon, the coherence and unity of the text, and the structure and organization of the text (Fitzgerald & Graves, 2004).

Although many of the same considerations for evaluating the levels of difficulty for textbooks apply to all learners, Fitzgerald and Graves (2004) give specific suggestions for English language learners:

- As content area text readings are introduced, check English language learners' understanding of key terms.
- Consider having ELL students read summaries or shorter subsections of text rather than lengthy reading assignments.
- Decide whether the examples in the text will clarify understanding or will create an overload of information.
- Supply students with an outline of the text prior to reading.
- Consider the relevance of the material to ELL students' background information.

**HOW USABLE IS THE TEXT?** ◆ To determine how usable a text is, you will need to consider its organizational features and its presentation of material. Your responses to the following questions will help you decide whether you are dealing with a **considerate text** or an *inconsiderate* one. For example, your responses may reveal the extent to which relationships among ideas in the text are clear, the logical organization between ideas, and the use of *signal words* (connectives) to make relationships explicit. To determine if a text is *considerate* and *user friendly*, ask yourself these questions (Irwin & Davis, 1980):

Does the table of contents provide a clear overview of the content of the textbook?

Do chapter headings clearly define the content of the chapter?

Do chapter subheadings clearly break out the important concepts in the chapter?

Do topic headings provide assistance in breaking the chapter into relevant parts?

Does the glossary contain all the technical terms used in the textbook?

Are graphs and charts clear and supportive of the textual material?

Are illustrations well done and appropriate to the level of the students?

Are the sentence lengths appropriate for the level of students who will be using the text?

Are important terms in italic or boldfaced type for easy identification by readers?

Do end-of-chapter questions check the reader's literal, interpretive, and applied levels of comprehension?

Is an adequate context provided to allow students to determine meanings of technical terms?

**HOW INTERESTING IS THE TEXT?** ◆ Textbooks should appeal to students; the more relevant the text, the more interesting it will be. Illustrations and pictures should have appeal, and they will when they depict persons that students can relate to. Do the cover design and other artwork convey up-to-date, culturally diverse images? Are type sizes and faces varied? Does the boldface lettering of headings contrast with the lightface lettering of the main narrative? Italics and numbering of words and phrases in lists are two other devices that can help make the printed page come alive for elementary as well as middle school students. In addition to the questions just raised, consider these as you analyze a textbook for interest:

Is the writing style of the text appealing to the students?

Are the activities motivating? Will they make students want to pursue the topic further?

Does the book clearly show how the knowledge being learned might be used by the learner in the future?

Does the text provide positive and motivating models for both sexes as well as for all racial, ethnic, and socioeconomic groups?

Does the text help students generate interest as they relate experiences and develop visual and sensory images?

Once the information accrues about factors contributing to textbook difficulty, you are in a position to use professional judgment. As we will examine next, the more traditional readability formula can be a complement to a teacher's judgment instead of a substitute for it.

## Readability

When teachers judge instructional content area materials, they frequently assess **readability.** Readability formulas can help *estimate* textbook difficulty, but they are not intended to be precise indicators. Of the many readability formulas available, the most popular ones are relatively quick and easy to calculate. They typically involve a measure of sentence length and word difficulty to ascertain a grade-level score for text materials. This score supposedly indicates the reading achievement level students would need to comprehend the material. Readability formulas can also be accessed via the computer by typing or scanning a passage or book. You do, however, need to be aware of limitations associated with using readability formulas.

LIMITATIONS ◆ Readability formulas yield scores that are simply estimates, not absolute levels, of text difficulty. These estimates are often determined along a single dimension of an author's writing style: vocabulary difficulty and sentence complexity. They are measured by word and sentence length, respectively. These are two variables most often used to predict the difficulty of a text. Nevertheless, they only *indirectly* assess vocabulary difficulty and sentence complexity. Are long words always harder to understand than short ones? Are long sentences necessarily more difficult than short ones?

Keep in mind that a readability formula doesn't take into account the experience and knowledge that young, middle school, linguistically and culturally diverse, or struggling readers bring to content material. The reader's emotional, cognitive, and linguistic backgrounds aren't included in readability estimates. Thus several factors that contribute to a reader's ability to comprehend text are not dealt with: purpose, interest, motivation, emotional state, environment, culture, and ability. Keeping these limitations in mind, we next examine a readability formula more closely.

FRY READABILITY GRAPH ◆ There are over 100 readability formulas in existence, many of which are used by industry and large commercial companies (Fry, 2002). The Flesch Kincaid Reading Ease Formula, for example, provides a readability score that is often cited on computers. One fairly quick and simple readability formula that educators use is the Fry Readability Graph, developed by Edward Fry (1968, 1977). Fry used two variables to predict difficulty and determine grade-level scores for materials from grade 1 through college: sentence length and word length. The total number of sentences in a sample passage determines sentence length, and the total number of syllables in the passage determines word length.

Three 100-word samples from the selected reading material should be used to calculate its readability. Grade-level scores for each passage can then be averaged to obtain an overall readability level. The readability graph in Figure 14.2 on page 462 is useful in predicting the difficulty of material within one grade level when the accompanying directions for the Fry formula are followed.

Keep in mind that, in addition to using readability formulas, classroom teachers often use a system of *leveling trade books* for the purpose of matching students with appropriate

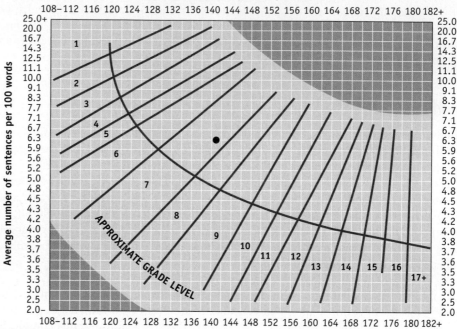

**Figure 14.2  Fry Readability Graph**

**Graph for Estimating Readability—Extended**

**Expanded Directions for Working the Readability Graph**

1. Randomly select three sample passages and count out exactly 100 words each, starting with the beginning of a sentence. Do count proper nouns, initializations, and numerals.

2. Count the number of sentences in the 100 words, estimating length of the fraction of the last sentence to the nearest one-tenth.

3. Count the total number of syllables in the 100-word passage. If you don't have a hand counter available, an easy way is simply to put a mark above every syllable over one in each word, then when you get to the end of the passage, count the number of marks and add 100. Small calculators can also be used as counters by pushing numeral 1, then pushing the + sign for each word or syllable when counting.

4. Enter graph with *average* sentence length and *average* number of syllables; plot dot where the two lines intersect. The area where the dot is plotted will give you the approximate grade level.

5. If a great deal of variability is found in syllable count or sentence count, putting more samples into the average is desirable.

6. A word is defined as a group of symbols with a space on either side; thus, *Joe, IRA, 1945,* and *&* are each one word.

7. A syllable is defined as a phonetic symbol. Generally, there are as many syllables as vowel sounds. For example, *stopped* is one syllable and *wanted* is two syllables. When counting syllables for numerals and initializations, count one syllable for each symbol. For example, *1945* is four syllables, *IRA* is three syllables, and *&* is one syllable.

STANDARD
2.1

reading material based on their reading achievement. Leveled books take into consideration such factors as the number of words on a page, the type size and layout of the page, how closely illustrations support the vocabulary, how much repetition of words and phrases there is, and how appropriate the content is for the age level of the reader (Fry, 2002). Hence, rather than being limited to using textbooks, teachers can take advantage of trade books that enhance their students' knowledge of content subjects. Next, we discuss the importance and value of using trade books to enhance content area reading.

# Using Literature and Nonfiction Trade Books Across the Curriculum

The use of children's literature and nonfiction **trade books** in elementary and middle school classrooms extends and enriches information provided in content area textbooks. Often textbooks cannot treat subject matter with the breadth and depth necessary to develop ideas and concepts fully. Literature and nonfiction trade books have the potential to capture children's interest and imagination in people, places, events, and ideas. And they have the potential to develop in-depth understanding in ways that textbooks aren't equipped to do.

According to Moss (1991), informational book selections should be made on the basis of the "five A's": the *authority* of the *author*, the *appropriateness* of the book for the children in the classroom, the literary *artistry*, and the *appearance* of the book. *Eye Openers II*, by Kobrin (1995); *Strategies That Work*, by Harvey and Goudvis (2000); and *Teaching with Picture Books in the Middle School*, by Tiedt (2000), provide brief synopses and teaching ideas for hundreds of high-quality nonfiction trade books.

Nonetheless, having a wide array of literature and nonfiction trade books available for content area learning is necessary but not sufficient to ensure that children make appropriate use of trade books. Teachers must plan for their use by weaving trade books into meaningful and relevant instructional activities within the context of content area study. In this section, the focus is not only on the uses and benefits of literature and nonfiction trade books across the curriculum but also on the preparation of units of study and strategies for using information texts.

STANDARD 2.3

**HOMEWORK EXERCISE: CASE STUDY**

Go to the Homework and Exercises section in Chapter 14 of MyEducationLab to view the video "Literature and the Reading Process" about how a teacher chooses articles and literature to use with students.

## Some Uses and Benefits of Literature and Nonfiction Trade Books

There are many benefits to using trade books and **literature across the curriculum,** either in tandem with textbooks or in units of study around a thematic unit. For one, trade books and other literature provide students with intense involvement in a subject; for another, they are powerful schema builders; for a third, they may be used to accommodate a wide range of student abilities and interests. With trade books, children may choose from a variety of topics for intensive study and inquiry. One benefit for the teacher, of course, is that literature may be used instructionally in a variety of ways. Picture books, for example, can provide elementary and middle school students with valuable background knowledge regarding diverse cultures. Hence picture books can provide students with a greater appreciation for the multicultural world in which we live.

DIVERSITY

**INTENSE INVOLVEMENT** ◆ A textbook compresses information. Intensive treatment gives way to extensive coverage. As a result, an elementary or middle school textbook is more likely to mention and summarize important ideas, events, and concepts than to develop them fully or richly. Brozo and Tomlinson (1986) underscored this point by illustrating the content treatment of Hitler, the Nazis, and the Jews in a fifth-grade social studies textbook.

Hitler's followers were called Nazis. Hitler and the Nazis built up Germany's military power and started a campaign against the Jews who lived in that country. Hitler claimed that the Jews were to blame for Germany's problems. He took away their rights and property. Many Jews left Germany and came to live in the United States. The Nazis

Trade books and informational texts provide students with intense involvement in a subject.

began to arrest Jews who stayed in Germany and put them in special camps. Then the Nazis started murdering them. Before Hitler's years in power came to an end, six million Jews lost their lives.

A textbook, as you can surmise from this example, often condenses a subject to its barest essentials. The result often is a bland and watered-down treatment of the subjects, which is particularly evident in today's history texts (Sewell, 1987). The paragraph on Hitler's treatment of the Jews is a vivid example of the "principle of minimum essentials" in textbook practice. The passage cited represents the entirety of this particular text's coverage of the Holocaust. Though it may be accurate, it takes one of the most tragic and horrifying events in world history and compresses it into a series of colorless and emotionless summarizing statements. On the other hand, trade books are an excellent vehicle for content study because they generate intense involvement in a subject. Kletzien and Dreher (2004) point out that young children are motivated by reading nonfiction and for "some children informational text provides a way into literacy that stories cannot" (p. 2).

**SCHEMA BUILDING** ◆ Intense involvement in a subject generates background knowledge and vicarious experience that make textbook concepts easier to grasp and assimilate. As a result, one of the most compelling uses of trade books is as schema builders for subjects under textbook study. Soalt (2005) suggests that combining the reading of nonfiction informational texts with fictional texts about the same topic not only helps students build background knowledge, but also prepares and motivates them to read a variety of genres.

The transition to content area reading is smoother when students bring a frame of reference to textbook study. Reading literature strengthens the reading process because reading about a topic can dramatically improve comprehension of related readings on the same topic. The background knowledge acquired in the natural reading of trade books helps students comprehend related discourse (Soalt, 2005).

STANDARD
1.4

**ABILITIES AND INTERESTS** ◆ When teachers use trade books in tandem with textbooks, there's something for everyone. A teacher can provide students with trade books on a variety of topics related to a subject under investigation. Books on related topics are written at various levels of difficulty. Greenlaw (1988) maintained that one of the benefits of trade books is that children can select books on a reading level appropriate to their abilities and interests. It is also clear that children of all ages find informational text motivating. Mohr (2003), for example, found that first graders had a strong preference for nonfiction trade books. Moss and Hendershot (2002) found that middle school students were highly motivated by sharing informational texts with their peers. Roser and Keehn (2002) discovered that fourth graders demonstrated "a kind of energy" (p. 425) when they were given the opportunity to engage in inquiry and talk about nonfiction texts.

**VOCABULARY BUILDING** ◆ It is well recognized that students need multiple exposures to new vocabulary words in order to learn them. This is particularly true of learning new content vocabulary which is often technical and difficult to pronounce. When teachers integrate trade books into their teaching of content, they provide students with opportunities to read new vocabulary in multiple contexts and trade books often use synonyms for new words (Soalt, 2005).

Gregg and Sekeres (2006) suggest teaching new content vocabulary using realia—actual objects—and demonstrations. They recommend providing time for students to physically experience new ideas and concepts before introducing them to the new vocabulary in texts. Boyd and Ikpeze (2007) demonstrated how seventh-grade students wrote and performed skits that exhibited their understanding of new vocabulary. When students have opportunities to observe and experience new concepts in real life, they will be more motivated to read about them.

In essence, when fictional and nonfiction trade books are integrated into content area instruction, students have opportunities to become intensely involved with the subject matter, build their background knowledge by using meaningful text, tap their interests and abilities, and learn new and often difficult vocabulary. In the Research-Based Practices featured in Box 14.2 you will find guidelines for selecting literature to augment content area instruction. Lesson development suggestions are featured in Figure 14.3 on the next page. Next we discuss three models that will help you decide how to integrate literature into the content areas.

---

**BOX 14.2**

### *Research-Based Practices*

### Guidelines for Choosing Literature to Enhance Content Area Reading Instruction

- Do the books—fiction or nonfiction—present accurate information? Even though fictional literature can include storylike narratives, the information that is discussed related to the actual content of a lesson should be true. It is essential that informational texts present authentic information. Consider the expertise of the author(s).
- If the students will be using the books independently, consider the readability levels. Otherwise, for those books that are too difficult for children to read, think about the possibilities of reading sections of those books aloud. Consider the format of the informational books that you select. Do they include a table of contents, glossary, bold text, and other useful organizational features or are those unnecessary to capture the purpose of your book selections?

- Evaluate the design of the books: the nature of the illustrations, photographs, and placement of the information on the pages. Do the books you have selected have an appealing style that would interest the students? Is the language engaging?
- Consider the state content area curriculum of the subject you are teaching when you select books. Be sure your book selection enhances specific content that you need to teach. In addition, refer to the professional organizations of your content area for related children and young adult literature to enhance your content teaching: National Council of Social Studies (NCSS), National Council of Teachers of Mathematics (NCTM), and National Science Teachers Association (NSTA).

*Source:* Adapted from *Using Literature to Enhance Reading Instruction: A Guide for K–5 Teachers,* by R. Olness (Newark, DE: International Reading Association, 2007).

## Figure 14.3   Lesson Guidelines for Engaging Readers in Content Area Lessons Using Literature

1. *Select the standards(s)* that you plan to teach based on your content area. It can be helpful to select a theme that addresses several standards. Examples of a social studies theme for first graders might include community helpers, neighborhoods, families, or community jobs.

2. *Decide on your purpose* for using literature and how you will use the literature to enhance the content of your lessons. Consider the specific goals that you want to address by using the literature you have selected. Are your goals to activate prior knowledge? Build background knowledge? Teach vocabulary associated with the content area? Share concepts in more vivid ways?

3. *Gather your books.* For beginning teachers, an efficient way to gather books is to enlist the help of a local children's librarian. By calling ahead, you can request that a collection of books be gathered by giving the librarian your needs and criteria; for example, "I need 20 books about communities that would be appropriate for first graders. Some of the books should be on a first or second grade reading level for independent reading; others can be for read-alouds; please balance the collection with approximately a third of the books being fictional; the others should expose the students to real-life community issues." As teachers continue to teach specific grade levels, writing grants that support literature-based content area instruction is another option. Browse the Martha Holden Jennings web site for educators (http://mhjf.org/grants_educators.html) for classroom grants you may tap to help you gather content area literature resources.

4. *Develop a plan.* For example will you use a read-aloud for each aspect of your theme? Will you select books in which the students can do independent reading? How will you introduce the children to the literature? Will you conduct book talks in which you briefly share the nature of each book?

5. *Consider your assessment strategies* based on using literature in your content area classroom. Will your students conduct poster sessions about what they learned? Will they conduct their own book talks that address the content? Will they develop artistic representations of what they learned? Will they gather journal entries for which you have developed specific criteria? Although there are a myriad of ways to assess student learning outcomes when teachers engage their students with literature-based content learning, you need to establish guidelines at the outset to ensure that your students are demonstrating the standards that you expected them to learn when you planned your lessons.

## Planning to Use Literature and Informational Text in Content Area Learning

**STANDARDS 2.1, 2.2**

**BUILDING TEACHING SKILLS: READING**

Go to the Homework and Exercises section in Chapter 14 of MyEducationLab to read the article "Getting Started: Manageable Literacy Practices" to develop an understanding of how to help students use all text effectively.

In order to effectively use literature and informational text to teach the content areas, teachers need to thoughtfully plan. Will you use read-alouds? Cooperative learning groups? Research strategies? How will you scaffold student learning? Smith and Johnson (1994) offer three models to consider when planning literature-based instruction in content studies: the single-discipline model, the interdisciplinary literature model, and the integrative literature model. Although these models are not set in stone, they do provide useful frameworks for planning instruction.

**THE SINGLE-DISCIPLINE MODEL** ◆ According to Smith and Johnson (1994), this model is typically based on a theme identified as important for the grade level; the theme may be based on standards identified in a required curriculum. Once identified, either a single narrative text or multiple texts, called *text sets*, are selected as the primary source of information about the theme. There are several advantages to using multiple texts. Students can read various points of view regarding the theme. Multiple texts allow students to choose what they read. There is also collaborative learning about the subject

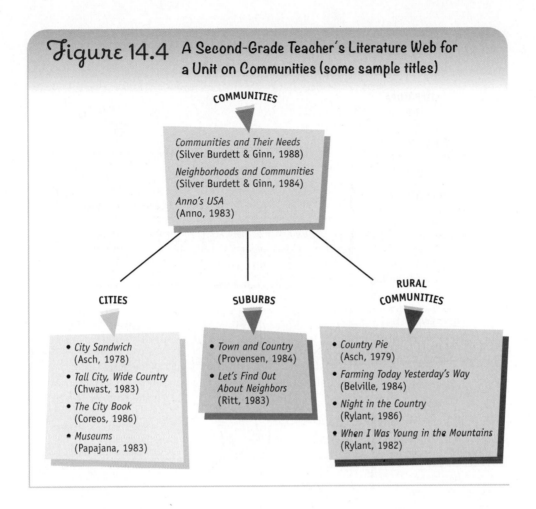

**Figure 14.4** A Second-Grade Teacher's Literature Web for a Unit on Communities (some sample titles)

COMMUNITIES

*Communities and Their Needs*
(Silver Burdett & Ginn, 1988)

*Neighborhoods and Communities*
(Silver Burdett & Ginn, 1984)

*Anno's USA*
(Anno, 1983)

**CITIES**
- *City Sandwich*
  (Asch, 1978)
- *Tall City, Wide Country*
  (Chwast, 1983)
- *The City Book*
  (Coreos, 1986)
- *Museums*
  (Papajana, 1983)

**SUBURBS**
- *Town and Country*
  (Provensen, 1984)
- *Let's Find Out About Neighbors*
  (Ritt, 1983)

**RURAL COMMUNITIES**
- *Country Pie*
  (Asch, 1979)
- *Farming Today Yesterday's Way*
  (Belville, 1984)
- *Night in the Country*
  (Rylant, 1986)
- *When I Was Young in the Mountains*
  (Rylant, 1982)

matter. Finally, students with varying reading and language abilities are provided with different books. The content area textbook serves as a resource. Figure 14.4 illustrates a **literature web** that uses multiple texts about communities.

**THE INTERDISCIPLINARY MODEL** ◆ This model incorporates two or more disciplines as the students learn about a central theme. Smith and Johnson (1994) provide an example of the interdisciplinary model in which the theme was "movement in U.S. history." Using the book *Constance: A Story of Early Plymouth* by Patricia Clapp, the disciplines studied included math (calculating the distance of the Old World to the New World), social studies (comparing Native American rituals to the religion of the pilgrims), and art (constructing models of villages or ships). Figure 14.5 on page 468 illustrates a sixth-grade teacher's web for an interdisciplinary unit on the middle ages.

**THE INTEGRATIVE LITERATURE MODEL** ◆ This model also focuses on a central theme. However, the nature of the unit revolves around skills that go beyond subject areas such as problem solving, critical thinking, values, and social action skills. For example, keeping with the theme "movement in U.S. history," the students might graph conflicts that occurred in the book *Constance: A Story of Early Plymouth*, critically think about individualism versus teamwork in their own lives, and examine health care issues "then and now" (Smith & Johnson, 1994).

Developing a unit of study involves deliberate teacher planning to set a tone for students that encourages them to actively engage in learning around a content theme or topic. It allows a rich opportunity to make reading useful by bridging the gap between children and the difficulties they often have understanding content area textbooks. In the next section, we take a closer look at additional considerations to think about when engaging students with informational texts in the content areas.

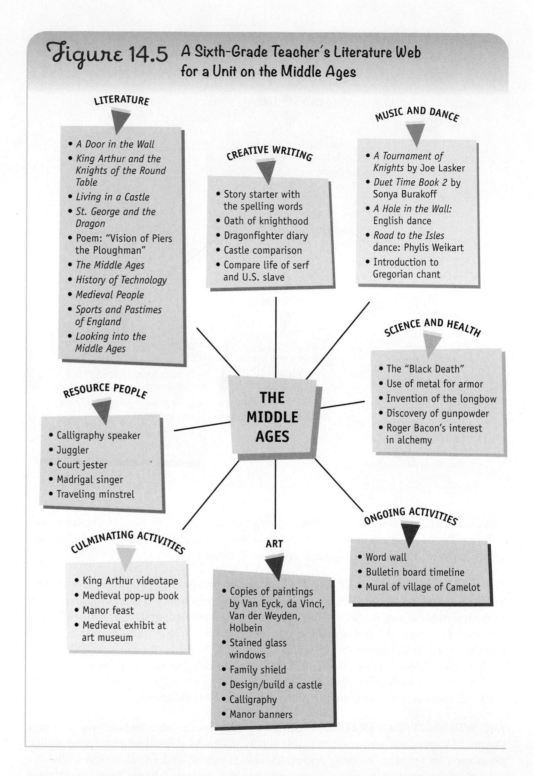

**Figure 14.5** A Sixth-Grade Teacher's Literature Web for a Unit on the Middle Ages

## Additional Considerations for Implementing Literature and Informational Text in the Content Areas

**INFORMATIONAL TEXT TYPES** ◆ You should be aware of the different types of informational texts that are available. Generally, there are three types of informational or nonfiction text types: narrative informational, expository informational, and mixed- or combined-text trade books (Chapman & Sopko, 2003; Kletzien & Dreher, 2004). In **narrative informational texts** the author typically tells a fictional story that conveys factual information. For example, in the book *Charlie Needs a Cloak* by Tomie dePaola, a make-believe shepherd goes through the steps of shearing a sheep and washing, carding, and spinning wool to make his cloak. This type of text often works well as a read-aloud and can be a motivating lead-in to a topic of study. **Expository informational books** do not contain stories; they contain information that typically follows specific text structures such as description, sequence, cause and effect, comparison and contrast, and problem solving. In addition, they often contain features such as a table of contents, a glossary, lists of illustrations, charts, and graphs. Whereas narrative informational texts are typically read from beginning to end, expository books do not have to be read in any particular order. **Mixed-text informational books,** sometimes referred to as *combined-text trade books,* narrate stories and include factual information in the surrounding text. For example, in *The Magic School Bus: Inside the Human Body* by Joanna Cole, the author takes the reader through an imaginary adventure through the human body; surrounding the story are true facts and illustrations about the body. With books of this type it is important to help the students distinguish fact from fiction. As mentioned earlier, when a combination of texts is used, this is referred to as a *text set.*

**READING THE TEXTS** ◆ Whether you use one informational text or multiple books, you will need to decide how you will engage the students with them. One strategy that Kletzien and Dreher (2004) recommend for young children is to use informational texts as read-alouds. They suggest developing a read-aloud chart for display in the classroom in which you list the books that you read aloud and have the children classify them as fiction or informational. To assist struggling readers or ELL students, Smith and Johnson (1994) suggest pairing students of different reading abilities, tape-recording informational texts so that they can be listened to, or using kaleidoscope reading in which children read different selections of the informational text and share what they have learned. Stien and Beed (2004) suggest how a literature circle setting can be adapted for the purpose of engaging students in talk about informational text. Roser and Keehn (2002) describe how to implement book clubs—small groups of children reading, followed by whole class and small group inquiry—using informational texts. Needless to say, there are a wide variety of ways teachers can engage students in reading informational texts as they study content area subjects.

**STRATEGIES FOR TEACHING READING COMPREHENSION WITH INFORMATIONAL TEXTS** ◆ In Chapter 10, we discussed specific strategies for teaching reading comprehension. Although many of the strategies—such as QARs, reciprocal teaching, and think-alouds—can be implemented with fiction as well as informational text, it is important that teachers think about teaching reading comprehension and explicitly teach students how to understand, connect to, and read nonfiction text. Below, we discuss several important components of teaching reading comprehension and share alternative reading comprehension strategies that explicitly address reading comprehension skills that teachers can use to enhance students' understanding of informational text.

**Hands-On Activities and Background Knowledge**   Introducing students to content material through hands-on activities can be motivating. The activities can be done with the whole class or in small groups. These firsthand experiences need not be elaborate; often simple demonstrations work well. For example, Fitzgerald and Graves (2004) share a prereading activity about *waves* in which the students line up in front of the classroom and recreate a wave scenario by "standing up and sitting down—much like fans do at a football game" (p. 33). After practicing the wave scenario, Fitzgerald and Graves suggest that the teacher can elaborate on wave formations and preteach concepts prior to reading textbook information about waves. We suggest that an activity of this sort is an excellent example of how to introduce the concept prior to reading trade books about waves. Fitzgerald and Graves point out hands-on activities are especially valuable for use with ELL students.

The relationship between background knowledge about a topic and reading comprehension is well documented (Pressley, 2000). Think About It! is a strategy in which a guest speaker shares knowledge about the topic under study prior to reading about the topic in trade books (Fitzgerald & Graves, 2004). The following day, the teacher writes several main categories about the topic on the chalkboard and, working in small groups, the students brainstorm what they learned about each topic from the speaker. A scribe for each group records the information, which is subsequently shared with the whole class. Fitzgerald and Graves suggest that this prereading activity is especially useful for ELL students because it focuses attention on the main ideas that the students will read about in the unit of study and *provides* background information about the topic.

Manitone and Smead (2003) describe activities during which middle school students experienced the music, dance, art, and poetry of the Harlem Renaissance prior to reading about the jazz era in Gail Carson Levine's *Dave at Night*, the true story of a young boy from an orphanage who sneaks out to explore the world of jazz during the night. Manitone and Smead describe the encounter thus: "We took the time. . . . We wanted our students to feel as much of the magic of those times as we could recreate in our little school" (p. 46). By providing firsthand experiences, the teachers helped build schema for the story so that they could more fully appreciate the life and times of the Harlem Renaissance.

Manitone and Smead (2003) also suggest numerous artistic activities for building background knowledge prior to reading informational books. For example, prior to reading a book about an Amish girl, *The Journey* by Sarah Stewart, second graders used disposable cameras to develop photo journals of significant events in their lives so that they would have an appreciation for connecting prior knowledge to the girl's experiences.

**Making Connections**    Closely related to background knowledge is the importance of providing students with the opportunity to make connections as they read informational text. As we discussed in Chapter 10, Harvey and Goudvis (2000) suggest that as students read content material, they use sticky notes to indicate sections of the text in which they have a connection. Wooten (2000) suggests that teachers and students can graph connections with sticky notes as they read or are read to. In Box 14.3 we have adapted Wooten's steps for graphing.

*Common threads* is a prereading activity that helps students make personal connections to what they are reading (Fitzgerald & Graves, 2004). Prior to reading historical fiction or information in which a problem is presented, the students brainstorm similar problems that have occurred in their own lives, as well as the solutions to those problems. For example, prior to reading Ching Yeung Russell's *First Apple*, a story of a young Chinese girl who encounters many obstacles as she tries to purchase an apple for her grandmother as a gift, middle school students brainstormed obstacles they had overcome. Fitzgerald and Graves acknowledge that students often like to talk about their own experiences; however, they recommend using caution with English language learners who may be reluctant to talk about their families and their personal lives. Regardless of the ways in which teachers help students make connections to informational text, it is important to realize that this is a crucial component of learning about subject matter.

**Determining the Structure of Informational Text**    As we mentioned earlier, expository informational books typically are written to reflect a variety of text structures: sequence, compare–contrast, cause and effect, and description, and they often contribute to difficulties in reading comprehension for students. It is critical that teachers work with students so that they understand the various structures they will encounter when reading expository text. Dymock (2005) recommends modeling how to diagram a text structure through graphic organizers. The visuals assist students in recognizing the organization of the expository text. As teachers work with students they need to model how to match the text structure with the graphics. Figure 14.6 shows four graphic organizers that

BOX **14.3**  STEP-BY-STEP *Lesson*

## Graphing Connections

Wooten (2000) maintains that personal responses to informational text can be graphed over a school year, providing teachers with enlightening assessment information about students' development as thinkers as they read. Here, we adapt her strategy, step by step, so that teachers can implement the strategy in a lesson.

1. Select a narrative informational book that engages the students in the upcoming topic of study. Tiedt (2000) provides an excellent resource of picture books for middle school teachers.
2. Read the book aloud.
3. Reread the book and do a think-aloud as you model connections to the story, as well as the facts, such as: "This reminds me of . . . I never realized that . . . I've always wondered about this." As you think aloud, write snippets of your thoughts on sticky notes and place the notes on large chart paper.
4. Provide the students with sticky notes and reread the narrative informational text again. After or during the read-aloud, the students should record *their* connections and questions on the sticky notes.
5. Next, have the students work in small groups to categorize their connections using the sticky notes that have been placed on the chart paper.
6. As a large group, discuss the categories. Help the students pick categories that have emerged as a class and record them on chart paper as a large graphic organizer. Engage the students in thoughtful questions: "Why this category?" "Why not *this* as a category?" "Let's make some group decisions about our categories." "How do they help us think about what we know about this topic?"
7. As thoughts and ideas are generated, guide the students in reading about the topic based on prior experiences.
8. Develop a postreading chart that compares prior experiences with new information.

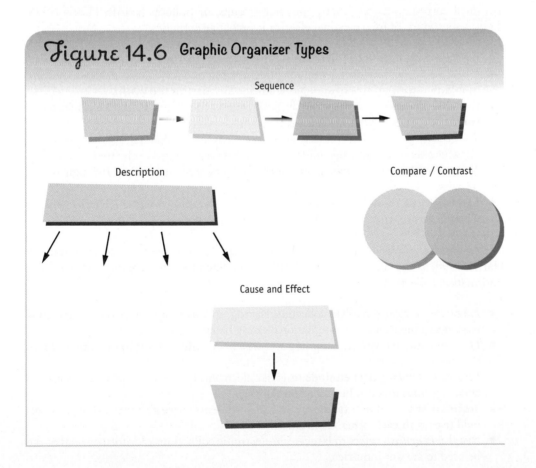

*Figure* **14.6** Graphic Organizer Types

Sequence

Description

Compare / Contrast

Cause and Effect

reflect expository text structure. Introducing students to graphic organizers that reflect the structure of expository texts or sections of the texts is a worthwhile strategy. Once students become familiar with the patterns, they can research topics and create their own informational texts (Harvey & Goudvis, 2000; Stead, 2002).

In addition to discovering the patterns of expository text, it is essential that students know how to determine the important information. Manitone and Smead (2003) suggest a variety of activities that incorporate the arts to help students understand essential information. Using improvisational drama, for example, in which students pantomime or role-play important information, helps them think "from within the situation . . . [and] identify important ideas" (p. 82). In addition, Manitone and Smead suggest quilting activities, poetry, and songwriting to develop the notion of main ideas as students read informational text.

In this section we have highlighted the importance of including literature and informational text in content area learning. Next we explore how electronic text can enhance students' understanding of information.

## Learning with Electronic Texts

In earlier chapters, we discussed the different forms electronic texts may take, such as pages on the World Wide Web, e-mail and discussion groups, word-processed documents, and interactive software programs using CD-ROMs.

Judi Harris (1998) classifies three general categories of electronic text and refers to them as "telecomputing tools" that can be used to design instructional activities across the K–12 curriculum. These tools involve *"interpersonal exchange, information collection and analysis,* and *problem solving"* (p. 22). *Interpersonal exchanges* are projects in which students can electronically talk with other students or groups. These interactive projects can occur as e-mail correspondences, chatrooms, newsgroups, or bulletin boards. Harris (1998) describes six kinds of interpersonal electronic exchange activities:

- *Keypal projects,* in which individuals are matched with partners in a different location.
- *Global classrooms,* in which groups of students from one part of the world study common topics with groups of students from another part of the world.
- *Electronic appearances,* during which special guests communicate with a classroom of students.
- *Telementoring,* in which content area specialists from universities, businesses, or elsewhere serve as electronic mentors to students regarding specific topics of inquiry.
- *Question-and-answer activities,* in which students tap the experts through online services.
- *Impersonations,* in which participants take on a different persona, such as a character from literature, and communicate from that point of view.

*Information collection and analysis* is less of an activity structure and is characterized by Harris (1998) as a process of "teleresearch" (p. 30). She identifies five types of electronic information collection:

- *Information exchange* involves collecting, sharing, and discussing electronic information related to a theme such as international eating habits.
- *Database creation* involves compiling and organizing information so that other groups of students can use it.
- *Electronic publishing* is when students create electronic publications such as newspapers and magazines that can be shared on the Web.
- *Telefieldtrips* are online expeditions in which students share either real-life or virtual field trips with each other electronically.
- *Pooled data analysis* refers to large-scale electronic collections of information that can be used to answer inquiries.

*Problem-solving* design tools, according to Harris (1998), hold the most promise for enriching the curriculum. Harris identifies seven electronic problem-solving activities:

- *Information searches* provide students with clues and reference points that allow them to conduct research by means of the Internet.
- *Peer feedback activities* are those in which students electronically exchange feedback regarding each other's work. For example, students can critique each other's written compositions by means of electronic files.
- *Parallel problem solving* involves having students from different locations around the globe compare and contrast their thoughts and solutions to a common problem by means of technology.
- *Sequential creations* are artistic electronic publications in which students around the globe write collaboratively. The creative writings might include visual images.
- *Telepresent problem-solving activities* involve students from various locations collaborating in real time. Students can chat about issues and topics of inquiry, or they might create multimedia presentations in real time through videoconferencing technologies.
- *Simulations* allow students to experience virtual worlds online. They are collaborative projects in which students undergo activities that seem real, such as being in outer space.
- *Social action projects* are those in which students take on humanitarian issues and attempt to solve problems by means of electronic collaborations.

Needless to say, there are an endless number of ways that teachers can use electronic text to engage students in content area learning. Later in this chapter, we elaborate on how teachers can design electronic lessons to meet their curricular content area needs as they guide students through inquiry projects using electronic text.

Next we look at strategies designed to help students learn from traditional texts. The strategies are appropriate with expository texts but in many cases can be adapted to stories as well as electronic texts.

# Strategies Before Reading

Teachers can help students learn new ideas by giving them a frame of reference as they get ready to read. A frame of reference is actually an anchor point; it reflects the cognitive structure students need to relate new information to existing knowledge. The student "wave" experience we shared earlier is an example. Helping students organize what they know and showing them where and how new ideas fit are essential for learning to take place.

## Previewing and Skimming

Previewing the format of a textbook is an excellent way to help students get a "picture" of the content of a course. Garber-Miller (2007) offers a number of motivating ways to do just that, including gamelike activities such as "Name That Feature" and "Textbook Scavenger Hunts." In Figure 14.7 we share modifications of some of Garber-Miller's strategies.

Another way to start previewing with a group of children or young adolescents is to model some questions that all readers ask to prepare for reading. **Previewing**, after all, should help students become aware of the purposes of a reading assignment. "What kind of reading are we going to do?" "What is our goal?" "Should we try to remember details or look for the main ideas?" "How much time will this assignment take?" "What things do we already know about _____ [the solar system, for example]?" "What do we still

HOMEWORK EXERCISE: VIDEO

Go to the Homework and Exercises section in Chapter 14 of MyEducationLab to watch the video "Before and During Reading Strategies" about how one teacher motivates her students to read a book about butterflies.

## Figure 14.7    Strategies for Text Previewing

- **Textbook Scavenger Hunt.** Provide prompts such as the following and have students work individually or in small groups to locate the information:

  Who are the authors of the book and where are they from?

  On what page will you find out about _____?

  What is the definition of _____?

  In the summary of Chapter _____, what do the authors say about _____?

  How many subtopics are there in Chapter _____?

  Prompts should be designed based on the features of the text.

- **Sticky Note Votes.** Have the students skim through the book and place sticky notes next to features they think will be helpful when they read the text. Next, divide the class into small groups to compare and contrast their findings. Next, have them rank-order the findings according to importance by voting. Each group can share with the class as discussion occurs about each feature.

- **Textbook Sales Pitches.** Divide the class into groups of three. Have each group skim the book for at least three interesting features. They can use sticky notes to highlight the features. Next, have each group develop a scenario in which they act as salespeople for the textbook. Allow time for each group to share its scenario while the rest of the class asks questions of the salespeople.

- **What's Old/What's New.** Divide the class into small groups and assign a chapter to each. Have students preview the chapters listing special features. Next, have them mark each item as a feature they have seen before in other texts as "old," and features they find unique as "new." List each feature in columns as the groups share and discuss any differences among the groups.

need to find out?" These questions prepare students for what's coming. Raising questions and setting purposes is the beginning of efficient processing of information. It calls for further explicit instruction in previewing.

First, select a subject area in which your textbook contains aids that are obviously visual. The textbook writer has incorporated a number of organizational and typographic aids as guideposts for readers. Point out how the table of contents, preface, chapter introductions or summaries, and chapter questions can give readers valuable clues about the overall structure of a textbook or the important ideas in a unit or chapter. Previewing a table of contents, for example, not only creates a general impression, but also helps readers of all ages distinguish the forest from the trees. The table of contents give students a feel for the overall theme or structure of the course material so that they may get a sense of the scope and sequence of ideas at the very beginning of the unit. You can also use the table of contents to build background and discuss the relatedness of each of the parts of the book. Model for students the kinds of questions that should be raised: "Why do the authors begin with _____ in Part One?" "If you were the author, would you have arranged the major parts in the text differently?" "Why?"

Here are some rules or steps to follow when previewing:

- Read the title, converting it to a question.
- Read the introduction, summary, and questions, stating the author's main points.
- Read the heads and subheads; then convert them to questions.
- Read the highlighted print.
- Study the visual materials; what do pictures, maps, and other displayed elements tell about a chapter's content?

Learning to identify the visual aids included in a textbook can help students organize the information before and while reading, as well as while reviewing the material.

**SKIMMING** ◆ Learning how to skim content material effectively is a natural part of previewing. *Skimming* involves intensive previewing of the reading assignment to see what it will be about. To help students get a good sense of what is coming, have them read the first sentence of every paragraph (often an important idea).

An effective motivator for raising students' expectations about their assigned text material is to direct them to skim the entire reading selection rapidly, taking no more than two minutes. You might even get a timer and encourage the students to zip through every page. When time is up, ask the class to recall everything they've read. Both you and the students will be surprised by the quantity and quality of the recalls.

Previewing and skimming are important strategies for helping students develop knowledge of textbook aids and for surveying texts to make predictions. They help get a general understanding as students learn how to size up material, judge its relevance to a topic, or gain a good idea of what a passage is about.

## Organizers

To prepare students conceptually for ideas to be encountered in reading, help them link what they know to what they will learn. An **organizer** provides a frame of reference for comprehending text precisely for this reason—to help readers make connections between their prior knowledge and new material.

There's no one way to develop or use an organizer. They may be developed as *written previews* or as *verbal presentations*. Whatever format you decide to use, an organizer should highlight key concepts and ideas to be encountered in print. These should be prominent and easily identifiable in the lesson presentation. Another key feature of an organizer activity should be the explicit links made between the children's background knowledge and experience and the ideas in the reading selection.

An organizer may be developed for narrative or expository text. It can be used for difficult text selections when the material is unfamiliar to students, including those from diverse backgrounds, because of limited schemata. Organizers can also assist students as they learn to sort through complex information on the Web. An organizer can be constructed by following these guidelines:

- Analyze the content of a reading selection, identifying its main ideas and key concepts.
- Link these ideas directly to students' experiences and storehouse of knowledge. Use real-life incidents, examples, illustrations, analogies, or anecdotes to which student readers can relate.
- Raise questions in the organizer that will pique interest and engage students in thinking about the text to be read.

Key concepts or main ideas in the material being studied can also be displayed as a **graphic organizer,** in which key technical terms are arranged to show their relationships to each other.

Ms. Mark designed a graphic organizer to show her third graders vocabulary in relation to more inclusive vocabulary concepts they would meet in their study of birds. Before constructing this activity, Ms. Mark listed the key concepts in her 4-week unit "Birds Are Special Animals." She then followed the steps suggested by Barron (1968) for developing an organizer and introducing it to her students.

1. *Analyze vocabulary and list important words.* Ms. Mark found these key terms in *The Life of Birds*, edited by Donald Moyle:

   | | |
   |---|---|
   | prehistoric birds | protection |
   | development | language |
   | behavior | ornithology |
   | migration | difference |

2. *Arrange the concepts to be learned.* Ms. Mark first chose the word *ornithology* as the most inclusive concept, superordinate to all the others. Next she classified the terms immediately *under* the superordinate concept and coordinated them with each other.
3. *Add any other vocabulary terms that you believe students understand.* Ms. Mark added terms such as *protect, animals,* and *help.*
4. *Evaluate the organizer.* The interrelationships among the key terms looked like Figure 14.8 and made sense to Ms. Mark and her third graders.
5. *Introduce students to the learning task.* Ms. Mark created as much discussion as possible among her third graders as she presented the vocabulary terms. She drew on their understanding and previous experiences with birds as well as on class activities over the previous few days that introduced the unit (e.g., some preassessment and an anticipation guide).
6. *As you complete the learning task, relate new information to the overview.* Using this overview as a study guide throughout the bird unit, Ms. Mark encouraged students to discuss what information was still needed and where it might best be located on the graphic organizer.

Teachers can also design graphic organizers to help students understand key concepts about subject matter from online information sources located on the Web. In addition to organizing main ideas and vocabulary, teachers can add related web sites to the organizer.

## Anticipation Guides

By creating anticipation about the meaning of what will be read, teachers facilitate student-centered purposes for reading. An **anticipation guide** is a series of oral or written statements for individual students to respond to before they read the text assignment. The statements serve as a springboard into discussion. Students must rely on what

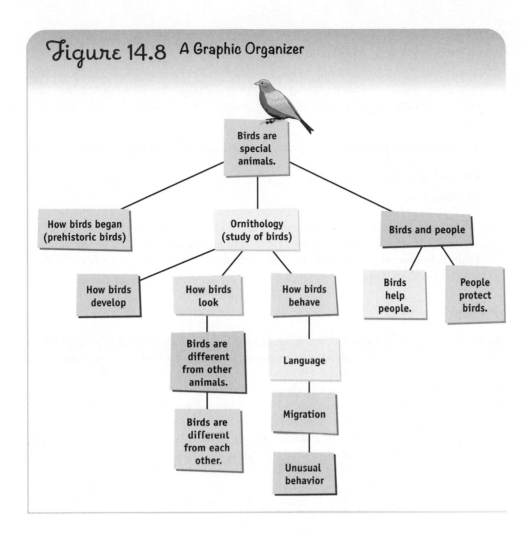

**Figure 14.8**  A Graphic Organizer

they already know to make educated guesses about the material to be read: They must make predictions.

For example, a fourth-grade class was learning about plants in the environment. The teacher, Ms. Henderson, wanted to help students discuss what they knew and believed about the unit in order to raise their expectations about the content matter before reading the text. Above all, she was determined to involve students actively. Here are the guidelines that Ms. Henderson followed in constructing and using anticipation guides:

1. Analyze the material to be read. Determine the major ideas, implicit and explicit, with which students will interact.
2. Write those ideas in short, clear declarative statements. These statements should in some way reflect the world that students live in or know about. Therefore, avoid abstractions whenever possible.
3. Put these statements into a format that will elicit anticipation and prediction making.
4. Discuss readers' predictions and anticipations prior to reading the text selection.
5. Assign the text selection. Have students evaluate the statements in light of the author's intent and purpose.
6. Contrast readers' predictions with the author's intended meaning.

Using these guidelines, Ms. Henderson pinpointed several major concepts, put them in the form of short statements, and wrote each one on the board. After some initial discussion about what students might already know about plants in the environment,

Ms. Henderson distributed two 3-by-5-inch pieces of construction paper (one green and one yellow) to each child and explained:

> On the yellow paper, write "unlikely," and on the green paper, write "likely." I will read each of the statements on the board; you will think about it and decide whether it is "likely" or "unlikely." Then, after 15 seconds, I will say, "Go," and you will hold up either your yellow *or* your green card.

The anticipation guide for this activity included several statements, including these:

> A dandelion is always a weed.
> All plants make their own food.

The information in each of the statements was developed in two short chapters in the students' text. After each statement or pair of statements, Ms. Henderson encouraged the children to discuss the reasons for their responses with questions such as "Why?" "Why not?" or "Can you give an example?"

## Brainstorming

As a prereading activity, **brainstorming** is especially helpful in getting students to generate ideas they can use to think about the upcoming reading material. The brainstorming procedure involves two basic steps: (1) identifying a broad concept that reflects the main topic to be studied in the assigned reading and (2) having students work in small groups to generate a list of words related to the broad concept within a specified length of time.

Brainstorming sessions are valuable not only from an instructional perspective but from a diagnostic one as well. Observant teachers discover what knowledge their students possess about the topic to be studied. Brainstorming also helps students become aware of how much they know, individually and collectively, about the topic.

Some teachers assign a hypothetical problem to be solved before reading a selection or perhaps a real-life school-related problem. Others simply select a major concept in the reading material and get students actively involved in brainstorming. Mr. Davis, a sixth-grade teacher, used the latter model to develop a brainstorming activity for a story by Robert Zacks, "The Nest."

Mr. Davis began by telling his sixth graders they would soon be reading a story called "The Nest." But first, he said, they would work with one of the major concepts of the story, *restrictions*. He divided the class into small groups, using an alphabetical scheme. (Other times he may choose the groups or let students form their own groups.) Once the groups were formed, Mr. Davis used a three-step brainstorming activity.

1. In your groups, brainstorm as many ideas as possible in 3 minutes that relate to the concept *restrictions*. Have one member of your group record your ideas.
2. As a group, put the ideas into categories (groups) wherever they seem to be related. Be prepared to explain the reasons behind the grouping of ideas.
3. Following class discussion on how ideas were grouped, examine your own work again and, using these ideas and others gained from the other groups, predict what you believe the story might be about. Be sure to consider the title of the story somewhere in your predictions.

The activity took about 20 minutes and required intermittent teacher direction. Mr. Davis, for example, followed step 1 with a brief oral direction for step 2. Before moving on to step 3, he initiated a class discussion in which groups shared their ideas for grouping ideas into categories and the logic behind the categories. This gave both individuals and groups a chance to react to the various categories. Although a teacher may offer some suggestions to a group that is bogged down in the categorizing process, we caution that this be done sparingly and only to keep the process going.

After step 3 of the brainstorming activity is complete and predictions have been generated, the story is usually assigned. It would, however, also be possible to extend the prereading phase. To illustrate, Mr. Davis might have asked students to complete a survey of parents, grandparents, and other adults about restrictions they faced earlier in life and which ones bothered them the most. By involving family members, he could have helped the students appreciate the diverse family backgrounds from which they come.

# Extending Content Learning Through Reading and Writing

Next we examine some teaching strategies that can be used in content areas to increase concept learning: point-of-view guides, idea circles, I-Charts, and Internet inquiry. All of these strategies can be used with textbook material, informational books, narrative stories, and electronic text.

**HOMEWORK EXERCISE: VIDEO**

Go to the Homework and Exercises section in Chapter 14 of MyEducationLab to watch the video "Content Area Literacy" and consider why content area literacy is a lifelong skill.

## Point-of-View Guides

As noted earlier, at times children and young adolescents may find learning with textbooks difficult. The wide range of abilities in most classrooms requires that teachers employ strategies for better comprehension of textbook content. Middle school students are expected to understand increasingly complex information, and many are not prepared for the intense demands of textbook reading. The International Reading Association's position statement on adolescent literacy (Moore, Bean, Birdyshaw, & Rycik, 1999) highlights the importance of providing students with explicit strategy instruction in the content areas. Because comprehension usually occurs when readers *use existing knowledge to reconstruct meaning* from text, teachers need to use strategies that *effect the reconstruction process*. Effecting the reconstruction process involves expanding readers' views, theories, or ideas. A point-of-view guide is designed to activate students' prior knowledge by having them elaborate on what is read through the use of alternative perspectives.

**Point-of-view guides** are questions presented in an interview format. Students are instructed to role-play, writing in the *first person* to ensure that different perspectives are being taken, elaborating whenever possible with information from their experiences. In answering the interview questions, students actively contribute their own experiences to the role, which ultimately enhances their recall and comprehension. These questions allow students to elaborate and speculate. The purpose of the point-of-view guide is to develop mental elaboration (students add their own information as they read) and mental recitation (students put new information in their own words, merging text-based and reader-based information). In this way, students learn the content of the reading selection. An example of a point-of-view guide, used in a social studies lesson on the Boston Massacre, appears in Figure 14.9 on the following pages. In the figure, you can see how Billy, a fifth grader, responded to the guide. In this case, the teacher used the guide with the "think-pair-share" strategy: After the children had read the passage, the teacher asked them to *think* about the question, to *pair* with another student and talk about how they would answer the question, and then to *share* by writing down their response.

Now let's turn our attention to another strategy that encourages students to integrate learning, idea circles.

## Idea Circles

**Idea circles** are small peer-led group discussions of concepts fueled by multiple text sources. Idea circles are similar to the literature circles discussed in Chapter 12 in that

## Figure 14.9  Point-of-View Guide, Social Studies, Grade 5

**The Boston Massacre**

*Text Passage:* On March 5, 1770, Boston did explode. A group of colonists had gathered at Boston Customs House. The group, led by Crispus Attucks and others, began to throw snowballs at the British soldier on duty. Soon eight other British soldiers arrived. "Come on, you rascals," the mob yelled. "You lobster scoundrels. Fire if you dare." For a while, the soldiers did nothing.

The group grew larger and larger. Fearing for their safety, the soldiers began to panic. Suddenly, in the confusion, a soldier fired. Then the other soldiers fired. When the smoke cleared, Attucks and two other men lay dead. Two more would die later from their wounds.

Colonial leaders called the event the Boston Massacre. A **massacre** is the killing of a number of defenseless people. Colonists used the shooting as **propaganda**, information used to win support for a cause. By calling the incident a massacre, the colonists suggested that having British troops in the colonies was dangerous. (*Build Our Nation*. Boston: Houghton Mifflin, 1997, p. 250)

*Question 1: Imagine yourself as the British soldier who first fired your gun. Pretend you are talking to your friends after the incident, telling them what happened. What were the reasons for firing your gun? How did you feel when the colonists were yelling at you and throwing snowballs at you? How did you feel and what did you do when the other British soldiers began firing also?*

Dear Tom,

I think I started a war with Britain and the colonists. The colonists were calling us names and throwing snowballs at us. There soon was a huge crowd. That was when I was scared and started to fear for my life. It just got to the point where I was so scared that I started to fire. When the smoke cleared I had realized what I had done. That night I thought to myself and said, "I didn't have to take that from them. I had the gun and had to show them who was in control." So I think I was right to show them who was boss. I also think it was wrong for me to fire at them. That is why I had to talk to someone about it.

Sincerly, Billy Kaiser

(Continued)

## Figure 14.9   *(Continued)*

*Question 2: Imagine you were the colonist who followed Crispus Attucks and yelled out to the British soldiers. You admired Attucks, and one of the other colonists was a close friend of yours. Pretend you are talking to your friends after the incident, telling them what happened. What would you say? Why do you think the incident occurred?*

Dear Tom,

    That incident that happened yesterday was wrong. We were defenseless and they just fired at us. I lost my best friend in that incident. I also lost the person I admired Crispus Attucks. I need to get revenge on them. They invaded my colony, took over my life, and killed my friend. They won't get away with this. If I have to I will fight. They can't invade our territory and kill our friends! It isn't right. Someone has to put a stop to this.

        Sincerely, Billy Kaiser

they are composed of three to six students and are peer led, with interaction rules explicitly discussed and posted. In idea circles, students discuss a concept. Because the students read different informational books, they bring unique information to the idea circle. In the circle, they discuss facts about this concept and relations among the facts and explanations. The teacher provides a chart to guide collaborative discussion, such as the one on lakes in Figure 14.10 on page 482. The goal of the idea circle needs to be communicated explicitly. Teachers should tell students what they are expected to accomplish in an allotted time for discussion. The desired product may be individual or collective. Either way, if the desired end product is articulated well at the beginning of the discussion, less time will be spent arguing over what to do, and more time will be invested in actually doing it (Guthrie & McCann, 1996).

Idea circles can be easily adapted to reading content information on the Web. Teachers can design questions for middle school students based on selected web sites. Here is how a Web-based idea circle works. Each small group is given a chart similar to the format in Figure 14.9. The group also receives an accompanying sheet with the same number of related web sites as there are members of the group. Each group member selects a web site from the list, making sure that everyone has selected a different site. The students are instructed to browse the Web in search of answers to the questions on the chart. After an allotted amount of time or class periods, the students share their findings in small discussion groups. When teachers develop different questions about related topics for each group, the students in each group can pool their information and design a PowerPoint presentation for the rest of the class.

In preparation for such an extended use of idea circles, teachers will find useful resources for planning on the World Wide Web. SBC's Knowledge Network Explorer is an excellent example of such a resource for teachers (see the web site at the end of this chapter). Using a concept called "filamentality," the web site allows teachers to select a topic of inquiry, specify goals, and search for related Internet sites.

**Figure 14.10**   Chart to Guide Collaborative Discussion in an Idea Circle

**Subject:** Social Studies          **Topic:** Lakes          Grade 4

Ask your friends and family members if they have ever gone to a lake. What did they do there? Write your responses here. We will share these responses with the class as a whole.

Find the following information using your book about lakes. It is possible that the book you are using will not include all of the answers. You may have to get some of this information from others in the idea circle.

What is a lake?

What is a freshwater lake? Give an example of one. What is a saltwater lake? Give an example of one.

What are lakes used for?

What about lakes and pollution?

## Curriculum-Based Reader's Theater

Another way to engage students in learning content from a textbook is to adapt reader's theater, discussed in an earlier chapter, by developing scripts that are based on curriculum content (Flynn, 2004, 2005). This strategy involves having the students read sections of text and working in small groups, rewrite the main ideas in the form of an entertaining play. The benefits of a **curriculum-based reader's theater** are threefold: increased fluency, enhanced understanding of content, and motivation to read.

Read what one teacher had to say after using a curriculum-based reader's theater:

> My class really enjoyed doing the readers' theater on the American Revolutionary War. I was a little worried in the beginning that the practice sessions we took to create and rehearse the script would take away from the time my students would need to learn the curriculum objectives required by our school system. But when I saw how enthusiastic the children were and how even my reluctant readers spoke their lines, I felt strongly that learning was taking place. (Flynn, 2004, 2005)

In the Step-by-Step Lesson featured in Box 14.4 we adapt Flynn's (2004, 2005) directions for conducting a curriculum-based reader's theater. See Figure 14.11 for an excerpt of a script about Mars.

## I-Charts

A common pitfall for elementary and middle school students in completing research projects is copying pages of unorganized facts out of encyclopedias using a note card system. **I-Charts,** as explained by Sally Randall (1996), were created to organize note taking, encourage critical thinking that builds on students' prior knowledge, and increase metacognitive awareness. Using I-Charts helps students identify what they want to know,

BOX 14.4

## STEP-BY-STEP *Lesson*

### Implementing a Curriculum-Based Reader's Theater

1. Select the content and provide students with the text pages or other content-based resource. Read the selection aloud or provide time for independent reading. Following the reading have the students brainstorm important facts that should be included in the script. The teacher can record the list on the board and clarify any missing information or any details that are unnecessary.

2. Discuss the nature of script writing in terms of location, narrator, character dialogue, plot, lines to be read as a group, and hand motions.

3. Divide the class into small groups and invite the students to write a script; encourage creative settings with appropriate, imaginative dialogue, humor, emotion, facial expressions, and body language. Circulate among the groups to guide the process and to ensure that the information is accurate. This becomes the first draft.

4. Make transparencies of the initial drafts and do whole class readings. During this step, editing takes place with suggestions from all students. Allow time for final drafts to be written. If word processing is used for the script writing, editing may take place more efficiently than hand-writing each draft.

5. Allow time for each group to select parts. At the outset, encourage the students to include parts that are limited to the number of persons in the group or should be read by all. Have the students highlight their parts and rehearse.

6. Other rehearsals should take place in which the students focus on expression, volume, body language, and so on. After practicing several times, the students are ready for the performances. Each group stands or sits in front of the class and the play is read. Alternatives include inviting parents to the performances, sharing with other classes or grade levels, or performing for staff members.

Other options include the following:

- Model an initial curriculum-based script that you have written based on text selection.
- Conduct an initial curriculum-based script that the whole class writes together while you transcribe the script on a screen with a word processing program.
- After the class has experienced the process, assign or allow the students to select the sections of the text for writing the script so that each group performs a different fact-based play.

*Source:* Based on "Curriculum-Based Readers Theatre: Setting the Stage for Reading and Retention," by R. M. Flynn, 2004, 2005, *The Reading Teacher, 58,* pp. 360–365.

---

## *Figure* 14.11 Partial Sample of Curriculum-Based Reader's Theater Script on Mars

*Setting: Outer Space*

*Characters: Earth, Moon, Mars, Comet, Crater*

Earth: Gee, you guys sure have more craters than I do! I'm SO jealous! (exaggerated body language)

Moon: Not to worry, Earth. It's REALLY not all that great.

Mars: Right on. Craters leave scars on us when objects from outer space crash!!!

ALL: Ouch! (Loud)

Earth: Yeah, I remember when a comet fell on me. Rather painful. Left a dent.

ALL: Ouch! (Loud)

Comet: Oh, brother, Earth. It wasn't THAT BAD! It was sort of exciting to all those on Earth.

Crater: Yeah, Comet, I remember you made the headlines on that Earth thing they call a lewspaper.

Earth: I think you mean NEWSPAPER!

Crater: Whatever. Comet was SO famous!

Earth: Well, anyway, I still am a bit jealous of all of your craters, Mars and Moon.

Moon: Well, I'm jealous of all of the water you have! Almost three-fourths of you is water!

ALL: YEAH! YEAH! Water, water everywhere! Almost three-fourths of Earth is water!!!!!!!
(Shout as a cheer and repeat three times with cheering actions.)

organize the information read, and determine if they have adequately answered their research question.

In using I-Charts, a teacher should introduce the process by guiding the whole class on the same topic with differing subtopics on each I-Chart. The procedures for using I-Charts can be found in the Research-Based Practices featured in Box 14.5.

When examining sources of information, students are encouraged to keep the I-Chart in front of them while they skim each new source to determine if it is helpful. As they read a source, they pull the chart with the subtopic matching the information they were reading and record the information. As they read new information, they pull out the corresponding I-Chart. This enables students to think critically about the relevance of each piece of information to their subtopics and eliminates random copying of unorganized data. Even with this structure, students occasionally slip up and include under one subtopic information that belongs under another (Randall, 1996).

Completed I-Charts can be used to teach outlining for research reports. Each of eight to ten subtopics on an I-Chart becomes a Roman numeral. Important facts found on the I-Charts complete the rest of the outline. Sometimes subtopics need to be divided when they are too broad or combined when too closely related. In this way, I-Charts contribute to the outline for the final paper or project. I-Charts can also be used to guide Internet inquiry. In addition to I-Charts, there are a variety of ways teachers can assist students in conducting research using the Internet. In the next section, we describe several ways for teachers to organize Web-based inquiry.

## Internet Inquiry

At the very least, when students use the Internet for learning about content area subjects, they need to understand that the organizational patterns of web sites differ significantly from those of textbooks. Information, for example, is made available through a menu that is displayed on a homepage rather than a table of contents. Instead of locating information using an index, a homepage often provides hyperlinks to related topics of inquiry. Students can easily get lost on the Web as they "surf" for information, and it is not uncommon for them to drift away from the original topic (Roe, 2000).

When teachers engage their students in **Internet inquiry,** they also need to consider the difference between knowledge and information. Judi Harris (1998) synthesizes a thought-provoking argument. According to Harris and others, "knowledge is the result of the process of knowing, which can only occur when learners actively construct what they know, using information in this process" (pp. 28–29). In other words, as teachers guide students in Internet inquiry, they need to ensure that students are not simply consumers of information but are instead learning how to use information technology to actively learn.

In order to assist teachers in developing instructional activities using the Internet that are purposeful and curriculum based, Harris suggests several steps to designing a Web-based project that are adapted in the following list:

1. Teachers should choose curriculum-based goals that could not be reached using traditional approaches to instruction, or at least not as well.
2. Teachers need to select an activity structure for organizing the online project. As discussed earlier in this chapter, an activity structure can be in the form of interpersonal exchange, information collection and analysis, or problem solving.
3. Teachers should review sample projects designed by other teachers.
4. Teachers should consider the details of the project, including the title, the length of time it will take, deadlines, the procedures or tasks the students will perform, and ways in which the students will collaborate.
5. Teachers should decide whether the project will be shared with other K–12 teachers and, if so, how?
6. Teachers should plan a tangible way to end the project. Will the students design a PowerPoint presentation, a written report, a videotape, or a display?

## BOX 14.5

*Research-Based Practices*

# Using I-Charts for Guiding the Research Project

1. Have each child write a topic proposal. A proposal explains the topic that interests the student about which he or she wants to learn more. For example, if the unit of study is mammals, that topic might be how a whale, a particular mammal, adapts to its environment, the ocean. In the proposal, students would explain their interest, list what they already know, and detail where they think they will find more information.

2. The students should brainstorm questions to which they would like to find answers. The questions must be ones that cannot be answered yes or no. It is helpful for this step to be done in groups of three or four, even when students choose different topics, such as different mammals. This significantly increases background knowledge and enthusiasm.

3. Give the students ten copies of blank I-Charts (see the accompanying blank I-Chart). One copy of the I-Chart is used for each subtopic research question. The I-Charts can be kept in a notebook.

4. Students should find their sources of information by searching libraries, by conducting interviews with experts, and by requesting letters to agencies. The Internet and CD-ROMs can also be used as sources of information.

5. In the middle section of the I-Chart, after completing notes on all available information from one such source, students should draw a line on the chart after the last recorded fact for that source (see the I-Chart on Whales on page 486). On the left, the sources are numbered in the order the student uses them. The references are recorded on a separate sheet.

6. As the students read sources of information, they should also find and write down interesting related facts and key words near the bottom of the chart. New questions to research often become new subtopics to include in the project.

---

### I-Chart

Name:                          Topic:

Subtopic:

What I already know:

| Bibliography number: | |
|---|---|
| | |
| | |
| | |

Interesting related facts:

Key words:

New questions to research:

*(Continued)*

# Research-Based Practices *(Continued)*

**I-Chart on Whales**

Name: Class Example          Topic: Whales

Subtopic: What do whales eat?

What I already know: Whales live in the ocean. They are mammals. They have blow holes. There are different kinds of whales.

Bibliography number:

| | |
|---|---|
| 1 | Some whales have teeth. They eat mostly fish and squid. Some whales do not have teeth. They have baleen plates in their mouths. They eat mostly krill. Krill are small shrimplike animals. |
| 2 | Baleen is a tough material that grows in fringes from the whale's upper jaw.<br><br>A blue whale may eat 8,000 pounds of krill each day. That would be the same as 16,000 servings of spaghetti in a day.<br><br>Killer whales have teeth and eat warm-blooded animals such as other whales, dolphins, seals, sea lions, and other kinds of fish. |
| 3 | Toothed whales use echolocation to navigate and to find their food. |

Interesting related facts: Like all mammals, baby whales get milk from their mothers. They might drink 600 quarts in a day. There are 63 species of toothed whales and 11 species of baleen whales.

Key words: baleen, prey, pod, echolocation

New questions to research: How long do toothed whales live?
How long do baleen whales live?

Bibliography for the I-Chart on Whales

1. *Dolphins and Whales,* by Stephen Savage, 1990, Chartwell Books.
2. *Giants of the Deep,* by Q. L. Pearce, 1992, RGA Publishing Group, Inc.
3. *S.O.S. Whale,* by Jill Bailey, 1991, W. H. Smith, Publishers, Inc.

*Source:* Based on "Information Charts: A Strategy for Organizing Student Research," by S. N. Randall, 1996, *Journal of Adolescent and Adult Literacy, 39,* pp. 536–542.

## BOX 14.6 — New Literacies

### USING THE INTERNET FOR DEVELOPING COMPREHENSION SKILLS

When students use the Internet to locate information based on a content area topic they experience new levels of reading comprehension. According to Coiro (2003):

> Some tasks on the Internet ask readers to extend their use of traditional comprehension skills to new contexts for learning. . . . Others, like electronic searching and tele-collaborative inquiry projects, demand fundamentally different sets of new literacies not currently covered in most language arts curriculums. (p. 463)

In addition, according to Solomon (2002) as discussed by Coiro, students use higher-order thinking skills when they develop Web-based presentations and reports. The instructional role of the teacher in lessons that feature technology is more of a facilitator than one who imparts knowledge. Teachers need to model strategies for accessing and synthesizing information, but each student will essentially gather unique information and formats for summarizing what he or she has learned.

Moreover, if teachers are to scaffold Web-based learning, they must practice. They need to experience using technology as a new means of gathering information and they need to observe the strategies they employ when using the Internet. We suggest that teachers work with one another as they plan technology-based lessons and discuss with each other the procedures for locating information they use. If teachers observe and discuss collaboratively, chances are they will gain insight into the new literacies that emerge during the process of searching the Web.

Underlying these guidelines is the importance of teacher planning and organizing Internet inquiry. Haphazard Web surfing can be counterproductive, whereas carefully orchestrated activities can result in creative and high-level critical thinking skills.

WebQuests, first developed by Bernie Dodge and Tom March at San Diego State University, are another way to organize Internet inquiry. The **WebQuest** model features systematic searching and focuses on supporting students' learning through synthesis, evaluation, and analysis. At the end of this chapter, we invite you to browse useful Web-Quests designed by teachers.

As teachers include Internet inquiry in purposeful ways to enhance content area learning, they will undoubtedly realize that this form of electronic text lends itself to new ways of defining literacy and subject matter learning. New skills will need to be honed. Skills such as skimming, scanning, evaluating sources of information, and synthesizing content take on new meaning when Web searching is included in content area learning. See the New Literacies Box 14.6 for a commentary on how using the Internet broadens our understanding of reading comprehension.

## WHAT ABOUT STRUGGLING READERS AND Content Area Texts?

Many students find content area texts difficult, but struggling readers find textbooks particularly daunting. Even though they may prefer nonfiction to fiction, the technical vocabulary, density of concepts, limited background knowledge, and lengthy reading assignments of content area books provide struggling readers with challenges in which they may feel frustrated, helpless, and resistant.

In order to assist struggling readers with textbooks, Ambe (2007) suggests using trade books and other resources to introduce concepts and new vocabulary before textbook reading. Offering students choices of related trade books that are written on a lower reading level can motivate students to read about otherwise challenging concepts. Brainstorming what students know about a topic prior to reading the trade books helps set the stage for introducing new vocabulary that the students may be unfamiliar with. Semantic maps are useful for this purpose. Guided reading, including the directed reading–thinking activity (DR–TA) (Stauffer, 1975), is also beneficial for struggling readers. When students are asked to read short selections to make predictions, they are less intimidated than when they are assigned to read an entire chapter.

While struggling readers often attend pull-out tutoring sessions that focus on skills unrelated to content learning, we suggest that reading tutors should consider using materials related to content classroom learning. By doing so, they will be helping students who struggle with content books to learn the subject matter while improving their overall reading.

# WHAT ABOUT STANDARDS, ASSESSMENT, AND Content Area Texts?

In the content areas, students need to be able to understand literal text, summarize important information, make inferences, and read critically. Although the nature of textbooks varies depending on the content, it is critical that students have a wide range of reading skills if they are to grasp the knowledge base and content standards of a subject area and, in many instances, apply that knowledge.

Vacca and Vacca (2008) provide teachers with an instructional framework that is useful as teachers develop lessons that address content standards and assessment considerations. We synthesize their plan here:

- First, consider the standards and benchmarks that you want to address. Take into account how some benchmarks overlap or complement each other.
- Second, consider the expectations that you have concerning what the students should know or be expected to do based on the standards and benchmarks.
- Third, decide what instructional strategies you will use to engage the students in actively learning the content. How will you organize your lessons? Will they include paired-learning, small group interaction, independent activities?
- Fourth, select the materials you will use for instruction. Will you primarily use the textbook? If so, how? Will you use trade books, electronic resources, hands-on manipulatives, guest speakers?
- Fifth, how will the students demonstrate what they know? Will you assess knowledge with a test? A project? A presentation? A portfolio entry? A journal entry? Will the students be engaged in self-assessment or peer-assessment?

In addition, we suggest that teachers consider how they will address differentiated instruction including modifications for ELLs, as well as how they will provide the students with choices during the instructional and assessment phases of the lessons.

# Summary

Elementary and middle school children often experience their first difficulties with reading when they encounter textbooks in content areas. The transition to content area reading should not pose major obstacles, although textbooks are inherently difficult for most students. In classrooms where children are guided to use literature, informational books, and electronic texts, children are more likely to make the transition to content area texts naturally and with ease. They learn to approach and appreciate many genres of texts, including the textbook.

To understand what makes a textbook difficult, several factors that contribute to the readability of a text were explained. Also, we explored the uses and benefits of using literature, nonfiction trade books, and electronic texts across the curriculum. Historical and realistic fiction, biographies, and informational books provide children with intense involvement in a subject. Using these different genres of books is a schema builder and can accommodate different reading abilities and interests in the classroom. Moreover, units of study provide teachers with the structure needed to coordinate literature study within the context of meaningful activity. Instructional strategies with electronic text can include interpersonal exchanges, information collection and analysis, and problem-solving activities.

Various strategies were presented to show how teachers can facilitate textbook study and learning. Some strategies to implement before reading included previewing, organizers, anticipation guides, and brainstorming. Other strategies were explained that can be used to improve the learning of concepts. Point-of-view guides help children reconstruct content learning by using their personal outlook. Students work in idea circles to discuss concepts and how they are related, drawing from different informational sources. I-Charts and Internet inquiry searches are ways teachers can guide students to pursue questions of interest as they learn.

## Teacher Action Research

1. Select a content area and access the standards for your state that delineate the benchmarks for each standard that are expected for a particular grade level. Next, access the specialized professional association (SPA) standards that correspond with the content area that you selected. Develop a table that compares and contrasts your state's expectations for the grade level you selected with the SPA that is associated with your content area. Write a commentary or develop a graphic representation that reflects your observations about the similarities and differences. Share with your classmates or colleagues as a springboard for discussion about standards.

2. Select a content area and access Web-based resources that can be used to enhance specific content area standards and benchmarks. Browse the web sites for practical resources and lessons that are available. Develop a chart of useful Web resources based on this activity. The chart might look something like this:

| Social Studies Grade 3 | | |
|---|---|---|
| Standard: _____(Fill in)_____ | | |
| Benchmark(s): _____(Fill in)_____ | | |
| **Topic of Study** | **Web Site** | **How Could I Use This Web Site?** |
| Learning about natural regions | www.mcps.k12.md.us/ curriculum/socialstd/ grade3/ Grade_Three.html | Use lesson for the third week of September on this site. Lesson has hands-on activity using oranges. Good idea. |

3. Select a content area and interview two teachers in two diverse school settings (for example, teachers in classrooms with high and low incidences of ELLs, respectively, or high and low numbers of multicultural students, or high and low poverty rates). Develop a questionnaire in which you ask the teachers if and how they differentiate instruction for their students in the content area that you have selected. Synthesize your findings by comparing and contrasting the teachers' responses.

4. Select a topic from a content area book. Divide the topic into subtopics. Locate children's literature—fiction and nonfiction—that could be used to teach the subtopics. Plan a lesson based on one of the subtopics and teach it to a group of children. Take anecdotal records in which you record the students' reactions to the lesson. Write a reflection about what you observed.

5. Develop a role playing scenario with a colleague in which you demonstrate the difficulties that students have with reading content area texts. Write your scenario as a script between two students. See the scenario at the beginning of this chapter to get you started. If you are a teacher, perform your scenario at a faculty meeting as a springboard for discussion about the difficulties students actually have when they read textbooks. You might take a leadership role by sharing your observations of how students struggle when reading *your* textbook. If you are a teacher candidate and do not yet have a classroom, use the scenario as a springboard for discussion on how you can assist students with learning content beyond the textbook.

**THROUGH the LENS of a Literacy Coach**

6. Observe a content area teacher who is using a chapter in a textbook to conduct a lesson. How does the teacher introduce the lesson? Can you tell what the purpose of the lesson is? Does the teacher activate prior knowledge? Does the teacher introduce any vocabulary associated with the chapter? How do the students read during the lesson? Do they read silently? Orally? Independently? With a partner? In small groups? Does the teacher have an activity that follows the reading? If so, what are the students instructed to do? Did you find the lesson motivating? Did you understand the lesson? What suggestions might you have for the teacher?

## Related Web Sites

*Bill Chapman's Classroom Tools*
**www.classroomtools.com**
Chapman includes activities for helping students validate online information.

*iearn*
**www.iearn.org/projects/project_list.html**
Contains numerous Web-based projects in which students can participate with communities around the world.

*Kathy Schrock's Guide for Educators—Critical Evaluation Surveys and Resources*
**http://school.discovery.com/schrockguide/eval.html**
Includes Web resources for helping students critically evaluate information on the Internet.

*KET's Internet Classroom Projects*
**www.ket.org/Education/IN/projects.html**
KET provides access to Internet classroom projects for all areas of the curriculum.

*Knowledge Network Explorer*
**www.kn.pacbell.com/index.html**
This Filamentality tool will help you compile a hot list to make your personal web page.

*National Council for the Social Studies*

**www.ncss.org**

This professional organization documents the national standards per grade level for social studies teachers. In addition, the following web site annotates notable social studies literature for classroom use by themes: www.socialstudies.org/resources/notable.

*National Council of Teachers of English*

**www.ncte.org**

This professional organization documents the national standards per grade level for English language arts teachers. In addition, the following web site includes numerous resources for literacy coaches: www.literacycoachingonline.org.

*National Council of Teachers of Mathematics*

**www.nctm.org**

This professional organization documents the national standards per grade level for mathematics teachers. In addition, the following web site offers many lessons and resources for integrating children's literature and mathematics: www.nctm.org/search.aspx?q=mathematics%20and%20children's%20literature.

*National Science Teachers Association*

**www.nsta.org**

This professional organization documents the national standards per grade level for science teachers. In addition, the following web site suggests children's literature that links to science: www.carolhurst.com/subjects/curriculum.html.

*Pitsco's Ask an Expert*

**www.askanexpert.com**

After you or your students think of a question, this site provides access to hundreds of experts on topics by category or a key word search. The experts also have excellent web sites related to topics of inquiry, including frequently asked questions. If your question is not answered on the expert's web site, you can e-mail your question.

*Study Guides and Strategies*

**www.studygs.net**

This site includes dozens of links to study strategies that can be adapted for elementary and middle school students. The suggestions are printable and user friendly, and can be applied to all of the content areas. The guides can also be translated into many languages.

*The WebQuest.Org*

**http://webquest.org/index.php**

Not only does this page include links to information on designing WebQuests, but it also includes examples of WebQuests, organized by grade level and subject area, for teachers to use.

Now go to the Vacca et al. *Reading and Learning to Read*, Seventh Edition, MyEducationLab course at **www.myeducationlab.com** to

- Take a pretest to assess your initial comprehension of the chapter content
- Study chapter content with your individualized study plan
- Take a posttest to assess your understanding of chapter content
- Engage in multimedia exercises to help you build a deeper and more applied understanding of chapter content

## CHAPTER 15

# Managing and Organizing an Effective Classroom

Standards found in this chapter:
- 2.1
- 2.2
- 2.3
- 4.1
- 4.2
- 4.4
- 5.2
- 5.3

## In this chapter,
### YOU WILL DISCOVER:

- What features make up a cooperative learning-centered classroom environment
- The teacher's roles in facilitating interactive literacy experiences and explicit instruction
- How individualized instruction influences effective reading instruction
- Characteristics of classroom communities and multiage classrooms
- Ideas for organizing and managing the classroom through learning centers, record keeping, and portfolio systems
- Technological features and instructional considerations of the classroom of tomorrow

## Concept Map

### MANAGING AND ORGANIZING AN EFFECTIVE CLASSROOM

**IMPROVING INSTRUCTION**

Classroom Teachers of Reading | Collaborative and Cooperative Learning

**INDIVIDUALIZING INSTRUCTION**

Groups | Materials

**PUTTING IT ALL TOGETHER**

Multiage Classrooms | Creating a Physical Environment

Technology in the Literate Classroom

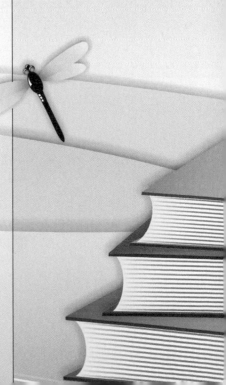

A teacher in a split third- and fourth-grade classroom in a suburban elementary school decided to broaden her reading program to a more literature-based approach. Colleen VanderSchie had been reading about using collaborative learning and natural texts to teach children to *want to read* as well as how to read. The more she read and the more she talked with her principal about her multiage, multiability students, the more intrigued Colleen became with her idea.

University students visiting Colleen's classroom for their field experience a few months later found the third and fourth graders in the middle of reading and language arts time. They had finished reading a selection and were engaged in a cooperative group assignment.

Students relied on one another, according to the observation field notes submitted by the prospective teachers, for interpreting instruction and for solving problems. Although Colleen circulated among the groups and was available to offer assistance, the students seemed to prefer to collaborate in their groups, resorting to asking the teacher for help only when they continued to be confused or unsure.

*Quincy:* I need Mrs. VanderSchie.
*Santos:* No, you don't. I'll show you how to do it.
*Quincy:* I don't think she wants you to write them down.
*Santos:* Yeah, that's what these lines are for.
*Quincy:* What are details?

*Santos:* Little tiny things. Not the main idea, but little things that make you think of it.
*Quincy:* Characteristics of a whale. What are characteristics of a whale?
*Santos:* I'll go get a dictionary. What do we need to look up?
*Quincy:* Characteristics of whales.
*Maylee:* C-H, you need C-H-A. Use the guide words.
*LaWanda:* Yeah, use the guide words, you guys!
*Santos:* Here it is! I found it!

Most surprising to the university students making field observations was the patience and the respect with which children who were not friends and who might avoid one another on the playground or in other settings worked together happily and productively in this setting. Individual friendships, preferences, and gender differences did not appear to affect the collaborative group dynamics. The most able readers were not consistently group leaders. Students of all ability levels were observed participating in the reading activities on  an equal basis. The collaborative nature of the project appeared to provide a low-risk setting in which children felt comfortable and confident to participate in reading and reading-related activities. In this environment for learning, children's ability levels were not obvious; they did not appear to be a factor in cooperative learning.

When teachers like Colleen take control of the physical arrangement of their classrooms, the grouping of students for instruction, and the way they approach activities and select and use materials, they are managing the classroom. Images of how teachers view their role (technician, expert, learner, etc.) vary, depending on how they view the reading process and, in turn, their instructional beliefs, concerns, and emphases. To manage their classrooms effectively, teachers need to consider a number of important variables shown in the Concept Map. Teachers must conceptualize and organize classroom instruction; select classroom materials and technology, approaches, and activities; and achieve a physical organization in which all the pieces fit together.

## Improving Instruction

Teachers make, verify, and rethink numerous decisions about instruction. They deserve relevant, up-to-date information if they are to be expected to make good decisions about classroom management and organization. Often it is the confluence of newer, research-based strategies with older, traditional ideas that helps teachers make intelligent decisions about comprehensive instruction and best practices. Learning more about what teachers know and do to create classroom environments in which best practice can flourish is important.

## Classroom Teachers of Reading

To put into practice their knowledge about reading and learning to read, classroom teachers must demonstrate that they are competent professionals who perform multiple roles. As they grow throughout their careers, teachers will acquire more and more expertise; they will have opportunities to reflect on and inquire into their own practice. As introduced in Chapter 1, belief systems help bring into focus what teachers know, believe, and value. What are some guidelines for classroom teachers to follow to look more closely into their roles? What are some instructional practices you are already implementing? Are there certain practices and contexts that most professionals generally agree are facilitating when it comes to instruction in reading?

**STANDARDS** ◆ According to the International Reading Association (2003), there are five broad standards, or guidelines, that literacy professionals use in developing effective instructional programs: *foundational knowledge; instructional strategies and curriculum material; assessment, diagnosis, and evaluation; creating a literate environment;* and *professional development.* In relation to managing and organizing an effective classroom, teachers need at least a basic understanding of and ability to take action in a large number of important areas:

- Use instructional grouping options as appropriate for accomplishing given purposes.
- Use a wide range of instructional practices, approaches, and methods, including technology-based practices, for learners at different stages of development and from differing cultural and linguistic backgrounds.
- Use a wide range of curriculum materials in effective reading instruction for learners at different stages of reading and writing development and from different cultural and linguistic backgrounds.
- Use a wide range of assessment tools and practices that range from individual and group standardized tests to individual and group informal assessment strategies, including technology-based assessment tools.
- Communicate results of assessments to specific individuals.
- Use students' interests, reading abilities, and backgrounds as foundations for the reading and writing program.
- Use a large supply of books, technology-based information, and nonprint materials representing multiple levels, broad interests, and cultural and linguistic backgrounds.
- Model reading and writing enthusiastically as valued lifelong activities.
- Motivate learners to be lifelong readers.
- Display positive dispositions related to reading and the teaching of reading.

**INSTRUCTIONAL PRACTICES** ◆ As the research base is built about comprehensive instruction and how teachers manage and organize effective classrooms, there is disagreement over "*how* teaching is conducted and who decides how teachers practice" (Freppon & Dahl, 1998, p. 248). This is often political and connected to curriculum mandates to "fix" school failures. A reality that deals more directly with classrooms and students is how teachers "mediate the research they know according to many factors (e.g., continuous changes in their own learning, students' needs, daily classroom events)" (p. 248).

As teachers, we need to analyze our own attitudes and behaviors, asking whether they are conducive to helping students form positive attitudes. What verbal and nonverbal signals do we send? What is the environment like in our classrooms? What expectations are we communicating? It is incumbent on classroom teachers to identify the instructional practices they are using that take students' attitudes, interests, and needs into account. Use the Instructional Practices Inventory in Figure 15.1 to do a quick self-assessment. Check *yes* if you are already implementing a numbered practice; check *perhaps* if you are interested in finding ways to implement the practice; check *no* if you are not implementing or not interested in the practice.

## Figure 15.1  Instructional Practices Inventory

| | YES | PERHAPS | NO |
|---|---|---|---|
| 1. I am aware of my students' attitudes toward certain aspects of reading. | | | |
| 2. I plan reading activities that students tend to like. | | | |
| 3. I use reading materials in which my students can succeed. | | | |
| 4. I use materials related to the interests and needs of my students' norm group. | | | |
| 5. I provide situations in which the usefulness of reading is apparent, such as reading that is necessary in order to do a certain desired project or activity. | | | |
| 6. I model reading, either orally or silently, so that my students can see that I value reading. | | | |
| 7. I provide for recreational reading in my classroom. | | | |
| 8. I use reading material found in the students' everyday life. | | | |
| 9. I encourage *parents* to improve attitudes toward reading by reading to their children, providing reading materials, and being examples themselves by reading in front of their children. | | | |
| 10. I avoid using reading as a punishment. | | | |
| 11. I use bibliotherapy—I guide my students into books that deal with their problems and relate to their world. | | | |
| 12. I am enthusiastic when I teach reading. | | | |
| 13. I am positive in my approach; I emphasize students' abilities instead of constantly referring to their errors and inadequacies. | | | |

Have you ever wondered what "the experts" in the field of literacy might say are practices worth incorporating into classroom instruction? Rona Flippo (1998) provided a summary of contexts and practices that would facilitate learning to read, as agreed on by 11 experts. In relation to contexts, environment, purposes for reading, and materials, these contexts and practices would facilitate learning to read:

- Focus on using reading as a tool for learning
- Make reading functional
- Give your students lots of time and opportunity to read real books as well as time and opportunity to write creatively and for purposeful school assignments (e.g., to do research on a topic, to pursue an interest)
- Create environments, contexts in which the children become convinced that reading does further the purposes of their lives
- Encourage children to talk about and share the different kinds of reading they do in a variety of ways with many others
- Use silent reading whenever possible, if appropriate to the purpose
- Include a variety of printed material and literature in your classroom so that students are exposed to the different functions of numerous types of printed materials

Sometimes, despite professional guidelines and preferred practices, teachers find that pressures outside school are overwhelming. Efforts to create responsive, well-organized, effective classrooms don't always work out. Family relationships, nutrition, illness, abuse, addictions, economic hardship, cultural miscommunication, and community pressures can and do override school and classroom-based factors. They are not, however, excuses for inaction. The key for teachers is to make certain that expectations are high and opportunities to succeed are many.

Teachers want to improve their instructional practice. As we learned in Chapter 2, effective teachers develop a comprehensive program by immersing students in integrated reading and writing activities and providing explicit instructional support to show students how to use skills and strategies. To juggle performance-based assessments, authentic texts and contexts, and learners with diverse needs, teachers need a basic knowledge of how to individualize and socialize within their classrooms. They need information about cooperative learning and collaboration in order to develop classroom communities in which their students can be effectively taught, through immersion in integrated language arts and provision of explicit strategy instruction.

## Collaborative and Cooperative Learning

The social aspects of reading and learning to read are obvious when one considers the reading process as a communication skill. **Cooperative learning,** described by Slavin (1999) as consisting of programs that "foster the hum of voices in the classroom" and "encourage students to discuss, debate, disagree, and ultimately to teach one another" (p. 193), has been a popular concept since the 1970s. Students work together in small groups to help one another in achieving an academic goal. To this end, classroom management and organization must begin to prepare students to be flexible so that they can recognize and adapt to competitive, cooperative, and individualized interaction situations (Kagan, 1989). Taking both the student and the classroom into account, **collaborative learning** is a cooperative learning environment in which students work effectively together to complete literacy tasks. This can also occur with the utilization of technology. Grabe and Grabe (2004) emphasize that technology is not a tool that promotes isolation. Rather technology can enhance student interaction through well-designed collaborative activities. Classroom settings that provide opportunities for collaboration encourage primary and middle school students to be active, engaged learners.

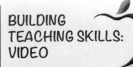

**BUILDING TEACHING SKILLS: VIDEO**

Go to the Homework and Exercises section in Chapter 15 of MyEducationLab to watch the video "Cooperative Learning" and think about the role a teacher must play in cooperative learning activities.

When collaborative learning programs succeed, all students are engaged in a collaborative learning process. Providing students the opportunity for student–student interactions is important for the enhancement of literacy development, especially for students from diverse backgrounds. Garcia (2002) reports that students from linguistically and culturally diverse backgrounds benefit from classrooms that allow students to interact with each other through collaborative learning activities.

Classrooms for both primary and middle school students should be organized to encourage cross-cultural interactions and collaborative activities that encourage students to work together in order to complete a single task. Rae and Mercuri (2006) stress that a cooperative learning environment helps students handle racial and social issues as well as break down social barriers and motivate students. This type of collaboration encourages students to ask more difficult questions of one another, challenge each other's answers, and seek assistance from each other more often (Garcia, 2002).

We know that the same features that characterize collaborative and cooperative learning are associated with environments that encourage creativity and intrinsic motivation: feelings of safety, acceptance, support, and belonging (Baloche & Platt, 1993). Thanks to Vygotsky's (1978) studies on internalizing language and thinking as we interact with each other socially, we have a variety of ways to look at the importance of the social context of learning.

According to Vygotsky, the best role for the teacher is to mediate between what students are able to do on their own and what they are able to do with support, prompting, and encouragement. Teachers can use this understanding of the role of the social context of thinking and learning to help them organize classroom instruction that will support learners, including those from diverse backgrounds, as they construct new meanings through reading and writing.

Teachers are renewing their focus on creating authentic classroom situations that help students become engaged, active learners and gain competence in reading and writing. Guthrie and Wigfield (2000) believe "that engaged readers in the classroom or elsewhere coordinate their strategies and knowledge (cognition) within a community of literacy (social) in order to fulfill their personal goals, desires, and intentions (motivation)" (p. 404). Collaboration and interaction among students during classroom literacy instruction gives them rich opportunities to practice and to refine new literacy learning. Students need to make choices about the type of work they do, negotiate small groups, make rules, delegate tasks to the groups, and decide on appropriate outcomes. Motivation and enthusiasm for learning come from opportunities for students to make their own choices about tasks and to work together to read, listen to a book or tape, research the Internet, or engage in writing activities. They practice strategies the teacher models, often assisting and coaching each other as they work.

**COOPERATIVE LEARNING AND THE TEACHER'S ROLE** ◆ Developing social skills for successful group work is a prerequisite when collaborative learning is a new experience for students. The classroom teacher needs to create activities that encourage and model (1) getting to know and trust group members, (2) communicating accurately and unambiguously, (3) accepting and supporting one another, and (4) constructively resolving conflicts to make mutual achievement of the goals possible (Johnson & Johnson, 1989–1990). The teacher's role becomes one of facilitator and agent for change in a collaborative classroom.

When the teacher is not the sole authority for interpretation in the classroom, when children are assisted in constructing their own reading and writing processes, students learn to connect their life experiences with literacy activities in expanded ways. Pearson (1993) found that even young children can engage in self-directed discussions about books and reading that cover all aspects of comprehension and can evaluate the quality of their writing and their comprehension without direct teacher supervision.

Often readers bring experiences from their own lives to their reading, giving them a logical and valid response that may be different from the teacher's or from other students' responses. If only the teacher's experiences and interpretations shape school literacy experiences, students with different cultural and academic backgrounds may find they have little or no opportunity to connect their own experiences with their reading and writing.

For example, Cynthia Lewis (1993) describes a student in her class who understood how to do the kind of close reading of texts required in school but used his own "interpretive lens" to build meaning. His view helped him construct a response that did not fit Lewis's cultural expectations, as he sympathized with the klutzy and bumbling guest in a story while showing disdain for the rich but insincere host. Lewis notes that teachers must be aware of how social identity informs our communication and our interpretations. Reading and writing in school should involve helping children learn ways to stretch the boundaries of the familiar and already known, but teachers also need to legitimize the knowledge and experience that students of diverse backgrounds bring to literacy tasks.

Ruth Nathan (1995) sensed that her third-grade students loved projects and therefore capitalized on their curious and social nature "to grab their attention and focus their drive to belong and to communicate with their classmates" (p. 82). Her role is to facilitate the project so that the group efforts are authentic. For example, she says that "big projects *require* that teachers share the burden of parceling out jobs" (p. 84). One of the major benefits of working on a project together is meeting the basic human need to belong. So whether they are working on astronomy, environment, animal habitats, timelines, or food, students begin to exhibit behaviors that we value: "lots of risk-taking with drawing, writing, and talking to others; frequent, independent journeys to the school library . . . ; students begging to work together during lunch break; kids asking to present their projects to other grades" (p. 85). And above all, in meeting the test of truly collaborative and cooperative learning, students bonded with each other in a mutually built, safe environment in which their teacher saw her role as an active agent for change.

**EXPLICIT INSTRUCTION AND THE TEACHER'S ROLE** ◆ There are times in a collaborative learning environment when the teacher purposefully supports literacy learning by showing students how to use skills and strategies that will lead to independent learning. As discussed in Chapter 2, effective teachers exercise flexibility in their use of approaches and strategies. They may center instruction on cooperative groups and projects yet provide literacy scaffolds with questions, explanations, demonstrations, practice, and application. The teacher's role shifts to capitalizing on teachable moments, or opportunities to provide **explicit instruction**; this involves explaining and modeling. For English language learners, Garcia and Beltran (2003) stress that explicit language teaching is essential. However, they voice their disappointment that the practice does not always happen, citing inadequate instructional time for English learning.

When teachers make instruction explicit, they may do so in conjunction with literature-based, integrated language arts approaches. A good illustration of this is Pat Meehan's (1998) description of how her own teaching philosophy changed from one of "running the class" to one of "teacher-learner in harmony with the other learners in my classroom" (p. 316). She says:

> Today I teach students to use reading strategies purposefully. I no longer teach skills as an "added extra," nor do I ask standard comprehension questions. I grab opportunities within the context of reading literature as a vehicle to teach skills strategically. In this way I also model techniques . . . students need a repertoire of comprehension and decoding/encoding strategies in order to respond flexibly in their reading and writing. (p. 319)

Explicit instruction typically is characterized by skill building and error correction (Krashen, 2004a). However, in a meaning-centered classroom, explicit instruction is not about isolated phonics drills or extensive practice of discrete skills on worksheets. Rather, teachers focus explicitly on the strategies that proficient readers and writers use to make sense of texts, modeling the strategies themselves, and on ways to think about using them flexibly in actual reading and writing situations. A minilesson is an excellent way for teachers to provide explicit instruction. Lasting a few minutes (no more than 10), minilessons follow this pattern: (1) creating an awareness of the strategy, (2) modeling the strategy, (3) providing practice in the use of the strategy, and (4) applying the strategy in authentic reading situations. When teachers take advantage of opportunities to explain and model, students develop understandings about strategy use as they build procedural knowledge of skills and strategies.

# Individualizing Instruction

The term *individualizing*, more than *individualized*, connotes the process of providing differentiated instruction to students. It reflects the accumulation of previous knowledge and direct experiences in reading classrooms over the years. Many teachers of reading subscribe to this process, which originated as the **individualized instruction** approach. Its relevance today is due in part to the inclusion movement, which worked to meet the needs of and adapt the curriculum for students having special needs. Often misunderstood, the term *individualized instruction* means different things to different people. To some, it means programmed, prescriptive instruction; to others, it means flexible grouping for instruction.

**STANDARD 2.1**

**BUILDING TEACHING SKILLS: READING**

Go to the Homework and Exercises section in Chapter 15 of MyEducationLab to read the article "Orchestrating Multiple Intelligences" and develop greater understanding of the importance of adapting instruction for individual needs.

## What Is Individualized Instruction in Reading?

This is a key question for anyone interested in classroom organization because it can help clarify the major ways we choose to deliver reading instruction: in small groups, as a whole class, or one to one.

Individualized instruction evolved out of a 150-year-old U.S. goal of providing free schooling for everyone. Its biggest impetus came with the development of reading tests in the early part of the twentieth century. It spawned many experiments in education such as ability grouping, flexible promotions, and differentiated assignments. Many of the plans followed the ideas outlined in the Dalton and the Winnetka plans, which allowed children to work in reading and content areas at their own pace (Smith, 1965, p. 194).

Gradually, individualized instruction went beyond children's learning rates and reading achievement. The child's interest in reading, attitude toward reading, and personal self-esteem and satisfaction in reading expanded the goal of instruction (Smith, 1965, p. 378). Terms associated with individualization ranged from *individual progression* in the 1920s to *individualized instruction in reading* to *self-selection in reading* to *personalized reading*. Today, we might add *objective-based* and *prescriptive learning*.

An interesting irony is that procedures used in the original individualized classrooms did not vary widely. Read the following classic description; does it conjure up a reasonable picture of individualized instruction in your mind?

> Each child selects a book that he wants to read. During the individual conference period the teacher sits in some particular spot in the room as each child comes and reads to her. As he does so, she notes his individual needs and gives him appropriate help. Finally she writes what the child is reading, his needs, and strengths on his record card. Then another individual conference is held,

Personalizing instruction allows the teacher to assess a student's progress on an ongoing basis, thereby allowing the teacher to respond to the student's unique learning needs.

and so on. If several children need help on the same skills, they may be called together in a group for such help. (Smith, 1965, p. 379)

This scenario does, after all, seem like a plausible description of individualized instruction. How it's actually applied in reading classrooms around the country is another matter entirely. In practice, two variations of the original individualized approach to instruction are often found in today's classroom: (1) Individualized procedures are one part of the total program (i.e., one day a week), or (2) parts of individualized reading are integrated into another reading approach (i.e., self-selection during free reading). Individualization can refer to instruction that is appropriate for the student regardless of whether it occurs in a one-to-one, small group, or whole class setting. According to Yanok (1988), individualization is a process of personalizing teaching to provide instruction that recognizes and responds to the unique learning needs of each child.

Although individualized instruction as an approach or a program for reading instruction is not as widespread as others, its influence on reading teachers has been pervasive because assessment of individual readers' strengths and weaknesses is at the very core of effective reading instruction. This tenet cuts across the delivery of reading instruction, regardless of classroom organization pattern.

## Influences of Individualized Instruction

Models of prescriptive and of personalized individualized programs, from skills management systems to literature–thematic units, have been popular off and on over the years. Among the many historical influences of individualized instruction, *groups* and *materials* evolved out of a long tradition yet still help shape the delivery of contemporary reading instruction.

GROUPS ◆ The practice of creating and disbanding groups of differing sizes, abilities, and interests of students for the purpose of providing instruction has been part of classroom management and organization since the 1920s. Yet as students were "tracked" and then assessed strictly according to their "ability," one of the effects was to limit opportunities. Children from minority backgrounds and low socioeconomic groups were "placed disproportionately in low-track, remedial programs" (Oakes, 1999, p. 228).

Today, **grouping** is used to organize teaching in content areas and for interdisciplinary instruction across subjects, such as social studies and science, mathematics and language arts. Although small groups are in operation throughout the day in many classrooms, reading instruction is most closely associated with grouping. The term *grouping* is narrow. A broader term is **patterns for learning.** "Patterns for learning include grouping practices used in classrooms that are dynamic and flexible. Grouping may be whole, small, pairs, triads, cooperative, heterogeneous, homogeneous, self-paced, individualized, or interest based" (Carnahan & Cobb, 2004, p. 2). No grouping pattern has more value over the other because they provide different experiences with different outcomes (Ford, 2005). Grouping depends on the teacher's beliefs, learning goals, and the student's needs.

When grouping students, teachers need to be aware that there are consequences to placing students in groups. It is important to match the patterns for learning with the instructional purpose. Ford (2005) discusses five instructional grouping strategies in order to keep all students engaged in meaningful work:

1. Allow meaningful small group and individual work to flow out of whole class instruction.
2. Set up meaningful small group and individual work that allows for connections across learners and flexibility in how learners read and respond to texts (e.g., literature circles, workshops).
3. Use parallel processes that allow for meaningful small group and individual work away from the teacher (e.g., schoolwide writing workshop).
4. Provide ongoing independent work that flows from classroom instruction.

5. Allow for small group and independent-inquiry projects as an ongoing alternative for engaging learners away from the teacher (e.g., districtwide infrastructure for inquiry projects). (pp. 28–29)

No matter what grouping practice is utilized it is important to be flexible in classroom organization. Some groups are in existence for a few minutes, and others last an entire class period; still others are ongoing. Students may split spontaneously into groups of three to five for the purpose of engaging in a discussion strategy; other groups work together through some questions and follow-up writing during their language arts period; a book study group meets every other day for two weeks. Sometimes a large group makes more sense. Silent reading time and freewrite time are occasions when the whole class participates. And there are times when one-on-one situations are best, such as student–teacher conferences for book sharing or response to writing.

When setting up groups, instructional management is key. Carnahan and Cobb (2004) define **instructional management** as "the system established within a classroom to facilitate maximum learning. Components of a management system can include effective use of time, use of instructional resources, and expectations for behavior" (p. 2). When establishing effective patterns of learning, it is important to create a classroom environment that encourages students to take literacy risks. They need to feel empowered to participate in active learning, share learning responses, and experience an increase in reading motivation (Ruddell & Unrau, 2004). In addition, to contribute to the effective environment, it is important for the teacher to explain to the students how and why groups are formed, the nature of the activity, and the length of time a student will be in a group. Finally, it is necessary to teach procedures and routines to all students at all ages about student movement, voice levels, responsibilities, and collaboration. Directions, whether verbal or written, must be clear and comprehensible. Maryjo Hepler, a teacher and gifted coordinator, shares her views in Box 15.1 on flexible grouping and provides her insights on managing a literate classroom.

Just as Maryjo Hepler pointed out, teachers' beliefs and decisions are major influences on successful patterns of learning. Teachers must decide and plan for instructional interactions that best fit the instructional goals and learners' needs and abilities. The accessibility and selection of materials also influence the instructional process and patterns for learning.

**MATERIALS** ◆ Using a wide variety of **materials** for reading instruction is accepted practice across most school districts, as discussed in Chapters 13 and 14. Originally, variety in materials was needed to accomplish the main purpose of matching students with materials on their own reading level. This quickly expanded with the development and availability of widely diverse materials to meet students' interests and instructional objectives as well. From reference books to videos and CD-ROMs, classroom materials move from shelf to groups of readers or individuals engaged in all types of learning configurations. This also includes whole class instruction. Fisher and Ivey (2007) affirm the need for a variety of materials and texts in multiple forms, especially when the teacher uses a single text for whole class instruction. They believe that it is difficult to locate one book that addresses the needs of all students. With comprehensive instruction, teachers employ a broad range of materials to explicitly demonstrate a strategy or facilitate the reading of personally selected books, short stories, poems, or nonfiction.

Record keeping—especially the amount of time it requires—is a major issue related to materials. Teachers might use computer programs that accompany their basal reading and language arts series, or they might develop a portfolio system of their own, in which students take responsibility for their own completed and in-progress work. Nevertheless, the necessity of keeping classroom records on individual readers' overall and daily performance entails keeping track of the materials used in all facets of the instructional program, including strategy instruction, projects and activities, groups, test scores and other benchmarks of progress, and recommendations for short-term and future placements. Teachers always seek more efficient yet meaningful ways of accumulating, recording, and synthesizing the different components in their teaching and learning environment. How do the parts come together in a classroom community?

## BOX 15.1

# Viewpoint

## Thoughts About Flexible Grouping

Maryjo Hepler

When grouping strategies are used in the classroom, they can significantly increase students' mastery of content. They also provide a variety of activities that can give the lessons new life and a welcome change from lecture or question–response instructional methods. Allowing students to work in groups ensures that they will learn to work cooperatively, collaboratively, and independently.

Flexible grouping means that the group participants change throughout the year. Sometimes students select the work groups and sometimes the teacher selects them. Groups can be formed based on individual learning needs. Students can be grouped according to interest, achievement level, or activity preference. Other times, groups can be created for special needs, learning styles, learning rate, or ability. The teacher can even match the tasks to meet the specific needs of students by offering different assignments to different groups.

Many teachers don't use grouping strategies because they "tried it once and it didn't work." Mostly we discover that it wasn't the strategy that was unsuccessful, but the management techniques that were missing from the procedure. Clear guidelines for group functioning must be taught in advance of group work and be consistently reinforced. I recommend that primary grades "practice" group procedures before beginning. The guidelines must include the equitable sharing of tasks, roles, and responsibilities of each member, and how and when to ask for the teacher's assistance. Each group will need to know where to work, what to study, and approximately how much time is allotted for each task. Skills in group work must also be taught. How to offer an opinion, how to treat members, and how to arrive at an agreement should be discussed before assigning groups. Groups will be more likely to succeed with these practices.

Generally, the best course of action for using groups in a unit is to pretest the students, introduce the major concepts, and reinforce them with activities and discussion. A midtest could be given to provide help in forming the groups. At this point in the curriculum, students learning needs tend to vary significantly. This is when group work is most beneficial. After each group has completed its task, the final evaluation could be administered.

Groups can be used for discovery learning, experiments, or brainstorming. Groups will also enhance problem solving, critical thinking, and creativity, and can help to create a sense of community in the classroom. Different projects can be assigned to different groups designed to showcase the strengths of individuals or build on their weaknesses. Flexible grouping allows for quick mastery of ideas and additional exploration by students who have higher ability.

Gifted students thrive in flexible groups. When groups are heterogeneously formed, there should not be a large gap in abilities. Students should be homogeneously grouped for objective material. You should group students randomly when the tasks are open-ended or creative. Students who struggle can be successful if placed in a carefully formed group to match their needs. It is a great way to build leaders and provide role models.

A good rule of thumb is to never give group grades. Each student should be assessed individually on his or her contribution to the final project. Group assignments should always be completed in class to ensure cooperative work. This is not a time for the teacher to sit and grade papers. The instructor must be interacting with the groups, keeping them focused and observing their work.

If it seems as though using flexible grouping in the classroom is a lot more complicated than lecturing, it is because it is true! But the benefits in mastery, motivation, and engaged students make it all worthwhile.

# Putting It All Together: Organizing a Classroom Community

The social nature of reading and writing and the importance of contextual factors in literacy instruction call for teachers to organize their classrooms into nurturing and supportive **communities of learners.** For teachers like Colleen in the chapter's vignette, literacy approached collaboratively quickly becomes a useful tool for thinking, learning, *and* enjoyment, just as she had hoped. Reading and writing are the focal activities that students and their teacher use every day to learn about themselves and about the larger world they inhabit.

*Community* is a quality of an inspirational classroom, according to Merrill Harmin (1994), where students are in "comfortable relationships with other students and with persons of authority" (p. 4). They also listen, respect one another, and solve problems in this environment, which brings out the best in them and their teacher. They do *not* isolate, disconnect, or reject; neither do they become self-centered or resentful.

**HOMEWORK EXERCISE: VIDEO**

Go to the Homework and Exercises section in Chapter 15 of MyEducationLab to watch the video "Classroom Arrangements" and consider how room arrangements have evolved as educational practices have changed.

How do we foster the positive feelings and motivation within readers and writers? Considering the variety of desirable attributes and depending on the needs of learners, take the following 12 guidelines into account for designing literacy-enhancing instructional environments (Ruddell & Unrau, 2004, pp. 971–972).

- Provide for the exploration of student identity and schemata through activities and interactions to bolster reflection and self-discovery.
- Design an environment that builds self-worth.
- Promote a climate that fosters a sense of mastery and competence.
- Help students to see that the acquisition of knowledge, skills, and strategies is incremental to becoming self-regulated.
- Activate and extend students' background knowledge.
- Model reflectivity and metacognitive processes.
- Design tasks that involve real-life issues, community-related interests, and are seen as useful.
- Establish expectations that are in line with students' abilities and provide support for attainment.
- Encourage the flexibility to view experience from multiple perspectives and encourage an aesthetic stance in response to reading.
- Use students' sociocultural values and beliefs as resources for constructing an environment that reflects students' orientations while developing understanding of and tolerance for alternative value and belief systems.
- Allow students to gain a sense of ownership and share in the interpretation of texts.
- Select texts that are suitable to students' task engagement and allow students to internalize knowledge and skills to become independent, self-regulating, and self-reliant learners.

STANDARD 4.4

These 12 instructional guidelines can help teachers reflect on their beliefs in organizing a classroom community to promote literacy engagement and motivation.

In addition, Garcia (2002) recommends that the following teacher practices be reflected in the learning communities in order to meet the needs of diverse learners:

- Bilingual and bicultural skills and awareness
- High expectations of diverse learners
- Treatment of diversity as an asset to the classroom
- Curriculum development that addresses cultural and linguistic diversity
- Ongoing professional development on issues of cultural and linguistic diversity and practices that are most effective

STANDARD 2.2

DIVERSITY

Creating such communities means that teachers must think of classrooms as learning places rather than as workplaces. But moving to such a community takes time. The teacher must help students by planning and setting up routines. Students need to be initiated into the kind of inquiry and collaborative work this definition of learning requires. Teachers need to help students value "thinking, questioning, discussion, learning from mistakes, trying new ideas, responding and challenging ideas, and appreciating diversity" (Clyde & Condon, 1992, p. 92). Multiage classrooms may hasten their initiation.

## Multiage Classrooms

Many school districts are implementing multiage classes. For our purposes in examining an effective classroom, we need to discover three major things: What is a **multiage classroom,** what are its major features, and what do teachers do that best supports literacy instruction in such a classroom?

A multiage classroom is a single learning community that meets the numerous needs of its student members, grouped across age levels. The classrooms that are considered multiage must meet several requirements: Students are grouped across age levels; they form a single learning community, meeting the academic, social, emotional, physical, and aesthetic needs of its members (Kasten & Lolli, 1998). Clusters of traditional grade levels and ages observed might be K–1 or 3–4, or classes of 6- to 8-year-olds or 9- to 11-year-olds. Teachers might form teams of two, teaching anywhere from 35 to 50 students in one large room. The ages, grades, and teaching combinations are variable.

Some major features have come to be associated with multiage classrooms; Kasten and Lolli (1998) investigated the theories behind nine features, claiming that all but the first cannot be replicated in typically graded classrooms:

1. A stable, nurturing environment is created when children are placed longer with the same teacher and group. [This is similar to "looping."]
2. Learners respond to roles as helpers and recipients when interacting with diverse ages.
3. Having multiple encounters with concepts, even those "untaught," prepares the way for future learning.
4. Cross-age tutoring occurs both implicitly and explicitly.
5. Individual paces are accepted and accommodated, making learning suited to developmentally appropriate practice and constructivist theory.
6. Nurturing, altruistic behaviors increase as competitive, aggressive behaviors decrease.
7. When students have opportunities to "be younger and older" in different years, birth-order effect is diminished in classrooms.
8. Social development and self-esteem are enhanced.
9. Decisions about promotion can be flexible with fewer grade-level benchmarks. (pp. 24–25)

A research team reported findings about how ten primary-grade teachers created multiage classrooms to meet the needs of a wide variety of readers and writers. These teachers "believed that children benefit from being part of a classroom community for multiple years" (McIntyre et al., 1996, p. 386). Their instruction most supported the children's literacy development in three ways: (1) Teachers created classroom contexts that provided many opportunities for interaction and conversation, a social dimension enabling children to learn concepts, strategies, and skills from each other; (2) teachers differentiated instruction for various groups of children as needed; and (3) teachers provided explicit instruction for specific children for specific purposes, helping all become more metacognitive about what they were learning.

The social and psychological aspects of the classroom community are emphasized throughout this chapter. When combined with the physical component, all three become the foundation of a literate classroom environment. What are the **physical characteristics** and how does the teacher create a physical environment?

## Creating a Physical Environment

What actually goes on in any classroom, multiage or traditionally graded, once the door is closed? Colleen and other experienced teachers readily acknowledge that within the walls of their classrooms, there is a certain degree of autonomy impervious to outside pressures. An expression of this autonomy is the physical arrangement or organization of classroom furniture, materials, and space.

Arranging desks, tables, chairs, technology equipment, and materials can contribute greatly to the organization of an entire semester or yearlong reading program. The physical structure put into place by the reading teacher can support the goals or underlying structure of the reading program. It can work for the teacher as much as any other component in the total program and total classroom environment.

When you do step back and look carefully at your reading classroom, what do you see? One perspective to take as you look around the room is to examine it for *space usage*, or books, nooks, and crannies. For example, do you see a space suitable for a reading loft? Such a loft might hold four or five readers on top and house a minilibrary underneath. Is there any room for a reading fort made of empty carpet-roll tubes? How about creating student "offices" by using partitions to divide a table into three or four separate areas? If these aren't feasible ways to use space, you might consider establishing several special reading spots, such as a chair, carpet, cupboard, or sofa.

Still another scan of your classroom might be made with *storage techniques* in mind. Boxes, crates, CD-ROM stacks, labeled shelves, bulletin boards, and Peg-Boards are multipurpose and inexpensive. Boxes and plastic crates make good filing cabinets; students, too, might like their own filing drawers. Thorough and visible labeling helps students know where to return materials in the room. Storing materials is important in all classrooms because students of all ages and levels need designated spots in which to put their belongings and work.

We asked a fifth-grade teacher whose classroom we admired and whose teaching always seemed to be carried out with purpose and reflection to describe how her unusual reading classroom is organized and why. She does so in Straight from the Classroom in Box 15.2.

The physical environment teachers of reading create can set the stage for a productive program. As use of children's or adolescents' literature in classrooms grows, teachers

**BOX 15.2**

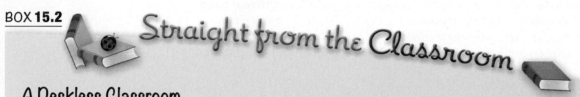

*Straight from the Classroom*

## A Deskless Classroom

### WANDA ROGERS

A fascinating experience in class arrangement took place in my classroom one year—all because a father of one my students worked for a cardboard box factory.

He came to me one day with the free offer of 50 heavy-duty, double-strength cardboard boxes approximately 2 feet square in size. Could I use them? The price was right, so of course I said yes.

Now, how could I use this terrific gift? The answer came to me one day when a student said, "Mrs. Rogers, I haven't sat in my own seat since the first 5 minutes of today!" I gave this some thought and realized that with the flexible grouping we were constantly using, the children actually did spend very little time at their own desks. So I asked, "Why not do away with desks?" And we did.

Each student was given a box that was to house books, supplies, and so on. We stacked the boxes two tall, and they provided instant dividers to make separate spaces in the room for small groups to meet.

Much of our class instruction was done in small groups with different groupings for each subject. By removing "desk ownership," we eliminated territorial problems. No more did we hear, "Jim wrote all over my desk during reading class." "You can't sit here. I don't want your cooties all over my desk." "Mrs. Rogers, Judy stole my pencil out of my desk when she was sitting there."

Desks were viewed as workbenches and storage areas for learning activities equipment and materials. By removing student–desk associations, the desks themselves became more flexible for rearranging to meet different organizational needs.

An unexpected benefit was that students became more involved. Because they no longer had a desk for retreat where they could while away time unproductively or daydream, they tended to "find something to do" when they finished a task—kibbitz with other students, use the library or resource center, take a book to a corner, or involve themselves in a listening or hands-on activity in special areas set up for that purpose. They learned to move themselves from one task to another, rather than "sit in *their* seats" and wait to be told what to do by the teacher.

One of the best advantages was that it opened new vistas of classroom organization for me as a teacher. I found myself less restricted and more creative and efficient. I could arrange the management of an activity without the confines of "desk ownership."

**REFLECTIVE INQUIRY**

◆ Why did Wanda feel more creative when she changed the way desks were used?

◆ How closely connected are classroom organization and management?

◆ How would you use the cardboard boxes?

find ingenious ways to make books accessible to their students. They manipulate physical space, materials, and time to make books, as well as computers, a natural part of their classroom environment. Some of the ideas to help organize classroom communities for whole class, small group, or independent activities are learning centers, room diagrams, student schedules, record keeping, and portfolio systems.

LEARNING CENTERS ◆ Several advantages to setting up **learning centers**—classroom areas set aside for student learning—are that they allow more pupil movement; more and diverse opportunities for students to work in small groups or independently; and more pupil choice, commitment, and responsibility.

Why teachers choose to use learning centers is important, because their purpose should determine the type of center. Provisions for flexible grouping, individual work, research, and group or committee work are essential for centers in classrooms that foster optimal literacy development for each student (Flood & Lapp, 1993). Such an environment encourages collaborative and social aspects of literacy learning and allows the teacher to plan for various reading and writing activities. Even in the smallest of classrooms, a center for quiet reading and research and a center for groups to meet and talk can usually be arranged, if only by placing desks together or setting up a few computer stations to make collaborative work areas.

In developing learning centers it is important to plan because good planning gets results. Establishing a routine and predictable daily schedule is essential. It is recommended that the teacher demonstrate the various activities and model the student's role in the centers. Additionally, it is important to demonstrate to the students how to work independently and what collaboration means. Finally, it is necessary to select the appropriate materials to match the instructional activity and students' abilities.

Supplementing textbooks and basal readers with dictionaries, newspapers and magazines, literature, nonfiction trade books, online stories, art supplies, electronic materials, and students' own previously published writing gives students sources to use in developing their ideas for reading and writing. All of these sources can be housed in learning centers organized in creative configurations.

**HOMEWORK EXERCISE: VIDEO**

Go to the Homework and Exercises section in Chapter 15 of MyEducationLab to watch the video "Planning for and Managing Learning Centers" and think about the considerations that have to go into arranging learning centers in your classroom.

STANDARD 2.1

STANDARD 2.3

Classroom learning centers allow more diverse opportunities for students to work alone or in groups, establishing choices, commitment, and responsibility.

ROOM DIAGRAMS ◆ One of the most useful ideas for organizing any classroom, whether you have learning centers or other formats, is a diagram of the classroom. A **room diagram** serves three simple yet essential purposes: (1) It helps the teacher keep track of where and how various activities are taking place and with whom; (2) it helps parents and other teachers acclimate to your classroom, whether they are visiting or presiding over another class or study hall (it becomes a handy seating chart); and (3) it gives students an opportunity to see what is available for them to do now and anticipate what other activities are in store for them.

Room diagrams are just as useful to teachers beginning to use activity centers as they are to teachers who long ago stopped using traditional formats. To illustrate, the room in Figure 15.2 is a traditional elementary classroom in which learning centers are separated from regular instructional areas either around the periphery or off to one side. Figure 15.3 outlines a room in which learning or activity areas for collaborative learning are the focal point of the classroom community.

STUDENT SCHEDULES ◆ The secret to effective implementation of classroom learning centers is teacher organization and the scheduling of students to designated activities. Arranging **student schedules** is time-consuming. In order to develop an *individual schedule* (see Figure 15.4 for a 5-week unit), teachers need to consider where and when and in what combinations they want students at the various stations. A student who needs extensive work in a particular area such as composition or listening is given more time at that numbered station. All students, regardless of their strengths and weaknesses, usually want equal time at certain popular areas such as games or free-reading stations.

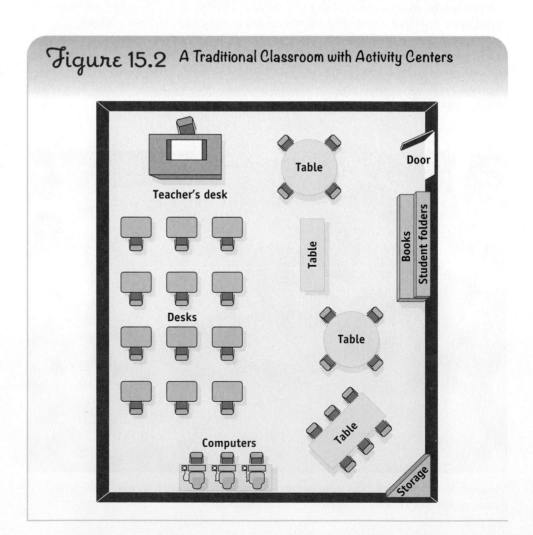

**Figure 15.2**  A Traditional Classroom with Activity Centers

## Figure 15.3   A Learning-Center Classroom

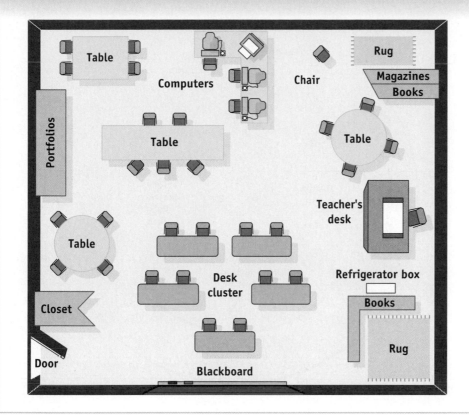

## Figure 15.4   Individual Student Unit Schedule (January 4 to February 1)

Name: _____

*Special comments:* Use time at Station 2 to finish the introduction to your portfolio.

| WEEK | MONDAY | TUESDAY | WEDNESDAY | THURSDAY | FRIDAY |
|------|--------|---------|-----------|----------|--------|
| A | — | 1 | 2 | 3 | 7 |
| B | 7 | 3 | 9 | 6 | 5 |
| C | 8 | 1 | 4 | 5 | 2 |
| D | 6 | 4 | 4 | 8 | 5 |
| E | 9 | 8 | 1 | 4 | 3 |

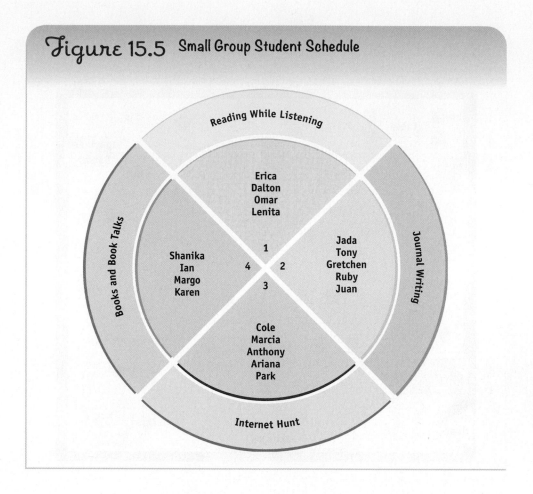

**Figure 15.5**  Small Group Student Schedule

In addition to, or instead of, individual student schedules, teachers may develop *small group schedules* to rotate groups of students to different stations. This type of schedule is often called *rotational*. Figure 15.5 illustrates a schedule designed for second graders to follow during their language arts hour each morning for a week to 10 days. The names of stations that the teacher believes are important enough to merit a block of time during language arts are put in the outer, stationary circle. Names of students are listed in the inner circle, which can be rotated daily or more or less frequently. In some cases, teachers let the students decide when to go to the next station or center.

A third way of scheduling students is through *contracting*. Ideally, this is a written agreement between student and teacher in which the student makes a commitment to assume responsibility for a learning experience. Successful contracting is a process that begins during student–teacher conferences. First, the interests of the student are determined through discussion or observation and discussion. Next, the teacher confers with the student about what type of follow-up will benefit this area of interest, and a contract is drawn up and signed. Materials are searched for and organized as the student carries out the plan of study. The teacher helps by answering questions and giving explicit instruction as needed, when the opportunity presents itself. This process continues until the contract is completed or modified and the student's goals are achieved.

Contracts between teachers and students then are the most individual and personal of schedules. Two sample contracts are illustrated in Figure 15.6, the one on top for use with a primary grader and the one on the bottom for a middle school student.

**RECORD KEEPING** ◆ Keeping track of books and stories read by students and materials used by students, or **record keeping**, is a problem for many teachers. It is not feasible for teachers to take on the task of recording who read what, at what level, and what it was

## Figure 15.6  Individual Student Contracts

My name: _____    Today is: _____

1. I will read _____ stories in the library corner.

2. I will write _____ times a week in my journal.

3. I will put _____ key words in my word bank.

4. I will search _____ Internet sites.

    Signed, _____
                  (me)

    _____
       (teacher)

Name _____    Date _____

    I'm interested in finding out about _____.
To do this, I will spend _____ hours a week at
the _____ and _____ hours at the _____.
    From my notes, I will prepare a _____
and do a _____, which I will share with
the class on _____.

    Signed, _____
                  (me)

    _____
       (teacher)

all about. Parent volunteers and teacher aides are ideal assistants. However, the most valuable assets to any organized classroom are the students themselves.

Any classroom that has a reading corner or that includes sustained silent reading in its reading program should also have a system to record what students are reading. One system is to have cards or charts attached to the inside back cover of a student folder (or portfolio or reading journal) as shown in Figure 15.7.

## Figure 15.7  Individual Reading Chart

### WHAT HAVE I BEEN READING?

| Date | Title | Author | Rating +/− | # pp. |
|------|-------|--------|-----------|-------|
| Mar. 13 | Lon Po Po: A Red-Riding Hood Story from China | Ed Young | + | 87 |
| Apr. 2 | Mufaro's Beautiful Daughters | John Steptoe | + | 206 |

Technology can also provide students and teachers with easily accessible ways to chart their self-selected reading and store information in an uncomplicated and understandable manner. Electronic record keeping, publishing programs, spreadsheets, portfolios, organizers, and reading software with a record-keeping component are also available.

PORTFOLIO SYSTEMS ◆ Collecting students' work and recording their literacy growth for documentation and assessment purposes in a **portfolio system,** described in Chapter 6, also helps in planning and organizing instruction. When students are evaluated not just on the "correct" answers they give but on their engagement in higher levels of thinking, improvement in problem solving, and attitudes toward learning, portfolios have the capacity to reinforce curricular and instructional goals. As Hopkin and colleagues (1997) point out, portfolios provide "a tool that clearly communicates information about a student's progress within our specified curricular program. Student portfolios are highly beneficial as transfer documents and, as such, become a practical vehicle to contain our curriculum" (p. 413). In traditional or electronic format, portfolios can become catalysts to link parents and the school and to link teachers and other colleagues.

Whereas student work makes up the bulk of a student-generated assessment portfolio, a *teacher's portfolio* needs to include other types of information as well. This portfolio can consist of a loose-leaf binder with a page for each student and room for adding artifacts and other pertinent data such as anecdotal records, observations during lessons, and perhaps surveys from parents, peers, or self about attitudes and aptitudes. Using self-adhesive labels, the teacher can easily write notes about a student as needed and transfer them later to a notebook page or an observation form.

A similar idea to the teacher's portfolio is the **teacher's log,** organized especially for assessment, with several pages for each student on which to record observations and narratives (Flood, Lapp, & Nagel, 1993). Teachers can use such logs to record not only reading and writing activities but social behaviors as well.

In addition, both student and teacher could fill out a self-evaluation form (see Figure 15.8). They might do this individually and then compare their responses in a conference. The form could be oriented toward the actual classroom activities or serve as a summative statement placed at the end of a student's portfolio.

Creating an environment that relies on physical, psychological, and social characteristics helps to "put it all together" in order to organize a literate classroom community. The classroom community of today and tomorrow includes the integration of technology.

Throughout this text we have stressed the importance of technology integration and utilization. We have pointed out that use of technology and the role it has in literacy development depend on teachers' beliefs. We have also focused on technology integration and use in instruction and assessment. In order to continue to prepare students for the technological challenges of this century, new technological literacies, management, and technology-based instruction are necessary and will be discussed next.

## Technology in the Literate Classroom

The nature of literacy has changed and been redefined. In order to be considered literate in today's world, students need to be proficient in information and communication technology (International Reading Association, 2002a). The International Reading Association continues to emphasize that students have rights related to technology development, and it is imperative for teachers to support students in developing new technological literacies.

New literacies generated by information and communication technology such as word processing, publishing, and media software, as well as e-mail and the Internet, have had an effect on reading and reading instruction (see Box 15.3 on page 514). Utilizing information and communication technology requires the development of new skills,

## Figure 15.8   Self-Evaluation Form

Name: _____        Date: _____

*Directions:* Answer *yes* or *no* in each box.

Centers

| | 1 | 2 | 3 | 4 | 5 | 6 | 7 | 8 | 9 | 10 | 11 |
|---|---|---|---|---|---|---|---|---|---|---|---|
| 1. Did I improve in this activity? | | | | | | | | | | | |
| 2. Did I understand and follow directions? | | | | | | | | | | | |
| 3. Did I write neatly and accurately? | | | | | | | | | | | |
| 4. Did I do as much as I could? | | | | | | | | | | | |
| 5. Did I learn anything new? | | | | | | | | | | | |

6. The activities I did my best work on were _____ and _____.

   It was my best work because _____.

7. The activities I had difficulty with were _____ and _____.

   They were difficult because _____.

8. The activity I like most is _____.

9. The activity I dislike most is _____.

   Comments about my portfolio: _____

strategies, and insights. Although some teachers are concerned about the traditional literacies and do not want to focus instructional time on new literacies, nevertheless, in order to be technologically literate, Leu (2002b) believes that students need to:

- *Learn how to learn* new technologies of literacy
- Develop the ability to critically evaluate information
- Learn how to locate, evaluate, and use information and communication technology
- Develop social learning strategies in order to communicate effectively
- Develop cultural understandings when they engage in collaborative activities and research
- Build on the traditional literacies of reading and writing

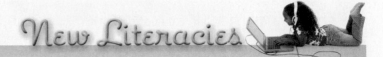

## INCORPORATING TECHNOLOGY

Being able to read, write, and think in new ways requires teachers to focus on knowledge construction and critical thinking in instructional contexts where students are active and engaged readers. Lewis and Fabos (2005) suggest asking students to think about out-of-school digital literacies and compare them to in-school literacies. Through metadiscussions "students can be guided to analyze the features of semiotic systems with which they interact across contexts" and "the semiotic processes they use to carry out these interactions" (p. 496). The need for flexible reading practices across genres and modes will further add to the development of new literacies (Kress, 2003). To facilitate the development of these skills and strategies the teacher needs to create a well-managed literate classroom community that incorporates technology.

The literate classroom is changing. Since computers are readily accessible in most schools, it is not uncommon for students to have access to computer labs and multiple computers in the classroom. In classrooms with access to one computer, it is especially important to think about room arrangement and management. Placing the computer in a central location where the screen can be viewed by the whole class is important. Teacher demonstrations, student presentations, and Internet usage are all facilitated by a central placement. In addition to whole class access, it is important that each student have computer time individually, with a peer, or in a small group. This can be aided by developing student schedules and providing open times throughout the day for computer access. Providing time for individual or small groups is important for teaching the new literacy technologies especially for children from less advantaged homes where their access is limited. Grabe and Grabe (2004) report that access to technology outside the school influences the skills students bring to school and the work they can do on their own. Therefore, knowing the students' backgrounds and the skills they bring is essential for classroom management.

Navigating and assessing information from the Internet are two literacies that have emerged from information and communication technologies. The use of the Internet is a common yet motivational experience for many students. Internet use, however, needs to be well managed. To ensure quality from the plethora of web sites, teachers as well as students need to be able to locate and identify appropriate material. Evaluating individual web sites involves critical thinking skills. Students need to know how to find, analyze, and judge the validity of the information to effectively use the resources available (Leu, 2002a). Critical thinking skills, therefore, become the basis for various formal and informal web site evaluations and checklists. A user-friendly web site that provides various links for Internet evaluation is Kathy Schrock's Guide for Educators at http://discoveryschool.com/schrockguide/eval.html. The links are based on four qualities to look for when evaluating web links: accessibility, accuracy, appropriateness, and appeal.

In addition to evaluating web sites, software and CD-ROM storybook evaluations are necessary. Valmont (2003) stresses that it is crucial for teachers to evaluate software in order to ensure alignment with the curriculum, educational soundness, and user friendliness. Research support on Web, software, and CD-ROM storybook usage has been mixed due to the various electronic features and the developmental levels of students. Therefore, to facilitate the evaluation process and selection of technology, reviews from media specialists, librarians, literacy coaches, and other teachers can be valuable resources. Additional information can be gathered from professional journals and demonstrations from publishers.

## Technology-Based Instructional Considerations

As information and communication technology become more accessible to teachers, technology has a greater impact on classroom organization and instructional practices. Teaching and learning are being defined by the technologies within the classroom environment. Technology has made reading materials easily available, changes the way in which reading takes place, provides individual learning opportunities, and encourages students to use good judgment in locating and using information.

Although the integration of technology for teaching and learning is increasing, the use and benefits of it depend on how much teachers value technology. The teacher's belief system will guide the integration of technology into teaching and learning practices. It is important that support and resources be provided for teachers as technology continues to change (Schrum, 1995). This support includes staff development in order to help ensure that teachers are prepared to integrate information and communication technologies into the curriculum (International Reading Association, 2002a). Literacy coaches can also provide teachers needed support as they develop technological skills and help them see the value in technology and new literacies.

Teachers need to know how to organize instruction in order to take advantage of technological benefits. Current practices in primary and middle school classrooms with technology build on keyboarding, a skill most students use or develop that introduces them to various other applications (Valmont & Wepner, 2000). Technologies that can be implemented into most primary and middle school classrooms are:

- E-mail
- Digitized pronunciations
- Word processing
- Hypermedia/multimedia
- Internet
- Smart boards
- Web cams
- Video

A selection of activities built on these technological understandings is listed in Figure 15.9. Additionally, refer to Box 15.4 for an explanation of teaching with the Internet.

As a result of these instructional practices, teachers should expect the following attitudes and behaviors from students:

### ATTITUDES

- Acts comfortable, confident, and capable when using the equipment
- Displays a positive attitude toward using technology and overcomes any "phobias" about technology
- Realizes the importance of working cooperatively with classmates
- Develops flexibility in working relationships with peers

---

### Figure 15.9  Technology-Based Instructional Activities

- E-mail a partner or book buddy
- Write own story or a collaborative story
- Create animated books
- Write language-experience books
- Read electronic tests
- Publish on the World Wide Web
- Research

- Create presentations
- Search the Web
- Participate in scavenger hunts
- Evaluate web sites
- Participate in virtual field trips
- Listen to talking books
- Generate WebQuests

BOX **15.4**

## Research-Based Practices

### The Internet Workshop

Information and communication technologies have had an impact on literacy development. The Internet is one such technology with increased classroom use. In order to utilize the Internet effectively, Leu and Leu (2000) describe an instructional strategy called Internet workshop.

The Internet workshop consists of independent reading on the Internet combined with a short workshop during which learned information is shared. Leu and Leu point out that Internet workshop has many variations, but it generally contains the following procedures:

1. Locate Internet sites related to topics being studied.
2. Design activities utilizing the Internet sites.

3. Complete the Internet activity.
4. Share and exchange information gathered during the workshop session. Also, discuss questions not answered and other topics of interest that resulted from the reading. Set the stage for the next Internet workshop.

*Source:* Adapted from *Teaching with the Internet: Lessons from the Classroom,* 3rd ed., by D. J. Leu Jr. and D. D. Leu (Norwood, MA: Christopher-Gordon, 2000).

BEHAVIORS
- Exhibits fluency with specific equipment
- Demonstrates a facility for gathering, sorting, analyzing, synthesizing, translating, and presenting information
- Shares knowledge with others
- Engages in literacy tasks
- Engages in cooperative or collaborative learning with classmates
- Stays on task and uses time productively

As teachers, we need to ask ourselves how to maximize students' learning and harness their enthusiasm. Moreover, are the children overwhelmed? Do they experience information overload? Are we reasonable in balancing how much of the curriculum should be taught using technologically sophisticated means? Sometimes material that is available doesn't fit naturally into a particular unit of study or project. If that is the case, do not include it. Electronic materials must fit naturally and logically with the curriculum for them to be meaningful—a major consideration for teaching and learning.

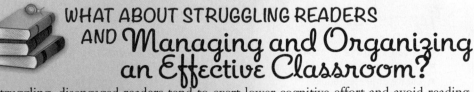

## WHAT ABOUT STRUGGLING READERS AND Managing and Organizing an Effective Classroom?

Struggling, disengaged readers tend to exert lower cognitive effort and avoid reading. Rarely do they enjoy reading during free time or become absorbed in literature. In contrast, engaged readers believe in their abilities and are motivated to read for personal goals; they take responsibility for their learning. Engaged readers seek to understand and are strategic in the comprehension process. They also interact with peers socially to help them construct meaning.

Motivation is the foundational process for engaged readers. Increasing competence is motivating, and increased motivation leads to more reading and writing. In order to facilitate literacy development for struggling readers, the teacher should incorporate the following classroom practices:

- Create a low-risk environment with real-world experiences.
- Provide a variety of interesting materials.
- Provide opportunities for the use of technology.
- Include heterogeneous and flexible grouping opportunities.
- Create a collaborative learning community.
- Provide indirect and explicit instruction.
- Encourage peer learning and sharing.
- Develop independence by facilitating strategy development.
- Have high expectations for all students.
- Integrate the use of technology.

How the classroom is managed and organized affects student learning. Students are motivated when classrooms provide opportunities for social learning. Active, engaged learning for all learners is essential; therefore, readers—especially struggling readers—need to be in an active learning environment where individual differences are respected. In addition, children need to understand the social and cultural practices that children from diverse groups bring to the classroom. They should have the opportunity to interact with others to develop literacy skills. The classroom must become a community of learners.

## WHAT ABOUT STANDARDS, ASSESSMENT, AND Managing and Organizing an Effective Classroom?

Knowing how to use information and communication technologies (ICT), such as the Internet, is integral to literacy in the twenty-first century. Practically all of the national education associations in the various academic disciplines have developed content standards or statements of principle that implicitly or explicitly acknowledge the proficient use of technologies for information and communication.

The International Reading Association and the National Council of Teachers of English (1996) are explicit in their standards for using ICT: "Students use a variety of technological and information resources . . . together and synthesize information to create and communicate knowledge."

State content standards, likewise, underscore the ability to put technologies to use for learning. But, for the most part, states continue to rely on paper-and-pencil tests to assess students' abilities to meet content standards. Donald Leu (2002b), one of the leading scholars associated with the new literacies, argues that proficiency assessments will need to be refined in the ever-changing world of ICT: "The challenge will be to develop assessment systems that keep up with the continually changing nature of literacy so that assessment data provide useful information for planning" (p. 326). He points out a major flaw in statewide proficiency assessments related to reading and writing: "Not a single reading assessment in the United States currently evaluates reading on the Internet and not a single state writing assessment permits the use of anything other than paper and pencil technologies" (p. 326).

## Summary

In this chapter, we considered what teachers need to do to manage and organize their classrooms effectively for reading instruction. The guiding principles can be traced back through the evolution of cooperative learning and individualized instruction. Collaborative learning, the social nature of reading and writing, and the teacher's role in creating a classroom community contribute to improved instruction to meet the overall goal of producing independent readers. We paid close attention to the role of classrooms teacher, central to understanding all other factors in an effective classroom. Teachers organize and manage their classrooms through daily decision making, guided by professional standards and best practices.

We considered the ways in which teachers put everything together to create an environment and described characteristics of classroom communities and multiage classrooms. Whether facilitating collaborative learning, patterns for literacy, or pro-

viding explicit instruction, teachers want to create a classroom environment conducive to learning. How they schedule students, balance activities and materials, and test and keep records differs from teacher to teacher. Just as teachers individualize in various ways, so their classroom environments vary from straight-row traditional to flexible-seating open arrangements. Learning centers and their organization were illustrated, along with room diagrams, schedules, record keeping, and portfolio systems. Management of technology, technology-based instruction, and new literacies were also discussed.

In the end, each individual teacher must decide on the best way to manage and organize the classroom in light of students' abilities and needs, priorities, reading program, instructional approach, and technological support. The way we balance all these and other variables in the social, psychological, and physical context contributes to our reputations as effective teachers.

## Teacher Action Research

1. Describe how you would organize your classroom to support the goals of your reading program. Develop a room diagram to illustrate how you would arrange furniture, materials, equipment, student activities, storage, and so on. Label the diagram and share it with another colleague or student in the class.

**STANDARD 5.3**

2. Interview two elementary or middle school teachers, preferably from different schools, asking them how they group children for instruction in reading and language arts. Or interview two of your fellow students and ask how they would group children. Analyze the results, and determine the most prevalent reasons for grouping children for the purposes of reading instruction.

3. Visit a classroom where the teacher uses technology. How does the use of technology affect instruction in this class? What kinds of literacy activities seem to work best with the technology? What doesn't work as well with the technology? Describe or illustrate the placement of technologically advanced equipment in the room.

4. Describe how you will manage motivation to read and write in your classroom.

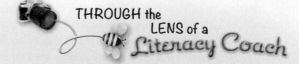

THROUGH the LENS of a Literacy Coach

5. You are asked to design a literate classroom and see the literacy coach for assistance. The coach encourages you to visit other classrooms and ask yourself how other teachers have organized their classrooms to make them effective. What evidence of this was seen? How might this information be used to organize your own literate classroom? Create a drawing and write up the essential components of your new literate classroom.

## Related Web Sites

*Education Week on the Web*

**www.edweek.org**

Education Week on the Web is an online educational newspaper that provides articles, news, archives, special reports, hot topics, and information related to the field of education.

*International Reading Association*

**www.reading.org**

By accessing this page, a link can be found to the Standards for Reading Professionals.

*The Internet Public Library*

**www.ipl.org**

The Internet Public Library provides links to informational and educational resources for youths and teens.

*Learning Point*

**www.learningpt.org**

Learning Point provides information for schools and teachers related to literacy, with links to information about facilitating instruction and curriculum, customized training, and evaluation of literacy programs and student achievement data.

*National Institute for Literacy*

**www.nifl.gov**

The National Institute for Literacy is a federal agency that provides leadership on literacy issues. The site provides links to research, policies, and information relating literacy to assessment, early childhood, childhood, adolescence, adulthood, and program reviews.

*PBS Newsroom Headlines*

**www.pbs.org**

The activities and lessons relate to the educational programming presented on PBS, as well as providing information about television for teachers, teaching with technology, lessons, and activities.

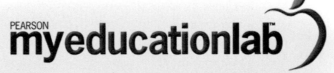

Now go to the Vacca et al. *Reading and Learning to Read*, Seventh Edition, MyEducationLab course at **www.myeducationlab.com** to

- Take a pretest to assess your initial comprehension of the chapter content
- Study chapter content with your individualized study plan
- Take a posttest to assess your understanding of chapter content
- Engage in multimedia exercises to help you build a deeper and more applied understanding of chapter content

# Beliefs About Reading Interview

## Determining Your Beliefs About Reading

To determine your beliefs about reading, study the sample responses in this appendix. Then compare each answer you gave to the interview questions in Box 2.1 in Chapter 2 to the samples given here. Using the form in Figure A.1, categorize each response as *bottom-up* (BU) or *top-down* (TD). If you cannot make that determination, check NI, for *not enough information*.

---

### Figure A.1    Rating Sheet for Beliefs About Reading Interview

|  | RATING SCALE | | |
| --- | :---: | :---: | :---: |
|  | BU | TD | NI |
| 1. Instructional goals | | | |
| 2. Response to oral reading when reader makes an error | | | |
| 3. Response to oral reading when a student does not know a word | | | |
| 4. Most important instructional activity | | | |
| 5. Instructional activities reader should be engaged in most of the time | | | |
| 6. Ordering of steps in a reading lesson | | | |
| 7. Importance of introducing vocabulary words before students read | | | |
| 8. Information from testing | | | |
| 9. How a reader should respond to unfamiliar words during silent reading | | | |
| 10. Rationale for best reader | | | |

---

## Table A.1  Rating Chart

| | |
|---|---|
| **Bottom-up:** | Gave 0 or 1 top-down response (the rest are bottom-up or not enough information) |
| **Interactive:** | Gave 3 to 5 bottom-up responses |
| **Top-down:** | Gave 0 or 1 bottom-up responses |

Ask yourself as you judge your responses, "What unit of language did I stress?" For example, if you said that your major instructional goal is "to increase students' ability to associate sounds with letters," then the unit of language emphasized suggests a bottom-up response. Bottom-up responses are those that emphasize *letters* and *words* as the predominant units of language.

By contrast, a top-down response would be appropriate if you had said that your major instructional goal is "to increase students' ability to read library books or other materials on their own." In this response, the unit of language involves the entire selection. Top-down responses emphasize *sentences, paragraphs,* and the *selection itself* as the predominant units of language.

An example of a response that does not give enough information is one in which you might have said, "I tell the student to figure out the word." Such a response needs to be probed further during the interview by asking, "How should the student figure out the word?"

The following rating sheet will help you determine roughly where you lie on the continuum between bottom-up and top-down belief systems. After you have judged each response to the interview questions, check the appropriate column on the rating sheet for each interview probe.

An overall rating of your conceptual framework of reading is obtained from Table A.1, showing where you fall on the reading beliefs continuum in Figure 2.1 in Chapter 2.

## Guidelines for Analyzing Beliefs About Reading Interviews

*Directions:* Use the following summary statements as guidelines to help analyze your responses to the questions in the interview.

### Question 1: Main Instructional Goals

BOTTOM-UP RESPONSES

Increase children's ability to blend sounds into words or ability to sound out words.

Increase knowledge of phonetic sounds (letter–sound associations).

Build sight vocabulary.

Increase ability to use word attack skills.

TOP-DOWN RESPONSES

Increase students' ability to read independently by encouraging them to read library or other books that are easy enough for them on their own.

Increase enjoyment of reading by having a lot of books around, reading aloud to children, and sharing books I thought were special.

Improve comprehension.

Increase ability to find specific information, identify key ideas, determine cause-and-effect relationships, and make inferences. (Although these are discrete skills, they are categorized as top-down because students use higher-order linguistic units—phrases, sentences, and paragraphs—in accomplishing them.)

### Question 2: Teacher Responses When Students Make Oral Reading Errors

BOTTOM-UP RESPONSES

Help students sound out the word.

Tell students what the word is and have them spell and then repeat the word.

TOP-DOWN RESPONSES

Ask "Does that make sense?"

Don't interrupt; one word doesn't "goof up" the meaning of an entire passage.

Don't interrupt; if students are worried about each word, they won't be able to remember what they read.

Don't correct if the error doesn't affect the meaning of the passage.

If the error affects the meaning of the passage, ask students to reread the passage, tell students the word, or ask, "Does that make sense?"

## Question 3: Teacher Responses When Students Do Not Know a Word

BOTTOM-UP RESPONSES

Help students sound out the word.

Help them distinguish smaller words within the word.

Help them break down the word phonetically.

Help them sound out the word syllable by syllable.

Tell them to use word attack skills.

Give them word attack clues; for example, "The sound of the beginning consonant rhymes with _____."

TOP-DOWN RESPONSES

Tell students to skip the word, go on, and come back to see what makes sense.

Ask, "What makes sense and starts with _____?"

## Questions 4 and 5: Most Important Instructional Activities

BOTTOM-UP RESPONSES

Working on skills.

Working on phonics.

Working on sight vocabulary.

Vocabulary drill.

Discussing experience charts, focusing on the words included and any punctuation needed.

Tape-recording students reading and playing it back, emphasizing accuracy in word recognition.

TOP-DOWN RESPONSES

Actual reading, silent reading, and independent reading.

Comprehension.

Discussion of what students have read.

Book reports.

Tape-recording students reading and playing it back, emphasizing enjoyment of reading or comprehension.

## Question 6: Ranking Parts of the Directed Reading Procedure

BOTTOM-UP RESPONSES

The following are most important:

   Introduction of vocabulary.

   Activities to develop reading skills.

The following are least important:

> Setting purposes for reading.
>
> Reading.
>
> Reaction to silent reading.
>
> Introduction of vocabulary when the teacher stresses using word attack skills to sound out new words.

TOP-DOWN RESPONSES

The following are most important:

> Setting purposes for reading.
>
> Reading.
>
> Reaction to silent reading.

The following are least important:

> Introduction of vocabulary.
>
> Activities to develop reading skills.

## Question 7: Introducing New Vocabulary Words

BOTTOM-UP RESPONSES

Introducing new vocabulary is important because students need to know which words they will encounter in order to be able to read a story.

Previewing new vocabulary isn't necessary; if students have learned word attack skills, they can sound out unknown words.

Introducing new words is useful in helping students learn which words are important in a reading lesson.

Vocabulary words should be introduced if students don't know the meanings of the words; otherwise it isn't necessary.

TOP-DOWN RESPONSE

Vocabulary words need not be introduced before reading because students can often figure out words from context.

## Question 8: What a Reading Test Should Do

BOTTOM-UP RESPONSES

Test word attack skills.

Test ability to name the letters of the alphabet.

Test sight words.

Test knowledge of meanings of words.

Test ability to analyze letter patterns of words missed during oral reading.

Test visual skills such as reversal.

TOP-DOWN RESPONSES

Test comprehension: Students should be able to read a passage orally, look at the errors they make, and use context in figuring out words.

Test whether students are able to glean the meanings of words from context.

Answer questions such as the following: Do students enjoy reading? Do their parents read to them? Do their parents take them to the library?

Have students read passages and answer questions.

Have students read directions and follow them.

## Question 9: What Students Should Do When They Come to an Unknown Word During Silent Reading

BOTTOM-UP RESPONSES

Sound it out.

Use their word attack skills.

TOP-DOWN RESPONSES

Look at the beginning and the end of the sentence and try to think of a word that makes sense.

Try to think of a word that both makes sense and has those letter sounds.

Skip the word; often students can understand the meaning of the sentence without knowing every word.

Use context.

## Question 10: Who Is the Best Reader?

| **Reader A** | **Reader B** | **Reader C** |
|---|---|---|
| Miscue is similar both graphically and in meaning to the text word. | Miscue is a real word that is graphically similar but not meaningful in the text. | Miscue is a nonword that is graphically similar. |

BOTTOM-UP RESPONSES

Reader C, because *cannel* is graphically similar to *canal*.

Reader B, because *candle* is a real word that is graphically similar to *canal*.

TOP-DOWN RESPONSE

Reader A, because *channel* is similar in meaning to *canal*.

# The DeFord Theoretical Orientation to Reading Profile (TORP)

Name: _____

*Directions:* Read the following statements and circle one of the responses that will indicate the relationship of the statement to your feelings about reading and reading instruction. SA = strongly agree; SD = strongly disagree.

| Select *one* best answer that reflects the strength of agreement or disagreement. | SA | A | — | D | SD |
|---|---|---|---|---|---|
| 1. A child needs to be able to verbalize the rules of phonics in order to ensure proficiency in processing new words. | 1 | 2 | 3 | 4 | 5 |
| 2. An increase in errors is usually related to a decrease in comprehension. | 1 | 2 | 3 | 4 | 5 |
| 3. Dividing words into syllables according to rules is a helpful instructional practice for reading new words. | 1 | 2 | 3 | 4 | 5 |
| 4. Fluency and expression are necessary components of reading that indicate good comprehension. | 1 | 2 | 3 | 4 | 5 |
| 5. Materials for early reading should be written in natural language without concern for short, simple words and sentences. | 1 | 2 | 3 | 4 | 5 |
| 6. When children do not know a word, they should be instructed to sound out its parts. | 1 | 2 | 3 | 4 | 5 |
| 7. It is a good practice to allow children to edit what is written into their own dialect when learning to read. | 1 | 2 | 3 | 4 | 5 |
| 8. The use of a glossary or dictionary is necessary in determining the meaning and pronunciation of new words. | 1 | 2 | 3 | 4 | 5 |
| 9. Reversals (e.g., saying "saw" for "was") are significant problems in the teaching of reading. | 1 | 2 | 3 | 4 | 5 |
| 10. It is good practice to correct a child as soon as an oral reading mistake is made. | 1 | 2 | 3 | 4 | 5 |
| 11. It is important for a word to be repeated a number of times after it has been introduced to ensure that it will become a part of sight vocabulary. | 1 | 2 | 3 | 4 | 5 |
| 12. Paying close attention to punctuation marks is necessary to understanding story content. | 1 | 2 | 3 | 4 | 5 |

|  | SA | A | — | D | SD |
|---|---|---|---|---|---|
| 13. It is a sign of an ineffective reader when words and phrases are repeated. | 1 | 2 | 3 | 4 | 5 |
| 14. Being able to label words according to grammatical function (e.g., nouns, verbs, objects, etc.) is useful in proficient reading. | 1 | 2 | 3 | 4 | 5 |
| 15. When coming to a word that's unknown, the reader should be encouraged to guess at meaning and go on. | 1 | 2 | 3 | 4 | 5 |
| 16. Young readers need to be introduced to the root form of words (e.g., *run, long*) before they are asked to read inflected forms (e.g., *running, longest*). | 1 | 2 | 3 | 4 | 5 |
| 17. It is not necessary for a child to know the letters of the alphabet in order to learn to read. | 1 | 2 | 3 | 4 | 5 |
| 18. Flash-card drills with sight words are an unnecessary form of practice in reading instruction. | 1 | 2 | 3 | 4 | 5 |
| 19. The ability to use accent patterns in multisyllable words (phó to graph, pho tó gra phy, and pho to grá phic) should be developed as part of reading instruction. | 1 | 2 | 3 | 4 | 5 |
| 20. Controlling text through consistent spelling patterns (e.g., "The fat cat ran back. The fat cat sat on a hat.") is a means by which children can best learn to read. | 1 | 2 | 3 | 4 | 5 |
| 21. Formal instruction in reading is necessary to ensure the adequate development of all the skills used in reading. | 1 | 2 | 3 | 4 | 5 |
| 22. Phonic analysis is the most important form of analysis used when meeting new words. | 1 | 2 | 3 | 4 | 5 |
| 23. Children's initial encounters with print should focus on meaning, not on exact graphic representation. | 1 | 2 | 3 | 4 | 5 |
| 24. Word shapes (word configuration) should be taught in reading to aid in word recognition. | 1 | 2 | 3 | 4 | 5 |
| 25. It is important to teach skills in relation to other skills. | 1 | 2 | 3 | 4 | 5 |
| 26. If a child says "house" for the written word *home*, the response should be left uncorrected. | 1 | 2 | 3 | 4 | 5 |
| 27. It is not necessary to introduce new words before they appear in the reading text. | 1 | 2 | 3 | 4 | 5 |
| 28. Some problems in reading are caused by readers dropping the inflectional ending from words (e.g., jump*s*, jump*ed*). | 1 | 2 | 3 | 4 | 5 |

## Determining Your Theoretical Orientation

To determine your theoretical orientation, tally your total score on the TORP. Add the point values as indicated on each item, *except for the following items:*

5, 7, 15, 17, 18, 23, 26, 27

For these items, reverse the point values by assigning 5 points for strongly agree (SA) to 1 point for strongly disagree (SD):

| SA | A | — | D | SD |
|---|---|---|---|---|
| 5 | 4 | 3 | 2 | 1 |

Once your point totals have been added, your overall score on the TORP will fall in one of the following ranges:

| Theoretical Orientation | Overall Score Range |
| --- | --- |
| Phonics | 0–65 |
| Skills | 65–110 |
| Whole language | 110–140 |

*Source:* Adapted from "Validating the Construct of Theoretical Orientation in Reading Instruction," by Diane E. DeFord, 1985, Spring, *Reading Research Quarterly, 20*(3), pp. 351–367. Copyright © 1985 by the International Reading Association. Reprinted with permission of the International Reading Association (www.reading.org).

# Reading and Writing Accomplishments of Young Children by Grade Level

## Kindergarten Accomplishments

- Knows the parts of a book and their functions.

- Begins to track print when listening to a familiar text being read or when rereading own writing.

- "Reads" familiar texts emergently (i.e., not necessarily verbatim from the print alone).

- Recognizes and can name all uppercase and lowercase letters.

- Understands that the sequence of letters in a written word represents the sequence of sounds (phonemes) in a spoken word (alphabetic principle).

- Learns many, though not all, one-to-one letter–sound correspondences.

- Recognizes some words by sight, including a few very common ones (*a, the, I, my, you, is, are*).

- Uses new vocabulary and grammatical constructions in own speech.

- Makes appropriate switches from oral to written language situations.

- Notices when simple sentences fail to make sense.

- Connects information and events in texts to life and life to text experiences.

- Retells, reenacts, or dramatizes stories or parts of stories.

- Listens attentively to books teacher reads to class.

- Can name some book titles and authors.

- Demonstrates familiarity with a number of types or genres of text (e.g., storybooks, expository texts, poems, newspapers, and everyday print such as signs, notices, labels).

- Correctly answers questions about stories read aloud.

- Makes predictions based on illustrations or portions of stories.

- Demonstrates understanding that spoken words consist of sequences of phonemes.

- Given spoken sets such as "dan, dan, den" can identify the first two as being the same and the third as different.

- Given spoken sets such as "dak, pat, zen" can identify the first two as sharing a same sound.

- Given spoken segments can merge them into a meaningful target word.

- Given a spoken word can produce another word that rhymes with it.

- Independently writes many uppercase and lowercase letters.

- Uses phonemic awareness and letter knowledge to spell independently (invented or creative spelling).

- Writes (unconventionally) to express own meaning.

- Builds a repertoire of some conventionally spelled words.

- Shows awareness of distinction between "kid writing" and conventional orthography.

- Writes own name (first and last) and the first names of some friends or classmates.

- Can write most letters and some words when they are dictated.

## First-Grade Accomplishments

- Makes a transition from emergent to "real" reading.

- Reads aloud with accuracy and comprehension any text that is appropriately designed for the first half of grade 1.

- Accurately decodes orthographically regular, one-syllable words and nonsense words (e.g., *sit, zot*), using print–sound mappings to sound out unknown words.

- Uses letter–sound correspondence knowledge to sound out unknown words when reading text.

- Recognizes common, irregularly spelled words by sight (*have, said, where, two*).

- Has a reading vocabulary of 300 to 500 words, both sight words and easily sounded out words.

- Monitors own reading and self-corrects when an incorrectly identified word does not fit with cues provided by the letters in the word or the context surrounding the word.

- Reads and comprehends both fiction and nonfiction that is appropriately designed for grade level.

- Shows evidence of expanding language repertory, including increasingly appropriate use of standard, more formal language registers.

- Creates own written texts for others to read.

- Notices when difficulties are encountered in understanding text.

- Reads and understands simple written instructions.

- Predicts and justifies what will happen next in stories.

- Discusses prior knowledge of topics in expository texts.

- Discusses how, why, and what-if questions in sharing nonfiction texts.

- Describes new information gained from texts in own words.

- Distinguishes whether simple sentences are incomplete or fail to make sense; notices when simple texts fail to make sense.

- Can answer simple written comprehension questions based on material read.

- Can count the number of syllables in a word.

- Can blend or segment the phonemes of most one-syllable words.

- Spells correctly three- and four-letter short vowel words.

- Composes fairly readable first drafts using appropriate parts of the writing process (some attention to planning, drafting, rereading for meaning, and some self-correction).

- Uses invented spelling/phonics-based knowledge to spell independently, when necessary.

- Shows spelling consciousness or sensitivity to conventional spelling.

- Uses basic punctuation and capitalization.

- Produces a variety of types of compositions (e.g., stories, descriptions, journal entries), showing appropriate relationships between printed text, illustrations, and other graphics.

- Engages in a variety of literary activities voluntarily (e.g., choosing books and stories to read, writing a note to a friend).

## Second-Grade Accomplishments

- Reads and comprehends both fiction and nonfiction that is appropriately designed for grade level.

- Accurately decodes orthographically regular multisyllable words and nonsense words (e.g., *capital, Kalamazoo*).

- Uses knowledge of print–sound mappings to sound out unknown words.

- Accurately reads many irregularly spelled words and such spelling patterns as diphthongs, special vowel spellings, and common word endings.

- Shows evidence of expanding language repertory, including increasing use of more formal language registers.

- Reads voluntarily for interest and own purposes.

- Rereads sentences when meaning is not clear.

- Interprets information from diagrams, charts, and graphs.

- Recalls facts and details of texts.

- Reads nonfiction materials for answers to specific questions or for specific purposes.

- Takes part in creative responses to texts such as dramatizations, oral presentations, fantasy play, etc.

- Discusses similarities in characters and events across stories.

- Connects and compares information across nonfiction selections.

- Poses possible answers to how, why, and what-if questions.

- Correctly spells previously studied words and spelling patterns in own writing.

- Represents the complete sound of a word when spelling independently.

- Shows sensitivity to using formal language patterns in place of oral language patterns at appropriate spots in own writing (e.g., decontextualizing sentences, conventions for quoted speech, literary language forms, proper verb forms).

- Makes reasonable judgments about what to include in written products.

- Productively discusses ways to clarify and refine writing of own and others.

- With assistance, adds use of conferencing, revision, and editing processes to clarify and refine own writing to the steps of the expected parts of the writing process.

- Given organizational help, writes informative well-structured reports.

- Attends to spelling, mechanics, and presentation for final products.

- Produces a variety of types of compositions (e.g., stories, reports, correspondence).

## Third-Grade Accomplishments

- Reads aloud with fluency and comprehension any text that is appropriately designed for grade level.

- Uses letter–sound correspondence knowledge and structural analysis to decode words.

- Reads and comprehends both fiction and nonfiction that is appropriately designed for grade level.

- Reads longer fictional selections and chapter books independently.

- Takes part in creative responses to texts such as dramatizations, oral presentations, fantasy play, etc.

- Can point to or clearly identify specific words or wordings that are causing comprehension difficulties.

- Summarizes major points from fiction and nonfiction texts.

- In interpreting fiction, discusses underlying theme or message.

- Asks how, why, and what-if questions in interpreting nonfiction texts.

- In interpreting nonfiction, distinguishes cause and effect, fact and opinion, main idea and supporting details.

- Uses information and reasoning to examine bases of hypotheses and opinions.

- Infers word meanings from taught roots, prefixes, and suffixes.

- Correctly spells previously studied words and spelling patterns in own writing.

- Begins to incorporate literacy words and language patterns in own writing (e.g., elaborates descriptions, uses figurative wording).

- With some guidance, uses all aspects of the writing process in producing own compositions and reports.

- Combines information from multiple sources in writing reports.

- With assistance, suggests and implements editing and revision to clarify and refine own writing.

- Presents and discusses own writing with other students and responds helpfully to other students' compositions.

- Independently reviews work for spelling, mechanics, and presentation.

- Produces a variety of written works (e.g., literature responses, reports, "published" books, semantic maps) in a variety of formats, including multimedia forms.

---

*Source: Preventing Reading Difficulties in Young Children,* edited by C. E. Snow, M. S. Burns, and P. Griffin. Copyright © 1998 by the National Academy of Sciences. Reprinted with the permission of the National Academy Press, Washington, DC.

# Trade Books That Repeat Phonic Elements

## Short *A*

Flack, Marjorie. *Angus and the Cat.* Doubleday, 1931.

Griffith, Helen. *Alex and the Cat.* Greenwillow, 1982.

Kent, Jack. *The Fat Cat.* Scholastic, 1971.

Most, Bernard. *There's an Ant in Anthony.* William Morrow, 1980.

Nodset, Joan. *Who Took the Farmer's Hat?* Harper & Row, 1963.

Robins, Joan. *Addie Meets Max.* Harper & Row, 1985.

Schmidt, Karen. *The Gingerbread Man.* Scholastic, 1985.

Seuss, Dr. *The Cat in the Hat.* Random House, 1957.

## Long *A*

Aardema, Verna. *Bringing the Rain to Kapiti Plain.* Dial, 1981.

Bang, Molly. *The Paper Crane.* Greenwillow, 1985.

Blume, Judy. *The Pain and the Great One.* Bradbury, 1974.

Byars, Betsy. *The Lace Snail.* Viking, 1975.

Henkes, Kevin. *Sheila Rae, the Brave.* Greenwillow, 1987.

Hines, Anna G. *Taste the Raindrops.* Greenwillow, 1983.

## Short and Long *A*

Aliki. *Jack and Jake.* Greenwillow, 1986.

Slobodkina, Esphyr. *Caps for Sale.* Addison-Wesley, 1940.

## Short *E*

Ets, Marie Hall. *Elephant in a Well.* Viking, 1972.

Galdone, Paul. *The Little Red Hen.* Scholastic, 1973.

Ness, Evaline. *Yeck Eck.* E. P. Dutton, 1974.

Shecter, Ben. *Hester the Jester.* Harper & Row, 1977.

Thayer, Jane. *I Don't Believe in Elves.* William Morrow, 1975.

Wing, Henry Ritchet. *Ten Pennies for Candy.* Holt, Rinehart & Winston, 1963.

## Long *E*

Galdone, Paul. *Little Bo-Peep.* Clarion/Ticknor & Fields, 1986.

Keller, Holly. *Ten Sleepy Sheep.* Greenwillow, 1983.

Martin, Bill. *Brown Bear, Brown Bear, What Do You See?* Henry Holt, 1967.

Oppenheim, Joanne. *Have You Seen Trees?* Young Scott Books, 1967.

Soule, Jean C. *Never Tease a Weasel.* Parents' Magazine Press, 1964.

Thomas, Patricia. *"Stand Back," Said the Elephant, "I'm Going to Sneeze!"* Lothrop, Lee & Shepard, 1971.

## Short *I*

Browne, Anthony. *Willy the Wimp.* Alfred A. Knopf, 1984.

Ets, Marie Hall. *Gilberto and the Wind.* Viking, 1966.

Hutchins, Pat. *Titch.* Macmillan, 1971.

Keats, Ezra Jack. *Whistle for Willie.* Viking, 1964.

Lewis, Thomas P. *Call for Mr. Sniff.* Harper & Row, 1981.

Lobel, Arnold. *Small Pig.* Harper & Row, 1969.

McPhail, David. *Fix-It.* E. P. Dutton, 1984.

Patrick, Gloria. *This Is . . .* Carolrhoda, 1970.

Robins, Joan. *My Brother, Will.* Greenwillow, 1986.

## Long *I*

Berenstain, Stan, and Jan Berenstain. *The Bike Lesson.* Random House, 1964.

Cameron, John. *If Mice Could Fly.* Atheneum, 1979.

Cole, Sheila. *When the Tide Is Low.* Lothrop, Lee & Shepard, 1985.

Gelman, Rita. *Why Can't I Fly?* Scholastic, 1976.

Hazen, Barbara S. *Tight Times.* Viking, 1979.

## Short *O*

Benchley, Nathaniel. *Oscar Otter.* Harper & Row, 1966.

Dunrea, Olivier. *Mogwogs on the March!* Holiday House, 1985.

Emberley, Barbara. *Drummer Hoff.* Prentice Hall, 1967.

McKissack, Patricia C. *Flossie & the Fox.* Dial, 1986.

Miller, Patricia, and Iran Seligman. *Big Frogs, Little Frogs.* Holt, Rinehart & Winston, 1963.

Rice, Eve. "The Frog and the Ox" from *Once in a Wood.* Greenwillow, 1979.

Seuss, Dr. *Fox in Socks.* Random House, 1965.

## Long *O*

Cole, Brock. *The Giant's Toe.* Farrar, Straus, & Giroux, 1986.

Gerstein, Mordicai. *Roll Over!* Crown, 1984.

Johnston, Tony. *The Adventures of Mole and Troll.* G. P. Putnam's Sons, 1972.

Johnston, Tony. *Night Noises and Other Mole and Troll Stories.* G. P. Putnam's Sons, 1977.

Shulevitz, Uri. *One Monday Morning.* Charles Scribner's Sons, 1967.

Tresselt, Alvin. *White Snow, Bright Snow.* Lothrop, Lee & Shepard, 1947.

## Short *U*

Carroll, Ruth. *Where's the Bunny?* Henry Z. Walck, 1950.

Cooney, Nancy E. *Donald Says Thumbs Down.* G. P. Putnam's Sons, 1987.

Friskey, Margaret. *Seven Little Ducks.* Children's Press, 1940.

Lorenz, Lee. *Big Gus and Little Gus.* Prentice Hall, 1982.

Marshall, James. *The Cut-Ups.* Viking Kestrel, 1984.

Udry, Janice May. *Thump and Plunk.* Harper & Row, 1981.

Yashima, Taro. *Umbrella.* Viking Penguin, 1958.

## Long *U*

Lobel, Anita. *The Troll Music.* Harper & Row, 1966.

Segal, Lore. *Tell Me a Trudy.* Farrar, Straus, & Giroux, 1977.

Slobodkin, Louis. *"Excuse Me—Certainly!"* Vanguard Press, 1959.

*Source:* "Using Children's Literature to Enhance Phonic Instruction," by Phyllis M. Trachtenburg, 1990, May, *The Reading Teacher, 43*(9), pp. 648–654. Copyright © 1990 by the International Reading Association. Reprinted with permission of the International Reading Association (www.reading.org).

# Annotated Bibliography of Read-Aloud Books for Developing Phonemic Awareness

**Brown, M. W. (1993).** *Four fur feet.* **New York: Doubleday.**
> In this simple book, the reader is drawn to the /f/ sound as the phrase "four fur feet" is repeated in every sentence as a furry animal walks around the world. The same pattern is used throughout the story as we see four fur feet walk along the river, into the country, and so forth. The book must be turned around as the animal makes its way around the world.

**Buller, J., & Schade, S. (1988).** *I love you, good night.* **New York: Simon and Schuster.**
> A mother and child tell each other how much they love one another. When the child says she loves her mother as much as "blueberry pancakes," the mother responds that she loves her child as much as "milkshakes." The child says she loves her mother as much as "frogs love flies," to which the mother responds she loves her child as much as "pigs love pies." The two go back and forth in this manner until "good night" is said. The rhyme invites the listener to participate and continue the story.

**Cameron, P. (1961).** *"I can't," said the ant.* **New York: Coward-McCann.**
> Household items discuss the fall of a teapot from the counter in a kitchen and the means by which to put it back. In a series of brief contributions to the conversation, each item says something that rhymes with its own name. " 'Don't break her,' said the shaker" and " 'I can't bear it,' said the carrot."

**Carle, E. (1974).** *All about Arthur (an absolutely absurd ape).* **New York: Franklin Watts.**
> Arthur, an accordion-playing ape who lives in Atlanta, feels lonely and travels from Baltimore to Yonkers making friends. In each city, he makes a friend whose name matches the initial sound of the city, from a banjo-playing bear in Baltimore to a young yak in Yonkers.

**Carter, D. (1990).** *More bugs in boxes.* **New York: Simon and Schuster.**
> This pop-up book presents a series of questions and answers about make-believe bugs that are found inside a variety of boxes. Both the questions and answers make use of alliteration: "What kind of bug is in the rosy red rectangle box? A bright blue big-mouth bug." Following a similar pattern is the author's Jingle Bugs (1992, Simon and Schuster), which has a Christmas theme and makes use of rhyme: "Who's in the chimney, warm and snug? Ho, ho, ho! It's Santa Bug!"

**Deming, A. G. (1994).** *Who is tapping at my window?* **New York: Penguin.**
> A young girl hears a tapping at her window and asks, "Who is there?" The farm animals each respond, "It's not I," and she discovers that it is the rain. The book is predictable in that each pair of animals rhymes. The loon responds, followed by the raccoon. The dog's response is followed by the frog's.

**de Regniers, B., Moore, E., White, M., & Carr, J. (1988).** *Sing a song of popcorn.* **New York: Scholastic.**
> A number of poems in this book draw attention to rhyme and encourage children to experiment. Also included are poems that play with sounds within words. In "Galoshes" the author describes the slippery slush "as it slooshes and sloshes and splishes and sploshes" around a child's galoshes. In "Eletelephony" sounds are mixed up and substituted for one another: "Once there was an elephant, / Who tried to use the telephant. . . ."

**Ehlert, L. (1989).** *Eating the alphabet: Fruits and vegetables from A to Z.* **San Diego, CA: Harcourt Brace Jovanovich.**
> Fruits and vegetables are offered in print and pictures for each letter of the alphabet in this book. The following are displayed for B, for instance: blueberry, brussel sprout, bean, beet, broccoli, banana.

**Emberley, B. (1992).** *One wide river to cross.* **Boston: Little, Brown.**
> This Caldecott Honor Book is an adaptation of the traditional African American spiritual about Noah's ark. Through the use of rhyme, the author describes the animals gathering on board one by one (while "Japhelth played the big bass drum"), two by two ("The alligator lost his shoe"), and so on up to ten, when the rains begin.

**Fortunata. (1968).** *Catch a little fox.* **New York: Scholastic.**
> A group of children talk about going hunting, identifying animals they will catch and where they will keep each one. A frog will be put in a log, a cat will be put in a hat, and so forth. The story concludes with the animals in turn capturing the children, putting them in a ring and listening to them sing. All are then released. The music is included in this book. A different version of this story that includes a brontosaurus (who is put in a chorus) and

*armadillo (who is put in a pillow) is J. Langstaff's (1974)* Oh, A-Hunting We Will Go, *published by Atheneum, New York.*

**Galdone, P. (1968).** *Henny Penny.* **New York: Scholastic.**

*A hen becomes alarmed when an acorn hits her on the head. She believes the sky is falling, and on her way to inform the king she meets several animals who join her until they are all eaten by Foxy Loxy. This classic story is included here because of the amusing rhyming names of the animals. A more recent release of this story is S. Kellogg's* Chicken Little *(1985), published by Mulberry Books, New York.*

**Geraghty, P. (1992).** *Stop that noise!* **New York: Crown.**

*A mouse is annoyed with the many sounds of the forest and implores the cicada to stop its "zee-zee-zee-zee," the frog to stop its "woopoo," until it hears far more disturbing sounds—the "Br-rrm" and "Crrrrrr RACKA-DACKA-RACKA-SHOONG" of a bulldozer felling trees. The presentation of animal and machine sounds makes this book useful in drawing attention to the sounds in our language.*

**Gordon, J. (1991).** *Six sleepy sheep.* **New York: Puffin Books.**

*Six sheep try to fall asleep by slurping celery soup, telling spooky stories, singing songs, sipping simmered milk, and so on. The use of the /s/ sound, prevalent throughout, amuses listeners as they anticipate the sheep's antics.*

**Hague, K. (1984).** *Alphabears.* **New York: Henry Holt.**

*In this beautifully illustrated book, 26 teddy bears introduce the alphabet and make use of alliteration. Teddy bear John loves jam and jelly. Quimbly is a quilted bear, and Pam likes popcorn and pink lemonade.*

**Hawkins, C., & Hawkins, J. (1986).** *Tog the dog.* **New York: G. P. Putnam's Sons.**

*This book tells the story of Tog the dog who likes to jog, gets lost in the fog, falls into a bog, and so forth. With the exception of the final page, where the letters* og *appear in large type, the pages in the book are not full width. As the reader turns the narrower pages throughout the text, a new letter appears and lines up with the* og *so that when Tog falls into the bog, for example, a large letter* b *lines up with* og *to make the word* bog. *This is a great book for both developing phonemic awareness and pointing out a spelling pattern. Also by the authors are* Jen the Hen *(1985),* Mig the Pig *(1984), and* Pat the Cat *(1993), all published by G. P. Putnam's Sons.*

**Hymes, L., & Hymes, J. (1964).** *Oodles of noodles.* **New York: Young Scott Books.**

*Several of the poems in this collection make use of nonsense words in order to complete a rhyme. In "Oodles of Noodles," the speaker requests oodles of noodles because they are favorite foodles. In "Spinach" the authors list a series of words each beginning with the /sp/ sound until they finally end with the word* spinach. *Words include* spin, span, spun, *and* spoony. *Many of the poems point out spelling patterns that will be entertaining with an older audience.*

**Krauss, R. (1985).** *I can fly.* **New York: Golden Press.**

*In this simple book, a child imitates the actions of a variety of animals. "A cow can moo. I can too." "I can squirm like a worm." The rhyming element combined with the charm of the child's imaginative play makes the story engaging. On the final*

*page, nonsense words that rhyme are used, encouraging listeners to experiment with sounds themselves: "Gubble gubble gubble I'm a mubble in a pubble."*

**Kuskin, K. (1990).** *Roar and more.* **New York: Harper Trophy.**

*This book includes many poems and pictures that portray the sounds animals make. Both the use of rhyme and presentation of animal sounds ("Ssnnaaaarrll" for the tiger, "Hsssssss . . ." for the snake) draw children's attention to sounds. An earlier edition of this book won the 1979 NCTE Award for Excellence in Poetry for Children.*

**Lewison, W. (1992).** *Buzz said the bee.* **New York: Scholastic.**

*A series of animals sit on top of one another in this story. Before each animal climbs on top of the next, it does something that rhymes with the animal it approaches. For instance, the hen dances a jig before sitting on the pig. The pig takes a bow before sitting on the cow.*

**Martin, B. (1974).** *Sounds of a powwow.* **New York: Holt, Rinehart & Winston.**

*Included in this volume is the song "K-K-K-Katy" in which the first consonant of several words is isolated and repeated, as is the song title.*

**Marzollo, J. (1989).** *The teddy bear book.* **New York: Dial.**

*Poems about teddy bears adapted from songs, jump rope rhymes, ball bouncing chants, cheers, and story poems are presented. Use of rhyme is considerable, from the well-known, "Teddy bear, teddy bear, turn around, Teddy bear, teddy bear, touch the ground," to the less familiar, "Did you ever, ever, ever in your teddy bear life see a teddy bear dance with his wife?" and the response, "No I never, never, never . . ." Play with sounds is obvious in the poem "Teddy Boo and Teddy Bear" in which the author says, "Icabocker, icabocker, icabocker, boo! Icabocker, soda cracker, phooey on you!"*

**Obligado, L. (1983).** *Faint frogs feeling feverish and other terrifically tantalizing tongue twisters.* **New York: Viking.**

*For each letter of the alphabet, one or more tongue twisters using alliteration is presented in print and with humorous illustrations. S has smiling snakes sipping strawberry sodas, a shy spider spinning, and a swordfish sawing. T presents two toucans tying ties, turtles tasting tea, and tigers trying trousers.*

**Ochs, C. P. (1991).** *Moose on the loose.* **Minneapolis, MN: Carolrhoda Books.**

*A moose escapes from the zoo in the town of Zown and at the same time a chartreuse caboose disappears. The zookeeper runs throughout the town asking citizens if they've seen a "moose on the loose in a chartreuse caboose." No one has seen the moose but each has seen a different animal. Included among the many citizens is Ms. Cook who saw a pig wearing a wig, Mr. Wu who saw a weasel paint at an easel, and Mrs. Case who saw a skunk filling a trunk. Each joins in the search.*

**Otto, C. (1991).** *Dinosaur chase.* **New York: Harper Trophy.**

*A mother dinosaur reads her young one a story about dinosaurs in which "dinosaur crawl, dinosaur creep, tiptoe dinosaur, dinosaur seek." Both alliteration and rhyme are present in this simple, colorful book.*

**Parry, C. (1991). *Zoomerang-a-boomerang: Poems to make your belly laugh*. New York: Puffin Books.**

Nearly all of the poems in this collection play with language, particularly through the use of predictable and humorous rhyme patterns. In "Oh My, No More Pie," the meat's too red, so the writer has some bread. When the bread is too brown, the writer goes to town, and so forth. In "What They Said," each of 12 animals says something that rhymes with its name. For instance, a pup says, "Let's wake up," and a lark says, "It's still dark."

**Patz, N. (1983). *Moses supposes his toeses are roses*. San Diego, CA: Harcourt Brace Jovanovich.**

Seven rhymes are presented here, each of which plays on language to engage the listener. Rhyme is predictable in "Sweetie Maguire" when she shouts "Fire! Fire!" and Mrs. O'Hair says, "Where? Where?" Alliteration makes "Betty Botter" a tongue twister: "But a bit of better butter—that will make my batter better!" Assonance adds humor to "The Tooter" when the tooter tries to tutor two tooters to toot!

**Pomerantz, C. (1993). *If I had a paka*. New York: Mulberry.**

Eleven languages are represented among the 12 poems included in this volume. The author manipulates words as in "You take the blueberry, I'll take the dewberry. You don't want the blueberry, OK take the bayberry. . . ." Many berries are mentioned, including a novel one, the "chuckleberry." Attention is drawn to phonemes when languages other than English are introduced. The Vietnamese translation of the following draws attention to rhyme and repetition: "I like fish, Toy tik ka; I like chicken, Toy tik ga; I like duck, Toy tik veet; I like meat, Toy tik teet."

**Prelutsky, J. (1982). *The baby Uggs are hatching*. New York: Mulberry.**

Twelve poems describe unusual creatures such as the Sneepies, the Smasheroo, and the Numpy-Numpy-Numpity. Although some of the vocabulary is advanced (the Quossible has an irascible temper), most of the poems will be enjoyed by young children who will delight in the humorous use of words and sounds. For instance, "The Sneezysnoozer sneezes in a dozen sneezy sizes, it sneezes little breezes and it sneezes big surprises."

**Prelutsky, J. (1989). *Poems of A. Nonny Mouse*. New York: Alfred A. Knopf.**

A Nonny Mouse finally gets credit for all her works that were previously attributed to "Anonymous" in this humorous selection of poems that is appropriate for all ages. Of particular interest for developing phonemic awareness are poems such as "How Much Wood Would a Woodchuck Chuck" and "Betty Botter Bought Some Butter."

**Provenson, A., & Provenson, M. (1977). *Old Mother Hubbard*. New York: Random House.**

In this traditional rhyme, Old Mother Hubbard runs errand after errand for her dog. When she comes back from buying him a wig, she finds him dancing a jig. When she returns from buying him shoes, she finds him reading the news.

**Raffi. (1987). *Down by the bay*. New York: Crown.**

Two young children try to outdo one another in making up rhymes with questions such as, "Did you ever see a goose kissing a moose?" and "Did you ever see a bear combing his hair?" Music is included.

**Raffi. (1989). *Tingalayo*. New York: Crown.**

Here the reader meets a man who calls for his donkey, Tingalayo, and describes its antics through the use of rhyme and rhythm. Phrases such as "Me donkey dance, me donkey sing, me donkey wearin' a diamond ring" will make children laugh, and they will easily contribute additional verses to this song/story.

**Sendak, M. (1990). *Alligators all around: An alphabet*. New York: HarperTrophy.**

Using alliteration for each letter of the alphabet, Sendak introduces the reader to the alphabet with the help of alligators who have headaches (for H) and keep kangaroos (for K).

**Shaw, N. (1989). *Sheep on a ship*. Boston: Houghton Mifflin.**

Sheep sailing on a ship run into trouble when facing a sudden storm. This entertaining story makes use of rhyme (waves lap and sails flap), alliteration (sheep on a ship), and assonance ("It rains and hails and shakes the sails").

**Showers, P. (1991). *The listening walk*. New York: HarperTrophy.**

A little girl and her father go for a walk with their dog, and the listener is treated to the variety of sounds they hear while walking. These include "thhhhh . . . ," the steady whisper sound of some sprinklers, and "whithh whithh," the sound of other sprinklers that turn around and around. Some phonemes are elongated as in "eeeeeeyowwwoooo . . . ," the sound of a jet overhead. Some phonemes are substituted as in "bik bok bik bok," the sounds of high heels on the pavement.

**Silverstein, S. (1964). *A giraffe and a half*. New York: Harper & Row.**

Using cumulative and rhyming patterns, Silverstein builds the story of a giraffe who has a rose on his nose, a bee on his knee, some glue on his shoe, and so on until he undoes the story by reversing the events.

**Staines, B. (1989). *All God's critters got a place in the choir*. New York: Penguin.**

This lively book makes use of rhyme to tell of the places that numerous animals (an ox and a fox, a grizzly bear, a possum and a porcupine, bullfrogs) have in the world's choir. "Some sing low, some sing higher, some sing out loud on the telephone wire."

**Seuss, Dr. (1963). *Dr. Seuss's ABC*. New York: Random House.**

Each letter of the alphabet is presented along with an amusing sentence in which nearly all of the words begin with the targeted letter. "Many mumbling mice are making midnight music in the moonlight . . . mighty nice."

**Seuss, Dr. (1965). *Fox in socks*. New York: Random House.**

Before beginning this book, the reader is warned to take the book slowly because the fox will try to get the reader's tongue in trouble. Language play is the obvious focus of this book. Assonance patterns occur throughout, and the listener is exposed to vowel sound changes when beetles battle, ducks like lakes, and ticks and clocks get mixed up with the chicks and tocks.

**Seuss, Dr. (1974). *There's a wocket in my pocket*. New York: Random House.**

A child talks about the creatures he has found around the house. These include a "nooth grush on my tooth brush" and a "zamp *in the lamp." The initial sounds of common household objects are substituted with other sounds to make the nonsense creatures in this wonderful example of play with language.*

**Tallon, R. (1979).** *Zoophabets.* **New York: Scholastic.**

*Letter by letter the author names a fictional animal and, in list form, tells where it lives and what it eats. All, of course, begin with the targeted letter. "Runk" lives in "rain barrels" and eats "raindrops, rusty rainbows, ripped rubbers, raincoats, rhubarb."*

**Van Allsburg, C. (1987).** *The Z was zapped.* **Boston: Houghton Mifflin.**

*A series of mishaps befall the letters of the alphabet. A is crushed by an avalanche, B is badly bitten, C is cut to ribbons, and so forth. Other alphabet books using alliteration include G. Base's* Animalia *(1987), published by Harry N. Abrams; K. Greenaway's (1993)* A Apple Pie, *published by Derrydale; and J. Patience's (1993)* An Amazing Alphabet, *published by Random House.*

**Winthrop, E. (1986).** *Shoes.* **New York: HarperTrophy.**

*This rhyming book surveys familiar and some not-so-familiar types of shoes. The book begins, "There are shoes to buckle, shoes to tie, shoes too low, and shoes too high." Later we discover "Shoes for fishing, shoes for wishing, rubber shoes for muddy squishing." The rhythm and rhyme invite participation and creative contributions.*

**Zemach, M. (1976).** *Hush, little baby.* **New York: E. P. Dutton.**

*In this lullaby, parents attempt to console a crying baby by promising a number of outrageous things including a mockingbird, a diamond ring, a billy goat, and a cart and bull. The verse is set to rhyme (e.g., "If that cart and bull turn over, Poppa's gonna buy you a dog named Rover") and children can easily innovate on the rhyme and contribute to the list of items being promised.*

# Recommended Books for Multicultural Reading Experiences

## African and African American Books

### Folklore

Aardema, Verna. *Bimwili and the Zimwi.* (P)

———. *Bringing the Rain to Kapiti Plain.* (P)

———. *Oh, Kojo! How Could You!* (I)

———. *Why Mosquitoes Buzz in People's Ears.* (P–I)

Bryan, Ashley. *All Night, All Day: A Child's First Book of African American Spirituals.* (P–I–A)

———. *What a Morning! The Christmas Story in Black Spirituals.* (P–I)

Climo, Shirley. *The Egyptian Cinderella.* (P–I)

Grifalconi, Ann. *The Village of Round and Square Houses.* (P–I)

Hamilton, Virginia. *The All Jahdu Storybook.* Ill. Barry Moser. (P–I)

———. *The People Could Fly.* Ill. Leo Dillon and Diane Dillon. (I)

Keats, Ezra Jack. *John Henry.* (I)

Lester, Julius. *How Many Spots Does a Leopard Have?* (I)

———. *John Henry.* (I)

———. *The Tales of Uncle Remus: The Adventures of Brer Rabbit.* (P–I)

McKissack, Patricia. *The Dark.* (I)

Mollel, Tololwa. *The Princess Who Lost Her Hair: An Akamba Legend.* (P–I)

San Souci, Robert. *Sukey and the Mermaid.* Ill. Brian Pinkney. (P–I)

Steptoe, John. *Mufaro's Beautiful Daughters.* (P)

## Poetry

Adoff, Arnold. *All the Colors of the Race.* (I)

———. *Black Is Brown Is Tan.* (P)

———. *In for Winter, Out for Spring.* (P–I)

———. *My Black Me: A Beginning Book of Black Poetry.* (P)

Brooks, Gwendolyn. *Bronzeville Boys and Girls.* (P–I)

Bryan, Ashley. *Ashley Bryan's ABC of African American Poetry.* (P–I)

———. *Sing to the Sun.* (P–I)

Chocolate, Debbi. *Kente Colors.* (P–I)

Clifton, Lucille. *Everett Anderson's Goodbye.* (P)

———. *Everett Anderson's Nine Month Long.* (P)

———. *Some of the Days of Everett Anderson.* (P)

Feelings, Tom. *Soul Looks Back in Wonder.* (I–A)

Giovanni, Nikki. *Spin a Soft Black Song.* (P–I)

Greenfield, Eloise. *"Honey, I Love" and Other Love Poems.* (P–I–A)

Grimes, Nikki. *Come Sunday.* (P–I)

———. *Meet Danitra Brown.* (P–I)

Johnson, Angela. *The Other Side: Shorter Poems.* (P–I)

Johnson, James. *Lift Ev'ry Voice and Sing.* (P–I–A)

Myers, Walter. *Dean Harlem.* (I–A)

Price, Leontyne. *Aïda.* Ill. Leo Dillon and Diane Dillon. (A)

Steptoe, Javaka. *In Daddy's Arms I Am Tall.* (P)

Winter, Jeanette. *Follow the Drinking Gourd.* (P–I)

---

P = primary; I = intermediate; A = adolescent

## Picture Books

Barber, Barbara. *Saturday and the New You*. Ill. Anna Rich. (P–I)

Bryan, Ashley. *Beautiful Blackbird*. (P)

Clifton, Lucille. *The Boy Who Didn't Believe in Spring*. (P)

———. *Everett Anderson's Christmas Coming*. (P)

———. *Three Wishes*. Ill. Michael Hays. (P)

Collier, Bryan. *Uptown*. (P–I)

Cosby, Bill. *Little Bill Books for Beginning Readers*. Ill. Varnette P. Honeywood. (P–I)

Crews, Donald. *Bigmama's*. (P)

Daly, Nikki. *Something on My Mind*. (P)

Flowers, Art. *Cleveland Lee's Beale Street Band*. Ill. Anna Rich. (P–I)

Greenfield, Eloise. *Grandpa's Face*. (P)

———. *She Come Bringing Me That Little Baby Girl*. (P)

Grifalconi, Ann. *Darkness and the Butterfly*. (P)

———. *Osa's Pride*. (P)

Hamilton, Virginia. *Drylongso*. Ill. Jerry Pinkney. (I)

Hoffman, Mary. *Amazing Grace*. Ill. Caroline Binch. (P)

Hopkinson, Deborah. *Sweet Clara and the Dream Quilt*. Ill. James Ransome. (P–I)

Howard, Elizabeth Fitzgerald. *Aunt Flossie's Hats (and Crab Cakes Later)*. Ill. James Ransome. (P)

Igus, Toyomi. *I See the Rhythm*. Ill. Michele Wood. (P–I)

Johnson, Angela. *One of Three*. Ill. David Soman. (P)

———. *Tell Me a Story, Mama*. Ill. David Soman. (P)

Keats, Ezra Jack. *A Snowy Day*. (P)

———. *Whistle for Willie*. (P)

King, Corretta Scott. *I Have a Dream*. (I–A)

Kurtz, Jane. *Trouble*. Ill. Durga Bernhard. (P–I)

———, and Christopher Kurtz. *Only a Pigeon*. Ill. E. B. Lewis. (P–I)

Lester, Julius. *What a Truly Cool World*. Ill. Joe Cepeda. (P–I–A)

London, Jonathan. *Ali, Child of the Desert*. Ill. Ted Lewin. (P–I)

McKissack, Patricia. *Flossie and the Fox*. (P)

———. *Mirandy and Brother Wind*. Ill. Jerry Pinkney. (P–I)

Mitchell, Margaree. *Uncle Jed's Barbershop*. Ill. James Ransome. (P–I)

Myers, Walter Dean. *Brown Angels*. (P–I)

Nelson, Vaunda. *Almost to Freedom*. (P)

Nolen, Jerdine. *Thunder Rose*. (P)

Pinkney, Brian. *Max Found Two Sticks*. (P)

Pinkney, Gloria Jean. *Back Home*. Ill. Jerry Pinkney. (P)

Polacco, Patricia. *Chicken Sunday*. (P)

———. *Mrs. Katz and Tush*. (P–I)

Ringgold, Faith. *Tar Beach*. (P–I)

Siegelson, Kim. *In the Time of the Drums*. Ill. Brian Pinkney. (P)

Steptoe, John. *Stevie*. (P)

Tarpley, Natasha. *I Love My Hair*. Ill. E. B. Lewis. (P)

Walker, Alice. *To Hell with Dying*. Ill. Catherine Deeter. (I–A)

Weatherford, Carole Boston. *Moses: When Harriett Tubman Led Her People to Freedom*. Ill. Kadir Nelson. (P–I)

Williams, Sherley Anne. *Working Cotton*. Ill. Carole Byard. (P)

Wilson, Beth. *Jenny*. Ill. Dolores Johnson. (P)

## Fiction

Curtis, Christopher Paul. *Bud, Not Buddy*. (I)

Davis, Ossie. *Just Like Martin*. (I)

Draper, Sharon. *The Battle of Jericho*. (I)

———. *Copper Sun*. (I–A)

Greenfield, Eloise. *Koya De Laney and the Good Girl Blues*. (I)

Hamilton, Virginia. *Cousins*. (I)

———. *Drylongso*. Ill. Jerry Pinkney. (I)

———. *M. C. Higgins, the Great*. (I–A)

———. *Planet of Junior Brown*. (I–A)

———. *Zeely*. (I)

Johnson, Angela. *Heaven*. (I)

Kurtz, Jane. *The Storyteller's Beads*. (I–A)

Myers, Walter Dean. *Fast Sam, Cool Clyde, and Stuff*. (I–A)

———. *Hoops*. (A)

———. *Motown and Didi*. (A)

———. *Somewhere in the Darkness*. (A)

———. *Won't Know till I Get There*. (A)

———. *The Young Landlords*. (A)

Smothers, Ethel Footman. *Down in the Piney Woods*. (I–A)

Taylor, Mildred. *The Road to Memphis*. (A)

———. *Roll of Thunder, Hear My Cry*. (A)

Woodson, Jacqueline. *Locomotion*. (I)

Yarbrough, Camille. *Cornrows*. (P)

## Nonfiction

Anderson, Laurie. *Ndito Runs*. (P–I)

Bunting, Eve. *Smoky Nights*. (I–A)

Feelings, Muriel. *Jambo Means Hello*. (P–I)

Lester, Julius. *From Slave Ship to Freedom Road*. (I–A)

McKissack, Patricia, and Frederick McKissack. *Black Hands, White Sails.* (P–I)

———. *A Long Hard Journey: The Story of the Pullman Porter.* (I)

Musgrove, Margaret. *Ashanti to Zulu.* (P–I)

Myers, Walter Dean. *Now Is Your Time! The African-American Struggle for Freedom.* (I–A)

Pinkney, Andrea Davis. *Let It Shine! Stories of Black Women Freedom Fighters.* Ill. Stephen Alcorn. (P–I)

Sabuda, Robert. *Tutankhamen's Gift.* (P–I)

## Biography

Angelou, Maya. *Kofi and His Magic.* (P–I)

Collier, Bryan. *Freedom River.* (I)

Cooper, Floyd. *Coming Home: From the Life of Langston Hughes.* (I)

Freedman, Florence B. *Two Tickets to Freedom: The True Story of Ellen and William Craft, Fugitive Slaves.* (I–A)

Hamilton, Virginia. *Anthony Burns: The Defeat and Triumph of a Fugitive Slave.* (I–A)

Haskins, James. *Bill Cosby: America's Most Famous Father.* (I)

———. *Diana Ross, Star Supreme.* (I)

Krull, Kathleen. *Wilma Unlimited.* (P–I)

Lester, Julius. *To Be a Slave.* (I–A)

Ringgold, Faith. *My Dream of Martin Luther King.* (P–I)

## Asian and Asian American Books

### Folklore

Birdseye, Tom. *A Song of Stars.* Ill. Ju-Hong Chen. (P)

Climo, Shirley. *The Korean Cinderella.* (P–I)

Coerr, Eleanor. *Sadako.* (I–A)

Demi. *The Empty Pot.* (P)

Louie, Ai-Ling. *Yeh-Shen: A Cinderella Story from China.* Ill. Ed Young. (P–I)

Mahy, Margaret. *The Seven Chinese Brothers.* (P)

San Souci, Robert. *The Samurai's Daughter.* (I)

Tan, Amy. *The Moon Lady.* (I)

Yacowitz, Caryn. *The Jade Stone: A Chinese Folktale.* Ill. Ju-Hong Chen. (I)

Yep, Laurence. *The Butterfly Man.* (I)

———. *The Rainbow People.* (I)

———. *Tongues of Jade.* Ill. David Wiesner. (I)

## Poetry

Baron, Virginia Olsen. *Sunset in a Spider Web: Sijo Poetry of Ancient Korea.* (I–A)

Behn, Harry. *Cricket Songs.* (I–A)

Demi. *In the Eyes of the Cat: Japanese Poetry for All Seasons.* Ill. Tze-Si Huang. (P–I–A)

Lee, Jeanne. *The Song of Mu Lan.* (P–I)

Liu, Siyu, and Orel Protopopescu. *A Thousand Peaks.* (P–I)

## Picture Books

Ashley, Bernard. *Cleversticks.* Ill. Derek Brazell. (P)

Baker, Keith. *The Magic Fan.* (P)

Bang, Molly. *The Paper Crane.* (P)

Breckler, Rosemary. *Hoang Breaks the Lucky Teapot.* Ill. Adrian Frankel. (P)

Coutant, Helen, and Vo-Dinh. *First Snow.* (P)

Friedman, Ina. *How My Parents Learned to Eat.* (P)

Garland, Sherry. *The Lotus Seed.* Ill. Tatsuo Kiuchi. (P–I)

Ho, Minfong. *Peek!* Ill. Holly Meade. (P)

Levinson, Riki. *Our Home Is the Sea.* Ill. Dennis Luzak. (P–I)

Say, Allen. *Bicycle Man.* (P)

———. *El Chino.* (P–I)

———. *Emma's Rug.* (P–I)

———. *Grandfather's Journey.* (I)

———. *The Lost Lake.* (I)

———. *Tree of Cranes.* (P–I)

Tejima. *Ho-limlim: A Rabbit Tale from Japan.* (P–I)

Turner, Ann. *Through Moon and Stars and Night Skies.* Ill. James Graham Hale. (P–I)

Wells, Rosemary. *Yoko.* (P)

Yashima, Taro. *Crow Boy.* (P–I)

———. *Momo's Kitten.* (P)

———. *Umbrella.* (P)

———. *Youngest One.* (P)

## Fiction

Merrill, Jean. *The Girl Who Loved Caterpillars.* Ill. Floyd Cooper. (I)

Mochizuki, Ken. *Baseball Saved Us.* (I)

Namioka, Lensey. *Yang the Youngest and His Terrible Ear.* (I)

Napoli, Donna Jo. *Bound.* (I–A)

Uchida, Yoshiko. *The Best Bad Thing.* (I)

Uchida, Yoshiko. *The Happiest Ending.* (I)

———. *The Invisible Thread.* (I)

———. *A Jar of Dreams.* (I)

Wong, Janet. *The Trip Back Home.* (P–I)

Yep, Laurence. *Child of the Owl.* (I–A)

———. *Dragonwings.* (I–A)

———. *Mountain Light.* (I–A)

———. *Sea Glass.* (I–A)

## Nonfiction

Banish, Roslyn. *A Forever Family.* (I)

Brown, Tricia. *Lee Ann.* Photos by Ted Thai. (I)

Fugita, Stephen, and Marilyn Fernandez. *Altered Lives, Enduring Community.* (I)

Hoyt-Goldsmith, Diane. *Hoang Anh: A Vietnamese-American Boy.* Photos by Lawrence Migdale. (I)

Maruki, Toshi. *Hiroshima no Pika.* (I–A)

McMahon, Patricia. *Chi-Hoon: A Korean Girl.* (P–I)

Meltzer, Milton. *The Chinese Americans.* (A)

Schlein, Miriam. *The Year of the Panda.* Ill. Kam Mak. (P–I)

Waters, Kate, and Madeline Slovenz-Low. *Lion Dancer: Ernie Wan's Chinese New Year.* (P–I)

Wolf, Bernard. *In the Year of the Tiger.* (I)

## Biography

Huynh, Quang Nhuong. *The Land I Lost: Adventures of a Boy in Vietnam.* (I)

Kashiwagi, Hiroshi. *Swimming in the American.* (I)

Lord, Bette Bao. *In the Year of the Boar and Jackie Robinson.* (I)

## Hispanic American Books

### Folklore

Aardema, Verna. *Borreguita and the Coyote.* Ill. Petra Mathers. (Mexico) (P–I)

———. *The Riddle of the Drum: A Tale from Tizapan, Mexico.* (P–I)

Alexander, Ellen. *Llama and the Great Flood.* (Quechua story from Peru) (I)

Anaya, Rudolfo. *Roadrunner's Dance.* Ill. David Diaz. (P)

Belpre, Pura. *Once in Puerto Rico.* (I)

———. *The Rainbow-Colored Horse.* (Puerto Rico) (P–I)

de Paola, Tomie. *The Lady of Guadalupe.* (Mexico) (P–I)

de Sauza, James. *Brother Anansi and the Cattle Ranch.* (Nicaragua) (P)

Hall, Melisande. *Soon Come: A Ptolemy Turtle Adventure.* (P–I)

Hayes, Joe. *A Spoon for Every Bite.* (P–I)

Jaffe, Nina. *The Golden Flower.* (P–I)

Joseph, Lynn. *A Wave in Her Pocket: Stories from Trinidad.* Ill. Brian Pinkney. (I)

Kurtycz, Marcos. *Tigers and Opossums: Animal Legends.* (Mexico) (I)

Schon, Isabel. *Doña Blanca and Other Hispanic Nursery Rhymes and Games.* (P–I)

Vidal, Beatriz. *The Legend of El Dorado.* (I)

Wolkstein, Diane. *Banza: A Haitian Story.* Ill. Marc Tolon Brown. (P)

### Poetry

de Gerez, Toni. *My Song Is a Piece of Jade: Poems of Ancient Mexico in English and Spanish.* (I–A)

Delacre, Lulu. *Arrorró, Mi Niño: Latino Lullabies and Gentle Games.* (P)

———. *Arroz con Leche: Popular Songs and Rhymes from Latin America.* (P–I)

Joseph, Lynn. *Coconut Kind of Day.* (P–I)

Soto, Gary. *A Fire in My Hands.* Ill. James Cardillo. (I)

———. *Neighborhood Odes.* Ill. David Diaz. (I)

### Picture Books

Belpre, Pura. *Santiago.* Ill. Symeon Shimin. (P)

Bunting, Eve. *How Many Days to America?* Ill. Beth Peck. (I–A)

Cannon, Janell. *Verdi.* (P–I)

Cruz, Martel. *Yagua Days.* (P)

Czernicki, Stefan, and Timothy Rhodes. *The Sleeping Bread.* (P)

Dorros, Arthur. *Abuela.* Ill. Elisa Kleven. (P)

———. *Isla.* (P–I)

Ets, Marie Hall, and Aurora Latastida. *Nine Days to Christmas: A Story of Mexico.* (P)

Galindo, Mary Sue. *Icy Watermelon/Sandria Fria.* Ill. Pauline Rodriguez Howard. (P)

Garza, Carmen Lomas. *Family Pictures: Cuadros de Familia.* (P–I)

Gershator, David, and Phillis Gershator. *Bread Is for Eating.* Ill. Emma Shaw Smith. (P–I)

Havill, Juanita. *Treasure Nap.* Ill. Elivia Savadier. (Mexico) (P)

Isadora, Rachel. *Caribbean Dream.* (P)

James, Betsy. *The Dream Stair.* (P)

Jordon, Martin, and Tanis Jordan. *Amazon Alphabet.* (P–I)

Marvin, Isabel. *Saving Joe Louis.* (P)

Politi, Leo. *Pedro, the Angel of Olvera Street.* (P)

Reich, Susanna. *Jose! Born to Dance.* (P–I)

Roe, Eileen. *Con Mi Hermano: With My Brother.* (P)

San Souci, Robert. *Cendrillon: A Caribbean Cinderella.* Ill. Brian Pinckney. (P–I)

Tompert, Ann. *The Silver Whistle.* Ill. Beth Peck. (P)

## Fiction

Cameron, Ann. *The Most Beautiful Place in the World.* Ill. Thomas B. Allen. (P–I)

Carlson, Lori M., and Cynthia L. Ventura (eds.). *Where Angels Glide at Dawn: New Stories from Latin America.* Ill. José Ortega. (I)

Joseph, Lynn. *The Color of My Words.* (I)

Mohr, Nicholasa. *El Bronx Remembered.* (A)

———. *Felita.* (I)

———. *Going Home.* (I–A)

———. *In Nueva York.* (A)

———. *Nilda.* (A)

Paloma, Juanito. *Downtown Boy.* (I)

Ryan, Pam. *Becoming Naomi Leon.* (I–A)

Soto, Gary. *Baseball in April and Other Stories.* (I)

———. *Taking Sides.* (I–A)

## Nonfiction

Ancona, George. *Bananas: From Manolo to Margie.* (P–I)

———. *Carnaval.* (P–I)

Anderson, Joan. *Spanish Pioneers of the Southwest.* (P–I)

Brown, Tricia. *Hello, Amigos!* Photos by Fran Ortiz. (P–I)

Brusca, Maria Christina. *On the Pampas.* (I)

Cherry, Lynn. *The Shaman's Apprentice.* (P–I)

Emberley, Rebecca. *My House: A Book in Two Languages/ Mi Casa: Un Libro en Dos Lenguas.* (I)

Grossman, Patricia, and Enrique Sanchez. *Saturday's Market.* (P–I)

McDonald's Hispanic Heritage Art Contest. *Our Hispanic Heritage.* (P)

Meltzer, Milton. *The Hispanic Americans.* (A)

Perl, Lila. *Piñatas and Paper Flowers: Holidays of the Americas in English and Spanish.* (I–A)

Shalant, Phyllis. *Look What We've Brought You from Mexico.* (I)

Thomas, Jane. *Lights on the River.* (I)

Zak, Monica. *Save My Rainforest.* Ill. Bengt-Arne Runnerstrom. Trans. Nancy Schimmel. (I)

## Biography

Codye, C. *Luis W. Alvarez.* (I–A)

de Treviño, Elizabeth Borten. *El Guero.* (I–A)

———. *I, Juan de Pareja.* (A)

———. *Juarez, Man of Law.* (A)

Gleiter, Jan. *David Farragut.* (A)

———. *Diego Rivera.* (A)

Shorto, R. *David Farragut and the Great Naval Blockade.* (A)

# American Indian Books

## Folklore

Bierhorst, John. *Doctor Coyote.* (I)

———. *The Ring in the Prairie: A Shawnee Legend.* (I)

de Paola, Tomie. *The Legend of the Bluebonnet.* (P)

———. *The Legend of the Indian Paintbrush.* (P–I)

Dixon, Ann. *How Raven Brought Light to People.* Ill. James Watts. (P–I)

Goble, Paul. *Beyond the Ridge.* (P–I)

———. *Buffalo Woman.* (P–I)

———. *Crow Chief: A Plains Indian Story.* (I)

———. *Death of the Iron Horse.* (P–I)

———. *Her Seven Brothers.* (P–I)

———. *Iktomi and the Berries: A Plains Indian Story.* (P–I)

———. *Iktomi and the Boulder: A Plains Indian Story.* (P–I)

———. *Iktomi and the Buffalo Skull: A Plains Indian Story.* (P–I)

———. *Iktomi and the Ducks: A Plains Indian Story.* (P–I)

———. *Star Boy.* (P–I)

Goldin, Barbara. *The Girl Who Lived with the Bears.* (P–I)

Harris, Christie. *Once upon a Totem.* (I–A)

Highwater, Jamake. *Anpao: An American Indian Odyssey.* (I–A)

Kusugak, Michael. *Hide and Sneak.* (P–I)

MacGill-Callahan, Sheila. *And Still the Turtle Watched.* Ill. Barry Moser. (P)

Martin, Rafe. *The Rough-Face Girl.* Ill. David Shannon. (P–I)

Monroe, Jean Guard, and Ray Williamson. *They Dance in the Sky.* Ill. Edgar Stewart. (I–A)

Osofsky, Audrey. *Dreamcatcher.* (P)

Oughton, Jerrie. *How the Stars Fell into the Sky.* Ill. Lisa Desimini. (P–I)

Renner, Michelle. *The Girl Who Swam with the Fish: An Athabascan Legend.* (P–I)

Rodanas, Kristina. *Dragonfly's Tale.* (P–I)

Siberell, Anne. *The Whale in the Sky.* (P–I)

Taylor, C. J. *How Two-Feather Was Saved from Loneliness.* (P–I)

Wisniewski, David. *Rain Player.* (P–I)

## Poetry

Baylor, Byrd. *The Other Way to Listen.* (P–I)

Begay, Shonto. *Navajos: Visions and Voices Across the Mesa.* (I)

Bierhorst, John. *A Cry from the Earth: Music of the North American Indians.* (P–I)

Bruchac, Joseph, and Jonathan London. *Thirteen Moons on Turtle's Back: A Native American Year of Moons.* Ill. Thomas Locker. (P–I)

Clark, Ann Nolan. *In My Mother's House.* Ill. Velino Herrera. (P–I)

Jones, Hettie. *The Trees Stand Shining: Poetry of the North American Indians.* Ill. Robert Andrew Parker. (P–I)

Wood, Nancy. *Dancing Moon.* (I–A)

———. *Many Winters.* (I–A)

——— (ed.). *The Serpent's Tongue: Prose, Poetry, and the Art of the New Mexico Pueblos.* (I)

## Picture Books

Baker, Olaf. *Where the Buffaloes Begin.* Ill. Stephen Gammell. (P)

Baylor, Byrd. *Hawk, I'm Your Brother.* (P–I)

Bruchac, Joseph. *Between Earth and Sky: Legends of Native American Sacred Places.* Ill. Thomas Locker. (I)

Buchanan, Ken. *This House Is Made of Mud.* Ill. Libba Tracy. (P–I)

Bunting, Eve. *Cheyenne Again.* Ill. Irving Toddy. (P–I)

Joosse, Barbara. *Mama, Do You Love Me?* Ill. Barbara Lavallee. (P–I)

Parsons-Yazzie, Evangeline. *Dzání Yázhí Naazbaa': Little Woman Warrior Who Came Home: A Story of the Navajo Long Walk.* Ill. Irving Toddy. (P)

Steptoe, John. *The Story of Jumping Mouse: A Native American Legend.* (P)

Yolen, Jane. *Encounter.* Ill. David Shannon. (I–A)

———. *Sky Dogs.* Ill. Barry Moser. (P)

## Fiction

Dorris, Michael. *Morning Girl.* (I)

Erdrich, Louise. *The Birchbark House.* (I)

Hobbs, Will. *Bearstone.* (I–A)

O'Dell, Scott, and Elizabeth Hall. *Thunder Rolling in the Mountains.* (A)

Rohmer, Harriet, Octavia Chow, and Morris Vidaure. *The Invisible Hunters.* Ill. Joe Sam. (I–A)

Spinka, Penina Keen. *Mother's Blessing.* (I)

Strete, C. K. *Big Thunder Magic.* (P–I)

———. *When Grandfather Journeys into Winter.* (I)

Wosmek, Frances. *A Brown Bird Singing.* (I)

## Nonfiction

Cherry, Lynn. *A River Ran Wild.* (P–I)

Freedman, Russell. *Children of the Wild West.* (I–A)

———. *Indian Chiefs.* (I–A)

Hoyt-Goldsmith, Diane. *Pueblo Storyteller.* Photos by Lawrence Migdale. (I)

Kendall, Russ. *Eskimo Boy: Life in an Inupiaq Eskimo Village.* (I)

Regguinti, Gordon. *The Sacred Harvest: Ojibway Wild Rice Gathering.* Photos by Dale Kakkak. (I–A)

Yolen, Jane. *Encounter.* Ill. David Shannon. (P–I–A)

## Biography

Ekoomiak, Normee. *Arctic Memories.* (Inuit in Arctic Quebec) (I)

Freedman, Russell. *Indian Chiefs.* (I–A)

Matthaei, Gay, and Jewel Grutman. *The Ledgerbook of Thomas Blue Eagle.* (I–A)

## Books on Other Cultures

Appelt, Kathi. *Bayou Lullaby.* Ill. Neil Waldman. (P)

Archambault, John, and David Plummer. *Grandmother's Garden.* (P)

Bunting, Eve. *Terrible Things.* (P–I–A)

Chin-Lee, Cynthia, and Terri de la Pena. *A Is for Americas.* (P)

Conrad, Pam. *Animal Lingo.* (P)

Durrell, Ann, and Marilyn Sachs (Eds.). *The Big Book for Peace.* (P–I–A)

Goldin, Barbara. *The World's First Birthday: A Rosh Hashanah Story.* (P–I)

Hooks, William. *The Three Little Pigs and the Fox.* Ill. S. D. Schindler. (P–I)

Igus, Toyomi. *Two Mrs. Gibsons.* Ill. Daryl Wells. (P)

Kimmel, Eric. *Baba Yaga: A Russian Folktale.* Ill. Megan Lloyd. (P)

Krensky, Stephen. *Hanukkah at Valley Forge.* Ill. Greg Harlin. (I)

Lacapa, Kathleen, and Michael Lacapa. *Less Than Half, More Than Whole.* (P–I)

Mayer, Marianna. *Baby Yaga and Vasilisa the Brave.* Ill. K. Y. Craft. (P–I)

Polacco, Patricia. *The Keeping Quilt.* (P–I)

Rosen, Michael. *Elijah's Angel: A Story for Chanukah and Christmas.* Ill. Aminah Robinson. (P–I)

Rosenblum, Richard. *Journey to the Golden Land.* (I–A)

Vagin, Vladimir. *Here Comes the Cat.* (P–I)

Wisniewski, David. *Golem.* (I)

Zusak, Markus. *The Book Thief.* (I)

# Appendix G

# International Reading Association Standards for Reading Professionals

## STANDARD 1: Foundational Knowledge

*Candidates have knowledge of the foundations of reading and writing processes and instruction. As a result, candidates:*

**1.1** Demonstrate knowledge of psychological, sociological, and linguistic foundations of reading and writing processes and instruction.

**1.2** Demonstrate knowledge of reading research and histories of reading.

**1.3** Demonstrate knowledge of language development and reading acquisition and the variations related to cultural and linguistic diversity.

**1.4** Demonstrate knowledge of the major components of reading (phonemic awareness, word identification and phonics, vocabulary and background knowledge, fluency, comprehension strategies, and motivation) and how they are integrated in fluent reading.

## STANDARD 2: Instructional Strategies and Curriculum Materials

*Candidates use a wide range of instructional practices, approaches, methods, and curriculum materials to support reading and writing instruction. As a result, candidates:*

**2.1** Use instructional grouping options (individual, small-group, whole-class, and computer based) as appropriate for accomplishing given purposes.

**2.2** Use a wide range of instructional practices, approaches, and methods, including technology-based practices, for learners at differing stages of development and from differing cultural and linguistic backgrounds.

**2.3** Use a wide range of curriculum materials in effective reading instruction for learners at different stages of reading and writing development and from different cultural and linguistic backgrounds.

## STANDARD 3: Assessment, Diagnosis, and Evaluation

*Candidates use a wide variety of assessment tools and practices to plan and evaluate effective reading instruction. As a result, candidates:*

**3.1** Use a wide range of assessment tools and practices that range from individual and group standardized tests to individual and group informal classroom assessment strategies, including technology-based assessment tools.

**3.2** Place students along a developmental continuum and identify students' proficiencies and difficulties.

**3.3** Use assessment information to plan, evaluate, and revise effective instruction that meets the needs of all students, including those at different developmental stages and those from different cultural and linguistic backgrounds.

**3.4** Communicate results of assessments to specific individuals (students, parents, caregivers, colleagues, administrators, policymakers, policy officials, community, etc.).

## STANDARD 4: Creating a Literate Environment

*Candidates create a literate environment that fosters reading and writing by integrating foundational knowledge, use of instructional practices, approaches and methods, curriculum materials, and the appropriate use of assessment. As a result, candidates:*

**4.1** Use students' interests, reading abilities, and backgrounds as foundations for the reading and writing program.

**4.2** Use a large supply of books, technology-based information, and nonprint materials representing multiple levels, broad interests, and cultural and linguistic backgrounds.

**4.3** Model reading and writing enthusiastically as valued lifelong activities.

**4.4** Motivate learners to be lifelong readers.

## STANDARD 5: Professional Development

*Candidates view professional development as a career-long effort and responsibility. As a result, candidates:*

**5.1** Display positive dispositions related to reading and the teaching of reading.

**5.2** Continue to pursue the development of professional knowledge and dispositions.

**5.3** Work with colleagues to observe, evaluate, and provide feedback on each other's practice.

**5.4** Participate in, initiate, implement, and evaluate professional development programs.

*Source:* Professional Standards and Ethics Committee, International Reading Association. (2003). *Standards for Reading Professionals—Revised 2003.* Copyright © 2003 by the International Reading Association. Reprinted with permission of the International Reading Association (www.reading.org).

**academic and cognitive diversity**  The situation that results when children learn faster than, slower than, or differently from what is expected in school.

**active comprehension**  Using prior knowledge, schemata, and metacognition to construct textual meaning; fostered by using questioning during reading.

**additive approach**  A thematic approach that addresses multicultural issues.

**aesthetic stance**  Attention is focused on personal response to what is read.

**alphabetic principle**  Principle suggesting that letters in the alphabet map to phonemes, the minimal sound units represented in written language.

**American Standard English**  The grammar, vocabulary, and pronunciation that are appropriate for public speaking and writing.

**analogy**  A comparison of two similar relationships.

**analogy-based instruction**  Sometimes referred to as *analogic phonics*, analogy-based instruction teaches children to use onsets and rimes they already know to help decode unknown words.

**analytic phonics**  An approach to phonics teaching that emphasizes the discovery of letter–sound relationships through the analysis of known words.

**anecdotal notes**  Brief, written observations of revealing behavior that a teacher considers significant to understanding a child's literacy learning.

**anthologies**  Bound collections of stories and poems in reading programs.

**anticipation guide**  A series of written or oral statements for individual students to respond to before reading text assignments.

**antonyms**  Words opposite in meaning to other words.

**aptitude hypothesis**  The belief that vocabulary and comprehension reflect general intellectual ability.

**authentic assessment**  Asking students to perform tasks that demonstrate sufficient knowledge and understanding of a subject.

**autobiographical narrative**  An instructional strategy to help students and teachers reflect upon personal knowledge.

**automated reading**  A reading approach in which students listen individually to tape-recorded stories while reading along with the written text.

**automaticity**  The automatic, almost subconscious recognition and understanding of written text.

**basal reading approach**  A major approach to reading that occupies the central and broadest position on the instructional continuum. Built on scope and sequence foundations and traditionally associated with bottom-up theory, basal programs have been modified in recent years with the inclusion of language experience and literature activities.

**belief systems**  Theoretical orientations and philosophical approaches to the teaching of reading.

**best practice**  Thoughtful, informed, state-of-the-art teaching in which literacy-related practices are theoretically sound and supported by research.

**big books**  Enlarged versions of children's storybooks, distinguished by large print and illustrations, designed to offer numerous opportunities for interaction.

**book-talks**  Discussion opportunities for children to engage in conversations about their responses to reading books from class core study, reading workshops, or literature circles.

**bottom-up model**  A type of reading model that assumes that the process of translating print to meaning begins with the printed word and is initiated by decoding graphic symbols into sound.

**brainstorming**  Prereading activity that identifies a broad concept reflecting the main topic to be studied in an assigned reading and organizes students in small groups to generate a list of words related to the topic.

**buddy journal**  Written conversations between children in a journal format; promotes student interaction, cooperation, and collaboration.

**categorization**  Critical manipulation of words in relation to other words through the labeling of ideas, events, or objects.

**checklist**  A list of categories presented for specific diagnostic purposes.

**choral reading**  Oral reading, often of poetry, that makes use of various voice combinations and contrasts to create meaning or highlight the tonal qualities of a passage.

**circular story maps**  A visual representation using pictures to depict the sequence of events leading to the problem in a story.

**class relationships**  Conceptual hierarchies organized according to the superordinate and subordinate nature of the concepts.

**collaborative learning**  Learning in an environment in which students work effectively together to complete literacy-related tasks.

**communities of learners**   Classrooms that are conceptualized as a nurturing and supportive environment.

**community of readers**   The conceptualization of children, in alliance with their friends and teacher, working together in classrooms where school reading imitates adult reading; an effect created by literature-based reading programs.

**comprehensive approach**   An approach to instruction that adheres to the belief that teachers need to possess a strong knowledge of multiple methods for teaching reading so they can create the appropriate balance of methods needed for the children they teach.

**concept**   A mental image of anything; can be used as the basis for grouping by common features or similar criteria.

**concept circles**   A vocabulary activity in which students identify conceptual relationships among words and phrases that are partitioned within a circle.

**considerate text**   A textbook distinguished by its user friendliness, particularly in regard to organizational features and presentation of material.

**constructivism**   Learning theory associated with Jean Piaget that describes meaning-making as cognitively constructing knowledge by using prior knowledge and experience in interaction with the environment.

**contextual search**   A dictionary-related activity in which prediction of word meaning comes from reading the word in different contexts. The dictionary is used for verification of predictions.

**contributions approach**   A multicultural approach that typically includes culturally specific celebrations and holidays.

**controlled vocabulary**   Vocabulary taught progressively by controlling the number of new words students will encounter in each reading lesson.

**cooperative learning**   Learning that occurs as students work together in small groups to help each other achieve an academic goal.

**core books**   Collection of books that forms the nucleus of a school reading program at each grade level; usually selected by a curriculum committee.

**criterion-referenced tests**   Informal tests devised to measure individual student achievement according to a specific criterion for performance (e.g., eight words out of ten spelled correctly).

**cross-age reading**   A routine for fluency development that pairs upper-grade readers with younger children.

**cross-checking**   Using letter–sound information and meaning to identify words.

**cultural diversity**   Situation that results when a student's home, family, socioeconomic group, culture, and society differ from the predominant culture of the school.

**curriculum-based reader's theater**   A strategy in which students work in small groups to create sections of content text in the form of an entertaining play.

**curriculum compacting**   An alternative way to accommodate gifted students in which the curriculum is compressed.

**decision-making and social-action approach**   A multicultural approach that provides students with opportunities to undertake activities and projects related to cultural issues.

**decodable text**   Text that is written with a large number of words that have phonetic similarities; there is typically a match between the text and the phonics elements that the teacher has taught.

**decoding**   The conscious or automatic processing and translating of the printed word into speech.

**definitional knowledge**   The ability to relate new words to known words; can be built through synonyms, antonyms, and multiple-meaning words.

**desktop publishing**   Using software programs that combine word processing with layout and other graphic design features that allow children and teachers to integrate print and graphics on a page.

**developmentally appropriate practice**   The matching or gearing of the reading curriculum to children's developing abilities.

**diagnostic test**   Formal assessment intended to provide detailed information about individual students' strengths and weaknesses.

**dialect**   A set of rule-governed variations of a language.

**dialogue journal**   A journal written as a conversation between child and teacher that emphasizes meaning while providing natural, functional experiences in both writing and reading.

**differentiating instruction**   Adapting teaching for all learners to meet individual needs.

**digital portfolio**   A multimedia collection of student work stored and reviewed in digital format.

**directed reading–thinking activity (DR–TA)**   An activity that builds critical awareness of the reader's role and responsibility in interacting with the text through the process of predicting, verifying, judging, and extending thinking about text material.

**discussion web**   A strategy used in cooperative learning that requires students to explore both sides of issues during postreading discussions before drawing conclusions.

**double-entry journal**   A two-column journal format that gives students an opportunity to identify passages from texts and explore in writing why those passages are interesting or meaningful.

**dramatic play**   Unstructured, spontaneous, and expressive classroom activities requiring little planning.

**efferent stance**   Attention is focused on accumulating information from the text.

**electronic texts**   Texts that are created and read on a computer screen.

**embedded phonics instruction**   Often called *holistic, meaning-centered instruction,* embedded phonics teaches phonics within the context of stories that make sense to the children.

**emergent literacy**   Children's literacy learning conceptualized as developmental, with no clear beginning or end, rather than as proceeding in distinct sequence. Thus children begin to develop literacy through everyday experiences with print long before they enter school.

**environmental print** Print that surrounds children in their everyday lives such as traffic signs, restaurant signs, charts, and labels.

**evaluative questions** Questions that focus on making a judgment about what is read.

**exceptional children** Children who differ from the norm and who generally require an individualized program to meet their needs.

**explicit** Based on stated information.

**explicit instruction** Teacher-centered or teacher-facilitated instruction.

**explicit strategy instruction** Instruction that makes clear the *what, why, when,* and *how* of skill and strategy use.

**expository-informational books** Books that contain information that typically follows specific text structures such as description, sequence, cause and effect, comparison and contrast, and problem solving.

**extension (integrating across the curriculum)** Using activities such as art, music, and writing as catalysts to extend ideas and concepts initiated during a formal lesson.

**family literacy** How family interactions influence the language development of young children and provide the context in which they learn to read and write.

**fluency** The ability to read easily and well.

**fluency development lesson (FDL)** An instructional framework designed to develop oral reading fluency. It incorporates the use of various repeated reading techniques such as choral reading and paired reading routines.

**focused question card strategy** A peer writing technique in which students develop questions that focus on what they want to say.

**formative assessment** An assessment that is used to gather information for teachers to adapt instruction to meet students' needs.

**free response** Active involvement or participation in reading through discussion or writing that includes inferential, evaluative, and analytic thinking about a book based on the reader's response.

**graphic organizer** Any diagram of key concepts or main ideas that shows their relationships to each other.

**graphophonemic cues** Letter–sound information that readers process during reading.

**grouping** The creation and disbanding of groups of differing sizes, abilities, and interests for the purpose of providing specific instruction.

**group share session** Discussion period intended to help students reflect on the day's work. As part of a writing workshop plan, the session focuses on specific writing concerns.

**high-frequency words** Words that appear often in printed material.

**high-stakes testing** The practice of using a single test score for making education-related or personnel decisions.

**I-Chart** A chart that helps students research, organize, and integrate information from multiple text sources.

**idea circle** A *literature circle* in which readers engage in discussions of concepts they have been exploring in trade books and other types of texts.

**image making** A strategy that uses visual images to evoke knowledge.

**immediate word identification** The rapid recognition of words; a process often triggered by a reader's well-developed schemata for different words.

**implicit** Based on unstated assumptions in conjunction with given information.

**inclusion** Incorporating the diverse needs and abilities of all students into classroom instruction.

**individualized instruction** Any strategy or instructional plan that allows students to work at their own pace and level.

**inferential questions** Questions in which the reader uses background knowledge and information from the text.

**inflected endings** Suffixes that change the tense or degree of a word. Examples include /s/, /es/, /ies/, /d/, /ed/, /er/, /ier/, /est/.

**informal assessment** Informal measures of reading that yield useful information about student performance without comparisons to the performance of a normative population.

**informal reading inventory (IRI)** An individually administered informal test, usually consisting of graded word lists, graded reading passages, and comprehension questions that assess how students orally and silently interact with print.

**inquiry learning** A process in which students engage in experimentation and problem solving as they research issues and interests, gathering information from a variety of sources.

**instructional aids** Charts, workbooks, skill packs, cards, game boxes, and other devices that accompany a basal reading program.

**instructional conversations** A teaching strategy in which the teacher scaffolds learning through divergent questions and students are encouraged to express their reactions to content on a personal level.

**instructional management** The system established within a classroom to facilitate learning. Components of a management system typically include effective use of time, use of instructional resources, and expectations for behavior.

**instructional scaffolding** Providing enough instructional guidance and support for students so that they will be successful in their use of reading strategies.

**instrumental hypothesis** Belief in a causal chain between vocabulary knowledge and comprehension; that is, if comprehension depends in part on the knowledge of word meanings, vocabulary instruction should influence comprehension.

**integrated instruction**    Another name for *literature units*.

**integrated language arts approach**    An instructional approach in which reading, writing, listening, speaking, and viewing activities are connected through the use of literature.

**interactive model**    A type of reading model that assumes that translating print to meaning involves using both prior knowledge and print and that the process is initiated by the reader making predictions about meaning and/or decoding graphic symbols.

**interactive reading**    Teachers and children reading books together, collaborating to construct meaning and enjoy stories.

**interactive writing**    Shared writing activity in which children are invited to volunteer to write parts of a story.

**Internet inquiry**    An instructional strategy designed to help students engage in research on the Internet based on the questions they raise or their interests in various topics of study.

**interviewing**    Periodic communication with individual students to assess reading interests and attitudes, self-perceptions, and understanding of the language-learning process.

**invented spellings**    Spellings children use early in their reading and writing development as they begin to associate letters to sounds.

**key pal correspondence**    The electronic equivalent of pen pals.

**key words**    Words charged with personal meaning and feeling selected for use in helping beginning readers identify words quickly and easily.

**kidwatching**    See *observation*.

**knowledge hypothesis**    The suggestion that vocabulary and comprehension reflect general knowledge rather than intellectual ability.

**KWL**    (What do you *know*? What do you *want* to find out? What did you *learn*?) Three-step teaching model designed to guide and motivate children as they read to acquire information from expository texts.

**language-experience activities**    Activities using the natural language of children and their background experiences to share and discuss events; listen to and tell stories; dictate words, sentences, and stories; and write independently.

**language-experience approach (LEA)**    A major approach to reading, located on the holistic side of the instructional continuum, tied closely to interactive or top-down theory. Often considered a beginning reading approach, connections between reading and writing are becoming more prevalent in classrooms.

**learning centers**    Classroom areas set aside to offer students more and diverse opportunities to work in small groups or independently and more student choice, commitment, and responsibility.

**levels**    Sequential arrangements of readers, teacher's editions, and ancillary materials for each grade level in basal reading programs.

**linguistic awareness**    Understanding the technical terms and labels needed to talk and think about reading.

**linguistic diversity**    The diversity that results when a student's first language, or language of communication at home, is not the language of instruction in the school.

**linguistic instruction**    A traditional approach to teaching phonics popular in the 1960s.

**literacy club**    The group of written language users with whom a child interacts.

**literacy coach**    An individual who provides professional development opportunities and resources. In-class coaching and support provide a variety of professional development activities while in a nonevaluative role.

**literacy development**    The stages of language experience.

**literacy event**    Any powerful, authentic instance of the use of language to convey meaning and understanding between a writer and reader.

**literacy play center**    Designated classroom area designed around familiar contexts or places and furnished with props to provide an environment in which children may play with print on their own terms.

**literal questions**    Questions that are based on explicitly stated information in the text.

**literate environment**    An environment that fosters and nurtures interest in and curiosity about written language and supports children's efforts to become readers and writers.

**literature across the curriculum**    Weaving an array of literature into meaningful and relevant instructional activities within the context of content area study.

**literature-based instruction**    A major approach to reading that encourages students to select their own trade books, with the sessions followed by teacher–student conferences at which students may be asked to read aloud from their selections; used by teachers who want to provide for individual student differences in reading abilities while focusing on meaning, interest, and enjoyment.

**literature-based reading program**    Reading program based on instructional practices and student activities using literature, books, novels, short stories, magazines, plays, and poems that have not been rewritten for instructional purposes.

**literature circle**    Discussion or study group based on a collaborative strategy involving self-selection of books for reading; each group consists of students who independently selected the same book.

**literature journal**    Journal that invites readers to respond to literary texts; less structured than reading logs and other journals.

**literature unit**    A lesson organized around book collections featuring unifying elements such as genre, author, or conceptual theme.

**literature web**   Any graphic device that illustrates the relationships among the major components in a unit of study.

**macrocloze stories**   Stories given to students with passages deleted from the text; students read the stories and discuss the missing text either orally or in writing.

**materials**   Reference books, catalogs, paperback books, magazines, and ancillaries provided in the classroom to meet students' interests and to offer instructional variety.

**metacognition**   Awareness of one's own cognitive processes, including task knowledge and self-monitoring of activity.

**minilesson**   A brief, direct instructional exchange between teacher and students to address specific, observed learning needs of students.

**miscue analysis**   Informal assessment of oral reading errors to determine the extent to which readers use and coordinate graphic–sound, syntactic, and semantic information.

**mixed-text informational books**   Sometimes referred to as *combined-text trade books;* stories are narrated and factual information surrounds the story.

**morpheme**   The smallest meaningful unit of a word. For example, /un/ is a morpheme that means *not.*

**multiage classroom**   A single learning community meeting the numerous needs of its student members, grouped across age levels.

**multigenre project**   A paper that is a collection of genres that reflect multiple responses to a book, theme, or topic. Examples of genres are postcards, letters, posters, and comic strips.

**multiliteracies**   Fluid representations of knowing beyond traditional text. Examples are drama, painting, photography, and technological representations.

**multimedia authoring**   Using software programs that allow students to produce text, color pictures, sound, and video in combination.

**multiple-meaning words**   Words for which readers must rely on context in order to determine meaning.

**narrative informational texts**   Books in which the author typically tells a story that conveys factual information.

**new literacies**   The knowledge, skills, strategies, and dispositions needed to use and adapt to the constantly changing information and communication technologies.

**norms**   Average scores of a sampling of students selected for testing according to factors such as age, sex, race, grade, or socioeconomic status; basis for comparing the performance of individuals or groups.

**observation**   Informal assessment by classroom teachers to document growth in learning by watching and recording students' literate behaviors.

**onset**   The initial part of a word (a consonant, consonant blend, or digraph) that precedes the vowel.

**oral recitation lesson (ORL)**   Lesson that makes use of direct instruction and student practice, including reading in chorus, as a means of incorporating fluency into daily reading instruction.

**organizer**   A frame of reference established to prepare children conceptually for ideas to be encountered in reading.

**orthographic knowledge**   Knowledge of common letter patterns that skilled readers use rapidly and accurately to associate with sounds.

**paired reading**   Structured collaborative work involving pairs of children of the same or different reading ability to foster reading fluency.

**paired-word sentence generation**   Teaching strategy that asks students to take two related words and create one sentence that correctly demonstrates an understanding of the words and their relationship to one another.

**patterns for learning**   Grouping practices used in classrooms. Grouping may be whole, small, pairs, triads, cooperative, heterogeneous, homogeneous, self-paced, individualized, or interest based.

**phonemic awareness**   An understanding that speech is composed of a series of written sounds; a powerful predictor of children's later reading achievement.

**phonemic segmentation**   The ability to isolate and identify sounds in words.

**phonograms**   Letter clusters that help form word families or rhyming words; see also *rime.*

**physical characteristics**   Attributes that may refer to the visual and organizational structure of a classroom, including the placement of desks, learning centers, and book centers.

**plot scaffold**   An open-ended script in which students use their imaginations to create characters, a setting, a problem, and a solution.

**point-of-view guide**   An instructional activity for supporting comprehension in which readers approach a text selection from various perspectives or points of view.

**portfolio**   A compilation of an individual student's work in reading and writing, devised to reveal literacy progress as well as strengths and weaknesses.

**portfolio assessment**   Informal evaluation of a portfolio to determine a student's literacy development; a process in which teachers and students make decisions and reflect on collaboratively chosen work samples.

**portfolio system**   A systematic plan and organization for collecting students' work and recording literacy growth for documentation and assessment purposes.

**predictable texts**   Literature that is distinguished by familiar or predictable characteristics of setting, story line, language patterns, or rhyme and consequently can promote fluency.

**predictogram**   A strategy that develops students' meaning vocabulary through the use of story elements.

**prereading activities**   Activities designed to help students activate prior knowledge, set purpose, and/or engage their curiosity before reading.

**pretend play**   The spontaneous creation of stories—including setting, characters, goal, plot, and resolution—during children's play.

**previewing**   Establishing purposes and priorities before reading to help students become aware of the goals of a reading assignment.

**professional knowledge**   Knowledge acquired from an ongoing study of the practice of teaching.

**psycholinguistics**   The study of the mental faculties involved in acting on and interacting with written language in an effort to make sense of a text.

**question–answer relationships (QARs)**   A comprehension strategy that enhances children's ability to answer comprehension questions by teaching them how to find the information they need to respond.

**questioning the author (QtA)**   A comprehension-centered instructional strategy designed to show readers how to question the author's intent while reading.

**readability**   The relative accessibility or difficulty of a text. Sentence length and word difficulty are among the elements used in formulas that assign grade-level readability scores for text materials.

**read-aloud**   Generally a group event in which literature is read orally.

**reader-response theory**   The belief that responsibility for constructing textual meaning resides primarily with the reader and depends to a great extent on the reader's prior knowledge and experience.

**reader's theater**   The oral presentation of drama, prose, or poetry by two or more readers.

**reading journal**   A journal used in conjunction with literary texts. After a period of sustained reading, teachers use prompts to guide students' written responses to the text.

**reading readiness**   The level of physical, mental, and emotional maturity that children need to reach to benefit from reading instruction.

**reading workshop**   Method, introduced by Nancie Atwell, for integrating the language arts around literature through an organizational framework that allows readers to demonstrate reading strategies by responding to books and sharing meaning with their peers.

**reciprocal teaching**   An instructional strategy that builds readers' awareness of and expertise in the use of various comprehension skills and strategies.

**record keeping**   Tracking the books and stories read by students; records can be maintained by teachers or students.

**reinforcement**   Exercises involving similar and contrasting examples that are used to reinforce learning in basal programs.

**reliability**   Consistency of test results over time and administrations.

**repeated readings**   Reading short passages of text more than once, with different levels of support, to develop rapid, fluent oral reading.

**ReQuest**   Reciprocal questioning that encourages students to ask their own questions about material they have read.

**response protocol**   A framework for teacher responses to English language learners when they respond to teacher questions.

**response to intervention**   An approach to early intervention that provides struggling readers with assessments and placements based on responses to instruction.

**retelling**   An assessment in which students identify and discuss integral parts of a story.

**rime**   The part of the letter pattern in a word that includes the vowel and any consonants that follow; also called a *phonogram* or *word family*.

**room diagram**   An illustration of the classroom organization and layout.

**running records**   Method for marking miscues of beginning readers while they read.

**scaffolded instruction**   Instruction in which teachers model strategies step by step and provide guided practice, followed by independent practice and application.

**schemata**   Mental frameworks that humans use to organize and construct meaning.

**scope and sequence**   General plan in basal reading programs for the introduction of skills in sequential or vertical arrangement.

**scrambled stories**   Stories separated into parts and jumbled; students read the stories and put them back in order.

**scribbling**   One of the primary forms of written expression; the fountainhead for writing that occurs from the moment a child grasps and uses a writing tool.

**self-assessment**   An assessment in which students identify their strengths and weaknesses to help provide a plan for intervention.

**self-monitoring**   Being aware of miscues, the pronunciation of unknown words, and comprehension processes during reading to develop the ability to correct oneself.

**self-selection strategy**   A strategy that helps students monitor their own vocabulary growth by selecting unknown vocabulary words.

**semantic cues**   The prior knowledge and experience that readers bring to a reading situation.

**semantic mapping**   A strategy that shows readers and writers how to organize important information.

**shared reading**   Strategy allowing all children in a classroom or small group to participate in the reading of a story, usually through the use of a big book with large print and illustrations.

**skill building**   The introduction, repetition, and reinforcement of skills at all levels of basal reading programs.

**sociolinguisitics**   The study of the everyday functions of language and how interactions with others and with the environment aid language comprehension and learning.

**spelling-based instruction**   Instruction that focuses on teaching students strategies for studying words they read and write; it is based on the idea that students need to be working on words that represent their levels of development.

**stages in the writing process**  Sequential activities involved in the production of written texts, including rehearsing, drafting, revising and editing, and publishing.

**standardized reading test**  A formal test of reading ability administered according to specific, unvarying directions; usually norm-referenced and machine-scored.

**storybook experiences**  Read-alouds, readalongs, interactive reading, interactive writing, rereadings of favorite texts, and independent reading and writing.

**story frames**  Skeletal paragraphs represented by a sequence of spaces tied together with transition words and connectors signaling lines of thought; frames can emphasize plot summary, setting, character analysis, character comparison, and problem.

**story grammar**  The basic elements that make up a well-developed story, such as plot and setting.

**story impressions**  Prereading strategy that helps students anticipate what stories could be about, using content fragments to make predictions.

**story map**  An analysis of a story's organizational elements; used to strengthen instructional decisions.

**story schema**  The underlying structure and relationships in a story that act as catalysts for constructing meaning and distinguishing important ideas and events.

**storytelling**  The act of telling a story orally without the use of text.

**strands**  Areas of skills developed at increasingly higher levels throughout basal reading programs.

**structural analysis**  A word recognition skill that involves identifying words in meaningful units such as prefixes, suffixes, and root words. Structural analysis also includes being able to identify inflected endings, compound words, and contractions.

**student schedule**  Organization of an individual student's activities in different learning-center areas based on the student's strengths, weaknesses, and interests.

**subordinate**  Inferior in rank, class, or status.

**superordinate**  Superior in rank, class, or status.

**support reading strategy**  A strategy designed to develop the ability to read fluently by combining several instructional elements.

**survey test**  Broad type of test that measures general performance only.

**sustained silent reading (SSR)**  Structured activity in which children are given fixed time periods for reading self-selected materials silently.

**synonyms**  Words similar in meaning to other words.

**syntactic cues**  Grammatical information in a text that readers process, along with graphophonemic and semantic information, to construct meaning.

**synthetic phonics**  A building-block approach to phonics intended to foster the understanding of letter–sound relationships and develop phonic knowledge and skill.

**teacher's log**  Observational record of student reading and writing activities and social behaviors organized especially for assessment.

**technology-based instruction**  An instructional approach that utilizes computers and their many capabilities.

**thematic instruction**  Another name for literature units.

**think-alouds**  A comprehension strategy in which students talk about their thoughts as they read aloud.

**think sheet**  List of questions used to elicit responses about texts for discussion purposes.

**top-down model**  A type of reading model that assumes that the construction of textual meaning depends on the reader's prior knowledge and experience.

**trade books**  Literature and informational books widely available in bookstores; used by teachers to supplement or replace sole dependence on textbooks in reading or content area instruction.

**transformative approach**  A multicultural approach that provides students with opportunities to read about cultural concepts and events that are different from their own, make judgments about them, think critically, and generate conclusions.

**units of language**  Categories of written language, ranging from the smallest unit, letters, to the largest unit, the whole text selection, that are emphasized for instructional purposes.

**uses of oral language**  Language functions that can and should be adapted to print at the beginning of instruction.

**validity**  The accuracy with which a test measures what it is designed to measure—the most important characteristic of a test.

**vocabulary**  The panoply of words we use, recognize, and respond to in meaningful acts of communication.

**vocabulary-building skills**  Linguistic skills that allow children to construct word meanings independently on the basis of context clues.

**vocabulary development**  Introduction and repetition of words for reinforcement in basal reading programs.

**WebQuest**  An electronic model in which Internet inquiry is organized to support student learning.

**whole language**  A theoretical perspective that focuses on the integration of all the language arts—reading, writing, speaking, and listening—to create child-responsive environments for learning that are supported by literature-based instruction.

**word banks**  Boxes of word cards that individual students are studying as they relate to phonics, spelling, or vocabulary learning.

**word knowledge rating**  A strategy that helps students develop an awareness of how well they know vocabulary words by rating themselves on their knowledge of words based on a continuum.

**word part connections**  A dictionary-related activity in which the unknown word is broken into word parts. The dictionary is used to verify the meaning of the word and/or word part.

**word processing**    Using computers to create and publish texts.

**words**    Labels for concepts.

**word sorts**    Vocabulary development through categorization activities with groups of words.

**word walls**    Words compiled on sheets of shelf paper hung on the wall of a classroom. Word walls are used by teachers to engage students in word study for a variety of instructional purposes.

**writing notebooks**    Places where students can gather observations, thoughts, reactions, ideas, unusual words, pictures, and interesting facts for future writing.

**writing process**    The stages of writing, including rehearsing, drafting, revising and editing, and publishing.

**writing workshop**    Classroom writing time during which students are given the structure and direction they need to understand, develop, or use specific writing strategies in planning and revising drafts.

# References

Aaron, R. L., & Anderson, M. K. (1981). A comparison of values expressed in juvenile magazines and basal reader series. *The Reading Teacher, 35*(3), 305–313.

Adams, M. J. (1990). *Beginning to read: Thinking and learning about print: A summary.* Urbana: University of Illinois, Center for the Study of Reading.

Agnew, A. T. (1982). Using children's dictated stories to assess code consciousness. *The Reading Teacher, 35*(4), 448–452.

Ahlness, M. (2005). Giving it away: The Earth Day groceries project. In R. A. Karchmer, M. H. Mallette, J. Kara-Soteriou, & D. J. Leu, Jr. (Eds.), *Innovative approaches to literacy education: Using the Internet to support new literacies* (pp. 28–43). Newark, DE: International Reading Association.

Allen, R. V. (1976). *Language experiences in communication.* Boston: Houghton Mifflin.

Allington, R. (2004). Setting the record straight. *Educational Leadership, 61,* 22–25.

Allington, R. L. (1977). If they don't read, how they gonna get good? *Journal of Reading, 21,* 57–61.

Allington, R. L. (1983). Fluency: The neglected reading goal. *The Reading Teacher, 36,* 556–561.

Alvermann, D. E. (1991). The discussion web: A graphic aid for learning across the curriculum. *The Reading Teacher, 45,* 92–99.

Ambe, E. B. (2007). Inviting reluctant adolescent readers into the literacy club: Some comprehension strategies to tutor individuals or small groups of reluctant readers. *Journal of Adolescent & Adult Literacy, 50,* 632–639.

Ammon, P., Simons, H., & Elster, C. (1990). *Effects of controlled, primerese language on the reading process* (Technical Report No. 45). Berkeley, CA, and Pittsburgh, PA: Center for the Study of Writing. ERIC Doc. No. ED 334542.

Anderson, R. C., & Freebody, P. (1981). Vocabulary knowledge. In J. T. Guthrie (Ed.), *Comprehension and teaching: Research perspectives.* Newark, DE: International Reading Association.

Anderson, R. C., Hiebert, E. H., Scott, J., & Wilkinson, I. A. G. (1985). *Becoming a nation of readers.* Washington, DC: National Institute of Education.

Anderson, R. C., Higgins, G. D., & Wurster, S. R. (1985). Differences in the free reading books selected by high, average, and low achievers. *The Reading Teacher, 39,* 326–330.

Anstey, M., & Bull, G. (2006). *Teaching and learning multiliteracies: Changing times, changing literacies.* Newark, DE: International Reading Association.

Armbruster, B. B., Echols, C., & Brown, A. L. (1982). The role of metacognition in reading to learn: A developmental perspective. *Volta Review, 84,* 45–56.

Armbruster, B. B., & Nagy, W. E. (1992). Vocabulary in content area lessons. *The Reading Teacher, 45,* 550–551.

Ashton-Warner, S. (1959). *Spinster.* New York: Simon & Schuster.

Ashton-Warner, S. (1963). *Teacher.* New York: Simon & Schuster.

Ashton-Warner, S. (1972). *Spearpoint: Teachers in America.* New York: Knopf.

Atwell, N. (1993). Foreword. In L. Patterson, C. Santa, K. Short, & K. Smith (Eds.), *Teachers are researchers* (pp. vii–x). Newark, DE: International Reading Association.

Atwell, N. (1998). *In the middle: New understandings about writing, reading, and learning* (2nd ed.). Portsmouth, NH: Heinemann.

Baines, L. (2000). Same facts, different audience. In L. Baines & A. J. Kunkel (Eds.), *Going Bohemian: Activities that engage adolescents in the art of writing well* (pp. 78–80). Newark, DE: International Reading Association.

Baloche, L., & Platt, T. J. (1993). Sprouting magic beans: Exploring literature through creative questioning and cooperative learning. *Language Arts, 70,* 264–271.

Banks, J. A. (2001). *Cultural diversity and education: Foundations, curriculum, and teaching* (4th ed.). Boston: Allyn & Bacon.

Banks, J. A. (2002). *An introduction to multicultural education* (3rd ed.). Boston: Allyn & Bacon.

Barone, D. (1996). Whose language? Learning from bilingual learners in a developmental first-grade classroom. In D. J. Leu, C. K. Kinzer, & K. Hinchman (Eds.), *Literacies for the 21st century: Research and practice* (pp. 170–182). Chicago: National Reading Conference.

Barr, R., & Sadow, M. W. (1989). Influence of basal programs on fourth-grade reading instruction. *Reading Research Quarterly, 24,* 44–71.

Barrentine, S. J. (1996). Engaging with reading through interactive read-alouds. *The Reading Teacher, 50,* 36–43.

Barron, R. (1969). The use of vocabulary as an advance organizer. In H. L. Herber & P. Sanders (Eds.), *Research in reading in the content areas: First report* (pp. 29–39). Syracuse, NY: Syracuse University Reading and Language Arts Center.

Baumann, J. F., & Heubach, K. M. (1996). Do basal readers deskill teachers? A national survey of educators' use and opinions of basals. *Elementary School Journal, 96*(5), 511–526.

Baylor, B. (1972). *When clay sings.* New York: Scribner.

Bear, D. R., Helman, L., Templeton, S., Invernizzi, M., & Johnston, F. (2007). *Words their way with English language learners: Word study for phonics, vocabulary and spelling instruction.* Upper Saddle River, NJ: Pearson.

Bear, D. R., Invernizzi, M., Templeton, S., & Johnston, F. (1996). *Words their way: Word study for phonics, vocabulary, and spelling instruction.* Upper Saddle River, NJ: Prentice Hall.

Bear, D. R., Invernizzi, M., Templeton, S., & Johnston, F. (2000). *Words their way: Word study for phonics, vocabulary, and spelling instruction* (2nd ed.). Upper Saddle River, NJ: Prentice Hall.

Bear, D. R., Invernizzi, M., Templeton, S., & Johnston, F. (2008). *Words their way: Word study for phonics, vocabulary, and spelling instruction* (4th ed.). Upper Saddle River, NJ: Pearson.

Bear, D. R., & Templeton, S. (1998). Explorations in developmental spelling: Foundations for learning and teaching phonics, spelling, and vocabulary. *The Reading Teacher, 52,* 222–242.

Beck, I. L., & Juel, C. (1995). The role of decoding in learning to read. *American Educator, 19*(2), 8, 21–25, 39–42.

Beck, I. L., & McKeown, M. G. (1983). Learning words well: A program to enhance vocabulary and comprehension. *The Reading Teacher, 36,* 622–625.

Beck, I. L., & McKeown, M. G. (1991). Social studies texts are hard to understand: Mediating some of the difficulties, *Language Arts, 68,* 482–490.

Beck, I. L., McKeown, M. G., Hamilton, R. L., & Kucan, L. (1997). *Questioning the author: An approach for enhancing student engagement with text.* Newark, DE: International Reading Association.

Beck, I. L., McKeown, M. G., & McCaslin, E. (1983). All contexts are not created equal. *Elementary School Journal, 83,* 177–181.

Beck, I. L., McKeown, M. G., McCaslin, E., & Burket, A. (1979). *Instructional dimensions that may affect reading comprehension: Examples of two commercial reading programs.* Pittsburgh, PA: University of Pittsburgh Language Research and Development Center.

Beck, I. L., McKeown, M. G., & Omanson, R. (1987). The effects and uses of diverse vocabulary instructional techniques. In M. McKeown & M. Cartis (Eds.), *The nature of vocabulary acquisition.* Mahwah, NJ: Erlbaum.

Beck, I. L., Perfetti, C. A., & McKeown, M. G. (1982). Effects of long-term vocabulary instruction on lexical access and reading comprehension. *Journal of Educational Psychology, 74,* 506–521.

Bennett-Armistead, V., Duke, N., & Moses, A. (2005). *Literacy and the youngest learner.* New York: Scholastic.

Benton, M. (1984). The methodology vacuum in teaching literature. *Language Arts, 61,* 265–275.

Betts, E. A. (1946). *Foundations of reading instruction.* New York: American Book Company.

Beyersdorfer, J. M., & Schauer, D. K. (1989). Semantic analysis to writing: Connecting words, books, and writing. *Journal of Reading, 32,* 500–508.

Bissex, G. (1980). *GNYS AT WRK: A child learns to write and read.* Cambridge, MA: Harvard University Press.

Blachowicz, C., & Fisher, P. (1996). *Teaching vocabulary in all classrooms.* Columbus, OH: Merrill.

Blachowicz, C., & Fisher, P. (2004). Vocabulary lessons. *Educational Leadership, 61*(6), 66–69.

Blachowicz, C., & Fisher, P. (2005). *Teaching vocabulary in all classrooms* (3rd ed.). Columbus, OH: Merrill-Prentice Hall.

Blachowicz, C. L. (1986). Making connections: Alternatives to the vocabulary notebook. *Journal of Reading, 29,* 643–649.

Blachowicz, C. L. Z., & Fisher, P. (2000). Vocabulary instruction. In M. Kamil, P. Mosenthal, P. Pearson, & R. Barr (Eds.), *Handbook of reading research* (Vol. 3, pp. 503–523). Mahwah, NJ: Erlbaum.

Black, P., Harrison, C., Lee, C., Marshall, B., & Wiliam, D. (2004). Working inside the black box: Assessment for learning in the classroom. *Phi Delta Kappan, 86*(1), 8–21.

Blair, T. R., Rupley, W. H., & Nichols, D. W. (2007). The effective teacher of reading: Considering the "what" and "how" of instruction. *The Reading Teacher, 60,* 432–438.

Blume, J. (1970). *Are you there, God? It's me, Margaret.* New York: Dell.

Bomer, K. (2005). Missing the children: When politics and programs impede our teaching. *Language Arts, 82,* 168–176.

Bond, G., & Dykstra, R. (1967). The cooperative research programs in first-grade reading. *Reading Research Quarterly, 2,* 135–142.

Booth, D. (2001). *Reading and writing in the middle years.* Portland, ME: Stenhouse.

Boyd, F. B., & Ikpeze, C. H. (2007). Navigating a literacy landscape: Teaching conceptual understanding with multiple text types. *Journal of Literacy Research, 39,* 217–248.

Bradley, J. M., & Talgott, M. R. (1987). Reducing reading anxiety. *Academic Therapy, 22,* 349–358.

Bransford, J. D., & Johnson, M. K. (1973). Considerations of some problems of comprehension. In W. C. Chase (Ed.), *Visual information processing* (pp. 383–434). New York: Academic Press.

Bredekamp, S. (1987). *Developmentally appropriate practice.* Washington, DC: National Association for the Education of Young Children.

Bromley, K. (1989). Buddy journals make the reading–writing connection. *The Reading Teacher, 43,* 122–129.

Bromley, K. (2007). Nine things every teacher should know about words and vocabulary instruction. *Journal of Adolescent & Adult Literacy, 50,* 528–537.

Brown, A. L. (1985). Metacognition: The development of selective attention strategies for learning from texts. In H. S. Singer & R. B. Ruddell (Eds.), *Theoretical models and processes of reading* (3rd ed., pp. 501–526). Newark, DE: International Reading Association.

Brown, S. C., & Kysilka, M. L. (2002). *Applying multicultural and global concepts in the classroom and beyond.* Boston: Allyn & Bacon.

Brozo, W. G., & Tomlinson, C. M. (1986). Literature: The key to lively content courses. *The Reading Teacher, 40,* 288–293.

Buikema, J. L., & Graves, M. F. (1993). Teaching students to use context clues to infer word meanings. *Journal of Reading, 36,* 450–457.

Bulion, L. (2006). *Hey there, stink bug!* Watertown, MA: Charlesbridge.

Bunting, E. (1989). *The Wednesday surprise.* New York: Clarion.

Bunting, E. (1994). *A day's work.* New York: Clarion.

Bus, A., Van Ijzendoorn, M., & Pellegrini, A. (1995). Joint book reading makes for success in learning to read: A meta-analysis on intergeneration transmission of literacy. *Review of Educational Research, 65,* 1–21.

Butler, A. (1988). *Shared book experience.* Crystal Lake, IL: Rigby.

Butler-Pascoe, M. E., & Wiburg, K. M. (2003). *Technology and teaching English language learners.* Boston: Allyn & Bacon.

Calkins, L., Montgomery, K., & Santman, D. (1998). *A teacher's guide to standardized reading tests: Knowledge is power.* Portsmouth, NH: Heinemann.

Calkins, L. M. (1983). *Lessons from a child.* Portsmouth, NH: Heinemann.

Calkins, L. M. (1994). *The art of teaching writing*. Portsmouth, NH: Heinemann.

Cambourne, B. (2001). Conditions for learning. *The Reading Teacher, 54*, 784–786.

Carlisle, J. F., & Stone, C. A. (2005). Exploring the role of morphemes in word reading. *Reading Research Quarterly, 40*, 428–447.

Carnahan, D., & Cobb, C. (2004). *A conceptual model of adolescent literacy*. Retrieved July 2, 2007, from www.learningpt.org/literacy/adolescent/model.php

Carnine, D., Silbert, J., & Kame'enui, E. T. (1990). *Direct instruction reading* (2nd ed.). Columbus, OH: Merrill.

Chall, J. (1967). *Learning to read: The great debate*. New York: McGraw-Hill.

Chapman, V. G., & Sopko, D. (2003). Developing strategic use of combined-text trade books. *The Reading Teacher, 57*(3), 236–239.

Chappuis, J. (2005). Helping students understand assessment. *Educational Leadership, 63*(3), 39–43.

Charron, N. N. (2007). "I learned that there's a state called Victoria and he has six blue-tongued lizards!" *The Reading Teacher, 60*, 762–769.

Chomsky, C. (1970). Reading, writing, and phonology. *Harvard Educational Review, 40*, 287–309.

Chomsky, C. (1976). After decoding, what? *Language Arts, 53*, 288–296, 314.

Chomsky, C. (1979). Approaching reading through invented spelling. In L. B. Resnick & P. A. Weaver (Eds.), *Theory and practice of early reading* (Vol. 2, p. 43). Mahwah, NJ: Erlbaum.

Christenson, T. A. (2002). *Supporting struggling writers in the elementary classroom*. Newark, DE: International Reading Association.

Christian, D. (1997). *Vernacular dialects in U.S. schools*. Retrieved June 2, 2007, from www.cal.org/resources/digest/christ01.html

Clark, K. F., & Graves, M. F. (2005). Scaffolding students' comprehension of text. *The Reading Teacher, 58*, 570–580.

Clay, M. (1992). *Early detection of reading difficulties* (3rd ed.). Portsmouth, NH: Heinemann.

Clay, M. (2005). *An observation survey of early literacy achievement*. Portsmouth, NH: Heinemann.

Clay, M. M. (1979a). *Concepts about print test*. Portsmouth, NH: Heinemann.

Clay, M. M. (1985). *The early detection of reading difficulties: A diagnostic survey with recovery procedures*. Portsmouth, NH: Heinemann.

Clay, M. M. (1988). Exploring with a pencil. *Reading Today, 6*(20), 179–185.

Clay, M. M. (1991). *Becoming literate: The construction of inner control*. Portsmouth, NH: Heinemann.

Clay, M. M. (2001). *Change over time in children's literacy development*. Portsmouth, NH: Heinemann.

Cleary, B. P. (2006). *A lime, a mime, a pool of slime: More about nouns*. Brookfield, CT: Millbrook.

Clyde, J. A., & Condon, M. W. F. (1992). Collaborating in coursework and classrooms: An alternative for strengthening whole language teacher preparation cultures. In C. Weaver & L. Henke (Eds.), *Supporting whole language: Stories of teacher and instructional change* (pp. 87–104). Portsmouth, NH: Heinemann.

Clymer, T. (1963). The utility of phonic generalizations in the primary grades. *The Reading Teacher, 16*, 252–258.

Coaches, controversy, consensus. (2004 April/May). *Reading Today, 21*(5), 1.

Coiro, J. (2003). Exploring literacy on the Internet: Reading comprehension on the Internet: Expanding our understanding of reading comprehension to encompass new literacies. *The Reading Teacher, 56*, 458–464.

Cole, J. (1990). *The magic school bus: Inside the human body*. New York: Scholastic.

Confrey, J. (1990). What constructivism implies for teaching. In R. B. Davis, C. A. Maher, & N. Noddings (Eds.), *Constructivist views on the teaching and learning of mathematics* (pp. 107–124). Reston, VA: National Council of Teachers of Mathematics.

Connelly, F. M., & Clandinin, D. J. (1988). *Teachers as curriculum planners: Narrative of experience*. New York: Teachers College Press.

Coody, B., & Nelson, D. (1982). *Teaching elementary language arts*. Belmont, CA: Wadsworth.

Cooper, P., & Gray, P. (1984). *Teaching listening as an interactive process*. Paper presented at the International Reading Association Annual Convention, Atlanta.

Cornett, C. E. (2006). Center stage: Arts-based read-aloud. *The Reading Teacher, 60*, 234–240.

Cowley, J. (1991, October). Joy of big books. *Instructor, 101*, 19.

Cramer, R. L. (1975). Reading to children: Why and how. *The Reading Teacher, 28*, 460–463.

Cramer, R. L. (1978). *Children's writing and language growth*. Columbus, OH: Merrill.

Cullinan, B., & Galda, L. (1994). *Literature and the child* (3rd ed.). New York: Harcourt Brace.

Cummins, J. (1986). Empowering minority students: A framework for intervention. *Harvard Educational Review, 56*, 18–36.

Cummins, J. (1989). *Empowering minority students*. Sacramento, CA: Association of Bilingual Education.

Cummins, J., Brown, K., & Sayers, D. (2007). *Literacy, technology, and diversity*. Boston: Allyn & Bacon.

Cunningham, J. W., Cunningham, P. M., Hoffman, J. V., & Yopp, H. K. (1998). *Phonemic awareness and the teaching of reading: A position statement from the board of directors of the International Reading Association*. Newark, DE: International Reading Association.

Cunningham, P. (1987). Action phonics. *The Reading Teacher, 41*, 347–249.

Cunningham, P. (1999). What should we do about phonics? In L. B. Gambrell, L. M. Morrow, S. B. Neuman, & M. Pressley (Eds.), *Best practices in literacy instruction* (pp. 68–89). New York: Guilford Press.

Cunningham, P. M. (1995). *Phonics they use: Words for reading and writing* (2nd ed.). New York: HarperCollins.

Cunningham, P. M. (2000). *Phonics they use: Words for reading and writing* (3rd ed.). New York: Longman.

Cunningham, P. M. (2005). *Phonics they use: Words for reading and writing* (4th ed.). New York: Pearson.

Cunningham, P. M., & Allington, R. L. (1999). *Classrooms that work: They can all read and write* (2nd ed.). New York: Longman.

Cunningham, P. M., & Cunningham, J. W. (2002). What we know about how to teach phonics. In A. E. Farstrup & S. J. Samuels (Eds.), *What research has to say about reading instruction* (pp. 87–109). Newark, DE: International Reading Association.

Cunningham, P. M., & Hall, D. (1998). *Month-by-month phonics for third grade.* Greensboro, NC: Carson-Dellosa.

D'Alessandro, M. (1990). Accommodating emotionally handicapped children through a literature-based reading program. *The Reading Teacher, 44,* 288–293.

Dale, E. (1965). Vocabulary measurement: Techniques and major findings. *Elementary English, 42,* 895–901.

Daniels, H. (1994). *Literature circles: Voice and choice in one student-centered classroom.* York, ME: Stenhouse.

Darling-Hammond, I., & Bransford, J. (Eds.). (2005). *Preparing teachers for a changing world.* San Francisco: John Wiley & Sons.

Davey, B. (1983). Think aloud: Modeling the cognitive processes of reading comprehension. *Journal of Reading, 27,* 44–47.

Davidman, L., & Davidman, P. T. (2001) *Teaching with a multicultural perspective: A practical guide* (3rd ed.). New York: Longman.

Davis, D. C. (1973). *Playway: Education for reality.* Minneapolis: Winston.

Davis, F. B. (1944). Fundamental factors of comprehension in reading. *Psychometrika, 9,* 185–197.

DeFord, D. E. (1985). Validating the construct of theoretical orientation in reading instruction. *Reading Research Quarterly, 20,* 366–367.

Deighton, L. (1970). *Vocabulary development in the classroom.* New York: Teachers College Press.

dePaola, T. (1973). *Charlie needs a cloak.* New York: Simon & Schuster.

Diaz, C. F. (2001). *Multicultural education for the 21st century.* Boston: Longman.

Dillard, J. M. (1983). *Multicultural counseling: Toward ethnic and cultural relevance in human encounters.* Chicago: Nelson-Hall.

Dix, S. (2006). I'll do it my way: Three writers and their revision practices. *The Reading Teacher, 59,* 566–573.

Dowhower, S. L. (1987). Effects of repeated reading in second-grade transitional readers' fluency and comprehension. *Reading Research Quarterly, 22,* 389–406.

Dowhower, S. L. (1989). Repeated reading: Research into practice. *The Reading Teacher, 43,* 502–507.

Downing, J. (1979). *Reading and reasoning.* New York: Springer-Verlag.

Downing, J. (1982). Reading: Skill or skills? *The Reading Teacher, 35,* 534–537.

Dray, M. (2005). *Dougal the garbage dump bear.* La Jolla, CA: Kane/Miller.

Drucker, M. J. (2003). What reading teachers should know about ESL learners. *The Reading Teacher, 57*(1), 22–29.

Duin, A., & Graves, M. (1987). Intensive vocabulary instruction as a prewriting technique. *Reading Research Quarterly, 22,* 311–330.

Dupuis, M. M., & Snyder, S. L. (1983). Develop concepts through vocabulary: A strategy for reading specialists to use with content teachers. *Journal of Reading, 26,* 297–305.

Durkin, D. (1966). *Children who read early.* New York: Teachers College Press.

Durkin, D. (1980). *Teaching young children to read* (3rd ed.). Boston: Allyn & Bacon.

Durkin, D. (1988). *A classroom observation study of reading instruction in kindergarten* (Technical Report No. 422). Champaign: University of Illinois, Center for the Study of Reading.

Durrell, D. D. (1958). Success in first-grade reading. *Journal of Education, 148,* 1–8.

Durrell, D. D. (1963). *Phonograms in primary grade words.* Boston: Boston University Press.

Duthie, C., & Zimet, E. K. (1992). "Poetry is like directions for your imagination!" *The Reading Teacher, 46,* 14–24.

Dymock, S. (2005). Teaching expository text structure awareness. *The Reading Teacher, 59,* 177–182.

Edwards, P. A., & Danridge, J. C. (2001). Developing collaboration with culturally diverse parents. In V. J. Risko & K. Bromely (Eds.), *Collaboration for diverse learners: Viewpoints and practices* (pp. 251–272). Newark, DE: International Reading Association.

Ehri, L., Nunes, S., Willows, D., Schuster, B., Yaghoub-Zadeh, Z., & Shanahan, T. (2001). Phonemic awareness instruction helps children learn to read: Evidence from the national reading panel's meta-analysis. *Reading Research Quarterly, 36,* 250–287.

Ehri, L. C. (1991). Development of the ability to read words. In R. Barr, M. L. Kamil, P. Mosenthal, & P. D. Pearson (Eds.), *Handbook of reading research* (2nd ed., pp. 383–417). New York: Longman.

Ehri, L. C. (1992). Reconceptualizing the development of sight word reading and its relationship to reading. In P. Grough, L. C. Ehri, & R. Trelman (Eds.), *Reading acquisition* (pp. 107–143). Mahwah, NJ: Erlbaum.

Ehri, L. C. (1994). Development of the ability to read words: Update. In R. Ruddell & H. Singer (Eds.), *Theoretical models and processes of reading* (4th ed., pp. 323–358). Newark, DE: International Reading Association.

Ehri, L. C. (1995). Teachers need to know how word reading processes develop to teach reading effectively to beginners. In C. N. Hedley, P. Antonacci, & M. Rabinowitz (Eds.), *Thinking and literacy: The mind at work.* Mahwah, NJ: Erlbaum.

Eisner, E. (1997). Cognition and representation: A way to pursue the American dream? *Phi Delta Kappan, 78,* 349–353.

English, K. (1999). *Francie.* New York: Farrar Straus Giroux.

Farnan, N., Flood, J., & Lapp, D. (1994). Comprehending through reading and writing: Six research-based instructional strategies. In K. Spranenberg-Urbschat & R. Pritchard (Eds.), *Kids come in all languages: Reading instruction for ESL students* (pp. 135–157). Newark, DE: International Reading Association.

Farr, R., & Tone, B. (1998). *Assessment portfolio and performance* (2nd ed.). Orlando, FL: Harcourt Brace.

Fawcett, G. (1990). Literacy vignette: The gift. *The Reading Teacher, 43,* 504.

Fielding, L. G., Wilson, P. T., & Anderson, R. C. (1986). A new focus on free reading: The role of trade books in reading instruction. In T. Raphael (Ed.), *The contexts of school-based literacy* (pp. 149–160). New York: Random House.

Fisette, D. (1993). Practical authentic assessment: Good kid watchers know what to teach next! *The California Reader, 26*(4), 4–9.

Fisher, D., & Ivey, G. (2007). Farewell to a farewell to arms: Deemphasizing the whole-class novel. *Phi Delta Kappan, 88*(7), 494–497.

Fitzgerald, J. (1993). Literacy and students who are learning English as a second language. *The Reading Teacher, 46,* 638–647.

Fitzgerald, J. (1999). What is this thing called balance? *The Reading Teacher, 53,* 100–107.

Fitzgerald, J., & Graves, M. F. (2004). *Scaffolding reading experiences for English-language learners.* Norwood, MA: Christopher-Gordon.

Flesch, R. (1955). *Why Johnny can't read—And what you can do about it.* New York: Harper & Brothers.

Fletcher, R. (1996). *A writer's notebook: Unlocking the writer within you.* New York: Avon.

Flippo, R. (1998). Points of agreement: A display of professional unity in our field. *The Reading Teacher, 52,* 30–40.

Flood, J., & Lapp, D. (1993). Are there "real" writers living in your classroom? Implementing a writer-centered classroom. *The Reading Teacher, 48*(3), 254–258.

Flood, J., Lapp, D., & Nagel, G. (1993). Assessing student action beyond reflection and response. *Journal of Reading, 36,* 420–423.

Flynn, R. M. (2004, 2005). Curriculum-based readers theatre: Setting the stage for reading and retention. *The Reading Teacher, 58,* 360–365.

Ford, M. (2005). *Differentiation through flexible grouping: Successfully reaching all readers.* Retrieved July 2, 2007, from www2.learningpt.org/catalog/item.asp?SessionID=155983050&productID=237

Fosnot, C. (1996). *Constructivism: Theory, perspectives, and practice.* New York: Teachers College Press.

Fountas, I. C., & Pinnell, G. S. (1996). *Guided reading.* Portsmouth, NH: Heinemann.

Fowler, G. L. (1982). Developing comprehension skills in primary students through the use of story frames. *The Reading Teacher, 36,* 176–179.

Fox, B. J. (1996). *Strategies for word identification: Phonics from a new perspective.* Columbus, OH: Merrill.

Fox, B. J. (2003). Teachers' evaluation of word identification software: Implications for literacy methods courses. In M. B. Sampson, P. E. Linder, J. R. Dugan, & B. Brancato (Eds.), *Celebrating the freedom of literacy: The twenty-fifth yearbook of the College Reading Association* (pp. 266–279). Texas A&M University-Commerce.

Fox, B. J. (2004). *Word identification strategies: Phonics from a new perspective* (3rd ed.). Upper Saddle River, NJ: Pearson.

Fox, B. J., & Wright, M. (1997). Connecting school and home literacy experiences through cross-age reading. *The Reading Teacher, 50,* 396–403.

Fractor, J. S., Woodruff, M. C., Martinez, M. G., & Teale, W. H. (1993). Let's not miss opportunities to promote voluntary reading: Classroom libraries in the elementary school. *The Reading Teacher, 46,* 476–484.

Freeman, D., & Freeman, Y. (1993). Strategies for promoting the primary languages. *The Reading Teacher, 46,* 551–558.

Freeman, D., & Freeman, Y. (2003). Teaching English learners to read: Learning or acquisition? In G. Garcia (Ed.), *English learners: Reaching the highest levels of English literacy* (pp. 34–54). Newark, DE: International Reading Association.

Freeman, D. E., & Freeman, Y. S. (2006). Teaching language through content themes: Viewing our world as a global village. In T. A. Young & N. L. Hadaway (Eds.), *Supporting the literacy development of English learners: Increasing success in all classrooms* (pp. 61–78). Newark, DE: International Reading Association.

Freeman, Y., & Freeman, D. (2004). Preview, view, review: Giving multilingual learners access to the curriculum. In L. Hoyt (Ed.), *Spotlight on comprehension: Building a literacy of thoughtfulness* (pp. 453–459). Portsmouth, NH: Heinemann.

Freppon, P. A., & Dahl, K. L. (1998). Balanced instruction: Insights and considerations. *Reading Research Quarterly, 33,* 240–251.

Friend, M., & Bursuck, W. D. (2002). *Including students with special needs: A practical guide for classroom teachers* (3rd ed.). Boston: Allyn & Bacon.

Fry, E. (2002). Readability versus leveling. *The Reading Teacher, 56*(3), 286–291.

Fry, E. (2004). Phonics: A large phoneme-grapheme frequency count revised. *Journal of Literacy Research, 36*(1), 85–98.

Fry, E. B. (1968). A readability formula that saves time. *Journal of Reading, 11,* 513–516, 575–578.

Fry, E. B. (1977). Fry's readability graph: Clarifications, validity, and extension to level 17. *Journal of Reading, 21,* 242–252.

Fry, E. B. (1980). The new instant word list. *The Reading Teacher, 34,* 284–290.

Fry, E. B. (1990). A readability formula for short passages. *Journal of Reading, 33,* 595.

Fry, E. B. (1998). The most common phonograms. *The Reading Teacher, 51,* 620–622.

Fuchs, D., & Fuchs, L. S. (2006). Introduction to response to intervention: What, why, and how valid is it? *Reading Research Quarterly, 41,* 93–99.

Galda, L., Ash, G. E., & Cullinan, B. E. (2000). Children's literature. In M. L. Kamil, P. B. Mosenthal, P. D. Pearson, & R. Barr (Eds.), *Handbook of reading research* (pp. 361–379). Mahwah, NJ: Erlbaum.

Galda, L., & Beach, R. (2004). Response to literature as a cultural activity. In R. B. Ruddell & N. J. Unrau (Eds.), *Theoretical models and processes of reading* (pp. 852–869). Newark, DE: International Reading Association.

Gambrell, L. B. (1985). Dialogue journals: Reading–writing interactions. *The Reading Teacher, 38,* 512–515.

Gambrell, L. B. (1996). Creating classroom cultures that foster reading motivation. *The Reading Teacher, 50*(1), 14–25.

Ganske, K., Monroe, J. K., & Strickland, D. S. (2003). Questions teachers ask about struggling readers and writers. *The Reading Teacher, 4*(2), 118–127.

Garber-Miller, K. (2007). Playful textbook previews: Letting go of familiar mustache monologues. *Journal of Adolescent & Adult Literacy, 50,* 284–288.

Garcia, E. (1999). *Student cultural diversity: Understanding and meeting the challenge* (2nd ed.). Boston: Houghton Mifflin.

Garcia, E. (2002). *Student cultural diversity: Understanding and meeting the challenge* (3rd ed.). Boston: Houghton Mifflin.

Garcia, G., Pearson, P. D., & Jimenez, R. (1990). *The at-risk dilemma: A synthesis of reading research.* Champaign: University of Illinois, Reading Research and Education Center.

Garcia, G. E. (2000). Bilingual children's reading. In M. L. Kamil, P. B. Mosenthal, P. D. Pearson, & R. Barr (Eds.), *Handbook of reading research* (Vol. 3, pp. 813–834). Mahwah, NJ: Erlbaum.

Garcia, G. G., & Beltran, D. (2003). Revisioning the blueprint: Building for the academic success of English learners. In G. Garcia (Ed.), *English learners: Reaching the highest levels of English literacy* (pp. 197–226). Newark, DE: International Reading Association.

Garcia, J., & Florez-Tighe, V. (1986). The portrayal of Blacks, Hispanics, and Native Americans in recent basal series. *Equity and Excellence, 22*(4), 72–76.

Gardiner, S. (2001). Ten minutes a day for silent reading. *Educational Leadership, 59*(2), 32–35.

Gardner, H. (1993). *Multiple intelligences: The theory in practice.* New York: Basic Books.

Gaskins, I. W., Ehri, L. C., Cress, C., O'Hara, C., & Donnelly, K. (1997). Procedures for word learning: Making discoveries about words. *The Reading Teacher, 50,* 312–327.

Gee, J. (2004). Reading as situated language: A sociocognitive perspective. In R. B. Ruddell & N. J. Unrau (Eds.), *Theoretical models and processes of reading* (pp. 116–132). Newark, DE: International Reading Association.

Gentry, J. R., & Henderson, E. H. (1980). Three steps to teaching beginning readers to spell. In E. H. Henderson & J. W. Beers (Eds.), *Developmental and cognitive aspects of learning to spell: A reflection of word knowledge* (pp. 112–119). Newark, DE: International Reading Association.

Gersten, R., & Dimino, J. A. (2006). RTI (Response to intervention): Rethinking special education for students with reading difficulties (yet again). *Reading Research Quarterly, 41,* 99–108.

Giff, P. R. (1980). *Today was a terrible day.* New York: Viking.

Gilles, C. (1990). Collaborative literacy strategies: "We don't need a circle to have a group." In K. G. Short & K. M. Pierce (Eds.), *Talking about books: Creating literate communities* (pp. 58–68). Portsmouth, NH: Heinemann.

Gillespie, J. (2005). "It would be fun to do again": Multigenre responses to literature. *The Reading Teacher, 48,* 678–684.

Glazer, S. M., & Brown, C. S. (1993). *Portfolios and beyond.* Norwood, MA: Christopher-Gordon.

Goatley, V. (1997). Talk about text among special education students. In S. I. McMahon & E. Raphael (Eds.), *The book club connection* (pp. 119–137). New York: Teachers College Press.

Goff, P. (1998). Where's the phonics? Making a case for its direct and systematic instruction. *The Reading Teacher, 52,* 138–141.

Goodman, K. S. (1973). Psycholinguistic universals in the reading process. In F. Smith (Ed.), *Psycholinguistics and reading* (pp. 21–27). Austin, TX: Holt, Rinehart and Winston.

Goodman, K. S. (1975). Do you have to be smart to read? Do you have to read to be smart? *The Reading Teacher, 28,* 625–632.

Goodman, K. S. (1986). *What's whole in whole language?* Portsmouth, NH: Heinemann.

Goodman, K. S. (1988). Look what they've done to Judy Blume! The basalization of children's literature. *New Advocate, 1,* 18–28.

Goodman, Y. M. (1978). Kid-watching: An alternative to testing. *National Elementary Principal, 10,* 41–45.

Goodman, Y. M., & Burke, C. L. (1972). *Reading miscue inventory manual: Procedure for diagnosis and evaluation.* Old Tappan, NJ: Macmillan.

Gordon, C. J., & Braun, C. (1983). Using story schemata as an aid to reading and writing. *The Reading Teacher, 37,* 116–121.

Goswami, U. (1986). Children's use of analogy in learning to read: A developmental study. *Journal of Experimental Child Psychology, 42,* 73–83.

Goswami, U., & Bryant, P. (1990). *Phonological skills and learning to read.* Mahwah, NJ: Erlbaum.

Gough, P. (1985). One second of reading. In H. Singer & R. Ruddell (Eds.), *Theoretical models and processes of reading*

(3rd ed., pp. 26–27). Newark, DE: International Reading Association.

Grabe, M., & Grabe, C. (2004). *Integrating technology for meaningful learning.* New York: Houghton Mifflin Company.

Graves, D. H. (1983). *Writing: Teachers and children at work.* Portsmouth, NH: Heinemann.

Graves, D. H. (1994). *A fresh look at writing.* Portsmouth, NH: Heinemann.

Graves, D. H., & Sunstein, B. S. (1992). *Portfolio portraits.* Portsmouth, NH: Heinemann.

Graves, M. F., & Watts-Taffe, S. M. (2002). The place of word consciousness in a research-based vocabulary program. In A. Farstrup & S. Samuels (Eds.), *What research has to say about reading instruction* (pp. 140–165). Newark, DE: International Reading Association.

Gray-Schlegel, M. A., & King, Y. (1998). Introducing concepts about print to the preservice teacher: A hands-on experience. *The California Reader, 32*(1), 17–21.

Greenlaw, M. J. (1988). Using informational books to extend the curriculum. *The Reading Teacher, 42,* 18.

Gregg, M., & Sekeres, D. C. (2006). Supporting children's reading of expository text in the geography classroom. *The Reading Teacher, 60,* 102–110.

Griffith, P. L., & Olson, M. (1992). Phonemic awareness helps beginning readers break the code. *The Reading Teacher, 45,* 516–523.

Gruenberg, R. (1948). *Poor Mr. Fingle. More favorite stories.* New York: Doubleday.

Gunning, T. G. (2000). *Best books for building literacy for elementary school children.* Boston: Allyn & Bacon.

Guthrie, J. T., & McCann, A. D. (1996). Idea circles: Peer collaborations for conceptual learning. In L. B. Gambrell & J. F. Almasi (Eds.), *Lively discussions! Fostering engaged reading* (pp. 87–105). Newark, DE: International Reading Association.

Guthrie, J. T., & Wigfield, A. (2000). Engagement and motivation in reading. In M. L. Kamil, P. B. Mosenthal, P. D. Pearson, & R. Barr (Eds.), *Handbook of reading research* (Vol. 3, pp. 403–433). Mahwah, NJ: Erlbaum.

Gutknecht, B. (1991). Mitigating the effects of negative stereotyping of aging and the elderly in primary grade reading instruction. *Reading Improvement, 28,* 44–51.

Hadaway, N. L., & Young, T. A. (2006). Changing classrooms: Transforming instruction. In T. A. Young & N. L. Hadaway (Eds.), *Supporting the literacy development of English learners: Increasing success in all classrooms* (pp. 6–21). Newark, DE: International Reading Association.

Haggard, M. R. (1986). The vocabulary self-collection strategy: Using student interest and world knowledge to enhance vocabulary growth. *Journal of Reading, 29,* 634–642.

Hall, A. K. (1995). Sentencing: The psycholinguistic guessing game. *The Reading Teacher, 49,* 76–77.

Hall, B. (2004). *Literacy coaches an evolving role.* Retrieved June 8, 2007, from www.carnegie.org/reporter/09/literacy/index.html

Halliday, M. A. K. (1975). *Learning how to mean: Exploration in the development of language.* London: Arnold.

Hancock, M. R. (1993a). Exploring and extending personal response through literature journals. *The Reading Teacher, 46,* 466–474.

Hancock, M. R. (1993b). Exploring the meaning-making process through the content of literature response journals:

A case study investigation. *Research in the Teaching of English, 27,* 335–369.

Hanna, P. R., Hanna, J. S., Hodges, R. E., & Rudorf, E. H. (1966). *Phoneme-grapheme correspondences as cues to spelling improvement.* Washington, DC: U.S. Department of Health, Education, and Welfare.

Hansen, J. (1981). An inferential comprehension strategy for use with primary children. *The Reading Teacher, 34,* 665–669.

Hansen, J. (1987). *When writers read.* Portsmouth, NH: Heinemann.

Harmin, M. (1994). *Inspiring active learning: A handbook for teachers.* Alexandria, VA: Association for Supervision and Curriculum Development.

Harris, J. (1998). *Design tools for the Internet-supported classroom.* Columbus, OH: Merrill.

Harris, T. H., & Hodges, R. E. (1995). *The literacy dictionary: The vocabulary of reading and writing.* Newark, DE: International Reading Association.

Harris, V. (1993). Bookalogues: Multicultural literature. *Language Arts, 70,* 215–217.

Harste, J. C., & Burke, C. L. (1977). A new hypothesis for reading teacher research. In P. D. Pearson & J. Hansen (Eds.), *Reading: Theory, research, and practice* (pp. 32–40). Clemson, SC: National Reading Conference.

Harste, J. C., Woodward, V. A., & Burke, C. L. (1984). *Language stories and literacy lessons.* Portsmouth, NH: Heinemann.

Harvey, S., & Goudvis, A. (2000). *Strategies that work: Teaching comprehension to enhance understanding.* York, ME: Stenhouse.

Hayes, J. (2007a). *Activities for newcomers.* Retrieved June 5, 2007, from www.everythingesl.net/inservices/september.php

Hayes, J. (2007b). *Creating an atmosphere of acceptance.* Retrieved June 5, 2007, from www.everythingesl.net/inservices/nurturing.php

Heffernan, L. (2004). *Critical literacy and writer's workshop: Bringing purpose and passion to student writing.* Newark, DE: International Reading Association.

Henderson, E. (1990). *Teaching spelling* (2nd ed.). Boston: Houghton Mifflin.

Henry, G. (1974). *Teaching reading as concept development.* Newark, DE: International Reading Association.

Hepler, S. I. (1982). *Patterns of response to literature: A one-year study of a fifth- and sixth-grade classroom.* Unpublished doctoral dissertation, Ohio State University, Columbus.

Hepler, S. I., & Hickman, J. (1982). "The book was okay. I love you": Social aspects of response to literature. *Theory into Practice, 21,* 278–283.

Herman, J., & Baker, E. (2005). Making benchmark testing work. *Educational Leadership, 63*(3), 48–54.

Herman, P. A. (1985). The effect of repeated readings on reading rate, speech, and word recognition. *Reading Research Quarterly, 20,* 553–565.

Herrington, A. J. (1997). Developing and responding to major writing projects. In M. D. Sorcinelli & P. Elbow (Eds.), *Writing to learn: Strategies for assigning and responding to writing across the disciplines.* San Francisco: Jossey-Bass.

Herrmann, B. A. (1988). Two approaches for helping poor readers become more strategic. *The Reading Teacher, 42,* 24–28.

Heward, W. L. (2000). *Exceptional children: An introduction to special education* (6th ed.). Columbus, OH: Merrill.

Hickman, J. (1983). Classrooms that help children like books. In N. Roser & M. Frith (Eds.), *Children's choices.* Newark, DE: International Reading Association.

Hickman, P., Pollard-Durodola, S., & Vaughn, S. (2004). Storybook reading: Improving vocabulary and comprehension for English language learners. *The Reading Teacher, 57,* 720–730.

Hilbert, S. B. (1993). Sustained silent reading revisited. *The Reading Teacher, 46,* 354–356.

Hitchcock, M. E., & Tompkins, G. E. (1987). Basal readers: Are they still sexist? *The Reading Teacher, 41,* 288–292.

Hittleman, D. (1973). Seeking a psycholinguistic definition of readability. *The Reading Teacher, 26,* 783–789.

Hoffman, J. V. (1985). *The oral recitation lesson: A teacher's guide.* Austin, TX: Academic Resource Consultants.

Hoffman, J. V., McCarthy, S. J., Elliot, B., Bayles, D. L., Price, D. P., Ferree, A., & Abbott, J. A. (1998). The literature-based basals in first-grade classrooms: Savior, Satan or same-old? *Reading Research Quarterly, 33,* 168–197.

Hoffman, J. V., Roser, N. L., & Battle, J. (1993). Reading aloud in classrooms: From the modal to a "model." *The Reading Teacher, 46,* 496–503.

Hoffman, J. V., Sailors, M., Patterson, E. U. (2002). Decodable texts for beginning reading instruction: The year 2000 basals. *CIERA Report #1-016.* Ann Arbor, MI: Center for Improvement of Early Reading Achievement.

Holdaway, D. (1979). *The foundations of literacy.* Portsmouth, NH: Heinemann.

Holdaway, D. (1982). Shared book experience: Teaching reading using favorite books. *Theory into Practice, 23,* 293–300.

Hopkin, M., Hopkin, M., Gunyuz, P., Fowler, A., Edmison, R., Rivera, H., & Ruberto, L. (1997). Designing a user-friendly curriculum guide for practical application in an integrated language arts classroom. *The Reading Teacher, 50,* 410–416.

Huck, C. S., Hepler, S., & Hickman, J. (1987). *Children's literature in the elementary school* (4th ed.). Fort Worth, TX: Holt, Rinehart and Winston.

Hunt, L. C. (1970). Effect of self-selection, interest, and motivation upon independent, instructional, and frustrational levels. *The Reading Teacher, 24,* 146–151.

Hunt, N., & Marshall, K. (1999). *Exceptional children and youth* (2nd ed.). Boston: Houghton Mifflin.

Hymes, D. (1974). *Foundations in sociolinguistics: An ethnographic approach.* Philadelphia: University of Pennsylvania Press.

Hymes, J. L. (1958). *Before the child reads.* Evanston, IL: Row & Peterson.

Ignoffo, M. (1980). The thread of thought: Analogies as a vocabulary building method. *Journal of Reading, 23,* 519–521.

Ikpeze, C. H., & Boyd, F. B. (2007). Web-based inquiry learning: Facilitating thoughtful literacy with WebQuests. *The Reading Teacher, 60,* 644–654.

International Reading Association. (1998). *Standards for reading professionals.* Newark, DE: International Reading Association.

International Reading Association. (1999a). *High-stakes assessment in reading.* Newark, DE: International Reading Association.

International Reading Association. (1999b). *Using multiple methods of beginning reading instruction: A position statement from the International Reading Association.* Newark, DE: International Reading Association.

International Reading Association. (2000a). *Making a difference means making it different: Honoring children's rights to excellent reading instruction.* Newark, DE: International Reading Association.

International Reading Association. (2000b). *Providing books and other print materials for classroom and school libraries: A position statement of the International Reading Association.* Newark, DE: International Reading Association.

International Reading Association. (2000c). *A tour and an invitation.* Retrieved June 8, 2007, from www.readingonline .org/newliteracies/lit_index.asp?HREF=wattspailliotet1/ tour.html

International Reading Association. (2001). *Second-language literacy instruction: A position statement of the International Reading Association.* Newark, DE: Author.

International Reading Association. (2002a). *Integrating literacy and technology in the curriculum: A position statement of the International Reading Association.* Newark, DE: International Reading Association.

International Reading Association. (2002b). *What is evidence-based reading instruction: A position statement of the International Reading Association.* Newark, DE: International Reading Association.

International Reading Association. (2003). *Standards for reading professionals—Revised 2003.* Newark, DE: International Reading Association.

International Reading Association. (2004). *The role and qualifications of the reading coach in the United States: A position statement of the International Reading Association.* Newark, DE: Author.

International Reading Association. (2005). *Literacy development in the preschool years: A position statement of the International Reading Association.* Newark, DE: Author.

International Reading Association and National Association for the Education of Young Children. (1998). *Learning to read and write: Developmentally appropriate practices for young children: A joint position statement of the International Reading Association and the National Association for the Education of Young Children.* Newark, DE: International Reading Association. Urbana, IL: National Council of Teachers of English.

International Reading Association and National Council of Teachers of English. (1996). *Standards for the English language arts.* Newark, DE: International Reading Association.

Invernizzi, M., Juel, C., & Rosemary, C. A. (1997). A community volunteer tutorial that works. *The Reading Teacher, 50*(4), 304–311.

Ioga, C. (1995). *The inner world of the immigrant child.* Mahwah, NJ: Erlbaum.

Irvin, J. L. (1998). *Reading and the middle school student: Strategies to enhance literacy.* Boston: Allyn & Bacon.

Irwin, J. W., & Davis, C. A. (1980). Assessing readability: The checklist approach. *Journal of Reading, 24*, 124–130.

Isakson, M. B., & Boody, R. M. (1993). Hard questions about teaching research. In L. Patterson, C. M. Santa, K. Short, & K. Smith (Eds.), *Teachers are researchers.* Newark, DE: International Reading Association.

Ivey, G., & Fisher, D. (2006). When thinking skills trump reading skills. *Educational Leadership, 64*(2), 16–21.

Jacobi-Karna, K. (1995). Music and children's books. *The Reading Teacher, 49*, 265–269.

Jimenez, R. T. (2004). More equitable literacy assessments for Latino students. *The Reading Teacher, 57*, 576–578.

Johns, J. L. (1985). *Basic reading inventory* (3rd ed.). Dubuque, IA: Kendall-Hunt.

Johns, J. L., & Ellish-Piper, L. (1997). *Balanced reading instructions: Teachers' visions and voices.* Dubuque, IA: Kendall-Hunt.

Johnson, D. W., & Johnson, R. T. (1989–1990). Social skills for successful group work. *Educational Leadership, 47*(4), 29–33.

Johnson, J., Christie, J., & Wardle, F. (2005). Play, development and early education. Boston: Allyn & Bacon.

Johnston, F. R. (1998). The reader, the text, and the task: Learning words in first grade. *The Reading Teacher, 51*, 666–675.

Johnston, F. R. (1999). The timing and teaching of word families. *The Reading Teacher, 53*, 64–75.

Johnston, P., & Costello, P. (2005). Principles for literacy assessment. *Reading Research Quarterly, 40*(2), 256–267.

Juel, C. (1988). Learning to read and write: A longitudinal study of fifty-four children from first through fourth grade. *Journal of Educational Psychology, 80*, 437–447.

Juel, C., & Minden-Cupp, C. (2000). Learning to read words: Linguistic units and instructional strategies. *Reading Research Quarterly, 35*, 458–492.

Kagan, S. (1989). *Cooperative learning: Resources for teachers.* San Juan Capistrano, CA: Resources for Teachers.

Kame'enui, E. J. (1993). A special issue on innovations in literacy for a diverse society. *The Reading Teacher, 46*, 539.

Kame'enui, E. J., Simmons, D. C., Clark, D., & Dickson, S. (1997). Direct instruction reading. In S. A. Stahl & D. A. Hayes (Eds.), *Instructional models in reading.* Mahwah, NJ: Erlbaum.

Kamii, C. (1991). What is constructivism? In C. Kamii, M. Manning, & G. Manning (Eds.), *Early literacy: A constructivist foundation for whole language.* Washington, DC: National Education Association.

Kamil, M. L., & Pearson, P. D. (1979). Theory and practice in teaching reading. *New York University Education Quarterly, 10*, 10–16.

Kara-Soteriou, J., Zawilinski, L., & Henry, L. A. (2007). Children's books and technology in the classroom: A dynamic combo for supporting the writing workshop. *The Reading Teacher, 60*, 698–707.

Karchmer, R., Mallette, M., Kara-Soteriou, J., & Leu, D. (2005). *Innovative approaches to literacy education: Using the Internet to support new literacies.* Newark, DE: International Reading Association.

Kasten, W. C., & Lolli, E. M. (1998). *Implementing multiage education: A practical guide.* Norwood, MA: Christopher-Gordon.

Keegan, B., & Shake, K. (1991). Literature study groups: An alternative to ability grouping. *The Reading Teacher, 44*, 542–547.

Keene, E. O., & Zimmerman, S. (1997). *Mosaic of thought: Teaching comprehension in a reader's workshop.* Portsmouth, NH: Heinemann.

Kieffer, R. D., & Morrison, L. S. (1994). Changing portfolio process: One journey toward authentic assessment. *Language Arts, 71*, 411–418.

Kinch, A., & Azer, S. L. (2002). *Promoting early childhood literacy: Highlights of state efforts.* Washington, DC: National Association for the Education of Young Children.

Kinzer, C. K. (2005). The intersection of schools, communities, and technology: Recognizing children's use of new literacies. In R. A. Karchmer, M. H. Mallette, J. Kara-Soteriou, & D. J. Leu, Jr. (Eds.), *Innovative approaches to literacy education: Using the Internet to support new literacies* (pp. 65–82). Newark, DE: International Reading Association.

Kist, W. (2005). *New literacies in action: Teaching and learning in multiple media*. New York: Teachers College Press.

Klein, G. (2006, May 1). "iPods, Podcasts latest teaching tool in classrooms." *PotomacNews.com*. Retrieved July 19, 2007, from www.potomacnews.com/servlet/Satellite?pagename=WPN/MGArticle/WPN_BasicArticle&c=MGArticle&cid=1137835724174

Klein, M. L. (1985). *The development of writing in children: Pre-K through grade 8*. Upper Saddle River, NJ: Prentice Hall.

Klesius, J. P., & Griffith, P. H. (1998). Interactive storybook reading for at-risk learners. *The Reading Teacher, 49*, 552–560.

Kletzien, S. B., & Dreher, M. J. (2004). *Informational text in K–3 classrooms: Helping children read and write*. Newark, DE: International Reading Association.

Klinger, J. K., & Edwards, P. A. (2006). Cultural considerations with response to intervention models. *Reading Research Quarterly, 41*, 108–117.

Knickerbocker, K. L. (Ed.). (1985). *Interpreting literature* (7th ed.). Fort Worth, TX: Harcourt Brace College Publishers.

KnowledgeWorks Foundation. (n.d.). *KnowledgeWorks Foundation: Empowering communities to improve education*. Retrieved September 3, 2007, from www.kwfdn.org

Kobrin, B. (1995). *Eye openers II: How to choose and use children's books about real people and things*. New York: Penguin.

Koskinen, P., & Blum, I. (1986). Paired repeated reading: A classroom strategy for developing fluent reading. *The Reading Teacher, 40*, 70–75.

Koskinen, P. S., & Blum, I. H. (1986). Repeated oral reading and acquisition of fluency. In J. A. Niles & L. A. Harris (Eds.), *Changing perspectives on research in reading/language processing and instruction. Thirty-Third Yearbook of the National Reading Conference* (pp. 183–187). Rochester, NY: National Reading Conference.

Koskinen, P. S., Blum, I. H., Bisson, S. A., Phillips, S. M., Creamer, T. S., & Baker, T. K. (1999). Shared reading, books, and audiotapes: Supporting diverse students in school and at home. *The Reading Teacher, 52*, 430–444.

Kostelnik, M. J., Soderman, A. K., & Whiren, A. P. (2004). *Developmentally appropriate curriculum: Best practices in early childhood education* (3rd ed.). Upper Saddle River, NJ: Pearson/Merrill/Prentice Hall.

Krashen, S. (2003). Three roles for reading for minority-language children. In G. Garcia (Ed.), *English learners: Reaching the highest levels of English literacy* (pp. 55–70). Newark, DE: International Reading Association.

Krashen, S. (2004a). False claims about literacy development. *Educational Leadership, 61*, 18–21.

Krashen, S. (2004b). *The power of reading*. Portsmouth, NH: Heinemann.

Kraus, C. (1983). The influence of first-grade teachers' conceptual frameworks of reading on their students' perceptions of reading and reading behavior. Ph.D. diss., Kent State University.

Kress, G. (2003). *Literacy in the media age*. London: Routledge.

Kuhn, M. R., & Stahl, S. A. (2000). *Fluency: A review of developmental and remedial practices* (CIERA Rep. No. 2-008). Ann Arbor, MI: Center for the Improvement of Early Reading Achievement.

Kurtz, J. (1998). *The Storyteller's Beads*. San Diego, CA: Harcourt.

Kymes, A. (2005). Teaching online comprehension strategies using think-alouds. *Journal of Adolescent & Adult Literacy, 48*, 492–500.

Labbo, L., Love, M., & Ryan, T. (2007). A vocabulary flood: Making words "sticky" with computer-response activities. *The Reading Teacher, 60*(6), 582–588.

Labbo, L., & Teale, W. (1990). Cross-age reading: A strategy for helping poor readers. *The Reading Teacher, 43*, 362–369.

Labbo, L. D. (2000). 12 things young children can do with a talking book in a classroom computer center. *The Reading Teacher, 53*(7), 542–546.

Labbo, L. D. (2004). Author's computer chair. *The Reading Teacher, 57*(7), 688–691.

Labbo, L. D., Eakle, A. J., & Montero, M. K. (2002). Digital language experience approach: Using digital photographs and software as a language experience approach innovation. *Reading Online, 5*(8). Retrieved July 31, 2007, from www.readingonline.org/electronic/elec_index.asp?HREF=labbo2/index.html

Ladson-Billings, G. (1992). Reading between the lines and beyond the pages: A culturally relevant approach to literacy teaching. *Theory into Practice, 28*, 312–320.

Laier, B. B., Edwards, P. A., McMillon, G. T., & Turner, J. D. (2001). Connecting home and school values through multicultural literature and family stories. In P. Ruggiano Schmidt & A. W. Pailliotet (Eds.), *Exploring values through literature, multimedia, and literacy events* (pp. 64–75). Newark, DE: International Reading Association.

Lamme, L. L. (1984). *Growing up writing*. Washington, DC: Acropolis.

Landt, S. (2006). Multicultural literature and young adolescents: A kaleidoscope of opportunity. *Journal of Adolescent & Adult Literacy, 49*(8), 690–697.

Lapp, D., Fisher, D., Flood, J., & Cabello, A. (2001). An integrated approach to the teaching and assessment of language arts. In S. Hurley & J. V. Tinajero (Eds.), *Literacy assessment of second language learners* (pp. 11–26). Boston: Allyn & Bacon.

Lauritzen, C. (1982). A modification of repeated readings for group instruction. *The Reading Teacher, 35*, 456–458.

Lazar, A. M. (2004). *Learning to be literacy teachers in urban schools: Stories of growth and change*. Newark, DE: International Reading Association.

Lehman, B., Freeman, D., & Allen, R. (1994). Children's literature and literacy instruction: "Literature-based" elementary teacher's belief and practices. *Reading Horizons, 35*(1), 3–29.

Leland, C., & Fitzpatrick, R. (1994). Cross-age interaction builds enthusiasm for reading and writing. *The Reading Teacher, 47*, 292–301.

Lenhart, L., & Roskos, K. (2003). What Hannah taught Emma and why it matters. In D. M. Barone & L. M.

Morrow (Eds.), *Research based practice in early literacy* (pp. 83–100). New York: Guilford Press.

Lenters, K. (2004/2005). No half measures: Reading instruction for young second-language learners. *The Reading Teacher, 58,* 328–336.

Leslie, L., & Jett-Simpson, M. (1997). *Authentic literacy assessment.* New York: Longman.

Leu, D., Kinzer, C., Coiro, J., & Cammack, D. (2004). Toward a theory of new literacies emerging from the Internet and other information and communication technologies. In R. B. Ruddell & N. J. Unrau (Eds.), *Theoretical models and processes of reading* (pp. 1570–1613). Newark, DE: International Reading Association.

Leu, D. J. (2000). Literacy and technology: Diectic consequences for literacy education in an information age. In M. L. Kamil, P. B. Mosenthal, P. D. Pearson, & R. Barr (Eds.), *Handbook of reading research* (Vol. 3, pp. 743–770). Mahwah, NJ: Erlbaum.

Leu, D. J., Castek, J., Henry, L. A., Coiro, J., & McMullan, M. (2004). The lessons that children teach us: Integrating children's literature and the new literacies of the Internet. *The Reading Teacher, 57,* 496–503.

Leu, D. J., Jr. (2002a). Internet workshop: Making time for literacy. *The Reading Teacher, 55,* 466–472.

Leu, D. J., Jr. (2002b). The new literacies: Research on reading instruction with the Internet. In A. E. Farstrup & S. J. Samuels (Eds.), *What research has to say about reading instruction* (pp. 310–336). Newark, DE: International Reading Association.

Leu, D. J., Jr., & Kinzer, C. K. (2000). The convergence of literacy instruction with networked technologies for information and communication. *Reading Research Quarterly, 35*(1), 108–127.

Leu, D. J., Jr., & Leu, D. D. (1999). *Teaching with the Internet: Lessons from the classroom* (2nd ed.). Norwood, MA: Christopher-Gordon.

Leu, D. J., Jr., & Leu, D. D. (2000). *Teaching with the Internet: Lessons from the classroom* (3rd ed.). Norwood, MA: Christopher-Gordon.

Levine, G. C. (1999). *Dave at night.* New York: HarperCollins.

Levine, S. G. (1984). USSR: A necessary component in teaching reading. *Journal of Reading, 27,* 394–400.

Lewis, C. (1993). "Give people a chance": Acknowledging social differences in reading. *Language Arts, 10,* 454–461.

Lewis, C., & Fabos, B. (2005). Instant messaging, literacies, and social identities. *Reading Research Quarterly, 40*(4), 470–501.

Lexile. (n.d.). *The Lexile framework for reading: Matching readers to text.* Retrieved September 3, 2007, from www.lexile.com/EntrancePageFlash.html

Liberman, I. Y., Shankweiler, D., Fisher, F. W., & Carter, B. (1974). Explicit syllable and phoneme segmentation in the young child. *Journal of Experimental Child Psychology, 18,* 201–212.

Lipsky, D. K., & Gartner, A. (1997). *Inclusion and school reform: Transforming America's classrooms.* Baltimore: Paul H. Brookes.

Littlewood, W. (1984). *Foreign and second language learning.* New York: Cambridge University Press.

Livingston, N., & Kurkjiam, C. (2003). Timeless and treasured books. *The Reading Teacher, 57,* 96–103.

Lobel, Arnold. (1979). *Days with frog and toad.* New York: HarperCollins.

Locke, D. C. (1989). Fostering the self-esteem of African-American children. *Elementary School Guidance and Counseling, 23,* 254–259.

Long, C. (2007). Podcasting the 1600s: Old world meets new when student podcasts bring the Jamestown settlement to life. *NEA Today.* Retrieved July, 19, 2007, from www.nea.org/neatoday/0703/features6.html.

Lynch, E. W. (2006). Developing cross-cultural competence. In E. W. Lynch & M. J. Hanson (Eds.), *Developing cross-cultural competence: A guide for working with children and their families* (pp. 41–77). Baltimore: Paul H. Brooks.

Lyon, G. R., & Chhabra, V. (2004). The science of reading research. *Educational Leadership, 61,* 12–17.

Lyons, C., & Pinnell, G. (2001). *Systems for change in literacy education: A guide to professional development.* Portsmouth, NH: Heinemann.

MacArthur, C. A., & Haynes, J. B. (1995). Student assistant for learning from text (SALT): A hypermedia reading aid. *Journal of Learning Disabilities, 28,* 150–159.

MacGinitie, W. H. (1993). Some limits of assessment. *Journal of Reading, 26,* 556–560.

Machado, A. M. (1996). *Nina Bonita: A story.* Brooklyn, NY: Kane/Miller Book Publishers.

Mandler, J., & Johnson, N. (1977). Remembrance of things parsed: Story structure and recall. *Cognitive Psychology, 9,* 111–151.

Manitone, R. D., & Smead, S. (2003). *Weaving through words: Using the arts to teach reading comprehension strategies.* Newark, DE: International Reading Association.

Manuel, L. (2006). *The trouble with Tilly Trumble.* Waterbury, CT: Abrams.

Manzo, A. V. (1969). The request procedure. *Journal of Reading, 11,* 123–126.

Marchbanks, G., & Levin, H. (1965). Cues by which children recognize words. *Journal of Educational Psychology, 56,* 57–61.

Marsalis, W. (2005). *Jazz ABZ.* Cambridge, MA: Candlewick.

Marshall, J. (2001). Critical literacy and visual art: A living experience. In L. Ramirez & O. M. Gallardo, *Portraits of teachers in multicultural settings: A critical literacy approach* (pp. 87–103). Boston: Allyn & Bacon.

Martin, B., & Brogan, P. (1970). *Sounds of a powwow.* New York: Holt, Rinehart and Winston.

Martinez, M., Roser, N. L., & Strecker, S. (1998/1999). "I never thought I could be a star." A reader's ticket to fluency. *The Reading Teacher, 52*(4), 326–334.

Mathers, P. (1995). *Kisses from Rosa.* New York: Knopf.

McCaslin, N. (1990). *Creative drama in the classroom* (5th ed.). New York: Longman.

McCracken, R. A. (1971). Initiating sustained silent reading. *Journal of Reading, 14,* 521–524, 582–583.

McCracken, R. A., & McCracken, M. J. (1978). Modeling is the key to sustained reading. *The Reading Teacher, 31,* 406–408.

McDonald, F. J. (1965). *Educational psychology.* Belmont, CA: Wadsworth.

McDonnell, G. M., & Osburn, E. B. (1978). New thoughts about reading readiness. *Language Arts, 55,* 26–29.

McGinley, W. J., & Denner, P. R. (1987). Story impressions: A pre-reading/writing activity. *Journal of Reading, 31,* 248–253.

McIntyre, E., Kyle, D. W., Gregory, K. M., Moore, G. H., Wheatley, V. A., Clyde, J. A., & Houda, R. A. (1996).

Teaching young readers and writers in multi-age classrooms. *Language Arts, 73,* 384–394.

McKenna, M., & Picard, M. (2006/2007). Revisiting the role of miscue analysis in effective teaching. *The Reading Teacher, 60*(4), 378–380.

McKenna, M. C., Kear, D. J., & Ellsworth, R. A. (1995). Children's attitudes toward reading: A national survey. *Reading, Research Quarterly, 30*(4), 934–955.

McKeon, C. A. (1999). The nature of children's e-mail in one classroom. *The Reading Teacher, 52*(7), 698–706.

McKeon, C. A. (2001). E-mail as a motivating literacy event for one struggling reader: Donna's case. *Reading Research & Instruction, 40*(3), 185–202.

McKeon, C. A., & Burkey, L. C. (1998). A literature-based e-mail collaborative. In E. G. Sturtevant, J. A. Dugan, P. Linder, & W. M. Linek (Eds.), *Literacy and community: The twentieth yearbook of the College Reading Association* (pp. 84–93). Texas A&M University-Commerce.

McKeown, M. G., & Beck, I. L. (2004). Direct and rich vocabulary instruction. In J. F. Baumann & E. J. Kame'enui (Eds.), *Vocabulary instruction* (pp. 13–27). New York: Guilford Press.

McMahon, P. (2000). *Dancing wheels.* Boston: Houghton Mifflin.

McMahon, S. I. (1997). Book clubs: Contexts for students to lead their own discussions. In S. I. McMahon & T. E. Raphael (Eds.), *The book club connection* (pp. 89–106). New York: Teachers College Press.

McQuillan, J. (1998). *The literacy crisis: False claims, real solution.* Portsmouth, NH: Heinemann.

McTighe, J., & Lyman, F. T. (1988). Cueing thinking in the classroom: The promise of theory-embedded tools. *Educational Leadership, 45*(7), 18–24.

Meehan, P. (1998). Beyond a chocolate crunch bar: A teacher examines her philosophy of teaching reading. *The Reading Teacher, 51,* 314–324.

Mesmer, H. A. (2001). Examining the theoretical claims about decodable text: Does text decodability lead to greater application of letter/sound knowledge in first-grade readers? In J. V. Hoffman, D. L. Schallert, C. M. Fairbanks, J. Worthy, & B. Maloch (Eds.), *Fiftieth Yearbook of the National Reading Conference* (pp. 444–459). Chicago: National Reading Conference.

Mesmer, H. A. (2006). Beginning reading materials: A national survey of primary teachers' reported uses and beliefs. *Journal of Literacy Research, 38*(4), 389–425.

Mezynski, K. (1983). Issues concerning the acquisition of knowledge: Effects of vocabulary training on reading comprehension. *Review of Educational Research, 53,* 258–279.

Mike, D. G. (1996). Internet in the schools: A literacy perspective. *Journal of Adolescent and Adult Literacy, 40,* 4–13.

Moats, L. (2006, Winter). How spelling supports reading. *American Educator,* 12–22.

Moffett, J. (1975). An interview with James Moffett. *Media and Methods, 15,* 20–24.

Mohr, K. A. (2003). "I want that book!": First-graders' preferences for expository text. In M. B. Sampson, P. E. Linder, J. A. R. Dugan, & B. Brancato (Eds.), *Celebrating the freedom of literacy: The Twenty-Fifth Yearbook of the College Reading Association* (pp. 71–85). Texas A&M University-Commerce.

Mohr, K. A. J., & Mohr, E. S. (2007). Extending English-language learners' classroom interactions using the response protocol. *The Reading Teacher, 60,* 440–450.

Moll, L. C. (1989). Teaching second language students: A Vygotskian perspective. In D. M. Johnson & D. H. Roen (Eds.), *Richness in writing: Empowering ESL students.* New York: Longman.

Montali, J., & Lewandowski, L. (1996). Bimodal reading: Benefits of a talking computer for average and less skilled readers. *Journal of Learning Disabilities, 29,* 271–279.

Moore, D. W., Bean, T. W., Birdyshaw, D., & Rycik, J. A. (1999). Adolescent literacy: A position statement. *Journal of Adolescent & Adult Literacy, 43*(1), 97–112.

Mora, J. K. (2006). Differentiating instruction for English learners: The four-by-four model. In T. A. Young & N. L. Hadaway (Eds.), *Supporting the literacy development of English learners: Increasing success in all classrooms* (pp. 24–40). Newark, DE: International Reading Association.

Morphett, M. V., & Washburne, C. (1931). When should children begin to read? *Elementary School Journal, 31,* 496–503.

Morris, D., & Nelson, L. (1992). Supported oral reading with low-achieving second graders. *Reading Research and Instruction, 31,* 49–63.

Morrow, L. (2003). Motivating lifelong voluntary readers. In J. Flood, D. Lapp, J. Squire, & J. Jensen (Eds.), *Handbook of research on teaching the English language arts* (pp. 857–867). Mahwah, NJ: Erlbaum.

Morrow, L., Kuhn, M., & Schwanenflugel, P. (2007). The family literacy program. *The Reading Teacher, 60*(1), 322–333.

Morrow, L. M. (1985). *Promoting voluntary reading in school and home.* Bloomington, IN: Phi Delta Kappa Educational Foundation.

Morrow, L. M. (1990). Preparing the classroom environment to promote literacy during play. *Early Childhood Research Quarterly, 5,* 537–554.

Morrow, L. M., & Gambrell, L. B. (2000). Literature based reading instruction. In M. L. Kamil, P. B. Mosenthal, P. D. Pearson, & R. Barr (Eds.), *Handbook of reading research* (Vol. 3, pp. 563–586). Mahwah, NJ: Erlbaum.

Morrow, L. M., & Weinstein, C. S. (1982). Increasing children's use of literature through program and physical design changes. *Elementary School Journal, 83,* 131–137.

Moss, B. (1991). Children's nonfiction trade books: A complement to content area texts. *The Reading Teacher, 45,* 26–31.

Moss, B., & Hendershot, J. (2002). Exploring sixth graders' selection of nonfiction trade books. *The Reading Teacher, 56,* 6–17.

Moustafa, M. (1997). *Beyond traditional phonics.* Portsmouth, NH: Heinemann.

Moustafa, M., & Maldonado-Colon, E. (1999). Whole-to-parts phonics instruction: Building on what children know to help them know more. *The Reading Teacher, 52,* 448–458.

Mraz, M. (2000). The literacy program selection process from the perspective of school district administrators. *The Ohio Reading Teacher, 35,* 2, 40–48.

Munsch, R. N. (1980). *The paperbag princess.* Toronto: Annick Press.

Munsch, R. N. (1985). *Thomas' snowsuit.* Toronto: Annick Press.

Munsch, R. N. (1989). *Love you forever.* Toronto: Firefly Books.

Murphy, H. A. (1957). The spontaneous speaking vocabulary of children in primary grades. *Journal of Education, 146,* 1–105.

Nagy, W., (1988). *Teaching vocabulary to improve reading comprehension*. Urbana, IL: National Council of Teachers of English.

Nagy, W., & Scott, J. (2004). Vocabulary processes. In R. B. Ruddell & N. J. Unrau (Eds.), *Theoretical models and processes of reading* (pp. 574–593). Newark, DE: International Reading Association.

Nagy, W., & Scott, J. A. (2000). Vocabulary processes. In M. Kamil, P. Mosenthal, P. Pearson, & R. Barr (Eds.), *Handbook of reading research* (Vol. 3, pp. 269–284). Mahwah, NJ: Erlbaum.

Nathan, R. (1995). Parents, projects, and portfolios: 'Round and about community building in Room 14. *Language Arts, 72*, 82–87.

National Center for Education Statistics (NCES). (1995). *Listening to children read aloud: Oral fluency*. Retrieved on October 10, 2004, from http://nces.ed.gov/pubs95/web/95762.asp

National Institute of Child Health and Human Development (2000). *Report of the National Reading Panel. Teaching children to read: An evidence based assessment of the scientific research literature on reading and its implications for reading instruction* (NIH Publication No. 00-4769). Washington, DC: U.S. Government Printing Office.

National Institute of Education, Commission on Reading. (1985). *Becoming a nation of readers: The report of the commission on reading*. Washington, DC: National Institute of Education.

National Reading Panel. (2000). *Teaching children to read: An evidence-based assessment of the scientific research literature on reading and its implications for reading instruction*. Washington, DC: National Institute of Child Health and Human Development.

Neisser, U. (1976). *Cognition and reality: Principles and implications of cognitive psychology*. New York: Freeman.

Nelson, J. (1978). Readability: Some cautions for the content area teacher. *Journal of Reading, 21*, 620–625.

Neuman, S. (2006). How we neglect knowledge and why. *American Educator, Spring*, 24–27.

Neuman, S., & Roskos, K. (1998). *Children achieving: Best practices in early literacy*. Newark, DE: International Reading Association.

Neuman, S., Roskos, K., Wright, T., & Lenhart, L. (2007). *Nurturing knowledge: Building a foundation for school success by linking early literacy to math, science, art, and social studies*. New York: Scholastic.

Neuman, S. B., Caperelli, B. J., & Kee, C. (1998). Literacy learning: A family matter. *The Reading Teacher, 52*, 244–252.

Neuman, S. B., & Roskos, K. A. (1990). Play, print, and purpose: Enriching play environments for literacy development. *The Reading Teacher, 44*, 214–221.

Neuman, S. B., & Roskos, K. A. (1993). Access to print for children of poverty: Differential effects of adult mediation and literacy-enriched play settings in environmental and functional print tasks. *American Educational Research Journal, 30*, 95–122.

Neuman, S. B., & Roskos, K. A. (1997). Literacy knowledge in practice: Contexts of participation for young writers and readers. *Reading Research Quarterly, 32*, 10–32.

Niguidula, D. (2005). Documenting learning with digital portfolios. *Educational Leadership, 63*(3), 44–47.

No Child Left Behind Act of 2001, U.S. Public Law 107-110, 107th Cong., 1st session (2002).

Noden, H., & Vacca, R. T. (1994). *Whole language in middle and secondary classrooms*. New York: HarperCollins.

Nolte, R. Y., & Singer, H. (1985). Active comprehension: Teaching a process of reading comprehension and its effects on reading achievement. *The Reading Teacher, 39*, 24–28.

North Carolina Department of Public Instruction. (2004). *English language arts curriculum guide*. Retrieved October 17, 2004, from www.ncpublicschools.org/curriculum/languagearts

Northwest Evaluation Association. (n.d.). *Northwest Evaluation Association assessment system*. Retrieved September 3, 2007, from www.nwea.org/assessments/

Norton, D. E. (1980). *The effective teaching of language arts*. Columbus, OH: Merrill.

O'Day, S. (2006). *Setting the stage for creative writing: Plot scaffolds for beginning and intermediate writers*. Newark, DE: International Reading Association.

Oakes, J. S. (1999). Limiting students' school success and life chances: The impact of tracking. In A. C. Ornstein & L. S. Behar-Horenstein (Eds.), *Contemporary issues in curriculum* (2nd ed.). Boston: Allyn & Bacon.

Oberman, S. (1994). *The always prayer shawl*. Honesdale, PA: Boyds Mills Press.

Obiakor, F. E. (2007). *Multicultural special education: Culturally responsive teaching*. Upper Saddle River, NJ: Pearson.

Oczkus, L. D. (2003). *Reciprocal teaching at work: Strategies for improving reading comprehension*. Newark, DE: International Reading Association.

Ogle, D. M. (1986). K-W-L: A teaching model that develops active reading of expository text. *The Reading Teacher, 39*, 564–571.

Ohio Department of Education. (2001a). *Academics content standards: K–12 English language arts*. Columbus, OH: Ohio Department of Education.

Ohio Department of Education. (2001b). *What is the process for planning and delivering standards-based instruction?* Retrieved on October 22, 2004, from http://ims.ode.state.oh.us

Ohio Department of Education. (2004). *Early learning content standards: English language arts*. Columbus, OH: Center for Curriculum and Assessment and Center for Students, Families, and Communities.

Ohio Literacy Alliance (n.d.). *Quick and easy high school reading assessments*. Retrieved September 3, 2007, from www.ohioliteracyalliance.org/fluency/fluency.htm

Ohnmacht, D. C. (1969). *The effects of letter knowledge on achievement in reading in the first grade*. Paper presented at the annual meeting of the American Education Research Association, Los Angeles.

Olness, R. (2005). *Using literature to enhance writing instruction: A guide for K–5 teachers*. Newark, DE: International Reading Association.

Olness, R. (2007). *Using literature to enhance content area reading instruction*. Newark, DE: International Reading Association.

Opitz, M. F. (1999). Cultural diversity + supportive text = perfect books for beginning readers. *The Reading Teacher, 52*(8), 888–890.

Ovando, C. J., Collier, V. P., & Combs, M. C. (2003). *Bilingual and ESL classrooms: Teaching in multicultural contexts* (3rd ed.). Boston: McGraw-Hill.

Padak, N., & Rasinski, T. (2008). *Evidence-based instruction in reading: A professional development guide to fluency*. Boston, MA: Allyn & Bacon.

Palincsar, A., & Brown, A. L. (1984). Reciprocal teaching of comprehension-fostering and comprehension-monitoring activities. *Cognition and Instruction, 1*, 117–175.

Palmer, R., & Stewart, R. (2003). Nonfiction trade book use in primary grades. *The Reading Teacher, 57*, 38–47.

Paratore, J. R., & Jordan, G. (2007). Starting out together: A home–school partnership for preschool and beyond. *The Reading Teacher, 60*(7), 694–696.

Park, L. S. (2001). *A single shard.* New York: Dell Yearling.

Patterson, A. (1992). *A field guide to rock art symbols of the greater Southwest.* Boulder, CO: Johnson Books.

Pearson, D., Heibert, E., & Kamil, M. (2007). Vocabulary assessment: What we know and what we need to learn. *Reading Research Quarterly, 42*(2), 282–296.

Pearson, P. D. (1982). *Asking questions about stories.* New York: Ginn.

Pearson, P. D. (1984). Guided reading: A response to Isabel Beck. In R. C. Anderson, J. Osborn, & R. Tierney (Eds.), *Learning to read in American schools: Basal readers and content texts* (pp. 21–26). Mahwah, NJ: Erlbaum.

Pearson, P. D. (1993). Teaching and learning reading: A research perspective. *Language Arts, 70*, 502–511.

Pearson, P. D. (1996). Reclaiming the center. In M. Graves, P. Vanden Broek, & B. Taylor (Eds.), *The first R: Every child's right to read* (pp. 259–274). New York: Teachers College Press.

Pearson, P. D., & Gallagher, M. (1983). The instruction of reading comprehension. *Contemporary Educational Psychology, 8*, 317–344.

Pearson, P. D., & Johnson, D. W. (1978). *Teaching reading comprehension.* Austin, TX: Holt, Rinehart and Winston.

Peck, J. (1989). Using storytelling to promote language and literacy development. *The Reading Teacher, 43*, 138–141.

Perez, B. (2001). Communicating and collaborating with linguistically diverse communities. In V. J. Risko & K. Bromely (Eds.), *Collaboration for diverse learners: Viewpoints and practices* (pp. 231–250). Newark, DE: International Reading Association.

Perfect, K. (1999). Rhyme and reason: Poetry for the heart and head. *The Reading Teacher, 52*(7), 728–737.

Perfetti, C. A. (1985). *Reading ability.* New York: Oxford University Press.

Piaget, J. (1970). *The science of education and the psychology of the child.* New York: Orion Press.

Piaget, J. (1973). *The language and thought of the child.* New York: World.

Pikulski, J. J. (1994). Preventing reading failure: A review of five effective programs. *The Reading Teacher, 48*, 30–38.

Pilgreen, J. (2006). Supporting English learners: Developing academic language in the content classroom. In T. A. Young & N. L. Hadaway (Eds.), *Supporting the literacy development of English learners: Increasing success in all classrooms* (pp. 41–60). Newark, DE: International Reading Association.

Pils, L. (1993). I love you, Miss Piss. *The Reading Teacher, 46*, 648–653.

Pransky, K., & Bailey, F. (2002–2003). To meet your students where they are, first you have to find them: Working with culturally and linguistically diverse at-risk students. *The Reading Teacher, 56*(4), 370–383.

Pressley, M. (1996). Concluding reflections. In E. McIntyre & M. Pressley (Eds.), *Balanced instruction: Strategies and skills in whole language.* Norwood, MA: Christopher-Gordon.

Pressley, M. (2000). What should comprehension instruction be the instruction of? In M. L. Kamil, P. B. Mosenthal, P. D. Pearson, & R. Barr (Eds.). *Handbook of Reading Research* (Vol. 3, pp. 545–561). Mahwah, NJ: Erlbaum.

Pressley, M. (2006). *Reading instruction that works: The case for balanced teaching.* New York: Guilford Press.

Pressley, M., Rankin, J., & Yokoi, L. (1996). A survey of instructional practices of primary grade teachers nominated as effective in promoting literacy. *Elementary School Journal, 96*, 363–384.

Pressley, M., Wharton-McDonald, R., Rankin, J., Yokoi, L., & Ettenberger, S. (1996). The nature of outstanding primary grade literacy instruction. In E. McIntyre & M. Pressley (Eds.), *Balanced instruction: Strategies and skills in whole language* (pp. 251–276). Norwood, MA: Christopher-Gordon.

Professional Standards and Ethics Committee, International Reading Association. (2003). *Standards for reading professionals—Revised 2003.* Newark, DE: International Reading Association.

Puig, E. A., & Froelich, K. S. (2007). *The literacy coach: Guiding in the right direction.* Boston: Pearson Education.

Pullman, T. (2000). Wanted posters. In L. Baines & A. J. Kunkel (Eds.), *Going Bohemian: Activities that engage adolescents in the art of writing well* (pp. 75–77). Newark, DE: International Reading Association.

Rae, D., & Mercuri, S. (2006). *Research-based strategies for English language learners.* Portsmouth, NH: Heinemann.

Rand Reading Study Group. (2002). *Reading for understanding: Toward an R&D program in reading comprehension.* Santa Monica, CA: Science and Technology Policy Institute, Rand Education.

Randall, S. N. (1996). Information charts: A strategy for organizing student research. *Journal of Adolescent and Adult Literacy, 39*, 536–542.

Raphael, T. E. (1982). Question-answering strategies for children. *The Reading Teacher, 36*, 186–191.

Raphael, T. E. (1986). Teaching question–answer relationships, revisited. *The Reading Teacher, 39*, 516–522.

Raphael, T., McMahon, S., Goatley, V., Boyd, C., Pardo, L., & Woodman, G. (1992). Literature and discussion in the reading program. *Language Arts, 69*(1), 54–61.

Rasinksi, T. V. (2004). Creating fluent readers, *Educational Leadership, 61*, 46–51.

Rasinski, T. V. (2003). *The fluent reader: Oral reading strategies for building word recognition, fluency, and comprehension.* New York: Scholastic.

Rasinski, T. V., & Fredericks, A. D. (1991). The Akron paired reading project. *The Reading Teacher, 44*, 514–515.

Rasinski, T. V., & Padak, N. D. (1996). *Holistic reading strategies: Teaching children who find reading difficult.* Columbus, OH: Merrill.

Rasinski, T. V., & Padak, N. D. (2000). *Effective reading strategies: Teaching children who find reading difficult.* Columbus, OH: Merrill.

Rasinski, T. V., & Padak, N. D. (2001). *From phonics to fluency: Effective teaching of decoding and reading fluency in elementary school.* New York: Longman.

Rasinski, T., & Padak, N. (2004). *Effective reading strategies: Teaching children who find reading difficult* (3rd ed.). Upper Saddle River, NJ: Pearson.

Rasinski, T. V., Padak, N. D., Linek, W. L., & Sturtevant, E. (1994). Effects of fluency development on urban second-grade readers. *Journal of Educational Research, 87*, 158–165.

Rasinski, T., Padak, N., McKeon, C., Wilfong, L., Friedauer, J., & Heim, P. (2005). Is reading fluency a key for successful high school reading? *Journal of Adolescent & Adult Literacy, 49*(1), 22–27.

Read, S. (2005). First and second graders writing informational text. *The Reading Teacher, 59,* 36–44.

Readence, J. E., Bean, T. W., & Baldwin, R. S. (2004). *Content area literacy: An integrated approach* (8th ed.). Dubuque, IA: Kendall/Hunt.

Reid, J. F. (1966). Learning to think about reading. *Educational Research, 9,* 56–62.

Reinking, D. (1995). Reading and writing with computers: Literacy research in a post-typographical world. In K. A. Hinderman, D. J. Leu Jr., & C. K. Kinzer (Eds.), *Perspectives on literacy research and practice* (pp. 17–33). Chicago: National Reading Conference.

Reinking, D. (1998). Synthesizing technological transformations of literacy in a post-typographic world. In D. Reinking, M. McKenna, L. D. Labbo, & R. Kieffer (Eds.), *Handbook of literacy and technology: Transformations in a post-typographic world* (pp. xi–xxx). Mahwah, NJ: Erlbaum.

Reinking, D., & Rickman, S. S. (1990). The effects of computer-mediated texts on the vocabulary learning and comprehension of intermediate-grade readers. *Journal of Reading Behavior, 22,* 395–411.

Reinking, D., McKenna, M. C., Labbo, L. D., & Kieffer, R. D. (Eds.). (1998). *Handbook of literacy and technology: Transformations in a post-typographic world.* Mahwah, NJ: Erlbaum.

Reutzel, D. R., & Cooter, R. B. (1991). Organizing for effective instruction: The reading workshop. *The Reading Teacher, 44,* 548–554.

Reutzel, D. R., & Cooter, R. B. (2002). *Strategies for assessment and instruction: Helping every child succeed.* Upper Saddle River, NJ: Merrill Prentice Hall.

Reyhner, J. (1986). Native Americans in basal reading textbooks: Are there enough? *Journal of American Indian Education, 26,* 14–22.

Rhodes, L. K. (1981). I can read! Predictable books as resources for reading and writing instruction. *The Reading Teacher, 34,* 314–318.

Rhodes, L. K., & Shanklin, N. (1993). *Windows into literacy: Assessing learners K–8.* Portsmouth, NH: Heinemann.

Rigg, P. (1989). Language experience approach: Reading naturally. In P. Rigg & V. Allen (Eds.), *When they don't all speak English: Integrating the ESL student into the regular classroom.* Urbana, IL: National Council of Teachers of English.

Roberts, J., Jurgens, J., & Burchinal, M. (2005). The role of home literacy practices in preschool children's language and emergent literacy skills. *Journal of Speech, Language, and Hearing Research, 48,* 345–359.

Robinson, H. A., Faraone, V., Hittleman, D. R., & Unruh, E. (1990). *Reading comprehension instruction, 1783–1987: A review of trends and research.* Newark, DE: International Reading Association.

Rodríguez, L. J. (1999). *It doesn't have to be this way: A barrio story.* San Francisco: Children's Book Press.

Roe, B. D. (2000). Using technology for content area literacy. In S. B. Wepner, W. J. Valmont, & R. Thurlow (Eds.), *Linking literacy and technology: A guide for K–8 classrooms* (pp. 133–158). Newark, DE: International Reading Association.

Rog, L. J. (2007). *Marvelous minilessons for teaching beginning writing, K–3.* Newark, DE: International Reading Association.

Romano, T. (1987). *Clearing the way: Working with teenage writers.* Portsmouth, NH: Heinemann.

Romano, T. (2000). *Blending genre, altering style.* Portsmouth, NH: Boynton/Cook.

Rose, K. (1982). *Teaching language arts to children.* Orlando, FL: Harcourt Brace.

Rosenblatt, L. (1982). The literary transaction: Evocation and response. *Theory into Practice, 21,* 268–277.

Rosenblatt, L. (2004). The transactional theory of reading and writing. In R. B. Ruddell & N. J. Unrau (Eds.), *Theoretical models and processes of reading* (pp. 1363–1398). Newark, DE: International Reading Association.

Roser, N. L., & Keehn, S. (2002). Fostering thought, talk, and inquiry: Linking literature and social studies. *The Reading Teacher, 55*(5), 416–426.

Roskos, K., Tabors, P., & Lenhart, L. (2004). *Oral language and early literacy in preschool: Talking, reading, and writing.* Newark, DE: International Reading Association.

Roskos, K. A. (1986). *The nature of literate behavior in the pretend play episodes of four- and five-year-old children.* Unpublished doctoral dissertation, Kent State University, Kent, Ohio.

Roskos, K. A. (1988). Literacy at work in play. *The Reading Teacher, 41,* 562–566.

Rosow, L. (1992). The story of Irma. *The Reading Teacher, 45,* 525.

Routman, R. (1991). *Invitations.* Portsmouth, NH: Heinemann.

Ruddell, R., & Unrau, N. (2004). The role of responsive teaching in focusing reader intention and developing reader motivation. In R. B. Ruddell & N. J. Unrau (Eds.), *Theoretical models and processes of reading* (pp. 954–978). Newark, DE: International Reading Association.

Rumelhart, D. E. (1982). Schemata: The building blocks of cognition. In J. Guthrie (Ed.), *Comprehension and teaching: Research reviews* (pp. 3–26). Newark, DE: International Reading Association.

Rupley, W. H., Logan, J. W., & Nichols, W. D. (1999). Vocabulary instruction in balanced reading programs. *The Reading Teacher, 52,* 336–346.

Russell, C. Y. (1994). *First apple.* Honesdale, PA: Boyds Mills.

Sample, K. (2005). Promoting fluency in adolescents with reading difficulties. *Intervention in School & Clinic, 40*(4), 243–246.

Samuels, S. J. (1972). The effect of letter–name knowledge on learning to read. *American Educational Research Journal, 1,* 65–74.

Samuels, S. J. (1976). Hierarchical subskills in the reading acquisition process. In J. T. Guthrie (Ed.), *Aspects of reading acquisition.* Baltimore, MD: Johns Hopkins University Press.

Samuels, S. J. (1979). Method of repeated readings. *The Reading Teacher, 32,* 403–408.

Samuels, S. J. (1988). Decoding and automaticity. *The Reading Teacher, 41,* 756–760.

Samuels, S. J. (1994). Toward a theory of automatic information processing in reading, revisited. In R. Ruddell,

M. Ruddell, & H. Singer (Eds.), *Theoretical models and processes of reading* (4th ed., pp. 816–837). Newark, DE: International Reading Association.

Samuels, S. J. (1996). Howling in the wind: Academics try to change classroom reading instruction. In M. Graves, P. Vanden Broek, & B. Taylor (Eds.), *The first R: Every child's right to read* (pp. 120–130). New York: Teachers College Press.

Samway, K. D., & Whang, G. (1996). *Literature study circles in a multicultural classroom.* York, ME: Stenhouse.

Sandmann, A. (2006). Nurturing thoughtful revision using the focused question card strategy. *Journal of Adolescent and Adult Literacy, 50,* 20–28.

Santa, C. M., Dailey, S. C., & Nelson, M. (1985). Free response and opinion proof: A reading and writing strategy for middle grade and secondary teachers. *Journal of Reading, 28,* 346–352.

Saul, E., & Dieckman, D. (2005). Choosing and using information trade books. *Reading Research Quarterly, 40*(4), 502–513.

Savage, J. F. (2004). *Sound it out! Phonics in a comprehensive reading program* (2nd ed.). New York: McGraw Hill.

Say, A. (1993). *Grandfather's journey.* Boston: Houghton Mifflin.

Scala, M. C. (2001). *Working together: Reading and writing in inclusive classrooms.* Newark, DE: International Reading Association.

Schickedanz, J. A. (1986). *More than the ABCs.* Washington, DC: National Association for the Education of Young Children.

Schickedanz, J. A. (1998). What is developmentally appropriate practice in early literacy? Considering the alphabet. In S. B. Neuman & K. A. Roskos (Eds.), *Children achieving: Best practices in early literacy* (pp. 20–37). Newark, DE: International Reading Association.

Schmidt, P. R. (1998a). The ABCs model: Teachers connect home and school. In T. Shanahan & F. Rodriguez-Brown (Eds.), *Forty-Seventh Yearbook of the National Reading Conference* (pp. 194–208). Chicago: National Reading Conference.

Schmidt, P. R. (1998b). The ABCs of cultural understanding and communication. *Equity and Excellence in Education, 31*(2), 28–38.

Schmidt, P. R. (1998c). *Cultural conflict and struggle: Literacy learning in a kindergarten program.* New York: Lang.

Schmidt, P. R. (1999). KWLQ: Inquiry and literacy learning in science. *The Reading Teacher, 52,* 789–792.

Schreiber, P. (1980). On the acquisition of reading fluency. *Journal of Reading Behavior, 12,* 177–186.

Schrum, L. (1995). Educators and the Internet: A case study of professional development. *Computers and Education, 24,* 221–228.

Schwartz, R. M. (2005). Decisions, decisions: Responding to primary students during guided reading. *The Reading Teacher, 58,* 436–443.

Searcy, B. (1988). Getting children into the literacy club— and keeping them there. *Childhood Education, 65,* 74–77.

Seuss, Dr. (1960). *One fish, two fish, red fish, blue fish.* New York: Beginner Books.

Sewell, G. T. (1987). *American history textbooks: An assessment of quality.* New York: Educational Excellence Network, Teachers College, Columbia University.

Shanahan, T. (1988). The reading–writing relationship: Seven instructional principles. *The Reading Teacher, 41,* 636–647.

Shanahan, T. (1990). *Reading and writing together. New perspectives for the classroom.* Norwood, MA: Christopher-Gordon.

Shanahan, T., & Neuman, S. B. (1997). Literacy research that makes a difference. *Reading Research Quarterly, 32,* 202–210.

Shanklin, N. L., & Rhodes, L. K. (1989). Comprehension instruction as sharing and extending. *The Reading Teacher, 42,* 496–501.

Sharpley, A. M., & Sharpley, C. F. (1981). Peer tutoring: A review of the literature. *Collected Original Resources in Education 5*(3), 7–11.

Shatz, E. K., & Baldwin, R. S. (1986). Context clues are unreliable predictors of word meanings. *Reading Research Quarterly, 21,* 429–453.

Shen, F. (2005). iPods fast becoming new teacher's pet. *The Washington Post,* p. B01.

Shiel, G., & Cosgrove, J. (2002). International perspectives on literacy: International assessments of reading literacy. *The Reading Teacher, 55*(7), 690–692.

Simmons, D. C., & Kame'enui, E. J. (2006). *Guide to evaluating a core reading program grades K–3.* National Center to Improve the Tools of Educators (NCITE) and Institute for the Development of Educational Achievement (IDEA). Eugene: University of Oregon.

Simons, H., & Elster, C. (1990). Picture dependence in first-grade basal texts. *Journal of Educational Research, 84,* 86–92.

Simpson, M. (1987). Alternative formats for evaluating content area vocabulary understanding. *Journal of Reading, 31,* 20–27.

Singer, H. (1978). Active comprehension: From answering to asking questions. *The Reading Teacher, 31,* 901–908.

Singer, H., & Ruddell, R. (Eds.). (1985). *Theoretical models and processes of reading* (3rd ed.). Newark, DE: International Reading Association.

Slapin, B. (1992). *How to tell the difference: A checklist for evaluating children's books for anti-Indian bias.* Philadelphia: New Society.

Slavin, R. E. (1999). Synthesis of research on cooperative learning. In A. C. Ornstein & L. S. Behar-Horenstein (Eds.), *Contemporary issues in curriculum* (2nd ed., pp. 193–203). Boston: Allyn & Bacon.

Smith, F. (1977). The uses of language. *Language Arts, 54,* 638–644.

Smith, F. (1985). *Reading without nonsense* (2nd ed.). New York: Teachers College Press.

Smith, F. (1988). *Joining the literacy club: Further essays into education.* Portsmouth, NH: Heinemann.

Smith, F. (1989). Demonstrations, engagement, and sensitivity: The choice between people and programs. In G. Manning & M. Manning (Eds.), *Whole language: Beliefs and practices, K–8* (pp. 48–59). Washington, DC: National Education Association.

Smith, J. L., & Johnson, H. (1994). Models for implementing literature in content studies. *The Reading Teacher, 48*(3), 198–209.

Smith, L. B. (1982). Sixth graders write about reading literature. *Language Arts, 59,* 357–366.

Smith, N. B. (1965). *American reading instruction.* Newark, DE: International Reading Association.

Smith, R. J., & Johnson, D. D. (1980). *Teaching children to read*. Reading, MA: Addison-Wesley.

Smolen, L. A., & Ortiz-Castro, V. (2000). Dissolving borders and broadening perspectives through Latino traditional literature. *The Reading Teacher, 53*(7), 566–578.

Snow, C. E., Burns, M. S., & Griffin, P. (1998). *Preventing reading difficulties in young children*. Washington, DC: National Academy Press.

Soalt, J. (2005). Bringing together fictional and informational texts to improve comprehension. *The Reading Teacher, 58*, 680–683.

Sowers, S. (1982). Six questions teachers ask about invented spelling. In T. Newkirk & N. Atwell (Eds.), *Understanding writing: Ways of observing, learning, and teaching*. Chelmsford, MA: Northeast Regional Exchange.

Spangenberg-Urbschat, K., & Pritchard, R. (Eds.). (1994). *Kids come in all languages: Reading instruction for ESL students*. Newark, DE: International Reading Association.

Spearitt, D. (1972). Identification of subskills in reading comprehension by maximum likelihood factor analysis. *Reading Research Quarterly, 8*, 92–111.

Spellings, M. (2007). Key policy letters signed by the Education Secretary or Deputy Secretary. Retrieved May 29, 2007, from www.ed.gov/print/policy/elsec/guid/secletter/070423.html

*Spotlight on Literacy*. (2000). New York: MacMillan/McGraw-Hill.

Squire, J. R. (1984). Composing and comprehending: Two sides of the same basic process. In J. M. Jensen (Ed.), *Composing and comprehending* (pp. 23–31). Urbana, IL: National Conference on Research in English.

Stahl, S. A. (1983). *Vocabulary instruction and the nature of word meanings*. Paper presented at a meeting of the College Reading Association, Atlanta.

Stahl, S. A. (1986). Three principles of effective vocabulary instruction. *Journal of Reading, 29*, 662–668.

Stahl, S. A. (1992). Saying the "p" word: Nine guidelines for exemplary phonic instruction. *The Reading Teacher, 45*, 618–625.

Stahl, S. A., Duffy-Hester, A. M., & Stahl, K. A. (1998). Everything you wanted to know about phonics (but were afraid to ask). *Reading Research Quarterly, 33*, 338–355.

Stahl, S. A., & Fairbanks, M. (1986). The effects of vocabulary instruction: A model-based meta-analysis. *Review of Educational Research, 56*, 72–110.

Stanovich, K. E. (1986). Matthew effects in reading: Some consequences of individual differences in the acquisition of literacy. *Reading Research Quarterly, 21*, 360–407.

Stauffer, R. (1975). *Directing the reading–thinking process*. New York: Harper & Row.

Stead, T. (2002). *Is that a fact? Teaching nonfiction writing K–3*. Portland, ME: Stenhouse.

Stein, N., & Glenn, C. (1979). An analysis of story comprehension in elementary school children. In R. Freedle (Ed.), *New directions in discourse processing* (pp. 53–120). Norwood, NJ: Ablex.

Stewart, O., & Tei, E. (1983). Some implications of metacognition for reading instruction. *Journal of Reading, 27*, 36–43.

Stewart, R. A., Paradis, E. E., Ross, B. D., & Lewis, M. J. (1996). Student voices: What works in literature-based developmental reading. *Journal of Adolescent & Adult Literacy, 39*(6), 468–477.

Stewart, S. (2001). *The journey*. New York: Farrar, Straus & Giroux.

Stewig, J. W. (1980). *Read to write* (2nd ed.). Austin, TX: Holt, Rinehart and Winston.

Stien, D., & Beed, P. L. (2004). Bridging the gap between fiction and nonfiction in the literature circle setting. *The Reading Teacher, 57*(6), 510–518.

Stokes, S. M. (1999). Empowering students with learning disabilities through language experience. In O. G. Nelson & W. M. Linek (Eds.), *Practical applications of language experience: Looking back, looking forward* (pp. 224–229). Boston: Allyn & Bacon.

Stoll, D. R. (1997). *Magazines for kids and teens*. Newark, DE: International Reading Association.

Stowell, L. (2000). Building alliances, building community, building bridges through literacy. In K. D. Wood & T. S. Dickinson (Eds.), *Promoting literacy in grades 4–9: A handbook for teachers and administrators* (pp. 77–96). Boston: Allyn & Bacon.

Strickland, D. S. (1996). In search of balance: Restructuring our literacy programs. *Reading Today, 14*(2), 32.

Strickland, D. S. (1998). *Teaching phonics today: A primer for educators*. Newark, DE: International Reading Association.

Strickland, D. S., & Ascher, C. (1992). Low-income African-American children and public schooling. In P. Jackson (Ed.), *Handbook of research on curriculum* (pp. 609–625). Old Tappan, NJ: Macmillan.

Strickland, D. S., & Morrow, L. M. (1990). Family literacy: Sharing good books. *The Reading Teacher, 43*, 518–519.

Strickland, R. (1962). *The language of elementary school children: Its relationship to the language of reading textbooks and the quality of reading of selected children*. Bloomington: Indiana University School of Education.

Sturtevant, E. G. (2001). What middle and high school educators need to know about language minority students. In J. A. Rycik & J. L. Irvin (Eds.), *What adolescents deserve: A commitment to students' literacy learning* (pp. 40–44). Newark, DE: International Reading Association.

Sutherland, Z. (Ed.). (1984). *The Scott, Foresman anthology of children's literature*. Glenview, IL: Scott, Foresman.

Swaby, B. (1983). *Teaching and learning reading*. New York: Little, Brown.

Taberski, S. (2000). *On solid ground: Strategies for teaching reading K–3*. Portsmouth, NH: Heinemann.

Taylor, B. M., Strait, J., & Medo, M. A. (1994). Early intervention in reading: Supplemental instruction for groups of low-achieving students provided by first grade teachers. In G. H. Heibert & B. M. Taylor (Eds.), *Getting reading right from the start: Effective early literacy interventions* (pp. 107–121). Boston: Allyn & Bacon.

Taylor, D. (1983). *Family literacy: Young children learning to read and write*. Portsmouth, NH: Heinemann.

Taylor, D., & Dorsey-Gaines, C. (1989). *Growing up literate: Learning from inner-city families*. Portsmouth, NH: Heinemann.

Taylor, H. P. (2000). *Secrets of the stone*. New York: Farrar, Straus & Giroux.

Taylor, N. E., & Vawter, J. (1978). Helping children discover the functions of written language. *Language Arts, 55*, 941–945.

Teachers of English to Speakers of Other Languages (TESOL). (2006). *TESOL revises PreK–12 English Language Proficiency Standards (March 2006)*. Retrieved May 31,

2007, from www.tesol.org/s_tesol/sec_document.asp?CID=1186&DID=5349

Teale, W. H. (1978). Positive environments for learning to read: What studies of early readers tell us. *Language Arts, 55,* 922–932.

Teale, W. H., & Sulzby, E. (1986). *Emergent literacy: Writing and reading.* Norwood, NJ: Ablex.

Thelen, J. (1986). Vocabulary instruction and meaningful learning. *Journal of Reading, 29,* 603–609.

Thorndyke, P. (1977). Cognitive structures in comprehension and memory of narrative discourse. *Cognitive Psychology, 9,* 77–110.

Thurstone, L. L. (1946). A note on a reanalysis of Davis' reading tests. *Psychometrika, 11,* 185–188.

Tiedt, I. M. (2000). *Teaching with picture books in the middle school.* Newark, DE: International Reading Association.

Tierney, R. J. (1998). Literacy assessment reform: Shifting beliefs, principled possibilities, and emerging practices. *The Reading Teacher, 51,* 374–390.

Tierney, R. J., & Shanahan, T. (1991). Research on reading–writing relationships: Interactions, transactions, and outcomes. In R. Barr, M. L. Kamil, P. Mosenthal, & P. D. Pearson (Eds.), *Handbook of reading research* (2nd ed., pp. 246–280). New York: Longman.

Tomlinson, C. A. (2001). *How to differentiate instruction in mixed-ability classrooms* (2nd ed.). Alexandria, VA: Association for Supervision and Curriculum Development.

Topping, K. (1989). Peer tutoring and paired reading: Combining two powerful techniques. *The Reading Teacher, 42,* 488–494.

Trachtenburg, P. (1990). Using children's literature to enhance phonic instruction. *The Reading Teacher, 43,* 648–654.

Trelease, J. (1989). *The new read-aloud handbook.* New York: Penguin.

Trelease, J. (2006) *The read-aloud handbook* (6th ed.). New York: Penguin.

Tunnell, M., Calder, J., Justen, J., & Waldrop, P. (1988). An affective approach to reading: Effectively teaching reading to mainstreamed handicapped children. *The Pointer, 32,* 38–40.

Tuttle, F. B. (1991). Responding to individual differences: Teaching the gifted. In J. Flood, J. M. Jensen, D. Lapp, & J. Squire (Eds.), *Handbook of research on teaching the English language arts* (pp. 372–379). Old Tappan, NJ: Macmillan.

Twain, M. (1897). *The innocents abroad or the new pilgrim's progress: Being some account of the steamship Quaker City's pleasure excursion to Europe and the Holy Land.* Vol. II. New York: Harper & Brothers.

Tyler, R. W. (1949). *Basic principles of curriculum and instruction.* Chicago: University of Chicago Press.

U.S. Census Bureau. (2004). *Population projections.* Retrieved May 24, 2007, from www.census.gov

U.S. Department of Education. (2007). *IDEA regulations: Disproportionality and overidentification (Febrary 2, 2007).* Retrieved June 6, 2007, from http://idea.ed.gov/explore/view/p/%2Croot%2Cdynamic%2CTopicalBrief%2C7%2C

U.S. Department of Education. (n.d.). *IDEA regulations: Identification of specific learning disabilities.* Retrieved June 6, 2007, from http://idea.ed.gov/explore/view/p/%2Croot%2Cdynamic%2CTopicalBrief%2C23%2C

Vacca, R. (2006). They can because they think they can. *Educational Leadership, 63,* 56–59.

Vacca, R. T., & Newton, E. (1995). Responding to literary texts. In C. N. Hedley, P. Antonacci, & M. Rabinowitz (Eds.), *Thinking and literacy: Mind at work in the classroom* (pp. 283–302). Mahwah, NJ: Erlbaum.

Vacca, R. T., & Rasinski, T. V. (1992). *Case studies in whole language.* Orlando, FL: Harcourt Brace.

Vacca, R. T., & Vacca, J. L. (2002). *Content area reading: Literacy and learning across the curriculum* (7th ed.). Boston: Allyn & Bacon.

Vacca, R. T., & Vacca, J. L. (2005). *Content area reading: Literacy and learning across the curriculum* (8th ed.). Boston: Allyn & Bacon.

Vacca, R. T., & Vacca, J. L. (2008). *Content area reading: Literacy and learning across the curriculum* (9th ed.). Boston: Allyn & Bacon.

Valdes, G., & Figueroa, R. A. (1994). *Bilingualism and testing: A special case bias.* Norwood, NJ: Ablex.

Valencia, S. W., & Buly, M. R. (2004). Behind test scores: What struggling readers really need. *The Reading Teacher, 57,* 520–530.

Valmont, W. J. (2003). *Technology for literacy teaching and learning.* Boston: Houghton Mifflin.

Valmont, W. J., & Thurlow, R. (Eds.). (2000). *Linking literacy and technology: A guide for K–8 classrooms.* Newark, DE: International Reading Association.

Valmont, W. J., & Wepner, S. B. (2000). Using technology to support literacy learning. In S. B. Wepner, W. J. Valmont, & R. Thurlow (Eds.), *Linking literacy and technology* (pp. 2–18). Newark, DE: International Reading Association.

Van Sluys, K., & Laman, T. T. (2006). Learning about language: Written conversations and elementary language learners. *The Reading Teacher, 60,* 222–233.

Vardell, S., Hadaway, N., & Young, T. (2006). Matching books and readers: Selecting literature for English learners. *The Reading Teacher, 59*(8), 734–741.

Veatch, J. (1968). *How to teach reading with children's books.* New York: Citation Press.

Veatch, J., Sawicki, F., Elliot, G., Flake, E., & Blakey, J. (1979). *Key words to reading* (2nd ed.). Columbus, OH: Merrill.

Venezky, R. L. (1978). Reading acquisition: The occult and the obscure. In F. B. Murray & J. J. Pikulski (Eds.), *The acquisition of reading.* Baltimore, MD: University Park Press.

Venezky, R. L., & Massaro, D. W. (1979). The role of orthographic regularity in word recognition. In L. Resnick & R. Weaver (Eds.), *Theory and practice of early reading* (pp. 85–107). Mahwah, NJ: Erlbaum.

Villaume, S. K., Worden, T., Williams, S., Hopkins, L., & Rosenblatt, C. (1994). Five teachers in search of a discussion. *Language Arts, 47,* 480–489.

Viorst, J. (1972). *Alexander and the terrible, horrible, no good, very bad day.* New York: Atheneum.

Virginia Department of Education. (2004). *K–5 reading textbooks adopted by the Virginia Board of Education.* Richmond, VA: Virginia Department of Education. Retrieved on October 22, 2004, from http://readingfirst.virginia.edu

Vukelich, C., & Christie, J. (2004). *Building a foundation for preschool literacy: Effective instruction for children's reading and writing development.* Newark, DE: International Reading Association.

Vygotsky, L. S. (1962). *Thought and language.* Cambridge, MA: MIT Press.

Vygotsky, L. S. (1978). *Mind in society.* Cambridge, MA: Harvard University Press.

Walley, C. (1993). An invitation to reading fluency. *The Reading Teacher, 46*, 526–527.

Walsh, K. (2003). Basal readers: The lost opportunity to build the knowledge that propels comprehension. *American Educator, 27*, 24–27.

Weaver, C. (2002). *Reading process and practice*. Portsmouth, NH: Heinemann.

Wells, M. C. (1993). At the juncture of reading and writing: How dialogue journals contribute to students' reading development. *Journal of Reading, 36*, 294–303.

Whaley, J. F. (1981). Story grammar and reading instruction. *The Reading Teacher, 34*, 762–771.

Williams, T. L. (2007). "Reading" the painting: Exploring visual literacy in the primary grades. *The Reading Teacher, 60*, 636–642.

Wood, A. (1984). *The napping house*. Orlando, FL: Harcourt Brace Jovanovich.

Wooten, D. A. (2000). *Valued voices: An interdisciplinary approach to teaching and learning*. Newark, DE: International Reading Association.

Wylie, R. E., & Durrell, D. D. (1970). Teaching vowels through phonograms. *Elementary English, 47*, 787–791.

Yanok, J. (1988). Individualized instruction: A good approach. *Academic Therapy, 24*, 163–167.

Yashima, T. (1976). *Crow Boy*. New York: Puffin.

Yep, L. (1977). *Child of the owl*. New York: Harper & Row.

Yokota, J. (1993). Issues in selecting multicultural literature for children and adolescents. *Language Arts, 70*, 156–167.

Yolen, J. (2000). *Not one damsel in distress: World folktales for strong girls*. San Diego, CA: Silver Whistle Books.

Yopp, H. K. (1992). Developing phonemic awareness in young children. *The Reading Teacher, 45*, 696–703.

Yopp, H. K. (1995). A test for assessing phonemic awareness in young children. *The Reading Teacher, 49*, 20–29.

Yopp, R. H., & Yopp, H. K. (1993). *Literature-based reading activities*. Boston: Allyn & Bacon.

Young, T. A., & Hadaway, N. L. (Eds.). (2006). *Supporting the literacy development of English learners: Increasing success in all classrooms*. Newark, DE: International Reading Association.

Zarrillo, J. (1989). Teachers' interpretations of literature-based reading. *The Reading Teacher, 43*, 22–28.

# Name Index

# Subject Index

# Credits

## Photo Credits

## Text Credits